de Gruyter Studies in Organization 53
Regulating Employment and Welfare

de Gruyter Studies in Organization

Organizational Theory and Research

This de Gruyter Series publishes theoretical and methodological studies of organizations as well as research findings, which yield insight in and knowledge about organizations. The whole spectrum of perspectives are considered: organizational analyses rooted in the sociological as well as the economic tradition, from a socio-psychological or a political science angle, mainstream as well as critical or ethnomethodological contributions. Equally, all kinds of organizations are considered: firms, public agencies, non-profit institutions, voluntary associations, inter-organizational networks, supra-national organizations etc.

Emphasis is on publication of *new* contributions, or significant revisions of existing approaches. However, summaries or critical reflections on current thinking and research are also considered.

This series represents an effort to advance the social scientific study of organizations across national boundaries and academic disciplines. An Advisory Board consisting of representatives of a variety of perspectives and from different cultural areas is responsible for achieving this task.

This series addresses organization researchers within and outside universities, but also practitioners who have an interest in grounding their work on recent social scientific knowledge and insights.

Editor:

Prof. Dr. Alfred Kieser, Universität Mannheim, Mannheim, Germany

Advisory Board:

Prof. Anna Grandori, CRORA, Università Commerciale Luigi Bocconi, Milano, Italy
Prof. Dr. Cornelis Lammers, FSW Rijksuniversiteit Leiden, Leiden, The Netherlands
Prof. Dr. Marshall W. Meyer, The Wharton School, University of Pennsylvania, Philadelphia, U.S.A.
Prof. Jean-Claude Thoenig, Université de Paris, I, Paris, France
Prof. Dr. Barry A. Turner, Middlesex Business School, London, GB
Prof. Mayer Zald, The University of Michigan, Ann Arbor, U.S.A.

Regulating Employment and Welfare

Company and National Policies
of Labour Force Participation at the End
of Worklife in Industrial Countries

Edited by
Frieder Naschold and Bert de Vroom

Walter de Gruyter · Berlin · New York 1994

Professor Dr. *Frieder Naschold*, Director of the Research Unit II, Technology-Work-Environment, at the Science Center Berlin (WZB), Germany

Dr. *Bert de Vroom*, Senior Sociologist, Institute for Law and Public Policy, University of Leyden, The Netherlands

With 38 figures and 110 tables

⊗ Printed on acid-free paper which falls within the guidelines of the ANSI to ensure permanence and durability.

Library of Congress Cataloging-in-Publication Data

Regulating employment and welfare : company and national policies of
  labour force participation at the end of worklife in industrial
  countries / edited by Frieder Naschold and Bert de Vroom.
      p. 15,5 × 23 cm. − (De Gruyter studies in organization ; 53.)
      Includes bibliographical references.
      ISBN 3-11-013513-2
      1. Labor policy − Congresses. 2. Public welfare − Congresses.
  3. Social security − Congresses. 4. Early retirement − Congresses.
  I. Naschold, Frieder. II. Vroom, Bert de. III. Series.
  HD4813.R33   1994
  331.1 − dc20   93-35001
                                                                       CIP

Die Deutsche Bibliothek − Cataloging-in-Publication Data

Regulating employment and welfare : company and national
policies of labour force participation and the end of worklife in
industrial countries / ed. by Frieder Naschold and Bert de
Vroom − Berlin ; New York : de Gruyter, 1994
  (De Gruyter studies in organization ; 53)
  ISBN 3-11-013513-2
  NE: Naschold, Frieder [Hrsg.]; GT

Typesetting: Converted by Jürgen Stephan, Digital Design, Berlin. − Printing: Ratzlow-Druck, Berlin. − Binding: D. Mikolai, Berlin. − Cover Design: Johannes Rother, Berlin. Printed in Germany.

Preface

The mode of regulation of work and welfare established in the period following the Second World War in highly industrialised countries, a vital element underpinning the success such countries have enjoyed in welfare and productivity development, is now coming under massive global adjustment pressure. This is giving rise to fundamental changes within the relevant actor systems – the state, collective organisations, firms and workers – and between the state at national level and global corporate structures.

These trends are the central focus of the present study. The analysis began with, and was motivated by, the massive use of "externalisation strategies" by firms and national states in continental Europe in response to the social dislocation resulting from cyclical and structural problems on the labour market. However, the research soon found itself confronted with the very different experiences of countries such as the USA, Japan or Sweden, with their heterogeneous modes of regulation of work and welfare.

The task of integrating the mass of empirical data, the variety of analytical concepts, theoretical approaches and political perspectives into a coherent whole called for quite extraordinary efforts on the part of our six national teams – from Great Britain, Japan, the Netherlands, the former Federal Republic of Germany and the former GDR, Sweden and the USA.

The research consortium, coordinated by the Science Centre, Berlin (WZB), met five times for extended working conferences in Berlin, Germany, and Leyden, the Netherlands. In addition, numerous bilateral discussions were held between the various national research teams.

We hope that these efforts have enabled us to present a study which, while it clearly does not meet the strict criteria of a systematic comparative analysis, undoubtedly goes far beyond a mere "additive" analysis of regulatory configurations at national level. It is to be hoped that this means that our research will not only provide a source of information on practical political discussions in this field – which are becoming ever more intense – but also will be able to make a direct contribution to the regulation of work and welfare within the context of state/firm interaction.

The success of international, cooperative research of this type, spread as this project was over four years, depends heavily on the quality and the consistency of its "infrastructure". Here we would very much like to record the indispensable help and support provided by the following persons and institutions, to all of whom go our thanks.

Without the engagement, initiative and social and organisational skills of Edith Narewsky at the WZB, the research project would never have got off the ground, nor would it have been successfully completed without the skill and hard work first of Linda Albrecht, and then of Gebhard Glock, aided by Anna Herr (all WZB). The same applies to the organisational and technical assistance by Thea de Beer and Anne-Marie Krens and to the stimulating support by Dr. Nick Huls, director, of the Ledyden Institute for Law and Public Policy. We are also in particular grateful for the intellectual support by the scientific council of the Leyden Institute. It recognised both the political and scientific relevance of this research project and allocated the necessary financial and organisational resources for the Dutch case study and the international meetings at Leyden. Andrew Watt (Berlin) has, as usual, produced an excellent translation of the texts originally written in German.

Equally vital was the support, theoretical as well as financial, offered by a number of national and international research-support institutions. Specifically, the German Project Leader would like to mention the Deutsche Forschungsgemeinschaft, the Volkswagen Stiftung and the Anglo-German Foundation. Thanks are also due for the assistance provided by the Japan-German Centre Berlin, the Departments of Research and Science, and Health and Social Security of the Berlin Senate, and the following firms: Schering; Dr. Kade; Siemens and the Berliner Sparkasse.

In the publishers, Walter de Gruyter & Co., represented by Dr. Bianka Ralle, we found a publishing house which brings together the best traditions of serious scholarly publishing and efficient, pragmatic support.

The whole research consortium would like to thank all the firms studied, their managements, workforces and works councils, together with the collective organisations and state institutions involved. With very few exceptions we received competent and friendly support in our intensive search for highly differentiated data and documentation and during our numerous interviews. In view of our commitment to maintaining the anonymity of both our interview partners and the data, we would here merely like to express our thanks to all the institutions involved.

As can be seen from the contents, this volume consists of three parts. The introductory chapter sketches out the frame of reference and the lines of enquiry underpinning the research network as a whole. The second part contains the national studies. Here the joint research agenda is supplemented by country-specific considerations and approaches. The detailed final section attempts to synthesise the national studies at the empirical, conceptual and theoretical levels.

With the aim of reinforcing the integrative aspect of the volume as a whole, a contribution by Martin Rein and Klaus Jacobs, who accompanied the entire project from inception to conclusion with their constructive criticism and helpful advice and mediation, has been included. They present a general picture of the patterns, past and future trends and the meaning of early retirement. We would also like to thank our colleagues Prof. Dr. Martin Kohli of the Free University Berlin, Prof. Dr. Ronald Dore, London School of Economics and Prof. Dr. C. J. Lammers, University of Leyden, for influential critical-constructive discussions.

On behalf of the research consortium

Frieder Naschold, Science Center Berlin (Wissenschaftszentrum Berlin für Sozialforschung)

Bert de Vroom, Leyden Institute for Law and Public Policy (Recht & Beleid), University of Leyden

October 1993

Contents

1 The Dialectics of Work and Welfare

Bert de Vroom and Frieder Naschold

1   Changing Labour Force Participation in Industrialised Countries

The starting point of our research project was the labour force participation trend – and the ensuing public discourse – in Europe, which have increasingly came to be dominated by the western early exit of older (male) workers leaving the labour market before the 'normal' age of retirement. This decline in participation in paid labour has revitalized the old normative debate on the broader socio-cultural meaning of work and non-work. Four well-known positions can be distinguished. Firstly, that participation in work is a necessary prerequisite of civilization and citizenship (Heilbroner, 1985: 22ff). According to this view exclusion from work implies an exclusion from rights, whereas the participation in labour is a matter of political emancipation. In this sense exit from the labour market – in particular non-voluntary exit – results in the lost of political influence. This has always been an important issue in the women's movement, and is becoming increasingly so for older age groups, like the "grey movements" in a number of industrialised countries. Affirmative action and anti-age discrimination legalisation are the political and legal reflections of this debate (Friedman, 1984). Another position, expressed within different sociological and philosophical traditions, sees work as a necessary precondition for self-expression and social contacts. Others, however, take the opposite position in the debate: exit from labour means escape from inhuman working conditions and work-related risks: exit means entry into a world of 'freedom'. Clearly, this presupposes a society that is able to combine the exit process with a relatively high level of welfare provision and citizenship, if exit is not lead to poverty and second-class citizenship. The fourth position in the debate stresses the exit from labour – or in other words retirement – as the expression of "an essential part of the societal process of individualization" (Kohli and Rein, 1991: 20). In this respect retirement is seen as part of the modern tri-partition of the life course: "By the 1960s (...) the tri-partition of the life course into a period of preparation, one of 'active' work, and one of retirement had become firmly established" (Kohli and Rein, 1991: 21). Notwithstanding the fact that the process of increasing early exit in the last decades has, undeniable, changed this modern life-time schedule, Kohli and Rein think that "the basic tripartition of the life course is still firmly in place" (Kohli and Rein, 1991: 22).

At the same time, the decreasing labour force participation of older age groups and the trend towards an aging society has also put the problems of the financing of social security programmes and the future supply of labour on the political agenda. The trend towards early exit has become one element in a normative and political debate, generating questions of control, regulation and even a quest for the reversal of the exit process. It is against the background of this political and normative debate on work – which clearly has a Western cultural bias – that we started our research project. However we are not so much interested in the normative debate as such; our scientific curiosity focuses on the logics behind this social process at the end of working life.

The choice of concepts, theoretical frameworks and research strategies is highly dependent on the way the social process we want to study is framed. So far, we have stressed the similarity in the labour force participation trend in industrialised countries. Notwithstanding this homogeneity, there are still important differences. The relative importance of *similarity or difference* depends on the level of aggregation. Starting from a high level of aggregation, that of the average OECD-country[1], the decreasing participation in paid employment is the striking feature. This development towards the so-called 'typical non-working OECD society' (Dahrendorf, 1988: 144), is the result of three different trends: (1) the increasing average age of entry into paid employment; (2) the decreasing average age of exit from paid labour; (3) a radical reduction of the average numbers of hours worked.

The 'typical OECD society', however, is a very artificial construct, which obscures important social, economic and political differences between industrialised societies and also differences in trends and patterns. In general, the trend towards the 'typical' OECD-society applies more to continental West European countries, whereas OECD-countries like the USA and in particular Japan display a substantial variance in participation profiles and trends. There is a world of difference between the 'logic of VUT' in the Dutch society and the 'logic of SHUKKO' in Japan.[2] The first reflects the development of industrial societies that combine already low levels of labour force participation with an explicit externalisation regime (of older workers). The second combines a comparatively high level of labour force participation with a purposive integration regime. But even within Europe we find sharp contrasts such as between Sweden and Germany.

In other words, on a lower level of aggregation similarities become dominated by country-specific differences. These dual aspects of both similarities and differences raise for the social scientist two intriguing questions: (1) what is the cause of the similarity and (2) what explains the differences? Our central hypothesis is that the different patterns must be explained by the interdependency between the developments of 'work' and 'welfare'. This analytical framework of the dialectics of work and welfare in different industrial societies has been the reference point of our comparative empirical research project. In doing this we go beyond the approach taken by the *Time for Retirement* research project, in which some of us also participated (Kohli et. al., 1991). In the *Time for Retirement* project the units of analysis were the instruments, the so-called pathways, at the macro level in different countries. This approach was very fruitful in explaining early exit trends by different (combined) financial provisions. However, this research focused mainly on externalisation which, in the final analysis, is explained by the 'pull-effect' of welfare-state institutions, whereas we have attempted to enlarge the question by looking at both the dynamics of externalisation and internalisation within the framework of the logics of welfare and work.

As a result our comparative approach differs also from other comparative studies, in that our focus is on the subsystemic, intermediate level of firms and sectors, instead of comparisons at only the macro or the micro level of the individual. Comparisons at only the macro level often result in unspecific statements and statistical artifacts. From this perspective the heterogeneity behind social changes becomes obscured, trends look like homogeneous processes in different subsystems. The intermediate level enables to integrate firm-state and firm-individual interactions in specific economic-political circumstances. This approach offers the opportunity to analyse the effects of both *institutional* and *organizational* effects – welfare-state provisions and production regimes respectively – on the social process of labour force participation at the end of the working life.[3] In the following we will elaborate our analytical framework (sec.2), the comparative method (sec.3). The last section of this chapter deals with the organisation of our cross-national research project (sec.4). In the concluding chapter in this volume we will come back to our analytical model and the results from the national case-studies.

2   The Dialectics of Work and Welfare

Instead of concentrating only on the (West European) concept of 'early exit' we start with the more neutral concept of labour force participation of older workers. Instead of asking 'why early exit', the question becomes what makes older workers 'to participate or not to participate' in paid labour. In the process of exchange and collaboration in the international research group this question was conceptualised in terms of *externalisation* and *integration*[4]. By externalisation we mean the social process in which workers leave paid labour. This research project focuses however, not on the general process of externalisation, but on a particular segment: the social process in which *older* workers (55 and over) leave paid labour before the 'normal' age of retirement[5]. This particular segment of the externalisation process is mostly referred to as 'early exit'. By integration we mean the social process by which workers enter and stay in paid labour until the normal age of retirement. Again, in this project we concentrate on the segment of older workers (55 and over).

Externalisation and integration are helpful concepts to describe the process of labour force participation of older workers, they are however not sufficient to explain this process. For this purpose we need an analytical framework. The analytical framework we have developed is based on the idea that the welfare-state regime of modern industrialised societies fulfils the fundamental task of regulating labour force participation through externalisation and integration.

Despite the fact that work and welfare are treated as separate units in day-to-day politics and academic disciplines, closer analysis reveals that the two systems form – in both historical and systematic terms – a close, albeit contradictory unit in the social development of modern industrial societies. Whatever their other differences all these societies were dependent at a relatively early stage in their industrial development on at least a minimum degree of public or social welfare (in the broad sense of the term) as a condition for growth and stability; guaranteeing the physical and mental reproduction of the labour force and for the social integration of the working class. At the same time, the expansion of industrial production and the growth of productivity generated the resources required to support collective inter-temporal, inter-sectoral and inter-personal distributive systems able to meet the numerous risks arising out of the production process and externalised by private firms.

On the supply side, the welfare-state system secured the provision of labour power (in both quantitative and qualitative terms), and, in its function as a transfer mechanism, stabilised collective social consumption and social integration in the face of a system of industrial work based on power relations and the extraction of labour.

The relationship between work and welfare has been theoretically and politically conceptualised in different ways (Esping-Andersen, 1990). Dominant for many years was the social-democratic view, emphasising extensive citizenship rights and the principles of universalism and equality. From this perspective the welfare-state was seen as ex post compensation for industrial development via the distributional side of industrial production. In the real world, the social-democratic welfare-state has produced highly differentiated social services and relatively high levels of benefit. The liberal concept, by contrast, emphasised the possibly dysfunctional effects of the welfare-state on the supply side of industrial production. This concept can be ideologically characterised by its primary reliance on the market; the welfare-state is to provide support only for those who are unable to provide for themselves in the marketplace. As a result the liberal welfare-state regime is characterised by a relatively limited package of social services and low levels of benefit.

Modern social-scientific analyses, however, tend to place the main emphasis on the dialectical relationship between work and welfare. This dialectic at the conceptual level is matched by one at the real-economic level. Welfare-state arrangements can indeed, in certain constellations, reduce flexibility and raise costs, initiating a vicious circle of work and welfare. Under different conditions, however, they may promote consensus and stimulate innovation, leading to a virtuous circle of work and welfare.

The empirical effect of work and welfare inderdependencies on the externalisation and integration of older workers is – we assume – the result of the concrete form of both the industrial structure and the welfare-state regime and its interrelation in a given socio-political context. Industrial structures can be defined as the aggregation of various firms, which may be classified as production regimes (2.2). Different production regimes exert externalisation or integration effects of varying strength on older workers. Welfare-state regimes, too, have an externalising or integrating impact, depending on the particular institutions developed in their historical development (2.1.). The interdependence between welfare-state regime and production regime is in the real world mediated by different firm-state relations, which may also have an effect on the particular externalisation/ integration pattern of industrialised countries (2.3).

2.1   Welfare-State Regimes and Externalisation or Integration Effects

Notwithstanding political differences between social-democratic, conservative or liberal welfare-states, in the historical development of the welfare-states two underlying work-related 'logics' can be distinguished: the 'logic of employment' and the 'logic of insurance'. The first logic is the result of the responsibility of industrial welfare-states to guarantee high and stable employment, not only as a precondition for industrial development but also a response to the increased 'general expectation of justice' in modern societies: the citizen's expectation of fair treatment, everywhere and in every circumstance (Friedman, 1985: 43). One result has been labour laws providing for greater job protection. Hiring and firing on the basis of race, sex, religion, physical handicap, and even – in some welfare states – age is prohibited by law. At the same time collective contracts between employers and unions have added various other protective measurements, such as seniority systems.

Modern welfare-states are not only responsible for the quantity of work, but also for the quality of life – including the quality of work. Alongside technological development and increased scientific knowledge new ideas of social and collective control over uncertainties and risks have developed.

"Technology has made the world over, and in so doing has vastly reduced certain kinds of uncertainty; it also opened the door to a vastly greater level of demands on government. Slowly people have come to expect more out of government, out of law, out of life" (Friedman, 1985: 50).

From a normative perspective as to what the state "should" do, the perspective changed to what the state "could" do. In former days workers who died of disease or by accident, or lost their job, received no compensation. Indeed: "People also did not expect compensation from anyone – not the employer, and not the state" (Friedman, 1985: 49), things 'just happened'. But new technological developments raised an 'expectation of recompense'. The increasing spread and depth of social insurance programmes in modern welfare states (the 'logic of insurance') is a direct reflection of this change in expectations. People still lose their jobs, still become sick or disabled at work, still grow old. But now various compensatory programmes and pension schemes guarantee, in modern welfare states, at least a basic income. For this reason the welfare-state has been labelled an 'insurance state', a 'no-risk state'.

There is however a duality between both logics, concerning the effect on labour force participation. Whereas the logic of employment basically stimulates entry into paid labour, the logic of insurance has the opposite effect: exit into the welfare-state. It is an empirical question – and one depending on particular political welfare-state constellations – which effect prevails in a given society. On an abstract theoretical level four different hypothetical outcomes can be distinguished, as in figure 1. The model is based on three propositions: (a) a growing economy, (b) people can only have one source of income from paid labour or social security and (c) choices are made on the basis of rational financial calculations and are not based on the intrinsic value of work or free time.

Theoretically we can have four different policy-systems[6], according to the relative importance of labour market policies and social security systems and the effect of their interplay. In a situation of low social security provision and relatively strong labour market policy the result will be, according to the above mentioned assumptions, *no-exit*. If a strong labour market policy goes together with a highly developed social security system, we probably will find exit and, at the same time, (re-)entry trends: *exit+entry*. In that case it might be that social security is strictly bound to re-integration in the labour process. The opposite is the case where we have a highly developed social security system, but at the same time no explicit integration policy. The result will be: *exit=exit*. If income based on social policy can 'compete' with paid labour, why you should try to get work? This combination might even be strengthened if social security income is based on a 'no-entry' obligation, as is the case in a number of welfare-states. The last case is *exit or entry*. It represents the situation where both integration policy and social security system are absent. In other words, it is the classical model of the 'market'. Exit or entry is mainly based on individual circumstances and choices.

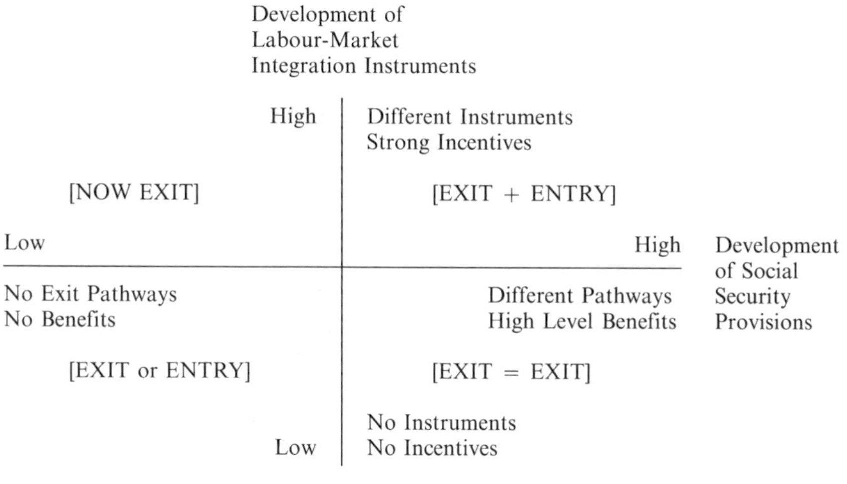

Development of
Labour-Market
Integration Instruments

	High	Different Instruments Strong Incentives	
[NOW EXIT]		[EXIT + ENTRY]	
Low		High	Development of Social
No Exit Pathways No Benefits		Different Pathways High Level Benefits	Security Provisions
[EXIT or ENTRY]		[EXIT = EXIT]	
	Low	No Instruments No Incentives	

Figure 1: The Two Logics of Welfare-State Regulation and Their Effect on Externalisation and Integration of Workers

2.2   Production Regimes and Age-Specific Risks

Firms are complex organisations in which labour and technology are combined in a particular organisational structure to produce products for
particular markets. We have labelled this complexity 'production regime'.
Firms are not isolated units, but operate within dynamic environments –
changing labour, product, and capital markets, political structures and
regulations. From the contingency studies in organisational sociology, we
know there is no one universal, effective production regime, but that
regimes may vary depending on particular environmental characteristics
and developments.

The basic question here is how different production regimes might be
related to internal labour 'markets', in particular the segment of older
workers. Or to reframe the question: can we distinguish production regimes
with respect to their age-specific integration and/or externalisation effects.
Concerning this question we can distinguish three dominant clusters of
production regimes in industrial societies: (1) the taylorist, fordist or mass
production regime type; (2) the diversified quality production and flexible
specialization regime, and (3) the innovation-oriented market-expansion
regime. From the relevant industrial and organisational sociology and
management literature one can draw two empirically and theoretically well-
founded hypotheses to develop an analytical typology of these production
regimes and their hypothetical relation to personnel trends, age-specific
risks and corresponding externalisation or integration strategies and effects
(figure 2).[7]

Taylorism, fordism or mass production is based on an extreme division of
labour and correlates with intensive production, high performance requirements and a strong polarisation effect on the workforce: i.e., low skill
requirements for the overwhelming majority of workers. This type of
production regime is assumed to cause increasing risks for aging workers, in
particular the threat of falling productivity and skill level. From the view-
point of economic efficiency, falling productivity and skill will stimulate an
externalisation strategy by firms. Where this production regime is paired
with a welfare-state regime dominated by the 'insurance logic', firms'
externalisation strategies will be reinforced by state policies. On the other
hand, explicit welfare-state integration policies and/or (expected) scarcity
on the supply side of the labour market and demographic trends may press
firms to develop an age-specific accommodation and prevention strategy to
keep older workers within the firm, overdetermining the effects of the
production regime itself.

The work structure in a diversified quality production or flexible specialisation regime is – contrary to the taylorist regime – relatively cooperative
and based on high skill levels. The work intensity and performance require-

ments are moderate and the personnel trends are in general characterised by a relatively stable workforce and low labour turnover rate. The risks for aging workers, in particular of falling productivity, are low compared to the taylorist regime. Combined with quasi-lifelong employment there is no necessity of pressure to externalise older workers nor to implement accommodation or prevention strategies.

The innovation-oriented market-expansion strategy is characterised by a continuous improvement of working structures and skills through job-rotation and by the polyvalent use of labour. The result is a polarised personnel structure: on the one hand a stable, core workforce, and on the other a flexible, peripheral workforce. This type of production regime is supposed to have a mixed effect on aging workers. The polyvalent use of labour and the polarised personnel structure will increase the risk of falling productivity of aging workers in the peripheral worker-groups and might stimulate externalisation of this group. Again, only welfare-state integration policies and/or labour market conditions and demographic trends may press firms in this case to develop accommodation and prevention policies. At the same time, the continuous improvement of working structures and skills might stimulate integration strategies or at least minimise pressure for the externalisation of aging core workers.

2.3   Firm-State Relations

Industrial societies may differ with respect to the relationship between firms and the state at both the economic and political level. The two extreme cases in this respect are 'state-centred' and 'market-centred' societies. In state-centred societies, we might expect hierarchical control by bureaucratic agencies using authoritative regulations to regulate industrial development and work. In these societies firms are not relatively autonomous actors; their strategies are dominated by state policies. In market-centred societies, relatively autonomous firms are the predominant actors. Labour force participation is the result of competition on labour markets. This type of society is combined with the liberal type of welfare-state. The process of externalisation/integration is, in theory, directly related to economic growth and particular production regime effects. In between these two contrasting regimes, we can distinguish some other types: the corporatist and the *kaisha* (large-firm-groupings) constellations. In corporatist constellations collective actors in the sense of functionally defined interest associations (of both firms and workers) and bureaucratic agencies regulate the process of externalisation and integration through inter- and intra-organisational concertation. There is no direct relation between the level of externalisation or integration and characteristics of production regimes or wel-

Production Regime	Work Organisation and Qualifications	Age-Specific Risks	Theoretical Effect
Taylorism, Fordism, Mass production	Extreme Division of Labour; Polarisation of the Workforce; Intensive Production; High Performance and Low Skill Requirements; High Labour-Force Turnover	Decreasing Productivity and Skill Level for Aging Workers	Either High Externalisation Effect or Explicit Firm Policy Towards Risk Prevention of Aging Workers
Diversified Quality Production, Flexible Specialisation	Relatively Cooperative and Innovative Work Structures; Moderate Work Intensity and Performance Requirements; High Skill requirements; Low Labour-Force Turnover	Relatively Low Risk of Decreasing Productivity and Skill for Aging Workers	No Strong Externalisation Effect on Aging Workers (Quasi Lifetime Employment Strategy of Firms)
Innovation-Oriented Market-Expansion Strategy	Permanent Improvement of Work Structure; Permanent Upgrading of Skills by Job-Rotation, Polyvalent Use of Labour-Force; Polarisation Into a Stable Core Workforce and a Flexible Peripheral Workforce	Risk of Decreasing Productivity for Elderly Workers from the Peripheral Group;	Low Externalisation Effect for Core Groups; (Pressure for Life-Time Employment Strategy); High Externalisation Effect for Elderly Workers in Peripheral Groups (no Need for Life-Time Employment Policy)

Figure 2: Production Regimes and Effects on Externalisation and Integration

fare-state institutions, but this level is, in principle, the result of bargaining and exchange between the different actors of the corporatist system. The ultimate outcome, is likely to depend on the precise nature of the corporatist system. In the literature on corporatism various typologies have been developed (Williamson, 1989). For our argument we need only make the distinction between national-level and meso-level corporatism. In the first type state influence is higher, whereas in the meso-level corporatism the influence of organised interests within a particular sectoral context is more important. The *kaisha*-constellation is based on the model of a vertically integrated pattern of firms, which act as a relative large corporate actor and which is able to regulate the internal labour market of this complex model. At the same time it can establish an inter-organisational concertation with state agencies (Samuels, 1987).

2.4   The Firm Level

So far we have conceptualised the dialectics of work and welfare – and in particular the externalisation and internalisation effects – as a result of the complex interdependency between welfare-state and production regimes. We now return to our basic research approach to analyse the dialectics and the effect on the employment at the end of the working life. We have chosen to take the firm as the unit of analysis: firms are so to speak the 'magnifying glass' through which we look to detect, illustrate and explain the logics behind the externalisation and internalisation of older workers in different socio-economic and political constellations.

Taking this firm-level approach we try to answer two simple questions: (1) what do firms do with their older workers? And (2) why do they do what they do?

The analytical tools used to address these questions is based on a firm-environment model in which the practices and strategies of firms are determined by the complex interplay of intra-organisational characteristics and environmental constraints and developments discussed above. In this model we have clustered the various contextual variables in two different types of environments: (1) the political environment, basically characterised by (a) welfare-state integration and externalisation policies and instruments and (b) socio-political constellations; (2) the socio-economic environment, characterised by labour market, demographic and overall economic and technological characteristics and developments.

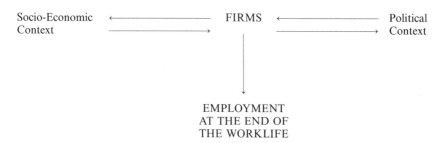

Figure 3: Firms and Environments

In order to address the first of our research questions, our case studies used firm-level information on participation (statistics, interviews and internal documents), in particular among older age-groups (55–59 and 60–64), differentiated by gender and class. Based on this information firm-level practices were analysed in terms of particular externalisation and internalisation developments and strategies.

The second question requires analysis of production-regime and welfare-state regime aspects and their effects on externalisation and internalisation practices at firm level. To this end the different country teams described and analyzed the welfare-state externalisation and internalisation programmes and instruments in detail. And on a more general level political constellations, labour-market, demographic and technological developments have also been described.

3   Comparing Contrasting Worlds

Our principal object of comparison are not countries as such, but the *social process* of externalisation and internalisation of older workers in paid labour, being part of a social, political and economic system. A number of approaches can be taken to comparative analysis (Dogan and Pelassy, 1984). There is a common distinction between the horizontal or cross-national approach and the vertical or historical one (Field, 1989: 5). In the former, the same issue is examined in more than one country, while in the latter the historical development of a particular phenomenon in one society is explored.

In some of the case-studies in this book, the vertical approach has been (partly) applied, but the main focus of the overall project has been cross-national comparison. Within this frame-work a choice has to be made between the 'most similar system' and the 'most different system' approach (Przeworski and Teune, 1970). Since the object of our research project is to understand the social process of externalisation/internalisation of older workers, to establish an interdependency between certain contextual variables and the particular manifestation of this social process, the second approach is the most useful. As we have seen, we not only expect a relation between welfare-state regimes and the externalisation/integration mix, but also between this mix and production regimes. For this reason the 'most different system' approach has been applied to both contrasting countries and contrasting production regimes.

A comparison between contrasting countries to explain the social process of labour force participation of older workers has to fulfil two conditions. Firstly, there should be a contrast between levels of labour force participation of this social category. Secondly, these contrasts must correspond with political-economic systems characterised by relevant systematic features. In other words, each country or set of countries must represent a particular conceptual type. To create a contrasting typology of (sets) of countries we have used the 'structured hypothesis' of the different firm-state relations as discussed above (2.3). The hypothesis is that each type functions in a specific way with regard to the social process of externalisation/internalisation. The countries selected in this project fulfil both conditions as illustrated in figure 4. In this figure the seven countries – Germany, the Netherlands, UK, USA, Sweden, Japan and the former East Germany – are classified according to the labour-force participation of older workers and the particular firm-state relation. These seven countries form five sets of contrasting cases: (1) East Germany (state-centred society combined with high labour force participation of older workers); (2) Sweden (corporatist society combined with high labour force participation); (3) Japan (large-firm-constellation combined with high labour force participation); (4) UK and USA (market-centred societies combined with a medium level of labour force participation of older workers; (5) Germany and the Netherlands (corporatist societies combined with low labour force participation). The difference between the two sets of corporatist countries with respect to the labour force participation might be explained by the different sub-types of corporatism. Sweden is an example of macro-level corporatism, whereas the Netherlands is a clear example of meso-corporatism. Germany is somewhere between the two models.

Participation of Older Workers	Firm-State Relation			
	State Centred	Corporatist	Large-Firm Centred	Market
High	DDR	Sweden	Japan	
Medium				USA UK
Low		BRD Netherlands		

Figure 4: Classification of Contrasting Countries by Firm-State Relations and the Average Labour Force Participation (1980–1990) of Older Workers (55–65)

Within these countries firms have been selected which represent the different types of productions regimes as discussed before.

4   The Organisation of Cross-National Research

We can distinguish between two extreme ways to organise cross-national research. One method is the so-called 'safari-research': the entire inquiry is made by a group of researchers from one country, collecting information in other countries, but analysing and reporting findings to the 'home basis'. In this strategy, the research design, the research method, the central concepts, measurement, and analysis are made from this central point. The second method is: "having the design, measurement, analysis and report made by coordinated (autonomous) researchers in each country" (Prins, 1990: 59).

Both strategies may fall into the trap of 'ethnocentrism'. The danger of the first one is that description and explanation are based on a supposedly 'universal concept', which usually turns out to be culturally determined. Dogan and Pelassy: "Every researcher, even a comparativist researcher, belongs to a culture, and that can limit his or her capacity to perceive" (Dogan and Pelassy, 1984: 9). One result might be that researchers see the world through the concepts of their own culture, or, to quote one of the members of our research team:

"It is curious that the central topic in our discussions changes according to the place where we come together; if we are in Germany the main topic is the 'state', in the Netherlands we always talk about the intermediary structure of society and when we arrive in the UK the market pops up as the central topic of discussion."

The danger of applying these culturally specific concepts to explain social processes in other countries might be the lost of the original context. It is precisely because societies across the world are infinitely varied that the use of universal concepts is inefficient to understand and explain what is going on in these different societies. On the other hand, the second method also runs into the risk of 'ethnocentrism': researchers that have a close relationship with the subject culture have the tend to "overemphasize their peculiarities, with the result that these writings deal more with the specificity of the culture than with comparisons" (Dogan and Pelassy, 1984: 9). Every researcher who has ever been involved in an international group of scientists is familiar with these impassioned contributions about the 'peculiarity' and 'uniqueness' of their own country. One way to escape from these two risks of ethnocentricity is to combine the two strategies. On the one side, relatively autonomous researchers who know their own society and use methods and concepts that make sense for those societies. On the other, both an organisational coordination and some kind of 'neutral conceptualisation' of the research question. This is the model we have followed in our research project: we discussed the general theoretical frame-work and concepts in a number of project meetings in Germany and the Netherlands, but the different national teams have followed their own research strategy within this overall frame-work. This has resulted in 'country-specific' research strategies which in a sense also reflect the national political-economic system. In our concluding chapter we have tried to bring together these different case-studies within the general logical framework of the dialectics of work and welfare.

Notes

1   According to its Convention the OECD - set up in 1961 - aims to promote the highest sustainable economic growth and employment and a rising standard of living in member countries. The original members were the West European countries and the United States. Japan, Australia and New Zealand became members through accession in later years (1964-1973).

2   VUT is a particular pre-retirement scheme in the Netherlands and has been used as a very popular pathway by both employers, workers and the state. The very broad use of this instrument - next to other pathways - explains the extreme pattern of externalisation in the Dutch case (*see* chapter 3 in this volume). SHUKKO, is a means used by large Japanese firms to replace (older) workers in their satellite firms. It can be seen as a particular way to keep (older) workers within the large-firm constellation (chapter 6).

3   Saetren (1985) has raised this point, the lack of focus on the subsystemic, intermediate level in many comparative policy studies.

4   On several places we also have used the term *internalisation* instead of integration. In some disciplines these term may express different things. In our project we use the terms interchangeable.

5   In most industrialised welfare states the 'normal' age of retirement is 65. Although this is not the case in every industralised country. Some countries have a lower (or higher) age of retirement for the whole working population, or for a specific segment of the working population (women, certain occupational groups, etc.). In order to facilitate comparison between countries, though, we stick to the common denominator of 65.

6   These different policy systems might not only differ between countries, but can also differ with respect to particular groups on the labour market (women, men, various age groups, migrants, etc.).

7   Cf. Abegglen and Stalk, 1985; Kern and Schumann, 1984; Monden, 1983; Piore and Sabel, 1984; Womack, 1990.

References

Abegglen, James C. and George Stalk (1985). *Kaisha, the Japanese Corporation*. New York: Basic Books.

Dahrendorf, Ralf (1988). *The Modern Social Conflict. An Essay on the Politics of Liberty*. London: Weidenfeld and Nicolson.

Dogan, Mattei and Dominique Pelassy (1984). *How to Compare Nations. Strategies in Comparative Politics*. Chatham, New Jersey: Chatham House Publishers.

Esping-Andersen, Gösta (1990). *The Three Worlds of Welfare Capitalism*. Princeton: Princeton University Press.

Field, Mark G. (ed.)(1989). *Success and Crisis in National Health Systems: A Comparative Approach*. New York: Routledge.

Friedman, Lawrence M. (1984). *Your Time Will Come: The Law of Age Discrimination and Mandatory Retirement*, New York: Russell Sage Foundation.

Friedman, Lawrence M. (1985). *Total Justice*. New York: Russell Sage Foundation.

Heilbroner, Robert (1985). *The Act of Work*. Washington: Library of Congress.

Kern, Horst and Michael Schumann (1984). *Das Ende der Arbeitsteilung? Rationalisierung in der industriellen Produktion: Bestandsaufnahme, Trendbestimmung*. München: Beck.

Kohli, Martin; Rein, Martin; Guillemard, Anne-Marie and Herman van Gunsteren (eds.) (1991). *Time for Retirement. Comparative Studies of Early Exit from the Labor Force*. Cambridge: Cambridge University Press.

Kohli, Martin and Martin Rein (1991). *The Changing Balance of Work and Retirement*. In: Martin Kohli et. al.: 1–35.

Monden, Y. (1983). *Toyota Production System*. Atlanta: Institute of Industrial Engineers.

Piore, Michael J. and Charles F. Sabel (1984). *The Second Industrial Divide: Possibilities for Prosperity*. New York: Basic Books.

Prins, Rienk (1990). *Sickness Absence in Belgium, Germany and the Netherlands. A Comparative Study*. NIA (dissertation).

Przeworski, A. and H. Teune (1970). *The Logic of Comparative Social Inquiry*. New York: Wiley.

Saetren, Haral (1985). *Comparative Public Policies: Some Methodological and Theoretical Notes from a Scandinavian Research Project*. In: *European Journal of Political Research* 13 (2): 227–234.

Samuels, Richard J. (1987). *The Business of the Japanese State: Energy Markets in Comparative and Historical Perspective*. Ithaca: Cornell University Press.

Williamson, Peter J. (1989). *Corporatism in Perspective*. London: Sage.

Womack, J.P. (1990). *The Machine that Changed the World*. New York: Rawson.

2 Early Retirement: Stability, Reversal, or Redefinition

Klaus Jacobs and Martin Rein

This essay concerns the decline of employment of men 55 to 64. This trend is one of the most dramatic economic transformations of labor markets and modern industrial economies. Whereas about 90 or more percent of men work in their prime years, in 1988 only about 50 to 60 percent of nonagricultural male workers were in employment. This decline in the employment of older men is widely believed to have signaled a new phenomenon, 'early retirement'. In an effort to understand this phenomenon, we examine past trends, identify the main national patterns of early exit, explore the industries in which age concentration occurs, and, finally, we review the competing meanings and possible future of early retirement.

1   The Significance of Early Retirement

There are good theoretical reasons for studying the phenomenon of early exit from the labor market of older workers aside from the obvious cost

implications for the level of welfare state spending.[1] The most important
reason is that it provides a window for understanding the way in which
social policy and labor markets interact. To explore this theme we locate
our analysis in a historical context of the idea of 'social wages'.[2] In the 1940s
analysts criticized the model of a labor market generating an original
distribution of income and social protection serving as a mechanism for
redistribution. These early analysts developed the theory of a 'social wage'
to show that social policy had entered into the market wage through a
system of transfers which supplemented wages in the form of fringe benefits
and reduced consumption expenditures in the form of price subsidies. They
argued that any measure of real wages must be based on total compensation
where earnings are combined with transfers and the variety of price subsidies that reduce the cost of the consumption of items such as medical care,
child care, housing, etc. According to this framework, the conventional
theory of redistribution as comprising original income, transfer income in
the form of social protection, and a redistribution of original market income
is misleading. Social policy does not redistribute original income, but is an
essential component of it. Viewed in this way, the system of social protection reinforces market incentives. While the idea of the social wage was
widely accepted, the conventional model of original market income and
redistribution through transfers continues to dominate intellectual thinking
about social policy.

The phenomenon of early retirement provides yet another window through
which to examine the close interdependence of social policy and markets.
Early retirement can be understood as a social invention by firms to use the
available social and public infrastructure to induce older workers to leave
work to enable firms to restructure their work force. The repertoire of firm
strategies varies from the use of supplements of the social infrastructure of
the state to substitutes where firm resources replace public programs. In
this view, the firm becomes a key actor in understanding the history of the
evolution of the welfare state. To our knowledge the history of the welfare
state has not systematically examined the interrelationship between the
state and the firm. This assertion does not deny the considerable historical
interest in welfare capitalism as a precursor to the welfare state. Our
argument is that the social policy of the firm continues to be an important
tool in industrial restructuring even in mature welfare states. It permits the
firm to undertake industrial restructuring in a 'bloodless' way, i.e., with
reduced industrial conflict.

Research on early retirement can provide the complementary rather than
antagonistic relationship between social policy and labor markets. Moreover, it is also especially important in trying to understand the evolution of
early retirement. The future will very much depend on whether the firm will
acquiesce to state initiatives to reduce early retirement, or whether the firm

will develop its own autonomous social policy and continue the trend. To grasp the future directions of the early exit of older male workers from employment we need to understand the complicated interplay between firm and state. The state's perspective is focused on 'can't afford' arguments about the cost of public social protection programs. The concern of the firm is about the impact of aging on average productivity levels and the aggregate wage bill.

The subject is also interesting for another reason. When we started our study of early exit, we recognized that retirement could not be limited to entry into the pension system of the welfare state. A broader concept of social policy was needed. We developed the concept of 'pathways' to retirement. A pathway comprised the creative packaging of unemployment, disability, sickness, means testing, welfare benefits, and other public and private income support programs as transitions into the public pension system (Kohli et al., 1991). Early exit, from the perspective of the labor market, represents a significant restructuring of the age, wage, and skill composition of the work force. Thus market and social policy issues were closely intertwined. In addition, changes in these processes also had a ripple effect on the tripartite division of the life course into a period of preparation for work, a working life, and retirement after complete exit from work.

These three interconnected perspectives: social policy (and especially the relationship between the state and firm), labor markets, and the organization of the individual life course are important if we are to understand the future evolution of both state and firm policies. Changes in one of these fields have direct and indirect impact on the others.

This framework helps us deal with the controversy that the emergence of the phenomenon of early retirement has created. Should the trend to early retirement actively be reversed by public policy? The answer looks different depending on the perspective we adopt. Early exit provides labor market flexibility, but it can financially overload the public social security system and create uncertainty about the organization of the life course.

We begin our analysis with a review of aggregate male labor force trends by age. We then disaggregate the data in terms of unemployment, part-time work, self-employment, and sectoral employment of men 55 to 65 years of age.[3] We focus on the labor market experience of men rather than women, despite the fact that there is evidence that a similar decline in the labor force of females is also occurring. In the case of women, however, there are different overlapping trends of both early exit from work at the end of the life course and growing entry in the prime years. The number of married women in the labor force has continued to rise in most countries. Whereas most men work for most of their lives, the labor force participation of women varies quite sharply across countries from a low of about a third in the Netherlands to over 80 percent in Sweden. In addition, the meaning of early retirement for men who, more or less, work continuously over their life course is different from women, many of whom leave work after child bearing and reenter later in the life course. From cross-sectional data it is often difficult to isolate those women who have remained outside of work in the years immediately preceding retirement and the low labor force participation of older women. It is also the case that women hold a different position in the labor market. In virtually all countries they are segmented in a limited number of occupations, and, in some countries such as Japan, are actively excluded from core lifetime jobs. There are, therefore, both technical and substantive reasons for treating women separately. The importance of studying women is not at issue, but, given the limitations of our data, we have elected in this overview to limit our analysis to the position of older men. Elsewhere we have documented these trends for both men and women and have described in great detail the evolution of labor force participation of older men (Kohli et al., 1991).

2   Labor Force Trends of Men 55 to 64.

If we look at the labor force participation of men 60 to 64 in 1990, we find very sharp divergence across countries with France and the Netherlands having less than a quarter of men in this age group in the labor force compared to Japan with almost three-quarters. Equally so, the rate of decline from 1970 to 1990 ranged from almost 70 percent in the Netherlands and France, to about 10 percent in Japan, and 20 to 25 percent in Sweden and the United States. In interpreting these rates of change, we need to pay attention to the differences at the beginning period in the labor force participation rates. The United Kingdom started at a much higher rate than the United States, and its rate of decline was sharper than that of the United States; but by 1990 the labor force participation between the two countries was quite similar, about 55 percent. Surprisingly, the United States had about the same labor force participation of men 60 to 64 in 1970 as Germany[4] and an even lower labor force participation rate than the Netherlands. These findings reinforce the need to take into account the levels at the base year when interpreting the rates of change.

When we examine the patterns of change in the 1970s and in the early and late 1980s, we see that in some countries the decrease was more pronounced in the 1970s than in the first part of the 1980s. This occurred in Sweden and the United States and, at a somewhat higher rate of change, in Germany. In other countries, it was the early 1980s that produced higher declines than those of the 1970s as in France, the Netherlands, the United Kingdom, and, to a lesser extent, in Japan.

The pattern between 1985 and 1990 shows that, with the exceptions of the

Table 1: Labor Force Participation Rates of Older Men below the "Normal" Retirement Age of 65; 1970−1990 in Seven Western Countries

Country	Age	1970	1980	1985	1990	Percent Change			
						70−90	70−80	80−85	85−90
Japan	60−64	81.5	77.8	72.5	72.9	−10.6	−4.5	−6.8	0.6
	55−59	91.2	91.2	90.3	92.1	+1.0	0.0	−1.0	2.0
Sweden	60−64	79.5	69.0	65.1	63.2	−20.5	−13.2	−5.7	−2.9
	55−59	90.8	87.7	87.6	87.7	−3.4	−3.4	−0.1	0.1
U.S.A.	60−64	71.7	59.8	55.1	54.9	−23.4	−16.6	−7.9	−0.4
	55−59	88.3	80.9	78.9	79.1	−10.4	−8.4	−2.5	0.3
U.K.	60−64	86.7	71.2	55.4	54.4	−37.3	−17.9	−22.2	−1.8
	55−59	95.3	90.1	82.2	81.0	−15.0	−5.5	−8.8	−1.5
Germany[a]	60−64	69.5	44.2	33.0	34.2[b]	−50.8	−36.4	−25.3	+3.6
	55−59	87.8	82.3	79.1	78.6[b]	−10.5	−6.3	−3.9	−0.6
France	60−64	68.0	47.6	30.8	22.7	−66.6	−30.0	−35.3	−26.3
	55−59	82.9	80.9	67.8	67.7	−18.3	−2.4	16.2	−0.1
Netherlands	60−64	73.7[c]	48.8	27.8	22.7	−69.2	−33.8	−43.0	−18.3
	55−59	86.6[c]	74.8	64.8	66.3	−23.4	−13.6	−13.4	2.3

Source: OECD Labour Force Statistics, Paris 1991; for Germany: Statistisches Bundesamt (Mikrozensus)
(a) West Germany (for 1990: the former West Germany)
(b) 1989
(c) 1971

Netherlands and France, the decline in the pattern of exit of men 60 to 64 was either reduced, stabilized, or slightly reversed. Of course, in no country has there been a dramatic reversal, returning the rate to the level it had reached in the early 1970s. Using labor force data for the United States by single years of age and examining long-run trends since 1968, Quinn concludes that "the trend toward earlier retirement may have stopped or perhaps even reversed. (...) For 8 of 10 ages (he tested) over age 61, participation rates are higher now than they were 5 years ago" (Quinn, 1993). Considerable caution is required in interpreting these data because these labor force estimates are continually revised by OECD as new information becomes available. It is not unusual to see significant changes in these rates as more recent and reliable data are made available. (*See* table 1 for a description of these findings.)

The pattern for men age 55 to 59 is somewhat different. For example, there has been virtually no decline in the labor force participation of men in this age group in Japan and almost none in Sweden. In the remaining countries the decline ranged from about 10 percent in the United States and Germany to almost a quarter in the Netherlands. In France and in the Netherlands one in three men age 55 to 59 is out of the labor force. Thus, we see evidence of an extension of the early exit pattern of men into the 55 to 59 age group, but the trend is much less pronounced than for those 60 to 64.

3   Disaggregating the Trends

One major interpretation of the decline of the labor force of older men is the growth of unemployment and structural change which pushed the older worker out of the core of wage and salary jobs. There is, however, as table 1 shows, considerable range in labor force participation of older men, from a little over a fifth in the Netherlands and France to almost three-quarters in Japan. Since the range is so wide between 'high early exit' and 'low early exit' countries, one might think that the pattern of expulsion of wage and salary workers is not a general phenomenon. This conclusion is premature. Labor force data do not permit us to address this question because it also includes the agricultural sector of the economy which is not overwhelmingly dominated by wage and salary workers and is driven by rather different processes of decline and restructuring from those in the manufacturing and the service sectors. In addition, table 1 includes information about those who are unemployed, self-employed, and those men who work part time. To disaggregate the labor force data reported in table 1, we start by examining the role of unemployment among older men.

4   Unemployment

The meaning of the unemployment of the elderly varies across countries. In many European countries, unemployment is a step in a well-defined pathway to early retirement. This is very clear in countries like Germany where a period of unemployment is a necessary pre-condition for early entry into the pension system. In these countries, therefore, those registered as unemployed people are clearly on a pathway to final exit from work, and re-entry is extremely unlikely. The 'unemployment' of older workers is not really unemployment interpreted as a period of transition in the loss of one job and the search for another. In countries where the duration of full unemployment benefits available for older men is about two-and-a-half years, as in Germany, and five years, as in France, it seems more appropriate to view unemployment as a step toward retirement. That the unemployment rate of older workers is not really a true measure of unemployment is also revealed

Tab. 2: Employment Activity Rates, Including and Excluding Agriculture.
The Importance of Agricultural Employment for Men;
in 1985, in Seven Western Countries

Country	Age	% Agriculture of Total Male Employment		Employment Activity Rate	
				Including Agriculture	Excluding Agriculture
Japan	60−64	26.0	(17.5)	67.4	49.9
	55−59	15.5		86.6	73.3
	15−64	6.8		81.0	75.5
Sweden	60−64[a]	12.0	(7.4)	61.7	54.3
	55−59[a]	9.7		85.6	77.3
	16−64[a]	7.1		83.5	77.6
U.S.A.	60−64	6.8		52.7	49.1
	55−59	4.6		75.5	72.0
	15−64	4.2		79.0	75.6
U.K.	60−64	4.5		49.6	47.4
	55−59	4.0		67.8	65.1
	15−64	3.1		73.5	71.3
Germany	60−64	13.5		29.8	25.8
	55−59	7.0		68.0	63.2
	15−64	4.5		73.9	70.6
France	60−64	34.5	(10.1)	29.4	19.3
	55−59	21.8		62.6	49.0
	15−64	9.0		71.3	64.9
Netherlands	60−64	17.7		26.7	22.0
	55−59	9.0		60.4	54.9
	15−64	6.4		65.4	61.2

Sources: Percent Agriculture: Census Data in Japan, Sweden;
EUROSTAT for France, Germany, the Netherlands, and the UK;
Employment Activity Rates: our own Calculations Based on OECD Data.
(a) 1980   CPS Data for the U.S.

by the variety of rule changes introduced to treat older workers as a special group. In some countries (France, Germany, the Netherlands, Britain), it was necessary for older workers to register as unemployed in order to receive unemployment insurance. This policy was later reversed. The unemployment trends are therefore a poor index of the real rate of unemployment of older men. In addition, as the maximum period for receiving unemployment insurance has been extended, entry into the unemployment pathway has led to retirement at an ever younger age. Changes in unemployment rules help account for the declining employment of men 55 to 59 in these countries. The meaning of unemployment in countries like the United States and Japan is different. In these countries the unemployment of an older worker does not necessarily imply that the worker is unlikely to return to work, and we do not find rule changes extending the duration of unemployment benefits only for older workers.

To improve our measure, we report the employment activity rate for 1985 in table 2, column 2. This measure includes only those individuals who are employed rather than the broader concept of labor force participant rates which include both those who are employed and those looking for work. By definition, the employment activity rate is lower than the labor force participation rate. We find that the range of experience in the countries we report is narrowed from 28 to 73 percent by the measure of labor force participation, to 27 to 67 percent when using employment activity rates.

To explore recent trends in employment activity rates, we did a special analysis of Eurostat data for Germany, France, the Netherlands, and the United Kingdom between 1983 and 1989 and compared these results with OECD data. We report in table 3 employment activity rates rather than labor force rates. The new data from Eurostat show that there is no evidence that early retirement in Europe has stopped or has been reversed as is the case in the United States. All four countries showed a clear decline in employment activity rates for men 60 to 64 ranging from 3 to 13 percentage points. The decline was from 39 percent to 33 percent in Germany; 27 percent to 19 percent in France; and 34 percent to 22 percent in the Netherlands. Only in Britain was the decline relatively small, dropping from 52 percent to 49 percent. In this age group, note the large discrepancy between Eurostat and OECD data for Britain and Holland. Employment activity rates for men 55 to 59 also declined in all four countries, but at a somewhat slower rate.

The German data is particularly important. OECD no longer reports German data due to a break in the time series; therefore, recent trends beyond 1987 cannot be analyzed. The Eurostat data for Germany, however, shows a picture of a continuing decline in the employment accounting of men in their late 50s as well as late 60s. Data from the German Mikrocensus also shows the same trend. A more careful analysis separating out employment and population shows that both population and employment increased only in Germany. There the population of men 60 to 64 increased by 24 percent and employment by 3 percent. The decline in the employment rate is therefore more due to a demographic change having to do with the increase in birth rates after World War I than with the trend to early retirement. The reason is not that in 1989 the cohort of 60 to 64 year old males (born between 1925 and 1930) is very large, but that the 1983 cohort (born between 1919 and 1924) is relatively small due to the casualty rates

Table 3: A Comparison of Changes in Male Employment Activity Rates between 1983 and 1989

	Germany		France		Netherlands		Great Britain	
	60 − 64	55 − 59	60 − 64	55 − 59	60 − 64	55 − 59	60 − 64	55 − 59
Eurostat								
1983	38.9	79.0	27.1	60.0	34.3	64.2	51.9	74.8
1989	32.5	72.5	18.5	56.3	21.8	61.9	49.1	72.2
Change	− 6.4	− 6.5	− 8.6	− 3.7	− 12.5	− 2.3	− 2.8	− 2.6
OECD								
1983	38.3	77.1	32.2	66.3	28.1	62.2	51.9	71.4
1989	−	−	23.2	62.5	23.5	61.6	51.2	68.1
Change			− 9.0	− 3.8	− 4.6	− 0.6	− 0.7	− 3.3

Source: Unpublished Eurostat Data
OECD Labor Force Data

inflicted on German men in World War II. You can see this if you compare the size of the male population with that of the female population. In 1983 for the age group 60 to 64, the male population is only about two-thirds of the female population (1.286 to 1.870), while in 1989 the proportion is 82 percent.

5 Agricultural Employment

We know that those people who work in agriculture are more likely to stay in the labor market than other groups. If the agricultural sector of older workers declines, this will have a ripple effect on the future employment activity rate of older men. These changes can affect the future pattern of early exit. The decline of agriculture in many of the countries is another factor which needs to be taken into account in understanding the future of early retirement. We need to separate structural change in the wage and salary sector from the equally dramatic transformation of the agricultural sector. Both of these changes affect the phenomenon of early exit.

A very different process of exit occurs in the agricultural sector. The restructuring that occurs in services and manufacturing leads to declining employment shares of older workers, but in agriculture the process is reversed. Older workers are more likely to be retained. Moreover, the process of restructuring agriculture has already occurred and is largely complete in most countries, while in most countries industrial restructuring is still going on. We therefore expect to find that agriculture accounts for a relatively high proportion of older male employment.

Table 2 also provides information on the impact that the exclusion of agriculture has on our understanding of employment activity rates. We report data for 1985, which is the most recent year that comparative data by age in the agricultural sector is available. In some countries, namely Japan and France, the agricultural sector accounts for between 26 and 35 percent of total employment of men 60 to 64 as compared with only from 5 to 14 percent in Sweden, the United Kingdom, the United States, and Germany. The Netherlands is still a high agricultural-intensive country for the employment of older workers. What is equally striking in this table is that in virtually all the countries, the percentage of employment in agriculture of men 55 to 59 is lower than the proportion of men 60 to 64. The difference is especially striking in those countries where the employment participation rate in agriculture of men 60 to 64 is very high.

When we look at the younger age group of men 55 to 59 years of age, a somewhat different pattern emerges. In France and the Netherlands we find that only half of all older men are employed in the civilian nonagricultural sector of the economy as compared with a range of from two-thirds to three-quarters in the other countries.

The exclusion of agriculture has a dramatic effect on the range of employment activity rates across our countries. Japan is no longer an outlier. Indeed, the employment rates, excluding agriculture, in the United Kingdom, the United States, Japan, and Sweden, converge within the surprisingly narrow range of 47 to 54 percent. Moreover, the difference between this group of countries and France, the Netherlands, and Germany is even more striking. Excluding agriculture, the range of the participation rate of men 60 to 64 in these European countries is only between 19 and 26 percent.

What emerges from the exclusion of agriculture is the narrowing of the range and the sharpening of two patterns of country experience in terms of the level of employment of older men.

6   Self-Employment

The same logic which leads us to exclude agriculture applies when we shift our focus from the sectors of the economy to the status of employment, i.e., wage and salary workers and the self-employed. Self-employment of older workers is governed by a different process and dynamic than employment of older workers in wage and salary positions. The self-employed in most countries are not automatically blanketed into the basic public pension system. Moreover, the rules governing access and benefit levels for unemployment, disability, and retirement differ for the self-employed and wage and salary workers. These measures affect the process of early retirement.

Table 4: Composition of the Labor Force of Older Men; 1989 in Seven Western Countries

Country	Age	Labor Force Participation (% of Population)	Unemployment Rate (% of Labor Force)	Self-Employment Rate (% of All Employed)	Part-Time Work Rate (% of Wage/ Salary Earners)
Japan	60–64	71.4	5.9	37.8	4.3
	55–59	91.6	2.6	26.3	1.3
Sweden	60–64	62.7	1.7	20.6	30.7[a]
	55–59	87.1	0.8	16.2	6.5[a]
USA	60–64	54.2	3.3	19.3	18.8[b]
	55–59	78.8	3.5	15.7	10.7[b]
UK	60–64	53.5	4.3	19.8	8.1
	55–59	77.4	12.1	20.1	2.9
Germany	60–64	34.2	6.4[c]	30.9	3.9
	55–59	78.6	9.0[c]	17.6	1.4
France	60–64	24.1	3.7	48.3	9.8
	55–59	68.0	8.1	33.8	5.8
Nether-lands	60–64	24.5	3.8	36.9	25.9
	55–59	65.3	5.6	17.5	15.2

Sources: Labor Force Participation Rates and Unemployment Rates:
OECD Labor Force Statistics, Paris 1991 (Women Labor Force Participation Rates Given by Statistisches Bundesamt (Mikrocensus).
Self Employment and Part-Time Rates: Own Calculations Based on Labor Force Survey (Japan), Labor Force Survey (Sweden).
Current Population Survey (USA), EUROSTAT (France, Germany, Netherlands, UK)
(a) % of all Employed Men (Including Self-Employed)
(b) % of Persons at Work in Nonagriculatural Industries
(c) 1987

We know, for example, that self-employed workers are more likely to continue at work as they age compared to wage and salary earners. This is, no doubt, in some measure related to the institutional pathways available to the wage and salary earners for exit.

But even more striking than the institutional rules with differences about entitlement to systems of social protection is that wage and salary workers enter into a contract with an employer which specifies among other things, the duration of their employment. In many European countries, there is a mandatory retirement age. For example, professors are expected to retire at age 65. A self-employed person is not bound, however, by such contracts and can continue to work as long as he chooses. This is an important factor accounting for the difference in the exit rates of the self-employed compared to wage and salary workers.

In table 4, we examine self-employment rates by age and show that they vary from about a fifth of total male employment for men 60 to 64 in the United States, the United Kingdom, and Sweden to almost a half in France. There is some correspondence between these self-employment rates and agricultural employment in countries where agriculture is important because the majority of men in agriculture tends to be self-employed.

How can we interpret why self-employment is so high for older people? As Quinn suggests, one interpretation is the so-called cohort effect where older men began their careers when self-employment was much more common than it is today (Quinn, Burkhauser and Myers, 1990). In virtually all these countries, self-employment is a declining status of employment, and older workers are over represented as compared to younger cohorts.

The second interpretation is that older workers stay longer in self-employment for a number of institutional reasons. For example, there is no mandatory retirement which forces the self-employed to exit from work because they have no labor contract with their employers. Anti-age discrimination legislation is common only in the United States. Mandatory retirement is more common in other countries.

Another interpretation discussed earlier is that there are many institutional mechanisms which provide exit routes from employment for wage and salary workers which are not customarily available for the self-employed. With fewer pathways for early exit open to them, they tend to remain self-employed.

Finally, and most interesting for our purposes, self-employment may be seen as a way of continuing work after leaving a wage and salary position. Sometimes this transition is made in combination with receipt of a private or public pension. Self-employment becomes a way of bridging jobs between work and retirement. This can occur if a person is laid off or fired from his career job and, because of the difficulty of finding opportunities for re-entering work, moves into self-employment. Because we have access only to cross-sectional data, it is difficult to disentangle which of these processes actually occurs.

While the self-employment rates of older men are high and range widely across our countries, we need to exercise more than a fair measure of caution in interpreting their contributions to the employment of all older men. One reason for caution is that the number of all persons employed, i.e., the denominator of the self-employment rate, varies considerably across countries. As shown in table 4, the highest self-employment rates of older men 60 to 64 are found in France, Japan, the Netherlands, and Germany where the employment rates vary from about 48 to 31 percent.

If we relate the number of self-employed to the total population in the

Table 5: Labor Force Participation of Older Men; 1989 in Seven Western Countries

Country	Age	Percent of Population					
		Wage/Salary Earners		Self-Employed	Unemployed Labor	Not in Force	
		Full-Time	Part-Time				
Japan	60 – 64	40.0	1.8	25.4	4.2	28.6	100.0
	55 – 59	64.8	0.9	23.5	2.4	8.4	100.0
Sweden[a]	60 – 64	33.9	15.0	12.7	1.1	37.3	100.0
	55 – 59	67.7	4.7	14.0	0.7	12.9	100.0
USA	60 – 64	34.2	8.0	10.1	1.8	45.8	99.9
	55 – 59	57.2	6.9	11.9	2.8	21.2	100.0
UK	60 – 64	37.8	3.3	10.1	2.3	46.5	100.0
	55 – 59	52.7	1.6	13.7	9.4	22.6	100.0
Germany	60 – 64	21.2	0.9	9.9	2.2	65.8	100.0
	55 – 59	58.1	0.8	12.6	7.1	21.4	100.0
France	60 – 64	10.8	1.2	11.2	0.9	75.9	100.0
	55 – 59	39.0	2.4	21.1	5.5	32.0	100.0
Netherlands	60 – 64	11.0	3.9	8.7	0.9	75.5	100.0
	55 – 59	43.1	7.7	10.8	3.7	34.7	100.0

Source: Our Calculations Based on Rates in Table 4.
(a) Under the Assumption that Part-Time Rate for all Employed (Including Self-Employed) is also Valid for Wage and Salary Earners.

age group, rather than to the employed population, we get a different understanding of the underlying processes. In table 5, we find that only in Japan does self-employment account for as much as a quarter of the employment of the total population of men 60 to 64. In all of the other countries, regardless of the differences in the rates, the share of self-employed people in the population is strikingly similar, moving within a very narrow range of 9 to 13 percent, and considerably lower than in Japan.

When we look at differences in self-employment by age, we find that, aside from Japan, the share of self-employment is higher in the younger age group 55 to 59. These findings are suggestive. Perhaps they indicate that both the cohort and the bridging argument may be less important than the earlier discussion suggests.

7   Wage and Salary Earners: Full and Part Time

Now we turn to the hard core of the wage and salary earners. As we stated above, this is the group toward which most theories about the declining labor force participation of older workers are usually directed. What emerges from this analysis is a clear dichotomy between two groups of countries – between 41 and 49 percent of the male population 60 to 64 in the United Kingdom, Japan, the United States, and Sweden, and, by contrast, employment rates of only 22 percent in Germany, 15 percent in the Netherlands, and 12 percent in France.

But even within the wage and salary group there are significant subgroups that already show signs of beginning the process of early exit, and these signals are especially common in some countries where the size of the wage and salary employment is still relatively large. The process of early exit may already begin when individuals change their career job and accept a 'bridging job' by changing their work status, the industrial sector in which they are employed, or reduce the number of hours they work, or the earnings they receive.

8   Part-Time Wage Work

Table 4 provides the information on employment activity rates for work for older male wage and salary earners. Part-time employment is particularly striking in Sweden, where over 30 percent of men 60 to 64 work part time. The United States also has high rates of part-time work. In 1987, almost 19 percent of males 60 to 64 work part time; however, about 14 percent of male wage and salary workers age 60 to 61 worked part time in the week of the survey compared to 24.2 percent of men 62 to 64.[5] Older male workers in the United States can retire at age 62 with an economic penalty. Disaggregating part-time employment by age shows that gradual exit is almost as important for some age groups in the United States as it is in Sweden. These numbers reflect the role that welfare state policy plays in creating part-time employment both in Sweden and the United States.

All of the other countries show low rates of part-time employment for men with the exception of the Netherlands. What is distinctive about the Netherlands is a large proportion of all men appear to work part time. It is therefore not surprising that older men also would work part time. We suspect these high part-time employment rates in the Netherlands are a statistical artifact rather than the emergence of a true part-time pattern of employment.[6]

In summary, we find that the proportion of wage and salary workers working part time differs among the countries. It is particularly high in

Sweden and the United States and much lower in all of the other countries. The Netherlands is an anomaly for which we have no institutional interpretation.

9   Patterns of Early Retirement

When we limit our analysis only to employed wage and salary workers, we find two quite distinct patterns. In the Continental countries of Germany, France, and the Netherlands, men move from full-time work to full-time retirement.[7] This means that there is, by and large, no partial exit or re-entry into employment at some later period of time. We call this pattern 'exit is exit' because it graphically illustrates that once a man leaves work, his opportunity to re-enter work is virtually non-existent.

What about the remaining countries where there is a much higher employment activity rate among wage and salary workers? What these countries share in common is that at least a substantial minority of older men combine work and retirement, or have their work redefined so that the job itself signals the beginning of a retirement process. But the different methods of how work and retirement are combined are quite varied. Here we want to call attention to the different processes that produce a similar outcome. In fact, we can distinguish three patterns, each based on a different logic. To describe these patterns we draw on information from sources other than the statistical series reported earlier. We will comment both on the principle on which each pattern rests and, when available, the actual practice which may diverge from the principle. We don't have enough data about the United Kingdom to classify its principles or practices. We suspect it is a hybrid form.

10   Sweden: Partial Retirement

In Sweden, the relatively high proportion of employment for older workers in wage and salary positions is created by a system of partial pension arrangements which permits an individual to get roughly about 75 percent or more of his previous earnings while working only half the number of hours. This system is both ambitious and costly. We can see from the evolution of its history how the development of a reduction in the level of benefits had an immediate impact on take-up rates. Understanding the practice of partial exit is clearly more complicated because when the higher benefit levels were restored only the cost of the program continued to rise, while the participation rates did not return to their previous high level.

Sweden is, of course, unique among other countries who have also tried to implement the Swedish system of partial retirement. But the system apparently seems to work only in Sweden where one finds a very strong commitment to the right to work which extends also to older men and even to those who are partially disabled and cannot find a job because of labor market conditions. There have been some changes, however, in this regard since the elimination of partial disability due to work-related conditions in 1990.

What is distinctive in the Swedish system of partial pensions is that individuals stay on their same job, and the employer reconstitutes it from a full-time to a part-time position. In this scheme there is an institutional commitment on the part of the employer to continue hiring the older worker and on the part of the state to create a special program to buffer the loss of income from a reduction in hours worked and earnings. As a result, we find that almost a third of all men 60 to 64 work part time in Sweden. While part-time employment for men 60 to 62 is high in the United States, there is no institutional commitment to find partial work. The responsibility to find part-time work falls on the individual and is not an obligation of the firm. We do not see a similar pattern and level of partial retirement in any other country.

For example, while Sweden and the United States are quite similar with respect to their still relatively high employment rates of older men, they differ strongly in terms of the 'society responsibility' for the exit process (and its consequences on the meaning of early retirement for the individual). In this matter Sweden has much more in common with Germany, although the institutional framing of the exit process is very different (gradual retirement and an emphasis on the 'right to work' in Sweden versus complete early exit as a well-earned entitlement in Germany).

11   Japan: Re-Employment

What distinguishes the Japanese pattern? Whereas the Swedish system emphasizes a change in the hours of work but a continuity of type of work, the Japanese system emphasizes a change in the status of work and a change in earnings. At a given age of termination of employment called the "teinen" age, at one time age 55 and later raised to age 60, virtually all wage and salary workers are expected to terminate their contracts with the firm. Rebick has shown that the "teinen" age arrangements increasingly apply to small as well as large firms. We conclude that most workers are covered by this arrangement. Workers are either reemployed by the firm, or are placed out to another affiliate or daughter firm. There are a variety of different levels that the parent firm can be involved in arranging for this placement. In general, the more the parent firm is involved, the better off the worker is economically. This system of out placement is known as "tienseki". It is sometimes also referred to as one-way "shukko" to distinguish it from the system of transfer while the worker is expected to return to the parent company (Rebick, 1993).

The core idea underpinning the Japanese system is the obligation of the firm to continue employment of workers on a full-time basis, but at lower earnings which can be supplemented with a public or private pension arrangement. In this sense the Japanese approach is similar to that of Sweden where firms have a social obligation to reemploy individuals, so the transition is an institutionally established principle and not merely an ad hoc arrangement where the initiative falls on the individual alone. This national pattern is by no means static, and many changes are observable within the framework of this system. For example, the "tienseki" system of transferring individuals was initially done largely for persons before they retired, but increasingly is used after the "teinen" age is reached as well. Perhaps even more striking is the growing proportion of unemployed individuals who are forced to find reemployment on their own initiative.

12   The United States: Multiple Options

The distinguishing characteristic of the American system is to support a variety of options that individuals can pursue on their own. There are at least two institutions which reinforce the support of these options. First, there is the public social security system which by its nature is designed to provide only a floor of social protection to prevent poverty and hardship. Unlike the European system, it is not designed by itself to promote for middle and higher income groups the continuity of lifestyles achieved before retirement. By and large, replacement rates compared to Europe are low, except for low-wage workers. Individuals need to supplement their public social security programs if they are to maintain their previous lifestyle. In fact, about half of all social security recipients rely on these benefits as their only source of retirement income.

The second institutional arrangement arises from legislation which eliminates mandatory retirement age and seeks to implement anti-age discrimination practice in firms. Of course, the legislation does not end age-linked hiring and firing, although it certainly reduces the extent to which age plays a role in this process. The point we want to stress here is that the existence of anti-age discrimination legislation works institutionally to support the range of individually chosen options.

The American system might, therefore, be described as follows. A majority of individuals follow the European pattern of 'exit is exit'. At some landmark point, close to the individual's birth date, individuals exit from the labor market and do not return. Many individuals supplement the minimum public pension with private pensions and savings so they are able to maintain their previous life styles by packaging pension arrangements and personal assets.

There is, however, a substantial minority of individuals who create ad hoc arrangements which work in different ways depending on the individual's situation. This generates a range of patterns rather than a definite national norm. The following variations are identifiable:

(a) Men move into other jobs that pay less and demand less of them. These are jobs characterized by easy entry and easy exit. This type of work has been referred to as bridging jobs (discussed below).
(b) Men remain in the same line of work or in the samefield, but diminish their investment in their career job. Of course, this can occur at any age; for example, the professor who stops writing after receiving tenure.
(c) Men gradually retire from work by acquiring a part-time position, which may be in their own field or, more typically, in a different industry or occupation.
(d) Men may reenter work after a period of retirement because the public and private pensions they received turn out to be inadequate to maintain the lifestyle they seek to maintain, or perhaps because the lack of work undermines their ability to realize a meaningful life, or for some combination of both financial and personal reasons.

Economists examining the Retirement History Survey in the United States have tried to reconstruct these different patterns. Quinn and Burkhauser followed men from 1969, when they were 58 to 63, until 1979. They showed that at least one quarter of wage and salary workers did not leave the labor market at the time they left their career jobs (Quinn, Burkhauser and Myers, 1990).

Based on these findings, Ruhm, Berkhauser and Quinn have developed the idea of a bridging job to describe the transition from full-time career jobs to complete retirement. These authors are critical of the view that the core idea of retirement is an abrupt process characterized by full withdrawal from paid work. A bridging job signals the onset of a 'job-stopping' process by older workers after they leave their primary career job.[8]

Ruhm in a recent study comparing the results of the Retirement History Survey in 1969 with the Harris Poll Survey in 1989 finds that in this 20-year period important differences have emerged. It looks as though people are retiring not only earlier, but more abruptly. This means that the period of bridge employment appears to be shorter. While the data are not conclusive, this new evidence of sudden retirement would appear to weaken the importance of bridging jobs in the exiting pattern of older men (Ruhm, 1992).

What can be deduced from these findings of the nature of work at the end of the working career? At the early phase of work, young workers search and eventually settle into a working career; at the last phase of the working life older workers search for a bridging job which permits them to gradually exit from work. One important difficulty with this concept, as noted from Ruhm, Quinn and Burkhauser's empirical study, is that about a third of the bridging jobs lead to upward income and status mobility. This masks two different processes: job advancement at the last stages of a career and the transition to retirement through reentry to a job with lower wages and/or fewer hours of work. The concept of a bridging job appears to have both theoretical and empirical difficulties.

The idea of bridging jobs for workers who are gradually exiting from work is, nevertheless, a provocative idea. If older workers start retirement gradually by redefining their job while they are still at work; if the process of job stopping is not random, but is concentrated in a limited number of industries; and if the process is as widespread as Ruhm, Quinn, and othershave suggested (despite Ruhm's more recent work), then we would expect to find a pattern of age-concentrated industries. There should be a disproportionately high share of older workers employed in a limited number of industries.

13   Age Concentration by Industry

If there are to a greater or lesser degree national policies and practices that affect the extent that work and the receipt of a pension are combined, then we would also expect to find different patterns of industry age concentrations in different countries. In the United States the evidence would seem to suggest that workers in a bridging job are likely to move out of the industry in which they were previously employed. If we assume that the kinds of industries that older workers could enter were not randomly distributed, then we might expect to find in these easy entry industries some pattern of age concentration. If, however, older workers stay in a declining industry, then their share of employment would increase because younger workers were not being hired. This, rather than mobility to a bridge job, brings about a change in the age composition of the industry. Unfortunately, from cross-sectional data we cannot distinguish movers from stayers and, therefore, cannot identify the process that produces age-concentrated industries.

In Sweden, by contrast, we would expect older workers to remain in the industries in which they were employed as they turn from full-time to part-time work. Here no systematic pattern of age concentration should emerge.

In studying this issue in the United States, Quinn finds no support for a pattern of age-concentrated industries. After examining whether the change in the industrial and occupational structure is related to the employment of older workers in these sectors, Quinn observes that a

"... comparison of these growth rates with the importance of elderly employment in these sectors, however, does not suggest that these compositional shifts have played a major role in the decline of older workers' labor force participation."

He goes on to say that

"... indeed the contrary is more nearly true. The most striking feature here is that ... the proportion of elderly across occupations (and industries) was remarkably similar ... there is simply not enough variation in elderly employment by industry to explain much. With the exception of agriculture, all the other industries have between 11 and 14 percent workers age 55 and over, and there is no apparent relationship between these growth rates and the modest differences in the percentage elderly, either recently or expected in the near future" (Quinn. 1993: 26-27).

Quinn, however, analyzed only 10 broad industry groupings. When we disaggregate industries at a 3-digit level and cross-classify these industries by sex and age, we reach a very different conclusion. The data reported are for the United States. We ranked industries by the share of employment of older workers 50 years of age and over. An age-concentrated industry employs a substantially greater share of all employed men aged 55 to 64 compared to its relative size, i.e., its share of total male employment. We set the cut-off point at 25 percent that an industry's share of older employed men has to exceed its share of male employment in order to be called "age concentrated". A low age-concentrated industry had 25 percent fewer older workers than its relative share of total male employment. We define three broad categories of age concentration. For the United States we find that almost a quarter of all industries are age concentrated. The industries employing older workers are reported in table 6 where we examined the age structure of the industry, the educational qualifications, the gender composition, part-time employment, earnings, relative position of male workers in the income distribution divided by quintiles. We find that almost a quarter of all industries are age concentrated. When we examine specific age-concentrated industries employing older workers, we see that 23 percent are located in social services (health education, and welfare), and 17 percent are in primary industries (agriculture, mining extraction, construction, etc.). In social services older men tend to work in industries that are largely female dominated.

These findings are provocative and not easily explainable. Even more surprising is that when we examine the age concentration of specific

Table 6: Selected Characteristics of Workers in Age-Concentrated Industries (United States) (Proportion of Workers Ages 50+ is 25 Percent Above the Mean of All Industries)

Occupational Groups	% Age Con*	% Total Emp	Number of Industries	Age <25	Age 65+	Educational Level		Low Earnings Quint	% Women	% Black
						Less HS	HS			
Services										
Business Services	1.9%	0.4%	304	6.7%	8.4%	3.2%	11.7%	14.1%	54.8%	2.8%
Transport & Com. Serv.	8.5%	1.9%	1.338	4.6%	2.6%	13.6%	46.1%	4.2%	27.4%	18.4%
Distributive Services	4.8%	1.1%	753	12.6%	8.7%	18.2%	36.5%	23.1%	46.7%	6.3%
Personal Services	15.7%	3.6%	2.463	9.4%	10.7%	18.2%	37.3%	18.4%	43.0%	9.9%
Social Services	9.1%	2.1%	1.438	6.9%	5.1%	9.9%	24.9%	9.7%	45.9%	12.4%
	22.6%	5.2%	3.557	5.8%	7.5%	10.2%	17.3%	11.0%	69.3%	11.3%
Manufacturing										
Primary Industries	17.2%	3.9%	2.712	13.6%	13.1%	33.9%	39.4%	27.1%	21.0%	6.5%
Traditional Manufac.	11.5%	2.6%	1.807	10.4%	2.8%	25.7%	44.4%	4.8%	24.7%	10.6%
Modern Manufacturing	8.6%	2.0%	1.359	6.3%	3.8%	8.1%	32.7%	3.0%	30.7%	7.8%
Total	100.0%	22.8%	—							
Total Cases			15.731	1.358	1.187	2.778	5.136	2.122	6.502	1.600
For All Groups			—		7.5%	17.7%	32.6%	13.5%	41.3%	10.2%
Entire Population		100.0%	69.031	10.996	2.798	12.004	26.085	9.581	24.619	6.606
For Entire Population			100.0%	15.9%	4.1%	17.4%	37.8%	13.9%	35.7%	9.6%

Source: Authors' Tabulations Based on Current Population Survey, 1989.
* Distribution of all Age-Concentrated Industires (SIC 3 Digit Industry Level) by Sector.

industries in Sweden and other countries, contrary to our expectations, we also find a similar grouping of age concentration. (Table not presented.) We also find, as expected, much less overall age concentration. Additional work is needed to explore this area.

14   The Concept of Early Retirement

The empirical evidence we report is disaggregated male labor force rates, implying exit patterns from these rates. We infer exit or retirement patterns from these rates on the assumption that re-entry into employment for older men is unlikely. Our review of country patterns in low exit countries raises questions about the validity of this assumption. To explore this question conceptually we need to address frontally the elusive issue of the meaning of retirement. The difficulty in conceptualizing retirement can be illustrated clearly by a puzzle posed by Fields and Mitchell. Consider the following example.

"Suppose you leave your life-long employer at age 61 with a year's terminal sabbatical. Starting at age 62, you become eligible for a private pension from your employer's pension fund which you accept. At age 65 you file for social security. You continue to earn a few thousand dollars a year as a part-time consultant. Have you retired? If so, at what age?" (cited in Atkinson and Sutherland, 1993)

How can we understand and resolve Field and Mitchell's puzzle? What is at issue at a conceptual level is different core ideas about the meaning of retirement. Is retirement an event signaled by an abrupt change in position, namely the entry into the public pension system? Retirement can be also understood as a process of gradual withdrawal from the world of work, combining in the process perhaps work and the receipt of a pension. The process can begin in a bridging job which starts a transition from a career job. Perhaps it is better understood as a status or role defined by the individual's own perception of the situation he defines himself in on the road between work and nonwork. The receipt of a public pension is not the same as labor market exit. The individual may or may not receive a pension in these definitions of retirement as a process or status. Naturally, research scholars asking different questions use different definitions.

Finally, a retirement ceremony marks a changed relationship to the world of work. It does not signal a withdrawal from work. This means that retirement must be defined as changes in the relationship to work at the end of the working life.

Three different types of empirical studies are based on these different conceptual approaches and definitions.[9] One approach views retirement as "leaving the labor force not to return." The second focuses on "sudden and discontinuous drop-in hours of work and pay (Burtless and Moffitt, 1984); and the third is based on self-assessed retirement (OECD, 1989). Each approach leads to somewhat different insights. This makes the task of comparative research about early retirement very frustrating. Empirical results are not comparable because each researcher employs a somewhat different definition of retirement. Hurd believes that this is one of the main reasons why empirical research has only been able to demonstrate a very modest impact of social security benefits on the retirement decision (Hurd, 1990).

Our aim is not to resolve inconsistencies of finding and definition, but to try to understand them. One source of inconsistency stems from the different perspective adopted by the inquirer. The quotation we started with seems, at least implicitly, to be asking the question of retirement from the point of view of the individual. From the individual's perspective, retirement means a change in the relationship to the people he works with and the meaning of work in general as he enters the last stage of his working career. But there are also alternative perspectives, namely that of the state and the firm. From the state's point of view, retirement begins when the individual makes a financial claim from the state for social security benefits. Entry into the public pension system provides a de facto meaning to the term retirement. This can be at age 60 in both France and in Germany (although in Germany access for men occurs only after a period of prolonged unemployment), or age 62 in the United States, or 65 in Britain. Considered from the perspective of the firm, retirement begins with a change in the firm's accounting procedure through which the individual is paid. When an individual retires, he is paid from a different operating fund such as a pension fund. The meaning of early retirement from the state's and the firm's point of view seems reasonably clear because of the financial implications in pursuing these pathways.

At the conceptual and empirical level, there is no way to separate core ideas about retirement from the penumbra of closely linked, but peripheral views. One way of intellectually dealing with the theoretical and empirical issues is to ground them in the concrete situation in which they are embedded. The meaning of the status of retirement depends on the institutional context. Even subjective, self-assessed meanings of retirement are best understood in the national institutional setting in which it is located. To illustrate this theme, we review a number of country studies, examine the very different conclusions they reach, and interpret whether their findings reconstitute the meaning of the life course.

What is the meaning of early retirement from the individual's perspective? Casey and Laczko identify the subjective view of the individual regarding his retirement status for Britain. They show that only one-third of men aged 60 to 64 who were not working in 1986 reported that they were retired, compared to one-half in 1979. Their interpretation is that the burden of unemployment is being disproportionally shifted to these men through a societal effort to reassign them an 'alternative role' as retired. "Yet the majority of older not working men do not embrace this role, and that as unemployment has risen the proportion who do has fallen" (Casey and Laczko, 1989: 523).

The Casey and Laczko interpretation of the individual's perspective in Britain portrays them as members of a new social group who are victimized by a process of exclusion from work. Because of labor market problems, they are forced to occupy a new 'intermediary status' in which they are "too old to work and too young to retire." It is the manual workers rather than the white collar workers who are likely to experience this intermediary status and feel they are being pushed out of the labor market and thus denied the chance to enjoy the positive social meaning that work provides. Casey and Laczko conclude, therefore, that the term "early retirement" is deceptive because it "deflects concern away from the labor market problems experienced by many older workers" (Casey and Laczko, 1989: 510). This interpretation means that in a work society, the marginalized, disadvantaged victims of the economy are no longer the manual workers assigned dirty jobs and low pay, but the older people who are excluded from the opportunities to work.

We do not wish to assess the merits of this argument, but it is important to point out that the interpretation of the statistics depends, in part, on whether one uses absolute numbers or shares. While, in the British case, the absolute number of all non-working men aged 60 to 64 almost doubled between 1979 and 1986, the number of men in this age group who defined themselves as being retired increased five-fold. This presentation of the same facts suggests a substantial increase in subjectively defined early retirement, but this comment is intended only as a digression. Our main point is that the answer to the question of what is retirement depends not only on the experience of these non-working men and the interpretation of the researchers but also, as we shall develop below, on the specific country context.

In Germany, as in Britain, with similar trends in labor force participation and unemployment in this age group the individual's perspective is quite different. Based on his study of the pre-retirement program in the chemical industry, Kohli found that

"... many workers would like to continue some work – if it were 'good work': less stressful and more self-controlled. But with the work they have, their preference is clear: the great majority of them accept early exit, and even view it as a blessing that sets them free from a work place that becomes increasingly hard to endure physically. ... Contrary to many beliefs, early exit from work is thus broadly popular with most of the actors involved" (Kohli, 1992: 100).

Reinforcing the subjective view is that the individual economic position of non-working men 60 to 64 is substantially worse in Britain when compared to Germany. Almost two-thirds of those whose main family income source is not factor income have low income (less than 60 percent of the median income) in Britain, while in Germany this proportion is less than one-quarter (Rainwater and Rein, 1993).

A French study carried out by Anne-Marie Guillemard (1990) shows that male French workers 60 to 64 see themselves as having been actively expelled from the labor market, and they reject the societal status of "retired". In the early 1980s, unemployment levels were very high among older men 60 to 64. Most were receiving unemployment insurance and saw themselves as actively looking for work. The French government in 1983 redefined the age of retirement to 60, largely because old age pensions paid about half of previous earnings; whereas, unemployment benefits covered about two-thirds. Thus, the French government could save money by lowering the age of retirement. Older French workers, unlike their British counterparts, continued, however, to see themselves as unemployed and rejected the status of retired. For example, many refused to use transportation subsidies available to those who were retired because they did not see themselves in this role.

A recent OECD study highlights trends in subjective retirement among men 60 to 64 years of age (OECD, 1989). In countries like Germany, there has been virtually no change in the self-definition of men 60 to 64 who are not in the labor market. In Germany over 90 percent report that they are retired, and the proportion has not changed over time. By contrast, there has been a decline in those who see themselves as retired in Britain and a rather sharp increase in the United States.

Without taking account of the institutional context of each country, we cannot understand the British men's view that they are in a suspended intermediary stage in which they are neither active nor inactive; German embrace of retirement as an earned entitlement in a moral economy; or the French resentment that the retirement status was notionally imposed on men searching for work. Pension replacement rates in Britain are low, and there is extensive reliance on mean-tested benefits; France lowered its retirement age from 65 to 60, thus redefining the unemployed as retired. In Germany, the value of the pension received at age 60 is 88 percent of the pension that would have been received if the individual retired at age 65. In addition, net replacement rates are consistently high (Rainwater and Rein, 1993: 125). It is, therefore, not surprising that German men embrace early retirement as an entitlement for a lifetime of work.

The specific country experiences are not only interpreted situationally, but as evidence for a much broader reinterpretation of the impact and meaning of these early exit pathways on the tri-partition of the individual life course. Two contrasting views can be juxtaposed. This disagreement is based on the above discussion of the different subjective responses to early retirement.

One view holds that the process of early retirement has destabilized the life course by substituting functional categories for chronological categories. The effect was to increase uncertainty, decrease the retirement system's control over the retirement process, and weaken the intergenerational contract. The growth of bridging pathways converted a standardized, orderly, predictable transition from work to retirement based primarily on age criteria into a de-standardized, heterogeneous process based on functional criteria. Since the chronological markers are becoming less visible, the end of the life course has, for individuals, been blurred. The threefold model, which laces everyone in a continuous, foreseeable trajectory of successive stage, statuses and roles, is coming apart. The life course is becoming variable, imprecise and contingent. Nowadays, no one working in the private sector knows at what age and under which conditions he (or she) will exit. Retirement as a social situation and a system of transfers no longer constitutes the horizon where everyone foresees the pathway he (or she) will one day take out of the labor force toward old age (Guillemard, 1990).

The alternative view concedes that the life course has become less standardized because early retirement is not a uniform practice. The tri-partition of the life course remains essentially intact. Age and functional categories combine to preserve the basic structure of the individual life course. We can see the process in a different perspective.

It is a story not of break-down and failure, but a story of success – success in keeping up the tri-partition of the life course by creatively using other welfare instruments than merely old-age pensions. We can see a kind of socio-political bricolage which redefines these other instruments or programs in terms of exit, and thus incorporates them into the retirement process (Kohli, 1990).

15   The Future of Early Retirement

Is the stability of the life course blurred and coming apart, or does a newly emerging bricolage creatively reinforce the tri-partition of the life course? From our analysis of trends, patterns, and meaning of early retirement, what picture emerges about the future evolution of early retirement? The trend to early retirement of men 60 to 64 has leveled off between 1985 and 1990. But in some countries, with 80 percent of all wage and salary workers already not employed, a slowdown is anything but surprising.

The more interesting question is not the trends which have already redefined the age structure of modern labor markets, but which of these two patterns will emerge in the future? Will 'exit-is-exit countries' change direction, raise the retirement age, and adopt a pattern of encouraging the combination of work and retirement because of the strong insistence of the state and the willing compliance by firms and individuals? A review of recent initiatives by states in virtually all countries shows a determined effort to slow down or reverse the trend to early retirement. If the firms believe it is in their interest tofollow such a policy, and if individuals experience economic hardship during the years of early retirement, then the convergence of these three forces could lead to a pattern which combines work and retirement. What we see, however, is a much more inconsistent pattern from which no clear trend is as yet discerned. In the United States, most private pensions are not indexed against inflation. In an inflationary period the value of these pensions will erode forcing workers to reenter work after spending some time out of the labor force simply because their pension is not adequate. If such individuals continue to seek part-time work, the United States will increasingly move toward a Swedish pattern of gradual exit, but in an American style with the responsibility for the transition falling on the individual. Ruhm's recent research suggests that early retirement is becoming more abrupt, rather than more gradual (Ruhm, 1992).

In Japan, if the state raises the age of receipt of a public pension to 65 while the "teinen" age continues at age 60, then there will be a five-year gap between work and retirement. It is interesting to ask whether Japanese firms will, as is done in the Netherlands, be willing in the future to provide private pensions as a bridge to a public pension as they have done in the past when the "teinen" age was 55. It appears that more workers are moving from "teinen" age to unemployment, suggesting a drift toward the American pattern and a weakening of the social responsibility of the firm.

The situation in Sweden is unclear. In 1990 the state has closed off the disability program for economic reasons, making it harder to exit via this route. At the same time there has been an expansion of private schemes, especially severance pay. This would suggest that as the disability pathway closes, severance pay might serve as a substitute. If instrument substitution occurred, Sweden could move in the direction of a Continental model where 'exit is equal to exit'. Another example of transition is that while the overall part-time employment in Sweden appears to be fairly stable over time, the share of partial retirement among all older men has declined from its high point. On the other hand, there has been an effort to eliminate partial pensions. Thus far this proposal has been defeated in Parliament, but with the high unemployment rates in 1993, a public policy to discourage the exit of older workers would exacerbate the problem of unemployment.

Will Continental countries, including Britain, follow the model of work and retirement? There is some evidence in Britain that private pensions are dropping the provision of an economic penalty for early retirement if the initiative comes from the firm. Rules covering the receipt of unemployment benefits combined with a pension are also being relaxed. Given the continued downturn in the economy in Britain, social policy will continue to be volatile. It is hard to imagine how the pattern of early exit without reemployment can be avoided, despite the introduction of new policy designed to remove the work test after age 65. Thus Britain will reluctantly follow the exit-is-exit path. Without an adequate pension system and limited opportunities to combine work and retirement, the social cost of early exit will lead to declining living standards as those who exit early become a new poverty class.

In the Netherlands wages are not rising in line with productivity because part of what would have been an increase in wages is diverted to cover the cost of the private early retirement 'VUT' scheme. At the moment the issue is being postponed in collective bargaining; but, if the Dutch economy continues to recover, one possible solution is the introduction of a public early retirement program. This would represent a sectoral crossover as policy moves back from private to public in order to relieve the latent intergenerational conflict.[10]

German unification has made the issue of early retirement more complicated. What we find is the invention of new pathways to early retirement in East Germany. An example is the use of "Kurzarbeit", not as short-time work, but as labor market exit. In July 1991, 2.6 million were unemployed or on short work. Moreover, East Germany has temporarily lowered its retirement age to 55 for some groups of workers in order to accommodate the problems of economic transformation. In such a turbulent environment, the experience in the East Germany may help change the development of policy in West Germany.

The attempt to develop a system of ideal national types, designed to capture an essential feature of the work and retirement system of each of the countries, has to be approached with caution because of the disparity between institutional norms and actual practice. This is another way of saying that the systems in each country are themselves being transformed, suggesting that the future of early retirement may involve a system of continuous redefinition and not merely one stable pattern. Perhaps other countries will adopt the American system which reinforces a variety of alternative ways of organizing work at the end of the life course without any single dominant national signature. A majority of Americans follow the Continental pattern of exiting completely from the labor market, never to return again; some individuals are able to work out arrangements with their firm where they are able to continue on their job with a lesser responsibility.

Surprisingly, a very large proportion of American males also seems to follow the Swedish pattern of gradual exit from employment.

Notes

1   For a detailed review of the vast literature on early retirement, *see* Guillemard and Rein (1993).
2   For a review of this history, *see* Rein and Rainwater (1987).
3   This analysis is a collaboration of an earlier paper (*see* Rein and Jacobs, 1993).
4   All German data in this chapter refer to West Germany respectively, after the German Unification in 1990, to the former West Germany.
5   Moreover, in the United States a substantial proportion of those who actually work part time in the survey week usually work full time but have reduced the amount of hours worked due to both economic and noneconomic reasons. For men 60 to 64, 19 percent work part time in the survey week, but only 14 percent report that they usually work part time. Some of the noneconomic reasons for the difference between actual and usual hours are sickness, holiday, bad weather, etc. We use the actual hours because the statistics usually made available from the EEC about usual hours contain errors.
6   Bert de Vroom, in correspondence with the author, reports that "a more precise (and positive) formulation of the central question about involvement in paid labour occurred after 1987. The result of the original framing of the question (combined with non-professional interviewers) was that many respondents with a paid job of less than 20 hours were classified/or classified themselves as non-participating in paid labour. The result of the new framed question has resulted in a very strong increase of the number of persons involved in paid labour for less than 20 hours/week. So, the massive increase of part-time jobs has hardly anything to do with a 'structural change' but is a statistical artifact."
7   Retirement is here defined as exit from work and entry into the welfare state or a public or private pathway leading to a public pension.
8   These economists who have worked on the concept of a "career job" differ on how best to define it. "Career job" can be defined either as the longest job held in the work career or as the job held for at least ten years. The different definitions yield different results about the size of the job bridging phenomena.
9   For a review of the literature, *see* Hurd (1990).
10 For a discussion of public-private crossovers in social protection, *see* Rein and Friedman (1992).

References

Atkinson, A. B. and Holly Sutherland (1993). *Two Nations in Early Retirement? The Case of Britain.* In: A. B. Atkinson and Martin Rein (eds.), *Age, Work, and Social Security.* London: Macmillan Press.

Burtless, Gary and Robert A. Moffitt (1984). *The Effect of Social Security Benefits on the Labor Supply of the Aged.* In: Aaron, Henry J. and Gary Burtless (eds.), *Retirement and Economic Behavior. Studies in Social Economics Series.* Washington, DC: Brookings Institution: 135–171.

Casey, B. and F. Laczko (1989). *Early Retirement, a Long-Term Unemployment? The Situation of Non-Working Men Age 55–64 from 1979 to 1986.* In: *Work, Employment and Society* 3 (4): 509–526.

Guillemard, Anne-Marie (1990). *The Unimportance of Aging.* A paper presented to the Transatlantic Research Conference on Age, Work and Social Security, Luxembourg, 13–15 June (Mimeo).

Guillemard, Anne Marie and Martin Rein (1993). *Comparative Patterns of Retirement: Recent Trends in Developed Societies.* In: *Annual Review of Sociology* 19 (1993): 469–503.

Hurd, Michael D. (1990). *Research on the Elderly: Economic Status, Retirement, and Consumption and Saving.* In: *Journal of Economic Literature* 28 (2): 565–637.

Jacobs, Klaus; Kohli, Martin and Martin Rein (1991). *The Revolution of Early Exit: A Comparative Analysis of Labor Force Participation Patterns.* In: Martin Kohli et al. (eds.), *Time for Retirement: Comparative Studies of Early Exit from the Labor Force.* Cambridge, N.Y.: Cambridge University Press: 36–66.

Kohli, Martin (1990). *Comment on Anne-Marie Guillemard's paper "The Unimportance of Aging",* presented to the Transatlantic Research Conference on Age, Work, and Social Security, Luxembourg, 13–15 June 1990.

Kohli, Martin (1992). *Labor Market Perspectives and Activity Patterns of the Elderly in an Aging Society.* In: W. van den Heuvel et. al. (eds.), *Opportunities and Challenges in an Aging Society.* Amsterdam: North-Holland: 90–105.

Kohli, Martin et al. (eds.) (1991). *Time for Retirement: Comparative Studies of Early Exit from the Labor Force.* Cambridge, N.Y.: Cambridge University Press.

OECD (1989). *Employment Outlook Report.* Paris: OECD: 66–68.

Quinn, Joseph F. (1993). *The Transition from Work to Retirement in the United States.* In: John Blackwell (ed.), *The Transition from Work to Retirement.* Paris: OECD.

Quinn, Joseph F.; Burkhauser, Richard V. and Daniel A. Myers (1990). *Passing the Torch: The Influence of Economic Incentives on Work and Retirement.* Michigan: W.E. Upjohn Institute for Employment Research.

Rainwater, Lee and Martin Rein (1993). *Economic Well-Being of Older Men in Six Countries.* In: A. B. Atkinson and Martin Rein (eds.). *Age, Work, and Social Security.* London: Macmillan Press, Ltd.: 115–131.

Rebick, Marcus (1993). *The Japanese Approach to Finding Jobs for Older Workers.* In: Olivia S. Mitchell (ed.), *As the Work Force Ages: Costs, Benefits, and Policy Challenges.* Ithaca, NY: The Industrial Relations Press.

Rein, Martin and Lee Rainwater (eds.) (1986). *The Public-Private Interplay in Social Protection: A Comparative Study.* Armonk, New York: M.E. Sharpe, Inc.).

Rein, Martin and Barry Friedman (1992). *Social Protection and Economic Change.* A paper prepared at the MIT Conference in honor of Albert Hirschman. (Mimeo).

Rein, Martin and Klaus Jacobs (1993). *Ageing and Employment Trends: A Comparative Analysis for OECD Countries.* In: Paul Johnson and Klaus F. Zimmermann (eds.), *Labour Markets in an Ageing Europe.* Cambridge, N.Y.: Cambridge University Press: 53–76.

Ruhm, Christopher J. (1991). *Bridge Employment and Retirement Transition.* Greensboro: University of North Carolina (Mimeo).

Ruhm, Christopher J. (1992). *Secular Changes in the Work and Retirement Patterns of Older Men.* In: *Journal of Labor Economics* 10 (1): 1–33.

3 The Netherlands: The Loreley-Effect of Early Exit

Willem Trommel and Bert de Vroom

1   Introduction

We have argued elsewhere that the process of early exit in the Netherlands
is stimulated by a whole range of existing and newly invented *exit opportunities* that have been labelled pathways (De Vroom and Blomsma, 1991).
Most industrialised countries dispose of a particular set of social-politicy
instruments which partially explains the different *degrees* of early exit
between countries (cf. Kohli et al., 1991); but these instruments as such
cannot explain the overall exit trend. What is more, the accent on pathways
might suggest that the exit process is a result of individual choices of
employees, obscuring at the same time structural features and the particular
role and responsibility of firms.

The central question of this contribution is: how and why in social reality
is early exit produced? How are social-politicy instruments, state policies,
economic and technological developments, firm strategies and individual
choices correlated? Can the ultimate outcome be characterised as a
purposive, rational exit policy, or is the whole process a 'perverse effect' of
social complexity?

To answer these questions, we firstly give an overall picture of the
structure and development of the Dutch 'non-working' society, and secondly we present the major results of case studies in four different firms: a
steel company, a bank, a public utility firm and an electrotechnical firm. The
processes of early exit that occurred in these firms during the eighties have
been reconstructed in detail.

The purpose is to clarify the interactions between the Dutch institutional
framework on the one hand, and the exit processes at firm level on the
other. Therefore we studied the economic and technological environment of
the selected firms, the development of their employment structures, the
production and personnel regimes, changing age profiles and the characteristics of the early-exit processes.

Concerning environmental constraints, production regimes, employment
developments and also the ways in which early-exit processes are shaped
and controlled, the selected firms display a high degree of heterogeneity.
Nevertheless, we found the same homogeneous and massive process of
early exit typical of the extreme macro pattern of the Netherlands. We
argue that the combination of social-economic constraints, social-political
instruments and firm strategies might explain the *origin* of the early exit
trend as a rational response. However, the *persistence* of the trend can be
(partly) classified as an autonomous, unintended mechanism. Like boats on
the river Rhine captured by the temptation of the singing *Loreley* long
before they reached their destination, workers in the modern welfare
society are lured into early exit pathways long before they reach the age of
65.[1]

2   The Dutch Non-Working Society

2.1   Low Participation and High Productivity

The Netherlands are an extreme example of the "typical OECD-society" (Dahrendorf, 1988): only a minority of the total population is involved in paid labour activities, while at the same time the level of productivity is relatively high.

Overall participation in terms of the *employment activity rate*[2] in the Netherlands is very low compared to other industrialised countries. From 1960 to 1988 participation decreased from 61% to 59%. By comparison the 1988 activity rates for the other countries in the research project: West-Germany 64%, UK 69%, Japan 71%, USA 72% and Sweden 81% (WRR, 1990: 59)[3]. Apart from the overall low figures, the low participation of women is another characteristic of Dutch society. In the last two decades, the participation of women has increased from 26% in 1960 to 44% in 1988, but this is still low compared to both the male activity rate (1988: 74%) and the general picture in most West-European countries.

The employment activity rate based on the number of *persons* does however distort the real involvement in labour activities measured in terms of the *number of hours* worked. In all industrialised countries we can observe an increase in part-time work in recent decades. Except for Sweden the Netherlands show the highest rate of the countries studied. Combined with other variables, the average number of annual working hours in Sweden and the Netherlands were among the lowest, 1,466 and 1,534, respectively (1987). In Germany, USA and Japan it was 1,620, 1,783 and 2,104 hours, respectively (SoZaWe, 1990: 38; OECD, 1990). The low number of working hours per employee implies a further reduction of labour force participation calculated in working years. In 1987 the level of participation in terms of working hours was 47% for the total labour force. Differentiated by gender it was 65% for men and 26% for women. By example, in West Germany the participation in terms of working hours for men and women in 1987 was 78% and 41%, respectively, and for the UK 74% and 37%.

In general, there is a significant correlation between the degree of part-time work and the level of labour force participation. Dutch society, however, represents an exceptional case. Notwithstanding the high level of part-time work, participation rates are low. Apart from possible statistical distortion[4] this unique pattern must be explained by the growing access of women to the labour market and, at the same time, a corresponding exit of (older) male workers. A far greater proportion of women than men work part-time: in 1988 57.5% and 14.5%, respectively (SoZaWe 1990: 39). The increasing part-time work among women is also reflected in the level of labour force participation of women. Measured in terms of the number of persons, the net labour participation of women increased from 26% in 1960 to 44% in 1988, while in terms of the total hours worked the net labour force participation of women hardly changed (1960 25%, 1988 26%) (WRR, 1990: 65).

So far the general pattern for men and women has been presented. How about the relation between age and participation? Apart from the age group 16–24 net labour force participation in terms of the number of persons is in the Netherlands lower than the OECD-average for every age group (WRR, 1990: 63). In the past two decades, one can observe an increase in labour force participation for the 25–54 age group, and adecreasing participation for the 55–64 age group similar to those in other OECD countries. However, compared to other countries the exit-rate in the Netherlands is much higher. Another particular characteristic of the Dutch pattern – as mentioned above – is that the increase of participation in the middle-aged groups is almost a direct effect of increasing *female* participation, whereas the process of early exit of the older age groups is predominantly a *male* phenomenon. As a result, by 1989 the net labour force participation of the male 55–64 age group in the Netherlands was lower than that of women in the same age group for the OECD (SoZaWe, 1990: 36).

The male exit trend – indicated as the level of non-participation – is illustrated in figure 1 for the period 1973–1989.

In 1985 the labour force participation of the male population between 55 and 64 years old was 53.8% in the Netherlands. [By comparison: United States: 59.7, Japan: 83.0, Germany 57.5, United Kingdom 66.4 and Sweden 76.0 (OECD)]. The dramatic fall of the participation rate between 1971 and 1985 (in 1971 the rate for males aged 55–64 was about 80%) was not restored during the subsequent period. Between 1985 and 1988 the relative growth of the participation rate of the total population between 55 and 64 was -.53%, whereas West Germany and Sweden showed a small increase (.05% and .16%, respectively) (OECD, 1990). For the time being it is not likely that the Netherlands will lose their exceptional position regarding the labour force participation of older workers. The high exit rates in age group 55–59 not only have tended to stabilise, the participation rate for the oldest age group (60–64) are even showing a further decline.

The female exit patterns are harder to detect than the male ones. The fact that female participation has increased for the last ten years (in the Netherlands and many other countries) implies that the participation rate is not a very reliable indicator for exit. Still, in spite of this cohort-effect the female participation rates for the oldest age groups indicate an exit process that resembles the male pattern. In 1971 the rate for the age group 55–59 was 17.7% increasing slightly until 1983; the rate then declined to 16.7 % in

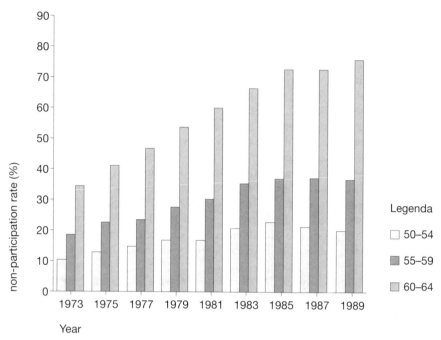

Figure 1: Non-Participation of Older Age Groups 1973-1989 (Male)

1988. Much more dramatic is the falling participation rate in age group 60–64: from 11.8% in 1971 the rate shows a steady decline to a level of 1.9% in 1988 (All data from OECD, Labour force statistics). As Kohli et al. (1991) argue, only a cohort analysis is able to give a more accurate picture of the underlying changes in female participation. However, Dutch statistics supply insufficient data for a reliable cohort analysis at the macro level. Based on long-term personnel data from our firm-level study we were able to perform a cohort analysis for a single case (*see* section 3). This analysis confirms an exit trend for older women.

2.2   Pathways into Early Exit: From Social Security to Bargaining

Given the formal structure and definition of the labour society, the puzzling question is how the growing and immense process of early exit is financed and legitimated. What, in other words, are the legitimised pathways that enable older workers to bridge the financial gap between exit from paid labour and a state-guaranteed old-age pension at the age of 65? In the Netherlands a number of different pathways have come into existence in the past decades, which can, according to their 'legal' status, be divided into public and private pathways.[5]

Public pathways are based on welfare-state social security regulations established in the fifties and sixties to fulfil demands for social justice and recompensation for injuries and loss of income. Since the early seventies various social security regulations have been combined to create particular pathways from work into retirement. After the reconstruction of the social security system in the eighties, there are still seven different social security exit pathways.[6] The disability pathway has become the main road of social security early exit and has created a picture of the Netherlands as a 'sick country' compared to other industrialised countries. In 1989 the number of recipients of a disability benefit for every thousand members of the working population was 139 in the Netherlands. In the United States, Sweden and Germany it was 43, 78 and 55, respectively. In all countries the number of recipients in the older age groups increased disproportionately from 1970 to 1989. But again, the Netherlands are an extreme case (Aarts and De Jong, 1991: 410).

In the eighties, early exit has gained increasing importance in collective bargaining between employers and trade unions. Two different programmes have been used for this type of early exit, whereby in a number of cases the bargained pathways also make use of social security regulations.

One bargained pathway frequently used in the eighties was mass dismissal in combination with the so-called *Social Plan* (SOP).[7] By using the (implicit) possibilities of unemployment regulations and the legal rules applying to dismissals, mass dismissals have become an early exit route for older workers.

The mass dismissal procedure contains a political dimension: according to law the employer is obliged to inform the trade unions about this matter. This legal obligation has stimulated collective bargaining between the firm and the trade union(s) on the social consequences of mass dismissals (Bakels and Opheikens, 1982: 115). The usual result is a so-called Social Plan that encloses a number of agreements on – among other things – the number of dismissals, outplacement activities, category of workers, level of financial compensation, etc.[8] Since 1987, there has been a tendency to give these *ad hoc* agreements a more structured character. From that year on a growing number of employers and trade unions have included the conditions of dismissal of older workers in collective agreements (SoZaWe, DCA, 1991).

As a result of bargaining on mass dismissals (laid down in Social Plans) older workers, in particular, have become the target group. Older workers who are not entitled to enter the disability pathway or the pre-retirement scheme, often enter such a 'social plan': the financial base is the unemployment benefit, supplemented by the employer. Since these older workers do not have to apply for another job, exit in this case becomes almost definitely exit.

Not only private firms but also the state as employer use older workers as solution for structural problems. Like private firms the state itself has also created a legal possibility for public servants of 55 and older to use an exit pathway in case of structural changes in state agencies. The use of this pathway is, as in the private sector, linked to a social plan. The financial base is the pre-retirement scheme for civil servants (Tweede Kamer, 1990-1991b).

Exit based on mass dismissals and social plans is – at the macro level – of only minor importance. Of much greater importance are the *Pre-Retirement Schemes* (VUT). These private exit routes have become very popular both with employers, trade unions and the state in coping with unemployment and/or economic problems at firm level. In the bargaining process between employers and the trade unions, these schemes have turned out to be very important means of exchange: a trade-off between wage demands and pre-retirement schemes for older workers has taken shape.

Pre-retirement is a form of social policy intended to offer certain categories of older workers a financially sounder and socially more acceptable way out of paid labour than through disability or unemployment. Simultaneously, the pre-retirement programme was meant to replace older workers by younger ones. So the scheme could be used as a tool in coping with the problem of unemployment.

In fact, pre-retirement schemes have become the most important exit route for male older workers (60–64), without structural effects on entry of younger unemployed workers (Van Ginneken, 1981; Bolhuis et al., 1987). This enormous increase of vut-awards in the Netherlands (*see* table 1) is largely the outcome of the downward pressure on the minimum age of entrance to the schemes. At the outset the pre-retirement schemes were exclusively directed at persons of 64 or 63 years of age. In 1988 entering a vut-scheme at the age of 61 or 60 was quite normal. Some schemes even have set the age limit at about 55.

2.3   Participation, Exit and State Policy

What has been the role of the state – as a regulator, as a policy maker and as an employer – with respect to the described labour-market developments and the increasing use of early-exit pathways?

During the eighties the *labour-market policy* of Dutch government shifted from a Keynesian to a neo-classical orientation. During the seventies government tried to cope with unemployment by creating 'additional public

Table 1: The Use of Different Pathways 1980–1988 (Male 55–59, 60–64). Number of
Participants as Percentage of Respective Age-Group (Males).

Year	Age-Group	Exit and Social Security		Exit by Bargaining[a] Pre-Retirement	Total
		Disability	Unemployment		
	55–59				
1980		30.0	0.8		30.8
1981		30.6	0.9		31.5
1982		31.2	1.2		32.4
1983		31.6	5.1		36.7
1984		31.9	7.0		38.9
1985		32.3	7.4		39.7
1986		32.1	7.6		39.7
1987		32.4	5.4		37.8
1988		32.8	5.7		38.5
	60–64				
1980		40.5	0.8		41.3
1981		41.7	0.9		42.6
1982		42.1	1.0	9.1	52.2
1983		42.6	8.3	13.6	64.5
1984		42.3	10.1	16.8	69.2
1985		42.0	11.1	21.3	74.4
1986		40.9	11.3	25.4	77.6
1987		39.8	10.2	29.5	79.5
1988		39.7	9.5	33.3	82.5
1989				35.3	

(a) There are no Exact Figures with Respect to the Number of Participants in Social
    Plans. These Numbers are Partly Included in the Unemployment Pathway.
Source: WRR 1990 and own Calculations.

works'; from 1982 on less emphasis was laid on employment policies and
more on measures to stimulate job seeking.

From 1975 until the late eighties, a whole range of instruments was
developed, either directed at the creation of employment (usually in favour
of specific groups like the long-term unemployed, women, school leavers,
etc.) or directed at the stimulation of effective employment seeking with
respect to certain groups of job searchers. The instruments in both categories usually consist of all kind of subsidies; in the first category of measures
the usual demand is that additional employment is created, in the second
category an employer may already get a subsidy if people from a specific
group are selected for a job.

From evaluation research (cited by WRR, 1987) it appears that the older
unemployed profited considerably from the 'additional public works' that
were realised in the seventies. From a review of evaluation studies concerning the 'job seeking measures' it also appears that the elderly were quite

well reached *until 1981/1982* (Stichting Weerwerk, 1989: 99). Since then, in particular the younger unemployed have benefited from the measures. This shift can partly be explained by the abolition of some measures that explicitly aimed at the re-employment of older workers. For example: in 1981 the '30% Wage subsidy regulation' was abolished, a measure that subsidised the labour costs of those unemployed that had poor employment chances due to age (>= 45 years). However, most recent measures[9] leave the possibility of appliance to the elderly; in practise the older unemployed are hardly reached by these measures. Since the agents who have to apply the measures (like the Labour Exchanges) strive for the highest participation rate, they tend to give priority to those job searchers that have the best chances.

Linked to the neo-classical emphasis on job seeking is the growing importance of training measures within the activities of the Labour Exchange. Some of these measures are explicitly directed at improving the labour-market chances of adults whose qualifications do not fit current market demands. In this field two obvious accents have been developed: women re-entering the labour market and young job searchers. Recently, also the ethnic minorities have received greater priority in training measures.

Data concerning the participation of the elderly in training activities point to a very weak representation of this group. The participation rate in any kind of training activitiy (1988) was 15.1% in the entire labour force but only 6.1% in the age group >= 50 years. Within firms the participation (1988) in training was 10.4 %, but only 5.2% in the age group >= 50 years (SoZaWe, 1989). Evaluating the training activities of the Labour Exchanges, Blomsma (1987) identifies only one measure that actually works out positively for the elderly: this measure (*SOB*), however, does not apply to the unemployed but to groups of workers that need training in order to retain their job.

Our first conclusion is that labour-market policies hardly have reached the older unemployed since 1982. This is partly a matter of intentional state policy (giving priority to women, ethnic minorities, school leavers, and so on), partly it is caused by the fact that the appliance of labour-market measures has developed very much into a 'market oriented practise', in which the elderly failed to compete successfully with other disadvantaged groups. A second conclusion concerns the fact that labour-market policy moved away from employment creation and concentrated on the re-employment of specific groups not including older workers. The (unintended) outcome of this approach has been that (re-)integration of the above mentioned has created on the other side an even higher pressure on the early exit of older male workers.

The state – *as employer* – has furthermore stimulated the process of early exit even more than the private sector. From 1980 to 1988 the proportion of age group 55–64 among the total active civil servants decreased from 10.6 to 7.0%. In 1981, 54% of all civil servants with a disability benefit (11,537) belonged to age group 55 and over. In 1989 this percentage decreased to 22% as a result of a tremendous increase in the use of Pre-retirement schemes: from 3,500 in 1981 to 19,339 in 1988 (WRR, 1990: 235). In 1989, 42% of all recipients of a private or public pre-retirement benefit belonged to the state sector (WRR, 1990: 238).

Moreover the state – *as regulator* – accepted until recently the use of social security regulations for age-specific exit. In 1987 Dutch government responded to the enormous increase of participants in the social security system with a reconstruction of the rules and norms of the different regulations. This reconstruction effected changes in the entrances and use of employment and disability programmes for most age groups except for older workers (55–64), which one also can observe in figure 2 and table 3. The practise of using social security for early exit is still common.

2.4   Norms and Structures

The puzzling question is: how can social security regulations, (partly) intended to promote re-integration into the labour process and not introduced as age-specific rules, be used as pathways for age-specific exit from the labour market?

One might argue that the enormous increase in participation in disability and unemployment schemes is a result of a worsening state of health of the working population or of severe economic problems. Several authors have argued and illustrated that this can only partially explain the increasing use of disability pathways. However, it can neither fully explain the age-specific character of the early exit process nor the relatively high level of the Dutch exit trend compared to other industrialised (welfare) countries.

In recent years, a growing number of scientific publications have addressed this question. Based on these contributions we argue that the extreme level of early exit on the macro level is a result of the particular *legal, organisational* and *institutional* structure of the social security system in the Netherlands. It is this complex configuration of rules, actors and institutions rather than an explicit state policy controlled by bureaucratic rationality, which – we argue – is responsible for the Dutch pattern of exit.

We will illustrate this by the use of the disability pathway. In this extremely frequently used pathway, detailed social security norms, private and public actors and a differentiated organisational structure come together.

Compared to other countries the legal structure of disability regulation in the Netherlands differs in a number of respects. Firstly, the level of benefit is relatively high. Until 1985 the maximum legal benefit level was 80% of the last earned wage. Since the second half of the eighties the legal level has been reduced to 70% and government has been pressing employers and trade unions to reduce the supplementing policy. The second characteristic of Dutch disability regulation is its detailed elaboration: seven different occupational disability categories are distinguished. As a result a person with an occupational disability of only 15% is entitled to enter the scheme. Thirdly, every worker is entitled to enter the disability programme from his or her first working day. The fourth and last particular characteristic is that the cause of disability is not relevant: a worker who has become handicapped outside the workplace is still entitled to receive an occupational disability benefit.

The legal structure not only sets a relatively low threshold to entry into this exit pathway. At the same time the legal structure is characterised by a high degree of complexity (large number of different variables), the social nature of a number of variables, and vagueness and ambiguity of the rules and goals. Both the complexity, the social variables and the vagueness have stimulated informal strategies of decision-making by social security agencies (Van der Veen, 1990: 267). In particular decision-making with respect to occupational disability is vulnerable to a 'social construction of social policy'. In contrast to the duration of unemployment, which is an administrative variable, occupational disability is a social variable: it depends on social (and economic) developments.

In this context, the interpretation of social security regulations becomes the object of informal strategies and norms. Based on empirical research into decision-making processes in these agencies, Van der Veen concludes that elderly people (with few chances on the labour market) will get an occupational disability pension more easily than others (Van der Veen, 1990: 265). The decision-making process can hardly be controlled by the state, since the organisational structure is highly differentiated and decentralised. At the same time, the implementation and control on the decentralised level is in the hands of private organisations of both employers and workers. The Dutch meso-corporatist structure of social-security, labour-market and labour-relations institutions have created a high level of accessibility and openness of policy decisions and implementation practises for employers, trade unions and different professionals at both the sectoral and regional level (Van Waarden, 1989; De Vroom, 1990).

The interest groups representing of labour and capital have a collective interest in the use of early-exit pathways and usually reject bureaucratic and administrative control of the use of social security programmes (Ganzevoort, 1984; WRR, 1990; Aarts and de Jong, 1991). The broad, social interpretation and flexible implementation of the law enables employers to get rid of problematic (more expensive and supposedly less productive) workers, e.g., older workers, almost 'for free'. Since, in particular, older workers need to be only marginal handicapped to get a full occupational disability benefit, the disability exit route was – and still is – a more attractive option for employers than starting a dismissal procedure for superfluous older workers.[10]

Since internal problems can be shifted to the social security system employers are not obliged to develop (costly) social and re-integration policies on firm level. Trade unions, on the other hand, have accepted the use of social security regulations for the exit of older workers: they could guarantee those 'excluded' older workers a relatively good benefit and at the same time could (theoretically) offer other groups (young workers, women) a chance on the labour market.

2.5   Summary

The Dutch 'work-society' is characterised by a very low labour force participation and at the same time a high level of early exit of, in particular, the male working population of 50 and over. This extreme exit process has – so far – been explained as a result of a combination of a differentiated pattern of exit routes, both public and private, and particular characteristics of the legal, institutional and organisational structure, which can be summarised in five aspects:

(a) Implementation and control of social security regulations by private, corporatist organisations in which employers and trade unions are represented; these interest organisations benefit from the way social security is used in this way;

(b) The decentralised, differentiated and professionalised system of agencies dealing with the daily decision-making process; these type of organisations and activities are difficult to control bureaucratically;

(c) Detailed rules and social elements which have created room for particular decisions and 'bargaining' situations between professionals and clients; it creates, in other words, room for a social policy of regulations (instead of administrative and bureaucratic control);

(d) A differentiated sectoral and regional institutional and organisational structure (meso-corporatism) with a high level of access and openness for professionals, employers, trade unions and local bureaucrats; this particular structure, based on short geographical and interpersonal relations, has created a social basis for informal bargaining and lateral collusion;

(e) As a result of the above-mentioned characteristics the process of early exit seems to be out of control of the state; at the same time the state

Table 2: Main Characteristics of the Studied Firms

	Steel Company	Electro-technical Firm	Bank	Public Utility Firm
Main Product	Steel	Telecom-munica-tions	Financial Products Services	Certificates Scientific Knowledge
Size (Employees)	17.000 (1988)	340 (1989)	2.200 (1988)	280 (1989)
Status	Private Dutch	Dutch div. of French Multinational	Private, Dutch	Private, Holded by Dutch Water Works; Task and Employment Status: Public
Employment Trend	Gradually Decreasing	Decrease (79−83); Increase (83−87); Largely Cut (88/90);	Gradually Increasing	Gradually Increasing
Studied Period	1976−1988	1979−88/89	1982−1988	1980−1989

– both as regulator and employer – does not have a great interest in changing the early-exit 'culture'.

3   Aging and Exit Patterns at Firm Level

3.1   Firm Characteristics, Economic Environment and Employment

We now move from the macro to the firm level, assuming that here the actual production of early exit takes place; at this level we study the interactions between national and sectoral regulations on the one hand, and corporate strategies on the other.

The four firms selected for empirical research are a Steel Company, a Bank, a Public Utility firm and an Electrotechnical firm (table 2). These firms differ in various respects; size, status, structure, employment, market-relation, external competition and management strategy.

The *Steel Company* is the largest of the four selected firms and also one of the largest employers in the Netherlands with about 23,000 employees in 1980. It is also the most important firm of the basic iron and steel industry[11] in the Netherlands, which in the early eighties consisted of only another three small firms (less than 100 employees) (CBS, 1982). As a powerful employer the Steel Company does not depend on collective action with other firms to negotiate with trade unions on labour conditions. Like other big employers, this company negotiates directly with the relevant trade unions. Although the company is a private enterprise, it received substantial financial support from the Dutch government at the beginning of the eighties.

The development of the firm and its personnel management are closely connected to the world steel crisis that started in the late seventies and continued during the first half of the eighties and had its effect on the internal policy of the firm. From 1976 on, management strategies have been directed at a financial reconstruction of the firm, reorganisation of the production process and at developing a series of productivity programmes. Until 1984 restructuring was characterised by crisis management, after that a more structural approach was developed. With the help of the Dutch government, extensive investments in new technologies were realised from 1984 on. In retrospect, what might have started as temporal solutions have in fact become a structural part of the companies management strategy. In the following pages we will describe the effect of these strategies on the overall employment structure and, in particular, the effect on elderly workers for the period 1976-1988. For empirical reference we will concentrate on a single plant, the *oxysteel factory*. At this plant a thousand workers find employment, most of them in blue collar jobs. The production regime of the Steel Company is based on mass production in a fordist manner; the physical character and the intensity of the work bring about high age-selective risks. However, the tradition of the firm's social policy had always offered different opportunities to cope with these risks; only recently can one observe a tendency to externalise the involved risks, based on a more 'flexible' perspective on social policy.

The *Electrotechnical Firm*[12], producing telecommunication equipment and hardware for the protection of railways, was part of an American multinational until 1988. During this period the firm had two plants, one specialised in mass production and one equipped for the production of small series of more complex apparatus. In both plants new technologies were introduced during the eighties so that the production became semi-automated. As a consequence the proportion of skilled work increased. In one of the plants a concept for 'flexible production automation' was devised and effected.

In 1987/1988, the firm was taken over by a French multinational which resulted in extensive reorganisations and substantial loss of jobs. The plant that produced the 'high-runners' was sold, the installation & service division closed and the business systems division turned into a separate firm. In the end a small production unit remained. At the end of the 'American period' the number of employees was about 1,050; since 1988/1989 the firm has employed only 330 workers.

In the period 1979-1989, the firm was confronted with two fundamental changes in its environment. Firstly, a technological development: digitalisation of products and the miniaturization of electronic components. Secondly, a change in market relations. Until the second half of the eighties the electrotechnical firm had a monopoly position. It was the main producer of telephone equipment for the state owned Dutch Telephone Company (PTT). In the second half of the eighties this public company was privatised. As a consequence the electrotechnical firm lost its monopoly and had to compete with other firms.

The firm reacted to the external developments by reconstructing the internal organisation and production process. Hardware-engineering became less important, whereas new technology know-how and software-engineering moved to the centre of the new production process. At the same time, automation and flexibility of the process became important elements of the firm's policy. One might say that the production regime of the firm developed from a fordist to a more innovation-based orientation, based on a more flexible concept of labour. The continuous pressure to raise skills might be seen as an age-selective risk.

The Public Utilities Firm is part of the sector 'Water Works and Supply'[13] and was founded by the public Water Works body as a task-specific firm: it was to develop and monitor quality standards and produce new scientific knowledge (research). In 1985 the firm employed 280 employees, equally split between the testing and research division. The firm has the legal status of a private company. However, according to the status of the employees and its state-licensed task it can be characterised as a public firm. This firm will have to cope with important external changes in the near future. As a result of the growing importance of an unified European Market (EG) and EG-regulations the firm might lose its certification and quality control task. The firm has already anticipated this predicted development by moving in a market-oriented direction. Management has developed a strategy based on selling relevant know-how on the market. This change might indicate a gradual transformation of (scientific) quality production into a market-oriented expansion strategy; theoretically this would bring about more age-selective risks, as a consequence of a more polyvalent use of labour.

The fourth selected firm is a *Savings Bank*.[14] The present bank is the result of an immense process of mergers which started in 1981 and which is expected to continue in the coming years. At this moment, 70 formerly autonomous savings banks have joined in the new united savings bank, which is now the biggest in its category. It has a dense network of more than 400 local and regional offices, particularly in the urban regions. As a result of the mergers employment increased from 1,991 in 1982 to 2,789 in 1988.

The merger process was a strategic response to the growing national and international competition in the banking sector. Scale-enlargement and rationalisation was one way of coping with falling profit margins. Another strategy of the different banks was diversification of services. Trade banks started offering saving facilities for private clients, while savings banks moved in the direction of trade. These different strategies can be traced in our particular *Bank*. The bank now offers products and services in such different sectors as travel, credit cards, mortgages, insurances, investments and so on. At the same time reorganisation and rationalisation policies were introduced. In 1986 the bank started a project aiming at concentrating all administrative procedures and cutting about 160 jobs in the early nineties. Automation of simple clerical jobs and up-grading the qualifications of sales jobs is another policy that will have effects on the employment structure. Again one can observe a gradual change from a purely fordist production regime into a more innovation-oriented one; new products and new, more flexible ways of using labour emerge which might lead to new age-selective risks.

The described structural changes and strategies are reflected in both *quantitative and qualitative* changes in the employment structure of the selected firms. Table 3 illustrates the absolute number, and the relative growth or decline of employment in the past decade. As can be seen the *Steel Company* has been involved in a continuous process of reducing the workforce after a period of expansion from 1966 to 1976 when the workforce increased from 17,600 to 24,500. After 1989 this process has continued (the 1990-level was ca. 16,000) and for the next five years the elimination of another 3,000 jobs is planned. The employment situation of the *Electrotechnical firm* has fluctuated greatly over the years. From the late seventies until 1983 an extensive reduction was realised. In the succeeding years, employment increased again until the French takeover led to a complete reconstruction of the firm in 1988/89 and a loss of about 700 jobs. Due to the process of mergers the *Bank* has experienced a considerable employment growth, amounting to ca. 40% in 6 years. The figures of the *Public Utility* firm illustrate a continuous growth, mainly as a result of the increased commercial activities.

An analysis of changes in the 'job-level-structure' of firms[15] (except the Public Utility firm) indicates a shift in the division of the work force over the various job levels within the firms. In the *Steel Company*, the share of the four lowest job levels declined from 34.8% to 11.2% between 1979 and 1988. According to the personnel management of the firm, this shift represents a general decline of unskilled work within the factory and the relative increase of jobs that require technical training on a low or medium level. A similar shift can be observed for the *Electrotechnical firm*, where the share

Table 3: Growth and Decline of Employment (Absolute and Proportional)

	Steel Company		Electro-technical Firm		Bank		Public Utility Firm	
	N	△%	N	△%	N	△%	N	△%
1978	22.657		1.138					
1980	22.838	− 0.8	983	−13.6			210	
1982	22.174	− 2.9	960	− 2.3	1.991		227	8.1
1984	20.793	− 7.2	1.072	11.6	2.315	16.2	231	1.7
1986	20.687	− 0.5	1.090	1.9	2.315		238	3.0
1988	18.299	−11.5	330*	−69.9	2.789	20.4	259	8.8

* Partly Realised in 1989

of the four lowest job levels fell from 49.5% to 22.4 % between 1979 and 1983. However, in contrast to the Steel Company, where a gradual process of upgrading took place during a period of 10 years, the dramatic decline of low skilled jobs in the Electrotechnical firm proceeded very rapidly and does not reflect a gradual upgrading process: it appears that in four years the share of the highest job levels increased from 7.8% to 16.2%. These figures point to a major reshuffling of jobs, an extensive replacement of low by highly skilled jobs. During this period new forms of labour were introduced in the firm – like highly qualified software engineers – while unskilled and low skilled jobs were eliminated. The employment structure of the *Bank* changed between 1985 and 1988 in the opposite direction: the share of the four lowest job levels increased from 26.7% to 35.5%. This shift must be ascribed to the process of mergers that led to a relative increase of the low skilled jobs while the highly qualified staff jobs increased in a much slower pace.

The previous explanation specified the relationship between economic and technological developments on the one hand, and the changes in employment on the other. One can observe both growing and declining employment and different types of qualitative change (downgrading as well as upgrading). These changes might have different effects on the developing age profiles. On the one hand, both a decreasing employment level and a stable or downgrading skill structure may result ceteris paribus in a trend towards an aging workforce. On the other hand, growing employment and upgrading of qualifications may have a rejuvenating effect. Furthermore the specific characteristics of (changing) production regimes might be relevant for the nature and intensity of age-selective risks and the ways firms deal with them.

These presumptions will be evaluated in three different steps. *Firstly*, this section continues with a description of the actual processes of aging and early exit. *Secondly*, section 4 deals with the questions if and how firms are able to control these processes. *Finally*, in section 5 we return to the strategic motives of the sample firms and check to what extent these are relevant for the exit trend in the Netherlands.

3.2   Aging and Old Age in the Selected Firms

Before describing the changes in age-structure we will first give an impression of the particular age-structures of the selected firms in 1985.[16] For this purpose we compared the age profiles of the firms with each other, with the sectoral[17] and with the national profile (*see* figure 2, a-d).

This comparison indicates a number of firm and sector-specific age profiles. Public Utilities and Basic Metals are rather 'old' sectors. The Steel Company is even older than its sector, the Public Utilities Firm is somewhat younger than the sector. These relatively old age profiles are related to the fact that these are traditional sectors with a very large share of male workers. While the proportion of female workers in the Dutch employed population is 33.7 (1985), this share is only 7.5 in the Basic Metals and 11.1

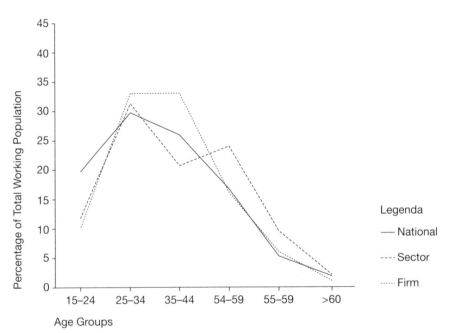

Figure 2a: Age Profile Public Utility Sector and Firm (1985)

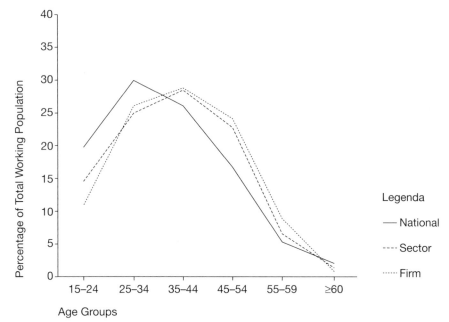

Figure 2b: Age Profile Basic Metal Sector and Firm (1985)

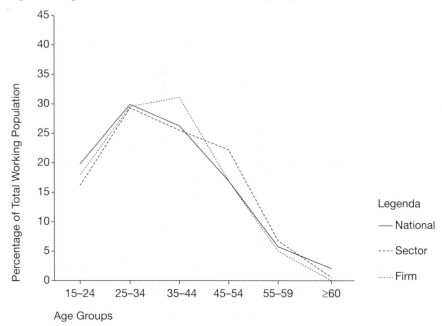

Figure 2c: Age Profile Electrical Engineering Sector and Firm (1985)

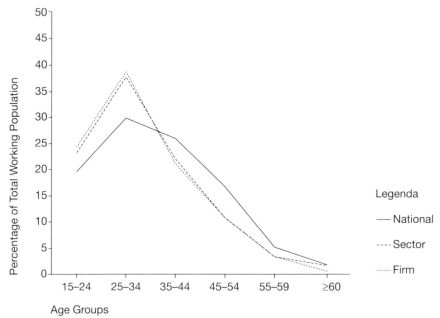

Figure 2d: Age Profile Banking Sector and Firm (1985)

in the Public Utilities. Indeed, the proportion of female workers in the Steel Company (1985) is only 6.0% and in the Public Utility Firm it is 19%. Both sectors are also characterised by a very low external mobility; workers are used to stay in their sector, and, in many cases in their firms, for a life-time. The turnover rates (1985) in both firms are between 5 and 6 %, which is far below the national average.[18]

The electrotechnical sector has a somewhat younger workforce than basic metals and public utilities. The share of female workers in this sector and in the sample firm is 15% (1985) which is not very high either. However, the yearly turnover rate in the electrotechnical firm is much higher than in the two previous firms (12.8 % in 1985): this permits a more rapid pace of rejuvenation, resulting in a younger age structure.

The banking sector is an extreme case, both compared to the other sectors and to the national age profile. Whereas the proportion of age groups 15–35 and >= 35 is fifty-fifty on national level, the proportion in the banking sector is 62% and 38% respectively (and for the selected bank 64% and 36%). This particular age structure can be explained by the high proportion of young female workers. The share of female workers is (in 1985) 44.0% and in the selected bank even 53.4 %. One may say that the bank illustrates a dual structure based on young female workers with

Table 4: The Bank, Age Structure and Gender (1985, Proportional)

	15−24	25−34	35−44	45−54	55−59	≥60
Male	7.4	36.9	32.1	16.1	5.8	1.6
Female	34.3	40.7	11.6	6.3	1.6	0.3

relative high turnover rates and a share of male workers who are more likely to climb the internal job ladder. This difference can be observed when we compare the male and the female age structure in the Bank (table 4).

From this table it is quite clear that the young age structure is mainly due to the large share of young females: almost 75% of all females are younger than 35.

From a longitudinal analysis of the changing age profiles in the selected firms the following conclusions can be drawn (see table 5).[19] The age profile of the two 'old' firms has grown even older between '82 and '88. Both in the *Steel Company* and the *Public Utility Firm*, the share of the 45–54 age group has increased. If we look at the trends over a longer period, it is also clear that the share of the 35–44 age group has slowly increased. In both firms the proportion of the youngest age group has declined; the long-term trend for the 25–34 age group is a steady decrease in the Public Utility Firm and a somewhat smaller decline in the Steel Company. The aging trend in both firms is mitigated by the fact that the trend does not extend to the oldest age group; the proportions of workers of 55 years and over has declined, a trend which can better still be observed if we look at the trend from the late seventies on (figure 3). So while the middle age groups increased in relative

Table 5: Changing Age Structures on Firm Level (Proportional) 1982, 1985, 1988

		15−24	25−34	35−44	45−54	≥55
1982	Steel	10.8	24.8	29.0	23.7	11.7
	Electro	7.2	38.4	28.0	16.3	10.1
	Bank	35.5	30.0	17.7	10.3	6.5
	Public Utilities	12.1	37.1	29.3	14.7	6.8
1985	Steel	11.1	26.1	28.9	24.2	9.7
	Electro	17.7	29.6	31.3	16.5	4.9
	Bank	24.6	38.9	21.1	10.9	4.4
	Public Utilities	10.1	33.2	33.2	16.2	7.3
1988	Steel	8.9	27.9	28.8	25.1	9.3
	Electro	4.4	32.5	36.0	24.1	3.0
	Bank	16.2	43.8	24.7	10.9	4.5
	Public Utilities	10.6	33.5	30.1	21.2	4.6

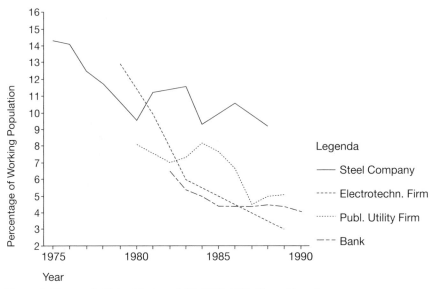

Figure 3: Shares of Older Workers (55) 1975–1990 (Four Fir ms)

terms the average age in the Steel Company hardly changed between 1977 and 1988 (39.6 in 1977; 39.4 in 1987), due to the decline in the proportion of workers over 55 years old.

The trend in the age structure of the *Electrotechnical Firm*, shows continuously growing shares of age groups 35–44 and 45–54 on the one hand, and an unstable development in the youngest age group on the other. The growth and decline in this age group (15–24) seem to be related to the overall employment trend at the firm. After the French takeover in 1988 and the extensive reconstruction of the firm the share of this youngest age group was still only 4.4%, whereas it was 17.7% three years earlier. Here, too, the aging trend is mitigated by a steady decline of the proportion of older workers of 55 years and over. Between 1979 and 1988 this group declined from 13% to 4%, while the share of workers of 60 years and over declined from 5% to zero.

The *Bank* is characterised by a decreasing share of the youngest age group (15–24), in favour of age group 25–34, and to some extent age group 35–44. It is not so much an aging trend here, but rather a process of getting 'less green'. From an analysis of the annual reports of another four big banks in the Netherlands, Tijdens (1990) concludes that exactly the same trend is going on in those banks. The large shift between the two youngest age groups is mainly caused by the increasing age of young females entering the firm.

Summarising the major trends in the age profiles of the selected firms, it appears that both the youngest and older age groups (>= 55) are decreasing; the work forces are tending to concentrate within age groups 35–44 and 45–54. No clear evidence can be found for the hypothesis that changing age structures reflect changing workforce levels. Aging can be found in situations of rising as well as declining overall employment, whereas in all cases a striking decline of the proportions of the oldest age groups can be observed.

3.3   The Early-Exit Process: Available Pathways

Before charactarising the early-exit processes in the selected firms we give an overview of the pathways used to shape the process. One can distinguish between three types of schemes: pre-retirement, social plans and disability schemes. Although some of these originate from national or sectoral regulation, several differences between the firms appear to exist, for example with respect to the level of benefits, the nature of participation (voluntary or compulsory) and the duration of a scheme.

3.3.1 Pre-Retirement

The Dutch state stimulated some experimental pre-retirement pathways in 1976/1977. The *Steel Company* participated in this project from 1977 till 1978. The firm and the unions agreed on a scheme, eligible to workers from the age of 63. The firm allocated 0.4% of the annual average wage payments to finance the pre-retirement benefits. During this experimental period the State guaranteed the financing of any extra costs, which might arise. At that time the attitude of the Steel Company towards an early exit pathway was very positive and outspoken:

"...full participation in the pre-retirement scheme would be desirable; an extension of the early-exit possibilities should be striven for. The firm holds the view that the Dutch government and the European Community should support the financing of an early-exit process for all workers of 60 years and over..." (Strategic Plan, 1977).

The company's interest in the creation and application of a voluntary pre-retirement pathway was not surprising. From 1977 on, this scheme turned out to be an effective instrument of workforce reduction. The firm argued that by doing so it could avoid the necessity of forced dismissals, which would not be in line with the social tradition of personnel policy at the firm.

After the experimental period the Steel Company and the unions agreed to continue and extend the schemes in the following years. In 1980, a second pre-retirement scheme was introduced for workers of 62 years old, followed by a third scheme in 1983 for workers of 60 and 61 years old.

After some years the financing of the scheme became a topic on the bargaining agenda, due to the increasing use of the pathway. Initially the firm met the costs alone, later the workers started to participate in financing. The Steel Company and the unions agreed that 40% of the costs would be paid by the workers, partly based on the argument that this would be paid back in the form of reducted working hours (on a life-time basis). The contribution of the workers consists of a very small percentage of their income (.25%) and of a larger share in the form of an 'unpaid salary rise'.

Financing the early-exit process remained an important issue and has been an incentive to search for other solutions. In the early eighties, the Steel company agreed with the unions about the so-called *Social Plans*; because these plans consist of early-exit pathways that were partly financed by the social security system – as we will discuss later – the firm was able to save around 80 million guilders on benefits. By this type of 'pathway management'[20], the firm realised that the welfare society could contribute to the financing of the firm-specific early-exit process.

The Steel Companies' attitude towards pre-retirement is nowadays very much the same as it was 15 years ago. Personnel reduction is still a policy end for which early exit is a useful instrument, it is just that the costs are still considered as a problem by the company:

"We are still in favour of the scheme, but we are worried about the costs since the cohorts of elderly workers are growing. If it could be afforded we would even establish the official pension age at 60... The continuation of pre-retirement in fact depends on whether we can agree with the unions on a new social plan that would lower the pre-retirement costs again..." (Interview with a personnel manager).

In *the Electrotechnical firm, the Public Utility firm and the Bank*, firm-specific pre-retirement schemes are lacking, but these firms do employ sectoral pre-retirement schemes. In the Banking sector, these schemes originate from 1979 when the age of eligibility was 62. In 1983 this was lowered to 60. The costs of the scheme are fully paid by the employer. In the Electrotechnical Industry, the age of eligibility was also lowered to 60 in 1983, but here the mode of financing was different: both employers and employees contributed to a fund from which the early-exit benefits are paid. Employment conditions at the Public Utility firm are largely based on those for civil servants, so the employees of this firm can use the opportunities of the pre-retirement regulation applying to the civil service sector, which

Table 6: Selected Firms and the Use of Social Plans

Firm	Social Plan	Period
Steel Company	I	1979/1980
	II	1981 – 1984
	III	1984 – 1986
	IV	1987 – 1990
Electro Firm	I	1980 – 1987
	II	1988 – 1990
Bank	I	1989 – ...

offers the opportunity of voluntary pre-retirement from the age of 60. The civil service sector pre-retirement scheme is financed by the pension fund of civil servants. To this fund both employers (the state) and civil servants contribute.

3.3.2 Social Plans

Three of the four selected firms have used the public unemployment scheme to create a firm-specific exit pathway, the so-called social plan. As illustrated in table 6, the Steel Company in particular has a long tradition in using this type of pathway.

The social plans of the selected firms all include an early-exit arrangement for elderly workers. The *financing principle* is always the same: the dismissed elderly worker receives a social security benefit that is supplemented by the firm to a level employer and unions have agreed on (usually the VUT level). So the dismissed worker is entitled to a guaranteed income until the official age of retirement at 65, consisting of a public and a private element. During this period, the public/private ratio changes as a consequence of decreasing social security benefits.

In most cases the age of eligibility is 57.5 years. Only in the second social plan of the Electrotechnical firm the age of entrance was fixed at 55 years. The application of a social-plan pathway is formally restricted to situations of collective dismissals following reorganisation of the labour process. Employees may only enter a social plan if their jobs are destroyed or taken over by (younger) collegues whose jobs will be destroyed. All social plans contain these formal requirements and need the approval of the director of the regional Employment Exchange. In practise, however, these formal requirements are not always strictly enforced, as the following quotations illustrate:

"The fact that you have arranged a good financial construction with the support of the unions is an extra argument for the Employment Exchange not to make a strong case of it, especially when you are talking about elderly workers" (personnel manager of the Bank).

"If you want to get rid of an older worker or if an older worker wants to make use of the Social Plan, you can always create a reorganisation... You know, nowadays organisations always change, so you can always think of a story that might be the case" (personnel manager of the Electrotechnical firm).

"You should look at the Social Plan as an extra option of personnel policy; the personnel manager should use this option in a creative manner. If an older worker has problems – in functioning at work or in a medical sense – the Social Plan might be a solution; you should be creative in constructing the arguments why this man should participate in the scheme" (personnel manager of the Bank).

We might conclude that most of the early-exit arrangements in Social Plans allow for the possibility of 'flexible application', what we have labelled situations of informal bargaining and lateral collusion (section 2). The most extreme case is the 1990 social plan at the Bank. In this plan no limitations are included with respect to duration or volume. The firm and the unions agreed upon the formulation:

"As a consequence of changing circumstances, insights and purposes, organisational changes will occur continuously. In this context... a Social Plan has been agreed upon by (name of the firm) and (name of the unions)..."

Sometimes restrictions are imposed, however. In the case of the Steel Company, for example, each Social Plan is limited to a maximum number of participants. We also saw that the scheme might be too costly for the firm if it was applied to the higher job levels. Finally, its application is often restricted by voluntarism: firms have to find ways to control participation in a quantitative and qualitative sense. Still, in spite of these restrictions, it seems firms can provide themselves with a rather flexible instrument of early exit by means of bargaining with the unions. The role of government in this process is limited. It provides the legal possibility of topping up social benefits; it accepts the age-specific practise of dismissing personnel and it frees the elderly unemployed from the obligation to look for work. However, the government is not involved in the process of shaping pathways.

The general rule in case of mass dismissals is 'first in last out'. Since this rule might create a problem for firms – they will end up with an elderly personnel structure – employers are allowed to spread the total number of dismissals over different age groups. Another solution is the so-called '55+ rule': the total number of dismissals is selected from the age group 55 and over. This solution is only accepted by the official agencies if (a) older workers accept their dismissal voluntarily and (b) if these workers are not entitled to enter a pre-retirement-scheme. The year 55 refers to the legal rule that unemployed workers of 55 and older are no longer obliged to search for work.[21] However, the older worker has to raise a formal objection against his dismissal in order to receive the unemployment benefit.[22]

3.3.3 Disability

In all selected firms the workers are insured against the risks of sickness and disability. However, differences exist with regard to the payment of extra-legal benefits. Until 1988 the Steel Company guaranteed the full income of every worker who had become (partially) disabled. This practice was motivated by social reasons:

"The idea was that the firm took responsibility for the well-being of the workers, since they were hired for a lifetime. Probably the improvement of public provisions has reduced the necessity for this practise" (personnel manager of the Steel Company).

Since 1988 the level of the supplements has been related to age; however, for the older workers this has not changed much. The Bank also pays supplements to older workers who enter the disability scheme; in this case the practice stems from the collective agreement in the banking sector. In the Bank it is also reported that the meaning of the extra-legal benefits changed during the eighties:

"It certainly originated from social reasons, related to the system of internal careers which was quite normal in the banking sector. But today it clearly has a function in smoothing an exit pathway'" (personnnel manager of the Bank).

3.4   The Use of Pathways

We now focus at firm-level differences with respect to the ways in which early-exit processes come into being (3.4.1). Furthermore, we look at differences that might be related to gender and age (3.4.2), and see to what extent reintegration in the labour process occurs (3.4.3).

Table 7: Early Exit Rates, Distribution of Early Exit over Pathways (in Percentages) and
          over Time, by Firm

	Early Exit Absolute	Distribution Over Pathways				Distribution Over Time
		Rate*	Disability	Pre-Retire-ment	Social Plan	
Bank	100	91.7	40	45	15	Flat Curve
Steel	6.456	73.2	37	34	29	Weakly Peaked
Electro	294	99.3	18	13	68	Highly Peaked
Public	25	83.6	8	92	–	Equal Growth

Bank: 1985–1990; Steel: 1989–1988; Electro-Technical Firm: 1980–1989; Public Utility
Firm. 1980–1989.
* Early Exit Rate Expresses the Share of Early Exit (of those Older than so) in Relation
  to Regular Pensioning.

3.4.1 Variety Between Firms

Table 7 summarises the main characteristics of the early-exit processes at
firm level.[23]

The first striking phenomenon is the high exit rate in all four firms. Early
exit has turned into a massive practise that has undermined the importance
of regular pensioning. Additional analysis shows that the strength of the
trend has not weakened through the years (i.e., during the eighties the
early-exit rate tended to increase in all firms).

Notwithstanding the uniformity of the trend we do find some differences
in early-exit rates. In this respect, it is worthy of note that the two 'oldest'
firms (Steel and Public Utilities) have lower rates; this fact might indicate
that large shares of older workers put a check on the strength of the trend.
We will come back to this point later. For the time being we conclude that
all four firms do show a massive process of early exit.

In spite of the uniformity in exit rates we find a striking variety in the use
of disability, pre-retirement and social plan pathways (table 9).

Some firms use a mix of instruments, while others employ just one
particular instrument. The Steel Company and the Bank are examples of
the first type. At the Steel Company all pathways are used in a 'balanced
way'. At the bank the distribution is a little less balanced; here the core
pathways are disability and pre-retirement. The social plan was only effective in 1990.

Quite different was the exit pattern in the Electrotechnical and the Public
Utility firms, where one exit instrument dominates the process. The Social
Plan is responsible for the major share of early exits at the Electrotechnical

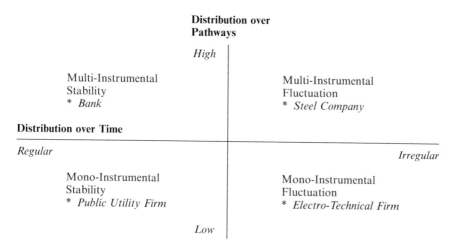

Figure 4: Early Exit: Distribution over Pathways and over Time

firm (68%), while the pre-retirement scheme in the Public Utility firm absorbs 77% of all exits.

The distribution of early exits over time also displays a striking variety. The bank has a very flat exit pattern over time. A slow increase in the number of early exits was found in the Public Utility firm. Quite different are the patterns in the electrotechnical firm and the steel company. The first one has sharp peaks in 1979/1980, 1983 and 1989/1990, the latter (more modest) ones in 1979, 1984 and 1987/1988.

The described variety in exit processes can be characterised along two dimensions (figure 4). *Multi-instrumental fluctuation* is typical for the early-exit process at the Steel Company. A balanced mix of different pathways underlies the process, which is also characterised by a fluctuating pattern over time. A more detailed analysis indicates that these fluctuations are mainly due to two instruments, the social plan and the pre-retirement scheme. *Mono-instrumental fluctuation* is particularly prevalent at the Electrotechnical firm, where the use of social plans produces very strong peaks in the levels of early exit. The Bank provides a clear example of *multi-instrumental stability*: different instruments contribute to a rather regular exit process. Finally, the Public Utility Firm is an example of *mono-instrumental stability*: one core instrument is used to shape a regular exit pattern over time.

Table 8: Cohort Analysis of Employed Persons, Age Group 50 Years and over (1985): Reconstruction of Situation in 1991

Age Cohorts	Employed 1985 Age ≥ 50	Employed 1991	Early Exit 1985 – 1991 Disability	Pre-Retirement	Social Plan*	Others**	TOTAL	Pension
'31 – '35	106	58%	20%	1%	8%	13%	42%	—
'26 – '30	82	24%	23%	38%	6%	9%	76%	—
< '26	20	—	20%	35%	—	—	55%	45%
Total	208	39%	21%	25%	7%	10%	7%	4%
-males	146	38%	18%	21%	8%	11%	58%	4%
-females	62	41%	29%	15%	3%	6%	53%	5%

* Only in 1990
** Deceases, Leave on Own Request, etc.

3.4.2 Gender and Age Differences

In section 2.1, we referred to the problem that an analysis of activity rates might not be appropriate for indicating female exit patterns. For that reason a *cohort* analysis of individual exit data from the bank will be presented. Since a large share of the workforce at the Bank consists of female workers this firm is an important case to control for gender effects. At the same time, we examine to what extent different age cohorts differ with respect to early exit.

Table 8 refers to all workers at the Bank who were 50 years and over in 1985. The table represents the status of this group six years later, at the beginning of 1991. The outcomes have been differentiated to three birth cohorts as well as to gender.

Of the employed age group 50 and over (in 1985) 39% were still working in 1991. For the cohorts 31–35 and 26–30 the 'survival rates' are 58% and 24% respectively. This difference is particularly due to the fact that the pre-retirement scheme does not affect the participation of those who are between 55 and 60 years old in 1991. The trends for the cohort born before 1926 give an interesting picture of the end of the working life at the Bank. In 1991 this group is over 65. If every worker were to leave the firm at the regular age of retirement we should have 100% cases of normal pensioning in 1991. As the table illustrates, only 45% did leave the firm on the basis of normal retirement, whereas 55% left by early exit. Compared to the development of the next older age group we see a sharp increase in early exit.

The survival rates of males and females indicate only a slight difference; 38% and 42% respectively. Much more obvious are the gender differences in the use of pathways. Males make more use of the pre-retirement scheme and the social plan, while females are more likely to enter the disability scheme. These differences can be ascribed to institutional barriers. Women are more often employed on a part-time basis and have relative short or disrupted labour biographies, which can bring disadvantages with respect to eligibility and/or the amount of benefits in pre-retirement and social-plan schemes. As a result early exit of women is more often channelled through the disability pathway which is also reflected in the national pattern (table 9).

3.4.3 Reintegration

The uniform and massive character of the early-exit trend is also reflected in the absence of reintegration policies during the eighties. In none of the firms was a well developed practise of reintegration observed. Indeed, in

Table 9: Disability Entry as a Proportion of the Male and Female Working Population, 1988–1990

	Males	Females	Total
1988	1.62	1.72	1.70
1989	1.66	1.91	1.79
1990	1.64	2.13	1.83

Source: Svr, CBS.

some cases (Steel, Bank) it was found that reintegration policies were reduced during those years. The Steel company used to have good facilities in this regard, but these were cut back during the eighties, as we will discuss later. The cohort analyses indicate that reintegration of older workers occurs only in incidental cases. At the bank 44 people (21%) of the initial cohort enter the disability scheme, but in only three cases reintegration was observed. At the national level 14% of the older workers (>= 55 years) who entered a disability scheme (1985) had reentered the workforce half a year later.[24]

3.5   Small Firms: An Exception?

It could be argued that the availability of early-exit pathways and the extensive use of them – we have identified – might be due to the relatively large size of the selected firms. Does the size of firms have an impact on the occurrence and the characteristics of the early-exit process? Table 10 shows the (changing) age structures in two sectors that are dominated by small firms.[25]

The catering industry can be characterised as a very 'green' sector. This is not only due to the large share of female workers, the age structure of males also shows an overrepresentation in the two youngest age groups. The sector largely depends on the recruitment of workers aged 34 or younger. Between 1979 and 1985 the number of male workers decreased; at the same time the share of older workers (>= 55 years) declined. The female population also shows a declining share of older workers, this, however, in a situation of increasing employment. For both male and female workers the declining shares of older workers, especially in age group 60–64, points to an early exit process.

The real estate agencies show a completely different age structure. The male population is characterised by large shares of the middle aged; this pattern resembles the 'old' age structures of the Steel Company and the Public Utility firm. Between 1979 and 1985 the male population experienced an aging trend that, however, does not continue in the two oldest age

Table 10: Age Structures in Catering Industry and Real Estate Agencies, 1979−1985

		15−24	23−34	35−44	45−54	55−59	60−64	
Catering Industry								
1979	M	34.4	32.2	16.8	11.9	2.8	1.9	(N = 36.300)
	F	40.5	27.9	18.8	8.0	2.4	2.4	(N = 25.100)
1985	M	36.4	35.4	17.1	8.0	2.3	0.8	(N = 34.300)
	F	42.3	25.3	20.7	9.3	2.1	0.3	(N = 32.600)
Real Estate								
1979	M	9.5	31.7	25.3	18.8	8.8	5.9	(N = 16.500)
	F	41.8	20.2	19.8	10.8	4.3	3.1	(N = 6.700)
1985	M	7.4	28.5	32.8	20.8	6.3	4.2	(N = 18.900)
	F	25.0	30.0	23.0	16.0	4.0	2.0	(N = 10.000)

groups. During this period the female population also aged somewhat. In this sector one can also point to an early-exit process that develops itself at least within the age group 60–64.

While the trend in small firms seems to develop in the same direction as in the larger ones, several sources indicate that the use of exit pathways is different. From a survey of 1200 small firms (<= 20 employees) it appears (for 1986) that the availability of a pre-retirement scheme is more likely as firms have more employees (EIM, 1986: 58). From macro data it appears that this observation can be generalised: in 1989 51% of the firms with less than 99 employees had a pre-retirement scheme while 90% of the large firms (>= 100 employees) had one (CBS, 1992: 89).

The fact that pre-retirement schemes are less common in small sectors seems to be 'compensated' by a more extensive use of unemployment and disability schemes. In the Netherlands the chance of becoming unemployed was 8.2% in 1986. However, this figure is much higher in some sectors that are traditionally dominated by small firms. The building industry for instance shows an unemployment chance of 24.5% in 1986, and the catering industry 24.7% (SoZaWe, 1987: 90). Furthermore, a survey of disability entries (1980) shows that small firms are more likely to 'produce' disability than the larger ones. While 49% of the insured persons work in small firms (<= 100 employees), 61% of the disability entries comes from these small firms (Aarts, Bruinsma and De Jong, 1982: 37).

One major consequence of small size is the lack of stable internal labour markets; the opportunities for work adaption and/or replacement of people are proportionally small. These circumstances might explain pathway variety between small and large industries. Small firms are more dependent on 'social justice pathways', but in the end it seems the level of early exit does not lag behind the trends at the larger firms.

4   Early Exit, Choice and Control

The four firms display a homogeneous exit trend, but at the same time a heterogeneous pattern of pathways used. Four different patterns were distinguished concerning the use of pathways and its distribution over time. Furthermore, variations were detected related to gender. Cases of reintegration appeared to be scarce. This heterogeneous pattern raises questions about the control of the exit process by the sample firms. Does a large fluctuation in the use of the exit process indicate a high level of control or 'pathway management' by the firm? What are the differences between mono-instrumental and multi-instrumental processes with respect to control?

The question is who actually controls the early exit process: the firm, another actor (state, trade union, bi- or tripartite institution), or is the use of pathways the consequence of particular individual characteristics or voluntary individual choices out of control of the firm? In other words: how is the use of pathways by individual workers related to purposive strategies of the firm?

4.1   Control of the Exit Process

Theoretically, a direct relation between exit and firm strategy exists to the extent that the firm is able to control the exit process, the extreme case where the firm can decide which particular employee and how many have to leave and when. But we can also imagine situations where exit is the result of individual choices or characteristics. If early-exit routes are produced on sectoral or national level as *public goods* than every employee (in a certain age category) may use these pathways, outside the control of the firm. Particular individual, social, psychological or physical characteristics can make individual employees eligible for particular forms of social insurances leading to exit on an individual basis without control by the firm.

The fundamental question is: who makes the choices for exit and who creates the pathways? To understand the actual process we have to make an analytical distinction between two dimensions: *exit* from the firm and *entry* into a particular pathway. Both actions might be controlled by different actors. In this respect a distinction can also be made between the *individual employee*, the *firm* and *external actors*. The last category refers to actors external to the firm, like the state, semi-state institutions, trade unions and bi- and tripartite institutions. We might expect these three actors to act on different levels. With respect to the *exit choice*, we suppose that it is either a choice of the individual employee or it is a choice (decision) of the firm. The *entry choice* to a pathway might be under control of the firm (in

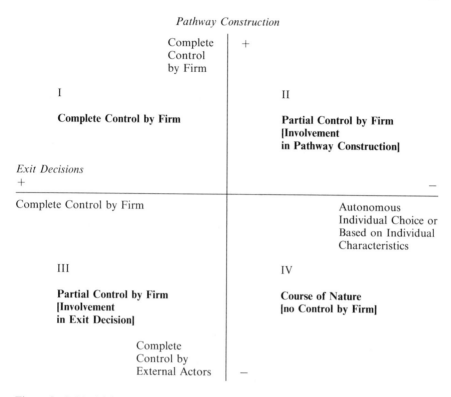

Pathway Construction

	Complete Control by Firm	+	

I

Complete Control by Firm

II

**Partial Control by Firm
[Involvement
in Pathway Construction]**

Exit Decisions
+

Complete Control by Firm

—

Autonomous
Individual Choice or
Based on Individual
Characteristics

III

**Partial Control by Firm
[Involvement
in Exit Decision]**

IV

**Course of Nature
[no Control by Firm]**

Complete
Control by
External Actors   —

Figure 5: A Model for Evaluating Pathway Construction and Exit Decisions by Firms

particular a firm-specific pathway) or of an external actor (sectoral or national pathways).

From the perspective of the firm we can now construct a scale on the two dimensions (figure 5): (1) the exit choice can vary between complete control by the firm and autonomous individual choice or particular individual characteristics (the horizontal axis); (2) the entry choice can vary between complete control by the firm and total control by external actors (the vertical axis). By combining the two dimensions four different relations between exit and firm strategy are generated. We have two extreme cases: exit is completely the result of purposive firm-strategy, the 'complete-control' case (I), and exit without any particular control by the firm, the 'course-of-nature' case (IV). In between we have two different possibilities: exit choices might be completely under control of the firm, but entry into specific pathways is controlled by other actors, so the firm is dependent on these actors to use exit as a management-tool (III) or exit choices are controlled by the individual, but choice of the pathway is under control of the firm (II).

How can firms control exit and entry choices? With respect to the individual exit choices firms might have a legitimated power to effect a *compulsory exit* for selected employees. Or firms might use positive or negative incentives – like financial, social and moral *incentives* – to influence the individual choices of employees. With respect to the entry side of pathways firms can control these choices if they have the power to decide directly who is allowed to enter the pathway. Firms also might have an indirect way of controlling entry by influencing the criteria by which employees may enter a particular exit route. Only when the firm has a private 'firm-owned' pathway, will the firm have complete control on entries. In cases where external actors are involved, the particular firm will have to rely on its power to influence collective bargaining agreements, government policies or the public discourse; or the firm might be represented in those institutions charged with implementing pathway regulations.

4.2   Control on Entry in Pathways

In general individual firms can hardly influence the process of creating the pre-retirement pathway since in most cases this is a matter for collective bargaining at sectoral level in which trade unions and employers' associations are involved. Individual firms that want to try to influence the results of this bargaining process are confronted with a number of barriers. Firstly, the firm must be able to present its own wishes on the internal agenda of the employers' association; the firm must therefore at least be a member of this association. Secondly, the firm is dependent on the political process of aggregating the different, and maybe conflicting, interests of other member firms within the association. In this aggregating process the individual wishes of singular firms are likely to be lost. Only powerful member-firms (usually the large firms) might be able to guide the aggregating process in the direction of their own interests. Thirdly, the individual firm will be dependent on the relative strength of its organisation confronting trade unions in the bargaining process.

The Public Utility firm and the Electrotechnical firm are relatively small firms and have only a marginal influence on sectoral bargaining processes. The Bank is a large firm and might have such an influence, but it must compete with other large banks in its employers' association. The only clear exception in this respect is the Steel Company. This firm is not dependent on sectoral schemes, but is directly involved in consultations with the trade union about creating private pre-retirement pathways. In the electrotechnical sector, to which the Electrotechnical firm belongs, a pre-retirement fund has been established to which employers and employees have to pay fixed contributions. However, just like the Steel Company, the Electrotechnical firm managed to agree with the unions on early-exit arrangements in social plans that could be applied over a very long period of time. Again these social-plan pathways are partly paid for by social security funds. In the case of the Electrotechnical firm most elderly workers go for an early exit along the social-plan pathway before they are eligible for the pre-retirement scheme. For this reason the sectoral pre-retirement fund pays restitutions to the firm; there again a firm appears to be able to save pre-retirement costs by establishing an alternative and cheaper pathway, in cooperation with the trade unions.

The head of the personnel department of the *Bank* says about the sectoral pre-retirement scheme:

"I don't say we couldn't live without it, but it helps a great deal in the context of renewing the organisation, it speeds up the process. We can replace more rapidly the obsolete management by a younger, more flexible one, the change in attitude towards a more client-centred one can be realised more quickly."

Nevertheless, the management of the Bank considers the pre-retirement pathway rather expensive since the employers bear all the costs. Two years ago the agreement in the sector was changed so that the benefits of pre-retirement participants are now related to their age: participants of 60 years old receive the lowest benefit and those of 64 the highest. On the other hand, the organisational need for early exit at the Bank has just increased. Like the Steel Company and Electrotechnical firm, the Bank managed to agree with the trade unions on a social plan with an early-exit arrangement beginning in 1989. So if the participation in the pre-retirement pathway has declined as a consequence of the changes in the sectoral agreement it seems the Bank has created itself an alternative with the additional advantage of lower costs. Although the firm is not able to influence the process of creating pre-retirement pathways, it seems it can still do some 'pathway management' by bargaining with the unions about a social plan and thus removing the disadvantages possibly arising out of changes to the sectoral pre-retirement agreement.

Finally the director of the *Public Utility firm* does not see a specific firm interest in the availability of a pre-retirement pathway:

"The PRS pathway happens to be there. I can see some advantages for the older workers, of course. You even might say it releases the firm from some of its responsibility for taking care of the elderly. But there is no firm policy behind it... We are aware of an aging trend and we are already thinking of strategies to cope with the consequences. How do we keep older scientists creative, for example. I don't know if early exit should be part of such strategies, because sometimes you don't want specific knowledge to leave the firm."

In the case of the Steel Company and the Bank, exit is only possible on a voluntary basis. Formally the firm cannot oblige elderly workers to leave the firm on social-plan terms. On the other hand, the individual worker has no right to early exit by means of the social plan: if the firm does not want him to go, permission to leave will not be given. In contrast, the two social plans of the Electrotechnical firm have a compulsory character: the firm has the authority to determine which workers are eligible for an early exit and which are not.

Usually the unions press the point of voluntarism; if forced dismissals are not strictly necessary they urge for a 'soft way of reorganising'. In a certain sense this means the firm has a control problem: how can it realise sufficient participation in the right places? This problem is partly solved by offering attractive supplements. Furthermore, the firm is usually allowed to apply the early-exit arrangements over a longer period of time. In the case of the Bank, a time limit has not even been set; in the case of the Electrotechnical firm, the unions accepted the fact that the first compulsory social plan was prolonged for many years on a 'voluntary' basis; in the case of the Steel Company, we see that every two or three years a new social plan is arranged.

4.3   Control on Individual Exit Choices

As mentioned above, participation in disability schemes is formally restricted to those who are medically (partly) incapacitated. Entering the disability scheme is formally not a matter of free choice but depends on individual characteristics like health and the labour-market position. In section 2, we described the way these variables are dealt with in the implementation agencies; we showed the importance of professional decision-making, informal strategies and norms. Before (sick) workers come into contact with professional bureaucracies, however, the firm already might have played a role in preparing the access to the disability pathway.

With respect to the participation in other exit pathways – which is, as we have seen, in many cases a formally voluntary decision- we might also wonder if firms can influence the process of decision-making. Our research in the four selected firms revealed a number of incentives used to stimulate early exit. We came across moral and social pressures and financial incentives. We also found that early-exit practices have grown into well accepted forms of enterprise social policy; the opportunity of early exit has become one of the professional tools of personnel managers, social, medical and psychological workers.

4.3.1 Moral and Social Pressure

Starting with an example from the Steel Company, let's see how a personnel reduction usually takes place in the day to day practise. All units of the Steel Company are instructed to develop plans and actions in order to save manpower. Consequently, the oxygen steel factory plans to reduce its staff, for example from 1000 to 990 jobs in a specific year. To fulfil this task the director of the factory discusses the different possibilities with the personnel manager. One of the strategies is now to check which workers would be eligible for entry into the social plan pathway during the next year. After that, two more questions will be discussed: do we want these people to leave and do we want their jobs to be abolished? The options resulting from this inventory lead to different actions. Suppose it is decided that it would be preferable if certain people used the opportunity of an early exit. Now the next question is if these people are willing to do so or if they can be convinced to do so.

The personnel manager will have '*social talks*' with potential social plan participants. He will point out any advantages of an early exit, and he might even argue that this exit is a kind of moral obligation towards the younger workers. A personnel manager of the Steel Company gives an example of such a procedure:

"...(I told him) 'you still have that boat haven't you... Wouldn't it be nice if you had lots of time for sailing and fishing... I'll bet your wife would be very happy, too. Besides I know you agree with me; we have to give those youngsters a chance...'"

Part of the social talk is also the *preparation for a jobless future*:
"I talked with all of them and made it clear they shouldn't see themselves as unemployed. I suggest they tell their friends and neighbours they got the opportunity of an early retirement. They should learn to see it as a right, they worked long enough for it. Economic recession is not their fault, I tell them, why not enjoy the unexpected freedom..." (social worker, Electrotechnical firm).

Sometimes more pressure is needed. A chief can make demands on people which he knows they cannot cope with; or he examines the sick leave of people and asks them critical questions about it. This strategy aims at '*self-normalisation*': it should give the elderly worker a feeling that he or she is not able to cope with all these changes, that their performance is not satisfactory anymore and that an early exit would probably be the best.

"Sometimes you have to show people their own limits. I know that they hate all that new technology stuff. Still it's inevitable, isn't it. I see them struggling and talk with them saying they might have lost some flexibility. I tell them I don't bother too much, they all did good jobs once, but times have changed. Well, usually they are happy we don't see it as weakness, it's a natural thing. Then usually they decide for themselves that the social plan would be a relief" (factory director of the Steel Company).

The normative force, pressing the use of exit opportunities, is not only the result of purposive social talks. When specific early-exit pathways are available over a longer period of time a 'blind process' of normalisation can arise. When, for example, the pressure to raise productivity increases, the limited capacities of some (older) workers are less likely to be tolerated:
"In former times elderly workers were much more accepted here. The firm had a family character: if elderly workers failed to do all their tasks well it was a natural thing that those tasks were modified or that the elderly were released from particular duties. It is a cultural change. Peers and chiefs make disapproving remarks now and hint at the exit opportunities" (trade unionist in the Steel Company).

It appears that normative pressures – initially meant to support staff reductions – easily reproduce themselves and become a relatively autono-mous force behind exit practises. When chiefs and colleagues make elderly workers feel they cannot do a satisfactory job anymore, they might well be induced into an exit pathway if they are eligible. Workers who are not might be tempted to look at medical incapacity, with regard to the (new) perform-ance standards. In different firms, we came across this tendency to redefine a worsening performance in medical terms. A director of the Bank explains:
"The boundaries between sick and healthy are highly arbitrary. It's really easy to enter the Disability Scheme if you are elderly and feel you are no longer able to cope with new performance standards. Now if chiefs, peers and personnel managers feel the same about it, in fact the decision has been made already..."

Finally, negative incentives are sometimes used to prevent people from staying:
"We show them we cannot offer a proper alternative if the job gets abolished; for a craftsman it is not an attractive perspective to be forced into an unskilled job, even if his income is guaranteed. Nor is it very appealing to

be transferred to another unit where nobody knows you. Those are strong arguments in favor of an early exit" (personnel manager of the Steel Company).

It appears that several pressures aiming at early exit can develop into a more or less stable and *age-related exit norm*. Gradually, steering the exit process becomes a legitimate practice irrespective of the formal rules that the pathways used are subject to.

4.3.2 Early Exit as Enterprise Social Policy

Many respondents in the Steel Company, the Electrotechnical firm and the Bank report that medical, social and psychological care for the workers have changed during the last decade. The opportunity of an early exit has become part of the enterprise social policy. Now this opportunity can be used directly to realise workforce reduction or productivity improvement:
"I'll give you an example. What should I do with a cranedriver who is 53 or 54 years old and whose performance is troubled by mental problems? The social plan might be a solution in three or four years, but will this opportunity still exist by then...? In former times we might have looked for a less demanding job, now we discuss the possibility of medical incapacitation. After all, such a solution might be in the interest of the factory" (team chief in factory of the Steel Company).

This logic is frequently explained and defended at the highest management level, though it is not made into official firm policy. The combination of troubled performances on the one hand, and the organisational need for change and productivity improvement on the other, lead to the promotion of early exit opportunities. Sometimes the elderly workers themselves want to be released from their duties, but it is also encouraged by (personnel) managers. Medical and social workers have grown accustomed to this practise and find themselves using the exit opportunities in their own practise. If the organisation is less willing to absorb people who have performance problems, early exit is a form of social care, they reason, even if an early exit is not strictly needed in a medical sense. '*You have to protect people against this new productivity fetishism*', one of the medical workers in the Steel Company says. A personnel manager of the Bank is very clear about this process of 'professional norm formation':
"Directors want to get rid of conservative forces, personnel managers want to help the directors, doctors have learnt they shouldn't want to change the organisation but just take care of the people working in it. Well, for all of them the disability scheme is a solution."

Organisational pressure can change the professional standards of those who were initially meant to improve medical and social working conditions. The acceptance of early exit as a form of social care smooths the way for organisational change. This change of professional standards can be explained as an unintended effect of the exit policies themselves. If professional workers are forced to change their practices – from an internalising into a more externalising role – they are also forced to seek new standards that legitimise this new role. Once these standards have been established they start functioning as a permanent force behind the exit process.

4.3.3 Financial Incentives

The Steel Company has always had the policy not to fire disabled workers even if they are fully incapacitated. The benefit of disabled workers was topped up to 100% by the firm. In 1988 this policy was abolished and the pension supplement made dependent on the age of the disabled worker. In practise older workers of 55 years and over still receive their full income until the official age of retirement. In the banking sector the same policy is in operation as a result of collective bargaining.

For social reasons the unions are very much in favor of this kind of policy. The implications for the Steel Company and the Bank are that 'exit' through disability of elderly workers is only a partial exit in financial terms. On the other hand, it also reduces the resistance of disabled workers against the disability schemes. In cases of doubt – and such cases do occur – the supplement offered by the firm might stimulate entrance into the disability schemes.

"Suppose you are 54 and not feeling too well. You might lose motivation, get sick and end up in the Disability Scheme with 70% of your income. It would be understandable if you tried to reach the VUT age or strived for participation in a social plan because of the better benefits. But in our situation it is more attractive to allow yourself to be judged disabled since there are hardly any financial disadvantages" (personnel manager of the Bank).

In incidental cases financial incentives are given to prevent people from taking an early-exit opportunity. A small salary rise might be attractive since many private pension systems are based on last earned incomes. However, this does not seem to be a widespread practise. Many personnel managers report that people usually take the decision to use the pre-retirement pathway long before they reached the age of eligibility. In other cases a salary rise is offered under condition of taking the early-exit opportunity after one or two years. This might be attractive since the benefits

		Involvement in Pathway Definition by Single Firms		
		High	Medium	Low
Control and Selection Employees for Exit by Single Firms	High	Social Plan **Firm E** (1983)		
	Medium	Social Plan **Firm B** **Firm S** **Firm E**	Disability **Firm B**	
		Disability **Firm S**		
	Low	PRS* **Firm S**	PRS **Firm B** **Firm E**	PRS **Firm P**
				Disability **Firm E** **Firm P**

* PRS = Pre-Retirement Scheme

Figure 6: Exit Control by Selected Firms

are also based on the last earned income. It is reported that negotiations about the financial terms of the projected exit are not common but do occur. In general, it is at higher income levels that financial incentives may have some importance.

4.4   Summary

Based on the model presented above (figure 6) we have classified the different pathways used in the four selected firms by the degree of control by the individual firms (figure 7). Involvement in pathway-definition is either high, medium or low. High involvement is the case if the firm directly bargained with the union or social security agency on the criteria to be used for a specific firm-level pathway, as was the case for the Social Plan in the electrotechnical firm. Involvement is classified as medium if the firm has a relatively strong position in sectoral bargaining through its employers' association, the case of the disability pathway for the Bank. If a firm is neither directly nor indirectly (or only very marginally) involved in sectoral bargaining, we have classified this type of involvement as low.

The other dimension is control on exit decisions: who will/must leave the firm? Again, we have three different possibilities. High control by the firm is the case when exit is formally compulsory and the firm can decide who has to leave. This is the case for the Social Plan in the Electrotechnical firm. If control is formally voluntarily, but in reality the firm uses various (informal) incentives to press individual workers in the direction of an exit choice, we have classified this type of control as medium. When the exit decision of workers is both formally and actually voluntary, exit control by the firm is low.

As can be seen from figure 6, the practise of early exit at firm level varies between firms with respect to the type and degree of control.

To summarise: the early-exit processes in our sample firms are not subject to one formal control regime. Informal processes at firm level tend to produce an exit norm that is reinforced by professional practices and the attitudes of chiefs and colleagues; early exit has become a 'natural' thing to do or to strive for. The question is why firms are prepared to accept such a 'Loreley-effect', even in cases where any instrumental utility seems to be lacking.

5   From Structural Pressures to Permanent Flexibility

Sectoral differences as well as firm-level differences regarding bargaining opportunities may explain variations in 'institutional behaviour'. In the previous section, we discussed several variations in this respect.

Variations may also stem from the economic and technological environment. Economic crisis, increasing competition, technological innovation and changing markets may bring about a need for *(1) radical staff reductions, (2) gradual decreases of the workforce, (3) changes in the qualitative structure of employment, and (4) more flexibility in personnel structures.* Early exit may fullfil a function in respect of these needs. However, like the institutional environment the economic and technological one is neither coercive nor decisive with respect to early exit. Here the production and personnel regime acts as an intermediate structure. In this section we concentrate on the ways external pressures are mediated and transformed into early-exit practises. Firstly, we will discuss the pressures mentioned above. Secondly, we examine how the resulting needs and their fulfilment partly depend on the production and personnel regimes of firms. It will be argued that early-exit practises not only have a meaning with respect to specific personnel problems but also that they have developed into regular tools of personnel policy that can be applied in the most varied of ways.

5.1   Economic Crisis

During the seventies and eighties many firms had to reorganize in order to reduce the costs of production. The recession implied in many cases that firms had to develop a 'master plan' how to withstand decreasing sales and falling profits. Such a plan can have many different ingredients one of which might be a strategy to reduce the workforce by a specific number. In 1975 the Steel Company was confronted with the most serious recession since the war. A few years later it would appear to be the first sign of a world steel crisis that lasted until the late eighties. The demand for steel and steel products collapsed, prices fell and in many places these basic industries were faced with a surplus of productive capacity.

Initially the firm reacted with temporary measures. However, after three years of rising losses the board decided that structural interventions were no longer avoidable. Saving in costs had to be realised amounting to 200 million guilders a year. Cutting the workforce by 2,000 jobs was one of the measures that were proposed in 1977. The VUT and SOP schemes were introduced in this year; the board of directors considered these schemes as the most important instruments to achieve personnel reduction.

The situation of the Electrotechnical firm in 1979 was comparable with the above. The firm lost some important orders during the period of recession and had to deal with a surplus of productive capacity. Here too the exit of elderly workers was a suggested solution; the board particularly promoted the creation of a social plan so that a large number of elderly workers (over 57.5 years old) could be dismissed in one go.

5.2   Productivity

In 1982 the board of the *Steel Company* published a new strategic plan in which the need for a sharp rise in productivity was defended. Extensive investments in new technologies were projected with the financial help of the Dutch government. On the base of these investments the firm made a start with the systematic development of *productivity programmes*. These programmes have been continued until today and have given rise to a permanent situation of redundancies. '*Making more steel with less people*' is still the guiding motto of the Steel Company. Since 1984 the process of workforce reduction has continued, while production and sales gradually grew. Between 1985 and 1990 an improvement in productivity has been realised of about 20%.

The continuous process of scale enlargement that characterised the economic behaviour of the *Bank* during the eighties, in fact arose from the same need for productivity increase. Of course the mergers that were realised had to bring advantages of large scale, the ongoing and steady process of early exit fulfilled a function in this respect. In this case, a purposive exit policy developed by the highest management level was not judged to be necessary until 1990.

Pressures to raise productivity not only have immediate effects on the required size of the workforce, they also give rise to changing work methods, integration of tasks and/or subcontracting of labour. As we will discuss later, such changes also appear to be relevant with respect to the position of older workers, especially when early-exit practises are strongly integrated within the personnel policies of firms.

5.3   Technological Change

As we have already pointed out, the *Electrotechnical firm* reduced its workforce in 1980 with the help of a social plan that set the rules for the early exit of elderly workers into an unemployment scheme. Once this reduction had been effectuated a period started in which the social plan became a permanent instrument of personnel management. While the Steel Company had to negotiate with the unions time and again about the realisation and the terms of a new social plan, the Electrotechnical firm was able to apply the same social plan until 1987. Although the unions accepted this practise they had hardly any influence on the way this instrument was applied. During this period the entire workforce aged 60 years and over left the firm, most of them into the unemployment scheme. In addition most of the workers between 57.7 and 60 years old made use of the opportunity the social plan offered.

What were the reasons underlying this extensive early exit process? A situation of crisis gave rise to the arrangement of the first social plan (1980). But next a complex of strategic considerations led to the continuation of an early-exit policy. At first, new activities had to be employed in order to compensate for the lost orders. The firm engaged in the development of a data communication network. This meant the firm had to gain another type of knowledge and qualifications: while the technology of telephone units was still based on ancient electronics in those years, in the new project microelectronics played an important role. But also the technology of telecommunications started to change and became subject to digitalisation. Hardware engineering lost its importance, the manufacture of large equipment with heavy cables and a lot of electronic connections was replaced by the construction of rather small units based on microelectronics. Software engineering became an indispensable part of the production process. This change in technology was (and is) a continuous process: the old technology was gradually displaced by a semi-digital phase before the digital phase definitely broke through.

From 1983 until 1987 the Electrotechnical firm seemed able to realise the required pace of innovation. It invested a lot and, in spite of the uncertainty of the market, it did reasonably well. This was partly due to the fact that the Dutch PTT functioned as a steady buyer of large numbers of telephone units. However, during this period the privatisation of the PTT turned into a political issue. Private status was finally realised in 1989, but before that the PTT had already started to change its policy concerning the purchase of equipment; it began to look for cheaper alternatives and the firm had to fear more competition. It had always produced high quality telephones for the PTT, yet it had to face the competition of the cheap products that became more and more popular in those years. Digitalisation had made it possible to produce these very cheap phones but in fact profitable production could only be realised on a very large scale and based on enormous investments in automation. Therefore, it was decided, after the French take over, that the Dutch division would not try to compete anymore on this market; the mass production of phones was moved abroad. A reorganisation of the firm was necessary, a new social plan was arranged for this purpose. A small production unit remained, especially equipped for the production of complex apparatus, according to the specific desires of clients.

In other words, to survive the structural changes which marked the 1980s the Electrotechnical firm was continuously pressed to realise technological innovation. With respect to the products, it became involved in data communication, it had to face the process of digitalisation in the field of telecommunications, and in the end it had to abolish the mass production of telephones and concentrate on high-tech apparatus based on software tuned to the preferences of individual buyers. The production process had to be adapted to those demands as did the qualification structure of the workforce. The firm was confronted with an urgent skill mix problem: again and again qualifications became useless while new ones were needed. The skill mix problem manifested itself on two dimensions:

- The nature of qualifications: knowledge of microelectronics was increasingly required; software specialists had to be recruited while knowledge and skills with respect to analogue technology and hardware engineering became less important or even useless.
- The level of qualifications: the production of complex apparatus based on microelectronics presumed a general upgrading of technological knowledge; the final abolishment of mass production of telephones led to a sudden decrease of low-skill work.

So the organisational change consists of two major pressures: less chances for the low and traditional qualified and a general force to upgrade one's knowledge and skills.

5.4   Internal Labour Markets and Age

When external pressures force firms to reduce or adapt employment, the institutional opportunities to do so become important. The more firms are able to carry out a 'hire and fire policy', the less problems they will have adapting their personnel structures to new demands. However, during the fifties and sixties many firms built up internal labour markets to make themselves less dependent on external recruitment. Since labour was scarce in those years the creation of internal personnel provision was one strategy to deal with labour market competition. Good social provisions, job security and attractive perspectives for the future had the aim of committing the workers to the employer. However, if external pressures arise, such systems might get dysfunctional and lead to the production of *bottlenecks* with respect to personnel recruitment.

The Steel Company provides a clear example of such bottlenecks. The firm is characterised by a very differentiated structure of career paths: all positions in the firm fit into one or more routes, some rather short, others rather long. Every step, from one job to another, is regulated: one should have x years of experience in the previous job and often one should have had additional training. On the basis of these job ladders the Steel Company builds its own internal labour market. It invests a lot in the training of its personnel, it creates workers with firm-specific qualifications. The firm offers the worker perspectives that usually last for many years. When you enter the firm at the age of twenty you might 'grow' until the age of 40 or so. But then in most cases the career does not develop any further.

This system of internal personnel provision offers the firm some specific advantages. It limits the necessary hiring activities, it offers the opportunity to create a firm-specific production process and it guarantees a regular refreshment of knowledge and skills on account of this internal mobility. The corresponding social policy might be described as rather good. During the sixties and the first half of the seventies, when the workforce gradually increased, all social instruments and activities were based on this concept of life- time employment. The firm had the character of a family, its personnel policy was directed towards social care, keeping the workers within the firm, even if their performance declined. The Steel Company never dismissed disabled workers; it created extensive opportunities for sheltered work or modification of tasks. It made allowances for those who lost their ability for night shifts, for the elderly workers it developed a system of reduced working hours, and any loss of income as a consequence of decreasing capacities was always largely compensated.

Now the system of an internal labour market can produce aging trends that are dysfunctional with respect to the required mobility. Older workers who have reached the end of their possibilities stay for another 20 or 25 years on the job, blocking the opportunities for in-coming workers. A combination of the need to reduce the workforce (and thus the opportunities for in-firm career development) and an aging workforce poses a grave threat to an internal labour market of this type.

To the firm this means it should look for measures to raise the mobility again; combining the reduction of the workforce with an early exit of older workers is a solution that can keep the concept of the internal labour market intact. To the unions this policy means they can maintain job security for a majority of the workers, they can maintain career opportunities for their members, and above all they can maintain the good social provisions that were once obtained.

At the Bank similar constraints stemming from the internal labour market are observable. The need for innovation asks for a new flow of personnel that is highly qualified and broadly usable. However, the simultaneous pressure to cut staff and enlarge productivity as well as the ongoing aging trend reduce the opportunities for renewal. Early exit helps to solve these tensions; it can contribute to the process of prising the internal market open.

5.5   Flexibility

During the eighties markets of goods and services became considerably less predictable. The uniform character of many products became more and more differentiated partly due to the possibilities microelectronics offer. Market demands seemed to change more rapidly and showed a much bigger variation in preferences. Mass production of a rather restricted assortment lost significance while the production of goods and services neatly tuned to the specifications of smaller groups of consumers or even individual buyers became more important. Flexibility joined price fixing and quality as weapons in the competitive struggle. The capability of firms to convert their products and production process according to changing market demands was now a deciding factor with respect to their performance. This need for flexibility has a qualitative as well as a quantitative aspect. Not only should the products continuously match the specific and changing wishes of consumers, firms should also reckon with significant peaks in the sale of (particular) goods.

This change can be summarised as the transformation of a sellers' market into a buyers' market. Not all markets and all firms are characterised by this change in the same way or to the same extent. The more potential markets are uncertain, the more firms are pressed to work on a flexible organisation of production.

The need for organisational flexibility is closely linked to organisational changes concerning technological innovation and raising productivity. In some respect the flexibility demand can be seen as a coordinating one: productivity programmes as well as technological projects should be executed in a way that they contribute to organisational flexibility. Striving for more flexibility seems to develop into an important element of corporate strategy.

In the *banking sector*, one can point at a strong diversification of the range of services offered to include such things as leasing, credit cards, different types of mortgage, travel, option trade, data communication, insurance and so on. The service to the client aims to be made-to-measure. No longer a limited set of standardised choices is offered, but preferably an offer that meets all the specific wishes of the client. The Bank, originally a savings bank with restricted services, is now involved in this process of flexibilisation.

In the *electrotechnical sector*, digitalisation of products created extensive opportunities for diversification. The high speed of technological change as well as the unlimited possibilities of digital technology gave rise to an uncertain market. Not only was the standardised nature of products breached, the size of the sales also lost predictability, because of the rapid pace of innovations. After the crisis of 1980 the Electrotechnical firm had to develop its strategy with respect to products and production, and although it tried to incorporate a great deal of organisational flexibility it was more than once forced to adjust its plans.

In the *production of steel*, the number of kinds and qualities gradually increased during the eighties. The Steel Company produces these various kinds and qualities to suit customers' requirements; production is more and more tailored to individual orders. An important tendency is the growing demand for 'stronger and lighter'. The Company tries to adapt its process to the desired specifications and even participates in the projects of steel-processing companies in order to be able to anticipate specific wishes. With a view to the growing number of alternatives for steel the firm also started an aluminium plant.

The *public utility firm*, facing increasing international competition, broadened the range of testing activities and increasingly employed consultancy practices.

The flexibility demand is partly a matter of technology. Firms can try to shape their production process in a way that rapid changes to other products or specifications can be realised. In 1984 the Electrotechnical firm, for example, built a new plant according to a design of 'flexible production automation': in a very short time the complete lay out of the plant could be reorganised to the needs of another type of production.

However, flexibilisation also implicates a number of formal organisational changes (cf. Mangum and Mangum, 1986), such as:
- creating functional flexibility by breaking down the barriers between jobs;
- upgrading of qualifications so that people can fulfill a variety of tasks;
- creating numerical flexibility by contracting out activities that are not firm
- specific or by enlarging the share of part-time workers, outworkers, or short-term workers.

Regarding the Bank we can point out the tendency to broaden the content of all jobs that have to do with sales and service; while simple administrative jobs are automated away or are assigned to temporary (female) workers, the jobs in which contact with clients is involved are upgraded: workers should have knowledge about all products of the firm and be able to act as an all round advisor. The bank aims at creating a well qualified core of all round advisors and sellers.

The concept of flexible production at the Electrotechnical firm aimed to create a 'multi skilled' group of 'flyers' on the one hand, and the use of a large group of temporary (female) workers on the other. During the eighties the firm arranged a pool of workers who had no regular contract but were available on demand. The personnel uncertainties induced by automation and market changes could in this way be reduced to some degree.

The Steel Company is particularly characterised by increasing efforts in the area of subcontracting. The reduction of the workforce is partly the result of these efforts. Although job security for all (younger) workers could be maintained during the eighties, the size of regular employment decreased gradually while all kind of subcontractors entered the firm.

Of all external pressures the need for flexibility is the most general one. Early exit appears to fullfil different functions with regard to this need. With the help of exit practises it is possible to flexibilise the core segment of the personnel structure, so that the ratio between regular and flexible work changes. Besides this, early exit can be interpreted as a continuous source of flexibility in a quantitative and qualitative sense. It not only offers the opportunity to adapt the size of employment to current needs, but it can also be applied again and again as a means of realising the social preconditions for organisational change. Still one may wonder if social policies that allow for a *massive* exit trend really contribute to the required flexibil-

ity; to some extent this mass character also indicates *rigidity*, as will be
discussed below.

5.6   Social Policy and the Myth of Flexibility

The experiences with external pressures like economic crisis, new technologies and changing market conditions might explain why firms might want to
make flexibility a more permanent feature of their social policies. This
endeavour is firstly reflected in a more business-like organisation of the
social function, as can be well observed at the Bank and the Steel Company.

During the eighties efforts were made in both firms to achieve a much
better integration of production management and social management. The
uniformity that had always been aimed for in personnel policy was given up
to some degree; the local professionals had to develop creativity in order to
support the innovative and productive ends of the line managers. In both
the Steel Company and the Bank substantial changes in social policy were
implemented:
- the formulation of new performance standards;
- the introduction of regular 'performance discussions';
- the breaking down of the automatism of climbing the job ladder; only
  really good performances should be considered; in other cases it might be
  necessary to stimulate external mobility (outplacement);
- the conceptualisation of the worker as an 'small businessman/woman';
  they should develop and discuss ambitions for the future, formulate their
  own productivity goals, and make their ideas known about possible
  improvements in work methods, about the type of supervision, etcetera.

Instead of social policy, personnel managers started to talk about 'human
resource management' which suggested a much closer link to corporate
interests. As we discussed in the previous section, social, medical and
personnel workers acted as the connecting link between early-exit schemes
and participation in these schemes. Fundamentally this practice did not fit
into the professional ethic of these workers, but now it became increasingly
legitimised within the framework of 'human resource management': it was
no longer tabu to suggest to people that they had better leave. Steering
efforts with respect to the early-exit opportunities became part of the
professional task, even if these exits were formally subject to the application of bureacratic rules. The human resource ideology stated that a
premature exit could serve not only the interests of the organisation, but
also those of the worker involved; the opportunity of an early exit was a
good thing in itself.

This shift in professional norms had implications for the presumed link between corporate interests and the early exit process. In a certain sense, the process developed into a rather autonomous piece of social policy, driven by new professional standards and reproduced by new images of the older worker and his 'right' to an early exit. The awareness that all this contributed to the personnel flexibility of the firm was only a vague one. This reflects the paradox that is related to the massive character of the exit process. Rational policies seem to have turned into 'rational myths': many believe that the early exit of older workers contributes to the flexibility of the labour process, but no one knows exactly why. Flexibility turned into rigidity. One might conclude that early-exit behaviour has taken an institutionalised form.

6   Conclusions

The uniform and massive character of the early-exit trend in the Nether-lands suggests that the early-exit process develops according to a uniform national pattern. Our firm-level studies, however, indicate a much more heterogeneous and differentiated pattern. Early-exit processes at firm level vary with respect to the differentiation of instruments and the differentia-tion over time. Different types of 'exit control' can be distinguished, according to the capacities of firms to influence the design of pathways and/ or the choices for exit. Since firms take different positions in the institu-tional sphere they also have different bargaining opportunities. Further-more, variations in the nature, the intensity and the spacing of external pressures may give rise to a heterogeneous pattern of needs, that requires different forms of personnel restructuring. In this respect it appears that the presence of strong internal labour markets heightens the pressure in case of necessary staff reductions. Finally, the way personnel policy is organised may lead to different ways of shaping the exit process.

In other words, a massive trend occurred although a specific national policy was lacking. We showed how a whole range of bargaining opportu-nities allowed for the privatisation and differentiation of public goods. However, to understand the general character of the phenomenon and its endurance over time we should focus on two other, related tendencies that were revealed by our analysis: the *institutionalisation* of early-exit practises and the *unintended character* of the trend.

6.1   Institutionalisation

Institutional theory has many faces (Scott, 1987). One can distinguish between the earlier and the more recent conceptions of institutions and institutionalisation, in which different emphases are elaborated. Borrowing some of the core elements of these conceptions we argue that the development of early-exit practises can well be described as a process of institutionalisation.

The initial and central concept refers to institutionalization as a 'process of instilling value' (Selznick, 1957). Or as Scott (1987: 494) puts it: "...institutionalization as a means of instilling value, supplying intrinsic worth to a structure or process that, before institutionalization, had only instrumental utility. By instilling value institutionalization promotes stability: persistence of the structure over time." In two of our cases (Steel and Electrical Engineering), one can quite well observe that early-exit practises moved away from their initial instrumental utility: the practises persist over time but their relationship to the main organisational goals becomes vague. Atchley (1982: 264) analysed 'retirement as a social institution' and distinguishes between several values that are incorporated in it.
Retirement:
a)   creates opportunities for younger workers
b)   reduces the cost of labour
c)   reduce the size of the labour force
d)   ties workers to jobs
e)   rewards workers for long and loyal service
f)   accommodates individuals' desires for retirement
g)   improves current worker morale by creating old-age security.

From our case studies it appears that some of these values are now strictly tied to the opportunity of early exit. Since the concept of regular pensioning at age 65 does not involve firm-specific values the general values related to retirement can easily be shifted to the concept of *early* withdrawal.

A second element in the process of institutionalisation dates from Meyer and Rowan (1977), who stress that social conventions may acquire a normative status over time: some practises get repeated over and over because it is 'the way it is always done'. In a similar way, Jepperson (1987) refers to institutionalisation as a 'particular set of social reproductive processes'. In our analysis, we showed how this process came into being within the practises of the professionals at the firms. The availability of voluntary exit opportunities, in particular, gave rise to different kinds of normative pressures; once generated these pressures remained effective, indicating that early exit not only serves an organisational goal but that it is a 'good thing' in itself. In the words of Meyer and Rowan (1977), early exit has taken a 'rule like status in social thought and action'.

This concept of institutionalisation explicitly calls attention to the role of the 'rationalised' beliefs and methods of the professionals in and around organisations. The intervention of these agents not only establishes early exit as 'something good' or 'something useful', but also as a practise that seems to be based in 'rational', scientific, objective standards.

A third core idea refers to a presumed tendency of organisations to adapt themselves to cultural elements like symbols, normative beliefs and cognitive systems. Unlike contingency theory – which calls attention to technical requirements, resource streams and so on – this concept stresses the need for adaption to "rationalized and impersonal prescriptions that identify various social needs" (Meyer and Rowan, 1977: 344). Dimaggio and Powell (1983) introduce the idea of *isomorphism* to understand the process of institutional homogenization between firms. They argue that organisations may derive an advantage from institutional adaption because it gives them a legitimate status. This argument might explain why firms are willing to adapt and stimulate exit opportunities even if they do not benefit directly from it.

As Lammers and Széll (1989) argue, the concept of institutionalisation does not necessarily involve formalisation. This might explain why the experienced right to an early exit also emerges in firms and sectors that did not show an increase in bargained exit opportunities. In those cases the early exits through the social security pathways are no longer exclusively the outcome of an unforeseen risk, but are also experienced as something that was earned in the past and serves positive values in the present.

Nevertheless, the prolongation of formal exit instruments in many firms and sectors has largely contributed to the processes of institutionalization. Some elements have been rather important in relation to the prolongation of early exit arrangements in the Netherlands. *Firstly*, it has always been suggested that schemes like pre-retirement and social plans would be temporary. This stressed the exceptional nature of the arrangements and legitimised them to some degree. *Secondly*, the voluntary character of many schemes prevented substantial resistance. How could one oppose to the prolongation of voluntary facilities? *Thirdly*, one of the initial motivations was the fight against youth unemployment. The use of early-exit schemes did keep the unemployment figures artificially low, even if few of the older workers' jobs were subsequently taken by younger workers. Thus, during the first half of the eighties a political argument to denounce the specific use of exit schemes was lacking. *Fourthly*, the pre-retirement schemes were often presented as a specific form of working hours reduction (on a life-time base). The fact that workers' associations were prepared to pay for it in the process of collective bargaining implied that actors gradually started to see the opportunity of an early exit as an acquired right. *Fifthly*, the idea that a new social right had been created was largely reinforced by the collective approach of the early-exit schemes. The logic of the welfare state was copied to some degree in arranging 'care facilities' at the sectoral level.

The state not only stimulated this during the first half of the eighties, in its role as employer it adopted the same policy itself. Now it seems that even in firms or sectors where 'bargained opportunities' are lacking still this right to an early exit is still felt.

6.2   Early Exit as an Unintended Outcome

Early exit may be seen as a rational strategy of firms, when structural pressures require personnel adaption. However, within the context of institutionalisation exit practises drift away from goal rationality. From our analysis we now conclude that the process of institutionalisation contributes to the arisal of exit practises that were not intended either by the management of firms, or by the planners of welfare state arrangements; on the other hand, those unintended practises reinforce the process of institutionalisation by establishing early exit as a 'normal social fact' (instead of a means of 'crisis management'). Beneath we discuss some examples of these mechanisms from our case studies.

We have already shown how an interplay developed between external pressures, organisational structure, institutional opportunities and social practises at the firms. Once the exit opportunities have been integrated in regular social, medical and personnel practises the relationship between organisational change and premature exit is no longer questioned every time. Premature exits on their turn can keep the process of organisational change going, and so a tacit agreement between different actors arises about the prolongation of exit opportunities.

An unruly process emerges when the initial motivations for exit policies lose significance. The process becomes self-evident and takes the character of a self-fulfilling prophecy. The exit practises themselves press for continuation. Though the schemes were never designed merely to get rid of the 'unproductive elderly workers', stereotype ideas about aging and productivity emerge from the 'bare facts themselves': if the organisational burden on the elderly increases, if the organisation in return offers escape opportunities and if the elderly start using them in large numbers, the stereotype image that older workers are not able to cope with higher productivity standards is confirmed. The social practises of professionals contribute to the reproduction of cultural images. If it is not thought necessary to train older workers (since they have the exit option it makes less sense to do so), the idea that the elderly are less 'trainable' gets reinforced. The same goes for the conceptualisation of the older worker as someone who is conservative and opposed to change and innovation. If every organisational change goes hand in hand with the premature exit of older workers, the image that the elderly cannot cope with change is easily reproduced.

Of course, one should not neglect the fact that older workers may indeed have specific performance problems. However, the availability of exit opportunities prevents policies being developed that reckon with eventual restrictions. In both the Steel Company and the Bank, it is reported that especially older workers suffer from the fact that the organisational opportunities for the replacement, reintegration or modification of tasks have diminished. In the past the Steel Company offered older workers with performance problems in their own jobs the opportunity to obtain a lighter one (cleaning service, staff catering, maintenance work, household chores, transport and so on). In the Bank, many elderly workers had the opportunity to finish their careers, if necessary, in relative easy, clerical jobs. Now, in order to improve productivity, the Steel Company has contracted out a lot of the activities mentioned above and concentrated on the core activities of the firm. The Bank gradually increased the number of cheap and flexible contract-workers for the easy jobs. Moreover a lot of the more routine work was also eliminated in both firms.

Changing work methods, higher productivity standards and job integration (putting more tasks in one job) increase the burden on older workers. Early exit develops into the *unintended effect* of all kinds of major and smaller organisational changes, as long as the exit opportunities take the place of policies that aim at creating better working conditions.

Summarising, the neglect of work policies and the contracting out of 'easy jobs' seem to be an unintended effect of early-exit practises that reinforces the need for these very practises. This effect contributes to the institutionalisation of the process; institutionalisation (and its production of normative pressures and stereotype images) is again a factor itself in realising unintended consequences.

6.3   A Loreley Effect

Together with the production of unintended outcomes, the tendency towards institutionalisation indicates a 'liberation' of the early-exit process: early exit shifts from being an instrument into being a goal in itself. In this respect, and contrary to normal retirement, early retirement has moved away from welfare state control, but is at the same time partly based on welfare state, social security regulations. On the other hand, the use of welfare state provisions for exit practises does not necessarily constitute a rational policy by firms or other sectoral actors. The origin of early exit might quite well be described as rational, but in the past two decades early exit has grown into a process of institutionalisation and has led to forms of reproduction that have no close link to rational policies or to instrumental attraction. It is this phenomenon we have labelled 'the Loreley effect of early exit'; it refers to the continuous 'suction' exerted by the exit option itself, without regard to the social, organisational or financial desirability and/or opportunities.

Still, one might argue that the *outcome* of the process has a rational character. From the perspective of corporate strategies we pointed to the ambiguous nature of this 'rationality'. The utility of the process is at least partly based on the myth, that early exit contributes continuously to organisational flexibility. We called this a rational myth because of the professional argumentation that exit from the labour market would reflect an objectively desirable value. Nevertheless, the outcome might be rational with respect to the inter-generational division of labour in society. We then looked at the phenomenon as a process of 'social closure' in the Weberian sense: participation chances and life chances are redistributed according to an age criterion (cf. Trommel, 1991). The Loreley metaphor stresses that this outcome was not planned – at least not as a permanent result – and that purposive acts of discrimination only played a minor role in the development of the trend: stereotype ideas about the capacities of older workers appeared to be the result of exit practices rather than their cause. From this point of view the redistributive outcome can only be labelled rational if political actors recognise it as such. We therefore conclude with an exploration of political attitudes towards the future of early exit in the coming years.

6.4 Future Trends

Some authors argue that the current early-exit trend will simply be reversed if labour market shortages occur. However, one may not only wonder when this will be the case – given the potential source of female labour on the one hand, and the ongoing processes of rationalisation on the other – one may also ask if it will be that easy to return to old practises. Our study indicates that flexibility has turned into a structural characteristic of economic and technological development. To many firms every source of personnel flexibility is welcome, especially to those that are involved in lasting processes of breaking open the internal labour market. Parallel movements in the direction of decentralised forms of (personnel) management establish a structural need for flexible tools of personnel policy; the gradual changes from 'uniform social policies' into a more differentiated and business-like form of 'human resource management' presume the permanent availability of different types of exit opportunities.

Moreover, it is very hard to see how the social image of an established right could be undermined in the short run. The organisational mechanisms of reproduction that rest on the process of institutionalisation (like stereotyping, imitation or the neglect of work policies) are rather stubborn and seem to guarantee the endurance of exit practises. A current issue in the public debate is the low labour force participation in the Netherlands. The social and political interest in this theme is reflected in different arguments. Firstly, the high inactivity rate brings about high social security costs. These costs must be financed by employees and employers pushing up labour costs. High labour costs in turn give employers the incentive to reduce their dependency on labour. Thus a vicious spiral arises of rising expenditures for social security, rising labour costs and declining participation rates. Most political parties are worried about the future financing of this typical socio-economic pattern. In 1990 the Scientific Council of Government Policy (WRR) published a report on the issue in which different recommendations were made to stimulate labour market participation.

Secondly, demographic trends bring the participation issue into the forefront and reinforce the discussion about the future costs of social care. Eventual shortages of labour in the future should be prevented, and furthermore we must reckon with an autonomous increase of social costs due to the aging trend. In this respect the importance of female labour force participation is often stressed, and some improvements concerning parental leave and day care centres have been realised. In comparison the labour force participation of the elderly is a minor issue at present.

Political action to raise participation has so far concentrated on the apparently easy exchange between 'work' and 'care'. In 1991 the disability scheme turned into a major political issue. Policy measures have been taken to reduce the access to the scheme by introducing restrictions on the amount and duration of benefits.[26] However, older workers (<= 50 years) have been excluded from these measures for social reasons.

In the course of public and political discourse it has become 'common knowledge' that the disability scheme has been used for years as a major tool of economic restructuring. It has directed attention to the role of employers and especially to that of the intermediate organisations that have to execute the disability legislation. These organisations are managed by collective employers' and employees' organisations and are now heavily criticised for being 'benefit factories' instead of organisations aiming at prevention and/or reintegration. However, a political attempt to restrict this form of corporatism has not been made and cannot be expected in the short run.

All in all there are no signs yet that political incentives are to be expected with respect to the labour force participation of the elderly. Examining the attitudes and policies of (collective) employers and employees the same conclusion might be drawn. In some respect the political attempts to cut back the meaning of 'social justice pathways' have paradoxal consequences with respect to labour force participation. On the one hand, the reduced availability of 'escape routes' should lead to higher participation rates, on the other hand, it re-establishes the need for bargained exit opportunities and the importance of corporatism. Already the employers and employees are collectively discussing the possibilities for compensating the income effects of the recent disability measures.

How should one judge the persistence of early exit patterns? Our suggestion that the process is 'out of control' does not necessarily constitute a negative judgement. One may argue that the Netherlands has managed to organise a rather efficient 'non-working society', based on a high level of productivity. Why should one object to low participation into paid labour if this can be combined with a relatively high level of welfare?

From an international comparative view it appears that the Dutch productivity per working year is indeed relatively high, but still not high enough to compensate for the high level of non-activity (Aarts and de Jong, 1991). Furthermore, it is true that one should not merely judge the productivity per working year, but the entire societal production: Bastianen et. al. (1991) estimate the loss of production due to the low participation rate at 30% of the GNP. They label this loss 'societal costs' and conclude that low participation is not efficient at all. In this approach, however, the (economic) value that individuals ascribe to free time is neglected. If one reckoned with these effects the authors admit that the low participation rates might very well be 'pareto-efficient'. Also neglected is the importance of participation in non paid labour, with respect to the functioning of the economic system. Surveys on time budgets show, for example, that males between 55 and 64 are relatively often involved in voluntary work (CBS, 1990). It might very well be that the high productivity within the formal economy is partly based on a high degree of voluntarism. These considerations with respect to the importance of free time and voluntary work may be arguments to keep the concept of an efficient non-working society intact.

One should not, however, neglect the social integrative function of paid labour as well as the opportunities it offers to shape life chances. As Dahrendorf (1988) argues, the labour society has not lost meaning although the time people spend on paid labour during their lifetime is still decreasing. As long as labour force participation offers much better chances for social participation and as long as the fate of unemployment can damage the social and psychological well-being of people, one cannot conclude that a fully satisfying non working society has emerged. In other words, one cannot simply assume that the division of labour and incomes and of free time and voluntary jobs conforms precisely to the division of individual needs. The question of the right division becomes, on the contrary, even more important as the scarcity of paid labour increases.

It is on this point that the conclusion drawn from our study comes in. It is true that the Dutch system may be seen as an efficient non-working

society from a macro-economic point of view, it is also true that many
individuals may attach great value to a premature exit from the labour
market, but our conclusion that the exit process is 'out of control' has
problematic consequences with respect to the question of societal division.
Society will not regain control on the matter by blocking the public
pathways into early exit; by that it only accepts that private actors become
increasingly involved in shaping the conditions of the process; as a consequence the outcome with respect to the division of jobs, benefits and free
time will have more and more an 'unintended' character. We may wonder if
collective values like 'the right to work', and the 'solidarity between generations' will survive, then.

Notes

1   Early exit does not necessarily lead to tragic events for the individual. The
    metaphor stresses the *unintended* character of the process and as a consequence
    the decline of public control on the process.
2   Activity rate: proportion of (potential) labour force actually involved in paid
    labour, based on the *number* of persons (unemployed persons excluded).
3   Based on OESO, *Historical Statistics*, Paris (different years).
4   The comparative high level of part-timers in the Netherlands might be partly the
    result of the interview method used there after 1985. Compared to the period
    before 1985 persons are now explicitly asked if they work 'also if it is for only
    a few hours a week or for a short period'. The consequence has been an increase
    in the number of very marginal jobs. For instance: of all women with a part-time
    job 33% have a job of less then 10 hours a week. Both among male and female
    part-timers we find numerous students with a small job (*moonlighting*). If the
    part-time figures are corrected for jobs of less then 10 hours, or for the age
    group 14-24, the increase of part-time work is only marginal. (CBS, 1987)
5   For an extended description: cf. De Vroom and Blomsma, 1991.
6   Consisting of different combinations of sickness, disability and/or unemploy-
    ment regulations.
7   Mass dismissals (=20 or more employees must be involved) was in particular a
    phenomenon in the early eighties. From 1980 to 1983 the number of individual
    employees involved in mass dismissals increased from 15,631 to 31,898. Since
    1983 the number has decreased to 12,819 in 1988. In the years 1989 and 1990 it
    was 3,604 and 3,294, respectively [Information from the Ministry of Social
    Affairs and Work (SoZaWe/DGA)].
8   In the Netherlands it is a normal practise in many sectors that employers
    supplement legal social security benefits up to 90-100% of the net income.
    Example: in 1989 the disability benefit in 62% of all firms (80% of total
    employment) is supplemented for a period of 1-2 years. In 30% the first year
    was supplemented to 100%. (SoZaWe, 1989: 5-9; 31-35) (*see* also Grobbee,
    1986: 81).

9   Of which the *1986 Wet Vermeend/Moor* is the most important.

10   Dismissal regulation, generally speaking, is based on 'administrative variables'; that means these regulations can be better controlled by bureaucratic agencies and are less vulnerable to 'social construction'.

11   According to the Dutch Sectoral Industrial Classification (SBI 1974) this sector has the sectoral code: SBI 331, which partly corresponds to the United Nations International Standard Industrial Classification ISIC 371. This subsector is part of the *Basic Metal Industry* (SBI 33, which correspondends roughly with ISIC 37 + 23).

12   SBI 3694 (part of 36, ISIC 390).

13   SBI 403; ISIC 420; part of the major division SBI 4 (public utility firms) and ISIC 4 (Electricity, Gas and Water) respectively.

14   SBI 8122; corresponds only partly to ISIC 8102.

15   This analysis is based on data obtained from the respective firms; these data concern the distribution of the workforces over the different job levels at the firms.

16   1985 was chosen for pragmatic reasons since for that particular year comparative data on all three levels and for all different age groups were available.

17   The two-digit SBI-level (*see* footnote 11).

18   From Caanen and De Neubourg (1990) it can be deduced that the total mobility out of the firms (into other firms, unemployment or exit from the labour force) was about 11% in 1985 for the Dutch working population.

19   These conclusions have been confirmed by a calculation of the trends per firm and age group over a number of successive years.

20   It is not argued here that the control of pathways is only motivated by financial arguments. However, through experience firms may learn that cheaper alternatives are available; future behaviour appears frequently to be steered by this new insight.

21   Until 1987 the limit was 57.5.

22   Here we face a striking contradiction: while the unions and the Ministry of Social Affairs press the point of voluntarism the legal rules prescribe that exit should be compulsory if one is to get unemployment benefit. Strictly speaking, voluntary dismissals do not fit into the language of social security; for the elderly an exception is made although the official rules - and a kind of ritual of obeying them - are maintained.

23   The data in this table cover the following periods: 1985-1990 (Bank), 1979-1988 (Steel), 1979-1989 (Electrotechnical firm), 1980-1989 (Public Utility firm). N represents the number of exit cases during the specific period. The early-exit rate expresses the share of early exits in relation to regular pensioning. The pathway segmentation shows the distribution of exit cases along the different pathways. The way in which exit cases are distributed over time is characterised on the 'spacing' dimension.

24   This figure also includes professional efforts at stimulating reintegration. So in reality the actual reintegration rate is even lower (SoZaWe, 1991a: 46, 47).

25   The catering industry consists of 99.6% small firms (<= 50 employees) that cover about 70% of the employed people in the sector (114,000 in 1990). Real estate

agencies also consist of 99.6% small firms; these firms cover about 85% of the employment in the sector (24,000 in 1990).

26   Besides that a further 30 measures were taken mainly aiming at reducing the *volume* of the scheme.

References

Aarts, L.; Bruinsma, H. and Ph. de Jong (1982). *Beschrijving van WAO-toetreders. Deelrapport Determinantenonderzoek WAO.* Svr, Zoetermeer.

Aarts, L. and Ph. de Jong (1991). *Arbeidsongeschiktheid in Nederland.* In: Socialisme & Democratie 48 (10): 409–415.

Atchley, R. C. (1982). *Retirement as a Social Institution.* In: Annual Review of Sociology Vol. 8 (1982): 263–287.

Bakels, H. L. and L. Opheikens (1982). *Schets van het Nederlandse arbeidsrecht.* Kluwer, Deventer.

Bastianen, R. D.; Butter, F. A. G. den and J. C. van Ours (1991). *De maatschappelijke kosten van non-participatie.* In: *ESB* (16-10-1991): 1028–1031.

Blomsma, M. (1987). *Evaluatie van arbeidsvoorzieningsmaatregelen,* Den Haag: HRWB.

Blomsma, M. and B. de Vroom (1988). *Vervroegd uittreden uit betaalde arbeid. Mogelijkheden en motieven in Zweden, de Verenigde Staten en Nederland.* Den Haag: HRWB.

Bolhuis, E. (1987). *De VUT met pensioen?* In: *Economisch Statistische Berichten:* 726–728.

Caanen, C. and C. de Neubourg (1990). *Numerical Labour Market Flexibility and Unemployment.* OSA-werkdocument Nr. W 69.

CBS (1982). *Algemeen bedrijfsregister (ABR).* Den Haag.

CBS (1987-1990). *Enquête Beroepsbevolking.* Den Haag.

CBS (1990). *Statistisch Vademecum Ouderen 1990.* Den Haag.

CBS (1992). *Statistisch Jaarboek 1991.* Den Haag.

Dahrendorf, R. (1988). *The Modern Social Conflict. An Essay on the Politics of Liberty.* London.

Dimaggio, P. J. and W. W.Powell (1983). *The Iron Cage Revisited: Institutional Isomorphism and Collective Rationality in Organizational Fields.* In: *American Sociological Review* 48 (April): 147–160.

EIM (1986). *Economisch Instituut voor het Midden- en kleinbedrijf, ATV in kleine bedrijven.* Zoetermeer.

Ganzevoort, J. W. et. al. (1984). *Het sociale zekerheidsnetwerk, voor wiens zekerheid?* In: R. J. L.Noordhoek et. al. (eds.), *Haalbaarheid van veranderingen in de sociale zekerheid,* Den Haag: 24–62.

Ginneken, P. J. van (1981). *VUT. Vervroegde uittreding in ontwikkeling.* Den Haag: SoZaWe.

Grobbée, J. J. J. (1986). *Co-referaat.* In: J. A. H. Bron et. al. (eds.), *Privatisering van de sociale zekerheid,* Den Haag: 79–87.

Jepperson, R. L. (1987). *Institutions, Institutional Effects and Institutionalism.* Stanford University and Yale University.

Kohli, M.; Rein, M.; Guillemard, A.M. and H. van Gunsteren (eds.) (1991). *Time for Retirement. Comparative Studies of Early Exit from the Labor Force.* Cambridge: Cambridge University Press.

Lammers, C. J. and G. Széll (1989). *Concluding Remarks. Organizational Democracy: Taking Stock.* In: C. J. Lammers and G. Széll (eds.), *International Handbook of Participation in Organizations.* Oxford University Press: 315–330.

Mangum, G. L. and S. L. Mangum (1986). *Temporary Work: The Flip Side of Job Security.* In: *International Journal of Manpower* 1 (1): 12–20.

Meyer, J. W. and B. Rowan (1977). *Institutional Organizations: Formal Structure as Myth and Ceremony.* In: *American Journal of Sociology* 83 (2): 340–363.

OECD Employment Outlook, 1990.

Paridon, C. W. A. M. van (1990). *Arbeidsmarktparticipatie in Nederland: plaatsbepaling in internationaal perspectief.* Den Haag: WRR.

Scott, W. R. (1987). *The Adolescence of Institutional Theory.* In: *Administrative Science Quarterly* 32 (4): 493–511.

Selznick, P. (1957). *Leadership in Administration.* New York: Harper and Row.

SoZaWe (1987-1991[a]). Ministerie van Sociale Zaken. *Rapportage Arbeidsmarkt.*

SoZaWe (1991[b]: 31). Ministerie van Sociale Zaken. *Bovenwettelijke uitkeringen in CAO's.*

Stichting Weerwerk (1989). *De reserves van de BV Nederland.* Nijmegen.

Trommel, W. A. (1991). *Het lied van de Lorelei; over leeftijdsspecifieke sluiting van de arbeidsmarkt.* Leyden Institute for Law and Public Policy. Working Paper Nr. 36.

Tweede Kamer (1990-1991)[b]. Kamerstuk 21 974, Nr. 3.

Tweede Kamer (1990-1994)[a], 21 814, Nr. 1–2, 1990/91. *Nota Ouderen in tel; een beeld en beleid rond ouderen:* 46–47.

Tijdens, K. (1990). *Veroudering en Doorstroming. Research Memorandum.* University of Amsterdam.

Veen, R. J. van der (1990). *De sociale grenzen van beleid. Een onderzoek naar de uitvoering en effecten van het stelsel van sociale zekerheid.* Leiden.

Vroom, B. de (1990), *Verenigde Fabrikanten. Ondernemersverenigingen van de voedings- en geneesmiddelenindustrie; tussen achterban en overheid.* Groningen.

Vroom, B. de and M. Blomsma (1991). *Exit in the Netherlands. An Extreme Case.* In: M. Kohli et. al.: 97–127.

Waarden, B. F. van (1989). *Organisatiemacht van belangenverenigingen. De ondernemersorganisaties in de bouwnijverheid als voorbeeld.* Amersfoort/ Leuven.

WRR (1987). *Activerend Arbeidsmarktbeleid.* Den Haag.

WRR (1990). *Een werkend Perspectief. De arbeidsparticipatie in de jaren '90.* Den Haag.

4 Germany: The Concerted Transition from Work to Welfare

Frieder Naschold, Maria Oppen, Holger Peinemann and
Joachim Rosenow

1 The Employment Patterns of Older Workers: Trends and Forms of Regulation

1.1 The Regulation of Retirement-Age Limits and Social Security in Old Age

The evolution of modern market economies has been closely linked to the development of systems of social security, both those of a contractual nature and those provided by the state. Such systems are designed to insure against the specific risks arising – for both employers and employees – from the coordination of the factors of production by the market. A central element of such systems is the provision of transfer payments, or pensions, which are linked to specific age limits and which compensate for the risks of invalidity and old-age. The establishment of such security systems as an integral part of state welfare policy leads to the development of a network of age limits which regulates the process by which workers leave the employment system and the associated financial transfer benefits. Such provisions for the risk of reduced ability to work due to invalidity or old-age, and the parallel historical development of retirement-age limits and benefit levels were established not only with a view to the social integration of the working class; they also provide the institutional precondition for labour and goods markets to function effectively and a basis for corporate personnel-optimisation strategies. The institutionalisation of age limits constitutes a central form of social regulation in modern societies, structuring workers 'biographies into three phases: preparation for working life, paid employment and retirement (Kohli, 1985).

At the same time, the systems developed by individual countries to provide security in old age and age-limit structures differ markedly from one another (Esping-Andersen, 1989). The characteristic mode of regulation of retirement-age limits in the Federal Republic, and the concept of social security in old age on which it is based have often been described from a social-policy perspective (Göckenjahn, 1988). Considering the matter from the perspective – generally ignored – of the fundamental relationship between production structure, labour-market risks and social security, the structural logic of the German system can be characterised in terms of three stages of development (cf. Rüb, 1989):

(1) The transition phase to a market economy with complementary welfare-state institutions in the course of the last third of the 19th century was marked by long daily working hours and life-long employment. The extensive mode of production and a labour market based on individual labour contracts generated the primary social risks of unemployment and invalidity. These risks were met by the public Poor Law system, offering a very low level of provision, and later by social insurance organised within the labour movement. Invalidity, alongside unemployment, became the most invidious social risk.

(2) The expansion of a fully developed social system based on the market economy and the start of more intensive production at the beginning of the 20th century led to a generalisation of the risks associated with invalidity and old age. It was against this background that complementary welfare-state institutions covering the risk of invalidity (for both workers and employers), and a fixed system of retirement-age limits were established. The system of age limits enabled employers to plan the use of labour power over time, to cope with labour-succession problems in a rational way and to stabilise their workforce levels. However, at this point the system of retirement-age limits did not provide all the conditions necessary for the consti-

tution of an autonomous retirement phase. Although on paper pension insurance established a normative differentiation between the risks of invalidity and of old age, in practice this amounted, notwithstanding the setting of retirement-age limits, to little more than coverage of the risk of invalidity: pensionable age was very high (in relation to life expectancy) and the level of pension benefits very low. It did not yet constitute a life-phase-retirement free of paid employment.

(3) From about the middle of this century the rise in the high level of pension benefits due to the policy of linking them to the growth of wage and salary income, and the simultaneous reduction and flexibilisation of pensionable age in the course of two major pension reforms (in 1957 and 1972), together with the secular rise in life expectancy has brought about a change in the function of retirement-age limits in the Federal Republic. Age limits for pension-entitlement, linked as they now are to an historically high level of pension benefits, no longer represent merely a condition for personnel planning and the rational treatment of the succession problem within firms. Through the state pension insurance, old age has become institutionalised as a financially secure retirement phase and, in this quality as an autonomous biographical phase, has become distinct from old-age provision seen merely as the coverage of a potential or actual risk of invalidity. The establishment of a pension-entitlement age and the level of pension benefits enable workers to maintain their standard of living in old age, at least where a full pension is paid. At the same time, due to the fact that individual pension levels are determined by the level and duration of insurance contributions paid out of earned income, security in old age is closely tied to the standard male employment relation based on continuous paid employment.

In the course of this evolution, the function of the state pension insurance system as a complementary institution within the developed market economy has undergone a fundamental change. The system of security in old age with its retirement-age limits is (a) no longer merely called upon to confront the classic problems of providing security against the risk of invalidity resulting from an historically specific production regime with its intensive use of labour power, and (b) no longer refer to the implementation of socially defined age limits to working life, limits which are necessary in order to stabilise internal labour markets. With retirement now seen as a financially secured non-economically active life-phase older workers are now seen as (c) providing employers with a highly flexible adjustment potential to changes in the demand for labour within the framework of a widely accepted social process. A retirement phase, institutionalised by social policy and enjoying wide social acceptance, makes older workers a highly flexible source of personnel adjustment. Their withdrawal from working life is no longer determined solely by invalidity and falling productivity in advancing years brought about by the taylorist production model, as is suggested both by the social-policy-oriented discourse on early retirement (Dohse et. al., 1982; Naegele, 1987, 1988), and the postulates of neoclassical economics (Lazear, 1979) on the link between falling productivity in old age and early retirement. The increasingly flexible forms of access to retirement resulting from state pension policies mean that such 'classical' functions of labour-market withdrawal in old age are now being overdetermined by additional 'motives': on the one hand, by firms' increased requirements for workforce adjustment arising in the context both of the historical transition from a taylorist regime of production with its intensive use of labour power to a flexible, integrative production regime, and of the effects of the cyclical fall in demand and structural crisis; on the other, by changes in the interests articulated by employees, for whom earlier retirement no longer represents merely the end of a career of physical and mental wear and tear, but the start of a separate phase of life.

This historical evolution in policy motives is linked with a mode of regulation of the transition from paid employment to retirement which, in the Federal Republic, is characterised by a multiplicity of direct and indirect pathways into retirement and which allows for very flexible regulation of actual age limits. Direct pathways are those which lead directly from paid employment into retirement, while indirect pathways involve an intermediate status, usually unemployment. The entire spectrum of pathways giving access to retirement is based on three distinct entry criteria, which constitute the cornerstones of the West German system of social security in old age. The three fundamental pathways are:

- retirement due to partial or total disability, the former preventing employment in a worker's existing occupation (Berufsunfähigkeit), the latter paid employment in general (Erwerbsunfähigkeit) for health reasons, which are independent of age; and early retirement at 60 for health reasons (for the severely handicapped);
- retirement linked to the state of demand for labour on the labour market: the so-called "59er provision" offering retirement via unemployment at 57.4 years of age (unemployment benefit followed by a pension) and at 60 entitlement to an "unemployment-pension" (Arbeitslosenaltersruhegeld); during the 1980s a number of specific retirement provisions, offering an indirect path into retirement from age 57 (Vorruhestandsregelung);
- age and group-specific retirement: for women a pension at age 60 (Frauenaltersruhegeld), full pension at 63 (flexible retirement age/flexible Altersgrenze) and at 65.[1]

In international terms these instruments all have features which can be seen as characteristic of the West German system, although to a varying extent: the provisions covering the risks of old age are all an integral part of an established core system of state social security rather than the result of ad hoc interventions by the state subject to historical fluctuation; those insured within the system have, on the basis of many years' insurance contributions a legal (property) right to benefits; the indexation of both contributions and benefits mean that pensions are both based on the insurance principle and are high enough to have the character of 'wage compensation'.

The relatively high level of benefits[2], the lowering of retirement ages for social-policy reasons, both constituent parts of established programmes initiated by the welfare state, and the fact that this has occurred on the basis of a political consensus among the most important social groups together constitute the characteristic features of the West German mode of regulation of security in old age and the structure of retirement-age limits. This system differs in important respects from the forms of regulation found in, for example, the English-speaking countries or in Japan.

1.2   Pathways into Retirement: Trends and Patterns

Since the mid 1970s the dominant mode of regulation of the state pension-insurance system in the Federal Republic has led to a more pronounced trend towards early retirement and falling participation rates among older workers than is the case in other developed market economies. These trends are briefly described below (for further details cf. Kohli et. al., 1991). The first trend of note is the relatively sharp decline, in international terms, of the 60–64 year old age group as a share of the working population (cf. figure 1).[3]

Although the trend towards an earlier end to working life (initially, and still primarily among male workers) can also be observed in comparable market economies (Great Britain, USA, the Netherlands, Sweden and Japan), the structures of labour-market withdrawal by older workers and the retirement volumes involved vary considerably. Together with the Netherlands and France, West Germany leads the international field in the trend to early retirement. Participation rates of older workers are highest in the USA and Japan. Since the mid 1970s retirement in the Federal Republic has been characterised by an acceleration of the early-retirement process and a reduction in the participation rates of older workers (including women). This is not the case in Japan or the USA.

These characteristics of labour-market exits by older workers in the Federal Republic are relatively homogeneous across the dividing lines between blue and white-collar segments and between branches, although, behind the surface similarities in the figures do exhibit relatively pro-

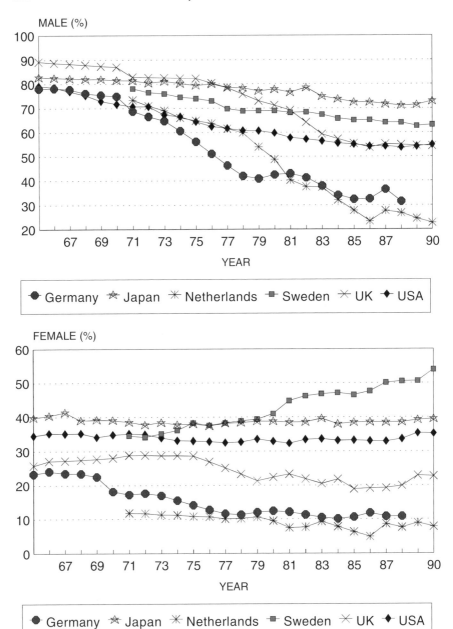

Source: OECD Labour Force Statistics,
         Paris (different volumes)

Figure 1: Labour Force Participation Rates by Age and Sex

Table 1: Early Retirement as a Proportion of all Retirements 1980 – 1989

	Total	Blue-Collar Workers	White-Collar Workers	Men	Women
Early-Retirement Share <63	68.7	69.3	65.7	66.5	69.5
Early-Retirement Share <65	76.5	76.8	76.2	82.8	70.6

Source: Amtliche Nachrichten der Bundesanstalt für Arbeit (ANBA), Nürnberg (Various Issues); Verband Deutscher Rentenversicherungsträger (VDR), Rentenzugangsstatistik, Frankfurt (Various Issues); own Calculations.

nounced gender-specific differences. This latter trend is due in large measure to the socially determined differences in occupational biographies between men and women.

1.2.1 Gender-Specific Differences

Since the beginning of the 1970s, the trend towards early retirement for men has gathered pace, and now seems to have stabilised at a level of about 80% of all retirements: only around one in five retirements occurs at the 'normal' retirement age of 65 or later (table 1).[4] As a result the average male retirement age has fallen from 61.6 to 59.3 years (1988) during the last two decades (cf. Jacobs et. al., 1991). Workers retire early under a number of different legal provisions: early retirement due to full or partial (i.e., occupationally specific) disability is the most important with over 40% of all retirements; early retirement due to the lack of demand for labour have risen steadily since the end of the 1970s and now account for 15% of retirements; a flexible pension at 63 (since 1973) is the pathway to retirement for just under 20% of male workers.

The structure of retirement in the Federal Republic is such that workers retiring early – especially men in the 60–64 year age group – simultaneously withdraw completely from paid employment and enter full-time retirement under the provisions of the welfare state system. The sharp fall in participation rates of this age group during the 1970s and 1980s – from almost 70% to 33% (cf. figure 1) – and their declining share of the active workforce are clear indications of this (cf. table 2).

The reasons for this specifically German pattern are to be seen not least in the lack – over a long period – of any provisions for, and the low level of acceptance of opportunities for a staged transition to retirement[5], together with the strict legal limits on pensioners wishing to top up their transfer benefits with earned income.[6] Last but not least, the strictly limited

Table 2: Employment Shares by Age Group (total workforce)

Year Ages from ... to	1966	1971	1976	1981	1986
15 – 19	9.5	8.1	8.6	8.1	6.8
20 – 24	10.3	11.0	11.0	12.3	13.7
25 – 29	13.0	9.9	10.9	10.8	12.1
30 – 34	10.9	13.5	10.9	11.1	11.1
35 – 39	10.5	11.5	14.2	11.0	11.1
40 – 44	10.0	11.1	11.4	14.0	10.7
45 – 49	7.9	10.2	11.1	11.0	13.2
50 – 54	8.2	7.6	9.6	10.0	9.9
55 – 59	8.7	7.3	5.9	7.4	7.5
60 – 64	6.7	6.1	3.8	2.4	2.5
65 – 69	2.5	2.3	1.3	0.7	0.5
70 – 74	0.9	0.8	0.6	0.4	0.3
75 and above	0.5	0.4	0.3	0.3	0.2
Total Employees	27.112	26.596	25.752	26.947	26.940

Source: Statistisches Jahrbuch für die Bundesrepublik Deutschland, Nürnberg (Various Issues).

number of part-time employment opportunities on offer in the Federal Republic is significant in this context. The German pattern of labour-market exit, characterised by an abrupt transition from full-time employment to full-time retirement differs markedly from other national forms of regulation which allow more highly differentiated forms of transition from working life to retirement.

Having said this, the retirement pattern for German women is rather different. Since the early 1970s the participation rates of older women (60–64) have also been on the decline, but from a much lower initial position than that of men (cf. figure 1). Looking at the figures for successive cohorts, this is also true of the 55–59 year olds.[7] This trend is, however, to a much lesser extent a reflection of a continuous increase in early-retirement rates: although 'normal' retirements as a share of all retirements fell from around 30% in the early 1970s to less than 10% in 1983, the figure subsequently rose to almost 50% by 1988 (Jacobs, Kohli and Rein 1991: 187). This discontinuity is due to a number of legal changes whose effects have been gender-specific, and which have served to make access to early retirement more difficult while at the same time easing the conditions for eligibility to a normal pension at 65.[8]

Gender-specific differences in the structure and extent of early retirement can only be adequately explained if reference is made to the socially dominant pattern of female integration into the labour market, to female occupational biographies and the way in which these interact with existing legal provisions for (early) retirement. Compared with other industrialised countries female participation rates are relatively low in the Federal Republic, and have increased comparatively slowly since the beginning of the 1970s. Despite the changes in female labour-market participation, the occupational biographies of women workers continue to be discontinuous and oriented to the short and medium-term. A survey conducted by a German research company (Prognos AG, 1989) has shown that 17% of single and 56% of married women have interrupted their career, and less than 40% intend to work until retirement. Subject to the prevailing situation on the labour market, women also often have to accept employment relations which are inadequately protected or which enjoy no social protection at all (e.g., part-time work). Together with the structural fact of pay discrimination against women, the result is that many women are unable to establish sufficient individual pension rights during their working lives to secure their income in old age. This means that women go down a wide range of pathways leading out of the employment system – compared with the relatively uniform pattern for men – depending on their (legal) position within the family and their level of autonomous economic security. Many working women do not have the option of taking early retirement:

a)   a large number of formerly working women have been unable to earn autonomous pension rights because they had paid contributions for an insufficient number of years (particularly up to 1984) or had opted to receive their pension entitlement as a lump sum on marriage;

b)   a second group of women finds – for the same reasons – that it cannot claim a pension until the age of 65 (this has been particularly often the case since 1985);

c)   a further group consists of women who, due to the insufficient level of welfare coverage of their employment relation, are forced to continue to work for as long as possible;

d)   last but not least, for many women labour-market exit does not mean entry into the retirement phase but entry (return) to 'family life' – as far as retirement and pension entitlements are concerned this is a sort of 'suspension' of contributions and benefits; retirement may then subsequently occur at 65 or, in some cases, via a disability pension.

The high level – until 1984 – of early retirement for women workers and the rising trend since the mid 1970s are linked to two typical modes of exit from the labour market:

–   Early retirement due to full or partial disability (representing over a long period almost half of all retirements, cf. Gather and Schürkmann, 1987) often represented (until restrictions were imposed in 1984) the only chance for women workers of claiming pension benefits at all.

–   The second possibility for women who have worked for many years has been to claim an early pension (at 60): in practice and depending on the prevailing situation on the labour market, labour contracts often define this as the 'normal' retirement age for women (Naegele, 1984).

1.2.2 Homogeneity across Economic Sectors, Differences between Enterprise-Size Groups

Taking the employment shares of the 60–64 year old age group in different sectors as an indicator of the volume of early retirement in each case, the volume and structure of the trend to early retirement in the Federal Republic appears to be relatively homogeneous across economic sectors, a finding which is in line with the "industrial-mix hypothesis" (Jacobs, Kohli and Rein, 1987). Statistical comparisons reveal that on average the 60–64 year-olds account for 1.9% of branch labour forces, and that variations around this figure are small. In only four branches does this group make up more than 4% of the workforce, i.e., more than double the average figure. Taking account of two additional structural characteristics does, however, reveal two slight deviations from the aggregate result:

– The non-profit sector (primarily state and public bodies) employs relatively larger numbers of older workers than do profit-oriented sectors.
  The average employment share of the 60–64 year olds in the non-profit
  sector was 2.8%; in the profit-sector it was only 1.7%. However, this
  difference is largely due to the influx of relatively large employment-
  cohorts rather than to lower early-retirement shares. Evidence from the
  public sector shows that here, as in other sectors, early retirement is the
  standard form of labour-market exit (Stubig and Wagner, 1991).
– Branches which experienced employment growth between 1980 and 1988
  tend (in about 80% of cases) to employ a slightly smaller proportion of
  older workers than contracting industries. This is due less to differences
  in early-retirement practices than to the fact that younger workers are
  attracted more than proportionately to growth industries (cf. Rosenow
  and Naschold, 1992).

Overall the very marginal segmentation of the employment shares of the highest age group between branches would seem to point to the existence of a general logic of regulation of early-retirement processes in West German firms as a whole. The differences that were identified are of marginal importance and do not represent sector-specific early-retirement trends.

In contrast to sector-specific disaggregation, analysis does reveal differences in early-retirement practices between enterprises of different sizes (large, medium-sized and small firms). Although the employment shares of

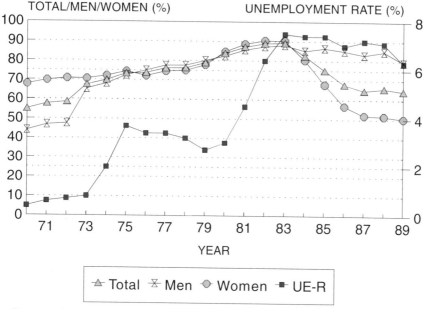

Source: Association of German Pension Insurers,
annual statistics and own calculations

Figure 2: Changes in Early-Retirement Shares 1970–1989

older workers are relatively homogeneous across enterprise size groups, this difference is the result of different conditions in each case (for further details *see* section 2). Our own analyses, together with studies by Schettkat (1989) show that large firms (and sectors dominated by them) make greater use of early retirement than smaller firms (and small-firm sectors). These differences are primarily the result of the organisational structure of small firms which enables them more easily to adjust their workforces without having to resort to early-retirement practices. In addition, industrial relations norms are such that the chances for workers to realise their interests with regard to early retirement correlate positively to enterprise size. Furthermore, enterprise-size-specific patterns of interaction between firms and the state mean that firms of different sizes make different uses of the various instruments and state transfer benefits available.

The relation between early retirement and changes in the level of unemployment is instructive for an analysis of the early retirement dynamic over time. Comparing early-retirement shares with the rate of unemployment over time, it is evident the two variables are clearly related but that the relation is not unambiguous and linear.

The increase in the early-retirement share occurred in the wake of the introduction of the so-called flexible pension (at 63), a provision of the Pension Reform of 1972, and thus occurred considerably earlier than the sharp rise in unemployment during the recession.[9] In other words, the major impetus for the increase in the volume of early retirement came from legal changes and from employee interest in retiring early. It was not until 1974/ 75 that the personnel adjustment strategies of firms began to have a major effect. These strategies entailed not only the reduction of staffing levels in response to the weakness of the business cycle, they were also the expression of far-reaching processes of restructuring within enterprises in the course of corporate reactions to changes in the international division of labour. Both these motives have been decisive in influencing early-retirement practices since the mid 1970s, although in recent years the early-retirement share has fallen slightly against the background of relatively stable unemployment rates. These findings show that macro-level arguments based on theories of the labour market have only limited explanatory value with respect to the extent and dynamic of early retirement. On the contrary, it is clear that the dynamic results from an interaction of three majors actors: the state, employers and workers, and that, as far as employers are concerned, it is not macro problems on the labour market which mark the point of departure but rather distinct restructuring and personnel adjustment processes.

1.3   Institutions and Social Actors: The Theoretical Approach

The analysis so far, conducted on the basis of aggregate statistical data, provides a point of departure for further inquiry. As we have seen, the Federal Republic is characterised by
- an early-retirement trend in line with continental-European (France, the Netherlands) developments and a characteristic pattern of labour-market exit: the employment dynamic of older workers is not characterised by integration (as in Sweden), or reinstatement and "shukko" (Japan), or by a second career (USA), but by a clear trend towards early retirements usually implying the transition from full-time paid employment to full-time pensioned retirement;
- this overall trend is subject to gender-specific variations, not, however, to branch-specific and only marginally to enterprise-size-specific differences;
- a public and controversial debate is under way as to whether this trend will continue in the future or if, as intended by the Pension Reform Law (Rentenreformgesetz) planned for 1992, it will be modified.

What causal factors lie behind these national trends, how is their dynamic, their continuities and discontinuities to be explained? This leads us on to an analysis of causal chains, the environment in which retirement trends unfold and the social actors behind them.

As is usual in the social sciences, the theoretical-conceptual discussion in this field has a choice of competing theories before it (cf. Naschold, Rosenow and Wagner, 1989):
– macro labour-market and demographical approaches;
– analyses of firms' behaviour within a neo-classical framework;
– analyses of the welfare state focusing on the "classic" state as the major actor;
– subject-theoretical perspectives concerned with social actors 'changing values.

Against the background of these competing theoretical approaches we favour a theoretical orientation for an empirical analysis of labour-market withdrawal by older workers and of early-retirement trends which is based on the following characteristics:
– The forms of labour-market withdrawal by older workers and of early-retirement trends should be reconstructed from the logic of action of the various social actors the state, employers, workers and non-state organisations and their interaction. The analysis should be centred around the interaction of the specific logics of firms and markets, on the one hand, with the logic of the state and its institutions, on the other. It is this analysis of the mode of interaction which represents the theoretical innovation and the increased epistemological potential of our approach.
– The corporate sector and the state are central actors whose actions are to be analysed in their institutional forms and not on the basis of a purely economistic or state-rationality calculation. Following neo-institutional and actor-theoretical approaches on this matter, we take employers 'production regimes and state policy regimes, both of which are to be conceived as specific regulatory frameworks as our point of departure.

Such a theoretical approach requires a specific methodological combination in order to ensure that empirical results can be generalised: although the reconstruction of the regulatory logic followed by employers and the state, and their interaction necessitates first and foremost qualitative methods of analysis, an evaluation of their potential general applicability is contingent on a comparison using aggregate statistical data on the relevant parameters. We therefore combine the analysis of aggregate statistical data indicating long-term trends at the macro and sectoral level, with firm-level case studies and analyses of state policies.

We proceed with an analysis of the logic of employer action with regard to their treatment of older workers (section 2). This is followed by consideration of the logic of state pension, labour-market and social policies and the way in which employer and state strategies interact (section 3). On the basis of the results so obtained, various scenarios for the "future of early retirement" will be described in the concluding section 4.

2   Employers' Age-structure Policies: On the Regulatory Logic of Firms' Behaviour

The general trend towards early retirement in the Federal Republic, identified in section 1 on the basis of aggregate statistical data cannot, due to the nature of the data, be used directly to draw conclusions on the behaviour of firms as 'economic subjects'. The age-structure policies of firms must therefore be analysed at a more appropriate level; that of firms as individual social actors. We use the term 'age-structure policies' to refer to all management activities which relate to workforce age structure, although we will be concentrating on retirement policy (in particular the use of retirement-age limits) and the conditions for their regulation.

The reconstruction of the regulatory trends and logic of firms' age-selective activities requires highly differentiated, qualitative and quantitative analyses of firms at the micro level. With this in mind we have conducted intensive studies of nine firms, differentiated by enterprise size, branch and product characteristics, using both qualitative and quantitative methods (on the underlying methodology cf. Rosenow and Naschold, 1992).

The analysis of the case studies presented below will show (a) the fundamental link between production regime and age-specific risks, (b) the importance for age-structure policies of regime characteristics and the

Table 3: Synopsis of the Firms' Case Studies

Firms		Sector	Workforce
Large	Small		
A		Public Service	5600
B		Engineering, Batch Production	2700
C		Engineering, Customised Production	3000
D		Electrical Engineering	250
E		private Services	1800
G		Steel	14300
	K	Metal-Working	120
	L	Printed Products	120
	M	Metal-Working	20

specific problems facing firms, and then, (c) the central regulatory characteristics and logics of firms' strategies.

2.1 Production Regimes and Age-Specific Risks

Of central importance for firm-specific policies towards older workers,
early-retirement practices and plant-level age-structures are the human
resource strategies adopted by firms in the context of their specific production regime. Unless these regulatory mechanisms are overdetermined by
other factors, they generate specific age-structure effects. Different regimes
with their associated human resource strategies are linked to heterogeneous
development options, age-specific productivity potentials and risks for older
workers, leading us to expect heterogeneous early-retirement practices.

Workforce age structures and firms' retirement policies are largely determined by plant-level personnel policy, i.e., the strategies adopted to recruit,
deploy, use and retire labour. Traditional management perspectives have
been transcended by a new theoretical discussion initiated by the debate on
the competitive advantages of Japanese firms (Womack et. al., 1990) and
the associated attempts at reform in Western countries (Kochan and
McKarsie, 1990). This new perspective has shown that human resource
options depend decisively on the strategic positioning of personnel functions within the firm's organisational structure. Human resource development itself is a function of many factors: the structural forms of the
horizontal and vertical division of labour within the firm's organisation, the
decentralisation of decision-making responsibilities on personnel matters,
the way in which it is embedded in the valorisation process within actual
production, the openness of the working structure for new ideas etc. Such
organisational and human-resource characteristics have far-reaching consequences for maintaining and developing the labour power of older workers,
and thus for their productivity and externalisation risks. Clearly, organisational and human-resource characteristics are themselves closely inter-
locked with the overall competitive strategies of firms, covarying with them
in a characteristic way (on this *see* also Rosenow and Naschold, 1992).

From this perspective – the relationship between competitive strategy,
the organisational characteristics of the production process and human-
resource management strategies – three characteristic production regimes
can be identified approximating to those in which firms operate under
today's competitive conditions (Womack et. al., 1990); each regime is
associated with specific risks for the employment of older workers:
– the taylorist production regime, in which the intensive use made of
  labour power leads to high risks of falling performance for (usually low-

skill) workers, combined with high fluctuation rates and risk of externalisation;

- the regime of diversified quality production (cf. Sorge and Streek, 1987),in
  which performance levels tend to remain high throughout working life,
  older workers are relatively highly skilled, long-term employment relations are predominant with low labour turnover, leading to a relatively
  low risk of externalisation;
- the regime of innovation-oriented market expansion (cf. Womack et. al.,
  1990), in which labour is seen as a central strategic (human) resource in
  the search for competitive advantage; the polyvalent use of skilled labour
  implies, on the one hand, considerable risks of performance decline, on
  the other, long-term employment contracts and low turnover rates.

Against the background of this typology we have conducted a study of a
sample of firms with a variety of production-regime characteristics. Its
purpose was to identify the link between production regimes, human
resource strategies and age-specific risks, and to compare the early-retirement practices of the firms. Analysis of the nine case studies has produced
three major findings which are of decisive importance in the context of
German early-retirement practices:

(1) None of the firms in the sample produces under the innovation-
oriented market-expansion strategy, a finding which is in line with other
studies on West German production structure (Jürgens and Naschold,
1992). The firms studied are distributed among the two remaining production regimes, whereby they exhibit a high degree of heterogeneity with
regard to human resource strategies, organisational development and overall business strategy. Within this overall heterogeneity the majority of firms
are concentrated in the quality-production, as opposed to the taylorist
regime; this too is characteristic of West Germany's core industrial sectors.
Even within this regime, though, the firms sampled exhibit a diversity of
characteristics (cf. table 4).

(2) The firms studied clearly revealed the expected link between production regime on the one hand and human resource strategies and age-specific
risks on the other. The taylorist production regime produces very considerable age-specific risks as reflected in deskilling and health problems with
increasing age, workforce instability and the tendency to externalise personnel considered "risky". The diversified quality production regime, by contrast, achieves substantial stability in terms of the skills and health interests
of personnel and of employment relations. The link between regime characteristics and age-specific risks against the background of corporate heterogeneity is summarised in table 4.

(3) Despite the heterogeneity of the regime-specific risks associated with
older workers in terms of their chances of maintaining work performance

Table 4: Production Regime, Personnel Trends and Age-Selective Risks

Production Regime, Personnel Trends and Age-Selective Risks

Firms		Production Regime	Personnel Trends	Age-Selective Risks
Large	Small			
A		Taylorism	Organisational Structure Based on Extreme Division of Labour	High Turnover Rates
D	K		Polarisation of Personnel Usage	Falling Productivity and Skill Levels in Old Age a Major Problem
			Intensive Production/High Performance Requirements	Older Workers Face Considerable Externalisation Risks,
			Low Skill Requirements	Precise Form Differs Between Segments
B	L	Diversified Quality Production	Working Structures Relatively Cooperative and Innovative	Low Risk of Falling Productivity
C	M		High Skill Level	Quasi-Lifelong Employment with a Low Risk of Externalisation in Old Age
E			Moderate Work Intensity/Performance Requirements	
F			Relatively Stable Workforces	
			Low Labour Turnover	
–	–	Innovation-Oriented Market-Expansion Strategy	Continuous Improvement to Working Structures and Continual Development of Skills Through Job Rotation	Serious Risk of Falling Productivity
			Polyvalent Use of Labour Brings with it Considerable Risks of Falling Productivity in Old Age	Lifelong Employment and a Low Risk of Externalisation for Core Workforce
			Stable Core Workforce	Differentiation Among Peripheral Worker Groups
			Flexible Peripheral Workforce	

Table 5: Early Retirement Shares of the Sample Firms and of the West German Economy as a Whole

Company (Retirement Period)	Early Retirement Shares <63 (%)	Early Retirement Shares <65 (%)	Early Retirement <63 (abs.)	Early Retirement <65 (abs.)	Retirement Cases	Employees 1989 (At Plant Level)
	1	2	3	4	5	6
Public Service Sector:						
"A" (80−88)	85.6	97.7	641	732	749	5692
"A": Blue Collar	85.0	97.8	467	572	585	4930
"A": White Collar	87.8	97.6	144	160	164	762
"A": Male*	83.9	98.1	537	628	640	5369
"A": Female*	89.6	96.8	138	149	154	485
Mechanical Engin. Industry:						
"B" (84−89)	78.6	92.7	151	178	192	2710
"B": Blue Collar	81.9	90.6	113	125	138	1590
"B": White Collar	70.4	98.1	38	53	54	1120
Mechanical Engin. Industry:						
"C" (80−89)	78.2	96.6	366	452	468	3047
"C": Blue Collar	83.2	99.5	163	195	196	1571
"C": White Collar	74.6	94.5	203	257	272	1476
"C": Male**	74.6	96.0	299	384	400	2760
"C": Female**	98.5	100.0	67	68	68	455
Electro Technical Industry:						
"D" (82/83/84/87)	75.0	93.8	12	15	16	245
Banking:						
"E" (80−89)	77.5	99.7	245	315	316	1809
"E": Male	54.2	99.3	83	152	153	830
"E": Female	99.4	100.0	162	163	163	979
Steel Industry:						
"G" (86−90)	97.2	100.0	669	704	704	14857
Overall Economy***	68.2	76.5	4359865	4901882	6406392	21619283
Blue Collar	69.3	76.8	2593967	2872801	3742049	10946975
White Collar	65.7	76.2	1560884	1811390	2376007	10672308
Male	66.5	82.8	2059164	2563082	3095819	12811173
Female	69.5	70.6	2300718	2338817	3312045	8808110

Notes:
  * The Data for Employees/Exits by Sex are Derived from a Different Source. Therefore you Will Find Small Differences Comparing these to the Total Data.
 ** The Male/Female Data for Empolyees Refer to 1990.
*** Employees on the Social Insurance Beneficiary List.
Early Retirement Shares < 63: Early Retirement Below 63 Years of Age in Percent of Total Retirement.
Early Retirement Shares < 65: Early Retirement Below 65 Years of Age in Percent of Total Retirement.
Sources: Case Studies; VDR-Statistics on Entries to the Pension System; Statistics of Employees on the Social Insurance Beneficiary List; Own Calculations.

and skill levels, the quantitative data reveal relatively homogeneous early-retirement practices, at least with respect to their volume effects. Once allowance is made for differences in enterprise size, they in fact correspond very closely to the early-retirement shares for the German economy as a whole. In other words, despite heterogeneous regime characteristics, skill structures, blue and white-collar-employment shares etc., all the firms studied made extensive use of early retirement as an instrument of person-nel adjustment (cf. table 5). Moreover, this occurred in the face of substan-tial qualitative differences in the problems facing the firms.

This 'overdetermination' of regime-specific risks associated with older workers by a personnel strategy which is implemented in widely differing contexts is described briefly with the help of the following five selected case studies (for further details cf. Rosenow and Naschold, 1992). In the subse-quent sub-section we will take a more analytical perspective, enabling us to draw more systematic conclusions. The five firms selected are fairly repre-sentative of the spectrum of regime conditions characteristic of the Federal Republic as a whole and also of the typical problem constellations facing firms – to which they respond by implementing early-retirement measures.

2.2 Case Studies: Production Regimes, Problem Constellations and Early-Retirement Practices by Firms

The *engineering company* C, with around 3,000 employees went through a period of considerable instability during the 1980s, suffering a substantial drop in profits. It produces high-value products, either singly or in small batches. Its customised quality production faces tough price and quality competition from domestic and, especially, from foreign competitors. The very high skill level of the – on average relatively old – workforce corre-sponds to a production structure oriented towards the use of highly skilled labour, with performance levels largely controlled by skilled workers them-selves. The risks of falling output and health damage (burn-out) for older workers are low, due to the considerable scope for self-regulation by the workers and the working structures which are open for further training and learning. Firm C thus embodies in an almost classic form the characteristics of the diversified quality production regime; long-term employment per-spectives and low risk of falling performance levels for older workers.

Despite the low age-specific risks characteristic of the regime, firm C made extensive use of early retirement during the 1980s, primarily to achieve personnel adjustment. The background to this finding is the prob-lem constellation facing large sections of the German engineering industry during this period – the sharp fall in sales during business-cycle downturns. The economic crisis of 1980 to 1984 was particularly severe for the firm, affecting as it did almost its entire product range. Faced with this situation management opted for a strategy of substantial job cuts in the short term, in both blue and white-collar areas. In stages, and using instruments such as natural wastage and redundancy for younger workers (below 45) in conjunction with early retirement, more than 700 jobs were shed, about 20% of the total labour force. The early-retirement programme centred around the state-subsidised "59er provision", supplemented by compensation payments made by the firm, and – to a lesser extent – early-retirement practices designed and financed solely by the firm. The cuts in the workforce brought about by early retirement were achieved almost entirely without conflict as they met with the assent of the works council. The positive attitude on the part of the works council is to be explained by the fact that the use of early retirement lessened the need for redundancies, retirement was on a voluntary basis and the relatively high pension levels ensured that worker acceptance was correspondingly high. Including the payments made by the company, net pension levels were about 75% of previous wages. Indeed, the 'demand' for early retirement by eligible workers actually exceeded 'supply'. These conditions for social acceptance are also characteristic of the second half of the 1980s in which early-retirement practices were maintained, despite the change in the external problem constellation. In order to stabilise its turnover position the management gradually and continually implemented rationalisation measures; the job cuts which this made necessary were again achieved through natural wastage and early retirement for older workers using the "59er provision". At times the works council requested that alternatives to this strategy of externalisation be sought with the aim of stabilising workforce levels and integrating older workers (e.g., product diversification), but this did not lead to a change in management strategies.

Similar processes of externalisation are to be observed in *firm E*, a *bank*, although – instructively – the basic problem constellation was slightly different. This company is also representative of the diversified quality production regime, this time in the service sector. A leading general bank with expanding turnover during the 1980s and a workforce of around 1,800 workers it offers a wide range of sophisticated services, many specific to different types of customer. Domestic competition is increasing in almost all product areas. The high level of skills and qualifications of the workforce – half of which are women, while the age structure roughly corresponds to the average – together with the extensive requirements made on all employee groups of whatever age continually to improve their skills and qualifications all reflect the integrated working structures in the context of rapid technological and organisational change. Working structures make relatively high demands on workers' performance levels, although there is scope for autonomous control of workloads. Labour turnover is high among younger workers – both men and women – while the remaining age groups enjoy considerable stability in terms of labour turnover and performance levels. Skill levels tend to rise continually irrespective of age group. The diversified quality production regime is here clearly reflected in a human resource strategy based on longterm employment relations and low age-specific risks.

Nevertheless, the company made extensive use of early retirement during the 1980s. This must be seen as a response to two successive and distinct problem constellations. Between 1980 and 1984 the continued improvements made to the product range were reflected in a considerable pressure to cut costs and rationalise production. Management responded to this situation by slowly but continually reducing staffing levels; this was achieved through natural wastage – which had an age-selective effect in that it affected mainly younger workers – and early retirement. Both instruments were used although there was no active cooperation between management and the works council: the latter merely acquiesced passively to the changes. The process occurred without conflict: management did not have to resort to coercion as most of the exits were based on voluntary retirement. In addition, the payment of a supplementary company pension led to an extremely high net pension level of over 90%, furthering workers 'acceptance of early retirement. Management steered and promoted the early-retirement process by – successfully – motivating older workers to apply for a disability pension. This shows that retirements on the basis of disability can also be steered by management and can be employed for human-resource management purposes. They have the great advantage – from a management perspective – of imposing no additional cost burden on the firm. The "59er provision", in which retirement occurs after a period of unemployment and is financed through state unemployment benefits and subsequently through a pension, was systematically avoided by the bank. This is probably due to the desire to avoid potential damage to the bank's reputation among its customers. Overall, the management pursued an almost exclusively "externalising" strategy during this period: product diversification, or the redeployment of workers within the company – "internalising" solutions to the problem constellation – were not part of the strategy.

Since 1985 the bank has continued with its early-retirement policy, despite a fundamental change in external conditions, which shows how compatible the externalisation strategy via early retirement is with the interests of employees and how the latter serves to stabilise the former. For, since 1985, it has not been the need to adjust to conditions on sales markets or workforce problems related to the output of services which represent the decisive problem constellation to which the firm must 'react', but rather employee interest in retiring early. The introduction of early-retirement practices by management during the early 1980s and the agreement on early retirement reached for the entire banking sector in 1984 had the effect of intensifying employee interest in retiring early. The agreement, originally signed by the employers in expectation of the continuing need to rational- ise, has now become an established part of 'enterprise social policy'. This entails considerable costs for the firm, but the fact that it corresponds to the wishes of the workforce enables it to be used to increase the "social integration" of employees within the firm. The firm has also benefited to the extent that the policy makes the personnel problems associated with mod- ernisation easier to solve: early retirement has tended to lead to the exit of employees who, in view of their lower skill or educational levels, had greater difficulty adjusting to the new product and process innovations.

A further example of the parallel existence of regime-typical low age- specific risks and the widespread use of early-retirement practices is the *steel firm G*. Firm G is an integrated steel works, part of a holding company with a total of 14,000 employees, and has been undergoing a process of contraction for many years. Production centres around high-quality steel. Given the overcapacity endemic in the industry as a whole, and its sensitiv- ity to changes in the overall economic climate, the firm is faced with a highly competitive market structure. The workforce is largely composed of rather young, male, semi-skilled personnel, with some more highly skilled steel workers. The limited opportunity for skill improvement and the traditional working structures broadly reflect the work-intensity practices which are agreed collectively. The firm finds itself confronted by a tension between structurally high age-specific risks on the labour market against the background of declining output of older workers on the one hand, and a highly juridified system of cooperative industrial relations, on the other, which restricts the use of simple externalisation strategies to deal with personnel problems. Despite these restrictions, the firm – and indeed the entire industry – makes extensive use of early retirement. This is the result of a problem constellation emanating from an industry-specific structural crisis tied to corporatist structures which require any personnel reductions to be "socially acceptable" and redundancies to be kept to a minimum.

Throughout the entire period studied, steel firm G has been affected by the structural crisis in the steel industry, a consequence of overcapacity world-wide. In 1986 the deepening crisis made it necessary to cut costs and production capacities; this was achieved in about equal proportions by structural measures (capital investment) and sweeping job cuts: the workforce was reduced by some 3,000. This was largely accomplished (to 70%) through early retirement by older workers. The actual instruments used ranged from the "59er provision", to social plans and the creation of a legally autonomous foundation, and there were combined in such a way that older workers, sometimes after a period of unemployment, were effectively able to retire at the age of 50. While such a large number of retirements cannot be said to have occurred without pressure, given the threat of closure hanging over the entire plant they met with a relatively high level of acceptance. Only a small proportion of the reductions were achieved through reorganisation and retraining measures aimed at younger workers. An innovative solution developed by the firm was the creation of a legally autonomous foundation in which the majority of workers made redundant were grouped. The aim here was to bring together the various financial measures available and to provide counselling and advisory services for older workers until they finally entered actual retirement. Some younger workers were also provided with further training or alternative employment possibilities. Financial support during the transition period between work and final retirement pension was a maximum of 90% of the last wage. While older, unemployed workers in the foundation were effectively merely waiting for final retirement, younger workers were offered some perspective of regaining employment as the firm was committed to a "moral guarantee of reinstatement". This form of collective redundancy was only possible due to cooperation and negotiations over a long period between management and the works council, the regional government, the local employment office and the trade unions. The final agreement was reached largely without conflict and was financed by state subsidies, money from the iron, steel and coal industry funds and by compensation payments made by the company itself. In principle this model also represents a strategy of externalisation, as alternatives, such as product diversification, integration of older workers by providing opportunities for further training etc., were not implemented or were of marginal importance. Nevertheless, in view of the measures implemented to reintegrate younger workers (retraining and subsequent redeployment within the company) the solutions adopted by firm G must be seen as innovative and as going far beyond the usual response by German firms to such problems.

Having described these three firms, with their relatively low age-specific risks on account of the nature of production, and their, nevertheless, extensive use of early-retirement practices, we now turn to those in the taylorist production regime, with their high age-specific risks and their equally extensive use of early-retirement practices.

The *public service firm A* employs about 5 600 workers performing street cleaning and refuse collection services; employment and turnover were relatively stable during the period studied. Although it has a monopoly in most areas, it is subject to some competitive pressure from private contractors. The use of unskilled labour and the high performance requirements are typical features of the taylorist production regime. The average age of the workforce is, at 48, relatively high and, with the exception of management staff, almost exclusively unskilled or semi-skilled. The lack of further-training opportunities comes with a high level of work intensity, to some extent produced by the workers themselves, in repetitive, demanding working structures. These regime characteristics imply a very high risk of reduced work capacity in old age and a tendency to externalise the personnel problems to which this gives rise.

The central human-resource problem faced by the firm is thus the declining working capacity of older workers combined with a relatively 'old' workforce. This problem is exacerbated by a gradual but continuous process of technical and organisational modernisation. Problems tend to be tackled by management, the works council and the employees together, resulting in, if not always cooperative, then at least routine and collusive behaviour on the part of all the actors concerned. From their different perspectives the three actor-groups attempt to solve these problems, whereby the strategy most often pursued is early retirement for reasons of disability; between 1980 and 1988 about 60% of the blue and white-collar workers leaving the workforce for retirement did so via a disability pension. Due to the opportunity to leave the employment system early and the high net pension level (together with the company supplement, up to 90%) this form of retirement is welcomed by employees. The firm itself benefits from the exchange of younger for older workers, easing its performance problems. Other advantages of the disability pension are that it is not subject to age restrictions of any kind and entails no costs for the firm. The high proportion of workers retiring for reasons of disability is also a reflection of cooperation between the actors directly involved and the pension insurance institution. Clearly the firm is fully exploiting the scope offered by the disability-pension provisions to meet enterprise goals. Measures to cope with performance problems internally are limited to a small number of jobs requiring less physical effort and limited opportunities for redeployment within the company.

The production structures in enterprise D, part of the *electrical engineering company D* of the same name, are also such that workers face considerable age-specific performance risks. Early-retirement practices are, however, primarily used to cope with a different problem altogether. The enterprise has been expanding for many years now and has a strong and improving market position. A workforce of about 250 employees produce a range of technically sophisticated, but relatively highly standardised products in medium to large batches. Both the level of mechanisation and the degree of vertical integration are low; the enterprise is dominated by assembly work with a highly developed division of labour and short cycle times. In terms of skills the workforce is highly polarised; a large proportion of the workforce is female, unskilled, young and foreign, with a much smaller number of skilled, male, usually older workers. Performance requirements are relatively high and are set largely unilaterally by management. Under these working conditions the risk of performance loss and health problems for older workers is high. There is a strong trend towards externalisation of these risks, although this usually occurs 'automatically': among the predominantly female workforce the working conditions lead to 'self-selection' and a high rate of turnover of those who are unable to keep pace with required performance levels. The dominant forms of exit – usually before the age of fifty – are transfer to another job or return to the role of housewife. This mode of labour turnover on the part of the female labour force is a consequence of the interaction of two significant factors: the predominant human resource strategies, particularly with regard to women workers, linked with the way in which low-skill labour is used and then replaced when performance problems arise, interacts with gender-specific working and social patterns which have their roots in the social division of labour. The social structure of gender roles has long meant that the role of housewife and mother has been dominant in female biographies; when problems arise it is therefore usually relatively easy to 'persuade' women workers to withdraw from the labour market or to change jobs.

Firms know that they can 'count' on such behaviour patterns; early-retirement practices are simply not required to externalise performance problems and help rejuvenate the workforce. Enterprise D nevertheless does make use of early retirement as an instrument of human resource strategy, although for very different purposes: early retirement is offered primarily to meet the interests of employees in retiring early and to ease the problems of social integration of the workforce. Here management makes selective early-retirement offers to workers who have been with the company for many years or to 'difficult employees'. The aim of this policy is to reduce the potential for social conflict within the enterprise and to provide a symbol – aimed at younger workers – that working hard for the company will be rewarded. The enterprise uses – as does the mother company – the state-subsidised "59er provision" for its 'social policy' initiatives in this area, supplemented by company bonuses.

2.3 The Regulatory Characteristics and Logic of Firms' Behaviour

The findings of our case studies, especially when viewed in the light of the quantitative data presented in section I showing consistently high early-retirement shares for the economy as a whole, enable a number of clear conclusions to be drawn concerning:
– the homogeneous age-selective externalisation strategies of West German firms in the face of heterogeneous problem constellations,
– the validity of explanations of early-retirement practices based on the declining productivity of older workers, and
– the central components of the regulatory logic of firms' behaviour.

2.3.1 Homogeneous Age-Selective Externalisation Strategies

(1) Our case-study findings clearly show that the differences in labour-market risks for older workers associated with different production regimes are overdetermined by a very consistent approach to workers near retirement age adopted by all firms. This represents an important modification to the production regime-hypothesis and points to the existence of regulatory conditions for age-structure policies in German firms which transcend production-regime boundaries. Irrespective of industry and production regime, all the firms studied did not view older workers as a vital human resource but rather as a 'flexibility potential' in order to realise their strategies of personnel adjustments. This potential is used in such a way that adjustment problems are dealt with by externalising (older) workers. Externalisation refers to a specific corporate problem-solving strategy by which problems are resolved primarily through labour-market exits (or at least firm-exits) rather than through internal changes in products, production structures and training processes. The term is used of the firm without making any statement regarding the social acceptability of such a strategy. The externalisation-bias of this dominant strategy is also reflected in the fact that none of the firms have made significant attempts to integrate older workers. Except for certain very limited efforts to develop age-specific working structures none of the firms had even attempted to initiate a systematic policy aimed at integrating older workers through redeployment, the creation of new, age-specific jobs or product diversification.

(2) West German firms pursue their homogeneous age-selective externalisation strategy not only in the context of different production regimes but also in the face of heterogeneous problem constellations. In other words, while the externalisation strategy dominates early-retirement practices, the latter are employed to cope with a whole range of diverse problems. As depicted in table 6, six distinct problem constellations were identified to which firms responded with the help of early-retirement practices. They range from structural crisis, modernisation problems associated with the introduction of new product and process technologies, through the problem of falling sales and firm-specific rationalisation processes to the productivity problems of older workers and employee interest in early retirement. This finding reveals an important problem-solving mechanism frequently employed by West German firms: problems facing the firm, of whatever nature, are conceived of as personnel problems which are then solved by externalisation. In this, older workers are seen as a potential for human-resource flexibility which can be realised quickly and at low cost in terms of social-integration considerations to solve a whole range of problems with which the firm sees itself confronted. This 'availability' of older

Table 6: Problem Constellations, Personnel-Adjustment Strategies and Instruments

Firms	Problem Constellations Facing Firms	Personnel-Adjustment Strategies	Instruments Externalisation		Internalisation	Net Pension Level for Those Retiring Early
			Withdrawal Through Early Retirement	Withdrawal of Younger Workers Via Natural Wastage, Resignation and Dismissal		State and Company Pension
Problem Constellations Linked to Sales Market						
Steel G	1 Industry-Specific Structural Crisis	Large-Scale Workforce Reductions	+	+	−	75%
Bank E*	2 Product/Process Innovation	Qualitative Personnel Restructuring	+	−	+	90%
Bank E**	3 Rationalisation	Continuing, Small-Scale Cuts in Workforce	+	+	−	
Engineering C	4 Cyclical Fall in Demand	Temporary Reduction in Workforce	+	+	−	75%
Problelm Constellations Linked to Internal Labour Market						
Public service A	5 Performance Problems Among Older Workers	Personnel Exchange	+		−	90%
Electrical Engineering D	6 Worker Interest in Early Retirement	Age-Selective Externalisation for Reasons of Social Integration	+			75%

+ Intensive Usage; − low or No Usage   * Phase 1   ** Phase 2
from Rosenow/Naschold 1993

workers must be considered a necessary condition for the dominance of externalisation strategies.

(3) The use of older workers as 'flexibility potential' for personnel adjustment in this way is greatly facilitated by a largely conflict-free social regulation of early-retirement practices and a relatively high pension level. Our research indicates that management's use of early retirement is usually accepted by the works council and, indeed, is not infrequently based on consensus and cooperation between management and the workers representatives. To the extent that early-retirement measures are under management control they are usually realised on a voluntary basis: employees then consider the option for early retirement to be their own decision and to offer relatively favourable opportunities. Of course, the pressure to reduce overall staffing levels can often restrict the 'optional' nature of early-retirement offers considerably; under conditions of such limited options early retirement can be seen as the result of a "constrained choice" on the part of workers.

(4) Our micro-level analysis of early-retirement processes involving older workers confirms the hypothesis, until now supported only by aggregate statistical data, that there exists a specifically national pattern of labour-market exit which transcends industry and enterprise-specific differences in the Federal Republic of Germany. The findings obtained from our case studies confirm that older workers (above 50) generally go straight from the firm into retirement, withdrawing completely from paid employment. It is relatively rare for workers of 50 years and above to leave the firm without entering retirement: of the exits into retirement the vast majority imply complete withdrawal from the employment system.

A good example is firm A, a public services enterprise. Exits of workers aged 50 and above who leave the firm without entering retirement account for a mere 3% of all exits by workers from this age group. Due to the high wage level the firm's employees are entitled to relatively high pensions, even if they retire early. Their interests are well represented by the works council, and workers above the age of 55 with at least 10 years tenure at the firm enjoy special protection against dismissal. Workers who decided to leave the firm without entering retirement would be exchanging age-group-specific rights of protection, a relatively good position within the enterprise and a comparatively high wage level for a substantial degree of social insecurity. Given that the special dismissal protection afforded older workers makes them difficult to fire, older employees have the option of waiting until they are able to take early retirement. Their high pension level places restrictions on their ability to take up paid employment in retirement and reduces the incentive to do so.

(5) A further finding from our case studies points to a levelling of age-structure differences between the firms as a consequence of early-retire-

ment practices. The expected differences in employment shares of older workers in firms operating in different production regimes were largely overdetermined by the homogeneous early-retirement practices of the firms. Consequently, no characteristic differences in employment shares of older workers, which could be interpreted as regime effects, were identified.

Any comparison of firms' age-structures is subject to serious methodological difficulties as such structures are contingent on a complex network of determinants, many of which, moreover, are subject to change over time (business cycle, structural crisis, demographic developments etc.), all of which must be taken into account. Nonetheless, if these 'period effects' are controlled for, a generalised trend towards an equalisation of age-structures becomes apparent (for older workers between 55 and 64, and the two subgroups, 55–59 and 60–64 year-olds) underlying the superficial appearance of differing age-structure characteristics among the firms studied. This is true not only of the firms studied, but also of the German economy as a whole. The employment shares of the upper age categories are declining to a low level: this is particularly the case in those firms in which the employment share of these groups is currently relatively high. Thus the differences between firms with regard to the employment-shares of older workers are declining over time[10] (cf. figure 3).

(6) The overall picture of homogeneous early-retirement practices and their extensive implementation must be modified slightly to take account of enterprise-size-specific differences; the picture as presented is, namely, slightly less true of small than of large firms. The three case studies conducted in small firms, each with different production-regime characteristics, clearly show that while early retirement is a relatively common form of labour market exit for older workers in small firms, too, early-retirement instruments tend not to be implemented strategically by management as a vehicle of personnel adjustment. A clear indication of this is provided by the fact that managements of small firms are often unaware of the conditions attached to the use of a number of central early-retirement instruments (e.g., the "59er provision"). Early retirement tends, therefore, to be initiated by employees themselves and is as a result less subject to management control. According to a study by Schettkat (1989) early-retirement shares are on the whole lower in smaller firms. The enterprise-size-specific differences in the use of early-retirement practices can be traced back to a number of structural factors: on the one hand, smaller firms have less severe adjustment problems as the natural wastage of a small number of employees produces, in relative terms, significant adjustment effects; on the other, the conditions are not as favourable for the use of early-retirement instruments as in larger firms. They tend to be less able, for example, to offer attractive terms to those retiring early as most small firms lack a company pension-insurance scheme and the liquidity to make supplementary pay-

Age	Total	Firm A	Firm C	Firm D	Firm E	Firm G
20–19	5.8	0.1	3.1	0.5	3.8	0.7
20–24	14.9	3.9	9.6	16.8	19.2	6.0
25–29	14.6	7.5	10.5	27.1	16.4	10.5
30–34	12.2	8.4	10.5	15.0	9.9	10.8
35–39	11.1	11.4	9.5	13.1	10.4	13.4
40–44	9.8	11.0	9.6	9.8	8.0	11.5
45–49	11.9	21.3	12.4	8.4	11.9	17.9
50–54	11.2	21.5	16.7	5.6	12.6	25.2
55–59	6.5	12.7	12.7	3.3	7.0	3.3
60–64	1.7	2.2	5.0	0.0	0.8	0.6
65+	0.3	0.0	0.2	0.5	0.2	0.0
	n=2161 in 1.000	n=5854	n=3215	n=245	n=1809	n=14000

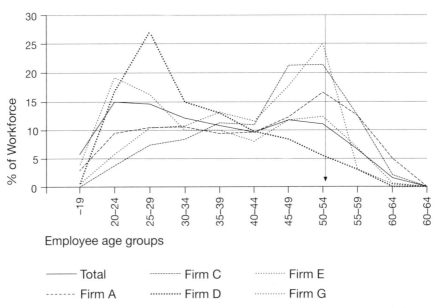

Figure 3: Age-Structure of Case-Study Firms and the German Economy as a Whole

ments of their own. Larger firms, by contrast, make considerable use of such incentives, especially for exits in which the initiative lies with management (such as the "59er provision"). Furthermore, due to the limited resources and skills invested in personnel planning and development (cf. Semlinger, 1989), smaller firms find it more difficult to take advantage of the state benefits and counselling services which are needed to make the fullest possible use of the early-retirement instruments available. Last but not least, the fact that it is usually more difficult for employees to exert collective pressure to realise their interests in smaller firms represents a further obstacle for the implementation of attractive early-retirement practices.

2.3.2 On the Validity of "Productivity-Theoretical" Explanations of Early-Retirement Practices

Several authors (cf., for example, Jacobs and Rein, 1990) have linked the trend to early retirement to a decline in firms' willingness to continue to employ older workers. This approach goes beyond a mere descriptive statement and amounts to a 'productivity-theoretical' explanation. Our case studies allow us to draw rather different conclusions concerning the link between employers' age-structure policies and demographic developments than those put forward by this approach, at least for the Federal Republic.

During the 1980s the firms studied (and also the corresponding industries and, indeed, the whole German economy) found themselves confronted by an age-structure problem which led to serious concern about productivity within firms' organisational structures: the increasing employment shares of older workers had the effect of blocking career ladders, damaging the career interests and thus restricting the performance levels of younger workers. Moreover, given the decline in the mobility of older workers, their increasing employment shares restricted the scope for personnel flexibility available to employers, slowing economic adjustment processes (cf. Weber, 1989; Pfeffer, 1985; Hutchens, 1993). Against this background, employers' early-retirement practices throughout the German economy during the 1980s were clearly oriented towards coping with the rising employment shares of older workers.

The scale of such age-structure problems is clear from the fact that the employment shares of older workers have remained stable, and in some cases have even increased, between 1980 and 1989, despite the high level of early retirement in this period (cf. table 7).

As can be seen from table 7, the employment share of workers between 55 and 64 years of age in the German economy remained relatively stable

Table 7: Changes in Employment Shares of the 55−64 Year Age Group in the Firms Studied, the Corresponding Industrial Categories and the German Economy as a Whole, 1980 to 1989

Firm/ Industrial Category	55−64 Year Age Group as a Percentage of Total Workforce		
	1980 (%)	1989 (%)	1980−89* (PP)
West German Total	8.7	8.2	−0.5
A	9.8	14.9	5.1
C	12.4	17.7	5.3
D	3.7	3.7	0.0
E	9.6	7.7	−1.9
G	4.7	4.1	−0.6
843 (A)	10.7	15.6	4.9
264 (C)	9.3	8.9	−0.4
348 (D)	8.0	6.9	−1.1
690 (E)	7.6	6.1	−1.5
170/200/211 (G)	9.9	8.6	−1.3

Notes:
* Change in Percentage Points.
In Firm A the First Year Studied was 1985.
In Firm C the Period Studied was 1984 to 1990.
In Firm D the Period Studied was 1982 to 1987 whereby the Figure for 1982 is Estimated.
In Firm G the Period Studied was 1986 to 1990.
Sources: Case Studies; Statistics of Employees on the Social Insurance Beneficiary List, Federal Employment Office; own Calculations.

between 1980 and 1989: indeed, in the largest segment, male employees, it increased slightly. In two of the firms studied (A and B) the employment share of older workers has increased, despite early retirement and in line with developments in their respective industrial categories (843 and 266). In enterprise D the share of older workers has remained constant while it has fallen slightly in the corresponding industrial category (348). Only in the service firm E, the corresponding category 690 and the steel firm G have the employment shares of older workers fallen slightly.

These findings enable us to draw the following conclusions regarding the problems facing firms and the dynamic underlying corporate early-retirement policies: the overall stability of the employment shares of older workers in the context of the increasing use of early retirement does not mean that employers in the Federal Republic are becoming increasingly unwilling to continue to employ older workers. Under conditions of rising employment-shares of older workers, early-retirement policies are not primarily aimed at rejuvenating the workforce and raising productivity, as the productivity-theoretical approach postulates, but at stabilising the employment shares of the upper age groups and thus maintaining an overall age-structure which is considered acceptable in terms of corporate organisational structures.

A concept often used to explain current early-retirement practices and based on a constellation of common solutions to common problems is grounded on the hypothesis of degressive productivity rates of older workers, and the resulting externalisation of productivity losses through corporate early-retirement strategies. In theoretical terms the argument is founded on the relationship assumed to obtain between long-term employment contracts, increasing discrepancies between productivity and pay trends with increasing age, and early retirement as a means of reducing this discrepancy. Specifically for the 1980s, the theory also incorporates the effects of the simultaneous heightening of international competition and the restructuring of productive capacity. Such a global increase in pressure on firms could, so the theory, provide the backdrop to homogeneous, collective reactions on the part of employers.

At first sight this approach seems plausible. Nonetheless, the empirical evidence and a number of theoretical considerations do not support it. Productivity and cost-oriented rationalisation strategies ought, if they are to achieve their aims, to involve different strategies for different groups of the workforce; blue versus white-collar, unskilled and semi-skilled workers as against highly qualified staff. According to our case studies, however, the incidence of early retirement scarcely differs between blue and white-collar workers (cf. table 5). This is true of the proportion of exits occurring both under 65 and under 63 years of age.

Our case studies also reveal considerable variation in personnel implementation strategies in the different firms within the framework of heterogeneous firm-specific production regimes. In addition to the enormous differences between workforce skill levels, forms of labour-use and the conditions for the development of skills, qualifications and work capacity in general, together with substantial variations in cost structures in the different branches, all the evidence indicates that the productivity levels of older workers also differ greatly from firm to firm. Assuming that early-retirement strategies have the aim of increasing productivity, such heterogeneous firm constellations could not generate homogeneous early-retirement policies; they would rather lead to differentially structured early-retirement effects. In both theoretical and empirical terms it is implausible to assume a generalised (i.e., irrespective of firms' human resource strategies), degressive productivity trend among older workers. Similarly, an explanation of empirically observable homogeneous early-retirement practices as representing a consequence of an underlying, generalised drop in productivity among older workers is unconvincing. Our findings show that the theoretical assumptions underlying this approach are insufficiently differentiated. While the finding that firms' early-retirement practices are largely homogeneous although they employ different human resource strategies does not preclude an argument based on productivity, such homogeneity would seem to point to a general logic of regulation, which cannot be reduced merely to the pressure to raise productivity levels.

2.3.3 The Regulatory Logic of Firms' Behaviour

So far the central empirical finding from our case studies – heterogeneous problem constellations and production regimes are transposed by firms into homogeneous personnel strategies and age structures – has been explained in terms of national forms of regulation which transcend firm and sector boundaries. Such an approach must not be equated with a neo-classical logic according to which firms adapt passively to the external dictates of the state, the labour market or demographic trends. On the contrary: firms are important actors contributing to the formation of the legal framework within which production occurs. They play a vital role in continually reproducing and legitimising this framework and, of course, in the day-to-day transposition of the normative and financial framework into the reality of production. We turn then to the 'regulatory logic' of the firms studied; the regulatory framework set by the state and the interaction between state and firms will be considered later in section 3. We have identified three central constellations constituting the mode of age-selective regulation which transcends firm-specific production regimes and forms an integral part of the overall national production regime: (1) the normative, regulatory framework – both statutory and collectively regulated – in the concrete form it takes at plant level and to the extent that it has age-selective effects; (2) the pattern of interaction between management and the works council – plant level industrial relations – with respect to age-structure policies, and (3) the specific constellation of firms in the national context (cf. Rosenow and Naschold, 1992, for further details).

(1) At firm level two forms of regulation emanating from the West German normative structure are decisive in influencing the dominant mode of early retirement at the level of the firm. From a management perspective these regulatory forms are seen as exogenous parameters which are then transformed into internal regulatory factors and which favour an age-selective externalisation strategy via early retirement:

(a) The Works Constitution Act, statutory and collectively negotiated dismissal protection norms and regulations, especially those applying to older workers militate against the use of adjustment strategies based on those forms of externalisation which are linked to redundancies determined by management and thus the use of its discretionary power. Typically, plant-level agreements contain selection guidelines which effectively restrict dismissals due to economic necessity to workers under the age of 45. Older workers (usually those above the age of – similar to the Swedish state – 5 and with at least 10 years' tenure with their current employer) are in addition also protected by dismissal protection provisions contained in (industry-wide) collective agreements. While it is very difficult for management to dismiss older workers, employees under 45 face the risk of dismissal according to the last-in-first-out principle. This axiom clearly hits younger workers hardest, in line with employers 'interests in holding on to employees with long tenure and with correspondingly high levels of (firm-specific) knowledge and experience.

(b) The other side of the coin of limitations on the use of dismissals, particularly in the case of older workers, is the availability of externalising, problem-solving options to meet personnel-adjustment requirements, normatively regulated by legal provisions on pensions and job creation, in the form of early retirement. Two factors complement each other here: the lack of state regulation and of impulses for a strategy of integrating older workers at plant level on the one hand, and the existence of substantial incentives for early retirement on the other. Thus while older workers are largely protected against dismissals, the availability of early-retirement options provides firms with a functionally equivalent instrument of workforce adjustment.

The availability of such externalising workforce-adjustment options and the incentives for their application are the result of structural characteristics of the state political regime. These are subsequently transformed by the production regime into an internal mode of regulation of workforce adjustments. State regulation offers firms a highly differentiated system of retirement options for their workers and provides significant incentives for externalising workforce-adjustment strategies. These retirement options, together with the additional transfer payments usually offered by the employer, provide managements with considerable flexibility in steering workforce exits via early retirement.

(2) The effects induced by this enterprise-oriented system of statutory and collectively negotiated norms are then specified and concretised by the procedures making up the system of industrial relations, i.e., the interaction between management and the works council (or trade union). Our case-study firms all show that, faced with firm-specific problems and the existing system of enterprise-oriented statutory regulation, the 'nexus' of the interests and parameters of action of both management and the works council lies in the empirically observed practice of early retirement for older workers.

In line with the predominantly cooperative pattern of industrial relations in the Federal Republic, this management strategy, which transcends firm and sector demarcations, leads primarily to the use of those instruments which minimise the potential for conflict in social relations within the firm – i.e., which maintain the social integration of the plant/firm as a system of social action – while simultaneously providing a relatively large potential for precise (in terms of both timing and quantities) control over workforce adjustments.

In the case of personnel adjustments to be realised via exits, our findings show that managements select a plurality of instruments, in particular those in which, on the one hand, exits can be considered in some sense "voluntary" and which meet with a relatively high level of worker acceptance and, on the other, those which allow the processes of workforce adjustment to be relatively accurately steered. Above and beyond 'natural wastage', in all the firms studied personnel adjustments were achieved using the following instruments: mutual agreement to terminate the employment contract; redundancies – where unavoidable – whereby this is usually restricted to younger workers (in both cases usually supported by financial incentives); the various early-retirement instruments, whereby a whole range of measures was employed according to the concrete situation. Due to the highly differentiated forms in which it can be implemented, early retirement enables substantial volume effects to be combined with accurate steering.

Employers often make use of these provisions despite the often substantial financial contributions they themselves have to make (for instance in the case of the "59er provision"). Due to the considerable interest on the part of workers in early retirement in Germany, and the high level of pensions, at least for those who have been in more or less continuous employment, the use of such provisions largely fulfills the criteria of social acceptability and effectiveness. Although they may involve considerable problems for individual workers, they enjoy widespread acceptance among employees and workers' representatives on works councils which are keen to minimise the risks of personnel adjustments where they have to be implemented. By contributing to workforce adjustment, early retirement secures the jobs of employees who will remain in paid employment for a long time to come, while not condemning older workers to unemployment but facilitating their transfer to an alternative status to paid employment, namely retirement. The various instruments of early retirement in the Federal Republic can be seen as an important weapon in the armoury of acceptable, consensual and effective strategies of externalising workforce adjustment problems.

This management strategy tends to accord with the practices and interests of the works council. Firstly, the relatively strong legal position of older workers, a consequence of the seniority regulations common in the Federal Republic, provides works councils with a powerful instrument with which to negotiate favourable terms (financial compensation) for early-retirement practices. Secondly, early retirement, given the high pension level, can be "sold" to the workforce in normative terms as a "contract between the generations": early retirement for older workers helps secure the jobs of younger employees. This provides works councils with a double legitimation for their policy – whether active cooperation or passive acceptance – towards early-retirement practices.

At the same time, it should be noted that this nexus of interests between management and works councils is a structure which needs the support of two fundamental pillars:

- the fact that a large proportion of the costs of externalisation can themselves be externalised – this is a problem which will be considered when we turn to the interaction between firms and the state – and
- the implicit "constrained-choice" nature of early-retirement options for employees. All our empirical evidence points to the fact that early-retirement practices in West German firms systematically and strategically exclude alternative options for individual workers: either socially integrative employment alternatives on the Swedish pattern or employment stabilisation via diversification and redeployment within the company on the Japanese model. Our findings show that, faced with this constrained option of early retirement, it was only in the initial stages, if at all, that workforces expressed doubts about – not to mention resistance to – early-retirement proposals. Sooner or later, workers came round to accept the proposals offered and in some cases actually took the initiative to demand that management provide early-retirement options.

(3) Finally, the homogeneous age-selective externalisation strategy of German firms is also determined by a constellation within the firm which is characteristic of the overall German model. German managements operate within a "social constitution of the firm" in which "hard commitments" regarding guaranteed employment up to a certain standard retirement age are not made. Externalisation, provided it occurs on socially acceptable terms and leads into a secure status (pensioned retirement), is not seen as a transgression against an employment norm which, nevertheless, is heavily oriented towards workforce stability. This "soft commitment" to employment stability is reflected in a highly differentiated pension system with a comparatively generous financial provision for retirement. Faced with this constellation, the parameters for management actions are determined within fairly narrow margins by the interest of the firm: on balance these support the age-selective externalisation logic. This is a fundamentally different constellation from that in Japan, where firms' strategy is strongly internalisation-oriented. In most Japanese companies the norm of employment stability is relatively "hard", even for older workers. Faced with this norm and the limited provision of state benefits for old-age pensioners, Japanese managements tend to take more account of the need to secure jobs, even

those of their older employees, than the direct interests of shareholders. A further factor is the more highly differentiated organisational structure of the larger Japanese firms which is used systematically to facilitate redeployment between different enterprises controlled by a single company.

Taken together these findings are of considerable theoretical interest. Rather than an economic causal logic behind early retirement, our results emphasise the importance of the social and institutional regulation of retirement impinging on the firm, in particular the potential for conflict and management's ability to control personnel adjustment processes as an overall system. Whereas the neoclassical line of argument explains the pressure for earlier retirement in terms of degressive productivity trends among older workers while pay levels simultaneously rise above productivity levels (efficiency wages), our findings suggest a more comprehensive approach based on social regulation by elements of a national production regime, which is in turn a product of state policies and the interaction of firms and the state. Such an approach does not, of course, deny the relevance of factors such as degressive productivity trends. Our findings show, though, that during the 1980s West German firms were not primarily pursuing a "productivity logic" in their use of early retirement (i.e., the externalisation of older workers with degressive productivity trends). Rather their strategy was one of workforce adjustment orientated closely towards social-integrative effects and effective control over the timing and volume of exits from the workforce. The role of the state in this overall regulatory framework is the subject of the next section.

3   The Interaction of Firms and the State: Retirement-Age Policies
      in the Federal Republic of Germany

The first two sections have provided an analysis of the German pattern of age-structure and age-limit trends largely in terms of enterprise production regimes in the context of labour-market and demographic trends. The analysis has already revealed the importance of a mode of regulation which transcends enterprise-types, the influence of statutory and collectively negotiated intervention and the interaction of the normative and financial framework provided by the state and the age-selective strategies of personnel adjustment pursued by German firms. This section will first consider the strategies, instruments and institutions of state age-structure policy (3.1) in order to identify the fundamental regulatory logic of the German state. It is against this background that we then attempt to identify the logic of interaction of employers, employees, their representative organisations and the state, and the policies of the various actors responsible for producing, reproducing and legitimising the trend towards early retirement in the

Federal Republic. For this purpose we draw on exemplary empirical material derived from our evaluation of documentary evidence and a series of expert interviews conducted at central, regional and local levels of the German administration responsible for social policy (3.2). In subsection 3.3, the material is then subjected to systematic analysis aimed at illuminating specific questions: the tri-partite nature, the consistency and selectivity of retirement policy in the Federal Republic, and the strategic positioning of both the state and firms in this constellation.

3.1   The Strategies, Institutions and Instruments of State Age-Structure Policies

It should be noted, first of all, that we do not mean by "state age-structure policy" merely those policies which explicitly seek to determine or to modify retirement policy, i.e., those which regulate the way in which workers leave the employment system and enter the system of social security. We also intend to consider the whole arsenal of strategies which have an indirect effect on firms' age-selective personnel policies.

The multiplicity of distinct strategies by the West German state can be explained with reference to three basic functions of state retirement-age policies:

- The social-policy and demand-side redistributive function of state retirement-age policies aims to influence – intertemporally and interpersonally – the distribution of life chances (work, income, skills and qualifications, health): it incorporates all policies (including those seeking to influence demographic and labour-market trends) to the extent that the social-policy component is the dominant interest.
- The supply-side, productivity function of state intervention aims at the comprehensive development of the efficient and cost-effective use of (in particular young, high-performance) labour-power potential, and the simultaneous filtering-out of workers whose health is impaired, whose performance levels have fallen and/or who are comparatively old.
- Concrete state strategies are developed and, above all, executed with the help of characteristic procedural forms. In most of the arenas of retirement-age policy mentioned above the political system in the Federal Republic is characterised by cooperative procedural regulations in labour relations and "concerted" (tri-partite) strategies between the state apparatus and representatives of employers and workers.

From the above sketches of the direct and indirect instruments of age-selective intervention the following overall picture emerges: the retirement-age policies of the West German state – the breadth and depth of which are

Table 8: Basic Functions of State Retirement-Age Policies in Comparison

Dimensions of State Strategies	States			
	FRG	USA	Sweden	Japan
Productivity Function	−	+	+ +	+ + +
Redistribution Function	+ + +	−	+ +	−
Cooperation Function	+ +	−	+ + +	+ +

considerable – are oriented primarily to the functions of redistribution and cooperation at the expense of the productivity function. The predominance of the transfer principle and procedural cooperation form the contours of the German pattern of retirement-age policies. It will be the task to show by means of examples that this pattern is largely coherent and in recent decades has remained relatively stable.

These three basic functions of state retirement-age policies, developed from analysis of the West German model, can also be transferred to the international comparative perspective, allowing us to identify and specify national strategies both similar to and different from that in the Federal Republic.

A comparison with Japan, the USA and Sweden will serve to illustrate the range of national-state strategy profiles, again in terms of a preliminary empirical study (cf. table 8).[11] Overall the clearly nationally specific profiles of state strategies indicate – at the present state of research – the relevance of the nation-state in providing a "home environment" (Porter, 1990) for corporate strategies and market developments.

In this strategic perspective the state and state institutions are seen as having – in principle – a whole range of instruments at their disposal. Following Ikenberry (1988: 122) we will distinguish between four types: organisational instruments, spending (fiscal) instruments, market instruments and information and advisory services. The West German repertoire of instruments and the relative importance attached to each type of instrument within the repertoire differs from those in countries such as Sweden, Japan or the USA.

– Organisational instruments involve direct intervention in job-design and in the way in which production and the use of labour is organised. In the Federal Republic such instruments are characterised by a specific asymmetry: they aim to develop the working potential of younger workers as comprehensively and as productively as possible (further training health and safety provisions etc.) and simultaneously to externalise older and/or less productive workers, smoothly but in a socially acceptable way (dismissal protection on the one hand and externalisation instruments on the other). Interventionist measures to restructure work processes on behalf of older workers, on the other hand, either do not exist or are not implemented in an offensive way. The one exception here is provided by state-run firms and the public administration where the state. in its role as employer, has to some extent performed an integrative function with respect to older workers.

- These asymmetrical organisational measures are linked to powerful fiscal instruments. The cornerstone of the West German retirement system is the provision of financial compensation for certain "risks" faced by the individual (e.g., old age), and this at a comparatively high level (maintenance of living standards as the guiding principle). Pensions (and other social benefits) are thus under certain circumstances an attractive alternative to paid employment and can be instrumentalised for firms' externalisation strategies. The precondition for this system to function is the relatively high compulsory contributions paid by both workers and employers.
- The third type of state policy – measures to influence market structures – is restricted almost exclusively to instruments of (age-selective) active labour-market policy, an area which is underdeveloped in the Federal Republic (compared, for example, with Sweden). Market-steering mechanisms such as an age-selective employment policy or, alternatively, a deregulation of age limits are systematically absent in Germany: market instruments are not part of the armoury of the German state in this area.
- The fourth type of instrument relevant in the present context are the information and counselling services provided by the state or the bodies responsible for administering the social security system and the cooperative procedural regulations and 'concerted' strategies. These instruments traditionally link up with the overall logic of externalisation and are heavily oriented towards the compensation of individual risks; they are of almost negligible importance when it comes to strategies based on problem-internalisation.

A comparison of the instruments used in the Federal Republic with those employed by other countries such as Sweden, the USA and Japan (cf. among other Samuels, 1987) – following the most-dissimilar-case approach – clearly reveals the profile of state policies towards older workers in Germany.

In Sweden, active labour-market and working-structure policies in the context of strong trade unions and a traditional shortage of labour condition the comprehensive – in comparison with the Federal Republic – internalisation strategies pursued by the majority of firms. These include the provision of "sheltered" jobs, humanisation of working structures and working conditions, offers of part-time employment linked to partial pensions and programmes to safeguard workers health and improve their

Table 9: Instrument Profiles of State Retirement-Age Policies in Comparison

State Instruments	States			
	FRG	USA	Sweden	Japan
Legal Norms	+ + +	+	+ + +	+ +
Transfer	+ + +	+	+ +	+
Market Instruments	−	+ + +	+ +	+ + +
Information and Advising Services	+	−	+ +	+

qualifications, all of which are constituent parts of Sweden's full-employment policy. Japan's age-selective regime is very much firm-oriented, based on a specific conception of the firm as an institution: most Japanese firms are part of a larger corporate network which is used systematically for inter-firm removals. Japanese managements are under heavy pressure to diversify production and expand market shares in order to safeguard or expand employment levels. This constellation does entail a degree of flexibility for personnel adjustment processes, which is facilitated by the Japanese regulatory system, both statutory and collectively negotiated. The distinguishing characteristic of the USA in this context is the under-instrumentation in the fields of organisational, fiscal, and advisory measures and the concentration on "decontrol instruments". While German firms face much heavier regulation than those in the USA, they do not have to cope with firm-centred or state-centred pressures to internalise their age-specific problems to the same extent as Japan and Sweden.

A third aspect, which is also significant for the different national strategies and their results – in the form of nationally specific forms of labour-market withdrawal by older workers – is the structure of political institutions and the division of labour and forms of cooperation existing between them. The German model of "statedness" – similar to the Swedish state – is relatively typical of continental Europe. It is based on a highly differentiated – both horizontally and vertically – network of state institutions; market processes are often overdetermined by non-market forms of coordination by state hierarchies and highly centralised social organisations (e.g., unions). This basic pattern of statedness provides the framework for arena-specific political structures. It differs substantially from the mode of statedness to be found, for instance, in Japan or the USA.

Analysis of West Germany's retirement policies against the background of its vertical (i.e., with respect to the different levels of hierarchical control) and horizontal (with respect to the different functions of the state) structure reveals the following country-profile for the Federal Republic. German age-structure policy combines a high degree of vertical differentiation, i.e., the involvement of both highly centralised and highly decentralised structures, with a high level of functional differentiation, i.e., the specific institutionalisation of individual arenas. This implies not only the existence of polyvalently articulated state and para-statal structures at the central level, differentiated ministerial structures, centralised trade unions and employers' federations, central forms of organisation of all the institutions charged with administering the various branches of the social insurance system and labour market policies. It also requires the establishment of a highly differentiated and vital network of institutions and organisations at regional and local level. These range from decentralised facilities run by state-level and local government, local employment exchanges and health insurance institutions, to the stations run by the pension and accident-insurance institutions at regional level. Compared with the German system, vertical differentiation in Japan and the USA is relatively low. These countries lack the local and regional cushion on which the German central welfare system rests – a form of local and meso-corporatism.

The way in which responsibility for dealing with the various age-structure problems is divided up between the various political institutions and levels is of decisive importance for the operative functioning of age-structure policy. This begs the question: what form does the political division of labour with respect to German age-structure policies take? The Federal Republic is distinguished by a strict division of responsibility for administering the different insurance risks. Almost according to taylorist preconceptions, institutional structures have crystalised in an historical process, each dealing with one of the risks of working life, this despite the fact that, particularly in old age, these risks often occur together. These institutions are not differentiated according to "ends" (i.e., different types of security provision, such as providing security in old age), but rather according to "cause" (i.e., the legal cause on which benefit entitlement is based, e.g., pension due to old age, pension due to industrial accident). This leads to serious demarcation and coordination problems in complicated cases (for example unemployment due to chronic sickness with a possible pension entitlement). The West German system with its strict division of labour has, however, produced an extraordinarily large number of effective linkages and interfaces which sometimes appear to enable problems to be dealt with on an inter-organisational basis, at least as far as compensation for the consequences of externalisation are concerned. Nevertheless, the organisational principles on which the system is based produce a number of disfunctionalities. The highly differentiated social security system, each section of which has its own interests, is an open invitation to pursue opportunistic policies in which problems and financial responsibilities are passed on from one area to the next. Moreover, the internal flexibility of the German institutions responsible for age-structure policies ties these institutions so closely together that they lose "external flexibility". The danger here is that the institutions gradually become incapable of making strategic changes of direction and accepting innovations. The structural lack of active labour-market policies is a good example of such resistance to change. The strength of state institutions can in this way turn into weakness and immobilism, revealing the "irony of state strength" (Ikenberry, 1986).

3.2 Strategic Action, Day-to-Day Policies and Non-Decisions

We take as our point of departure three distinct constellations of political decision-making and interaction between the state, firms and social organisations. Strategic action, by means of which the central parameters of retirement policy are produced and legitimated; day-to-day policies which break down these parameters, reproduce or modify them, and; non-decisions by means of which potential alternative solutions to specific problems go unused or unmentioned. Against the background of these three forms of interaction we will now present empirical material of an exemplary nature to elucidate further the interaction between the participating actors.

3.2.1 Strategic Action in German Retirement Policy

Three large-scale strategic actions in West Germany since the War have each taken the central parameters of the pre-War system of retirement policies, developed them further and modified them: the three major pension reforms of 1957, 1972 and 1992. The equivalent strategic action within the unemployment-insurance system was the Work Promotion Act of 1969 although it is not possible to go into this aspect of the problem in greater detail at this point.

The pension reform of 1957 laid the foundations for retirement-age policy in the Federal Republic of Germany. It established old-age pensions as social security in a recognised social status (retirement), rather than in the form of a universal basic pension; by linking pension levels to real-wage growth pensioners were no longer to be regarded as recipients of welfare but as quasi-wage earners (Müller, 1988). The system of financing, based on the insurance principle, determined the individual nature of security in old age, based on income levels during working life: the pay-as-you-earn basis. The Act also offered early-retirement opportunities at 60 for women and the unemployed. Taking over a number of traditions from the Weimar Republic, the law laid the foundation for the West German system of security in old age, including the possibility of early retirement in the sense of the direct passage from full-time employment to full-time retirement.

Early retirement for women workers was aimed at bringing the passage into retirement temporally into line with their spouses (who were older on average) (Jacobs et. al., 1991) and, above all, to compensate for the double burden borne by women in the form of paid employment and housework.

The reform of 1972 was initially greeted as the "most significant legal development in the field of social policy" since 1957. It confirmed the basic structure established in 1957 and initiated a series of important further developments (cf. Hermann, 1988). Of central importance for retirement-age policy was the – uncontroversial – introduction of the flexible retirement age. Against the background of considerable surpluses in the various pension funds and optimistic forecasts about coming economic trends, those who had paid contributions continuously throughout their working life, i.e., largely male workers, were offered the option of retiring early (at 63, the severely handicapped at 62). The early-retirement option was sweetened with additional financial incentives, in the form of the non-introduction of the controversially discussed actuarial deductions. The large number of eligible persons taking advantage of the early-retirement options (immediately after the new Act went into effect and before the rising unemployment from 1974/75) indicate that the initial intentions of the legislators – to soften rigid retirement ages for health and social reasons were largely realised in practice. As we shall see below this was not true of the flexible transition to retirement (1.2).

In the succeeding years, a number of legal changes had the effect of facilitating and supporting early retirement, not least with the aim of easing pressure on the labour market: the retirement age for the severely handicapped was reduced to 61 and then 60 years (1979/80), eligibility for the "unemployment pension" was eased (1982), and the law on early retirement enacted (1984).

The reform law of 1992 also builds on the tradition established by its two predecessors while bringing about a change of strategic direction in a number of respects. As far as retirement-age policy is concerned the legislative proposals have stirred up considerable controversy. The agreement reached at the end of 1989 comprises, besides other changes, the successive increase in retirement ages for all types of retirement – with the exception of that for the severely handicapped (60) – to 65, starting in 2001. A flexible form of early retirement – at 62 – is to be maintained, but at the cost of actuarial deductions amounting to 3.6% of the pension level per year. The trade unions and sections of the Social Democratic Party, in particular, have expressed their criticism of the plans to prolong working lives in this way. The policy has been defended with both financial and demographic arguments, and union and SPD pressure only managed to postpone implementation of the increase in retirement-age limits and to oblige the federal government to report on the current state of the labour market before they are actually raised.

All three major pension reforms followed approximately the same pattern of interaction between the political parties and the leading social actors: the "social partners", the representatives of employers and workers, were all involved in one way or another at all stages, preparing the ground for the reforms, making objections and counter-proposals, providing experts for discussion purposes right up to the fine print of legislative proposals. In this arena the German Employers' Federation (BDA) and the congress of the German trade unions (DGB) act as independend associations as well as in the function of partners in the different organisations responsible for running the various branches of the social insurance system. These are self-governing (non-state) bodies administered jointly by the unions and the employers.

Despite often fundamental differences and long, often highly conflictual negotiations in the run up to the three Acts, in the end the main actors have always managed to reach a compromise. A number of factors serve to promote this general willingness to compromise. There exists a general consensus that the German population's confidence in the pension system should not be unduly weakened. Pension security and the relative stability of the level of pension benefits should not be made to depend on changing political majorities and tactical, political or election considerations. A further factor promoting cooperation between the social partners is the joint financing of the pension schemes by employers and workers; they provide nearly 80% of the financial volume required. One effect of the parity between the social partners on the self-governing organs of the pension insurance system is to give the two sides, acting together, considerable influence over pension policy, leading them to seek fundamental agreement on basic aims and strategies vis a vis the public administration (ministerial bureaucracy etc.). The "pension consensus", routinely held up as "exemplary" in public discussions, is also based on the fact that conflictual problems, often of a very fundamental nature and for which a compromise is unlikely to be reached, are excluded from the arena and postponed. The evidence presented so far permits the provisional conclusion that the normative (and financial) prerequisites for the trend to early retirement, the conditions for externalisation strategies on the part of firms are created in the course of a broad process of social consensus-building.

3.2.2 Non-Decisions

The thrust of the West German retirement-age policy, its logics of externalisation and compensation, are clearly shown by the fact that any germs which may have existed of an active age-selective labour-market and labour policy based on the "work principle" have never flowered, or were actively prevented from so doing. International comparison, particularly the Swedish experience, reveals a whole gamut of potential instruments. In the Federal Republic, by contrast, while a number of work promotion measures refer explicitly to older workers, they are not actually conceived in an age-specific way. This is true both of government job-creation measures, the creation of alternative employment possibilities suited to older and less productive workers and subsidised by the employment exchanges, the programmes currently being implemented to deal with long-term unemployment and to further-training measures under the Work Promotion Act. The clearest evidence of the failure of German labour-market policy to integrate older workers is the "non-decision" to promote part-time employment. This is a particularly significant contributory factor to the German pattern of retirement: labour-market withdrawal marking the end of full-time paid employment and the beginning of full-time retirement. This point can be illustrated with regard to the following chronology of non-decisions:

– The legislator had more in mind than merely the reduction of de facto retirement ages when the flexible retirement ages were introduced in 1972. A reduction in working hours and the expansion of part-time working opportunities were supposed to permit workers "gradually" to leave the labour market while remaining entitled to the full pension amount. Thus initially no upper limit was placed on additionally earned income. But barely a year later a relative limit was set, followed, in 1977, by a fixed ceiling of DM 1,000. According to the socialdemocrat/liberal government of the day, this was to allow for the rising levels of unemployment from the mid 1970s on (cf. Hermann, 1988). This policy change led the flexible retirement age provisions to "mutate" into a buffer for labour market policy in the form of a general reduction in retirement ages.

– The non-existence of a part-time labour market effectively deprived the partial-retirement scheme for health reasons (occupational disability) of the preconditions needed for it to function. Two court decisions (1969 and 1976) brought the actual implementation of this form of retirement more closely into line with the concrete labour-market situation. Since then those who would be able to work part-time despite their occupational disability have been entitled to the full disability pension in view of the fact that suitable part-time jobs simply are not available. In practice this has led to a considerable expansion of early retirement for health reasons. When deciding on an application for a disability pension the employment office formally determines whether or not part-time work is available. The individual worker, or the medical staff employed by the pension-insurance institutions have no legal basis on which to

demand work suited to a worker's (reduced) abilities. Although objections have been raised for many years to the externalisation of those
capable of part-time work, the legal position remains unchanged.
- The so-called "Altersteilzeitgesetz" (roughly: old age part-time act) has
been in force since January 1989. Here the intention of the legislator was
to offer the labour market incentives to reemploy the long-term unemployed by reducing working hours for older workers. The law provides
for the working time of workers aged 58 and above to be reduced by half
at 65% of the previous wage level; the employer is entitled to a subsidy
of up to 35% provided he employs an additional formerly unemployed
worker. The law is generally agreed to have been a failure. No collective
agreements have been reached to "flesh out" the legal framework and
one state-level employment exchange studied reported that a mere 20
applications for subsidies under this law had been received from employers.
- A similar failure is already being prophesised for the part-time pension
envisaged under the Pension Reform of 1992, which the government has
introduced under the motto "Flexibilisation and Lengthening of Working
Life". The flexibilisation aspect is to be achieved among other things by
a part-time retirement pension which has been facilitated by the sim-
plifications on calculating pension levels which the Reform aims to bring
about. The legislator has, however, presumably as a consequence of the
failure of the part-time pension law, moved very half-heartedly in the
direction of collective bargaining by merely mandating the employers
and workers concerned to discuss and reach a consensus on this matter.

This overview clearly shows that none of the major social actors has been
willing to promote effective concepts for a flexible or staged transition from
employment into retirement. Neither employers and their federations nor
workers and their representative organisations have as yet considered a
reorientation of firms' personnel policies along these lines to be necessary
or even desirable. This all the more so in view of the fact that, as far as the
aim of easing the burden on the labour market is concerned, only complete
and early withdrawal by older workers from the labour market would
appear to be the suitable strategy. The lack of part-time employment
opportunities, for its part, legitimises the total exclusion from the labour
market of persons who would in fact be able and willing to earn (part of)
their living through part-time paid employment. Successive governments
have made brief references to this matter but have failed to provide the
necessary financial incentives to create part-time jobs and induce workers to
take them. A change of policy here would mean dropping the predominant
orientation of the German legal system to the standard male employment
biography, and would require part-time employment to be privileged

in actuarial terms. Had decisions to this effect been taken, they would have represented an important contribution to providing independent social-security cover for women workers at the same time.

3.2.3 Day-to-Day Policies

This sub-section considers the day-to-day practices and policies within the framework of which the existing range of instruments enabling workers to retire early is transposed into concrete reality and constantly modified. This process occurs in interaction between the firms and the state or, to be more precise, between actors from the corporate sector and those from the polit-coadministrative system. We shall seek to ascertain the extent to which the corporate externalisation logic complements the interests and normative parameters of the state bodies responsible for administering social policy.

The first point to note here is that the administration processes early-retirement applications "without a sound": the arena is so heavily regulated and routinised that administrative staff have very little scope to exercise discretion in individual cases. Applications are decided on the basis of fixed criteria and, if need be, are often passed on to other social-insurance institutions. In each case the administration determines the entitlements which have been earned over the years and fixes the appropriate level of benefit. This is especially true of the forms of retirement which are re-stricted to certain groups of people and are dependent on the duration of contribution payments. It is also largely true of early retirement for health reasons, with the one difference that in these cases the medical experts enjoy considerable discretionary power making it more difficult for employ-ees and employers to steer such retirements according to their own inter-ests.

The financial (as opposed to the health) conditions for entitlement to disability pensions (independent of age) do not represent much of a barrier to entitlement. Until 1984 all that was required was a total of five years' contributions during working life, and since then in three years' employ-ment during the last five years. As shown above (section 3.2.2), two legal decisions have added a labour-market component to the original health-related justification for granting a disability pension, so that a full pension is now ensured for those whose ability to work has been impaired. The process of transition from paid employment through a usually long period of illness (which under certain conditions can represent grounds for dis-missal) through attempts at occupational and medical rehabilitation and reintegration into the labour market and finally into retirement involves a complex network of cooperation between various institutions active in the relevant fields of social policy. It is the authorised medical experts, on the one hand, together with practicing doctors (as representatives of their patients' interests), on the other, who have the greatest say with regard to eligibility to this type of pension. The diagnosis and the evaluation of the still remaining capacity to work are factors which cannot be subjected to bureaucratic control. To the extent that unequivocal and objective criteria are lacking for a large number of illnesses and diagnoses, the doctor's report can be seen as the result of a bargaining process between the doctor and the patient. The evaluation of the degree of disability is still open at this stage, not only for the doctor to take account of the general labour-market situation but also for individual evaluation of reemployment chances by the insured patient, who, of course, is usually the initiator of the application for a disability pension.

As a result the disability pension is best seen as offering a degree of instrumentalisation which, depending on the labour-market situation, goes beyong actual legal provisions, particularly where alternative, socially acceptable exit-options are not available. The insurance institutions themselves are well aware of this fact: they admit that the influence exerted by the overall labour-market position is very high, particularly for blue-collar workers, with respect to actual, concrete medical reasons. Our interview partners pointed out that in a situation of mass unemployment, doctors often felt they had no choice but to opt for a socially legitimate status (disability pension) rather than unemployment.

The so-called "59er provision" (Arbeitslosenruhegeld – unemployment pension), is similarly complicated and subject to conflict. Here the evidence shows that, despite the complex statutory framework and the not inconsiderable requirements for interaction and coordination between the various actors, the smooth cooperation, against the background of the consensus on the strategy of externalisation, has in fact helped to reinforce and perpetuate the trend towards early retirement and has served to make this strategy more generally acceptable.

Unemployment totalling one year during the previous 18 months is the precondition for entitlement to the "unemployment-pension" at age 60 (hence the term "59er provision"). Given that, in the face of persistent mass unemployment, the period for which older workers are entitled to unemployment benefit has been steadily lengthened during the 1980s, the path into early retirement under this provision can now start when workers are just 57. In view of the far-reaching protection from dismissal enjoyed by older workers with long tenure, unemployment usually results from "mutual agreements" – between employer and older worker(s) – to end the employment relation. Compensation is then paid either on an individual or collective basis (social plan). It is in such cases that the pension administration has to conduct numerous checks as compensation payments may affect the level of benefits paid. The statutory regulations contain a number of clauses with the aim of preventing employees from leaving the employment system without good reason and of taking the compensation payments made by the firm into consideration when calculating the level of benefit entitlement.

According to our expert interviews, it is now common practice for the employment offices to advise works councils and managements on how to draw up the social plans in which the compensation payments are set out, so as to conform with the legal requirements in such a way that the affected workers do not suffer any material disadvantage.

In view of the continuing pressure on the labour market, and the fact that all the evidence shows that not only do older workers have no chance of finding a job under present labour-market conditions, they themselves lack the motivation to seek further employment, administrative staff also tend to opt for the consensus on the externalisation strategy. Experts often admit that the payment of unemployment benefit to older workers is a de facto form of early retirement, foreign to the overall system and totally "passive" (in contrast to "active" labour market policies) in that it does not contribute to solve the fundamental problem. They defend the use of such strategies by pointing to the fact that by making full use of the statutory provisions redundancies among younger workers – who, due to their shorter job-tenures, usually enjoy far less social security than their older colleagues – could be avoided. Both administrations and firms argue that the use of social plans (based on compensation payments from the social insurance system) is the only way out of the dilemma, representing a socially accept-able solution for the older workers affected.

The so-called "Rückerstattungsregelung" (reimbursement provision) in-troduced within the framework of the "59er provision" led to an interesting series of highly conflictual interaction processes which brought a note of conflict into the daily routine of many of those involved in early-retirement practices. At the beginning of the 1980s the Federal Ministry of Labour observed that the "59er provision" was not being used by firms merely to cope with periods of economic crisis, but that they were "misusing" it to rejuvenate their workforces, leaving the social insurance system to pick up the bill. It determined to prevent this abuse, to limit access to early retire-ment via the "59er provision" and to make it more expensive for employers.

In 1982 employers were required by law to reimburse the Federal Em-ployment Office and the pension institutions for the increased costs the latter incurred whenever the "59er provision" was implemented: exceptions were allowed in the case of firms under severe economic pressure. Initially both employers and the unions supported this measure in principle, not least because of their responsibility for the financial solidity of the pension insurance system through their activities in the self-governing administra-tion of these institutions. However, it became apparent that in practice, while small and medium-sized companies fulfilled the reimbursement requirements, larger firms put up massive resistance, whereby managements were often supported by the works councils as the reimbursement payments meant that fewer financial resources were available for making compensation payments to redundant workers under the social plans. In some cases of mass redundancies firms managed to gain exemption under the provisions for firms in difficult economic situation by exerting sufficient political pressure, making full use of their close contacts to the local employment offices or the Federal Ministry of Labour. Other large firms simply did not pay, but rather – at the cost of tying up considerable personnel resources – raised legal objections and sought to gain satisfaction through the courts. This went all the way to the Federal Constitutional Court whose verdict (1989) represented a phyrric victory for the social-insurance institutions as the legal stipulations introduced were such as to exceed the administrative capacity of the social-insurance system to process current cases, not to mention the backlog of cases of non-payment. This backlog now runs to around 240,000 cases representing DM billions in demands for payment. To sort out all these cases individually would require massive personnel resources not only in the social-insurance institutions but also within companies. In view of this the Federal Employment Office, the Federal Ministry of Labour, the employers' federation and the trade unions have reached a compromise under which the employers are to provide approximately 45% of the total sum demanded. The employers' federation has actually managed to raise DM 500 million as a lump-sum payment to the social insurance institutions to meet the latter's demands. This involved the participation of 70 large firms and represents "a feat of regulation the like of which has never been seen". In return the reimbursement provision has now (1991) been scrapped.

This example shows how the state has failed in its attempt to limit the extent to which firms can pass on the costs of their externalisation strategies to the social-insurance system. Large firms, in particular, enjoying the backing of their federation, have systematically undermined the legal provisions and, in the final analysis, have won the battle over the distribution of the cost burden of externalisation strategies. A successor provision is now under discussion to restrict abuse of the early-retirement system, but the stance of the employers seems to be steadfastly negative. They argue that the state – through its unemployment and pension laws – has shown older workers the "normal way" out of the employment system – in the form of early retirement. They also claim that it is no longer possible to distinguish between employer and employee interests in early retirement. This is shown by workers' willingness to participate in the 59er provision or social plans providing compensation for workers retiring early. Should it prove possible to reach agreement between the various social actors on a provision to succeed the scrapped reimbursement regulation then – this much is clear – it will be one which is substantially "cheaper" for the employers.

We now return to the foundation set up by the steel firm discussed in section 2.2, this time focusing on the mode of interaction between the most important actors. This will help illustrate the way in which the trend to early retirement is perpetuated and indeed reinforced, even within negotiated, tri-partite solutions initially aimed at inducing social innovations in personnel-adjustment processes.

The establishment of the foundation in which, as described above, the approximately 1,800 workers made redundant were assembled, was the result of a consensus-building process involving many actors. The fundamental interest shared by employees and their representatives at plant-level and above, by management, the economics ministry of the federal state involved and – subsequently, after a change of government – the socialdemocratic state government as a whole, and the local employment office was to avoid the closure of the plant as a whole. Given the regional predominance of the coal and steel industries this would have meant the loss of thousands of jobs in industries up-stream and down-stream from the plant itself. Considerable resistance was put up, however, during negotiations on the creation of so-called "employment and training company" by two organisations, both part of the public administration of the labour market in Germany, the BA (Federal Employment Office) and the LAA (State Employment Office).

The foundation aimed to provide advisory services for the redundant workers, allocate job-vacancies which became available elsewhere in the company and to develop further-training and job-creation programmes. The foundation draws on numerous sources to cover the costs of its programmes, the largest share being provided by the BA, which bears the costs of unemployment benefits for all the members of the foundation (topped up with money from the social plan) and also benefits for those participating in further-training and employment initiatives. The labour-market authorities, both the BA and the LAA, have insisted on a narrow and formalistic interpretation of the relevant legal provisions. It required the intervention of the trade-union representative within the self-governing administration of the labour-market authorities to enable about 80 jobs to be created in an employment and training company, after proposals had initially been flatly rejected. But the delay (the whole process took more than a year) and the way the authorities stuck to the letter of the law (opening the measures to the labour market as a whole) meant that the jobs created did not benefit the former steel workers to whose skills the programmes had originally been tailored.

The disagreements between the large majority of those in favour of the foundation and the labour market authorities at federal and state level had a number of different aspects. These included: the wish on the part of the labour market authorities to develop their measures autonomously; the fact that they were brought into the scheme rather late in the day, despite the fact that it was to be largely financed by benefit payments by them, and the limited room for manoeuvre at local level with respect to discretionary benefits. Whatever the precise reasons, in the final analysis narrow bureaucratic norm-orientation, sequential prolonged "ploughing through" the legal stipulations, and the individualised way in which problems were approached by the administration have been some of the main reasons why the germs of an innovative policy based on social integration, training and employment and aimed at solving labour-market problems not only at firm but also at regional level have not really come to fruition. The difficulties in implementing internalising measures is contrasted by the relative ease with which the foundation can be used as a "waiting-room" for early retirement at a subsequent date. For older workers, the large majority, the foundation has institutionalised a form of early exit from the labour force enabling, under certain conditions, workers effectively to retire at the age of 50. One of the incidental effects of the relatively generous provisions for early retirement contained in social plans in recent years is that younger cohorts of workers have become, as it were, "addicted" to the idea of early retirement.

3.3 Nationally Specific Forms and Conditions of the Interaction between Firms and the State

Against the background of the regulatory logic specific to both firms and the state in the Federal Republic, we now proceed to elaborate – in the form of a series of propositions – the characteristic forms and conditions of the interaction of firms and the state in the Federal Republic.

3.3.1 Stability and Consistency over Time

In recent years two hypotheses have been put forward concerning the intervention strategies employed by the German state in retirement age policy:

- Intervention by the German state with respect to retirement ages is characterised by an opposition between expansion and restriction, in other words by a fundamental "ambivalence" (Jacobs, Kohli and Rein, 1991).
- Retirement-age policies by the German state have gone through the

following orientations; from a social-policy to a labour-market to a growth-policy orientation (Nullmeier and Rüb, 1989).

On the basis of our case studies within the political regime of the Federal Republic and the evidence provided by our firm studies, we come to a different overall interpretation of the stability of West German retirement-age policies, placing a very different accent on state policy.

Retirement-age policy in the Federal Republic of Germany is dominated by the transfer principle, procedural cooperation, externalisation strategies by both firms and the state, all this against the background of the absence of an overall full-employment policy. The same applies to the "policy" of non-decision with regard to potential internalisation strategies. Particularly when compared with the "compactness" of externalisation strategies, it becomes clear how little chance there is for the erratic, unsystematic initiatives and concrete measures for internalising solutions to labour market problems to succeed, particularly in view of the lack of longer-term strategic and political developments and movements in the Federal Republic into which they could be integrated. In its substantive consistency and stability over the years neither corporate nor state age-structure policy can be considered ambivalent or the result of phased development. On the contrary, it is characterised by a purposeful, single-minded approach regarding the social-political aim of providing security in old age; to a surprisingly great extent German retirement-age policy is thus to be seen as the result of a consciously pursued strategy.

3.3.2 Cooperative Tripartite Approach

The findings from all three decision-making arenas point almost without exception to a dominant characteristic feature of German retirement-age policy since the Second World War: cooperation and consensus among the social groups involved, including employees, on questions of early retirement. Despite friction in the practice of granting individual pensions and the conflicts which accompany large-scale, complex social-plan provisions, at all relevant phases of strategic decision-making German retirement-age policy is distinguished by long-term cooperation and consensus between the major social actors involved.

As has been shown in the sections dealing with the various actors, the pattern of interaction in this cooperative consensual system is based on an integrated political system consisting of four levels:

– a compromise between the political parties in the arena of inter-party competition;

- consensus between the "social partners", the employers' federations and trade unions;
- the consensus between the specialist representatives of the social partners within the social-insurance system;
- the small network of political technocrats from all these arenas, together with the Federal Ministry of Labour representing the central nexus of the constellation as a whole.

In other words, the overall constellation of cooperative consensus consists of a network of different regulatory modi: the competitive democracy of the party system in the choice of strategies, state hierarchies in programming and implementation, relatively autonomous networks of legally equal – although, in terms of power, asymmetrically endowed – negotiating partners. This constellation allows a quality of consensus-building which goes beyond Pareto-optimal solutions (in which redistribution is not possible). The structure of the constellation allows for political solutions of a relatively complex nature in which macro-optical solutions are combined into a package which also considers questions of redistribution and compensation payments to potential "losers", which can then be enacted. The limits to the degree of optimisation which this constellation can achieve, on the other hand, are revealed by the structural selectivity of German retirement-age policies: the structurally constrained choices facing workers which are not offset by any form of compensation.

3.3.3 Selectivity and Constrained Choice

In the preceding sections, we have drawn attention to what we see as the most prominent feature of German retirement policies compared with those in other countries: the consistent use at all levels of an externalisation strategy leading to a high early-retirement share at a relatively high level of pension benefits. The other side of the same coin – at firm level – is the lack of internalising alternatives for both workers and managements. They face a constrained choice between variants which exclude non-exits from the labour market and staged withdrawal. The history of strategic "non-decisions" in this area described above clearly reveals the systematic deficiency in German retirement policy and the consequent constraints placed on individual options. In contrast to Sweden there has never at any time in the history of the German social-insurance system been a vision – not to mention operative strategies – of a "work-line". German policy has been dominated by a philosophy of age-selective transfer-benefits, the aim being to achieve the highest possible level of financial compensation outside working life. The Swedish example shows that it is only when the welfare state pursues corresponding long-term strategies, and these are supported by important social groupings that comprehensive internalisation measures can be generated. A glance at Japan, on the other hand, shows that German firms lack endogenous incentive mechanisms to develop internalising strategies. On the contrary, we have shown how it can be in the rational interest of firms to link statutory and corporate instruments in order almost systematically to externalise older workers for personnel adjustment reasons and how this can meet with the acceptance if not the active support of employees and works councils.

3.3.4 Networks and Instrument-Linkages

The interaction between firms and the state is shown most clearly by studying the linkages between the instruments used by both firms and the state to solve – jointly – the problems associated with older workers, and the way in which these instruments interact.

This summary of instrument linkages confirms the conclusions we have drawn and reveals a number of additional aspects of the mode of interaction between firms and the state:

– The externalisation instruments of the state are closely linked to those employed by firms. (The opposite is true for the instruments of internalisation, where fewer instruments have been developed and these have been far less frequently implemented.) Given the relative transparency of these instruments, the network of experts involved with the linkages is restricted to personnel managers, those employed in the benefits department of the employment offices and the pension-insurance institutions.

– From the marginal attempts made to implement internalising strategies in the Federal Republic and, above all, on the basis of evidence from Japan and Sweden, we know that the networks and instrument-linkages involved in internalising strategies are very different. Firstly, internalising strategies are almost always linked to measures of externalisation. This alone renders internalising networks and instrument-linkages more complex. But even looking at internalising instruments by themselves, and ignoring the link with externalising measures, we find that they are intrinsically more complex and sophisticated. Age-selective training and job-creation, restructuring work and diversifying production in order to stabilise workforce levels etc. all require the use of large numbers of highly differentiated instruments. The interactive steering constellation is rendered extremely complex due to the expansion and differentiation of the professional expertise required to run it. The lack of such an organisational and personnel infrastructure – which is only to be expected given the lack of a full-employment policy – is thus an additional factor conditioning the selectivity and the resultant structural limitations of steering capacity in the interaction between German firms and the state.

3.3.5 Power Relations between Firms and the State

The theoretical debate on the interaction between firms and the state circles around two opposing views: the "steering capacity" of the strong interventionist state, on the one hand, the "take-away" effect of dominant firms, sometimes known as the "chameleon effect" of a state instrumentalised by the corporate sector, on the other.

At first sight, our findings can be interpreted as providing evidence for both hypotheses. In the older-worker segment the system of incentives provided by the state has increasingly become a constitutive element vitally affecting corporate personnel policies: in other words, enterprise personnel strategy in this sphere has been increasingly subject to a form of étatisme. At the same time, conflicts such as that over the reimbursement provision and the substantial "take-away" effects involved in enterprise externalisation strategies point to corporate instrumentalisation of the state.

By comparing our findings on the regulatory logic of firms and the state we arrive at a far more complex picture of this interaction – and one which requires different forms of conceptualisation – than views based simply on the hierarchical state, self-regulating markets or autonomous networks and bargaining systems.

– German retirement policy is dominated by a multi-layered network of multi-lateral bargaining systems consisting of a limited number of large actor-systems which assume different roles in different situations.
– Within this multi-layered, multi-lateral bargaining system the state is not the guiding central force but a sort of arbiter in a complex bargaining process.
– At the same time, the multi-lateral bargaining systems which make up West German retirement policy always contain an element of hierarchical statedness: the state transfers huge financial resources with considerable redistributive effects, and it regulates the cooperative framework within which a number of these bargaining processes are conducted. The state, in its articulation as a competitive democracy between political parties, develops and mediates an overall orientation regarding the general policy direction. The primacy of the transfer over the work-line principle and the lack of a full-employment policy are due less to the initiative of firms and their representative organisations or to the trade unions than to the historical precipitation of the competition between

political parties in the Federal Republic, the results of which are enacted within the framework of hierarchical coordination.
– On the other hand, clear asymmetries do exist in the bilateral bargaining systems between employers (and their federations) and workers (and their unions/works councils). At first sight the results of our study seem to fit the pluralism or business-politics (Windsor, 1989) approach, according to which an optimal and stable equilibrium of interests results from the interaction of different interests which, in principle, bear equal rights and are of equal weight. However, our findings concerning the non-decisions and the selectivity of instruments in the political sphere and on the externalisation-dominated regime within firms show how distorted this "equalisation" of interests is in practice. Although the de facto exclusion of the strategic alternative of internalisation does not prevent a stable compromise being reached, it very forcefully confirms the structurally "privileged position" (Windsor, 1989) of the corporate sector in the retirement-policy arena in its interaction with the state.

To sum up: retirement policy in the Federal Republic of Germany is constituted on the basis of the common ground between all the participating actor-systems in a multi-lateral bargaining system, the nationally-specific selectivity of its instruments against the background of the privileged position of firms and in the context of the "guiding" function of the state as a sort of first among equals.

4   The Future of Older Workers' Employment

Our evaluation of future employment and retirement trends for older workers is based on a synthesis of our evaluation of past developments together with our expectations of future developments, more specifically, our interpretation of the relative stability of the externalisation strategy over time, supported by a consensus of all the major interested parties, on the one hand, together with legal reform strategies enacted against the background of socio-demographic and economic developments.

The Pension Reform Law which came into force in 1992 was passed by parliament in 1989, almost just when the process of German unification was getting under way. At that time the legal changes providing for an increase in retirement age limits aimed to adjust the pension insurance system to changing demographic constellations, to the rising average age of the population, in order to maintain the financial basis of the pension system in the long term without resorting to substantial increases in the contribution rates. The explicit orientation towards the future requirements of the labour market – the expected fall in the supply of labour from the youngest cohorts, forecasts of a shortage of skilled labour – was thus based on completely other expectations of different conditions than now exist following German unification: mass unemployment, particularly in the new federal states of the former GDR, a flood of workers migrating to West Germany and uncertain prognoses with regard to future (un)employment trends.

The trend begun in 1957 towards a reduction in retirement-age limits is now to be broken in a consensus decision accepted by the vast majority of parties and social groups with the Pension Reform 1992. The policy aims which provided the basis for previous attempts at reform – shortening the span of working life, 'humanising' work, easing the pressure on the labour market by facilitating exits by older workers, self-determination in the transition to retirement, or compensation for the double burden of work and family borne by women have rapidly become all but obsolete, a trend which has gone largely unnoticed.

The most significant elements of the new retirement-age policy which goes under the official label of the "flexibilisation and lengthening of working time" are:
– the successive raising of all the retirement ages currently in force with the exception of the flexible pension for the severely handicapped at age 60), beginning in 2001, to age 65, with the aim of establishing a single retirement age by the year 2017;
– the option of taking early retirement from age 62 at the cost of actuarial deductions from the benefit level (3.6% per year);
– the introduction of the "part-time pension" from age 62.

Although there can be no doubt that the Pension Reform 1992 initially means that the earliest possible retirement age for certain groups (in particular women and the unemployed) will be gradually raised, it remains to be seen whether the German state's intervention strategy of increasing the length of average working lives will in fact be implemented to any considerable extent. This is because the Reform is – with respect to the arsenal of potential steering instruments – at present an isolated measure lacking support in the social insurance systems a whole. The strategy also presupposes considerable adjustment and reorientation on the part of firms and workers. From the interaction of legislative impulses and adjustment reactions by social actors we expect limited volume effects in terms of an actual increase in average retirement ages. But these will be broken by substantial substitution effects, in particular in the form of increased recourse to disability pension as this is independent of age and takes account of the labour-market situation and some cost-shifting effects to the disadvantage of those employees who will still be able to afford to take early retirement. As regards structural characteristics we see no reason to believe that the fundamental characteristic of the German regime of early retirement – the complete transition from paid employment to pensioned retirement – will lose its predominant position.

Given the state of the labour market in the new federal states it must be open to doubt whether retirement ages can in fact be raised in accordance with the present timetable. It is there that the early-retirement provisions imported from West Germany and subsequently extended will be desparately needed in order to ease the pressure on the labour market in a socially acceptable way. It could, on the other hand, be the case that the massive redundancies in the new federal states will have feedback effects on West Germany which will have the effect of reinforcing existing trends. The discussion on the renewed extension of the short-time-working provision, which often marked the point of entry into labour-market withdrawal for older workers, to other crisis-hit industries can be seen as evidence for such a trend.

The unification process and the wave of East-West migration means that the labour-market shortages which had been forecast and which represented one of the assumptions on which the feasibility of raising retirement ages was based no longer constitute an argument for firms to dispense with their policy of externalising older workers. With the possible exception of certain highly specialised skill groups any labour shortages which might occur can be compensated relatively easily through geographical mobility.

Even if retirement ages are in fact raised as planned, the uncertainty and potential for conflict to which this will give rise are likely to be rather limited. This is because considerable scope will remain to utilise alternative instruments of labour-market exit, in particular disability pensions which are not (yet) affected by the Reform. Even the monetary disincentives in the form of actuarial deductions will become the subject of intensinse bargaining between employers and workers and are likely to be substantially modified using the multitude of options for cost sharing and cost shifting which exist.

The main reason for the evaluation advanced above is, however, that the Pension Reform 1992 lacks any complementary measures, neither in labour-market and working-structure policy nor in training or support for the provision of part-time employment with the aim of providing attractive employment relations both for firms and for older workers along the lines forseen by the Reform Law. As a result, few older workers will be encouraged to take account of the "part-time retirement pension" envisaged by the Act. Only one instrument remains: the financial "lever" of actuarial deductions from pension-benefit levels for those retiring early, which could force certain social groups with low pension entitlements to continue working until (or beyond) the standard retirement age.

The evidence seems to show that, despite limited quantitative effects, the basic conditions for the stability of the German early-retirement regime are not about to be swept away, nor is a long-term change of strategy from externalisation to internalisation-dominated approaches (not to mention their instrumentalisation) in sight. For the foreseeable future the concerted transition from paid employment into pensioned retirement is likely to remain the dominant age-selective regime in the Federal Republic of Germany.

Notes

1   The various pathways into retirement, often involving other state transfer benefits such as sick pay, social security, compensation for industrial accidents, unemployment benefit etc., and the various modi by which state benefits are topped up under collectively negotiated provisions at branch or plant level, are described in greater detail in Kohli, Jacobs, Rein, 1991 and Heinelt, 1991.
2   Average net pension levels - after 40 years' contributions - have climbed from 54.4% in 1970 to 64.3% of net wages in 1989. This does not include company pension schemes which are widespread, particularly in large firms. Cf. Verband der Rentenversicherungsträger (Association of Pension Insurers): *Rentenversicherung in Zahlen und Zeitreihen.* Frankfurt/M., 1990.
3   Age-specific participation rates are often used as an indicator for labour-market withdrawal by older workers. Such aggregate data do not, of course, permit us to consider individual transitions from work to retirement, but, given that transitions in the opposite direction are all but unknown, age-specific participation rates enable us to determine the proportion of an age group remaining in employment. In methodological terms it would be more correct to use age-specific cohort data, but such statistics are not available in sufficient quality to enable international comparisons to be made. Age-specific aggregate data are dealt with in detail in Jacobs and Kohli (1990).
4   The data on retirement presented in the following section are taken largely from the Verband der Rentenversicherungsträger (VDR - Association of Pension Insurers) and official data from the Federal Employment Office (Bundesanstalt für Arbeit) and our own calculations. Early-retirement shares are defined as all forms of retirement before the age of 65 as a proportion of all retirements. This includes (from 1984 to 1988) the legal provisions on early retirement but not the pensions paid to partially disabled workers, as they do not involve complete withdrawal from paid employment. The age-structure data by economic sector are based on surveys conducted by the Federal Employment Office. They only include those workers on the social insurance beneficiary list paying social insurance contributions.
5   The law on part-time work for older employees (Altersteilzeitgesetz) which

came into force in 1989 and which provides for older employees to work half-time while receiving about 70% of their last net income, is extremely rarely implemented in practice (according to our expert interviews).

6   In the case of flexible pensions at 63 (flexibles Altersruhegeld) this amounts to only DM 1,000 per month; in the case of the other forms of early retirement, DM 425 per month, the level below which (marginal) workers are not considered - for tax purposes etc. - as being in paid employment in the Federal Republic.

7   From a cross-sectional perspective, however, the participation rates of this group has increased slightly over time, a statistical complication which is due to the fact that the overall increase in the participation rates of women workers has more than compensated for the trend towards earlier retirement (cf. Jacobs et. al., 1987).

8   Of these the most important was the "Haushaltsbegleitgesetz" of 1984 which substantially restricted entitlements to full and partial disability pensions. In particular this involved cutbacks in the so-called non-insured (versicherungs-fremde) benefits, i.e., benefits previously paid out to those who were not in paid employment in the years running up to retirement, most of them women. At the same time the requirements for entitlement to "Altersruhegeld" (old-age pension) were reduced from an insurance period of 180 to one of 60 months. The net result of these legal changes was a significant shift in the retirement shares of disabled and normal retirements in favour of the latter of some 35%.

9   It is estimated that 70-80% of those entitled took advantage of the early retirement provisions against the background of the steadily worsening situation on the labour market (Kühlewind, 1986).

10   This applies not only to the five case studies presented above but to the entire sample of firms studied. Within this overall pattern of age-structures there do exist significant gender-specific differences in age-structure characteristics. The electrical engineering enterprise D, for instance, employs a considerably lower proportion of older workers than the other firms on account of the large proportion of women workers employed by the firm and their high rates of labour turnover (cf. the case study description above).

11   The typology can also be used to provide further fuel for the controversy surrounding the hypothesis that weakly interventionist states need not necessarily be weak themselves. This can be demonstrated using the example of the USA. The "weak" intervention of freeing market forces with regard to retirement age has had substantial effects on changes in such age limits, exit rates and forms (*see* Hutchens in this volume).

References

Dohse, Knuth; Jürgens, Ulrich and Harald Russig (eds.) (1982). *Ältere Arbeitnehmer zwischen Unternehmensinteressen und Sozialpolitik*. Frankfurt a.M.: Campus.

Esping-Andersen, Gösta (1989). *Labor Costs and Employment in the Service Economy*. In: Gianna Gianelli and Gösta Esping-Andersen, *Labor Costs and Employment in the Service Economy*. San Domenico: European University Institute (EUI working paper; 412).

Esping-Andersen, Gösta (1990): *The Three Worlds of Welfare Capitalism*. Cambridge: Polity Press.

Gather, C. and M. Schürkmann (1987). *Frauen im Übergang in den Ruhestand – ein problemloser Rückschritt in die Hausfrauenrolle?* In: G. Backes and W. Clemens (eds.), *Ausrangiert? Lebens und Arbeitsperspektiven bei beruflicher Frühausgliederung*. Bielefeld: AJZ Druck und Verlag GmbH: 124–149.

Göckenjahn, Gerd (ed.) (1988). *Alter und Alltag*. Frankfurt a.M.: Suhrkamp.

Herrmann, Christopher (1988). *Die Rentenreform 1972 – Bilanz und Perspektiven nach 15 Jahren*. In: *Deutsche Rentenversicherung* (1–2): 1–21.

Hutchens, Robert (1993). *The United States: Employer Policies for Discouraging Work by Older People*. In: Frieder Naschold and Bert de Vroom (eds.), *Regulating Employment and Welfare. Company and National Policies of Labour Force Participation at the End of Worklife in Industrial Countries*. Berlin: de Gruyter.

Ikenberry, G. John (1986). *The Irony of State Strength: Comparative Responses to the Oil Shocks in the 1970s*. In: *International Organization* 40 (1): 105–138.

Ikenberry, G. John (1988). *Reasons of State. Oil Politics and the Capacities of American Government*. Ithaca: Cornell University Press.

Jacobs, Klaus; Kohli, Martin and Martin Rein (1987). *Testing the Industry-Mix Hypothesis*. Discussion paper, Wissenschaftszentrum Berlin für Sozialforschung.

Jacobs, Klaus and Martin Kohli (1990). *Der Trend zum frühen Ruhestand – Die Entwicklung der Erwerbsbeteiligung im internationalen Vergleich*. In: *WSI-Mitteilungen* 43 (8): 498–509.

Jacobs, Klaus; Kohli, Martin and Martin Rein (1991). *Germany: The Diversity of Pathways*. In: Martin Kohli et. al. (eds.), *Time for Retirement: Comparative Studies of Early Exit from the Labor Force*. Cambridge, N.Y.: Cambridge University Press: 181–221.

Jürgens, Ulrich and Frieder Naschold (1992). *Arbeitsregulierung in der Bundesrepublik Deutschland im Spannungsfeld zwischen nationalen Gestaltungsstrategien und internationaler Produktivitätskonkurrenz*. In: Georg Simonis (ed.), *Politische Techniksteuerung – Forschungsfrage und Forschungsperspektiven*. Berlin (in preparation).

Kochan, Thomas A. and Robert B. McKersie (1990). *Human Resources, Organizational Governance and Public Policy: Lessons from a Decade of Experimentation*. Boston (Massachusetts): MIT (mimeo).

Kohl, Jürgen (1987). *Alterssicherung im internationalen Vergleich. Zur Einkommensstruktur und Versorgungssituation älterer Haushalte.* In: *Zeitschrift für Sozialreform* 33 (11/12): 698–718.

Kohli, Martin (1985). *Die Institutionalisierung des Lebenslaufs.* In: *Kölner Zeitschrift für Soziologie und Sozialpsychologie* 37 (1): 1–29.

Kohli, Martin et. al. (eds.) (1991). *Time for Retirement: Comparative Studies of Early Exit from the Labor Force.* Cambridge, N.Y.: Cambridge University Press.

Kühlewind, G. (1986). *Beschäftigung und Ausgliederung älterer Arbeitnehmer. Empirische Befunde zu Erwerbsbeteiligung, Rentenübergang, Vorruhestansregelung und Arbeitslosigkeit.* In: *Mitteilungen aus der Arbeitsmarkt- und Berufsforschung* 2: 209–232.

Lazear, Edward P. (1979). *Why is There Mandatory Retirement?* In: *Journal of Political Economy* 87 (6): 1261–1984.

Müller, J. Heinz (1988). *Die Rentenreform 1957 und heute – zugleich ein Beirag zur Notwendigkeit langfristiger Entscheidungen in der Sozialpolitik.* In: *Sozialer Fortschritt* 37 (7): 147–157.

Naegele, Gerhard (1984). *Frauen zwischen Arbeit und Rente – Anmerkungen zur Arbeitsmarkt- und Verrentungssituation von Frauen im mittleren und höheren Lebensalter.* In: *Info Frauenforschung (1/2/1984),* Institut Frau und Gesellschaft (ifg): 23–29.

Naegele, Gerhard (1987). *Frühverrentung in der Bundesrepublik Deutschland – Eine sozialpolitische Analyse.* In: Gertrud und Clemenz Backes (eds.), *Ausrangiert? Lebens- und Arbeitsperspektiven bei beruflicher Frühausgliederung.* Bielefeld: AJZ Druck und Verlag: 18–50.

Naegele, Gerhard (1988). *Zur Zukunft älterer Arbeitnehmer – Die Entscheidung für oder gegen die Alterserwerbsarbeit fällt in den Betrieben und ist dort zu beeinflussen.* In: *Soziale Sicherheit* 37 (6): 169–178.

Naschold, Frieder; Rosenow, Joachim und Gert Wagner (1990). *Zum Zusammenhang betrieblicher Personalpolitik und staatlicher Sozialpolitik.* In: Udo Bermbach et. al. (eds.), *Spaltungen der Gesellschaft und die Zukunft der Sozialpolitik.* Opladen: Leske und Budrich: 38–63.

Nullmeier, F. and F. Rüb (1989). *Das Rentenreformgesetz 1992. Eine erste sozialpolitische Analyse des interfraktionellen Gesetzentwurfs.* In: *Diskussionspapiere und Materialien aus dem Forschungsschwerpunkt 32.* Hannover: Institut für politische Wissenschaft.

Pfeffer, J. (1985). *Organizational Demography: Implications for Management.* In: *California Management Review* 28 (1): 67–81.

Porter, Michael E. (1990). *The Competitive Advantage of Nations.* New York: Free Press.

Prognos AG (1989). *Arbeitslandschaft bis 2010 nach Umfang und Tätigkeitsprofilen.* In: *Beiträge zur Arbeitsmarkt- und Berufsforschung* 131.1.

Rosenow, Joachim und Frieder Naschold (1992). *Humanressourcennutzung und Altersstrukturpolitik in bundesdeutschen Unternehmen – Zur sozialen Regulierungslogik der Frühverrentungspraxis.* Berlin: Sigma (in preparation).

Rüb, Friedbert W. (1989). *Die gesetzliche Rentenversicherung als Komplementärinstitution des Arbeitsmarktes. Eine historische und theoretische Annäherung.* Diskussionspapier Nr. 33 (Schwerpunkt Sozialpolitik). Universität Hannover.

Samuels, Richard (1987). *The Business of the Japanese State.* Ithaca: Cornell University Press.

Schettkat, Ronald (1989). *Innovation und Arbeitsmarktdynamik.* Berlin: de Gruyter.

Semlinger, Klaus (1989). *Vorausschauende Personalwirtschaft – Betriebliche Verbreitung und infrastrukturelle Ausstattung.* In: *Mitteilungen aus der Arbeitsmarkt- und Berufsforschung* 3: 336–347.

Sorge, Arndt and Wolfgang Streek (1987). *Industrial relations and technical change.* Discussion paper, Wissenschaftszentrum Berlin für Sozialforschung.

Stubig, Hans-Jürgen and Gert Wagner (1991). *Trend zum vorzeitigen Ruhestand.* In: *Bundesblatt* (11): 12–16.

Weber, W. (1989). *Der Einfluß demographischer Veränderungen auf die Arbeitsorganisation und Beschäftigungsstrategien.* Paderborn, Hannover (mimeo).

Windsor, D. (1989). *The Theory of Business Politics.* Paper prepared for the APSA Annual Meeting, Atlanta.

Womack, James P.; Jones, Daniel T. and Daniel Roos (1990). *The Machine That Changes the World.* New York: Rawson.

5 Sweden: Policy Dilemmas of the Changing Age Structure in a 'Work Society'

Gunnar Olofsson and Jan Petersson

0   Introduction: A Strong Policy Regime at Work

The Swedish Policy Regime of the postwar period took shape with a Social
Democratic government in power and a *pro-labour climate* on the labour
market. The labor market policy of the state was general in its range and
was administered by a strongly centralized Labor Market Board (AMS).
Centralized bargaining procedures in the labor market also strengthened
the tendency to national and standardized solutions in labor market polices.

The high labor force participation rates, and the commitment to full
employment, have made *labor scarcity* a basis of action for all parties within
the Swedish labor market, and not just an exception during economic
booms. Subsequently, the power of unions was strengthened and employers
as well as their organizations have had to operate within this framework.

In Sweden, firms act within the environment of a strong Policy Regime,
where state labor market and social policies decisively shape the personnel
policy of these firms. This Policy Regime is best understood through the
concept of a "Work Society", which promotes employment, on the one
hand, and avoids unemployment, on the other.

Firms and the employers' organizations sought to influence the way the
labor market policies were implemented and administered by participating
in corporatist labor market boards on local, county and national levels. On
personnel matters firms demonstrated a sort of "enforced decency", as a
way of adapting to the labor scarcity and the Social Democratic version of
a "Work Society", and for a long period there were few open protests from
employers. Of course, policies could be ignored, but they were not challenged. Acceptance and adaptation were reinforced by high economic
growth rates (at least up to the 1970s) and a favorable treatment, e.g., in tax
rules, of large firms.

The scenario changed in the early 1990s. The effects on the labor market,
with its rising unemployment and ending to labor scarcity, combined with a
new Liberal/Conservative government in 1991, will likely transform the
Swedish Policy Regime.

Evidently this process is contradictory, as the full employment philosophy
is still widely shared in all Swedish political circles and the labor market
policy is still favored by the new government. However, one might expect
that changes in the Policy Regime will occur by a process of "*penetration
from below*", that is to say, the effects of changing priorities and decisions
taken within firms. The new political majority can, given its pro-industry

orientation, be expected to support these pressures from firms and employers. The position of individual firms is further strengthened by the new policy of Swedish Employers' Confederation (SAF), which favors a decentralized bargaining model, thus giving more influence to actors at the level of the firm.

We expect therefore that many firms will try to break away from the enforced consensus that shaped the postwar period. It can be argued that this will have a serious impact on employment security and the protection of weaker groups, such as older workers, which can be the consequence of an increased capacity by firms to shape their personnel policy in line with management claims.

1   The Older Workforce in a 'Work Society'

International comparative early exit studies, have demonstrated two tendencies. On the one hand, there is a *gradual increase in exit* from the labor market among older males in all countries. On the other hand, the employment rates in the age group 55–64, show *large variations among countries.* The first tendency can be explained by the common features in qualifications and work capacities demanded of individuals in the production systems and the responses from the employees. Everywhere, there is an exit flow, produced by the increasing demands on the employees, but variations are not explained by different industry mixes among countries (cf. Jacobs, Kohli and Rein, 1991). They can only be understood in the light of the different socio-political regimes.

There are basically three dimensions by which countries differ as to their socio-political setting.

(a) Countries have different sets of priorities in economic policy (cf. Scharpf, 1987). Two significant goals are the *employment level and the unemployment ratio.* Countries differ on the value they put on unemployment and on labor market participation of the older workforce. In both these respects Sweden is a deviant case, within Europe, with a high labor force participation rate which has, at least until 1992, been coupled with a low unemployment rate.

(b) Countries also differ in their ambitions and *scope of policies* used to keep the older workforce employed, or attached to the labor market. These policies include:
– legal protection of older workers (ranging from anti-discrimination laws to employment protection for older workers);
– preventive measures trying to counteract major marginalizing processes and conditions, such as ill-health (due to the work environment), lack of training etc.;

- subsidizing regular employment for older workers;
- the construction of a secondary labor market, adapted to specific groups (cf. Japanese system, with age-specific parallel firms within the large corporations, which is a "private" solution; while the Swedish version of sheltered jobs is a "public" solution).

Generally, a high ambition on (a) is followed by a high ambition on (b). But there exists a third, separate issue:

(c) Countries can be more or less generous in the way employees are *compensated* when out of work and are supported between their exit from the labor market and their entry into the public pension system. Recently, social research has developed the pathway approach (cf. Wadensjö, 1991, on Sweden) to account for the ways in which this transition can be institutionalized. When the state compensates redundant employees, or sponsors the growth of supportive arrangements such as a broadening of disability pension which creates different pathways between work and pension, it thereby accommodates also the personnel decisions of firms.

Moreover, different priorities on the three dimensions generally lead to different outcomes:
- If employment is high and unemployment low, we should expect little age-specific exit pressure and practice (the reverse for high unemployment).
- If compensation is generous for older employees, we should expect that the age-specific exit pressures in firms are higher than if it is marginal or restricted.
- If policies to prevent exit of the older workforce are ambitious and systematic, we should expect smaller age-specific differentials in exit.

1.1   Some Traits of a 'Work Society'

The key to understanding the employment/unemployment patterns and the welfare system as a whole in Sweden, is the *primacy of work*. Since the 1930s, Sweden has had *a national commitment* to high, *all-encompassing employment* (cf. Therborn, 1985). As a result the Swedish labor market policy is geared towards this goal and economic, social and regional policies are linked and even subordinated to this commitment.

A varied spectrum of measures are used and coordinated in this haste for full employment. Important components of the "employment nexus" are policy measures:
- encouraging high labor-force participation rates;
- keeping unemployment low;

- making it easier for the disabled to have a job;
- enabling individuals to remain in their job until normal retirement age;
- encouraging women to enter the labor market.

The fundamental tenet in the Swedish labor market's "belief system" was the dilemma between economic efficiency (in firms) and the need for security (of employees) which could be resolved by a "labor market contract" between Capital and Labor. Full employment was the basic gain for the wage earning population, guaranteeing its income flow. Adaptation to the needs of firms, in terms of geographical and occupational mobility became the complementary price and income was further guaranteed in the intervals between jobs. This solution of combining economic efficiency and income security was thus not tied to a specific firm or job. It was precisely the result of a trade-off – a *generalized efficiency/mobility mix*.

1.2   A Short Background

Participation in working life has long been institutionalized as a central part of Swedish society. The history of Swedish unemployment policy has been analyzed with the concept of the "work-for-all strategy" as its central axis, that was pitted against the traditional emphasis on compensation in the form of unemployment insurance. This philosophy was established gradually in Swedish labor market policy during the first third of the 20th century. A specific feature was added in the inter-war period, when the participation in working life was institutionalized as a moral value for women, and implicitly for the population as a whole (cf. the classic manifesto *Kris i befolkningsfrågan*, by Gunnar and Alva Myrdal, 1934). A strong emphasis on womens' participation is found in major policy statements, especially in relation to family policy reforms (cf. subsidized public child care), during the 1960s and 1970s.
   Labor-force participation has since then, that is during the whole period of Social Democratic hegemony in Swedish politics, been systematically rewarded by state policies. Employment is stimulated through linking the social security systems to labor market outcomes. Benefits from sickness insurance, parental insurance, and the supplementary pension scheme are all directly related to labor market incomes. The income-related supplementary pension scheme (ATP) encourages labor-force participation by the older workforce. However, Sweden has a dual welfare system, where the secondary system has flat-rate benefits related to just being a citizen (cf. Marklund and Svallfors, 1987). The new and growing social security systems constructed or reformed in the 1950s to 1970s are, nevertheless, strong illustrations of an "industrial-achievement model of social welfare" (cf.

Titmuss, 1974), which played an important role in shaping the Swedish "Work Society".

The creation of a "Work Society" is symbolized and made effective by powerful labor market authorities. The Labor Market Board (AMS), launched in 1940, got its modern shape in 1948. The national board shapes policy, while Local Employment Offices act as the major executing agencies.

1.3   The Swedish 'Work Society' in an OECD Context

The work-for-all strategy is decisive in understanding the pattern of early exits in Sweden, and more generally, the situation of the older workforce. In an international perspective, Sweden has a very low unemployment rate and it has, over a long period, been consistently low, much lower than the OECD average (Therborn, 1985; OECD, 1991). In 1990 the open unemployment rate was 1.5%, while Germany had 5.1%, and Great Britain 6.9% (OECD, 1991). A long record of low unemployment and promotion of labor-force participation, which has been the Swedish case, makes labor a scarce resource. This then strengthens the position of marginal groups, such as women and older individuals, in the labor market.

As a consequence, the high *labor-force participation rate*, in Sweden, is remarkable for groups that generally do not have a strong position in the labor market. The particular *gender and age mixture* has become the distinguishing Swedish trait. In relation to the US, Great Britain and West Germany, for instance, Sweden is the only country in which labor-force

Table 1: Labour Force Participation Rates for Men and Women 55−64 Years of Age in Selected Countries 1970−1985

Country	Gender	1970	1975	1980	1985	Change 1970−1985
Sweden	Male	85.4	82.0	78.7	76.0	− 9.4
	Female	44.5	49.1	55.3	59.9	+15.4
Germany	Male	82.2	68.1	65.5	57.5	−24.7
	Female	29.9	24.8	27.2	23.9	− 6.0
UK	Male	91.3	87.8	81.8	66.4	−24.9
	Female	39.3	40.3	39.2	34.1	− 5.2
USA	Male	80.7	74.6	72.2	67.3	−13.4
	Female	42.2	40.7	41.0	41.7	− 0.5

Source: OECD 1988, Table c.3.

Table 2: Percentage of Older Women in the Labor Force by Age Group 1970–1985 in
Six Countries

Country			1970	1985	Change
Germany	Women	55–59	37.2	40.2	+ 3.0
		60–64	22.5	11.8	−10.7
Japan	Women	55–59	48.7	51.0	+ 2.3
		60–64	39.1	38.5	− 0.6
Holland	Women	55–59	18.4	20.7	+ 2.3
		60–64	12.7	8.9	− 3.8
Sweden	Women	55–59	41.1	74.4	+33.3
		60–64	24.7	46.4	+21.7
UK	Women	55–59	50.7	51.9	+ 1.2
		60–64	28.0	22.4	− 5.6
USA	Women	55–59	48.8	50.1	+ 1.3
		60–64	34.8	33.2	− 1.6

Source: Gordon, 1988: 103.

participation rates of older women have increased since 1970 (table 1). In addition, the decline in the employment rates for older men has been small in Sweden.

When we look closer into the figures on older women we find that Sweden is extreme in both the age groups 55–59 and 60–64.

1.4   The Emergence of a Part-Time Work Pattern

A Swedish feature is, no doubt, the existence of a part-time pension scheme established in 1976. Without a part-time "tradition" in the labor market, part-time pensioning is an unlikely reform. The scheme is presented in section 2.3.4 below, but one of its preconditions, the existence of part-time jobs, will be elaborated upon here.

In the mid 1960s around half a million individuals were employed part-time in Sweden, that is 6–7% of the population. Since that time, it has grown to the point that by the early 1980s the figures had more than doubled. This expansion correlated with women's growing share of the labor force. 75% of the growth in female employment was part-time. This growth is most marked within local government. Furthermore, part-time work has gained importance within the 60–64 age group, increasing its part-time work share, from 25% to 45%, over the above mentioned period.

Labor-force participation of women starts to increase with the expansion of the public sector, especially in health and caring tasks, which demanded more labor. Expansion of the public child care, but also of old age care, made it possible for more women to work outside the home. Women still cared for children and the old, not in the form of unpaid work within the family, but as paid work in the public sector. When the public welfare provision expanded, in an environment of labor scarcity, women were in a strong position to influence work-scheduling. Increasingly, women needed these services as they entered the labor market and the process became self-reinforcing.

This coincided with two further circumstances. First, women entered the labor market, this being a way to increase real household income in that period, due to the rising marginal income tax rates (cf. Tegle, 1985). Second, the tax reforms of 1970, when taxation of the incomes of husband and wife were separated, and the "married man's allowance" (the family-privilege of taxation) was abolished, made it even more rewarding for women to work.

To this development social security laws adapted, as well as further strengthened the development, creating incentives for more women to enter the labor market. The following reforms came about during the 1970s:
– Subsidized public child-care expanded.
– Paid parental leave increased, by several stages, during the 1970s; this made it easier for women with young children to keep their affiliation to the labor market.
– In 1975 a right for full or partial temporary leave, for education, was established.
– More flexible rules for parental leave came about in 1978 and 1979.

An econometric study on part-time work sums up what happened: "Demand for labor seems to have been adapted to changes in the composition of labor supply, i.e., a larger part of the labour force prefers part-time... The part-time proportion was greater in growing sectors" (Pettersson 1981: 7).

The "labor supply explanation" is strengthened by the fact, that firms in Sweden have no financial or wage-cost reasons to prefer part-time work. Wage cost taxes (mainly contributions to pensions and sickness insurance), are levied on the total wage, i.e., the hourly cost is the same for full- and part-time workers. In a similar way, all costs for occupational welfare (severance pay schemes, occupational pensions etc.) are levied on the total wage, although some benefits are denied to persons working less than 17 hours.

The pressure on firms to offer part-time employment has been reinforced by specific part-time oriented changes in social security regulations, especially the legislated rights for parents (in practice, mainly mothers) to work part-time if they have children aged below 12 years.

Significant parts of the private service sector also have part-time work,

Table 3: Part-Time Work among Female Salaried Employees in the Private Sector 1980 –
1990 (%)

Sector	1980	1985	1990
Manufacturing	43	43	34
Building	49	48	38
Retail Trade	41	38	31
Financial Services (Banking, Insurance etc)	–	–	44

Source: Statistiska meddelanden AM 62 SM 9101, p. 2.

because of time variations in the demand for their products or services and the nature of work (including shift-work). The most clear-cut case is retailing and we could add restaurants and hotels. In retail and distribution around 70% of the female workers worked part-time in 1990. Since women dominate these branches the share of part-time female work is about 50% (SCB, 1991).

However, in the private sector as a whole (retail included) the recent trend has been a decrease of part-time work. Now women work less part-time than in 1980 (table 3).

After 1983, full-time work increased and lowered marginal taxation rates in those years may be an explanation since it made it more advantageous to work full-time. In 1981, the replacement rate in the part-time pension scheme was temporarily lowered from 65% to 50% (cf. section 2.3.4 below) and the part-time pension became less attractive and less used.

Part-time work is not just the prerequisite for (and effect of) the high participation rates of women in the Swedish economy. Part-time work continues in older age groups. While it followed the general proportional decrease after 1980 (mentioned above) in the age span 55–59, it did not, however, in the case of the age group 60–64 (table 4).

Table 4: Female Full-Time and Part-Time Employees in the Age Groups 55 – 59 and
60 – 64 (100's)

Year	Women (55 – 59)		Women (60 – 64)	
	Full-Time	Part-Time	Full-Time	Part-Time
1987	838	884	422	721
1988	882	831	400	732
1989	872	798	422	695
1990	902	761	449	713

Source: AKU ("Arbetskrafts undersökningarna", Labour Force Survey), Unpublished Statistics.

Table 5: Full-Time and part-Time Work for Individuals Between 60−64 in 1990 (100's)

Age	Men		Women	
	Full-Time	Part-Time	Full-Time	Part-Time
60	232	69	133	161
61	206	85	110	162
62	179	87	77	156
63	145	82	70	128
64	126	71	59	106

Source: AKU ("Arbetskraft undersökningarna", Labour Force Survey), Unpublished Statistics.

If we look closer at the figures for 1990 and follow the proportions of full and part-time work for each year between 60 and 64 (table 5), we find that the importance of part-time increases with age, including males.

Our conclusion is that the "institutionalization" of part-time work in Swedish society has paved the way for the combination of part-time-pensions with part-time work for older ages. Since this part-time work pattern already exists, it is possible for former full-time workers to enter part-time work when they become older.

2   State Policies and the Older Workforce

2.1   The Policy Regime – Two Strategies

Within the Swedish Policy Regime, we can classify the different types of policies that have been used in the labor market and social policy fields. They form a *first layer of standardization* for decisions taken within firms and fall into two categories:

− *Prevention policies* that support employment of the older workforce.
− *Accommodation policies* that facilitate exits. They improve the economic terms for those who exit, thereby legitimizing firms' exit strategies.

Prevention follows the "work-for-all" strategy, and is essentially the more traditional "Swedish" way. Prevention strategies work at three levels:
− the older workforce is given special employment security;
− they encourage firms to take early steps to prevent actual exit situations from occurring, that is they prevent in the precise meaning of the term;
− they are found in the support of re-employment measures.

In the following, the Policy Regime is focused mainly through existing state policies. Minor negotiated benefits supplement many of these policies. A detailed description of the negotiated benefits is found in Edebalk and Wadensjö (1989). While the details on negotiated benefits are left out here, the essence of a corporatist model, which has wider importance for the functioning of state policies, is elaborated in section 3.

2.2   Prevention Policies

2.2.1 Employment Security

Historically, employment security was greater in the public sector. The goal of the 1975 reform – the *Act on Security of Employment* – was to make employment conditions more congruent between the private and the public sectors. Critics of the reform – the Employers' Confederation as well as some economists – argued that it would become an obstacle to an efficient labor market. Increased security of employment would imply that employees were "locked in", therefore diminishing the allocative efficiency of the market.

One consequence of the 1975 reform was that a *"first in/last out"* rule was institutionalized, but not made formally compulsory. In cooperation with the relevant unions the priority order could be reversed. Until the 1980s, this was more a formal possibility than practice. Moreover, there remains a loophole in redefining the contents of a specific job to dismiss those targeted by management. The first in/last out principle was a major boost in securing jobs for the older workforce in the private sector. Older employees were protected at the expense of the young. In addition, the notice period was also made longer for older workers than for younger. The Act on Security of Employment did therefore inhibit firms' freedom to form employment decisions only according to their own preferences.

A second more social policy-oriented legislation – the *Promotion of Employment Act* – increased the Labor Market Authorities' insight into and influence on firms' personnel decisions. The employers had to notify the Regional Labor Market Board when they planned to reduce the workforce by more than five employees. Of greater interest, the Act called for the creation of *Adaptation Groups* within firms, with representatives from management, unions and the authorities.

In one of the case studies (*see* Hospital below) the role of the Adaptation group in action is well illustrated. The group is responsible for taking care of employees who have been disabled, and/or sick for longer periods. The hospital has a special Adaptation group account in its budget, which can
– finance temporary transfers of personnel within the Health Care District;
– create individually targeted positions (few and hard to get);
– finance retraining and (re-)education.

One result of the Adaptation group institution is the creation of formalized Employment Policy Programs at the level of the firm, and not least within local governments and public bodies.

2.2.2 Work Environment and Rehabilitation

Work environment became a key issue and a general welfare priority of the State in the 1980s. There are many explanations for this but three circumstances reinforce this priority. (1) The knowledge that permanent exits drain the social insurance funds, has made the state more interested in work environment. (2) Firms find these issues increasingly important in their competition for employees. (3) Certain unions find it an important issue for recruiting and engaging members.

In recent years *rehabilitation* has become another key issue. At present, employers have to investigate the need for rehabilitation when an employee has been sick for more than four weeks. Rehabilitation is also closely linked to the establishment of company health care services. Until 1986, state grants were linked to medical care and company health care was nothing but medical attendance. In that year the rules for grants were changed to stimulate the wider aspects of health care and especially in areas of prevention and rehabilitation. A goal was set that 75% of firms would provide health care services. Firms could cooperate to share costs and in 1991 80% of all employees were entitled to such services (i.e., around 3 millions). But there has been a failure in attracting small firms, with only a fraction offering health care services. Besides, evaluation of the schemes show that medical care rather than prevention initiatives still dominates.

Previously, it was possible to receive disability pension without rehabilitation measures. However, rehabilitation is now enforced up to 60 and only those between 60–64 get a disability pension without any requirement of rehabilitation. Furthermore, the Act on Work Environment was modified in 1991, which meant that the goal of the work environment policy is now explicitly stated as prevention of "ill-health and work injuries". The section on rehabilitation in the Act on National Insurance is to be modified from 1992. The connection between work rehabilitation and work environment is stressed. The Social Insurance Offices have been given new coordinating powers and tasks (*see* Hospital below).

2.2.3 Employment Creation Measures

The Labor Market Authorities have a spectrum of measures that prevent permanent exit through employment creation. Some are relevant to the older workforce. In April 1991, workers aged 55–64 accounted for 10.4% of the registered unemployed. At the same time they accounted for far less in the more *general labor market programs*: in public temporary work (7.1%); in rehabilitation (1.8%); and in training (1.1%) (Source: *Labor Market Statistics*). No doubt, these programs were primarily directed towards the younger workforce.

Two other forms, sheltered jobs and subsidized employment, are more important for older workers since they are explicitly designed for weak groups in the labor market, i.e., individuals with reduced work capacity.

The state provides *sheltered jobs* at Samhall, a large state-owned conglomerate of workshops around the country. In latter years, it has increasingly been trying to meet market requirements. The share of the older workforce of those employed at Samhall can be studied in table 6.

Subsidized employment was, until 1980, identical with sheltered jobs in the public sector which were 100% subsidized. Since then, reforms in 1980 and 1991, have allowed for more flexibility. Through the 1980 reform an individual who was entitled to a wage-subsidy could be hired with a 90% subsidy for the first six months followed by 50% for two years and 25% for another two years. The main idea behind the differentiation was to gradually transfer wage costs to the employer, as the individual (hopefully) during his employment became qualified for his new position. Since 1991 no standardized decreases have been imposed. However, the wage-subsidy should last no more than four years.

These more flexible terms reflect a trend of decentralization and Local Employment Offices have been given more freedom in stating terms. In 1980, for instance, private firms were brought in as potential employers. In 1990, instead of a fixed number of subsidized positions, each office received a fixed budget at its own disposal. The money is not, however, transferable between programs without consultation with the Regional Labor Market

Table 6: Employment in Samhall and Subsidized Employment for the Age Group 55–64 over the Years 1985–1990

Year	Samhall			Subsidized employment		
	Male	Female	Total	Male	Female	Total
1985	4413	2968	26487	6040	4836	39321
1986	3801	2944	27666	6342	4958	41210
1987	3952	3028	28187	6448	5026	42810
1988	3725	2913	28716	6819	5198	44360
1989	3734	2968	30232	6836	5175	44915
1990	4198	3035	30548	6911	5226	45286

Source: Labor Market Board, Unpublished Statistics.

Board. Local strategies will more than likely begin to vary; including the priority given to older workers.

Table 6 shows that older workers make up more than 25% of the total number of those within the two job creation measures. Data from monthly inflow statistics show a smaller share of older workers (Source: *AMS Statistics*). The difference between inflow and stock figures indicates that the two measures are more permanent for older workers while seemingly more temporary for younger workers. Sheltered jobs and subsidized employment do not prevent exit from specific firms or jobs, but *prevent or delay exit from the labor market*. Thus they illustrate quite clearly another building block of the Swedish "Work Society".

2.3   Accommodation Policies

Benefit-related early exit, whether partial or total, have three major forms in Sweden:
- disability pension,
- early drawing of national pension,
- part-time pension.

The proportions of the three forms for the group 60–64, over the last 15 years, can be studied in table 7.

Table 7: Disability Pension, Early Drawing and Part-Time Pension for individuals 60 – 64 during the period 1976 – 1990

Year	Number of the Population (appr.)	Disability Pension	Early Drawing	Part-Time Pension
1976	481.300	96.700	8.303	14.560
1977	475.700	102.341	10.484	31.509
1978	470.300	105.432	11.472	41.913
1979	462.200	107.776	11.978	48.654
1980	473.200	114.971	13.374	67.837
1981	485.700	120.144	14.580	64.641
1982	492.800	123.226	16.174	61.732
1983	494.500	128.288	17.992	54.637
1984	494.964	135.453	18.036	47.204
1985	484.000	137.706	17.211	37.638
1986	467.400	138.420	16.321	32.180
1987	453.800	139.420	14.839	35.736
1988	444.400	141.103	13.345	38.472
1989	435.100	141.928	12.401	39.211
1990	427.300	141.839	12.121	38.068

Source: Statistics from SCB and RFV.

Table 8: Percentage of the Swedish Population between 60–64 Years of Age with Different Kind of Pension Benefits (december 1988)

Kind of Pension Benefit	Age in Years					Average 60–64
	60	61	62	63	64	
Complete Exit:						
Compl. Early Retirement*	24.7	25.2	29.1	32.2	34.6	28.5
Early Drawing	1.2	2.0	2.9	4.0	5.0	3.0
Partial Exit:						
Partial Early Retirement	3.6	3.9	3.9	3.8	3.5	3.7
Part-Time Pension	6.5	9.4	9.7	9.4	8.8	8.8
Total	32.4	40.5	45.6	49.6	52.0	44.1

Source: SOU 1989: 101, p. 92
* Handicap Pension Included

Disability pension far outnumbers the other two. Almost every third individual aged 60–64 has exited using this way. The number of women exiting with a disability pension is increasing. In 1971, for example, 39% of those exiting were women. In 1984 the proportion was 48% and by 1989 it had reached 53% (Source: RFV).

One can also distinguish between partial and total exit from the labor market (table 8).

2.3.1 The National Pension System

The pensions of Swedish wage earners have three components – the basic flat-rate pension, the public earnings-related pension and negotiated occupational pension benefits. The latter add a further 10% to pensions for average incomes. The use of exit options can not be fully understood except in relation to the public earnings-related pension system. This system was established in 1960 and operated from 1963. Payments were related to past work income and it was a PAYG (pay-as-you-go) system, financed by a payroll fee, paid by the employer. In the 1963, reform the statutory pension age was set at 67, in 1976 it changed to 65 years.

To be entitled to full compensation a person has to work for 30 years. Payments are further based on an average of the 15 best-paid years. Those who have not qualified for the "30 year rule" have strong incentives to work until they are 65 years old and their marginal benefit of doing so is substantial. This is the case for many women. The "15 year rule" creates incentives to continue work among those who expect their salaries to increase substantially over the last years of work. This is the typical "career" pattern, although not for manual workers. In addition, it is also important for those women who have shifted from part- to full-time work in their later years. These two rules function as an institutional barrier against early exits, since they encourage and reward the continuation of work of major groups. The rules are modified in the public sector, making later income years more important for the size of pension benefits.

2.3.2 Early Drawing of National Pension

The pension system has a built-in flexibility, today ranging between the ages 60 and 70, which yields access to early and deferred drawing of an individual's pension benefits. Benefits are reduced on an actuarial basis: 0.5 % times the number of months withdrawing early. Reduction of benefits are not limited to the years between withdrawal and the statutory age at 65, but are permanent. Pension benefits after 65 can also be lowered if years with good incomes are withdrawn that should have replaced earlier years with lower income. These are major disadvantages of the early-drawing scheme in the early-exit context.

Private and occupational pension schemes have increased dramatically in the 1980s, and will give major additions to regular pensions in the future. They may make early drawing a more favorable option, since the loss of income becomes less important. A second change, beginning in 1992 favors early drawing, when it will become possible to combine half early drawing with half early retirement (disability pension).

2.3.3 Disability Pension

Early retirement through disability pension historically have three main causes: work injury, health problem or unemployment.

Work injury insurance is, in Sweden as elsewhere, the oldest form of disability compensation. It is financed by a separate public fund – the Work Injury Fund. The idea is full compensation for lost work capacity.

Work-injury related early retirement has a higher compensation ratio than early drawing. Early retirement follows the general pension rules and a "future" income calculated for the years between the exit year and 65 is added to the pension calculation. This can have a significant impact on the pension if the last years are good income years. No reductions are built in, neither temporary nor after 65. The rather generous terms for early retirement pensions, due to disability, are connected to strict medical rules of eligibility. The pension is total or partial (2/3 or 1/2) depending on the reduction in the capacity to work. The pension is temporary or permanent (the latter is the focus of attention here). Benefits from work injury insurance and from early retirement are coordinated since 1976. As a rule, those entitled to work injury compensation benefits get a 100% compensation ratio. Of the 140,000 with early retirement in the 60–64 age group, around 30,000 were also entitled to work injury compensation in 1990 (Source: RFV).

In the early 1970s, early retirement expanded rapidly and in 1972 22% of the population between 60–66 received this kind of pension. The increase was, said the Minister of Social Affairs in 1979, "... a consequence of the development in the labour market in the form of rationalization, changing methods of work and increased demands on the labor force" (*quoted in* Hedström, 1980). The growth was sustained through a widening eligibility, which came about through two steps.

In 1973, the disability criteria were widened to include the *combination of high age and unemployment* as a cause. Thus this was deliberately directed at the older workforce. From the start, the age limit was 63 years and it came down to 60 years in 1976. This "unemployment pension" was abolished in 1990, in conditions of an "over-heated" labor market. Up till the early 1980s there were less than 4,000 cases a year. By the mid 1980s, it had increased to more than 10,000, and fell thereafter (Source: RFV).

The disability criterion was further extended in 1977. The focus shifted from the cause of disablement (work-injury) to disablement in itself (*health status*) (cf. Wadensjö, 1991: 296). Socio-medical handicaps were brought in on par with physical-medical injuries, i.e., strict rules were replaced by vaguer categories. Abuse of alcohol, for example, became an accepted cause. In health cases, age paves the way for a more generous assessment. It can be argued that cases that earlier were dealt with through the now abolished "unemployment pension" might in the future appear as health cases.

Hedström (1980) has followed those who received disability pension in 1975–78, within the Swedish level-of-living survey. In the year before (1974), 75% had been employed in a traditional working-class job and their health status had been very bad. The year before they received the disability pension they had been supported by sickness benefit for, on average, 200 days. Early retirement through disability pension is a *working class exit*.

Thus, different paths lead to the disability pension:
– The *work-injury path* starts with a period of sickness benefit/sick pay (social insurance and employer) and then moves over to work injury insurance benefit and disability pension retirement. The insurance part is the clue to the total compensation in the case of work-injuries.
– The *health path* starts with sickness benefit/sick pay and then moves over to disability pension.

– The *unemployment path* starts with a period of unemployment benefit and moves over to disability pension.

The point of the "pathway approach", much elaborated by Wadensjö (1991), is that exit from the firm occurs before the actual pensioning. In cases of sickness, exit cannot be planned in advance. In the case of an "unemployment pension" it became a standard part of employers' dismissal strategies. Instead of exiting through disability pension at 60, "black-pensioning" brought it down to a "58.3–pension" through the use of 450 days unemployment benefit which led directly into disability pension at 60.

2.3.4 Part-Time Pension

In 1976, a part-time pension reform made it possible for those between 60–65 years of age to exit part-time. A work requirement is set at a minimum of 17 hours a week, but a reduction of at least five hours is needed to qualify. A period of earlier employment of at least 10 out of the last 20 years (with income entitling to pension) and employment during at least 75 days during four of the last 12 months are further required.

The part-time pension benefit covers 65 percent of the income lost due to reduction in working hours. During the years 1980–87, the 65% compensation was lowered to 50%. If an individual has to move to a lower paid job the coming pension benefit is still calculated on his previous wage per hour, set equal to an average of his three highest incomes years during the last five. This average is inflation-proof.

Part-time pensions have increasingly been used among white-collar workers, as shown in table 9.

Table 9: Distribution of Part-Time Pensions between Workers and Salaried Employees 1979–1988

Category/Sex	1979	1981	1986	1988
Men in All	22.010	29.298	13.159	17.226
Salaried Employees	24%	30%	42%	45%
Workers	76%	70%	58%	55%
Women in All	10.807	16.645	11.336	12.627
Salarial Employees	38%	43%	55%	59%
Workers	62%	57%	45%	41%

Source: RFV, Delpensioneringen 1976–1988. Statistik rapport Is – R1989: 9, pp. 13–14.

The selective use of early retirement and part-time pensions has been increasingly recognized by management. In a report from a management consultant group affiliated to the Swedish Employers' Confederation, the experience was summarized as "... part-time pension is used for the most part by management and salaried employees, and far less among blue-collar workers" (Carlgren, 1989: 19–20).

When we look at the process of exit as a whole, the "class character" of different forms of exit is revealed, and the "choice" between options for individuals becomes largely illusory. Starting from unemployment or sick insurance, ending in the early retirement exit, is a pathway for a different group of individuals than the early-drawing or part-time pension schemes.

2.4   Qualifying the Interpretation of Sweden as 'Work Society'

In table 7 above, the three main institutionalized exit forms in Sweden were quantified. In this table, part-time pension and partial disability pension are classified as exit-policies. It is the standard form of representing the Swedish pattern (cf. Wadensjö, 1991).

Even so, in an international comparison it is the *part-time work aspect, rather than the partial exit aspect* of these two pension schemes that should be stressed. The point is that the individuals within these schemes still are partially employed. This can be interpreted as support of Sweden as a "Work Society", rather than as a haven for lavishly subsidized early exit. The point can be further illustrated through rearranging the data in table 7 (table 10).

Table 10: Two Interpretations of Work and Exit (1990) as a Proportion of the Population 60 – 64 Years

	Early Exit Perspective	Work Perspective
Disability Pension		
Full	124.303	124.303
2/3	2.114	—
1/2	15.422	—
Early Drawing	12.121	12.121
Part-Time Pension	38.068	—
Total Exit: Number	192.028	136.424
Total Exit: Percent	45%	32%

Source: Table 7 and Additional Statistics from RFV.

Table 11: Retirement Age Span in the Public Sector in Sweden in 1988

	Retirement Age Span			Total Population
	60−63	63−65	65−66	
Employed by the State	20%	15%	60%	550.000
Employed by Local Government	−	60%	40%	966.000

Source: SOU 1989: 101, pp. 96−97.

The "work interpretation" changes the exit percentage from almost half of the individuals in the age group 60–64 to less than a third. *The choice of interpretation certainly makes a difference to the contours of a "Work Society".*

A second argument strengthening the "Work Society" interpretation of Sweden is the increase of the statutory pension age within the public sector. Up till now many employees in the public sector, as an effect of established patterns and collective agreements, can retire with a full pension before 65, as shown in table 11. It can be noted that many individuals, and mostly women, have a right to retire well before 65, since women are in a clear majority amongst employees (almost 80%), in counties and local authorities.

Two kinds of changes are on their way. Firstly, the average pension age of those employed in the public sector has in fact been rising, because of individual choice. A rise in the average pension age from 63 to 64 years occurred between 1985 and 1990 [Source: Unpublished data from SPV (Statens Pensionsverk) and KPA (Kommunernas Pensionsanstalt)]. Secondly, the pension privilege of the public sector is gradually being dissolved. Today, the pension age for incoming state employees is 65 and only those employed before 1991 can retire at the early age. Furthermore, the pension agreement for those employed by local government is also being reconsidered and there is an increasing pressure on unions to trade in a low pension age for higher pension benefits.

3   Swedish Corporatism at Work

The analysis in section 2 demonstrates how Swedish labor market and social policies create an environment that shapes the behavior of firms. Yet, organized interests in the labor market are still powerful. Therefore, no exit related decision can be taken without consultation with unions, and in many cases the employers organizations are also involved. We actually end up with "action patterns", where firms respond within a logic of incentives and sanctions shaped by the state *and* a corporatist framework. Negotiated agreements and corporatist "thumb-rules" form a *second layer of standardization*.

Employer organizations, trade unions and state agencies have formed corporatist networks, especially in relation to the labor market institutions. These corporatist networks exist on three levels – the *national*, the *intermediate* and the *local* level. The combination of a long period of Social Democratic governing and the nexus of full employment has given the Swedish corporatist model a *pro-labor slant*. As a consequence, the behavior of employers organizations can be understood as behavior under "enforced decency". Still at the same time, cooperative problem-solving became characteristic for the Swedish model, which for a long period was consensualistic.

For the same reasons, it was a centralized model, and centralized wage-bargaining was the rule. In labor market policy the national and the intermediary levels have dominated. The so called Adaptation group is an example of a centrally imposed innovation; which is based on intermediary representation; with representatives from unions as co-implementors with management (cf. 2.2.1 above).

The corporatist layer has brought with it certain basic features. It tends to prolong the decision-making process within firms, while, at the same time, it smooths implementation. The presence of unions in decision making creates a conception of a "fair treatment", even when harsh firm decisions (such as personnel reductions) are taken. In this way corporatism generally *legitimizes* decisions of firms.

3.1   Two Corporatist Elements

In most areas of social security, Sweden has *public* and *general* (covering the whole, relevant population) solutions to "classic social problems" of occupational health, pensions, as well as sickness and unemployment.

However, there is also an important history of social security that originates from collective agreements between employers and trade unions, i.e., negotiated rights. These occupationally based solutions (cf. the sick pay schemes) were in several fields even a precursor of later public policies. In the inter-war and post-war period it was especially the white-collar unions that pushed forward in this field (cf. Nilsson, 1985).

In order to ease the effects of redundancies, the unions began to demand severance pay in the 1960s. The blue-collar *severance pay* (AGB) started in 1964, through the establishment of a special fund and this decision was initiated by LO and SAF. Those who were eligible were above 62 years, although later eligibility was set at age 55. In 1970, a similar scheme (AGE) was introduced for white-collar workers, for which arrangements of this kind previously had been individually settled. The severance pay eased a strategy of exit. It also seems to pave the way for individually set benefits, such as "golden handshakes" for top management as well as on lower levels (cf. Bank below).

The recession, in the late 1960s, made a significant number of white-collar employees unemployed. Their unions became increasingly aware of deficiencies in the existing labor market policy, which had a blue-collar bias. The white-collar unions made new measures for handling redundancies and relocation of their members an item on their bargaining agenda. The result was the creation of *Employment Security Funds* which started in 1972–74. The most important of them, the SAF-PTK fund began to operate in 1974, covering salaried employees in the private sector (Järnegren, Angelöw and Johansson, 1990). In 1983 the SAF-LO fund was established.

The SAF-PTK fund for the salaried employees is financed by a 0.35% pay-roll contribution. The activities of this fund increased from 224 million SEK, in 1986, to 868 million SEK by 1990. Subsequently, the number of employees covered by the activities of the fund has increased by the same rate. 35% of the employees that have been supported were between 50 and 65 years. 315 million SEK went to older employees in the form of severance pay and pensions. About 200 million SEK went into education for those made redundant. Another 300 million SEK were paid to companies for development, education and training, in order to avoid redundancy. In practice the last of these is coordinated with pension expenditures.

The SAF-PTK Security Fund intervenes in redundancy situations with the following options, often in the form of a package:
- part-financing pensions for those who exit (cf. Steel Mill below);
- supporting employees to start businesses of their own, i.e., transforming union members to self-employed entrepreneurs;
- providing income while employees participate in education (sometimes for quite long periods);
- counselling individuals/helping employees to find new jobs through a machinery that has more than 35 consultants working full-time.

The SAF-LO fund is financed by a 0.15% pay-roll contribution. In 1990, approximately 96.000 firms had joined the fund. In that year, the total support given was 112 million SEK. Its major activities have been the education of workers threatened by redundancy (cf. the upgrading effort in Steel Mill as shown below).

The initial role of the Employment Security Funds was to finance income losses in exit situations, but gradually the emphasis shifted from this *reactive response* (supporting the already unemployed) to *proactive intervention* (giving support in earlier stages of a process of personnel reduction and relocation). Corporatism stepped in more actively.

3.2   Transition from Central Corporatism to Firm-Level Corporatism

The Swedish employers have for several years tried to escape from the central form of corporatism. They have opted for a firm-level based form of managerial corporatism. In this model the state is noticeable as an absent friend (or sleeping partner) in the day to day business of bargaining and reorganization. Furthermore, labor and the unions are present as a bargaining partner, but mainly as a reactive/responding force.

In many countries, the intermediate level is the hub of the corporatist pattern (the Netherlands is a case in point). The Employers' Confederation has actively sought to shift the priority from the central to the local level. In Sweden, much of the wage-bargaining is, today, located at the intermediary level.

With the Employment Security Funds an important part of labor market and social policy is shifted away from the institutional corporatist state policy settings within the labor market authorities (national and regional labor market boards) to a local form of corporatism.

The Employment Security Funds reinforce trends towards decentralization and differentiation. An indication of the importance of the funds is the number of employees supported. During its 15 years of existence the SAF-PTK Fund has given support to around 110,000 white-collar employees. Out of these, 70,000 have received support to prevent lay-offs in a period of transition and adaption and 35,000 have received complementary money support in connection with exits. In 1990 the economic boom came to an end. In that year, expenditures from the SAF-PTK Employment Security Fund far outreached earlier years', and far exceeded its income.

During the later half of the 1980s, the Employment Security Funds seemed to have modified the Swedish model. Not just had firm-level corporatism been strengthened, but the responsibility and domain of the Labor Market Authorities was postponed to a later date in trying to help solve employment problems (e.g., counselling). This new rationale, also seen in the case of a closing supermarket (Olofsson and Petersson, 1992), is to leave the problem with corporatist institutions and social insurance until the individual enters open unemployment. Not until then does the State step in. This indication of a new division of labor, however, came about in a period of good times, where the funds took on but marginal problems. In the context of a recession in 1991/92, the undertakings of the funds have not grown in proportion to the worsening economic situation.

This indicates that the permanent role of the Employment Security Funds is rigidly defined and limited in size.

3.3   Social Steering through Redistribution with the Help of Funds

The institution of funds have been extensively used in Swedish labor market and social policies. During the 1980s this became an even more pronounced feature through the creation of the Work-Environment Fund, the Working Life Fund and the Employment Security Funds. Funds function as an *enforced re-distribution mechanism*. Firms (indirectly, partly the wage-earners) finance these funds, and the funds then reallocate ear-marked money back to the firms. The *steering element* is an important element in the Fund construction.

The fund technique has its obvious strength in the implementation of political goals within firms, since they are backed with financial incentives. It is a characteristic of the Social Democratic model. The neo-liberal critique of the fund technique argues that the "redistribution" of money in many cases only becomes "repay", and that funds implies a bureaucratic cost-burden. Steering is seen as a waste of resources, since firms themselves know best and legislation can be used to set the minimum standards. With the new Liberal/Conservative government, the "Fund-economy" might be on its way out (cf. 5.4).

3.4   Shifting Corporatist Patterns?

The gradual emergence of managerial, firm-level corporatist tendencies does not imply a total break with other forms of corporatist solutions. Rather, the *mix* changes. This change in managerial strategy endangers the well-established pattern of negotiations and consensus, with its well-defined roles for local trade unions. It opens up two alternatives, both strengthening management but giving different roles to local unions (cf. Brulin, 1989; Brulin and Nilsson, 1991).

Manual workers' unions have traditionally had a strong organization at the work-place, often with full-time officials (cf. Steel Mill, Hospital, Refuse Collection, HighTech below). In many cases, the white-collar unions have followed suit (cf. Bank, Hospital, and in many larger manufacturing firms). An important trend is that the *role of the local union in relation to the national unions increases* as a consequence of the new managerial strategy. Accordingly, this change of level of the main negotiating arena, will also affect the relative power positions of management and unions. It is well established that the logic of organization and basis of strength for Labor A and Capital differs (cf. Offe and Wiesenthal, 1980). Since Labor is organized reactively and based on numbers, its strength grows with centralization as well as with increasing scope of organization. If more importance is given to managerial power at the level of the firm, it strengthens the position of management in relation to the unions.

The second trend is that more employers now *try to bypass the influence of local unions*. Employers create a more flexible personnel policy, introduce new methods of salary and wage determination, foster specific "company cultures", involve the workers and employees in the company by selling shares at favorable prices etc. These widely spread policies are in part an adaption to changing methods of production, where the active involvement of the employees becomes strategic. In a broader socio-political sense, employers want their employees to identify more with the future of their own company (starting in the work group), and less with unions representing them as workers/wage-earners in general. The new managerial corporatism, linking employees directly to the firm, is the alternative to traditional trade-union based corporatism.

4   Five Swedish Case Studies

4.1   Introduction

In this section, we analyze the Swedish pattern in action, by studying how, on the level of firms, older employees are related to the labor market, to specific jobs and firms. This will be done by a close examination of five firms and public organizations. These case studies illustrate how the Swedish Policy Regime, filtered through corporatist networks, influenced the way the age-structure and early-exit dilemmas are handled in real situations.

The result becomes twofold. The case studies will, we believe, reveal the deep *penetration* of the Policy Regime (such as work-environment legislation and pension rules) into the internal work organization and personnel policy of the Production Regime. Yet they will also show a *rich variety of strategies and outcomes* in this setting. This variety can be explained by the interplay of numerous instruments, rules and co-operating actors that form "packages", unforeseen in advance.

The presentation of State policies was made with the help of a distinction between *prevention* and *accommodation* policies, both focusing the intentions of the State. In the case studies, these intentions are transformed into decisions of *internalization* and *externalization*. On the individual level, these strategies and decisions turn out as integration and compensation. The conceptual classification is summed up in the following scheme:

Conceptual Typology of the Older Worker
Problem: Strategy, Response and Result

	State/corpo-ratist Policy	Firm Decision	Individual Fate
Stay at job	Prevention	Internalization	Integration
Exit	Accommodation	Externalization	Compensation

Firms can shift the burden and the costs of older workers on to the state or the workers themselves, thereby externalizing both costs and the problem. On the other hand, the prevention policies of the state can induce, subsidize or legally prescribe firms to internalize costs and problems, thus making the firm the scene for preventive action. Consequently, the concepts of externalization and internalization are located at the level of the firm.

The concept and practice of compensation can be used to describe how, and in which forms individuals are compensated for their loss of work and thereby income. It includes income loss due to absence from work, to work accidents, ill-health, sickness etc. Generous compensation makes it easier for older workers to adjust to redundancy and for unions to accept age-specific dismissals. When the state compensates the redundant employees, or sponsors the growth of supportive arrangements (for instance, a broadening of the criteria for disability pension), it also accommodates for the actions of firms. By making redundancy and early exit economical and viable options, through the construction of compensation payments to individuals, the state encourages firms to get rid of the groups that were targeted for compensation. At the same time, individuals can use these compensatory mechanisms as escape routes from their work. Compensation can thereby be classified as state policies accommodating exits, which makes it easier for firms to undertake certain decisions and actions of externalization.

The counterpart to compensation, in the eyes of the individual, are all the efforts that are done to integrate him in the firm. This is sometimes forced on the firm by the state (e.g., the first in/last out rule), sometimes bought by the state (subsidized employment), and sometimes it is a wish of the firm to secure certain valuable individuals on its own (competence loss). Integration denotes a continuing attachment to the labor market and the wage or salary as a basic form of income. But it also, within the context of the Swedish "Work Society" and all the varieties of prevention policies at hand, points to the role of work as the basic form of attachment and participation of individuals in society.

4.2   An Overview of the Firms

Steel Mill: The steel company confronts decreasing demand and its problems have been reduction and structural change. The firm used early retirement as well as internal education to cope with its problems. The Employment Security Fund has supported the reconstruction, and close cooperation with the Local Insurance Office has been a necessary prerequisite.

Bank: The bank has been confronted with a problem in its age-profile, i.e., too many individuals in middle age – partly a consequence of its internal career practices. It has a pension arrangement of its own and has used topping-up practices to pension staff. The bank is concerned with work-environment issues of its more unqualified personnel.

High Tech: The hightech firm has been engaged in two major reconstructions. A long-term aim has been to erase the dividing line between blue- and white collar workers. The firm also has used support from the Employment Security Fund and from its mother company to construct a mix of early exit, internal mobility and education.

Refuse Collection: The refuse collection department faces a major problem of disabling work conditions and it has engaged in work environment reorganization efforts to cope with this. On the other hand, decentralization of the work organization has increased efficiency claims on the workforce. Disability pension has been used as a form of exit for the blue-collar workers.

Hospital: The hospital has many unqualified jobs characterized by disabling effects. It has started a prevention and rehabilitation program in cooperation with the Local Social Insurance Office to cope with these problems. In this matter, it has been somewhat of a pioneer. The hospital has further used disability pensioning quite extensively.

4.3   Case 1: A Steel Mill – Handling Redundancy and Exiting in a
      Large Company Dominating a Small Community

The Steel Mill is the dominant employer within its community and located in the classic industrial heartland region of Sweden called "Bergslagen". The main product is sheet steel in large plates and in thick shape, of high quality. Steel Mill previously produced both iron and steel of different qualities; bar iron, sheet iron, sheet steel etc. Production now is exclusively

Table 12: Total Number of Employed at Steel Mill 1975—1990

Year	Blue-Collar Workers		White-Collar Workers		Total
	No.	% of all	No.	% of all	
1975	1363	(79.6%)	349	(20.4%)	1712
1980	1171		291		1462
1985	955		285		1240
1990*	822	(71.6%)	326	(28.4%)	1148
Absolute Change:					
1975—1990	−39.7%		−6.6%		−32.9%

Source: Personnel Statistics.
* 1990: Situation at the End of July

in stainless steel. The narrower segment in production reflects the fact, that the firm has reshaped itself, and has witnessed a decline in size. Today, Steel Mill has a little over 1,000 employees, while twenty years ago there were around 2,700 employed. For the change in employment over the last fifteen years see table 12.

During the process of change, the age composition in the firm has changed. Developments between 1975 and 1990 are shown in table 13. Steel Mill reduced its staff in two large waves, one in the mid to late 1970s and a second in the early 1980s.

In fifteen years, the share of the blue-collar workers older than 55 years has diminished from 23.5% to 13%, while the share of those above 60 has fallen from 11% to 4.5%. The trend was the same among the white-collar

Table 13: Age Composition Among the Blue-Collar Workers 1975—1990

Age	Absolute Numbers				Percentages			
	1975	1980	1985	1990	1975	1980	1985	1990
−19	95	69	27	—	6.6	5.9	2.8	—
20—24	210	152	163	146	14.5	13.0	16.7	17.3
25—29	173	132	130	147	11.9	11.3	13.3	17.4
30—34	135	128	106	96	9.3	11.1	10.9	11.4
35—39	115	111	111	92	7.9	9.5	11.4	10.9
40—44	118	102	95	95	8.1	8.8	9.7	11.3
45—49	116	108	96	77	8.0	9.3	9.8	9.1
50—54	147	105	101	81	10.2	9.0	10.3	9.6
55—59	179	128	87	72	12.4	11.1	8.9	8.5
60—64	141	125	59	38	9.7	10.7	6.0	4.5
65—	20	4	0	0	1.4	0.3	—	—

Source: Personnel Statistics.

Table 14: Age Distribution among the White-Collar Workers 1975–1990 at Steel Mill

Age	Absolute Numbers				Percentages			
	1975	1980	1985	1990	1975	1980	1985	1990
−19	4	–	–	–	1.2	–	–	–
20–24	30	1	1	9	8.6	0.3	0.4	2.7
25–29	30	22	14	28	8.6	7.5	4.9	8.4
30–34	33	35	39	31	9.5	11.9	13.5	9.3
35–39	39	43	42	56	11.2	14.6	14.6	16.7
40–44	29	38	46	54	8.4	12.9	16.0	16.1
45–49	48	32	48	50	13.8	10.9	16.6	14.9
50–54	41	52	32	45	11.8	17.7	11.1	13.5
55–59	54	36	46	29	15.6	12.2	16.0	8.7
60–64	35	35	20	33	10.1	11.9	6.9	9.9
65–	4	–	–	–	1.2	–	–	–

Sources: Personnel Statistics.

workers. The share of those 55+ has diminished from ca. 27% to ca. 18%, i.e., with a third (table 14).

With the hard and demanding work in Steel Mill, most workers feel that they have had enough of work when they reach sixty. The local expression for leaving work at this age is "*going home*". At 60 many have been working for 40 years or more in the plant. The decline of Steel Mill affected the age structure of the community. The number of retired people increased by about 40% between 1975 and 1985. The proportion of those in the labor force commuting to other cities for work also increased during those ten years (from every sixth to every fourth person). Some younger individuals moved away.

4.3.1 Production Regime

The impetus of change in Steel Mill came from the product market, and it affected the company directly. It was, however, mediated by the situation of the Swedish steel industry in general, which was heavily subsidized by the state. Steel Mill – export oriented, with rapidly changing market conditions – was an active and initiating force in its own restructuring. During the process, both production and employment changed dramatically.

The change has been influenced by two aspects of its Production Regime. Firstly, Steel Mill is a local plant within a larger corporation and its policy is affected by its "mother company". Needless to say, newly acquired companies usually face a bleak future in a crisis. Secondly, there are special restrictions on the decisions of a local firm belonging to the Swedish "Bruk" tradition, such as Steel Mill. It is the dominating employer in the community, and the decisions of the firm must in some sense be judged as legitimate by the community. The company, therefore, cannot treat an older worker too unfairly if it still wants to recruit his son. Its dominating position further creates close cooperation with the Local Employment Office, not least from the point of view of the latter.

Steel Mill has witnessed a long process of restructuring and shrinking. Features of the Production Regime have pushed for gradual change. The changes, however, have come in waves. These occurred in the mid 1970s and in the early 1980s. Steel Mill is further witnessing a new phase of change in 1990/91. The basic strategy of the company, in the first two waves, was simply to lay off workers. This was coupled with a recruitment halt and internal replacements.

The lay-offs took two forms, which occurred at either end of the age scale. The last in/first out practice applied to the young. Laying off the older workers is, however, a strategy, which is more appealing to the company, as a rule. This strategy appeals to the criteria of qualifications, competence, productivity etc. Aging is increasingly seen in terms of a loss in productivity and not as a gain in knowledge.

Using the figures presented in table 12 and 13, we can calculate the "cohort survival rate" for the five-year age groups for three periods, i.e., how many remain in a given cohort after five years? We deduct the average "survival rate" of all workers at Steel Mill from the survival rates of the five year age groups. It is done in table 15.

In the first period, the young age groups were reduced by more than the average and the middle-aged groups were more likely to "survive". Al-

Table 15: "Excess Survival Rates" of Five Year Cohorts for Three Five-Year Periods. Blue-Collar Workers at Steel Mill

Age-Group	Period 1 1975 → 1980	Period 2 1980 → 1985	Period 3 1985 → 1990
20−24/25−29	−17.4	+1.7	+3.6
25−29/30−34	−6.3	−3.5	−12.7
30−34/35−39	+1.9	+2.9	+0.2
35−39/40−44	+8.4	+1.8	−1.0
40−44/45−49	+11.2	+10.3	−5.5
45−49/50−54	+10.2	+9.7	−2.2
50−54/55−59	+6.8	−1.5	−15.3
55−59/60−64	−10.5	−37.7	−42.9
Average Rate	80.3%	83.8%	86.6%

Source: Table 13.

Table 16: Number of Persons Using the Disability Pension Exit at Steel Mill 1977–1987

Year	Workers	Salaried Employees	Total
1977	46	35	81
1981–82	35	27	62
1983	76	5	81
1986–87	55	23	78

Source: Personnel Statistics.

though the situation stabilized, with fewer people leaving the company in the last two periods, the older age-groups have increasingly became smaller, and more likely to exit.

A series of labor market and social security measures, during the 1970s and 1980s, made it easier for workers around 60 years to adjust to unemployment. Unemployment compensation plus severance pay made the first year of unemployment rather unproblematic in pure economic terms. The degree of compensation was high. After 450 days – for older workers the right to unemployment compensation has been extended into 450 days – a worker could apply for and receive disability pension on "labor market conditions" (if chances of getting a new job were poor). This led to the so-called "black pensioning", the 58.3 year being the effective cut off point. This was the normal destiny for laid off workers around 60 years of age. Some could get a health disability pension, after a similar "career" (table 16). For the white collar workers the solution was a "pension package" (cf. below).

The outcome was the result of an interplay between the company and its strategy, the unions with their twin interests of protecting the middle-aged (who remained in their jobs) and the old workers. It was also the preference of many old workers themselves. Besides being satisfied with the pension terms, most workers own their homes in this community, thus strengthening their positive attitudes towards "going home". The possibilities allowed by the social security system were used according to an agreement between the different parties. The Local Employment Office and the Regional Labor Market Board were both part of the agreement, and they did not offer new jobs to these old unemployed workers. Extremely few (if any) of these workers have become dependent on social assistance.

For the white-collar workers in general the basic strategy was to subsidize their further education. Older individuals retired early with extra benefits from occupational schemes. For the white-collar workers on staff level, pension arrangements were even more advantageous than staying on the job.

4.3.2 1990/91 Considerations – Externalization and Internalization

The technical, supervisory and administrative apparatus is continually being reorganized, e.g., computerized. There are now problems in relocating older employees, and finding new jobs for some older routine office clerks and supervisors. Many of these want to "go home", and the company wants to reduce its staff.

Steel Mill presented a plan for pensioning 37 employees, born 1927–1931, which offered them early retirement in 1990–1991. They were guaranteed 80% of their wages in pensions. The calculus of the company was the following. If these 37 employees (clerks, supervisors, engineers etc.) stay on until they are 65 years, the total wage bill for them will be 39.5 million SEK (wages plus contributions to social security, pensions etc.). To "buy them a pension" from late 1990 will cost Steel Mill 21.5 million SEK. The company can then take the total costs in one year (which may be an advantage), and reduce it by 18 million SEK.

How can we explain this gain of 18 million SEK?
(a) The difference between hundred and eighty per cent (the pension offer) in wages is the first part of the answer.
(b) Social security contributions are markedly lower for pensions payments than for wages, which forms the second part.
(c) The third part is a subsidy from the SAF-PTK Employment Security Fund, which subsidizes Steel Mill's cost for the pensions by about 30%.

The part-time pension exit route is now rather seldom used. Only ten individuals at Steel Mill have part-time pensions. It was earlier possible to find new and suitable part-time jobs within the company. At present, the changes in the internal labor market has made this exit more difficult to use in practice.

With a slackening demand for Steel Mill's products, it has gone from a five to four shift pattern. Another way to handle the situation is to further train and educate the workforce.

The alternative used for white-collar employees is to raise their basic educational level. Those with low formal education will be educated up to high school level. Here the Employment Security Fund (cf. above) will pay the employee 80–90% of his/her earlier salary while in school. The company will then top this up to the former level.

For the blue-collar workers the alternative, in 1990, was eight weeks of full-time further education within the firm, after which the worker will be an "acknowledged/licensed steel worker". All workers will get this training, and up to 20 (or sometimes 40) are taken out of personnel staffing schemes each period. This device will make it possible for Steel Mill to keep the workers in employment. The County Labor Market Board will subsidize the internal education by 35 or 55 SEK per hour for each worker, if the alternative is unemployment. This vocational training for steel workers will also help Steel Mill as a company to be upgraded in the international classification of steel mills (the BSI standard). This upgrading is important in relation to the steel market and for the prices Steel Mill can ask for is products.

We find here a specific combination of personnel policy, promoted by labor market policy in Sweden, and the industrial and market profile of Steel Mill as a company.

4.3.3 Decentralization and Internal Job Shifts

Within a large plant like Steel Mill the traditional "soft exit" was internal job-shifts, such as:
- transfer from shift work to day work;
- change from production to maintenance, upkeep, service, transport, repair, and jobs in supply departments.

Certain categories of workers had to "take to the broom", when getting too old for their former jobs.

This can be seen as industry's own form of phasing out a part of the older workforce, what we might call an "internal gradual exit". It can also be interpreted as the later stages of an implicit long-term, in some cases life-time, employment contract. In this respect, it is part of the "Bruk" tradition – characteristic for companies interwoven with a specific community as a source for labor.

Today, there is no room in Steel Mill for physically fit men in the so-called "easy jobs". They have to be reserved for the handicapped, and for the older workforce, that is for those who get a negotiated replacement for physical, medical or social reasons. "Earlier you could get certain jobs with the 'rights of age'. But they have been reduced more than other kinds of jobs. Steel Mill is a harder and tougher place to be in now than before. The pressure has increased" (from an interview with a worker at Stell Mill).

Since 1982, Steel Mill has formed a "personnel pool", which is part of overhead costs and a "free" resource for the units in which they work. The persons belonging to the pool do not know that they are part of it – the pool is only seen in the internal bookkeeping. The personnel department highly favors this construction. They emphasize its social advantages, because it is possible to use for individuals, for whom they otherwise would have large problems in finding an internal transfer.

4.4   Case 2: A Bank – Regional Level and a Local Office of a large Swedish Bank

The Bank is hierarchic in its organization. Six levels exist: Concern – Group – Region – District – Office – Division. Decisions are taken at all levels, although when a thorough change is implemented it is prepared at the Concern and Group levels. On employment policy issues, for instance, Region has been the strategic level. Over the last five years, decision making has been increasingly decentralized. Today every Division has to be profitable. Still, the Regional level takes on coordination.

Around 1980, it was thought that computerization and over-all modernization would decrease employment in banking drastically. An employment prognosis forecasted reductions of more than 10.000 employees in the banking sector over the decade, but instead employment grew by approximately 20.000 employees. Rationalizations in routinized transactions were offset by new tasks.

A powerful expansion came with the emergence of the Swedish financial (money) market, starting in 1983, and with the revival of the stock-market from 1981 on. A deregulation of the loans-market in 1985 completed the scene. This development demanded more "back-office" work (as distinguished from "front-office" work). Besides, financial advising has grown rapidly. There are new market shares to be gained. A "unit-link" market is building up. "There actually never were any structural problems in banking, causing reductions in employment, just the fear" (Staff manager at the Region level).

Figures on employment are shown in table 17.

Table 17: Positions and Numbers of Employees in Bank 1985–1989, Stockholm Region

Year	Number of Positions	Number of Employees	Men	Women
1985	2.724	3.246	1.271	1.975
1986	3.563	3.651	1.456	2.195
1987	3.165	3.693	1.461	2.232
1988	3.159	3.643	1.411	2.232
1990	3.132	3.713	1.436	2.277

Source: Personnel Statistics.

4.4.1 Production Regime – Two Aspects of the Internal Organization

The internal career pattern within banking involves recruiting employees early and educating them within the bank. Education is both introductory, but also reoccurring and consists of four steps; the first two are basic and compulsory and the last two specialized and voluntary. They reach university level status. Almost 1/4 of all employees have presently reached such competence. At the same time, those who don't pass all the steps are stimulated to take over new tasks, which rely on acquired work-skills. The union complains that its a "man's world" and women, especially older women, are disadvantaged at the top of the career ladder. A new task, i.e., giving highly qualified professional advice, has slightly modified the standard pattern. Some specialists are brought in from outside, but the internal career pattern still shapes the employment policy of Bank.

A central problem of Bank is a high turn-over rate of employment at low levels. Basic tasks are getting increasingly standardized. Therefore, "front-office" work has become more monotonous and less attractive. The internal career pattern implies that entrance at this level is mostly open to young people. "Impatience" among younger entrants is one explanation to the increasing turn-over rate. On the other hand, those who have been in Bank 10–15 years tend to stay on, causing an increase in the average age. An employment freeze in the 1970s has made the age group of 30–35 small or even void in Bank. As a consequence, the importance of those above 40 years has been upgraded. "The older workforce is more loyal to the company" (the personnel manager), and an early exit of these "unskilled" and semi-skilled employees thus is a threat.

A second element in the management philosophy, is the idea of producing high achievement at the most productive age. This gives rise to "wearing out" at management level, since a rapid change of skills, associated with executive tasks, has occurred over the last ten years.

At the local office, "front-office" work is divided between a younger group below 25 (majority), and a middle-aged group aged 40 and upwards. Two women over 40 were recruited 2–3 years ago for such tasks.

Attitudes towards exit in Bank can then be stated: *Early exit is a threat at lower levels. Early exit is a must at higher levels.*

4.4.2 Handling Reorganization

Banks in Sweden have created their *own occupational pension system*, with own funds and own rules. The Bank pension system provides more flexibility and in some respects more generous terms than similar occupational pension systems. In banking, pension rules are formed through negotiations

Table 18: Early Drawing, Early Retirement due to Employment Reasons and Total Retirement in Bank

	Early Drawing		Early Retirement (Employment Reasons)		
	Male	Female	Male	Female	Retired
1985	–	1	9	4	70
1986	–	1	8	12	66
1987	–	1	4	10	61
1988	–	1	18	12	79
1989	–	–	12	6	64

Source: Personnel Statistics.

between the employers organization and the union of bank employees, which has high coverage. The latest reformulation dates to 1988/89. Opening up for exit on higher levels is done mainly through the use of early drawing of pensions and a bank version of early retirement. Table 18 shows the development of Bank Region in recent years.

Early drawing has been rarely used. On the other hand, there is a steady stream of early retirement due to employment considerations. While early drawing is an individual right, the bank subsidized early retirement pension and as such is an offer from the employer. In 1988/89 early drawing and early retirement were made more competitive, when Bank increased compensation rates: for early drawing from 65 to 72% and for early retirement from 70 to 72%. The last is still more favorable because the scheme gives no pension loss at all after 65. The age limit for early retirement is set to 55. The increase in numbers of early exits in the years 1988/89 is a reflection of these improved conditions. Extra pension payments above 72% can be given on an individual basis, but are rarely used. It is an exclusive right for managers, according to the union.

Private pension arrangements have been supported by Bank through good credit terms. Profit-sharing schemes have further emerged within banking. It is possible to sell some of the shares after five years' employment, and all of them at the age of 60. The combination of private pensions and profit-sharing schemes strengthens incentives of voluntarily early exit. Together they form *a pattern of individualized pension combinations in banking*.

At the local office, work tasks are very differentiated, which favours part-time work. It partly reflects the wishes of women and partly the needs of the employer. One individual works four days a week, one woman with a newly born child works half-time, one individual is free three days a month and one individual works a shorter day. At the time "this is it", since too much part-time work will cause competence problems for Bank (the managing director).

Part-time pensions (80%, 60% or 50%) exist in banking, starting at the age of 60. They are in general supported by the employer, but do often result in a transfer to a new position (mostly within the office). In mid 1990, only 35 persons in the whole region had part-time pensions. 21 of those were women. One explanation to the low frequency of part-time pensioning is the high volume of regular part-time work in Bank.

The opposite to exiting early is allowing "pensioners" to continue working when vacancies arise, e.g., at holidays. For instance 62 persons work after retirement (in mid 1990) and their conditions are individually settled. It is easy to keep contact with retired employees, since pension issues are handled within Bank. Bank looks favorably at a truly flexible retirement age for the future. It is well in line with the two main problems, i.e., the threat of exit on lower level, and the need of exit on higher level.

Early exits due to work-injuries or health causes also occur. In mid 1990, for example, 56 persons were registered as long-term sick, i.e., for over three months. They will probably get a disability pension. 34 individuals had half-time disability pension and 50 full-time in 1990; a majority of them were above 55 years of age. The terms are comparatively favorable. Bank supplements the sickness benefit, and for those who retire early, Bank guarantees a pension of 80% of the salary. There is a right to return to Bank if early retirement is canceled.

Preventive measures are undertaken by Bank. There is a collective agreement on work environment that regulates health issues and Bank supports sports on a broad scale. Bank has a counsellor, at Region level, who gives advice and help.

4.5   Case 3: High Tech – A Firm within a Multinational Company

The Swedish High Tech company is a plant and a "business area" within one of Sweden's larger international companies, with 90 percent of its sales going to countries outside Sweden. It has subsidiaries, retailers or agents in more than 140 countries worldwide. The company was restructured in 1982 and today, the company consists of three operating areas (the percentage proportions in brackets): Industry (50%) – Food (30%) – Agri(-culture) (20%).

Food is a high-tech business area. Furthermore, it is the fastest growing area of the company. Today it is one of the world's largest suppliers of equipment to the food processing industry, with shares of 10 to 40% depending on the product. Focus on design and sales of processes and plants is being gradually extended by a new strategy involving after-sales and customer service. The product range includes complete process lines and individual components for the food processing industry.

The Food business area has its Center of Competence at the chosen high-tech company. This center serves the market transacting companies around the world with technical and commercial support. Complicated construction tasks, coordinated purchase planning and management decisions are executed here. The tendency is, however, that extended competence is built up outside of Sweden.

4.5.1 Production Regime – Reoccurring Reconstructions and The advent of Just-in-Time Production

High Tech has witnessed two major problems in the 1980s. The first involves a *market pressure* to decrease delivery times, which is mainly a problem for the blue-collar workforce. This has been met through increased flexibility and readiness. On the other hand, it has created an increasing need to cope with slack time in production. High Tech has responded by broadening work skills.

Since 1980, the firm has faced difficulties in recruiting skilled workers. The counter measure has been to try to upgrade blue-collar work, i.e., include also white-collar tasks which, eventually, results in erasing the dividing line between the two groups. In this way "blue-collar" work also becomes more attractive. Since the company is basically selling technology, a profitability crises will be a white-collar problem. In practice, the main problem has been slow adaption of white-collar positions to changes.

To make recruitment of blue-collar workers easier and to increase flexibility, *work-teams* have been created. High Tech further believes that teamwork is a solution not only to the physical but also to psycho-social work environment problems. The teams have been provided with rights of self-determination. The optimal number of individuals in a team is seen as ranging between 8–12. Administrative work and planning has been decentralized to the teams, and they have decisive influence on recruitment. The number of supervisors have been reduced on this road to a new organization.

As the whole company has become more and more international in its approach, a general requirement that all personnel should know English has been formulated – in line with upgrading the claim on blue-collar competence. The reorganization makes strictly white-collar positions increasingly superfluous. The new work organization further increases the possibilities of promotion of skilled blue-collar workers and becomes a component in attracting them to High Tech.

The change has two effects on the older workforce. It makes replacements within the firm easier. It increases the importance of older, experienced employees, since they are thought to "stabilize" teams and younger workers are more prone to leave the firm.

4.5.2 Two Reorganizations – Causes, Decisions, Consequences

In 1982 High Tech was reorganized. Blue-collar workers had to re-apply for their old jobs or for a new one within High Tech. This led to a (modest) reallocation of employees and partly solved blue-collar inefficiency, but accentuated white-collar inefficiency.

Employment and age distribution at High Tech can be studied in table 19. The table further shows the increasing share of white-collar workers during the 1980s.

In 1985, the Swedish Government cut subsidies to agriculture, decreasing agricultural production within Sweden and causing a fall in demand for products of High Tech. Subsequently, profits went down. Finding the cause in circumstances linked to changes in government policy, legitimized the firm to take thorough action. By now, it was the white-collar problem which needed resolving.

In the 1982 reconstruction, the blue-collar problem was solved without using exit strategies. Internal strategies, i.e., replacements were one minor answer: the second was expanding the internal labor market. A firm was acquired in a town nearby and closer links were formed with a thermical production firm (belonging to the mother corporation) located in the same town as High Tech. Increased cooperation became the solution to slack problems and a fear of losing competence.

Table 19: Age Distribution of the Employees at HighTech 1982–1990

Year	White-Collar Workers			Blue-Collar Workers		
	55–59	60–64	Total	55–59	60–64	Total
1982	32	28	591	8	9	136
1983	32	24	598	9	7	144
1984	28	27	594	10	8	145
1985	30	27	600	8	8	148
1986	28	28	625	10	8	144
1987	27	12	529	9	6	146
1988	28	14	491	10	6	140
1989	27	19	483	12	8	124
1990	29	25	529	8	9	129

Source: Personnel Statistics.

In the 1986/87 reconstruction, the excess of the white-collar workforce was brought to a head and immediate internal measures were taken. New entrances were stopped. With a turn over rate of between 6–7% this would result in around 40 vacancies a year not being replaced. 15 individuals were (re)located abroad. However, since the firm wanted to reduce the number of white-collar employees drastically, other steps had to be taken. High Tech turned to the SAF-PTK Employment Security Fund for support in mid 1987. With financial support from the Fund, a strategy took form, with two major components.

The *first* component included offers of temporary paid education to white-collar workers in the age ranging from 25 to 45. This education was supposed to create greater skills in areas like Computing and Business Economics and increase internal mobility. In addition, education in itself implied a temporary reduction of the white-collar workforce. Those in education were also encouraged to start a business of their own, relying on new acquired skills, or to leave the company for another employer. This would give a permanent reduction. – When the offer appeared, 32 individuals took up the option. The Fund paid 50% of the costs and subsidized 25% extra if the individual took a job outside the company when the education was finished. The *second* component was an offer of early leave on generous terms, partly financed by the Fund. No future pension losses were to come about due to leaving early. In June 1987, this exit offer was given to 14 individuals, aged 63+; five accepted.

At the same time, planned reductions increased from 100 to 150 white-collar workers, to be completed by 1988. The result was a second exit offer in January 1988 and the age group was extended to 61–65. Favorable information from those who accepted the offer in 1987 was used as an extra argument. This time 30 individuals were eligible and 14 took the offer. In mid 1988 the planned reductions were almost completed (cf. table 19). Because of the participation of the Fund the Labor Market Authorities were not involved. The union supported the program from the start, with the added requirement that it had to be a general offer and no individuals in particular should be singled out. The company approved this. The disadvantage for the firm was that some employees regarded as valuable exited in the process, according to the personnel manager.

The company favors part-time retirement at 60 of white-collar workers, viewing it in the light of productivity gains. The attitude towards part-time pension of blue-collar workers is more reticent, since the loss of skills is pronounced; but it also reflects an over-heated labor market. However, almost 50% of the blue-collar workers in the relevant age group have such an arrangement.

As to internal prevention measures it could be added that preventive and work environment related health-care is expanding and managed within the

Table 20: Number of Employees at Refuse Collection 1985–1989

Year	Total Number	Refuse Collection	Supplies Repair	Street Cleaning	Admini- stration
1985	211	113	32	44	22
1986	206	112	32	44	18
1987	206	–	–	–	–
1988	206	–	–	–	–
1989	214	–	–	–	–

Source: Personnel Statistics.

company. One doctor, two nurses and half-time physiotherapist are employed by High Tech.

4.6 Case 4: Refuse Collection in a Large City – Reorganizing the Work Process to Avoid Early Exit

Refuse Collection is part of local government in a large city (230.000 inhabitants) and has the overall responsibility for household refuse, the transport from dustbins, containers and refuse chutes to the dustheap. The road works' department, however, is in charge of street cleaning. The number of employed at Refuse Collection is shown in table 20.

The largest part of the workforce is occupied in traditional refuse collection. The trucks transporting the refuse are operated by a team of two persons. The workers are divided into such regular teams (self-selected) and a pool of substitutes. Teams have fixed routes, and the members of the pool have to replace the regulars, when they are sick or absent. Wages are hourly paid. The teams are paid for eight hours per tour, and are free to work at their own pace. Most teams do their work in about six hours of intense work.

There is a special transport section of one-man trucks for container transport and delivery, including small lorries for working in large housing estates. For this group, wages are paid by the month. There are also certain job functions related to maintenance, garage and repair work etc. Finally, there is a "street section", where the main task is cleaning up sidewalks. The majority of blue-collar workers belong to the first group; still the core of Refuse Collection. Of these, about 90 are paid by the hour (i.e., in practice by a piecework system). The different sections, comprising mainly jobs for blue-collar workers, are coordinated and supplemented by an administrative section.

For the age distribution among the employed workers and staff see table 21.

Table 21: Age Distribution of Employees at Refuse Collection 1985 and 1990

Age-Group	Workers			Salaried Employees	
	1985	1990		1985	1990
−20	1	−		−	−
21−25	3	4		−	−
26−30	11	12		1	−
31−35	22	18		−	1
36−40	19	23		3	1
41−45	31	21		12	3
46−50	24	26		6	14
51−55	16	23		10	11
56−60	19	18		5	5
61−66	22	9		1	5
Total	168	154		38	40

Source: Personnel Statistics.

4.6.1 Production Regime and Strategies for Reorganizing Work

Refuse Collection is a monopoly operated by local government. This determines its attitudes and strategies. Its personnel policy is always expected to seek internal transfers; within the whole area of local government.

Refuse collection is physically demanding. The organization of the work together with payment by the hour have led to a situation of highly intense work. This is crucial in understanding the health problems of the workforce. More often than not, few men continue their work as regular refuse collectors beyond the age of 55–60 years.

The status of Refuse Collection as a public agency makes it impossible just to fire older workers, so Refuse Collection has, instead, developed three strategies for taking care of the older section of the workforce. The first, and in the long term, the most important strategy has been the *reorganization of the work process*. The trash bags have been replaced by bins on wheels (small containers in plastic or metal). This makes it impossible for the workers to load their barrows with several bags. The new bins must be steered by two hands (i.e., it becomes impossible to drag more than one at a time). The availability of the bins (and the reduction of damaging work conditions) has also been changed by administrative rules, i.e., by rules governing the shape of rooms for the bins (height, availability etc.). The board governing refuse collection and disposal is part of the political administration and open for pressure and arguments.

The second strategy has been a successful *broadening of the area of work and competence*. It has taken three main forms.

(1) *Container transport*
Container transport has grown in two areas: industrial waste and the collection of material for recycling (paper, glass, metal) from households. There is also a special service for collecting old household appliances, such as, refrigerators, cookers etc. One man operates a truck and the handling of containers is mechanized (using lifts etc.).

(2) *Integrated service for larger housing estates*
Refuse Collection takes over tasks that were previously done by caretakers, e.g., dealing with the garbage rooms (where the bins and cans are placed). For the Refuse Collection worker this is an upgrading of his work, with more varied tasks. Accordingly, the caretakers have also had their work upgraded and their services have become more visible (simple repair work, taking care of flowers, lawns, bushes etc.). It has also been in the interest of the landlords as they want the work of their caretakers to be visibly more important for tenants. This work is now being done by small new trucks, which are operated by one man. About 15 people are now employed in this service and it covers around 25% of the housing estates in the city. The work is physically less demanding than regular refuse collection and has no piece-work incentive built into it.

(3) *Sidewalk cleaning*
Cleaning of public roads and streets comes under the Road Works Department. However, cleaning of sidewalks and other areas, apart from the street, is the duty of the house owner (landlord). Refuse Collection has been rather successful in bidding for such contracts and jobs, and this constitutes the third road to renewal and the "street section" now employs about 20 persons. Transfer to the street section was the traditional exit for the older workers and is still valued as such.

All these new jobs are paid monthly (and there is no "time incentive" as in regular refuse collection). In this way the new jobs bring in a slower pace of work, with positive effects on health in the medium and long run.

4.6.2 Handling Exits in a Local Authority

A third strategy is the *use of different exit routes*. On the average, absence from work at Refuse Collection due to sickness, is about 12%. This is not regarded, neither by management nor the unions, as alarming, taking into considerations the demands of this work. There are, however, serious problems for several older workers. Long sickness periods often lead to disability pensions. However, there are no cases of disability pensions for labor market reasons, i.e, unemployment pension, for Refuse Collection workers. This exit is closed to a public sector agency.

The later part of a worker's career in Refuse Collection will follow any

Table 22: Type of Job Related to Type of Pension Exit. All Pension Exits 1976–1990
from Refuse Collection

Section within the Refuse Collection	Full Disability Pension	Half Disability Pension	Part-Time Pension	Early Pension
Refuse Collection	13	2	4	–
Street Cleaning	17	–	8	–
Supply/Repair	3	2	1	–
Administration	3	3	–	4
Total:	36	7	13	4

Source: Personnel Statistics.

of the customary exit pathways. If we relate the different exit options to the four major sections within Refuse Collection we get table 22.

The exit rate from the street section is markedly higher than from the others. This is what we should expect given the pattern of internal job shifts. These normally lead from regular refuse collection to:
– container transport,
– housing estates services,
– repair, supply, garage work (indoor),
– street section.

In the street section, wages are lower. One who voluntarily applies for a transfer to this section will get a lower wage. If, however, an individual is transferred due to health reasons he will continue to get the earlier wage. Many workers also anticipate such a transfer by voluntarily changing to a more mechanized job, such as, one-man truck or container transport; thereby getting an easier job and avoiding part of the wage reduction.

In theory, the local authority and all its departments, agencies and divisions, should function as a replacement and transfer area for those employed within Refuse Collection. This follows the normal practice of the Act on Security of Employment in the public sector. In reality this does not work and in the last ten years very few individuals from Refuse Collection have been replaced this way. What has happened is that every department or division will defend and reserve for "their own" the easy jobs and niches. The Road Works Department, for example, wished to take over the Street Division from Refuse Collection as a way of finding jobs for their older workers. This advance was rebutted by the elected board of Refuse Collection. Refuse Collection encounters the same resistance from other departments when it needs to find new jobs for their workers.

4.7   Case 5: A General Hospital – New Ways of Handling Disabling Work

The Swedish health care system is organized through public bodies. Hospitals, including psychiatric hospitals, nursing homes, and the majority of outpatient care are run by the counties. Costs for health care are financed by the county tax, a flat income tax, varying between 13–16% in different counties. Sickness insurance, and the major part of the medicine costs (medicines prescribed by doctors) are financed by a social insurance contribution, levied as a pay-roll fee (about 10%).

The county we have chosen employs about 30,000 people and is divided into "Health Care Districts", centered around a hospital. Our district employs about 6,000 and also administers a large psychiatric hospital, several nursing homes and several primary care outpatient facilities. The district is the employing agency and responsible for personnel policy. The central administration of the county has mainly regular staff functions (education, training, etc.). The size of the district is shown in table 23 through employment figures.

Table 23: Distribution of Employees in Hospital District in 1990

Category	Hospital Care District		County as a Whole	
1. Doctors	367		1,708	
2. Nurses	1,386		5,483	
3. Other Care Personnel of which:	2,421		10,660	
a) Asst. Nurses		1,608		5,532
b) Wardens		435		1,873
c) Orderlies		256		2,754
4. Medico-Technical	48		297	
5. Paramedical	254		1,630	
6. Maintenance of which:	741		3,298	
a) Cleaning		357		1,299
b) Kitchen		218		836
7. Administration	525		2,718	

Source: Personnel Statistics.

4.7.1 Work Organization

During the last decade patients in nursing homes, as well as in hospital clinics, have become harder to handle. They are in general older and demand more care and are not as agile as before. Caring work has thus become more "physical" and at the same time the number of support personnel has decreased. Some "intermediate wards", caring for patients, that could manage themselves, have been closed. Work has become more intense and concentrated. After a long phase of expansion of resources and growth in the numbers of employed, the situation is now one of realloca-tion, restructuring and intensification. To this should be added a change in the proportion of different categories within nursing. Consequently, the number of trained nurses is growing and the number of assistant nurses and orderlies are diminishing. This tends to shift some parts of work from the category of assistant nurses to trained nurses, which entails an intensifica-tion of the work for both categories.

The average age of the employees has slowly been rising and this has been due, in the main to expansion in the 1970s and a tendency for those over 50 to increase their hours of work (diminishing the need for new entrants). Today, however, the demand is for younger people and the schools, educating nurses and assistant nurses, are all geared to those coming directly from high school. Earlier the county organized "reactivat-ing courses" for nurses and others who had been away from work for years and courses for older people who wanted to be employed. This was in vogue 15 to 20 years ago, but no such course have been initiated in the last five to six years. Efforts to re-enlist nurses that have left the hospital sector, have not been successful.

Work injury is still a problem – and many members of the SKAF-union (organizing orderlies, nurses assistants, cleaning and kitchen personnel) are worn out before they reach 60. In the words of a local SKAF union representative: "They are worn out before 60. Every day someone is coming and reporting a work injury." Some of them will receive disability pensions when they are around 57–58 years. The administrative union (SKTF) stated their main problems as reorganization and computerization. With the pro-posed transfer of some work areas in old age care to the local authorities, there may be problems for some amongst the administrative personnel at Hospital. Some of these will have an offer of early retirement (from 60 years+). Computerization, on the other hand, demands new skills and further training. Some older personnel have experienced this change and see it as a difficulty.

Sickness is also problematic, with the average number of sick days per employee increasing dramatically, from 27 to 45 days between 1984 and 1989. The total number of sick days increased from 148,190 to 263,104, an

Table 24: Average Number of Sick-Days, and Long-Term Sickness among Different Categories of Employees at Hospital in 1989

Category	Average Sickdays	Long Sick Spells: % of Category	Average Days Absent per Longterm Sick Spell
1. Doctors	13.5	5.2%	171
2. Nurses	24.1	11.1%	141
3. Other Care Personnel of which:	46.0	20.2%	163
a) Asst. Nurses	39.2	17.2%	150
b) Wardens	54.5	24.3%	174
c) Orderlies	76.5	32.8%	170
4. Medico-Technical	37.5	9.8%	242
5. Paramedical	27.4	17.3%	108
6. Maintenance of which:	75.3	34.1%	167
a) Cleaning	88.9	39.8%	169
b) Kitchen	63.7	30.3%	154
7. Administration	38.9	19.4%	146
Average for all Employees:	45.3	—	162

Source: Personnel Statistics.

increase of 77.5% during the same period. Long-term sickness (> 32 days a year) accounted for more than 95% of this increase and is seen as an alarming problem. The whole picture is shown in table 24.

The sickness rate differs considerably between occupational categories. The harder the work and the less qualified the personnel, the higher the rates of absence (cf. the gap between group 1, 2 and 3, as well as the increase within group 3).

4.7.2 The Dialectics of Decentralization and Internal Mobility

In the last few years, the trend towards a more decentralized organization within the Health Care District has been featured. The personnel administration has shifted downwards to the level of the clinics, which have become the "basic units". Work schedules, budgets and hiring of personnel, are now decisions within the jurisdiction of the manager of the "basic unit" (in practice the head physician). In the future, further major personnel decisions, including the problems of the long-term sick and those in need of new jobs etc., will also be within the responsibility of the "basic unit".

The philosophy of Hospital management is that "basic units" should take care of their own problems and carry the costs of their work organization, such as work injuries, disability etc. Thus, management believes, they will be forced to take a long-term view of their working arrangements.

Decentralized responsibility has made it practically impossible to move between clinics and work units, so it has become increasingly more difficult for older employees, or those in need of "easy jobs", to be transferred to other clinics. Every "basic unit" wants to reserve their nice and easy jobs for their own employees, but it has also rendered normal mobility between units and clinics more difficult as a union representative explains: "They are building walls between the units."

Age-specific mobility differs amongst categories of employees. Most nurses stay in their normal nurse position, although some may take up a more administrative position (becoming head nurses, section administrators etc.). Even so a few try to transfer to out-patient clinics, which have only day schedules and weekend closing, that makes the job very attractive. The out-patient clinic is also appealing for assistant nurses and when there is an opening, between 30 and 40 individuals apply. The possibility to move is obviously limited. In addition, assistant nurses have the option for an individual career in nursing and they can receive paid training to become a qualified nurse. It should be noted, that there are few possibilities for internal mobility for the maintenance personnel. In another area, the administrative personnel works within an hierarchical organization. In the 1980s, Hospital tried to recruit many of the top career positions from outside, thereby partly blocking internal mobility. This pattern included top managers as well as engineers and supervisors but there is no parallel move out of Hospital to other sectors.

This "locking-in" was enhanced by changing rules for promotion. Previously, "experience", which was interpreted as the number of years worked, was the major qualification when applying for a new job or an internal transfer. An employee could, so to say, "earn" the right to a transfer. But this is no longer the case. Today, the emphasis is on training, formal education and suitability, including your personal style.

4.7.3 Dilemmas, Causes of Action and Means Used

The counties have defined two exit points in the pension system: one as an age span 63–65 and the other at 65. The occupational pension system in this sector offers incentives for many employees to work until the statutory age but many employees in fact leave before 63/65. Few people stay on until they reach the upper retirement age within their category. The typical exit for the long-term sick is the disability pension.

The dilemmas of Hospital may be found in the combination of an aging personnel, an aging group of patients and budgetary constraints. This leads to a rising intensity of work, which, in turn, creates rising rates of absenteeism due to exhaustion and sickness among the employees. These trends are visible in the exit patterns found in Hospital.

Before proceeding to examine the ways out, which involve a combination of preventive measures, let us first consider the facts about exit. The number of individuals achieving early retirement, due to disability, is very large, nearly as large as the number of those who retire at the statutory pension age. The increase in disability pensions has been very poignant since the early 1980s. Early retirement is most common amongst the nursing aides and the cleaning personnel. The Health Care District has a higher rate of disability pensions than other districts within the county. This may be due to better counselling from the pension officer or to the bad environment in the area (a consequence of several major polluting industries).

The SKAF representatives sometimes suggest that some older women among their members should try to get their sickness and injuries recognized as "work injuries", and demand compensation. But "quite often they answer that they don't want to do this because then '...they (i.e., the supervisor) will get angry with me'." The older women, for instance, do not want to raise this issue with the supervisor or manager and thereby expose themselves to the danger of being disliked or suspected of "scrounging", that is to say, exploiting the welfare system. "Many don't want to use the social insurance system we have, they will come to work, even if they are not able to have a decent life outside the job."

Another union officer gave a graphic description of the consequences of these set of attitudes:

"Sometimes we have meetings for our older members, to inform them about the pension agreement. Then you notice that half of those present will stand up or walk around every five or ten minutes. They have so much pain, in their back or in their shoulders that they can't sit still. But they will not report as sick and they will try to avoid, for as long as possible, taking up sickness benefit."

Certain older female workers feel strongly pressured to quit: "Many of my older colleagues will tell me, almost crying, that their supervisor tried to persuade them to look for and apply for other jobs; to quit 'their' clinic." Why is this? The major reason is that if they are old and sick they cause problems for the supervisor; economical as well as practical. "They want to get rid of them as soon as possible, to get rid of their responsibilities." This can be explained by the economic squeeze that is now put on basic units. If they have people with long-term sickness within them, the basic units must deal with that on their own because of the decentralized procedure.

The preventive efforts take place through the work environment and health policies and two major efforts can be distinguished.

The *Local committee for the work environment and occupational safety* is an organization present in all Swedish workplaces. It is composed of representatives from the employer and the unions concerned. Three (elected) union representatives are employed full time to cover this area and they are paid by the employer. There are 78 elected representatives responsible for the work environment in their units with another 50 in reserve. This is the formal machinery for discussions and negotiations relating to the work environment.

The *Adaptation group* is responsible for taking care of employees who have been sick for longer periods. It is the traditional internal institution handling sickness and exit problems. Hospital has a special fund (APG account) – part of the budget of the district – which is directed specifically to the problems of those employees who can not continue to work in their normal jobs. The 1990 budget for the Adaptation Group was about 7.5 million SEK.

The APG account is handled by a committee, where the unions have representation. During 1989 there were the following number of cases:
- 60 were transferred to other jobs,
- 7 were paid while getting an education or labor market vocational training,
- 9 were paid out of the central APG account, while continuing to work in their old units.

4.7.4 Decentralization and Rehabilitation Policies – The Work Environment Project

Today, decentralization of responsibility has begun and the APG account will probably be abolished. The question arises why? One answer is: As long as it exists there is a temptation for some units to shift the cost and the burden of sick and injured employees on to the APG account. The maintenance section for example has used the APG account more than others, which can be explained by their work situation and sickness patterns.

However, preventive efforts do not end with this. Hospital is attempting with extra effort, to put through its own "*work environment project*". The aim of this project is to teach administrators and the heads of the basic units how to set up a "rehabilitation plan". The clinics are made responsible for their personnel and must find jobs for them within the organization in case of sickness, work injuries etc. They will lose the easier way out of such dilemmas – for example the transfer to a central problem-solving unit (like the APG); or firing people. The basic units will have to plan for this new situation when an institution like the Adaptation group no longer exists. This project is a way for the central personnel management to force and induce, but also to help, the heads of the local units to act in accordance with the new work environment and rehabilitation legislation. The goal of the project, conducted with resources from the Working Life Fund (cf. section 5.4), is to create new routines for handling rehabilitation.

4.7.5 Collaboration between the Social Insurance Office and Hospital

During 1990 a new form of collaboration began between the Health Care District (as the employer) and the Regional Social Insurance Office. The background to this was a government proposal, which placed more emphasis on rehabilitation and reform of the work environment (cf. section 5.4). The new policy emphasizes on keeping people employed and not on accepting the rise in early retirement due to work injuries and sickness.

The work routines of the Local Social Insurance Office (SIO) were also changed at this time. Four SIO employees were allocated to Hospital, to handle its employees, especially its long-term sick cases. Each SIO officer usually handles a random sample of cases, based on their birth dates, but in the new procedure, the officers will try to connect the individual cases with their work. The aim of this change is governed by concerns of rehabilitation. Over time the SIO officers will get to know the specific work environment of their cases much better. In this way they can become involved in establishing new tasks for them at their workplace. The SIO officers are able to finance both retraining (e.g., in the education offered by the Labor Market Board) and rehabilitation schemes (such as special treatment of back injuries etc.).

During mid 1990 Hospital had a backlog of 143 people who had been reported long-term sick, i.e., who had received sickness benefit for more than six months. The immediate action of the SIO was to attempt to look more closely into these cases with the help of doctors and other specialists of the SIO. Some were soon recommended disability pensions, and some were put on a rehabilitation program.

The SIO (and the doctors) defines the criteria for receiving the disability pension. Hospital then will have to take action with regards to those that are judged able to go back to work. This will put new demands on Hospital as an employer and especially on the personnel department. In the future, the SIO's ambition is that their officers will contact each person when he/she has been reported sick for four weeks, or if they have repeated spells of short-term illness.

4.8   Concluding Remarks

The case studies have shed light on different age-related practices in Swedish firms and work organizations. We have focused on situations where age, as a variable, is seen as problematic, due to reorganizations, productivity crises, including patterns of work injuries and sickness. We have also demonstrated the presence in firms of prevention policies. Even more space has, however, been devoted to exit-related practices. This seems to be a paradox, given our insistence on the "Work Society" character of Sweden, and the special role we have accorded to the prevention policies, which aimed at internalizing the age-related dilemmas of the older workforce into firms.

Thus our case studies show *how the pressures towards exits* of the older workforce *are managed in firms*. Of course, exits occur on a wide scale. But our cases also show how they are being forestalled, as well as prevented, through concrete measures and if nothing else, they were being postponed and delayed; thereby slowing the exit rates. Thus, the case histories illustrate how the balance between accommodating and preventive policies is struck in practice.

However, one major aspect of prevention has been underestimated through our focus on firms. This is the labor market oriented prevention, what we will characterize as the *firm-external prevention*. By this we denote those policies that keep marginalized groups in the labor force, through subsidized employment and sheltered jobs, and the use of labor market training and education, to minimize open unemployment. Some exit routes from a specific job or firm, however, presuppose that the firm-external prevention policies exist as a next step. The Employment Security Fund often supports exit from one firm – but in combination with re-employment at another job, or retraining.

The cases illustrate *the combination of accommodation and firm-internal as well as firm-external prevention policies*, that together define the way Sweden deals with the older workforce and (early) exit situations. Furthermore, the cases give examples of emerging trends and dilemmas that modify the Swedish Policy Regime and have consequences for the Swedish model. Some of these trends and dilemmas will be dealt with in the concluding section of our chapter. We will discuss the effects of changing work processes, new managerial strategies and accentuated decentralization on the older workforce. This will point to the new direction in prevention policies – with the Social Insurance Office as coordinator and with "work environment" and "rehabilitation" as key items.

Table 25: Costs for Disability Pensions, Work Injury Annuities and Sickness Benefits 1980—1990. Milliard SEK (current prices)

| Year | Disability Pensions | Work Injury | | Sickness Benefits |
		Annuities	Sick Benefits	
1985	17.9	1.1	0.7	17.9
1986	19.7	1.3	1.6	20.0
1987	21.1	1.6	2.9	23.1
1988	23.3	2.2	4.7	31.1
1989	26.2	2.9	5.4	33.9
1990	–	3.7	6.2	34.9

Source: RFV
Note: In 1991 Sickness Benefits Costs Fell to 31.9 Milliards SEK; this can be Attributed to Changes in Sickness Insurance Regulations from March 1991.

5 Current Issues and Future Trends

5.1 The State Dilemma – Increased Costs

During the 1980s public costs for the major exit forms have grown significantly. Disability pensions and work injury life annuities are the main components of this "cost explosion". Sick benefits show the same sharp increase (table 25). Total costs for these schemes are straining the public budget, which has made a change in priorities a government issue.

Public costs can be cut *through closing some exit options and tightening eligibility to others.*

(1) The growing uneasiness with early retirement was shown when the combination of unemployment benefit for 450 days, followed by disability pension (i.e., "unemployment pension"), was abolished in 1990. At that time an over-heated labor market was the immediate precondition, but the decision to end unemployment pensions indicated a general change in attitudes towards early exit.

(2) Eligibility to the "health disability pension" has been tightened; stricter medical terms have applied since 1991 and a minimum age of 60 years has been enforced. This pension is planned to be phased in with the work injury insurance. By making it more difficult to qualify for the more generous work injury scheme, a certain transfer to the less costly disability pension system is expected to take place, thereby, reducing the total public costs.

(3) The state wants to direct a larger number of exit-prone individuals into the scheme of early drawing. Early drawing is in principle just an actuarial redistribution of the individual's pension benefits over more pension years and involves no extra costs to the state. If the alternative is a

state-financed early exit the state will gain substantial amounts, by directing more exits into the scheme of early drawing, thereby shifting the costs onto the individuals. This is planned in two steps.

(a) Some early retirement cases that formerly were "full" cases are hoped to end up as "half" cases, when it has become possible to combine half early retirement with half early drawing in 1992.

(b) The part-time pension has in 1992 been questioned. The non-socialist government wants to abolish it and half early drawing is mentioned as the distinct alternative.

To sum up the new trend: The state wants the number of exits to decrease, but if early exit occurs, the cost shall to a larger extent be born by the individual himself.

5.2   The Firm Dilemma – Decreased Internal Transferability

Today, Sweden witnesses changes, within industrial and service production, similar to those in other countries. Our case studies demonstrate that one common feature is the *decentralizing of the responsibility for profits and efficiency* to lower-level production units. This is obvious in all five cases. It includes the decentralization of personnel policy to the same units. Together, these circumstances determine the employment and personnel strategies of firms, which affect the older workforce. On the one hand, there is a pressure within the Swedish Policy Regime on firms to internalize certain public policy objectives. On the other hand, there is a spontaneous strategy by firms to externalize some of their problems.

The technical-organizational changes in firms tend to eliminate many socalled "*easy jobs*"; those that have been used as the internal gradual exit routes. Many of these "easy jobs" were located in intermediary functions within firms, such as, inventories, secretary pools, attendance, repairs etc. Workers, in the past, have been given lighter white-collar tasks or have been transferred to less burdensome manual jobs. Refuse Collection gives a picture of extensive transfers from regular refuse collection to container transport; housing estate services; repair, stock, garage work; and the "street division", in cases of disability or low productivity. They are all examples of more or less "sheltered" work. Steel Mill reveals the same. The general pattern is that individuals are moved from a special division to supporting, complementary tasks, in cases of disability or decreased productivity.

Decentralization makes the process of internal gradual exit much more difficult. Decentralization is linked to *local responsibility for profits and efficiency*. This makes lower levels within an organization less inclined to take responsibility for "problematic" employees (those with low productivity, sickness problems etc.) and they also want to preserve their "easy jobs" for their own employees, which makes internal replacements generally more difficult for these groups. The personnel programs of local governments, on the other hand, cover wide areas, and transfers have usually taken place between entities. Transfers are the standard solutions in the public sector. Due to decentralization, the personnel policy of replacement within local governments has almost collapsed.

Modern *"just-in-time" strategies* imply cutting down stocks of inputs, of intermediate products, and of finished products. The just-in-time strategies lead to demands for more flexibility, therefore team-work is the answer (cf. Steel Mill and High Tech) to this demand in the most competitive firms of our cases. This general trend penetrates public and private firms and bodies, less subjected to competition, but still under pressure to increase productivity and efficiency. In this process the "classical chain of command", not least the supervisor position tends to be made redundant. The intermediary level is out, the *"work-team"* is a new key concept.

The drive towards technical rationalization and organizational decentralization inclines to marginalize certain individuals:
- with low formal education,
- with limited ability to adapt to new conditions,
- not willing or able to learn new techniques in the way that firms want them to (cf. Steel Mill),
- not willing or able to participate in new and changing forms of organization (sometimes the case with older foremen and supervisors), especially relevant for older white-collar workers with routine jobs, for whom the changing boundaries between workshop and office might be socially problematic.

In firms, internal job shifts were the traditional solution for marginalized employees. Can work-teams be expected to cope with this problem – much the older worker's problem? The answer is in the negative. Low level units, such as work-teams, seem to externalize their personnel problems within the firm, but the level that could handle these claims is slowly disappearing.

Given the compressed Swedish wage structure and the rather high level of total labor costs, we should perhaps expect that the changes discussed above would lead to an even faster marginalization of older employees in Sweden than in other countries. Adaptation to declining competence and productivity of an employee can be compensated by a lower wage – and if that road is closed, the dilemma must be handled in other ways.

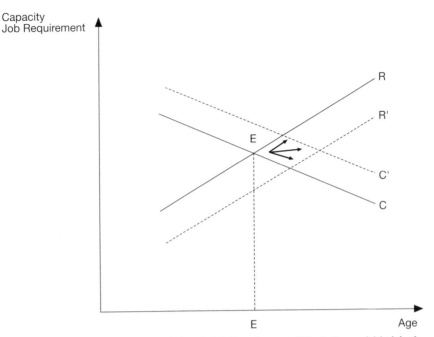

Chart 1: Age, Individual Capacity (C) and Job Requirement (R); A General Model of the Older Workforce Dilemma in Firms

5.3   Age, Capacity and Job Requirements – A Model for Understanding Exit Dilemmas in Work Organizations

The model in chart 1 links age of employees to (1) changes in the demands on capacity and (2) changes in job requirements. This, we suggest, is a likely pattern for *exit threatened employees* 50–65 in many work organizations.

Over a period of time, a job position in a work organization normally demands increased competence, work capacity, productivity etc. This is shown by the *job requirement line* (R) sloping upwards. At the same time work capacity, competence and productivity of the average employee in a given job declines over time – *the capacity line* (C) is sloping downwards. At a certain age the capacity of the individual falls short of the requirements. At this point (E) we find "the firm-preferred exit point". Beyond (E), with increasing age, the gap between (individual) capacity and job requirements widens (cf. the REC-angle in chart 1).

The problem that this widening gap implies can be solved in different ways. We regard the different solutions as *functional alternatives*. The problem is illustrated for one individual. For the firm it generally appears as a problem of the workforce as a whole.

We can distinguish three alternative solutions:

A) Externalizing the problem through exit,
B) Internal solutions to the problem through,
B1) Changing job requirements,
B2) Changing the capacity of employees (job-specific or general).

Externalization simply means that firms close the gap by dismissing individuals when they reach or approach their individual E-points. This is the *exit-solution*. When individuals reach this point, firms are even willing to subsidize exits. Steel Mill gave a concrete picture of how far a company is willing to subsidize an early exit for some of its employees. The same can be seen in the practice of early retirement at Bank. However, the State Dilemma formulated in section 5.1 above implies that we should expect the State to block "topped-up exits" from becoming the preferred solution. This is one way in which we can interpret the closing of the alternative of "unemployment pension".

Firm-internal solutions can shift the two lines in chart 1 (as shown by the dotted lines), thereby pushing the E-point to a later age. The complete success of an internal strategy implies pushing the point to the statutory pension age of the individuals.

The "spontaneous" firm internal solution is *internal transfers*. These can shift the requirement line (R) downwards, since the new job that the individual is transferred to generally implies easier tasks than the job he is leaving. It could come as a result of moving to a new position or to a part-time job. This might also lead to a shift of the capacity line (C) upwards, since a new job position can change the set of requirements that the individuals have to respond to, thereby increasing his job specific capacity. A new job might also increase motivation and thereby capacity.

Internal transfers have been part of the personnel policy of many larger firms. We talk of them as "spontaneous" because they have been part of personnel programs *without* intervention from the State. It has, as was shown in Steel Mill, been the traditional gradual internal exit route. Now, our case studies indicate that this solution is increasingly blocked through technical change and changes in the work organization within firms (cf. the Firm Dilemma in section 5.2).

Then, what internal solutions are left? We will now come to state-induced internal changes in the firms, i.e., changes coming about as results of *internalizing strategies*. They can also be illustrated through the model in chart 1.

(1) The requirement line can be lowered if the State *subsidizes jobs for*

specific groups of employees, e.g., older workers. This is part of existing prevention policies (cf. section 2.2.3 above). However, such a policy can become a cost problem for the State and it is therefore likely to remain a measure of minor importance.

(2) The capacity line can be shifted upwards by *upgrading* individual capacities through *internal education.* We have seen such efforts in action, partly stimulated by the State (cf. Steel Mill), partly (and recently) through initiatives by Employment Security Funds. *Vocational training* through the Labor Market Training Schemes (AMU) belong to this category.

Both these strategies often imply a change of job *and* firm. Getting a job with employment subsidy might involve a change of employer. Training and education often aim at giving the individual new possibilities of leaving the firm for a new job, or even becoming self-employed (cf. High Tech and Steel Mill). Standing alone, these programs will only be a minor element in solving the two dilemmas.

However, none of the so far described alternatives can obviously solve the older worker exit problem. Instead, new forms of prevention have been proposed, changing the *work environment* and efforts of *rehabilitation.* In relation to the exit problem in chart 1, successful prevention implies that the decrease in capacity is slowed down (cf. physical deterioration). Instead of shifting the capacity line (C) upwards in chart 1, we should rather illustrate this alternative through a decrease of the slope of C, i.e., giving it a flatter shape.

5.4   The Social Democratic Heritage – Renewed Emphasis on Prevention within Firms

Besides being a cost problem early exit has become a threat to the full-time, full-employment pillar of the "Work Society" ideology. The large number of early exits has led to a lowered average actual pension age of the Swedish workforce, even taking the rising actual pension age of public employees into account (cf. section 2.4). And this has not been due to a reform ideology from above, but due to practices from below, where firms, corporatist bodies and employees are the main actors.

Ambitions to reduce costs have created a *renewed emphasis on prevention policies*, especially regarding work environment and rehabilitation, forming a way out of the exit/cost dilemma and adhering to the "Work Society" logic. In 1988, the new direction was set out in the report "Early and coordinated rehabilitation" (SOU 1988: 41). The report emphasized cooperation between health and social services, as well as employment and insurance offices, together with firms. These actors were, in such a setting, supposed to plan more effectively for rehabilitation. In 1989 the Pension

Commission published a report on disability pensions and early exit, arguing that state policy ought to "...counteract the ongoing marginalization of
older workers from working life" (SOU 1989: 101, p.12). New laws regulating these two areas were passed by the Swedish Parliament in 1991 (cf.
Proposition 1990/91: 140 and 1990/91: 141). The goal is to *prevent exits
through reorganization of the work process and work organization*. The
argument was that preventive action could, if it was successful, decrease the
number of individuals having to exit due to disability and work injuries,
thereby reducing the costs of the compensation. We will point to two
characteristic and illuminating institutional developments in this field.

5.4.1 Preventing Sickness and Physical Deterioration as Causes for Early Exit – Designing a New Role for the Social Insurance Office

Social Insurance Offices (SIOs) have traditionally taken on a passive role in
exit related situations. They have given service, but not until the matter is
almost settled. With the new policy (that early retirement ought to decrease) the office has to take a new and more active role at an earlier stage.

This new formula can be seen in Hospital above, which is actually a pilot
project in renewing the role of SIO. SIOs normally handled their number
of cases randomly, but in the new procedure, they work with a group of
employees in the same firm. In practice, they try to connect the sickness
pattern of individual cases with the work environment. It is suggested that
over time the SIO officers will get to know the specific work environment
of their cases better and that they should be able to influence work
conditions, and even work organization, within firms. The SIO can use their
control over the financing of retraining and rehabilitation measures as a
way to influence changes in work organization.

In the new law on rehabilitation, the Social Insurance Offices have
become the coordinating public authority. The classic accommodating authority has now to proclaim prevention. This close cooperation between a
public agency such as the Social Insurance Office and a large employer
represents a new direction in Swedish policy. It is a case of *penetration of
Social Welfare Agencies into the work organization of firms*. This is the
organizational response to the new direction in prevention policies.

5.4.2 The 1990 Working Life Fund

An important new component in stimulating rehabilitation in the early
1990s, using subsidies to encourage changes within Swedish firms, is the
Working Life Fund, established in 1990.

This Fund is designed to be temporary, and to complement law-bound, compulsory measures within firms. A temporary work environment fee, paid by employers, during the period September 1989-December 1990, is the financial basis of the Fund. Starting to distribute financial support in early 1991, the Fund is supposed to have a life-time of around five to six years distributing around 2–2.5 milliard SEK a year. Support from the Fund is supposed to be linked to firm-based financial contributions. As a net calculation, the Fund will subsidize around 30% of the resulting firm-based programs.

The Fund is organized county-wise. It gives support to mainly work-rehabilitation (80–90%), though it also supports work-environment projects. Change in work-organization and education efforts to increase job-rotation are subsidized. The Funds support should be distributed in proportion to size of branches within private and public sectors, as well as amongst the two sectors. Almost all applications, that have not fallen outside of the Funds' field of operation have been approved during 1991.

5.5   Future Trends – Clashing Trends?

A Liberal/Conservative government took power in autumn 1991, proclaiming its adherence to the "work-for-all strategy", in a period of rapidly increasing unemployment. How will the new government deal with the "Social Democratic heritage" of extended prevention through work environment and rehabilitation?

Implementation of these goals through the use of Funds will probably be given less priority, because of the ideological resistance to state and trade union directed redistribution through Funds (cf. section 3.3). Pressures for changes from firms, e.g., externalization of problems, will be expected to meet less resistance, given the more pro-employer orientation of the new government (cf. Introduction).

The essence is still a situation of clashing trends, given the existing Policy Regime. On the one hand, the Swedish *state* aims at forcing and inducing firms to *internalize the exit problem* through rehabilitation and work environment reforms. On the other hand, the *lower level units within the firm* aim at *externalizing* redundant individuals. This creates a management dilemma, with far-reaching social consequences, which is a central paradox coming out of our case studies. It has been embedded in a strong Policy Regime, which keeps externalization within bounds, and thereby keeps the exit rate rather low.

It is hard to evaluate the relative strength of the forces mentioned. How strong will the pressures on firms to internalize the older workers be, i.e., keeping them employed? How strong will the pressures from within firms to externalize their "older worker problem" become? Experience from other countries suggests that the development of the unemployment rate, the volume of employment in society, or in broader terms the survival of the Swedish "Work Society" is the basic determinant. Existing evidence from comparative social research indicates that a recession with increasing unemployment, combined with decreasing State ambitions on prevention, will result in rising levels of early exit among the older Swedish workforce in the 1990s.

References

Brulin, Göran (1989). *Från den 'svenska modellen' till företagskorporativism? Facket och den nya företagsledningsstrategin.* Lund: Arkiv.
Brulin, Göran and Tommy Nilsson (1991). *Mot en ny svensk modell - Arbete och förhandlingssystem i förändring.* Kristianstad: Rabén & Sjögren.
Carlgren, Andreas (1989). *Att ta vara på de äldre i arbetslivet.* Lidingö: M-gruppen.
Edebalk, Per Gunnar and Eskil Wadensjö (1989). *Arbetsmarknadsförsäkringar.* Stockholm: DS 1989: 68.
Esping-Andersen, Gösta (1990). *The Three Worlds of Welfare Capitalism.* Cambridge: Polity Press.
Gordon, Margaret S. (1988). *Social Security Policies in Industrial Countries: A Comparative Analysis.* Cambridge, N.Y.: Cambridge University Press.
Guillemard, Anne-Marie (1989). *The Trend Towards Early Labour Force Withdrawal and the Reorganization of the Life Course: A Cross-national Analysis.* In: P. Johnson et. al. (eds), *Workers versus Pensioners. Integrational Justice in an Ageing World.* Manchester/New York: Manchester University Press: 163–180.
Hedström, Peter (1980). *Förtidspension – välfärd eller ofärd?* Stockholm: Institutet för Social forskning 1980-08-25.
Hedström, Peter (1987). *Disability Pension: Welfare or Misfortune.* In: R. Eriksson et. al. (eds), *The Scandinavian Model.* M. E. Sharp: Amok and London: 208–220.
Järnegren, Anders; Angelöw, Bosse and Lars G. Johansson (1990). *Övertalighet och arbetsmiljö.* Lund: Sociologiska institutionen, Rapport till arbetsmiljöfonden.
Jacobs, Klaus; Kohli, Martin and Martin Rein (1991). *The Evolution of Early Exit: A Comparative Analysis of Labour Participation Patterns.* In: M. Kohli et. al. (eds), *Time for Retirement.* Cambridge, N.Y.: Cambridge University Press: 36–66.

Johnson, Paul; Conrad, Christoph and David Thomson (eds.) (1989). *Workers versus Pensioners. Integrational Justice in an Ageing World*. Manchester/New York: Manchester University Press.

Kohli, Martin; Rein, Martin; Guillemard, Anne-Marie and Herman van Gunsteren (eds.) (1991). *Time for Retirement*. Cambridge, N.Y.: Cambridge University Press.

Kruse, Agneta and Lars Söderström (1989). *Early Retirement in Sweden*. In: W. Schmähl (ed.), *Redefining the Process of Retirement. An International Perspective*. Heidelberg: Springer Verlag: 39–61.

Laczko, Frank and Chris Philipson (1991). *Changing Work and Retirement*. Milton Keynes: Open University Press.

Marklund, Staffan and Stefan Svallfors (1987). *Dual Welfare*. Umeå: Research report no 94, Dept of Sociology, Umeå University.

Myrdal, Alva and Gunnar Myrdal (1934). *Kris i befolkningsfrågan*. Stockholm: Bonniers.

Nilsson, Tommy (1985). *Från kamratförening till facklig rörelse*. Lund: Arkiv.

OECD (1990). *Employment Outlook*, July 1990. Paris: OECD.

OECD (1991). *Employment Outlook*, July 1991. Paris: OECD.

OECD (1988). *Reforming Public Pensions*. Paris: OECD.

Offe, Claus and Helmut Wiesenthal (1980). *Two Logics of Collective Action: Theoretical Notes on Social Class and Organizational Form*. In: *Political Power and Social Theory* Vol. 1 (1980): 67–115.

Olofsson, Gunnar (1991). *Firms, the State and the Early Exit Pattern in Sweden*. Lund: Working paper.

Olofsson, Gunnar and Jan Petersson (1992). *Seven Swedish Cases*. Berlin: Working Paper, Wissenschaftszentrum Berlin für Sozialforschung (forthcoming).

Petersson, Jan (1990). *On Incentives to Early Exit*. Lund: Working paper.

Pettersson, Marianne (1981). *Deltidsarbetet i Sverige*. Stockholm: Arbetslivscentrum.

Proposition 1990/91: 140. *Arbetsmiljö och rehabilitering*.

Proposition 1990/91: 141. *Rehabilitering och rehabiliteringsersättning*.

Scharpf, Fritz W. (1987). *Sozialdemokratische Krisenpolitik in Westeuropa*. Frankfurt a.M.: Campus.

SCB [Statistika Centalbyran] (1991). *Statistika meddelanden AM 62 SM 9101*.

SOU (1988: 41). *Tidig och samordnad rehabilitering*. Stockholm: Allmänna förlaget.

SOU (1989: 101). *Förtidspension och rörlig pensionsålder*. Stockholm: Allmänna förlaget.

SOU (1991: 82). *Drivkrafter för produktivitet och välstånd*. Stockholm: Allmänna förlaget.

Sundström, Marianne (1987). *A Study in the Growth of Part-Time Work in Sweden*. Stockholm: Arbetslivscentrum.

Tegle, Stig (1985). *Part-Time Employment - An Economic Analysis of Weekly Working Hours in Sweden 1963-1982*. Lund: Studentlitteratur.

Therborn, Göran (1985). *Why are Some People more Unemployed than Others?* London: Verso.

Titmuss, Richard M. (1974). *Social Policy. An Introduction*. London: Allen & Unwin.

Wadensjö, Eskil (1991). *Early Exit from the Labour Force in Sweden*. In: M. Kohli et al. (eds.), *Time for Retirement*. Cambridge, N.Y: Cambridge University Press: 284–323.

6 Japan: Shukko, Teinen and Re-Employment

Takeshi Kimura, Ikuro Takagi, Masato Oka and Maki Omori

The overall project on "firms, the state and the changing age structure" started from the Western European continental view that the trend of workers' early exit from work to retirement is the predominant tendency and pattern in the employment and retirement structure of industrialized countries. The Japanese experiences however provide quite a different picture. While we can also see some minor trends of early exit among the elderly male workers aged over 60, the predominent trend here is apparently the increase of the mandatory retirement ("Teinen") age to 60 in the

Table 1: Change in Labor Force Participation Rate by Gender and Age Group between 1965 and 1988 (Annual Average, %)

Age G.	Males			Females		
	1965	1973	1988	1965	1973	1988
15 – 19	36.3	25.2	17.2	35.8	28.0	16.5
20 – 24	85.8	79.9	71.0	70.2	67.3	73.7
25 – 29	96.8	98.4	96.2	49.0	44.4	58.2
30 – 34	97.0	98.3	97.0	51.1	46.9	50.9
35 – 39	97.1	98.0	97.5	59.6	56.1	61.3
40 – 44	97.0	97.0	97.5	63.2	62.2	68.1
45 – 49	96.8	96.5	97.2	60.9	62.7	69.3
50 – 54	95.0	92.2	96.0	55.8	58.7	63.3
55 – 59	90.0	81.1	91.3	49.8	50.4	50.9
60 – 64	82.8	46.6	71.1	39.8	38.4	38.6
65 –	56.3		35.8	21.6	16.7	15.7
Total	81.7	82.1	77.1	50.6	48.2	48.9

Source: Office of Prime Ministry; Survey Report on Labor Force for the Fiscal Year 1989.

firms in the 1980s and the adjustment processes resulting from this regulatory shift.

Against the background of the rapid aging of Japanese society – with higher increase rates than in Western industrialized countries – the subject of this chapter is the responses to the changes in the age-configuration of the companies, the workers and the state caused by the rapid aging of Japanese society. The first response, which is ongoing, is the raising of the "Teinen" age, a company-ruled factor for Japanese workers' retirement. The focus is on why the "Teinen" age has been raised and how large Japanese companies, strengthening the rigidity in Japanese life-time employment thereby, are striving to keep flexibility in work organization. This will be discussed in Section 1, 2 and 3. The second possible response, which still remains much-debated, is the raising of the public pension eligibility age, a more important state-ruled factor for retirement. This will be discussed in the final section.

1   Country Introduction

1.1   Factors for Retirement in Japan

1.1.1 Labor Force Participation Rate for Older Males

See table 1. Although our focus is on the older male, the trends for the other age/gender groups are also to be mentioned. The rates for males and females in the youngest age group have drastically declined because more young people have preferred to go on to higher education. Since the 1970s the rates for females, except for those in the youngest and the oldest age groups, the members of the latter mostly being self-employed, have steadily risen. More women tend to stay in or re-enter the labor market, a trend similar to that in Europe and the U.S. More worthy of note in an international perspective is, first, the high rate for males aged 55–59 who used to be affected by the Japanese company-specific practice of "Teinen", and second, the declining but still high rate of males aged 60 and over, especially 60–64, who are generally covered by public old age pension schemes.

Moreover these rates and their trends are to be seen against the background of the rapid aging of the population and the rising percentage of older employees in the workforce. (See Table 2)

1.1.2 "Teinen" and Labor Force Participation Rate

All of the large companies and many of the medium-sized companies in Japan enforce a "Teinen" age at which to terminate employment for all of their regular employees. "Teinen" marks the end of the first and major stage of their working life. But it does not necessarily mean their final retirement from the labor market. The "Teinen" age used to be about 55. However, it effected only a slight reduction in the labor force participation rate for males aged 55–59 (see table 1). This means that the majority of those who left their company at "Teinen" found new employment in large companies on a non-regular basis or in small to medium-sized companies. Today 60 is the dominant "Teinen" age. But this raising has not increased further the rate for the age group. Moreover, many people continue to work after the new "Teinen" age of 60. Table 2 shows that the majority of them are working in small to medium-sized companies.

Table 2: Distribution of Older Male Employees by Size of Company (Number of Persons Engaged) in Selected Years (in ten thousands of persons and in percentage)

	Total	50 – 54aged	55 – 59aged	60 – 64aged	65aged
(1973)					
Total	2381 (100.0%)	144 (6.0%)	113 (4.7%)	80 (3.4%)	67 (2.8%)
Size	100.0%	100.0%	100.0%	100.0%	100.0%
1 – 29	729 30.6%	40 27.8%	38 33.6%	34 42.5%	33 49.2%
30 – 99	352 14.0%	21 14.6%	21 18.6%	16 20.0%	13 19.4%
100 – 999	448 18.8%	23 15.9%	21 18.6%	16 20.0%	11 16.4%
1000 –	551 23.0%	37 25.7%	17 15.0%	7 8.7%	5 7.4%
Gov.*	301 12.6%	23 16.0%	16 14.2%	8 10.0%	5 7.4%
Unemp.*	43 (100.0%)	2 (4.6%)	3 (7.0%)	3 (7.0%)	2 (4.6%)
(1978)					
Total	2493 (100.0%)	211 (8.4%)	119 (4.8%)	76 (3.0%)	69 (2.8%)
Size	100.0%	100.0%	100.0%	100.0%	100.0%
1 – 29	818 32.8%	59 28.0%	42 35.0%	35 46.0%	37 53.6%
30 – 99	374 15.0%	31 14.7%	22 18.3%	16 21.0%	13 18.9%
100 – 999	463 18.6%	34 16.1%	20 16.7%	13 17.1%	9 13.9%
1000 –	519 20.0%	49 23.2%	17 14.2%	5 6.6%	4 5.8%
Gov.*	319 12.8%	38 18.0%	18 15.0%	7 9.3%	6 8.7%
Unemp.*	81 (100.0%)	6 (7.4%)	7 (8.6%)	8 (9.9%)	4 (4.9%)
(1988)					
Total	2839 (100.0%)	288 (10.1%)	228 (8.0%)	112 (3.9%)	74 (2.6%)
Size	100.0%	100.0%	100.0%	100.0%	100.0%
1 – 29	885 31.2%	90 31.3%	74 32.4%	48 43.0%	43 58.1%
30 – 99	433 15.3%	45 15.6%	39 17.2%	22 19.6%	13 17.1%
100 – 999	595 20.9%	59 20.5%	45 19.2%	22 19.6%	11 14.4%
1000 –	594 20.9%	58 20.1%	36 15.8%	10 8.9%	3 4.0%
Gov.*	332 11.7%	36 12.5%	34 14.9%	10 8.9%	4 5.4%
Unemp.*	91 (100.0%)	7 (7.7%)	10 (11.0%)	14 (15.4%)	3 (3.3%)

* Gov. is Government Sector, and Unemp. is Unemployed.
Source: Ministry of Labor; Survey Report on Employment Structure for the Fiscal Year 1989.

1.1.3   Public Pension and Labor Force Participation Rate

The Japanese public pension scheme for private sector employees started very late and in its initial stage the benefit level was extremely low. This as well as a high percentage of self-employed among the older people explains the high rate of labor participation for males aged 60 and over in the past.

Today the scheme covers the majority of retired employees aged 60 and over and the benefit level is, on average, sufficient to support them. It is supposed that this as well as the decreasing percentage of self-employed has caused the decline in the rate. Despite this, many older people are working. One reason for this is that the scheme is designed for wage earners aged 60 and over to be eligible for partial benefit unless their earnings exceed a certain limit. We will return to this point later.

1.1.4 The Significance of the Difference in Size of Companies

In Japan, the size of the company in which one works directly relates to one's working conditions.

First, if one is a large company regular employee, one's employment will be guaranteed until the "Teinen" age and one's annual pay rise and promotion will be strongly age-oriented. At "Teinen" one will receive a lump-sum retirement allowance and thereafter benefit from the company pension. In the small companies, there is a contrasting picture as you will see in the case study. The turn-over rate is very high. The pay is much lower and the pay rise is only weakly age-oriented, as figure 1 shows. There is an extremely low retirement allowance or no allowance at all. There is no company pension.

Second, the age structure differs according to the company size as table 2 shows. Large companies have a younger workforce, since they have been in a privileged position to be able to secure young labor and to eject the older workers by "Teinen", while the small companies have had to depend on the older workers. Further, table 2 hints that many of the employees in large companies have re-entered the smaller companies for a second period of employment after they reached "Teinen".

1.1.5 Retirement: A Gradual Process

Accordingly, neither the "Teinen" age nor the public pension benefit age marked nor do mark Japanese workers' final retirement from working very clearly. Rather, after "Teinen" many of them stay in the company on a non-regular basis or re-enter the smaller company, with or without public pension benefit, until their final retirement. And, as a whole, they are retiring earlier and earlier.

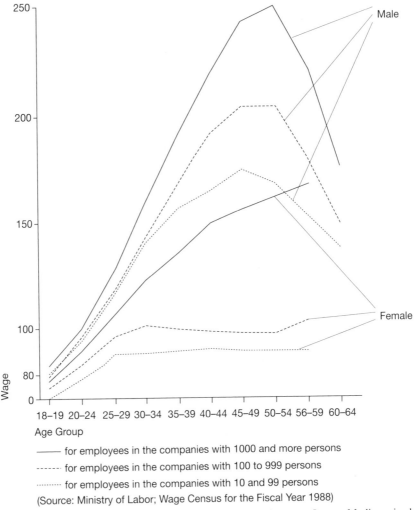

Figure 1: Differences in the Average Wage-Age Profile between Large, Medium-sized and Small Companies in 1988 (100 = the average wage for the large company males aged 20-24)

1.2   Company Regime: Life-time Employment and "Teinen"

1.2.1 Two Components of Life-time Employment

The well-known life-time employment in large Japanese companies has two components: employment security until the "Teinen" age and the treatment of regular employees on an age-oriented basis. First, large companies usually hire school leavers only and train and re-train the employees on the assumption that they will continue to work at the same company until "Teinen". "No firing" is a norm among large companies and the enterprise-based Japanese unions have assigned highest priority to employment security for the regular force.

Second, the level of pay annually rises for every regular employee, in addition to pay rises achieved by bargaining. Roughly speaking, the level of pay for an employee depends on (1) his length of service (accordingly, his age), (2) his location on the promotion ladder (two distinct ladders for white-collar and blue-collar workers) and (3) the rating of his performance and attitude by the senior. Factor (2) itself is composed of factors (1) and (3). Therefore, on the one hand, every regular employee more or less enjoys an annual pay rise and the opportunity for promotion as he ages. The employment security until the "Teinen" age and a firm prospect for an annual pay rise and promotion motivate a strong commitment and devotion to their company among Japanese workers. On the other hand, great differences in pay rise, the amount of bi-annual bonus and promotion according to the rating of the performance and attitude of the workers stimulate harsh competition among individual workers and groups of workers.

1.2.2 Aging and Productivity: Our Hypothesis

Traditionally this age-orientation has been interpreted by means of the hypothesis of individual productivity development with aging. However, from our case studies, the Japanese management seems to have a perception that the productivity of individual workers peaks out in their 40s or early 50s. This means that there is a disparity between the amount of pay for older workers and their individual productivity. In our hypothesis the large companies have solved this problem by assigning to the experienced older workers the role of team-supervisor; he must extract the maximal productivity from his team, on the one hand, by maintaining the harmony of the team and, on the other, by stimulating the competition among the team members by means of the rating of their performance and attitude.

This age-mix, a combination of a highly paid supervisor and low paid younger forces, might be more or less relevant also for the counterparts in other countries. However, it seems to be of strategic importance for the organization of large Japanese companies, which must by all means maintain the age-orientation to integrate their regular employees. This hypothesis can explain why a large Japanese company is organized like a pyramid with a large number of low managerial staff at the bottom and a small number of high managerial staff at the apex. The precondition for this age-mix to be maintained and function well is the increase in size of the labor force due to the incessant inflow of young and cheap workers, what really took place in the era of rapidly growing economy.

1.2.3 Flexibility in Work Organization

Another important feature of large Japanese companies is the extreme flexibility in their work organization.

First, over-time work is a traditional cushion to adapt to quantitative change in demand.

Second, personnel reshuffling takes place very frequently, in the form of short-term job rotation, seasonal and yearly transfers across sections and plants and even across companies ("Shukko"). The reshuffling is a means for training and re-training workers since Japanese companies aim to develop their employees' ability to adapt to various duties. At the same time, it is an integral part of the promotion ladder. But the reshuffling is, among others, an essential means to adapt to the changes in the demand structure and technology. Thus, a large company itself forms an "internal labor market" in which its workforce is incessantly moving.

Third, the regular employees are those covered by life-time employment as mentioned above. But regular female workers are only partly covered since they were and, in many cases, still are forced to quit on marriage, as the case of our regional bank will show. In addition, in a large company there are a large number of people working who belong to the other categories such as non-regular employees with the employment contract renewed annually, seasonal workers and part-timers. Recruited from the external labor market, they are placed out of life-time employment and form a cushion for adjustment.

1.2.4 Inter-company Relationship: "Quasi-Internal Labor Market"

"Shukko" refers to the practice where Company A puts its employee temporarily on the employment roll with Company B while retaining his status as a regular employee of Company A. Company A pays the difference if the wage in Company B is lower.

A large Japanese company usually has a host of subsidiaries (e.g., the biggest iron and steel company, Nippon Steel has more than 200). More than half of them are of small size with less than 100 employees and the working conditions for their regular employees are, generally speaking, worse and less age-oriented than those in their "parent companies". In addition, most of the workers on the production processes are part-timers.

These have been built or acquired in order to go into promising but risky business fields, to delegate the sales sections, to separate labor-intensive and unprofitable processes and so on. Moreover, there are a considerable number of sub-contractors which depend on the large company for their survival. The subsidiaries and the sub-contractors form a group centering on their parent company. Each company of the group might have some autonomy, but it is possible to say that, at least from the parent company point of view, division of labor is organized on a group-wide scale under the instructions and guidance of the parent company. Originally a parent company sent and still sends his employees on "Shukko" to its satellites to keep up the personnel ties with them and to give managerial and techno-logical advice and guidance. A parent company is, so to speak, the head and its "Shukko" workers form the nerve system to convey the instruction to and supervise the group companies, the hands and feet. Thus, from the parent company point of view, these satellites form a "quasi-internal labor market" in the sense that a portion of regular employees incessantly move across companies.

However, since the mid-1970s another version of "Shukko" has been developing for shedding the middle-aged and older workers from the parent companies, although it has never been explicitly distinguished from the original one.

1.2.5 "Teinen": Ejection of Older Workers

"Teinen" is for a company to terminate the employment of every regular employee at a specified age. It used to be about 55. A large company usually paid a leaver a lump-sum which was calculated on the basis of his final pay and length of service. Accordingly the lump-sum payment paid to the leaver at "Teinen" ("retirement allowance") amounted to the maximum possible, equivalent to 30–50 months pay. This large amount of money was a compensation for ejection by "Teinen".

In the 1960s, when successive pay improvements and higher numbers of employees increased the large companies' liability for retirement allow-ances, some companies began to substitute the annual payment for a portion of the lump-sum given at "Teinen". Two government measures gave decisive encouragement to this move. First, the contribution to the com-pany pension fund was given a tax write-off. Second, the 1966 legislation allowed individual companies to establish a Welfare Adjustment Pension Fund to operate the earning-related portion of the public Welfare Pension on the condition that the Fund provided benefit 30 percent higher than the statutory. So the public pension was fused with company pensions and a portion of the lump-sum payment became incorporated into the additional

Welfare Pension benefit. Since then many of the large companies have built up the fund. Today an average retiree from a large company benefits from a statutory and a company-added Welfare pension and/or a tax write-off company pension, in addition to the lump-sum retirement allowance at "Teinen".

1.3   State Regime

The following three age-related state policies will be discussed next: (1) the public old age pension schemes, (2) unemployment benefit and (3) the employment promotion policy for older workers by means of "Gyosei-shido" (administrative guidance), subsidy programs and legislations.

1.3.1 Public Pension Schemes

Before the 1985–86 reform, there were two main public old age pension schemes for the private sector. The National Pension scheme, established late in 1961, was to provide a fixed-sum to the self-employed who contributed 25 years. The Welfare Pension scheme, established in 1942, extended a fixed-sum plus earning-related benefit to the employees who contributed 20 years. (The result of the reform will be mentioned in the next subsection.) As to the Japanese public pension for the employees, Welfare Pension, three features are to be mentioned for comparison with its European counterparts.

First, the requirement for benefit is one's age, which was and still is today 60 as a provisional arrangement, but is not necessarily one's retirement. Firstly, since 1965 a wage earner of the age of 65 and over can receive full benefit unless his monthly earnings exceed a certain limit. If his earnings do exceed this he only receives 80 percent benefit. This rule is based on the actuarial principle. Secondly, since 1967 a wage earner aged 60–64 has been eligible for 80 percent benefit as long as his monthly earnings do not exceed the limit above. The percentage decreases to 50 percent and then 20 percent as his earnings approach the limit. This arrangement obviously has the effect of subsidizing low pay for the older workers. However, it is questionable whether it is effective in encouraging the older workers to work, because the earning-limit for 80 percent benefit is lower than the welfare-minimum for a couple. But there is some way out; for instance, since the bi-annual bonus is not counted, the low monthly pay can be compensated by it. No matter what the effect is, there are many people aged 60–64 receiving this partial pension. Thus, in 1987, while 5,724,000 retirees and workers aged

65 and over and 1,644,000 survivors of the retirees received the Welfare Old Age Pension, 403,000 workers aged 60–64 received the partial Welfare pension. The latter number is to be compared with the total number of the workers of the same age, 1,120,000 in 1988 in table 2.

Second, there is no European type of disability pension, but, instead, there is a "pension for handicapped employees", which is provided only for the seriously handicapped following a strict medical check and only while one is handicapped. A simple case of ill-health does not meet the requirement. In contrast to the European disability pensions, it is of no significance in terms of the number of beneficiaries. In 1987 the recipients of the Welfare Handicap Pension amounted to only 253,000 people aged 20 to 59.

Third, as was mentioned above, in most large companies the company pension is fused with the public Welfare Pension.

1.3.2 Unemployment Benefit

As a result of the successive reforms made in the 1970s in response to the employment difficulty for the middle-aged and older workers, the duration of benefit receipt has become strongly age-related. It is shorter for the younger and longer for the older. Today for the unemployed aged 55–64, the maximum duration is 300 days and, in special cases, 390 days. People aged 65 and over are not eligible.

This benefit affects the older people's choice between work and retirement to a greater extent after "Teinen" than before it. Thus a person who has reached "Teinen" has two choices; one choice is to receive the unemployment benefit based on his relatively high final wage for 300 days, in addition to the public pension benefit, and then retire completely from work or look for a job again. The second choice is to re-enter work on a non-regular basis with the partial pension for a while and then retire and receive the lower unemployment benefit based on the lower wage for a non-regular. In this sense the unemployment benefit seems to motivate the older workers from large companies to withdraw from work.

1.3.3 Employment Promotion Policy for the Older Workers

The state has made efforts to promote the employment of the older workers by inciting and regulating the companies to raise their "Teinen" age and to hire more older people through a variety of policy measures such as administrative guidance, subsidy programs and legislations. This is an unique feature of Japanese labor policy. But the age group targeted and the policy context have changed much in the course of time. So the policy history will be described in brief in the next subsection and the present policy will be discussed in the final section.

1.4   Change in the Regime: the Raising of the "Teinen" Age

1.4.1 The Stage of Life after "Teinen"

"Teinen" at 55 was a relic from pre-war times. After the war, life expectancy rose steadily and 55 was regarded as too young an age for retirement. Then the workers, particularly those in large companies, came to face two problems.

First, from 1962 on, the Welfare pension began to provide a full benefit, but its level was extremely low at 10 percent of the average wage for the insured. Therefore, the unions and the opposition party began to demand an improvement in the level of benefit in the early 1960s.

Second, the pension was available only at 60 so that there was a five year gap between the "Teinen" age and the pension age. Accordingly many workers were, after "Teinen", forced to seek new employment and found it in the small to medium-sized companies which were suffering from a shortage of young workers and depended on a relatively aged workforce, no matter what their "Teinen" age was. But the labor market conditions were unfavorable for the middle-aged and older workers even in the booming economy. And as the number of "Teinen" leavers swelled, the older workers experienced more and more difficulty in the labor market. (See the higher unemployment distribution for the middle-aged and older workers in table 2.)

This difficulty and the poorer working conditions in the small to medium-sized companies drove the unions of large company employees to demand the raising of the "Teinen" age in about the latter half of the 1960s.

1.4.2 State Policies and Company Responses

It seems that the state strategy for older workers until the mid-70s was "to promote the employment of people aged 55–59 and provide a public pension for those of 60 and over".

First, from the late 50s on, the state tried several times to increase the benefit but faced opposition from the large companies who were reluctant to bear the higher contribution added to the retirement allowance liabilities. When the 1966 legislation made it possible to fuse company pensions with the public scheme, this barrier was finally eliminated. The benefit was gradually increased and, in 1973, reached about 50 percent of the average gross wage of the insured and became related to the average wage rise.

Second, in the 1970s, the state launched a labor policy for the middle-aged and older workers. On the one hand, as was mentioned above, the duration of unemployment benefit receipt became age-related and was shorter for the younger to quicken their re-entry into the next job and longer for the older, to take into account their difficulty in finding employment. On the other hand, the state started to promote employment for the middle-aged and older workers. The 1971 legislation obligated employers to make efforts to employ workers aged 45 and over up to a certain percentage of their total workforce. In 1973 the state declared its intention to encourage employers to raise their "Teinen" age to 60 and arranged a subsidy program for it, which was to be financed by a special contribution by employers to the unemployment fund. In 1976, the 1971 legislation was amended so that employers were obliged to make efforts to employ workers aged 55 and over up to 6 percent of their total workforce and a subsidy program for this was established.

In the meantime some large companies had themselves decided to prolong the employment of their regular employees in response to the union demand. Thus, they began to re-employ a portion of their workers who had reached "Teinen" for a couple of years on a non-regular basis receiving a salary unrelated to age-orientation. Soon the re-employment scheme came to cover all of the workers at the "Teinen" age and the term of employment became longer (see the electric maker's case later). However, they refused to raise the "Teinen" age, namely, to enlarge the span of life-time employment. And the large companies in the iron and steel industry with relatively older age structure refused even to adopt the re-employment scheme.

1.4.3 Impacts of the Depressions

The deep depressions following the two oil-price rises changed the situation drastically. The labor market situation for the older workers extremely worsened . Thus, in 1979, while the annual average unemployment rate rose to 2.2 percent, the rates for males aged 55–59 and for those aged 60–64 went up sharply to 3.4 and 5.7 percent. And the age groups containing large numbers of workers were approaching the "Teinen" age. For the union the raising of the "Teinen" age became a pressing demand.

The state took decisive action. In 1979, right after the opposition parties failed to pass a bill for a compulsory "Teinen"" age of 60, the Ministry of Labor announced its intention to make the "Teinen" age of 60 universal by 1985 and referred to the Employment Council the problem of how to promote the raising of the "Teinen" age. And from 1981 onward the ministry started to give administrative guidance, encouraging companies to raise the age. The result of the council's seven year discussion was the 1986 Older Workers Employment Stabilization Act, the first legislation regulating the company practice of the "Teinen" age. It imposed on employers an obligation to make efforts to raise their "Teinen" age to 60 and over.

On the other hand, the slump in demand and drastic changes in the demand structure and technologies had been driving large companies for a far-reaching restructuring including a personnel policy. They depended increasingly on part-timers and dispatched workers, delegated more of the processes of production to their subsidiaries and promoted computerization. The personnel policy changed considerably. They began to decrease their regular workforce by stopping the mass hiring of senior high school leavers and, instead, employing a smaller number of university graduates, and by shedding out the surplus middle-aged and older regular employees by "Shukko".

It is amidst this restructuring that large companies accepted the union demand and the state request to raise the "Teinen" age to 60. In 1980 the managements and the unions of the five major companies in the iron and steel industry, a leading sector of that time, reached an agreement on raising the "Teinen" age step by step to 60, as the iron and steel company case will show. This presented a model and paved the way for the other industries and large companies. By the time of the 1986 Act, 60 had become the dominant "Teinen" age among large companies.

Why and how the "Teinen" age has been raised and what has been happening with it will be seen later in the case studies.

1.4.4 Change in the Policy Context

It seems that in the meantime the state had altered its strategy toward older workers. It has become evident that the rise in life expectancy and the decline in fertility are causing the rapid aging of the population which would bring about the solvency crisis in the public pension funds and the decrease in the labor supply. It seems that the state policy stance is now "to provide a job for those younger than 65 and a pension for those aged 65 and over".

First, in the late 1970s the state began to argue in favor of raising the pension eligibility age to 65 and in practice submitted a bill for it to Parliament but failed. And in 1985–86 a far-reaching public pension reform was put into practice. (1) The National Pension scheme and the fixed-sum portion of the Welfare Pension scheme were integrated into a new "Basic Pension scheme" to relieve the former from pressing solvency difficulties. On top of the Basic Pension fund, a new "Welfare Pension scheme" was set up to operate the earning-related portion. (2) The contribution rate was scheduled to be raised and the benefit was scheduled to be reduced gradually. Further, a 25 year contribution, instead of a 20 year one, became required. (3) The conditions for the independent Public Servant Pension schemes were scheduled to be assimilated to those for the private sector employees. (4) The eligibility age was increased to 65 in principle. However, persons aged 60–64 remained eligible for the new Welfare Pension benefit. In 1989 the state tried to raise the eligibility age for the new Welfare Pension benefit but withdrew the bill due to the political situation. It remains a controversial issue.

Second, the focus of the state labor policy has been shifting to males in their early 60s. In the early 1980s the state arranged a subsidy program for encouraging employers to lengthen the period of employment past the age of 60 by further raising the "Teinen" age or re-employing those older than 60. And the 1986 Act putting the "Teinen" age at 60 stipulated also the state's obligation to support companies to employ workers aged 60 and over. Further, the amendment made for the Act in 1990 imposed on employers an obligation to make efforts to employ those who reached the "Teinen" age of 60 in their company or its subsidiary.

How large companies are responding to this state labor policy and what is the prospect for the raising of the pension age will be discussed in the final section.

2   Case Studies

In this section the findings from five case studies based on in-depth surveys are briefly presented. Case report 1 on a general electric maker presents a typical example of why and how a large company has raised its "Teinen" age. This report includes a case report on one of its subsidiaries which was originally established to accept the older workers. Case 2, an iron and steel company, represents a typical case of a heavily depressed industry which has undergone serious restructuring. Case study 3 looks at banks, a typical white collar sector. Here the situation in a regional bank is analyzed in comparison with a large city bank. Case study 4 focuses on the manual workers in the public sector where the prototype for Japanese life-time employment is found. The last case study gives a sharply contrasting picture in a small company.

In addition, we carried out interviews with the personnel staff from a large watch maker, a giant electricity company and a major department store and the officials from the Ministry of Labor, some prefectural staff for local labor policy and the officials from JTUC (the Japan Trade Unions Congress). Other useful information was gained from the interviews which we made in the summer of 1989 with 100 persons who had retired or were retiring.

In Section 3 some generalizations from the surveys and interviews above will be attempted.

2.1   Case Study 1: A General Electric Maker and its Subsidiary

2.1.1 The Company and the Aging Problem

The company is one of the largest general electric makers in Japan. It was founded in the early 1920s as a member of a big business group. Traditionally it produced mainly heavy electric equipment, but now it produces not only electric machine tools for industry, but also tele-communication systems, computers, satellites and consumer appliances.

It was just after the 1973 oil crisis that the company showed great concern over the aging problem of its employees. In the great depression of 1975–76 the company stopped hiring school leavers, which was considered the final emergency measure to adjust the number of regular employees in the life-time employment system. Since the cohort of middle-aged employees was large, the average age of employees rapidly rose. The management realized the difficulty caused by aging and began to implement measures to combat the problem.

The first measure taken in 1977 was the "Welfare Vision" which included an intensive health care system aimed particularly at middle-aged and older employees. In 1978, a new qualification system was introduced especially aiming for the revitalization of middle and high aged employees. In 1979 a new subsidiary firm was established aiming to transfer unprofitable and labor-intensive business sections from the company together with their aged employees, on which we will see later.

In 1980 a new training course started for the employees aged 40 and those aged 55 to stimulate them in their approach to work and give them practical knowledge on preparing for after their retirement. At the same time various measures for improving working processes and promoting job changes for elderly workers were also introduced. In 1980 the trade union of the company started to request a raising of the "Teinen" age to 60. A brief history of the "Teinen" age of the company is as follows. Before 1947 the "Teinen" age was 50 for blue-collar workers and 55 for white-collar workers. In 1947 a "Teinen" age of 55 was applied to all employees. In 1957 the male "Teinen" age was raised to 56 but the female "Teinen" age stayed at 55. In 1962, although this "Teinen" age was not changed, the re-employment scheme for male employees after "Teinen" was introduced. This re-employment was available only for a small number of employees nominated by the management, but in 1972 it became available for all male applicants. Therefore, in principle, employment up to 60 years old had been realized for all male employees in 1972.

The claim for re-employment for all "Teinen" workers was, between 1970 and 1972, one of the most important demands of the Japanese Federation of Electrical Machine Workers' Unions (JFEMWU), which organized about 500 thousand workers in 200 enterprise unions. The measure taken by the company in 1972 was a response to this coordinated demand.

However ,the pay and working conditions for the re-employed workers were much lower than those for regular employees. In the 1980 spring offensive, the union of the company demanded the raising of the "Teinen" age to 60 as a coordinated demand of JFEMWU.

The request of the union was partly granted in the spring of 1982 by the raising of the female "Teinen" age to 56 and the offering of the re-employment scheme to all applicants. With regard to the raising of the "Teinen" age to 60, the management was reluctant at the initial stage because it believed that this might greatly affect its employment system and personnel policy. The management was especially nervous about the increase in labor costs and the delay in promotion for the younger generation. However, as the union suggested that it intended to concede some points, the management agreed to start negotiations. The main reason for the management's concession may have been strong pressure from the government since 1981 and the example of the iron and steel industry which had already reached agreement in the previous year. The joint research committee on the "Teinen" problem made up of the management and the union started in June 1982 and concluded in March 1984.

The important point of the agreement was the "57 Years Old Rule" on pay reduction and resignation from managerial posts. With regard to pay, it meant that the pay level of a 57 year-old fell to 70–80 percent of that of a 56 year-old and remained the same until the age of 60, except for a small increase to adjust to inflation. Therefore, it resembled the former re-employment scheme, though the application of an age-oriented wage system was extended by one year and some additional improvements in company pension etc. were made. The resignation rule from managerial posts at 57 aimed to avoid the delay of promotion for the younger generation. Therefore, in reality, the period of age-oriented treatment increased by only one year to an upper age of 56. The results of the negotiation indicate some basic elements of the managerial philosophy of the company. They are firstly to accept the request of the state, secondly to follow the example of other industries and companies, thirdly to keep good industrial relations as far as possible with its company-based union within the limits of managerial efficiency. A personnel officer expressed it as "the social responsibility of the large companies like our company". The union was also careful not to upset the stability and vitality of the company organization and conceded with modest gain.

In the following section, we will give a description and analysis of the practice of personnel change and its effects on the age structure in a middle-sized manufacturing plant of the company after the "Teinen" revision in 1984.

2.1.2 The Flow of Employees and Its Effects on the Age Structure in a Manufacturing Plant of the Company (1984–1989)

The plant, founded in 1954, produces mainly refrigerators, air-conditioners and compressors as important components of the products mentioned above. The total number of workers in the plant as of April 1989 was about 3,000 consisting of about 2,000 regular employees, about 400 seasonal workers and part-timers and about 600 employees of related companies.

Table 3 shows the flow of regular employees of the plant between 1984 and 1989. With regard to females, the main source of inflow was the hiring of school leavers and the main cause of outflow was retirement for reasons other than "Teinen". The main reason for retirement was marriage and child birth which has been the typical pattern of female workers. The

Table 3: Flow of Regular Employees in the Manufacturing Plant (1984–1989)

	Total	Male	Female
Total Inflow	(388)	(318)	(70)
(1) Employment of school leavers	226	171	55
(2) Employment other than above factors	40	31	9
(3) Transfer from other establishments	56	55	1
(4) Return from "Shukko"	65	60	5
(5) Return from temporary retirement, etc.	1	1	0
Total Outflow	(498)	(395)	(103)
(6) "Teinen" Retirement	52	50	2
(7) Retirement other than above factors	149	62	87
(8) Transfer to other establishments	103	98	5
(9) "Shukko" to subsidiary or related firms	186	178	8
(10) Temporary retirement through disease, etc.	8	7	1
Total Balance	(−110)	(−77)	(−33)
(a) Employment (1) + (2) −Retirement (6) + (7)	65	90	−25
(b) Transfer in the company	−47	−43	−4
(c) "Shukko" (4)−(9)	−121	−118	−3
(d) Temporary retirement (5)−(10)	−7	−6	−1

Table 4: Age Distribution of "Shukko" Workers of the Manufacturing Plant (April 1990)

Age Group	Number	Percentage
15–19	0	0.0
20–24	4	2.2
25–29	1	0.1
30–34	7	3.8
35–39	16	8.7
40–44	22	12.0
45–49	26	14.1
50–54	43	23.4
55–59	64	35.5
Total	184	100.0

decrease of 33 can be simply understood by the balance of employment and retirement. With regard to male employees, the factors were more complicated. As to inflow, the hiring of new school leavers accounted for 54 percent, but other factors like transfer from other establishments of the company (17.3 percent) and return from "Shukko" (18.9 percent) were not negligible. Transfer within the company and return from "Shukko" usually occur among employees in their 30s and early 40s. The hiring of persons other than school leavers was traditionally negligible, but in the labor shortage caused by the boom after the end of 1987, the plant assigned 26 young seasonal workers to regular employees. As for outflow, "Shukko" was the principal reason (45 percent), retirement including "Teinen" was the second reason (28 percent) and transfer within the company was the third reason (25 percent). 60 percent of the "Shukko" appointments occurred with workers in their fifties (table 4). The retirement for reasons other than "Teinen" includes the case of transfer to subsidiary and related firms. It is noteworthy to observe that the inflow promoted by the hiring of the school leavers and the outflow through "Shukko" were almost balanced.

Table 5 shows the age structure of the regular employees of the plant as of April 1984 and 1989. The average age of total employees rose 2 years in five years, becoming 40 years. As the average age of the company as a whole in 1960 was 30, it seems that the speed of aging accelerated between 1984 and 1989. It is remarkable that the average age of the plant's manual workers rose 5 years in as many years.

Looking at the column of female manual employees, the real number under 35 years old decreased by more than half. It was a result of personnel policy reducing the employment of new school leavers and substituting them with middle-aged house-wife part-timers. With regard to male manual employees, the contrast between the decrease in the number of employees

Table 5: Age Structure of the Manufacturing Plant in 1984 and 1989

Age group	Non-manual				Manual				Total	
	Male		Female		Male		Female		1984	1989
	1984	1989	1984	1989	1984	1989	1984	1989		
15 – 19	0	11	15	4	7	1	1	0	23	16
20 – 24	44	74	45	39	47	28	47	16	183	157
25 – 29	66	104	18	24	129	51	30	22	243	201
30 – 34	85	63	15	12	223	121	23	9	346	205
35 – 39	121	87	11	14	265	208	9	20	406	329
40 – 44	109	107	11	12	274	251	8	15	402	385
45 – 49	76	93	3	10	200	260	1	8	280	371
50 – 54	15	44	4	3	102	176	1	0	122	223
55 – 59	16	12	1	2	66	77	0	0	83	91
Total	532	595	123	120	1.313	1.173	120	90	2.088	1.978
Av. Age	37.7	36.2	28.8	31.4	37.7	43.3	28.2	32.7	37.9	39.7

under 45 and the increase in that of employees over 45 is very clear. The reasons are firstly the reduction in the hiring of school leavers, and secondly the aging of employees who were hired in large numbers in the midst of the high growth rate economy before the oil crisis. The hiring of school leavers was substituted by seasonal workers and part-timers.

As for female non-manual employees, the hiring at 18 years old for simple clerical work decreased, while the hiring of university graduates increased, which is reflected in the rise of the average age by 2.6 years. It seems the management had the intention of keeping the number in the 20–29 age group at the same level. The number of people in the over 50 age group was negligible.

On the other hand, the number of male non-manual employees increased by 63 (11.8 percent) and the average age fell by 1.5 years. The 20–29 age group clearly expanded which was a result of the strategic personnel policy hiring highly educated young staff in order to cope with rapid technological innovation and the changing industrial structure. Thus, the increase in the number of employees in the 20–29 age group vastly surpassed the increase of employees in the over-45 age group.

Meanwhile, the cohort analysis of male employees shows that the number of employees belonging to an age group began to decrease gradually at 40 years old and the tendency accelerated after 50 years old. If this decrease of older employees had not happened, the average age of the plant might have risen more rapidly. Observations on the practice of personnel change (table 3) and the age distributions of "Shukko" workers (table 4) suggest this tendency depends mainly upon the "Shukko" appointments. There were

Table 6: Age Structure of a Subsidiary Firm of the Manufacturing Plant as of April 1990

Age Group	Regular Employees		"Shukko" Men	Total
	Male	Female		
18−19	14	24	0	38
20−24	32	10	0	42
25−29	26	3	1	30
30−34	18	2	5	25
35−39	7	0	8	15
40−44	5	0	13	18
45−49	5	0	14	19
50−54	2	0	22	24
55−59	0	0	23	23
60−64	5	0	0	5
Total	114	39	86	239

21 subsidiary firms and 7 related firms which had accepted 184 workers from the plant as of April 1990. One subsidiary firm, in particular, had accepted 86 "Shukko" workers. We shall now observe this subsidiary firm to discover the reality of "Shukko" as an important personnel measure to cope with the aging problem.

2.1.3 The Reality of "Shukko" in a Subsidiary Firm of the Company

The firm was founded in 1979 as a 100 percent invested subsidiary of the large electric company mentioned above. The initial aims of the firm were the storage and shipping of parts and components of the above mentioned plant's products. This task had been under the charge of a section of the plant, but the management of the parent company decided to transfer this section to the new subsidiary in order to offer jobs to older workers and also reduce a labor-intensive, unprofitable section. The subsidiary firm was inaugurated on the site of the plant with 5 million yen paid capital and 33 employees. As most of them including the directors were aged "Shukko" men from the plant, the firm was originally a small elderly workers' company. In 1982 however, the firm began to produce electronic control substrates for air-conditioners and refrigerators of the plant. At the same time, the firm began to hire younger workers as its own regular employees. This meant that the firm enlarged its task from a simple customer service and also from a mere receiver of older workers from the plant. In early 1984, the firm built a new factory in a neighboring city to produce component parts of compressors with a modern manufacturing system called FM system and also to assemble electronic control boxes for air-conditioners.

The total number of employees as of April 1990 was 536 including 153 regular employees, 86 "Shukko" men from the plant and 297 seasonal and part-time workers.

Table 6 shows the age structure of regular employees and "Shukko" men. The regular employees aged over 35 had been tranferred from the plant and lost the status as regular employees of the parent company. The "Shukko" men aged over 50 were supposed to stay in the firm until "Teinen". The unique combination of younger regular employees and older "Shukko" men is clearly shown in the table. The firm expects the "Shukko" workers mainly to play the roles of coordinators or supervisors for seasonal and part-time workers. Therefore, the personnel section of the parent company is careful enough to select the right person for the task.

"Shukko" is surely a measure to drain the redundant manpower, but it is also a means of effectively utilizing the ability and experience of older workers in the company group. The firm has adopted almost the same employment system as the plant including the 60 years old "Teinen" rule and the "57 Years Old Rule". Although the pay level of the firm is 10 percent lower than that of the plant, the "Shukko" workers can earn the same income as the workers of the plant, since the plant compensates for the difference in pay.

One important difference in the employment systems of the firm and the plant is that the firm approved a special rule of employment extension for the "Shukko" workers from the plant who reached the "Teinen" age. This rule depends on an agreement between the management and the union of the parent company. It says that the employees of the parent company, who are sent on "Shukko" to subsidiary and related firms and reach the "Teinen" age during their "Shukko" period, have the right to apply for the extension of their employment in the subsidiary and related firms. These firms have a duty to employ them for three years and this employment contract can be extended two more years if both parties agree. It is an advantage for the "Shukko" men from the plant because the original employees of the firm do not have this right to apply for employment extension. This advantage might also be to make the "Shukko" appointment more acceptable for the older regular workers of the plant.

The effect of this special employment extension scheme is not so clear at the moment, because there were only five post-"Teinen" men working in the firm as of April 1990. The majority of the "Teinen" men chose to retire from the labor market and to live on their pensions. The reason for this behavior seemed to a personnel officer of the plant that they could feel little economic advantage in the scheme. That is, the reduced pension benefit for wage earners and the lock-in effect of the unemployment benefit, both mentioned above, seem to have prevented them from applying for the scheme. The officer said that if the economic disadvantages were removed or the public pension eligibility age was raised to 65 in the future, the scheme would be utilized by far more post-"Teinen" workers. One more reason for the retirement may be the rural nature of the location of the plant and the firm. Since a considerable number of employees own small plots of land, they can earn additional incomes by engaging in small farming or land leasing.

This is an argument from an economic point of view. However, there would certainly be another point of view to consider the value of the employment extension scheme. According to the personnel officer, a considerable number of retired men at the "Teinen" age told him that they would want to do some less demanding work for their health and social participation. At any rate, he anticipated that the firm should play an important role in absorbing older workers at the peak of the high age structure which will come in ten years time.

2.1.4 Concluding Remarks

This case study attempted to show a typical personnel practice of a large Japanese company group to cope with the increase in aged employees. The key word was "Shukko". "Shukko" does not originally refer to a personnel measure aimed specifically at older employees. However, especially in recent years, not only the company in our case study but also almost every large company in Japan has utilized it as an effective measure to drain redundant aged manpower into subsidiary and related firms without damaging life-time employment and the stable industrial relations with the company-based union. One of the aims of the "57 Years Old Rule" may have been to force older employees to accept the "Shukko" appointment. It was a revision of the age-oriented personnel system, but it also contributed to keeping the system workable for the younger generation.

As for older workers, "Shukko" does not simply mean a miserable life resembling exile, because the home company usually offers a position one rank higher to white collar workers and a longer employment opportunity to blue collar workers. Their salaries or wages are secured at least at the same level as those in the home company. Moreover, it can be a good opportunity for older workers to utilize their skills and experience which are still valuable in small-to medium-sized companies.

With regard to subsidiary firms like the firm in our case study, accepting "Shukko" workers might be an effective method of obtaining relatively well-trained and reliable manpower at lower costs. Thus, the "Shukko" system seems to have its own rational ground in a large company group like the company's one in our case study. However, it is workable only when there are proper vacant positions to accept older employees. The foundation of the subsidiary firm in our case study was a typical effort to make such vacant positions. It may be unthinkable in Western European terms, but it is a reality of present Japan. However, it would be a big question for the parent company's group in our case study or other large company groups whether they could afford sufficient positions for older workers in future.

2.2   Case Study 2: An Iron and Steel Company

2.2.1 Outline of the Company and the Related Union

The company is one of the five major iron and steel companies. It has six main factories located in Kyushu and the Kansai and Kanto regions. The value of sales was about 112 billion yen in 1989. In the same year the total number of regular employees was 28,857, of which , as will be discussed later, 8,837 had been sent on "Shukko" and that of the employees in the subsidiary companies was 9,738.

An enterprise-based union, which is a member of the Federation of Iron and Steel Workers' Unions (FISWU) exists in the company. As the union has concluded a union-shop agreement with the company, it organizes all the employees, both the white collar and blue collar workers, except those in managerial posts. It has its branches in the head office and every establishment of the company.

Generally speaking, in Japan, collective bargaining is carried out by the management and the union of each company and the resulting collective agreements are effective only within the company. Also in the iron and steel industry the labor-management relations are of a similar type. As FISWU, however, has been the most functional industrial federation of the unions in the private sector, it has formed the unified demands of the affiliated unions to improve such working conditions as the annual improvement in the wage level, the number of scheduled working hours, the "Teinen" age and/or the average amount of the retirement lump-sum. The managements of the five major companies, on their side, have preferred to standardize the basic working conditions in the industry, at least, within the five major companies. Thus, the institutions and/or the standards concerning the working conditions have tended to be common to these five companies, although collective bargaining itself has been carried out within each company and there has been some degree of "wage drift" or differences in the course of the operation of the institutions. In this sense the iron and steel industry is supposed to have had the strongest "industrial regime". It should be noted that FSIWU has played the role of the "pattern setter" for the unions in the other industries, in particular, in the annual joint spring offensive concern-

Table 7: Number and Average Age of Employees of the Iron and Steel Company

Year	Total of regular employees	Company workers in subsidiaries	K factory	
			Number of regulars	Average age
1973	30.615	25.894		
1974	30.359	24.497		
1975	30.669	24.973		
1976	30.549	19.269		
1977	29.616	15.952		
1978	29.200	16.531		
1979	29.947	17.647		
1980	29.675	17.854	2.396	37.17
1981	29.426	18.500	2.315	37.53
1982	29.353	16.781	2.383	38.46
1983	28.489	14.449	2.313	39.12
1984	27.337	14.887	2.231	39.62
1985	26.465	13.586	2.200	40.59
1986	25.205	11.472	2.135	41.18
1987	23.108	10.771	1.865	41.34
1988	21.136	10.638	1.365	41.36
1989	19.796	9.738	1.104	41.41
1990	20.020	−	935	41.98

ing the wage increase. In short, the institutions and/or levels concerning the working conditions in the iron and steel industry have been seen as a kind of social standard to be referred to by the other industries, although they have not always introduced the same institutions and/or levels.

2.2.2 The Age Problem for the Company and the Union

It is clear that, as table 7 shows, the number of regular employees in the company decreased after the mid-70s without compulsory dismissals. Also, as the average age became higher, under the seniority wage system, total payrolls increased more than the rise in the value of sales in the period just after the first oil shock in 1973. The transition of the demographic structure in the company was a result of a new personnel policy. The management has not at all intended to destroy the life-time employment system within the company, because it has considered that the system has been the key to maintain good relations between labor and management. Under this condition, the company stopped recruiting high school leavers for a few years and, instead, hired a smaller number of university graduates in order to, on the one hand, decrease the total number of employees without compulsory dismissals to cope with new market situation and, on the other hand, develop new technology-oriented programs.

According to the staff of the personnel section, however, the most important problem has not necessarily been the rise in the average age of the employees but the change in the age-mix of the workforce on the shop floor resulted from the higher percentage of middle-aged and older workers. The management has been concerned that the workforce on the shop floor is composed exclusively of workers belonging to the same generation. Thus, the management has had to solve the following three problems; firstly, maintaining the life-time employment system, secondly, suppressing the increase in the total payroll and thirdly, and maybe most importantly, keeping a suitable age-mix on the shop floor.

On the other hand, the union of the company, jointly with the other unions in the major iron and steel companies, first demanded the raising of the "Teinen" age to 60 in 1970. Documents of the unions, however, suggest that in the early 70s the demand was a matter of "principle". According to them it is only amidst the economic depression and worsened labor market condition just after the oil shock that this demand became most urgent. The union drive to increase the "Teinen" age was due to the fact that it had become very difficult for workers who had reached the "Teinen" age to find jobs outside the company. Then, as the documents show, the union adopted the attitude that, once the "Teinen" age increase had been realized, the union would accept certain poorer working conditions including the wage level for workers over 55 years old.

2.2.3 "Teinen" Increase and the Expansion of "Shukko"

The following is a brief history concerning "Teinen":
   1970   Union demanded "Teinen" increase (the "Teinen" age was 55 at that time).
   1980   The agreement between the union and the management to increase the "Teinen" age in the following stages;
          1981 to the age of 57,
          1984 to the age of 58,
          1986 to the age of 59,
          1988 to the age of 60.
          The plan was carried out completely as far as to the third stage but it was frozen for three years because the high Yen badly hit the industry.
   1991   The increase to 60 was completed.

Table 8: Change in the "Shukko" Distribution by Age Group (in real number and percentage)

Age Group	1986			1990		
	Total	Shukko	%	Total	Shukko	%
−20	149	0	0.0	170	2	1.2
21−35	1.494	0	0.0	1.005	35	3.5
26−30	2.419	0	0.0	1.410	102	7.2
31−35	4.801	0	0.0	2.727	335	12.3
36−40	5.717	18	0.3	5.664	941	16.6
41−45	6.072	58	1.0	5.455	1.368	25.1
45−50	3.647	113	3.1	6.153	2.384	38.7
51−	1.946	270	13.9	4.075	2.620	64.3
Total	26.245	459	1.7	26.659	7.787	29.2

There are some important points concerning this process. When the "Teinen" age was increased, the company changed the wage system. The wage for a 59 yeas old was designed to be the same as that he had received at 54; then the wages for employees aged 50 to 54 were reduced and employees aged 55 to 58 received wages lower than the previous wage level for a 54 years old. The promotion system was also changed; there was a rule for retiring from managerial posts, which meant that the employee in a middle or lower managerial post had to abandon his post at the age of 55 and could benefit from the company pension after his retirement from the company. We can see the system as a kind of early retirement system.

The most important phenomenon since the increase of the "Teinen" age has been the very rapid expansion of "Shukko", which is shown in table 8 and 9.

Of course, "Shukko" itself was not a product of the increased "Teinen" age. A white collar worker used to be transferred to the subsidiary firms, joint venture business or industrial associations, once or twice in his career, and return to the home company. For example, in 1973, about one thousand

Table 9: How Many Companies Had Accepted How Many „Shukko" Workers in 1990?

Kind of Companies	Number of Companies	Number of Shukko Men
Subsidiaries	108	5.994
Sub-Contractors	145	979
Other Companies	746	1.864
Total	999	8.837

out of some thirty thousand regular employees in the company had been
sent on "Shukko". For a white collar worker it was, to some extent, an
ordinal step on his promotion ladder within the company. However, since
the time of the "Teinen" increase the nature of "Shukko" has changed in
quality as well as in quantity. In the company, the percentage of "Shukko"
workers against the total registered regular employees was as much as thirty
percent and the majority of the "Shukko" workers were 55 years old or
over. At the same time, the blue collar workers as well as the white collar
workers have become involved in the "Shukko"" system. About one thousand companies have accepted "Shukko" workers from the case company,
of which 108 are its subsidiary or related companies. Some of them have a
workforce consisting almost entirely of "Shukko" workers. The sub-contractor companies, many of which are operating on the factory site of the
case company, also have accepted large numbers of "Shukko" workers. It
may be supposed that this acceptance would have caused many employees
of the sub-contractor companies to leave. As table 6 shows, the number of
workers in the subsidiaries has been decreasing together with that in the
parent company. Would the decrease then have been much less if they had
not accepted the "Shukko" workers?

We have obtained two contrasting answers from the interviews. According to the personnel staff of the head office the answer was "yes". They
guessed that the "Shukko" workers from their company have pushed the
people out of the subsidiaries. But according to the personnel staff of K
factory of the company the answer was "no". They said; "To simply replace
the low-paid workers of the subsidiary and the sub-contractor companies
with the high-paid regular employees of the parent company would be
rather uneconomic from the view point of the whole group.

Therefore, we have made efforts to find other receivers, which had had
no relation with our company, under the strong support of the prefectural
and the municipal administration". Such a thing was possible because the
factory had a strong economic influence in the region. Table 8 shows that
there are very many companies who, although they do not have strong
relations with the iron and steel company, have accepted "Shukko" workers. The personnel section of the company negotiates with the receiving
companies in order to transfer the older workers. If the working conditions
there are lower, the company gives compensation to the transferred workers. Usually "Shukko" for workers over 55 is a one-way ticket leading
eventually to retirement.

According to our interviewees, the expansion of "Shukko" has been
accompanied by both advantages and disadvantages. The company certainly
has to pay a portion of the wages for the "Shukko" workers to compensate
the wage differences, so this creates some burdens for the company. However, by means of "Shukko", the company has become able to regulate the

age structure of the company. At the same time, the company has become able to organize the labor force, on the group-wide scale, more flexibly.

2.3   Case Study 3: A Regional Bank and a City Bank

2.3.1 Banks in Japan

Japan has various sorts of private banking organs, among which the ordinary commercial banks have occupied an important position in the Japanese economy. There are two types of ordinary commercial banks, city banks of which there are 10 and regional banks of which there are about 80. The city banks have a large amount of credit with numerous depositors, finance large companies, locate branches in big cities on a nation-wide scale and employ large numbers of employees. The regional banks carry on business mainly in one region and are smaller in all aspects than the city banks.

The "Teinen" age is 60 in all of the city banks and in 80 percent of the regional banks. We selected a regional bank because of its appropriate size for a case study. Another reason is that the regional banks have been confronted with the aging staff problem earlier than the city banks, perhaps because the latter have expanded business more rapidly.

We interviewed the deputy chief of the personnel department of the regional bank several times and gathered detailed data on the age structure. We also had a chance to interview a person who had been employed in a city bank for more than 25 years and put on "Shukko" to its subsidiary company. His information is very useful for our conclusion.

The regional bank's antecedents were established in 1878 but the bank itself was founded in 1965. The head office is in a prefectural seat in the northern part of Japan and carries on business mainly in that prefecture where most of its 90 branches are located. The first step of the on-line real-time system began in 1970, the second in 1980 and the third in 1990. It has several subsidiaries.

2.3.2 Aging between 1984 and 1989

In the past the bank hired secondary school graduates for its male staff but today hires university graduates. Female secondary school and 2-year college graduates are recruited for simple clerical work. It is an unwritten rule for those female employees to quit the bank on marriage. The bank has begun to take a few female university graduates recently to whom the rule is not applied.

Table 10: Aging of Male Staff in the Regional Bank between 1984 and 1989

Age Group	1984 (A)	Cohort (B)	1989 (C)	(C)−(A)	(C)−(B)
20−24	86	−	72	−14	−
25−29	106	86	169	63	83
30−34	178	106	104	−74	− 2
35−39	158	178	175	17	− 3
40−44	163	158	155	− 8	− 3
45−49	219	163	161	−58	− 2
50−54	176	219	212	36	− 7
55−57	58	176	109	51	−67
Total	1.144	−	1.157	13	−
58−59	(12)	(58)	(18)	(6)	(−40)
60	(10)	(22)	(14)	(4)	(− 8)

In 1989 the bank employed 1,157 male staff, 684 female clerks and 57 male and female workers, in total 1,898. In addition, the bank employed 38 non-regular males and 108 female part-timers, most of whom had left the bank on marriage and re-joined later. The total number of regular employees and the percentage of the female regular employees was fairly stable in the 1980s, although the latter decreased in 1989 due to the office automation. The increasing percentage of the managerial employees in the total male staff is the most noteworthy point. It was 40 percent in 1970, increased to above 50 percent in 1977, reached 60 percent in 1984 and 64 percent in 1989. In our view this reflects the aging of male staff.

Table 10 shows the aging process in the bank, which includes the number of male staff in each age group in 1984 (A) and 1989 (C). Cohort (B) shows the expected numbers in each group in 1989 based directly on the numbers

Table 11: Inflow and Outflow of Male Staff in the Regional Bank between 1984 and 1989

Year	Hiring	Shukko			Quitting		
		Total	Subsidiaries	Others	Total	Teinen	Others*
1984	31	47	35	12	16	12	4
1985	35	59	42	17	20	15	5
1986	41	66	41	25	23	14	9
1987	25	64	38	26	30	25	5
1988	29	89	44	45	36	26	10
1989	37	85	43	42	51	46	5

* Death, Voluntary Quitting and Becoming Board Members

Table 12: Age Structure of the Regional Bank as of April 1989

Age Group	M. E	F. E	M. W	F. W	M. N	F. N
18 – 19	0 (0)	95 (0)	0	0	0	0
20 – 24	72 (0)	475 (0)	2	0	0	9
25 – 29	169 (0)	170 (0)	3	0	0	27
30 – 34	104 (2)	19 (0)	3	0	0	30
35 – 39	175 (146)	12 (0)	1	0	0	24
40 – 44	155 (148)	6 (0)	3	2	1	8
45 – 49	161 (154)	1 (1)	7	1	0	3
50 – 54	212 (196)	2 (1)	16	3	2	2
55 – 57	109 (101)	1 (0)	13	1	3	0
58 – 62					27	
63 – 67					5	
Total	1.157 (740)	686 (2)	48	7	38	103

Legenda: M. E: Male Regular Employees
          F. E: Female Regular Employees
          M. W: Male Manual Workers
          F. W: Female Manual Workers
          M. N: Male Non-Regular Employees
          F. N: Femal Part-Timers

* The Figures in ( ) Are for the Managerial Staff and Are Included in the Figures on the Left Side.

in 1984. The fourth column shows the balance between the age structure in 1984 and that in 1989 [(C)–(A)]. The last column shows the disparity between the actual number for 1989 (C) and the expected number for the same year (B). We find that the actual number in the 50 to 57 age group increased between 1984 and 1989 but the disparity [(C)–(B)] has a minus sign. On the other hand, the disparity is rather small under 49 years old.

This means that some male staff over 50 years old, especially over 52 years old, must have been put on "Shukko" in order to reduce the increasing number of male staff aged 52 and over. Table 11 also shows the increase of the Shukko" appointment during the five years.

As table 12 shows, there were a number of non-regular male employees aged 58 and over, most of whom had been re-employed after "Teinen". In 1989 the bank re-employed on a non-regular basis 11 of 46 male employees who had reached "Teinen". The number of the non-regular male employees for the years before 1989 is unavailable but seems to have increased.

2.3.3 "Teinen" and the Response to Aging

The "Teinen" age had been raised from 55 to 58 as early as 1969, but it was only in 1991 that the bank raised it to 60. (Our case study was done mainly when it was 58.) The 1986 legislation forced the bank to do so. When the "Teinen" age was 58, wage levels continued to rise until the "Teinen" age but the rate of increase decreased at the age of 50. The retirement allowance was paid on the basis of a special standard wage which depended on length of service. The deputy chief of the personnel department told us, "with the raising of the 'Teinen' age to 60, we will have to revise the pay and retirement allowance system based on age-orientation."

The bank has no early retirement scheme and has tried to secure the employment for male staff until the "Teinen" age in spite of having been faced with the serious problem of the aging of male staff. The highest managerial staff, on the one hand, and the non-managerial male staff, on the other hand, tend to stay in the bank until the "Teinen" age, but an increasing number of male staff over 55 years old have been sent on "Shukko" to the subsidiary companies and other companies, most of which are the bank's customers. When they are put on "Shukko", they receive the same amount of basic pay as they received in the bank. The bank pays the difference between the wage in the bank and that in the company receiving the "Shukko" workers; the difference sometimes amounts to 50 percent of the wage in the bank.

When the "Teinen" age was 58, a small number of employees stayed at the bank after the age of 58 as non-regular employees for about 2 years. Some of the staff on "Shukko" stayed at their receiving companies after the bank's "Teinen" age. Generally speaking, when male staff in the bank reached the age of 58, half of them retired from work and half continued working in the bank as non-regular employees, in a subsidiary company and so on. Some of the retirees returned to work after a period of rest. According to the deputy chief, the peak of aging was passing and the bank would face another kind of problem in the future. To fill up the vacancies after the highest age group containing a large number of employees retired, the bank would have to assign the male staff to the managerial posts at an earlier age. We can conclude that the move is beginning because we find that more young male staff were promoted to managerial posts in 1989 than in 1984.

2.3.4 The Case of a City Bank

The city bank has no early retirement scheme and its formal "Teinen" age is 60. But the personnel department has been arranging "Shukko" for most of the male staff with 25 and more years of service to subsidiary companies

and non-subsidiary companies. Since the non-subsidiary companies themselves have also been faced with the aging of employees and have hesitated
recently to accept the "Shukko" men from the bank, the bank has established many subsidiary companies recently not only for business expansion
but also for accepting the "Shukko" men. For example, the bank recruited
about 80 male university graduates including our interviewee in 1961. They
were about 51–52 years old in 1990. 10 of them had quitted the bank and
10 stayed in the bank, including two board members. About 60 had been
put on "Shukko" and half of them worked in the subsidiary companies. On
the other hand, the subsidiary company, in which our interviewee worked,
had about 500 male employees and 300 female employees. About 200 of the
male employees were "Shukko" men from the bank and some of them were
transferred to this company at the age of 55.

Only a few male staff stayed at the bank until the age of 60. But they
stayed there because of the bank having been unable to find a suitable
receiving company for them due to poor health and other reasons. As it is
more difficult to find a receiving company for non-managerial males than
managerial males, the bank has arranged a training course for the former.

All the regular employees of the bank receive the retirement allowance
at the age of 55 and wages are lowered at that age no matter whether the
employee has been put on "Shukko" or stays in the bank. The bank has set
the standard wage for the "Shukko" men both under and over 55 years old
in the subsidiary companies. The bank's welfare facilities are also available
for the "Shukko" men and even for the retirees.

When some older employees returned from "Shukko" to the bank for
various reasons the bank found another company to which the employees
were put on "Shukko" until they are 60 years old. The bank tries to find
even an employee aged 60 and over a new job if he wants to continue
working. Less than half of the bank's male staff retire completely in their
late 50s. The main reason why the remainder continue to work in their late
50s is probably to pay off housing loans.

The bank has two personnel departments, one of which deals with
employees under 55 years old and the other of which deals with those over
55, usually 55 to 60 and sometimes to 65. This division of work between the
two departments shows typically how the bank is utilizing its quasi-internal
labor market to secure employment for its elder male regular employees.

2.3.5 Some Concluding Remarks

The way the banks treat older male staff and operate a personnel policy is
very similar, regardless of the vast difference in the size of the banks. The
banks, regional as well as city, have made an enormous effort to secure

employment for male staff until the "Teinen" age or sometimes even for those over 60 years old. But most of the male staff must leave the banks before the "Teinen" age, work in the subsidiary companies and in most cases have their salary lowered after the age of 55. With regard to the banks' efforts for employment security, our interviewees stressed the "bank's social responsibility with regard to employment security". At the same time, we need to point out the important difference between the city bank and the regional bank. The former treats elder male staff in a systematic way and on a large scale. The city bank has a clearly defined policy and male staff tend to be selected for "Shukko" much earlier according to the policy than in the regional bank. The city bank can afford to establish subsidiary companies to absorb elder staff, but the regional bank can only do this to a much lesser extent.

2.4 Case Study 4: A City Administration and its Department of Refuse Collection and Disposal

2.4.1 City Administration Employment as a Whole Sub-heading within

The Structure of Employment

The city has a population of 283 thousands. The number of its regular employees has doubled from 1960 to 2,448 in 1988, a trend similar to that in the other municipalities. In the Japanese public sector, life-time employment is practiced in the true sense of the word. First, the independent laws regulating the public sector employment prevent the employers from laying off or dismissing their regular employees. Second, the treatment of regular employees including female and manual workers is strongly length of service-oriented in terms of annual pay rise and promotion, although there are some handicaps in promotion with the latter group.

Adding to the regular workforce, there are 22 part-timers and 110 non-regular employees with their contract annually renewed. Further, the city administration has established 4 institutions, to which it has delegated social welfare services and the care of city parks and sports and culture facilities. They employ 78 of their own regular employees and 34 non-regular employees. These workers are not covered by the laws above and are, therefore, out of the "public servant" category.

Career Pattern by Servant Category

City regular employees are categorized into manual and non-manual employees with separate recruitment. Although there is an age limit for entry to non-manual jobs, most of the applicants are new graduates. Most of the

Table 13: Age Distribution of the City Employees by Public Servant Category and Gender as of April 1985 and April 1988

Age Group	Male				Female			
	1985		1988		1985		1988	
Non-manual Employees								
18−19	11		5		2		3	
20−24	88		61		62		72	
25−29	230		168		103		77	
30−34	254		242		79		90	
35−39	245	(14)	276	(11)	68		69	
40−44	164	(54)	211	(56)	50		65	
45−49	157	(98)	151	(74)	55	(4)	52	(5)
50−54	158	(127)	143	(117)	38	(5)	39	(10)
55−59	73	(59)	126	(100)	18	(9)	23	(6)
Total	1.389	(352)	1.383	(358)	475	(18)	490	(22)
Av. Age	37.3 (49.3)		39.4 (50.3)		34.1 (53.0)		36.1 (52.3)	
Manual Employees								
18−19	2		5		0		0	
20−24	4		9		4		0	
25−29	30		21		2		4	
30−34	70		57		19		4	
35−39	80		87		27		25	
40−44	67		76		37		23	
45−49	63		56		38		37	
50−54	77		70		12		34	
55−59	69		74		3		9	
60−62	3							
Av. Age	43.0		43.0		41.5		45.1	

* The Figures in ( ) Are for the Managerial Staff and Included in the Figures on the Left Side.

males are from 4-year course universities and most of the females are from 2 year course colleges. They are frequently transferred between clerical duties and, in most cases, promoted to the managerial posts, though females are obviously handicapped in this respect. Although categorized as non-manual, firemen and kindergarten nurses are separately recruited and stay until "Teinen" within their job categories.

Manual employees work in garbage collection and disposal, sewage disposal, water supply and its charge collection, school care-taking and school

Table 14: Entries and Exits of the City Employees by Public Servant Category and Gender
(April 1985 to April 1988)

	Non-manual		Firemen	Manual		Total
	Male	Female		Male	Female	
Entries	80	80	14	54	2	230
Exits	77	64	11	65	10	227

lunch services. For entry to this category, there was earlier no age-limit.
Many of the applicants have job experience elsewhere. Their entry at a
higher age means fewer years of service, so, a disadvantage in terms of pay
rise and the amount of lump-sum retirement allowance and Public Servant
Pension benefit. To offset this disadvantage, an age-limit of 30 was recently
stipulated. This category of workers is still handicapped since the workers'
pay rise takes place more slowly and they are not qualified for the managerial posts.

Age Structure and its Determinants

See table 13 and table 14. City employees as a whole are aging. However,
there are some features specific to the public servant category and to
gender. As for the non-manual males, the exits of workers have been
balanced by the entries. Nevertheless, they are aging together with the
largest groups aged 30 to 45 as of 1988. The non-manual females are
relatively young but are more rapidly aging because the exits have occurred
much more among the younger group. The manual males are older but their
aging has leveleed off because of a relatively high rate of re-filling of
positions. The manual females are the most rapidly aging category because
of little re-filling.

As to the non-manual males, promotion is obviously age-related. As the
personnel staff put it, the promotion policy has been aimed at as many of
them as possible reaching the lowest managerial posts before "Teinen". In
this respect the staff point to two problems. First, "the largest age groups
will have less prospect for promotion to the managerial posts, which might
dampen their motivation to work." Six managerial posts added in the last
4 years might be a response to this problem. Second, as a result of the policy
above, "some people lacking ability and motivation are at managerial posts
and this has caused discontent among the younger employees."

More serious for the personnel staff is the problem of the surplus of older
firemen who were hired in large numbers at the service's inauguration. The
Ministry for Local Government has instructed the municipalities to transfer
the firemen to other jobs, but "it is impossible to re-train them for clerical
work".

Exit

In the past, there was no "Teinen" age enforced in the public sector. Instead, each employer provided its own age at which every public servant should resign. In the case of this city administration it was 58 for the managerial staff (to make room for the younger employees), 63 for the manual workers (to compensate for fewer years of service) and 60 for the other categories. In addition, what is today called the Early Retirement Scheme was available for employees aged 57 and over. The scheme was attractive because benefit from the Public Servant Pension began at the age of 55.

Prior to the enforcing of the 1986 Older Workers Employment Stabilization Act, a universal "Teinen" age of 60 was introduced to the whole of the public sector. At the same time, the city administration re-instituted its Early Retirement Scheme. The public employers pay a lump-sum allowance to the leaver, the amount of which is decided by his final basic salary multiplied by a certain number of months. The number of months relates to his length of service with an upper limit of 35 years. In the case of the city administration the maximal number is 62.7 months. The leaver at "Teinen" receives the lump-sum, which is calculated on the basic salary which is two grades above his actual final basic salary. This is the sole advantage for the leaver at "Teinen" since, in most cases, he has worked longer than 35 years before "Teinen". Moreover contributions exceeding 35 years do not affect his Public Servant Pension benefit any more.

The employees aged 50 and older with 25 or more years of service are eligible for the early retirement scheme. If you choose to retire early, you will receive a lump-sum allowance which is calculated on the basic salary two grades above his actual final basic salary and includes a supposed 2 percent annual pay rise until "Teinen". In the context of the whole public pension schemes reform, the benefit age from the Public Servant Pension is being raised to 60. This will reduce the advantage of early retirement to some extent. However, the "35 years of service" rule above might offset this.

Table 15 shows how the people left the city administration in the years from March 1985 to March 1988. Almost half the managerial employees made their exit through early retirement. We suggest that this is because there is a norm "to make room for the younger." But both the personnel staff and the union officials deny this. According to them, this is because "being at a managerial post is demanding". 23 females chose to retire early. "Older women, whose children have got jobs, tend to early retirement." "Younger women tend to quit mainly due to child bearing." In contrast, most of the manual male workers tend to stay until "Teinen", "to lengthen their years of service."

Table 15: Exit Routes of the City Employees by Pubic Servant Category and Gender
(March 1985 to March 1988)

	Mana.		Non-m.		Fir.	Manu.		Total
	M	F	M	F		M	F	
Teinen	25	4	2	3	1	49	1	85
E. R.	25	7	4	13	4	6	3	62
Others	6	0	15	37	6	10	6	80
Total	56	11	21	53	11	65	10	227

Legenda:	Mana.:	Managerial Employees
	Non-m.:	Non-Managerial Employees
	Manu.:	Manual Workers
	Fir.:	Firemen
	M:	Males
	F:	Females
	E. R.:	Early Retirement

After "Teinen"

The personnel section has arranged for about half the leavers at "Teinen" to be re-employed as non-regular employees by the city administration itself or the city-related institutions. The employment is on a yearly re-newed basis to a maximum of 3 years. Their jobs are easy but low paid. This low wage depends upon the Public Servant Pension providing 80 percent benefit for the older workers with an annual wage earning of below 1.5 million yen, which is slightly higher than the annual sum of monthly earning limit for 80 percent benefit from the Welfare Pension for the private sector. As the personnel staff put it, "they have chosen to continue working more for health reasons than to increase their earnings."

2.4.2 Department of Refuse Collection and Disposal

The Organization and Nature of Work

The department is responsible for the collection and disposal of home garbage and is staffed with 34 non-manual, 113 manual and 8 non-regular employees. Half the workload of collection is contracted out to 4 private companies with 53 workers. 76 of the workforce carry out the collection in areas under the direct management of the city. Teams of one truck with two men collect packed garbage regularly from 6.000 dustbins and transport them to 2 factories. In addition, city teams of one truck with three men collect home appliances when requested by the citizens. In the two facto-ries, combustibles are incinerated and incombustibles are broken into pieces, after materials for recycling have been selected out. The remainder is transported to the 3rd factory and buried in the ground. 57 of the workers in the factories are machine operators and drivers.

Recruitment, Transfer and Exit

Despite central government pressing municipalities not to re-fill the vacant manual jobs but to contract out the service, the city administration has re-filled the positions by hiring younger workers. The majority of them had job experience elsewhere and their average age of entry is in their late 20s. Transfer between manual jobs has seldom occurred. In the last 5 years, there were only two cases of personnel reshuffling between the school care-taking section and the refuse department. Due to the handicap in pay rise, employees tend to stay till "Teinen". From 1985 to 1989 19 manual workers left at "Teinen", 1 worker chose early retirement at the age of 55, 1 worker left voluntarily at the age of 53 and 3 workers died at the age of 45, 46 and 56. As a result of the union's negotiation, an improvement was made so that the salary for the manual workers near the "Teinen" age became equivalent to that of the lowest managerial staff. "This has increased their morale" and will strengthen their tendency to stay till "Teinen". Half the leavers at "Teinen" have found non-regular based job in the city administration or city-related institutions. The department itself employs three former employees as non-regular machine operators because of their skills.

The Age and Health Problem

The average age of the factory workforce is 43.6 and that for workers in refuse collection is 46.6. (The workforce in the private contractor companies is older with an average age of 49.0). It is for health reasons that the two refuse collectors were transferred to the school care-taking section, but in fact refuse collection work is not regarded as demanding enough to affect the health. The elder team member works as a leader and the harder work is carried out by the younger member. Less demanding jobs are assigned to the older and the unhealthy. Rather, the factory jobs are regarded as more demanding because they continue till midnight and some of the elder workers hope to move to the collection work.

According to the union officials, many of the collectors suffer from lumbago. However, this is also true for the other manual workers. The union officials told us: "since the causal relationship between lumbago and manual work has not yet been demonstrated, we can not, at present, press the employer for introducing a policy to improve the situation." According to them, "at any point in time, two or three persons are on leave of absence for long-term sickness". But, according to the union officials, the number is not especially high for the department and, after two weeks to a month of absence, all return. The up-take rate of paid leave (which private sector workers make use of for short-term sickness) is higher for the department workers at 68 percent compared with the average of 56 percent. But, according to the personnel staff, "it is higher not because the manual workers become sick more often but because they tend to exert their due right more." For foreign readers this story might need some explanation. The average up-take rate of paid leave for the private sector workers in Japan is as low as under 50 percent. The first reason is, that if a worker takes paid leave frequently, this is believed to unfavorably affect the rating of his performance and attitude by his supervisors. The second reason is that, since there is no scheme for leave for short-term illness, workers are believed to save their days of paid leave to be used up if they become sick. As the figure above shows, there is the same tendency among the public sector workers. So the manual workers in the public sector, who have no prospect of promotion, "exert their due right more." The tendency is, however, changing among the younger workers in the private as well as in the public sector. More younger workers are taking paid leave more freely than before.

2.4.3 Concluding Remarks

Presented here is a prototype of Japanese life-time employment, which covers female and manual workers on an equal footing with non-manual male workers as long as they are regular employees. Public sector employers are also faced with their own aging problem but they do not have a "Shukko" system, which is a powerful weapon for large company personnel policy in the private sector. The early retirement scheme plays a role in solving the aging problem but it depends utterly upon the older worker's own choice. Despite this, the problem does not look very serious because it may only be applicable to the public sector where no competition takes place such as that among private companies. In 1985 central government decided (1) to reduce the number of its regular employees, in particular not to re-fill the vacancies for manual jobs and to marketize the services and (2) to cease the annual pay rise at the age of 58. This decision was made under the rising political stream of "neo-conservatism" and is supposed to aim at making a small hole in the life-time employment system in the central government.

The Ministry of Local Government, a patron and watcher, has directed the local authorities to follow the central model and many of them have complied. In the city administration in our case study, the Ministry policy has not been fully pursued. Vacant refuse collection jobs have been re-filled and pay continues to rise until the "Teinen" age. It may be because union resistance has been effective.

2.5   Case Study 5: A Small Company

2.5.1 The Company

The original body of the company was inaugurated in 1963 in Yokohama by Mr.X. His first business concerned the assembly of transformers for X-ray generators. In 1974 he was successful in getting an officially authorized qualification to produce medical equipment and established a private company with his wife and father. His business grew steadily but the original factory site was not large enough to cope with this expansion in the 1970s. In 1978 he became a member of a newly established cooperative association consisting of 15 small to medium sized enterprises. The association aimed to borrow public money at low interest for moving into the Yokohama Kanazawa Industrial Complex which was constructed by the Yokohama municipal government on reclamated land in order to create good factory sites for small- to medium-sized enterprises located in the Yokohama area. In 1982 his company moved into the Kanazawa Industrial Complex and started production with ten workers including his wife, father, a younger brother and himself. The factory was a one-floor building with 300 square meters of floor space. In 1985 the private company was transformed into a joint stock company with 20 million yen paid capital and was renamed. In 1986 the factory was enlarged into a three-story building with 950 square meters of total floor space and the paid capital increased to 40 million yen.

The industrial sector of the company is concerned with the manufacturing of electric machinery and equipment. The products and their percentage of sales as of the 1989 fiscal year were small-sized X-ray equipment for medical use (70 percent), their parts and components (20 percent) and other electronic equipment (10 percent).

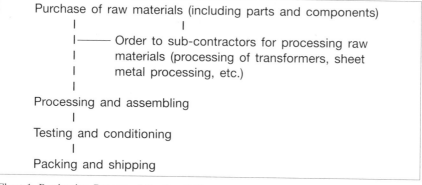

Chart 1: Production Process of the Small Company

The main production facilities and equipment were a coil winding machine, a drying machine, a generator of 60 HZ electricity, testing machines for X-rays and high voltage electric currents and a CAD system based on personal computers. The production process is shown in the flow chart below.

With regard to purchasing raw materials, the company has been buying X-ray tubes from T. Medical Co. Ltd. which has supplied 40 percent of the company's total sum of purchasing of raw materials including parts and components. The sum of orders to ten sub-contractors formed 40 percent of the total sum of shipped products. Total sales as of the 1989 fiscal year amounted to 340 million yen. There were ten customers and the top customer was T. Medical which formed 70 percent of the company's sales. These facts suggest that the case company, as a fact, has been a sub-contractor for T./Medical, although there is no capital relationship between the two companies. This special relationship with T./Medical is reflected in the personnel policy of the company which we will see later.

2.5.2 Age-Related Rules

Before the enactment of the 1986 Employment Act the company had no "Teinen" policy. However, it had an employment policy concerning workers over 55. This stipulated that the pay after 55 years old would not increased except for a small sum to adjust to inflation. There were two employees aged 58 and 61 in 1986. Therefore, the company's introduction of the "Teinen" age seemed to make it difficult to employ the 61 year old man on a regular basis. Mr. X, the owner director, decided to hire him as a "Shokutaku" worker whose pay was lower than that for regular workers but higher than that for part-time workers. In 1990 the company introduced a re-employment scheme which allowed all "Teinen" workers to be re-employed in the company. The term of contract was indefinite. The pay level of re-employed workers was 40–50 percent of that for a 55 year old worker. The company received a subsidy from the government, which will be mentioned later, for these re-employed workers.

2.5.3 Age Structure and Personnel Changes in 1984–1990

The age Structure of the company is shown in Table 16.

The number of employees as of April 1984 was 11 not including 5 directors. All the directors belonged to Mr. X's family. They were his father (77 years old), wife (50), brother (43), elder son (34) and himself (54). The father and wife were nominal directors. Among the 11 employers there

Table 16: Change in the Age Structure of the Small Company Between 1984 and 1990

Year	84	87	90	84			87			90		
Age G.	T	T	T	A	B	C	A	B	C	A	B	C
65 –	1	0	0	0	0	0	0	0	0	0	0	0
60 – 64	0	1	2	0	0	0	0	0	1	1	1	0
55 – 59	2	4	4	1	1	0	1	2	1	3	1	0
50 – 54	3	2	3	2	1	0	2	0	0	1	1	1
45 – 49	0	2	5	0	0	0	2	0	0	2	2	1
40 – 44	2	2	5	1	1	0	2	0	0	3	1	1
35 – 39	1	5	5	0	1	0	3	2	0	4	1	0
30 – 34	4	2	4	2	2	0	2	0	0	2	1	1
25 – 29	1	2	1	1	0	0	2	0	0	0	0	1
20 – 24	1	1	3	0	0	1	0	1	0	0	3	0
18 – 19	1	5	0	0	1	0	0	5	0	0	0	0
Total	16	26	32	8	7	1	14	10	2	16	11	5
Av. Age	42	38	43									

Legenda: T: Total Personnel Number
          A: Directors and Managers
          B: Operatives and Simple Clerical Workers
          C: "Shokutaku" Workers and Part-Timers

were three chiefs aged 57, 31 and 26 and seven operatives aged 59, 53, 43, 36, 31, 18f (f=female) and a young part-timer (a student aged 20). The average age of the 16 people was 42.

By April 1987 the total number had increased from 16 to 26. Between 1984 and 1987, 15 people joined and five left. With regard to directors, Mr. X's younger son (aged 27) took a position replacing the 80 year old father, and two new directors aged 50 and 42 joined. They were responsible for R&D and sales. The company invited them from T. Medical, its largest customer. In 1987 there were eight employees in the higher rank. Between 1984 and 1987 four new employees aged 40, 36, 36 and 30 joined, two were promoted from the operative rank and one aged 59 was lowered to the operative rank because he was approaching the "Teinen" age. Out of these eight men four including two new employees belonged to the R&D Section. This reflected Mr. X's desire to invest for the future. Out of the remaining four, three were group leaders of production and one was a sales leader.

With regard to operatives, out of seven people in 1984, three quitted at the ages of 34, 32 and 21f, two aged 46 and 39 were promoted to higher ranks, one retired at "Teinen" and was re-employed as a "Shokutaku" worker at the age of 62 and one was lowered from a higher rank. Four new employees aged 35, 19, 19, 18f joined the production group and three female school leavers aged 20, 18 and 18 joined the general affairs section as routine clerical workers. One aged 56 stayed in this rank.

As for part-timers and "Shokutaku"" workers, one part-timer aged 21 quitted, one operative aged 62 was transferred to "Shokutaku" rank because of "Teinen" and one "Shokutaku" worker aged 60 was hired.

In the period 1984–87, the average age of the company workforce fell about four years mainly because of hiring school leavers. In April 1990 the total personnel increased to 32. Between 1987 and 1990 , 14 people joined and eight left the company. A 57 year old male director from T. Medical also joined. As for the higher rank of employees, two men aged 58 and 38 were hired, two men quitted at the ages of 45 and 31 and six men stayed.

With regard to operatives, three females aged 22, 20 and 19 and one male aged 20 quitted. To replace them, five men aged 51, 46, 45, 33 and 18 were hired. A man aged 61 who had retired at "Teinen" was re-employed in 1990 after receiving unemployment benefit for ten months. Four people stayed.

As for the part-timers and "Shokutaku" workers, two "Shokutaku" men retired at the ages of 63 and 60. To replace them, five female part-timers aged 53, 46, 44, 32 and 28 were hired. Between 1987 and 1990 the average age rose sharply to 43 because of the exits of young operatives and the entries of middle-aged and older people.

2.5.4 Concluding Remarks

Some personnel characteristics of the case company between 1984 and 1990 can be seen in the following points:

1. Family Enterprise

Five family members of Mr. X have been the core of the company.

2. High turn-over rate of employees

Between 1984 and 1990, 24 people were hired and 12 people quitted not including part-timers and Mr./X's family members. Seven out of the 11 employees in 1984 had left by 1990. The turn-over rate was especially high in the younger generation. Six out of nine employees aged 18–20 quitted after one or two years of service and three men quitted at the age of 31. In contrast, the exit of workers between the age of 35 and the "Teinen" age was negligible; only one case. In order to cover the high turn-over rate of younger employees, the hiring of middle-and upper-aged operatives, "Shokutaku" workers and female part-time workers increased. "Life-time employment" could not be ffered in the company, even if Mr./X had wanted to do so.

3. Cases of aged retirement

There were three cases of quitting at retirement age between 1984 and 1990. The first person who had worked more than 10 years in the company faced the introduction of the "Teinen" age in 1986 at the age of 61. He received a small retirement lump-sum less than one million yen at that time but stayed two years more in the company as a "Shokutaku" worker and finally retired at age 63 in 1988. The second man who had also completed long service reached the "Teinen" age in 1988. He retired from the company with a retirement lump-sum and received unemployment benefit for 10 months. Then, in 1989, he came back to the company as a "Shokutaku" worker. In 1990 he was re-employed as a full operative at the age of 62 because of the change of personnel rule of the company mentioned above. The third man was a "Teinen" man from T. Medical and was hired by the company as a "Shokutaku" worker in 1987 but he retired after one year. We can say that "Shokutaku" and "re-employment" are the key words for the treatment of older workers.

4. Strong personnel relations with a main customer

The case company accepted three men as directors and a man as a sales manager from T. Medical between 1987 and 1990. The two directors who joined in 1987 at the ages of 50 and 42 were engineers and expected to be key persons for R&D. However, two further cases seem to be rather different.

It seems that a director who joined in 1989 at the age of 56 and a sales manager who joined in 1990 at the age of 58 were accepted in order to keep a close business connection among the two companies. This may be a typical pattern where elderly white collar workers are accepted from a large company which is usually a main customer for a small-to medium-sized enterprise. It seems that the above mentioned points would be more or less common characteristics for all small-to medium-sized enterprises in Japan. Most of them are playing the role of sub-contractor as well as the role of saucer for spilled aged manpower from large companies.

2.6   Summary

The following three points summarize the findings of the case studies.

(1) All the large companies including the regional bank have increased the period of employment for regular employees by raising the "Teinen" age to 60. At the same time, however, all the companies have altered the treatment of older employees. Firstly, the older employees have been placed out of the age-oriented system of pay rise and promotion. Secondly, many of them have been shed out to the subsidiary and related firms by

"Shukko". In some cases, special subsidiary firms have even been established only to accept the older "Shukko" workers from the parent company. A further development was also revealed. The electric maker has enforced a scheme to re-employ its post "Teinen" men on a non-regular basis for a number of years in order to respond to the labor shortage or to offer a longer term of employment. These arrangements are phenomena common throughout most large Japanese companies.

The cases of the city administration and the small company seem to be rather exceptional. The former had already had a de facto "Teinen" age. The newly introduced formal "Teinen" age of 60 has not affected the situation much. The age-oriented system of pay rise and promotion has been kept intact. The city administration has had no weapon to combat its aging problem with, apart from the early retirement scheme which is voluntary. The small company had already had to depend upon the workers aged over 60. Its introduction of the "Teinen" age of 60 has not changed the state of affairs much, apart from the fact that the workers aged over 60 are treated as non-regular "Shokutaku" workers.

(2) As a result, the regular employees of large companies enjoy employment security till the age of 60 and some of them even enjoy it past this age on a non-regular basis.

Some large companies are reported to have enforced the early retirement scheme. In this respect, a case we investigated should be mentioned here. A large electric machine company paid, in addition to a lump-sum retirement allowance on quitting, a monthly allowance amounting to 140–150 thousand yen to a person who had chosen to quit at an age between 55 and 59 and retired. This was a sum equivalent roughly to the national welfare minimum for a couple with two dependents. None of the companies in our case studies has arranged such a scheme. However, their workers who retired at the age of 55 or even 50 were made eligible for the company pension. Further, the service year after the age of 55 was not reflected in the amount of the retirement lump-sum and company pension. These arrangements seem to be effective in encouraging early retirement.

But, as was seen, the majority of the workers continue to work until "Teinen". The career pattern after "Teinen" varies. Workers may decide: (1) to retire from the labor market and to receive the public pension and the company pension, together with the unemployment benefit for 300 days, (2) to retire once and re-enter the labor market after the 300 day receipt of unemployment benefit, (3) to apply for the re-employment scheme and to continue to work, if the company has arranged such a scheme, and (4) to find a second job by themselves in small to medium-sized companies.

With respect to the benefit level of the public pension, the average monthly benefit for the total beneficiaries amounted, in January 1989, to

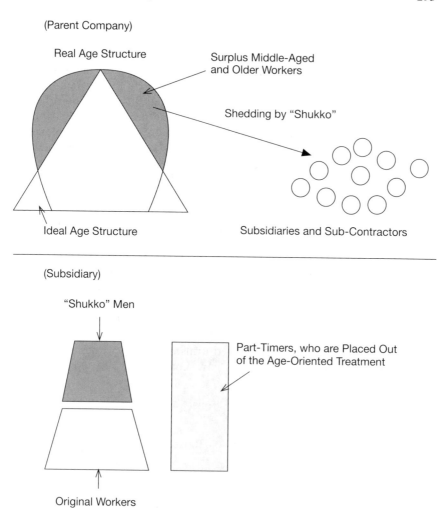

Figure 2: "Shukko" and Quasi-Internal Labor Market; A Conceptual Model

57.6 percent of the average gross monthly wage for the total employees (excluding bi-annual bonus). The benefit from the unemployment insurance fund is usually 60 percent of one's last basic pay. In most cases the pay level for the workers aged over 60 is below the earning limit for 80 percent public pension benefit.

Figure 2 presents an example for the age-income profile of the blue collar workers in large companies, the calculation for which is based on the case of the electric maker.

(3) Our main focus was on the destiny of regular male employees in large Japanese companies. However, they form only about a quarter of Japanese workers as a whole. Some words should be given to the remainder.

The regular female employees in large companies are, in most cases, forced to quit on marriage or child birth. It is usually a part-time job that they find when they return to the labor market. In the plants of large companies, there are a lot of seasonal workers and part-timers. The workers in small companies never enjoy an age-oriented system with employment security or enjoy it to a much lesser extent than large company employees. In the external labor market the older people are always handicapped. The unemployment rate is much higher for them. Those workers who left a large company at "Teinen" can find usually a job on non-regular or part-time basis.

With respect to this portion of Japanese workers our studies noted three phenomena. First, the regular female employees in the regional bank were, by an unwritten law, forced to quit on marriage. Second, in contrast to a very high turn-over rate among the younger workers in the small company, almost all the middle-aged and older people stayed in the company during the surveyed period. The reason for this seems to be that they were unlikely to find a better job. Third, the increase in the number of "Shukko" workers from the iron and steel company paralleled the decrease in the number of employees in its subsidiary and related firms. Our survey does not indicate where the people who left the firms have gone.

3   Process

3.1   Why Has the "Teinen" Age Been Raised?

3.1.1 What Were the Motives for the Individual Companies?

Our five companies including the city bank, though belonging to various industries, have all raised their "Teinen" age to 60 or introduced the "Teinen" age of 60 since 1980. However, the time of decision of the policy differs slightly between the companies. The iron and steel company was the first and the regional bank was the last. In our view, the differences reflect what directly motivated the individual company's decision.

The regional bank had already had a "Teinen" age of 58, an age higher than that in the other four. The reason for this high "Teinen" age is unknown. Since 1972 the electric maker had enforced the re-employment scheme guaranteeing employment till the age of 60 for all male workers, which was one of the coordinated claims of the unions of the 16 major electric maker companies affiliating

However, the decisive move to the raising of the "Teinen" age itself started with the agreement on raising it to 60 between the unions and the managements of the five major iron and steel companies. Two points are to be emphasized.

First, as was mentioned above, the negotiations between the most functional federation of unions and the association of employers in this industry have very often built up the standard concerning the working conditions which the large companies in the other industries have followed. The decision for raising the "Teinen" age in this key industry also influenced the attitude of other large companies.

Second, however, the large companies in this industry were never in a favorable position to raise the "Teinen" age. They suffered the most from the serious depression among industries and had a more aged workforce. Moreover, they had no re-employment scheme which might have been a stepping stone to the raising of the "Teinen" age. On the other hand, for the very reason of the deep depression, the unions' demand for a longer term of employment security was much pressing. It took over two years for both parties to reach agreement on it. The decision made in such a way was a very valuable model.

As the union documents suggest, the main driving force was, first of all, the unions' demand. But the negotiation and decision-making process in this industry coincided with the actions taken by the state in timing. For, as was also mentioned above, the Ministry of Labor declared its commitment to promoting the raising of the "Teinen" age in 1979 and started to give administrative guidance to individual large companies, according to its document, from 1981 onward. We might be able to regard the decision in the iron and steel industry as a concerted action between the managements, the unions and the state, although there is no evidence for this supposition.

The city banks' decision was obviously affected by this model. The electric maker's personnel staff referred, in addition, to the strong administrative guidance given by the state as a motive.

Prior to the enforcing of the 1986 Older Workers Employment Stabilization Act the state introduced a universal "Teinen" age of 60 into the whole of the public sector, an act which was intended as another model according to the officials from the Ministry of Labor.

The regional bank is the last of the regional banks which were driven to raise their "Teinen" age by the 1986 legislation. This legislation as well as a subsidy, which will be mentioned later, seems to have motivated the small company.

3.1.2 Why Has the "Teinen" Age Been Raised? Our View

Looking back, there could have been alternative responses to the employment difficulties among older workers. The public pension eligibility age could have been lowered or the duration of unemployment benefit receipt could have been prolonged. Then, there might have emerged the early retirement path in the Japanese version. However, the state did not follow this policy line for financial reasons. The only thing it did in this direction was the adding of 90 days to the duration of unemployment benefit receipt for the older unemployed in such regions or from such industries as the Minister of Labor designated to be "especially depressed". The workers, on their side, pressed their employers for a solution to the problem, but not the state. Both the state and the workers counted on the large companies' initiative.

The personnel staff of the large companies we interviewed gave us some insight into why the "Teinen" age was raised. The same two answers cropped up regularly; "stable industrial relations" and "the social reputation and sense of responsibility of the company".

The management of the large companies have attached the highest importance to maintaining stable industrial relations owing to life-time employment of regular workers. Therefore, it seems that the management came to the conclusion that a "Teinen" age lower than the pension eligibility age could not be held any longer if the morale of the regular core and the cooperative relations with the unions were to be maintained, especially at a time when the "Teinen" reachers faced serious employment difficulties. A "Teinen" age of 55 had become too low. The large companies reluctantly accepted the union demand and what the state thought should be a norm, for the sake of stable industrial relations.

3.1.3 Problems and Solutions

With the previous "Teinen" age, the large companies had already been suffering from the surplus of middle-aged and older employees which was paralyzing the well-functioning of life-time employment in terms of both pay cost and promotion. The raised "Teinen" age would amplify the problem further, with the age-orientation principle kept intact. As all the interviewees admitted, it is these points about which they held the greatest concern. What were the solutions and what did the unions concede for a longer term of employment security?

3.2   What Took Place with the Raised "Teinen" Age?

3.2.1 Changes in Age-Orientation

As our cases all indicate, the raised "Teinen" age was accompanied, first, by the change in the pay system. (At the time of our survey the regional bank was also examining a change in pay system for the new "Teinen" age.) Roughly speaking, the pay was re-designed to level off or rather to be reduced at the previous "Teinen" age of 55 (in the case of our electric maker, 57). In the iron and steel company, while pay continued to rise for the workers aged 55 and over, the wage system was reformed so that the pay level for employees aged 50 to 54 was reduced and the new pay level for those aged 59 was made roughly equal to the previous level for employees aged 54.

The promotion system was also changed. The new rule is, in most cases, that the middle and lowest managerial post holders lose their posts at the age of 55 (in the electric maker, 57). In short, although the duration of employment security has become longer, the age group concerned is not included in the age-orientated treatment. That is, the age-orientation principle ceases to be applied at age 55. This is the point of compromise between the unions who put highest priority on employment security until the age of 60 and the large companies who strive to avoid the difficulty which the aging of the workforce brings about.

3.2.2 Shedding the Middle-Aged and Older Workers by "Shukko"

Another common development is the drastic increase in the number of workers put on "Shukko". As was mentioned above, originally "Shukko" was a means for large companies to keep personnel ties with their satellite companies. In 1973, for instance, the iron and steel company had put a thousand out of its thirty thousand regular employees on "Shukko".

However, another version of "Shukko" has been developing in every large company case since the late 1970s and especially in connection with the raising of the "Teinen" age. In 1989 the iron and steel company had put a surprising nine thousand workers, indeed 30 percent of the total regular force, on "Shukko" and the overwhelming majority of "Shukko" men were middle-aged and older employees including a considerable number of blue collar workers. It is also noteworthy that the average age for the workers put on "Shukko" is decreasing.

Obviously "Shukko" has come to be utilized to shed the middle-aged and older workers out of the parent companies. This "Shukko" is a one-way trip. The middle-aged and older workers, once put on "Shukko", usually

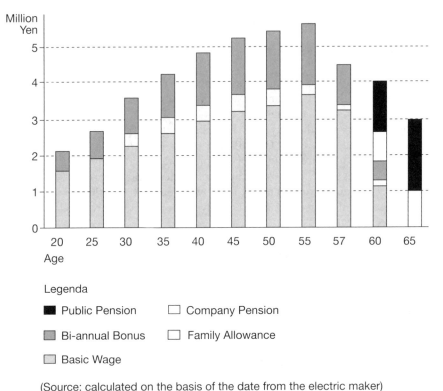

Legenda

■ Public Pension   ☐ Company Pension

▨ Bi-annual Bonus   ☐ Family Allowance

☐ Basic Wage

(Source: calculated on the basis of the date from the electric maker)

Figure 3: Age-Income Profile Model for Blue Collar Workers in the Case of the Electric Maker (annal income excluding overtime pay)

never return to the parent company, although their status as a regular employee of the parent company is guaranteed until the age of 60. In the city bank an employee with 25 years or more service has to be prepared to be put on "Shukko" at any time.

As our interviewee, who had once drafted the middle-aged and older workforce reduction plan when he was a member of the personnel staff of a giant electricity company, told us, "we strove to shed surplus middle-aged and older workers out by 'Shukko' in order to make the age structure of the parent company a pyramid-shaped one." Therefore "Shukko" is, today, an instrument of strategic importance to regulate the age structure of the parent company where redundancy-making is impossible. Why, however, do the large companies eject especially the middle-aged and older workers? Pay cost reduction is a likely motive, since the parent company has to bear only the difference in pay for "Shukko" men. But this alone does not explain the large companies' attachment to a "pyramid-shaped" age structure in the parent company. Rather it is better explained by our "age-mix" hypothesis that from the large Japanese company's point of view, a combination of a small number of older and experienced workers and a large number of younger workers is the most productive age-mix.

However, the solution of using "Shukko" to deal with the surplus problem also means passing on the difficulty from the parent company to its satellites. Are, then, the receiving companies like the subsidiaries and subcontractors a shelter for the surplus middle-aged and older people from the parent company's point of view? The answer is "yes and no". For, since the receiving companies usually belong to the small to medium-sized companies where the working conditions are much less age-oriented and the personnel policy is much less age-conscious than those in the large parent companies, it is relatively easy for them to accept the "Shukko" workers. In addition, these companies accept them only within the limits of their managerial efficiency. When the individual qualities of "Shukko" workers and the number of them exceed this limit, the parent company has to build up some subsidiaries only to offer jobs for their older "Shukko" men. But such subsidiaries are not simply a shelter but run their own business. One of such subsidiaries in an iron and steel company was farming eels! The subsidiary of the electric maker was even growing.

In the case of every large company, the personnel section negotiated with the receiving companies about pay, duty and other things for individual "Shukko" cases. The city bank even has an independent personnel section to control its "Shukko" men working in the bank's subsidiaries. Therefore, we can conclude that by "Shukko" the large companies do not only shed the middle-aged and older workers to their satellites but also transfer them in a quasi-internal labor market and endeavor to exploit individual workers' skill and ability as much as possible in the right place. Apart from some persons who were given promises of positions as board members, a small number of the workers aged 55 and over stayed within the city bank because they were those for whom the personnel section failed to find a suitable receiver for reasons such as ill health. In this case the bank itself fulfills the role of a shelter.

The on-passing of the surplus middle-aged and older workforce to the satellites is successful only as long as the size of total employment in the "quasi-internal labor market" is growing, as seems to have been the case for the electric maker, or at least maintained at the same level. The most depressed iron and steel company had to find receiving companies outside its quasi-internal labor market. The "Shukko" workers sent there were, so to speak, spilled out of the quasi-internal labor market.

3.2.3 More Flexible "Teinen" System

The previous "Teinen" age was a relatively strong standard in the sense that every employee had to cease working as a regular employee in his large company. The raising of the "Teinen" age has meant a significant change in the meaning of "Teinen".

First, many of the middle-aged and older workers are destined to leave the parent company by "Shukko" for ever, although their employment is secured.

Second, they are placed out of age-oriented treatment at, in most cases, the age of 55. In addition, the service years after this age are not reflected in the amount of the lump-sum retirement allowance and company pension. As is the case for the iron and steel company, employees aged 50 and over are able to retire and receive the company pension. Therefore, the older workers are less motivated to stay until the new "Teinen" age and the employer can encourage them to retire from the company before the "Teinen" age. In the extreme case of the city bank, every regular employee has to receive the lump-sum retirement allowance and leave the bank to retire or to work in one of its subsidiaries, except those people mentioned above.

Third, thus the new "Teinen" age means the age at which the older workers are finally thrown out of employment security. Faced with the present labor shortage many large companies have begun to re-employ a portion of their "Teinen" reachers on a non-regular basis. In this case the age of 60 is nothing more than a passing point in the gradual retirement process of these older workers (see Figure 2 in the previous section).

In conclusion, with the raising of their "Teinen" age, the large Japanese companies have introduced more flexible personnel management, while maintaining life-time employment.

3.2.4 The Case of the Small Company

Before introducing its "Teinen" age, the small company had hired some workers who were older than 60. The pay had been decided for individual workers and there had no systematic criteria. The pay had tended to rise according to age and length of service of the employees but peaked out at the age of 55. The introduction of the "Teinen" age has brought about no important change in this situation, apart from that the employees aged 60 and over were treated as "Shokutaku" workers. In 1990 Mr. X introduced a "re-employment" scheme and "re-employed" the "Teinen" reachers. However, it was mainly for the purpose of getting a state subsidy to promote re-employment, which will be mentioned later. He regretted "if we had arranged a 'Teinen' age of, say, 55 earlier, we would have been able to receive also the state subsidy for raising the 'Teinen' age."

This small company case also presents an example of the sub-contractors who have accepted "Shukko" men from their main customer. This company accepted two older "Shukko" men from its main customer "in order to keep a close business connection among the two companies." The acceptance had its own rational ground in this sense. However, the impact of the acceptance on the company's own workforce is not clear because many people joined and left the company during a short period.

3.3   The Role of the State

3.3.1 Methods of Instituting Policies

As was mentioned above, the state has encouraged and driven the employers to raise their "Teinen" age by giving administrative guidance, subsidizing the raising and legislating the 1986 Older Workers Employment Stabilization Act. Some words should be given to the significance of these methods instituting policies.

The Administrative Guidance: In order to obtain the desired effect when pursuing a certain policy, the Japanese government very often asks or presses the circles concerned to cooperate voluntarily with the policy, by means of circulating documents titled "Recommendation", "Government Interpretation of Law", "Instruction" and so on, and in some cases by itself joining the behind-closed-door negotiation among the parties concerned. This policy method particular to Japan, in other words, the persuasion or pressing by the government, is made in order to conciliate or coordinate different interests, to support a consensus to be formed among the parties concerned or to regulate the behavior of the circles concerned to go along with what the government wants to be a social norm. One example: right after the first oil crisis the government gave administrative guidance to all the gas stations to the effect that they should be closed on Sundays for the purpose of economizing on oil consumption. Almost all of them complied. In our case studies, it is the model formed in the iron and steel industry and the administrative guidance given by the government that affected our bank's and electric maker's decision. We can conclude that the administrative guidance given by the state fulfilled a significant role in the process of the consensus on the new "Teinen" age being established among large companies.

The Subsidy Program: From 1973 onward, the state operated a subsidy program which gave to the employers who raised their "Teinen" age from 55 a subsidy of an annual amount of 300 thousand yen per head for the first age group concerned. The amount was roughly equivalent to a tenth of the annual average wage of those days. Of course all our large companies received the subsidy. However, in view of its nature as a pump-primer, this program seems to have played a secondary role. The program expired in 1986. Our regional bank raised its "Teinen" age after it.

The 1986 Employment Act: By the time of the 1986 Act, most of the large companies had raised or decided to raise their "Teinen" age. In view of this fact, it is possible to assert that the role of the legislation was to establish the minimum "Teinen" age of 60 as a general aim for all the employers including those in small to medium-sized companies.

Today a "Teinen" age of 60 is the norm not only in the large companies but also in the small to medium-sized companies. In 1990 the "Teinen" age was 60 in 96.0 percent of the companies with 5.000 and more employees, in 87.1 percent of those with 1,000 to 4.999 employees, in 77.4 percent of those with 300 to 999 employees, in 77.7 percent of those with 100 to 299 and 67.3 percent of those with 30 to 99 employees. Smaller companies tend to have no "Teinen" age or a "Teinen" age lower than 60. The tendency is much stronger in the smallest companies with fewer than 30 employees, which the Ministry of Labor has placed out of its target. Despite depending more on the older workers, the employers of the smallest companies tend to be reluctant to introduce a "Teinen" age or raise the "Teinen" age. The reason might be that they fear they would be thereby forced to introduce a kind of employment security or provide a longer term of employment security and pay a retirement allowance or a higher allowance at "Teinen", that is, to strengthen the factors which promote life-time employment.

3.3.2 Japanese Features of the Labor Policy

In the labor policy field the Japanese state seldom imposes on the employers a universal, trans-sectoral compulsory standard by legislation. Rather the state very often tries to pursue a policy by supporting and leading the initiatives of employers toward the intended policy. To incite companies to raise their "Teinen" age, the state made use of policy instruments like administrative guidance and a subsidy program. The subsidy program was awarded to the companies but not to the workers. Since the subsidy was financed by extra contributions which employers paid to the unemployment insurance fund, the compliant were rewarded and the non-compliant were, in a sense, fined. In the discussion in the Employment Council on how to promote the raising of the "Teinen" age, the representative of the workers argued in favor of a universal and compulsory "Teinen" age while the representative of employers contended that it should be entrusted to the negotiation between the management and the union of each company. The

1986 Act, a result of the seven year discussion in the Council, did not establish the workers' right to work till the age of 60 but it, instead, imposed an obligation on the employers. The legislation, although seemingly very binding, has obligated them simply to make efforts to raise the "Teinen" age to 60. Non-compliant are not punishable. After several recommendations, a local employment agency makes their names public.

In short, Japanese labor policies have always been implemented via companies and counted on their initiatives.

4   Retirement in Future

4.1   The Present Policy Focus

In view of the foreseeable shortage of labor resulting from the rapid decline in the fertility rate since the 1970s, the present focus of the state policy for the older male workers is on promoting employment for those aged 60–64. As the high officials from the Ministry of Labor put it, "we can not avoid utilizing the older workforce in this rapidly aging society." That policy intention was declared in the 1986 Employment Act. In 1990 the act was revised so that it imposed on employers a new obligation, this time, to make efforts to prolong the employment of workers till the age of 64, either by raising the "Teinen" age further or by introducing the re-employment scheme for their "Teinen" reachers. The Ministry is expecting the large companies in particular to create employment opportunities for those aged 60–64 within their quasi-internal labor market.

In the 1980s there were a variety of subsidy programs for promoting the employment of workers between 60 and 64 but in 1990 they were reformed and integrated into the following three:
(1) An employer, who recruits handicapped workers including older people through an employment agency, can receive a subsidy amounting to a fourth (in the case of small to medium-sized companies, a third) of the wage for those workers for one year only.
(2) An employer, who institutes schemes to extend the employment period for those aged 60 and over by raising the "Teinen" age further or operating a re-employment program, can receive a lump-sum subsidy of 800 thousand yen to 10 million yen according to the number of total employees and the number of additional working years.
(3) An employer, whose company has a workforce of which over six percent of the workers are aged between 60 and 64, can receive an annual subsidy of 360 thousand (in the case of small to medium-sized companies, 480 thousand) yen for an employee in this category exceeding this percentage.

The Ministry of Labor has not made public how often the subsidy programs including those in existence in the 1980s have been used. This hints at their poor performance. In the case studies we found that the small company was subsidized for its "re-employed" older workers. But the electric maker's subsidiary which is operating a re-employment scheme for the "Teinen" reachers, did not take up this program. At any rate, the subsidy programs seem to have played a secondary role as the subsidy program for raising the "Teinen" age to 60 did.

As was mentioned above, the Ministry of Welfare and Health is intending to gradually raise the public pension eligibility age to 65 in view of the foreseeable solvency difficulty of the fund. The officials from the Ministry of Labor denied that this measure is part of their policies. But the raising would be extremely effective in driving the older people to the labor market.

4.2   Companies' Response

At the time of our survey, the city administration, the small company, the electric maker's subsidiary (only for the "Shukko" men) and the department store were operating re-employment schemes for their "Teinen" reachers. In every case, the re-employed workers received a wage below the earning limit for 80 percent pension benefit but the department store, in addition, paid the full wage to a small number of the workers with special skills. None of the companies planned to raise the "Teinen" age further. But the personnel staff of the iron and steel company forecast: "As we are entering a time with a severe labor shortage, we will sooner or later be forced to raise the "Teinen" age once again but in a more flexible form."

In the face of a shortage of labor due to the present booming economy, many large companies have begun to re-employ a portion of their "Teinen" reachers by selection. The pay for them is, in most cases, below the earning limit for 80 or 50 percent public pension benefit. To make the re-employment scheme more attractive for applicants, some large companies are re-designing the jobs and assigning easy work to them. In 1990, 39 percent of the companies with 5,000 and more persons, and 54 percent of those with 1,000 to 4,999 persons had some certain kind of re-employment scheme. The percentage was higher in the smaller companies which had had to depend upon an older workforce from the beginning. The companies will have to respond to the future labor shortage by depending more or less on older workers as well as on females and foreigners and/or by locating more plants abroad. The re-employment scheme will expand and it might lead to a further raising of the "Teinen" age.

The employers are facing a dilemma. On the one hand they will support the raising of the public pension age because they would, otherwise, have to bear a higher contribution. On the other hand, they are hiring the older workers at low cost due to the pay being based on the public partial pensions. The raising of the public pension age will deprive them of this top-up. Some of the largest companies, like our iron and steel company, might be able to pay the full wage to their re-employed older workers or go further to lengthen the employment of the regular employees by raising the "Teinen" age again. However, it is questionable how many of the other companies would be able to do this.

4.3 Workers' Attitude

When the government suggested the raising of the public pension age, the unions position was "we will oppose it unless the 'Teinen' age is raised to 65." A newly established national center of the unions, the Japan Trade Unions Congress ("Rengo") is preserving the same position. According to the officials from JTUC, "we fear mostly that there will be a new gap between the 'Teinen' age and the public pension age." This may suggest that most of the unions are prepared to accept the raised pension age if a longer term of employment security is given. However, as was seen, it is questionable whether every of large companies will be able to do it.

In our view, the workers' attitude toward work has been changing along with improvements in the public pension benefit. More of the older people now continue full-time work only until the age of 60 and then they retire or work shorter hours. As we saw, only a few post-"Teinen" men applied for the re-employment scheme in the electric maker. In the summer of 1989, we interviewed a hundred people who had retired or were soon retiring. The majority of them told us: "We don't want any more full-time work after 60. If we continue to work, we want easy and short-term work, bearing in mind our health." The development of public pensions has brought about a change in the life-style of the older people. More of them now enjoy retired life and work has been losing its traditional value among them.

There still remain older people who have to continue full-time work due to not being eligible for the public pension or receiving insufficient benefit. There are also a number of older people who have preferred to continue full-time work in order to receive a higher pension benefit in the future. On the whole, however, Japanese workers are retiring earlier and earlier. The raising of the public pension age would lead to a radical reversal of this tendency.

In our view, on the other side, the Japanese workers, too, are facing a dilemma. They will have to choose between paying a higher contribution at present and retiring early in the future or paying less at present and retiring late in the future. Taken together with the dilemma for employers, the only option might be an actuarially reduced pension available at the age of 60.

References:

Dore, R.P. (1973). British Factory-Japanese Factory: The Origins of Na-
    tional Diversity in Industrial Relations. Berkeley and Los Angeles:
    University of California Press.
Dore, R.P. (1986). Flexible Rigidities: Industrial Policy and Structural
    Adjustment in the Japanese Economy 1970-80 .London: The Athlone
    Press.
Ministry of Labor (1988). White Paper on Labor for Fiscal 1988 (Rodo
    hakusho, 1988 nendo). Tokyo.
Ministry of Labor (1988). Wage Sensus for Fiscal 1988 (Chinginsensasu,
    1988 nendo). Tokyo.
Ministry of Labor (1989) White Paper on Labor for Fiscal 1989 (Rodo
    hakusho, 1989 nendo). Tokyo.
Ministry of Labor (1989). Survey Report on Employment Structure for
    Fiscal 1989 (Shugyo kozo kihon chosa, 1989 nendo). Tokyo.
Office of Prime Minister (1988). Survey Report on Labor Force for Fiscal
    1988 (Rodoryoku chosa, 1988 nendo). Tokyo.
Shindo, M. (1992). Administrative Guidance (Gyosei shido). Tokyo: Iwanami
    Shoten.
Takagi, I., Kimura, T. and D. Gatu. (1986). Social Policy in Japan (Gaisetsu
    nihon no shakai seisaku). Tokyo: Daiichi Shorin.
Tanaka, H. (1980). Employment in today's Japan (Gendai koyo ron).
    Tokyo: Nihon Rodo Kyokai.
Tokunaga, S. (1984). The Structure of the Japanese Labor Market. In:
    S.Tokunaga and J.Bergmann (eds.), Industrial Relations in Transition.
    The Cases of Japan and the Federal Republic of Germany. Tokyo:
    University of Tokyo Press: 25-55.
Totsuka,H. and T. Hyodo (1991). The Changes and Perspectives in the
    Industrial Relations in the Japanese Automobile Industry (Roshi kankei
    no tenkan to sentaku, nihon no jidosha sangyo). Tokyo: Nihon Hyoron
    Sha.
Uzihara,S. (1985). The Enterprises Responses to the Demographic Changes
    (Koreika shakai ni okeru kigyo no taio). In: Tokyo University, Institute
    for Social Science (ed.), Welfare States, (Fukushi kokka). Vol. 5. Tokyo:
    University of Tokyo Press: 353-421.
Uzihara,S. (1989). Japanese Economy and Employment Policy (Nihon keizai
    to koyo seisaku). Tokyo: University of Tokyo Press.

Yamazaki,H. (1988). The Process of the "Far-reaching Reform" of the Welfare Pension Scheme (Kosei nenkin seido no bappon kaisei katei). In: Tokyo University, Institute for Social Science (ed.) Welfare States in Transition, (Tenkan ki nofukushi kokka). Vol. 2. Tokyo: University of Tokyo Press: 79-169.

Yokoyama, K. (1988). Japanese Social Security Policy Development since 1973 (Fukusi gannen iko no shakai hosho). In: Ibid: 3-78.

7 Former East Germany: From Plan to Market and the Dramatic Effect on Exit

Martina Schuster and Brigitte Stieler

0   Introduction: The Regulation of Age Structures

For several years now an international research team has been investigating the problems of state-firm interaction in the context of changing age structures. For the German team at least, the unification of Germany has had the effect of broadening its field of study, opening up new and interesting possibilities. This has led to the inclusion of social scientists from the Federal Republic's new Eastern states, the former GDR, charged with studying the specifics of age-structural regulation in the process of economic and political transformation. *The aim was to determine whether – and if so in what form – age-structural regulation existed within the context of the GDR's planned economy, what effects it had, and how it (and its effects) have been modified in the course of the transition to a market economy.*

The conclusions drawn on the process of transformation are likely to be of interest for other, formerly socialist countries. At the same time, causion is warranted not to generalise glibly from results in the former GDR. Due to the historical links between the Federal Republic and the GDR, and the admission of the ex-GDR into the highly developed market-economic system of the FRG, new age-structural forms of regulation have been constituted in a different way than is likely to be typical for the other East European countries. In view of this, this chapter deals with aspects of the age-structural activities of the state and firms in the transition to the market economy, some of which are typical of the former socialist countries as a whole, while others are specific to the GDR.

Not only in the market economy, but also under the centrally planned economic system, social actors (and in particular, the state, firms and individuals) were constantly engaged in a form of reciprocal action and reaction which can be characterised as a particular form of "regulation" (cf. Naschold, 1985).

The economic discipline in socialist countries, however, did not employ the term regulation, although it was used to refer to the market-economic systems. Indeed, within the social theory dominant in the socialist countries such a term is superfluous, as the planned economy's major claim was to have overcome the "blind forces of the market" (Engels) and to have replaced them with the conscious, purposeful moulding of social processes – planning – which was supposed to be based on a far-sighted, anticipatory awareness (assumed a priori to exist) of the requirements for social development. The gap between this theoretical claim and the reality of actual social processes was evident.

In practice, socialist economy and society were, of course, "regulated", and this in an administrative and bureaucratic fashion, which has proved to be one of the main barriers to innovation. The system was based on planning targets, instruments, algorithms and institutions, whereby planning responsibilities were distributed within an hierarchically structured system, which restricted the scope for decision making at the lowest levels of the hierarchy (firms and enterprises). The free play of market forces, of supply and demand, "under the counter" and the consequent deviation by individual actors from the dictates of the plan was inevitably seen as a threat to established structures and was therefore suppressed.

This constellation also applied to the subject under discussion here, the entry and withdrawal of individuals into and out of working life and their occupational, sectoral and locational allocation ("planned use of labour power"). The distinguishing feature of the overall constellation was the assumption of a principle – although not absolute – identity of interests between the different actors (individuals, firms, the state), which, however, existed far more in theory and than in practice.

This gave rise to a specific view of economic and, in particular, social policy, including the setting of a framework of regulatory conditions, such that age-selective practices by firms were practically non-existent while state age-structure policies were of only marginal importance. Individuals oriented their life plans to the age limits (retirement ages) set by the state. These age limits were influenced by economic considerations, political expectations and social interests. With the collapse of the political and economic system, this constellation, which had remained fundamentally stable decades, was subject to abrupt and far-reaching change.

The specificity of the resulting transformational process is to be seen not only in its historical uniqueness, but also in the fact that, alongside processes representing a gradual transformation to market-economic forms of regulation, fundamentally new statutory instruments of regulation were introduced overnight. This is not to mention those phenomena which were the "creation" of market-economic instruments of regulation, but which did not exist in their present form in the market economy (i.e., the FRG) before German unification. Examples are the foundation of the "Treuhandanstalt", the trust fund responsible for privatising formerly state enterprises in the new federal states, and a number of special provisions within the social-insurance system.

One of the results of these processes has been *the creation in East Germany of specific conditions for the regulation of age-structural change.* With respect to the social actors already mentioned, the transformational characteristics of these regulatory conditions can be summarised as follows.

The regulatory and control instruments previously implemented by the *state* have been abandoned, in many areas (e.g., the planning system) without replacement. New models of age-selective regulation (e.g., retirement-age limits) have been established, some more quickly than others. This process also involves the restructuring of the system of social security in old age, culminating in the adoption of the West German pension system in 1992.

Overnight, *firms* have become independent economic units required to adapt their economic activities to the requirements of the market-economic system. This process has occurred within the complicated framework of collapsing markets (especially in Eastern Europe), falling demand and new competition. Against the background of the changing forms of state regulation, highly differentiated age-selective strategies are proving to be significant variables of firms' personnel policies.

Individuals face a fundamental change in the factors on which they had until recently orientated their life-plans. New retirement-age limits have been set, new modes of labour-market withdrawal and forms of social security installed, which together place a question mark over life-perspectives in old age which were once considered secure, while offering other, previously unavailable alternatives. Individuals are having to react very quickly to the changes in the regulatory framework.

Against this background we present selected age-relevant aspects of state-firm interaction within the transition process to the market economy. Our presentation will follow the logic of the various levels of regulation, starting with the age-relevant policies of the state. It was the collapse of the centrally planned state regulatory mechanism which formed the precondition for new corporate strategies. Firms subsequently have to adapt to the new regulatory conditions "imported" from the West German state.

To understand the particular developments in the GDR it will be necessary to draw attention to, and explain some characteristic features of the centrally planned economic system. Reference will only be made to theoretical approaches, however, to the extent that they are necessary to illuminate the problem in question.

The empirical material on which this paper is based is derived from the evaluation of a number of case studies of firms conducted during the transition process and from relevant economic, aggregate-statistical data. The study was conducted under rigorous personnel, financial, data and time constraints and may be accordingly limited in its depth and coverage. The research in this field has been finished in December 1991. Yet, it reveals important contours and specific details of state-firm relations against the background of age-structural change and the transition to the market economy.

In the next section we describe the following trends over time: the age structure of the labour force, the extent of paid employment by older workers and the use made of existing modes of withdrawal from the labour market. Our aim is to provide an overall picture of the macroeconomic dimension of the system of regulation of old age.

1   Age-Structure Trends and Modes of Labour-Market Withdrawal in
     the Former GDR, 1980 to 1991

Due to *the state full-employment policy* and the strategy to promote female participation in the labour market, the GDR was characterised by a high

degree of congruence between demographic developments and the employment shares of different age groups in the labour force as a whole. The
problem of visible unemployment did not become relevant until the beginning of 1990, when it became statistically significant. Parallel to this, new
instruments of labour-market policy were created, opening "pathways" out
of the employment system which until then had not been available.

Even at this early stage we have already touched on a fundamental
problem of the following presentation: we must attempt to establish the
relationship between discrete stages of development which are substantively
and systematically non-comparable. This throws up the problem of the
availability of data in two respects: the general lack of an adequate data
basis, and also the fact that certain social phenomena either did not exist in
the former GDR or, at least, were such as to be inaccessible to statistical
description. For these reasons, we have attempted to find substitute indicators which provide at least the broad outline of the relations in which we are
interested, and which permit comparative interpretations to be made. Where
this restricts the validity of the conclusions drawn, the appropriate caveats
will be made.

1.1   Age-Specific Participation Rates

Although special pathways out of the employment system hardly existed
before 1989 and no evidence of age-selective strategies on the part of firms
can be identified, since the end of the 1970s *the trend among male workers
has been one of comparatively marginally falling participation rates* in the
upper age groups, while *the reverse is true for women workers.* Only in

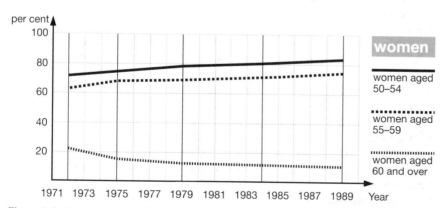

Figure 1: Labour-Force Participation Rates (Women)

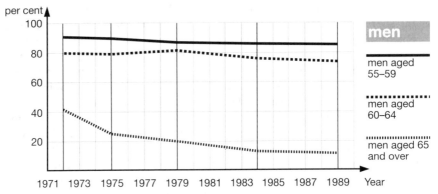

Figure 2: Labour-Force Participation Rates (Men)

excess of standard retirement age (65 years for men, 60 for women) a sharper decrease in participation rates for both sexes can be observed. Figure 1 and 2 illustrate these trends.

The slight decline of labour-force participation rates *is not caused by firm policy intentions*, but, primarily, influenced *by individual decisions* made as a result of disability.

The data currently available do not permit us to continue the time series to 1990 and 1991, as the results of the labour-force survey conducted in autumn 1990 did not include data on age structure.

In order to establish the influence of recent economic changes on participation rates in spite of the lack of official data, we turned to the results of the Socio-Economic Panel developed by the German Institute for Economic Research (table 1). Due to differences in statistical methodology, these figures are not comparable with the official statistics presented above.

According to the DIW's survey results, *during an 11-month period the following changes in participation rates* occurred among the older age groups.

Within the mere eleven months covered by the panel data a substantial reduction in participation rates of older workers is clearly evident, despite the fact that far-reaching structural changes did not, on the whole, begin until July 1990 (i.e., until after monetary union with the Federal Republic).

How is the position of women workers to be explained? Not a single woman reported being unemployed at the time of the survey, while 5 per cent of the 65–69 year-old age group continued to work despite pension entitlements. As the survey shows (cf. DIW, 1990: table 2005) these were usually unmarried women. Although this is not explicitly evident from the table, the figures hint at the trend, an innovation in the GDR, which is soon to become *the pathway* out of the employment system for workers over 55: pre-retirement (cf. section 1.5).

Table 1: Participation Rates of Older Workers, 1989 and 1990

Employment Status	Date	Age Group		
		55 – 59	60 – 64	65 – 69
of 100 Women in the Respective Age Groups ... were in				
1) Full-Time Employment	6/90	52	11	5
	7/89	56	11	8
2) Part-Time Employment	6/90	20	13	2
	7/89	25	17	2
3) Retirement/Early Ret.	6/90	21	89	98
	7/89	17	77	99
of 100 Men in the Respective Age Groups ... were in				
1) Full-Time Employment	6/90	82	66	10
	7/89	88	76	28
2) Part-Time Employment	6/90	2	3	4
	7/89	2	2	2
3) Unemployed	6/90	1	2	–
	7/89	–	–	–
4) Retirement/Early Ret.	6/90	15	30	96
	7/89	11	21	82

Source: Data from the Socio-Economic Panel (DIW, 1990).

The following *two points deal with two specificities of labour-force partici-pation in the former GDR* relevant to the foregoing tables and figures.

1.2   Female Employment

Occupational biographies and participation rates of women in the GDR differed fundamentally from those in West Germany. While this had economic reasons, it was, above all, a reflection of social policy. Female participation rates rose from a relatively low initial value in the 1950s to a level which – in terms of the countries involved in the research project – is only comparable to that in Sweden. This is shown in table 2.

Taking into account the fact that a further significant proportion of women were studying or undergoing vocational training, the figures give rise to over 91 per cent for 1989.

It is precisely this group – women workers – which has come under the

Table 2: Participation Rates of Women of Working Age in the GDR

Year	1955	1970	1980	1989
Percentage	52.5	66.1	73.2	78.1

Source: Frauenreport (Women's Report) 1990.

greatest pressure from the economic difficulties facing East German firms. Young women with small children, in particular, are now regarded a priori as "unreliable", and face discrimination when applying for jobs. The results of these new personnel strategies are beginning to be reflected in changing labour-market trends. 65 per cent of women in the DIW's Socio-Economic Panel reported that they were in employment in June 1990, compared with 66 per cent in July 1989. At the same time a mere 2 per cent were registered as unemployed at this point in time.

Now, however, women in the new federal states are more than proportionately affected by unemployment and their chances of re-entering the labour market are comparatively slim. In our view, this cannot be put down to voluntary withdrawal from the labour market: to be involved in working processes is an important content of life for women in the former GDR. The alternative occupation, confined exclusively to household chores, is not acceptable to many women (IASW, 1991: 19).

1.3   Labour-Force Participation by Pensioners

Continued paid employment beyond retirement age is another trend specific to the GDR which can only be explained with reference to the country's history and economic situation (table 3). This is clearly evident from the fact that after the collapse of the economic and political system during 1990 a clear discontinuity in this long term trend can be observed (even though employment by pensioners in the GDR had already begun to decline before 1989).

Alongside demographic changes, this fall in participation rates is due primarily to changes in the economic situation of pensioners and changing attitudes and values (cf. 2.1).

The highest proportion of "working pensioners" is to be found in the age group exceeding standard retirement age. In 1988 some 28 per cent of male workers between the ages of 65 and 69 continued to remain in employment. For the next age group (70–74) it was only 15 per cent. Of women aged between 60 and 64 a full 38 per cent were in employment, while in the next age groups the figure gradually declined to 10 and 8 per cent. A high level

Table 3: Participation Rates of Workers beyond Retirement Ages

Workers of Pensionable Age in Employment as a Proportion of all those of Pensionable
Age

Year	Total	Men	Women
1972	22.7	29.2	15.3
1975	18.1	24.7	15.2
1980	13.9	16.6	11.5
1986	10.3	11.8	9.8
1989	10.5	11.0	10.4

Source: Altenreport (Old-Age Report) 1990.

of differentiation, particularly for women, was thus registered for the length
of time after retirement age which individuals chose to remain in employment (cf. *Altenreport*, 1990).

Disaggregating the statistics by sector reveals that employment after retirement age in the GDR was concentrated in the sectors trade, agriculture and
forestry, engineering and automobiles and light industry: about 44 per cent of
all working pensioners were employed in these branches. Over-proportional
levels of employment for those of pensionable age were also registered in
light industry, domestic trade, post and telecommunications and in the
cultural sphere (cf. *Altenreport*, 1990).

This was due largely to the high proportion of working women of
pensionable age, whereby two motives for their continuing to work after
retirement age were dominant: the desire to supplement the comparatively
low level of pensions (this applied especially to jobs lower down in the pay
scale, which tended to be performed by women); and the desire for social
contact, particularly as many of the women in this age category lived alone.

A comparison of data for 1988 and 1990 shows that participation rates
above retirement age have also been affected by social and economic
changes (table 4).

Although the differences in statistical methodology limit the degree of
comparability between the two sets of figures, *the withdrawal of workers of
pensionable age out of paid employment is unmistakable* at the macro level.
Our case studies point to a "clear-out" of this group of workers in recent
months.

1.4   Sectoral Differences

As was to be expected, the age structure of workforces in the different
branches of the GDR varies only within relatively narrow limits (cf. appen-

Table 4: Employment of Workers above Pensionable Age (Selected Age Groups in percent)

Age Group/ Year	60—64		65—69	
	Male	Female	Male	Female
1988	—	38.1	28.2	10.0
1990	—	25.0	16.0	7.0

Sources: Alternreport, 1990; DIW, 1990.

dix, table A). This applies also to the employment shares of older workers, which are presented in the following synopsis (table 5).

The demographic components in the age structure of employment in 1989 are also clearly reflected in the structures in each branch. Furthermore, the overall distribution was heavily influenced by the sector employing the largest number of workers, the industrial sector accounting for over 40 per cent of employment in the former GDR.

The only sector with a significantly younger age structure than the economy as a whole was the construction industry. Agriculture and forestry and the post and telecommunications sector had comparatively old workforces, employees over 55 representing a higher proportion of the workforce than in other sectors. Particularly in agriculture, where workers in the upper age groups – the majority of them women – faced difficult working conditions, the process of economic restructuring has led to increased pressure on older workers.

1.5   Withdrawal from Paid Employment before Retirement Age

State policy in the GDR was based on a legal system whose point of departure was *the universality of work and the explicit duty to work*. In principle, there were – in contrast to a number of the former socialist countries, such as Bulgaria, Hungary and Poland- only one general and some categorial provisions *for workers to leave the labour force before reaching standard retirement age*:

1)   a disability pension and
2)   pre-retirement schemes for particular groups (e.g., miners).

It was not until the onset of economic problems *after 1989* that *the legal general provision for early retirement* linked to the provision of basic financial security *was established*.

Insufficient data is available to ascertain the extent of early retirement in

Table 5: Employment Shares of Older Workers by Sector, 1989 (in percent)

Sector	Total	Age Groups			
		55−59	60−64	>65	Sum of 3 Age Groups
GDR Economy	100	8.7	3.0	3.3	15.3
Industry	100	8.6	3.4	2.9	14.9
Construction	100	7.1	3.1	1.7	11.9
Agric./For.	100	11.5	4.3	3.4	19.2
Transport	100	8.8	4.3	2.2	15.3
Post & Tele.	100	10.7	2.7	6.0	19.4
Trade	100	8.2	1.7	4.9	14.8
Other Product. Sectors	100	8.1	2.7	2.8	13.6
Non-Product. Sectors	100	8.3	2.1	3.7	14.1

Source: Staatliche Zentralverwaltung für Statistik, own Calculations (The Division of the Economy into Sectors in the Former GDR is Different from that Employed in the Federal Republic, with the Result that Comparisons Must be Made with Caution).

the former GDR. We have thus opted to fall back on a substitute variable, retirement due to disability and on reaching the retirement age for miners as a proportion of retirements as a whole, as it can be assumed with some degree of certainty that the large majority of these retirements occur before the regular retirement age (table 6).

The volume of early retirements in the GDR was far lower than that in the Federal Republic, largely because only one pathway into retirement before

Table 6: Early Retirements[1] as a Percentage of all Retirements[2]

Year	Early-Retirement Share (%)		
	Total	Men	Women
1983	30.2	51.2	19.9
1984	28.7	52.6	20.0
1985	26.3	36.4	19.4
1986	28.2	39.0	20.7
1987	30.4	42.6	21.8
1988	31.2	45.8	21.8
1989	32.9	48.3	22.5

(1) New Disability and Miners' Pensions
(2) New Disability, Miners' and Old-Age Pensions, Excluding Accident and Special Pensions and Voluntary and Supplementary Insurance
Source: Figures Provided by the Social-Insurance Authorities.

Table 7: Exit from the Labour Market, November 1989 to April 1991

Early Exit	Retirement	Other Exit
Preretirement Scheme	Old Age Pension	Unemployed
409.000	130.000[1]	837.000
Transition Pension	Previously Employed Persons of Pensionable Age	Emigration (of Working Age)
100.000	250.000	320.000
Disability Pension		Working in West-Germany
65.000[1]		300.000
		Job-Creation Schemes
		85.000
		Others (Hidden Unemployment)
		100.000
574.000	380.000	1.642.000

(1) Estimated

the standard age limit existed. The number of disabled persons increased in recent years, but disability pensions remained relatively constant as a share of retirements as a whole, a fact which would appear to reflect the influence of demographic developments.

Disability primarily affected male, blue-collar workers, whereas women tended to retire at the "normal" time. It can be fairly safely assumed that this is linked to differences between the working conditions of male and female workers. In 1991 men of the 60–65 year-old age group formed the strongest unit within the age structure of the disabled pensioners.(cf. appendix, table B). This partly explains the recent decrease in labour-force participation rates for men (cf. 1.1). Concerning women in the same age structure the 50–60 year-old group was the strongest. Women comprised 125 000 persons whilst men made up 143 000. Women represented 47 per cent of the total population.

All in all, the recent low increase in early exit rates as well as the fact that early exit was normally *based on individual decisions do not point to an overall exit policy in the former GDR.*

The pre-retirement and Transition Pension (Altersübergangsgeld) provisions, introduced according to the labour-market situation in 1989/90 *opened up completely new pathways* out of the employment system. Due to the repeated changes in the group of people entitled to these pathways (cf. 2.4), it is not possible to formulate clear hypotheses at this point. In order to give an idea of the dimensions of this phenomenon, however, we present *a labour-market balance* for the GDR from November 1989 to April 1991 (Schuldt, 1991: 24).

As seen in table 7, early retirement accounts for about 50 per cent of all retirements, compared with about 30 per cent in the years before 1989. Moreover, if allowance is made for the fact that the relatively large proportion of previously employed workers of pensionable age will be a transitory phenomenon, early retirement accounts for about 70 per cent of all retirements, i.e., *an order of magnitude comparable with that in the old federal states*.

Of course, this finding can only indicate general trends. In our view though, and taking into account the results of the Socio-Economic Panel, it is valid to conclude that the phenomenon of early retirement has now reached a completely different qualitative and quantitative dimension in the former GDR than was the case before 1989.

2   Age-Related Policies by the State

2.1   The Logic of Age-Related State Policies in the Context of the Centrally Planned Economy

The logic of employment policy in the GDR was derived from and embedded in the economic and social, theoretical and practical, and, last but not least, in the political-ideological conception of the socialist model developed in the GDR. Within this model, the economy was a socialist centrally planned economy administered by the socialist state on the basis of decisions reached by the ruling party, the SED. According to the model the state was the "main instrument" for the realisation of the economic strategy pursued by the SED and was responsible for "organising the required behavioural patterns and activities" (*Sozialistische Volkswirtschaft*, 1989).

The system of controlling, planning and (national) accounting was organised by the state through the ministries, the managements of the industrial combines down to the individual enterprises and, parallel to this, from the state planning commission down to the administrative hierarchy (regional, local, town governments) according to uniform principles. The system was implemented to plan, realise and control economic and social policy according to the principles of "democratic centralism". As is well known, this system became increasingly bureaucratic-administrative, degenerating into a "command economy". State employment policy and, as we will see later, activities by firms in this arena, were developed – and had to develop – within this framework.

At the ideological level, the system was based on a number of fundamental paradigms and conceptions which had consequences for state activities affecting age structures. In this context the following are particularly relevant.

The *right to work* and, consequently, *full-employment* were explicitly guaranteed in the constitution of, and the laws governing work in the GDR. This was a basic principle, realised despite changing conditions throughout the life-span of the GDR, and based on a view of "work as a fundamental condition of the existence and development of human society" (Marx). This affected employment policy to the extent that each and every citizen capable of work, irrespective of his or her age, was to be provided with a suitable job. In this sense, it can be claimed that *the former GDR pursued a "non-age-selective employment policy".*

As a consequence workers as a rule did not withdraw from employment until they reached the standard retirement age; early retirement was restricted to disability pensions for those unable to work. Moreover, the possibility existed to continue working beyond retirement age (cf. section 1), even under certain conditions, for those drawing a disability pension. This in turn had consequences for firms' age-structural policies (cf. section 3).

Given this overall framework the GDR age structure of the labour force was affected by two different state policies:
(1) so-called labour-force policy,
(2) and social policy.

2.1.1 Age-Relevant State Action within the Framework
       of Labour-Force Policy

Age-relevant action by the state within the context of labour-force policy can be seen in *the aim of integrating all those capable of work into the labour process.* This was closely linked to *the persistent problem of the apparent shortage of labour.* There were many reasons for this phenomenon. The principle of guaranteed full-employment itself meant that workers were employed without regard to the efficiency of labour. But it was also due to inherent, systemic deficiencies in state incomes policy. Enterprises sought to maintain as large a wage-fund as possible, in order to have the resources to provide incentives and therefore applied for more new jobs than they needed. In the final analysis the economic system of performance assessment was insufficiently directed toward employing the various elements of the work force to the achievement of their highest work product potential. All these factors meant that older workers, and indeed pensioners, had no problem finding employment if they wished to continue working.

It is therefore only natural that working pensioners were explicitly considered as part of the pool of potential labour in the state's system of labour-force planning and accounting: this was also reflected at enterprise level in planning and costing procedures. This did not change significantly when the programme of "intensification of the economy" – i.e., increased rationalisation and automisation measures were introduced during the 1980s. The statutory system of labour-force use was, namely, based on the principle that labour made "redundant" through rationalisation and the introduction of new technology was to be re-employed in either the same, or if not possible, in another enterprise. It was a legal requirement that enterprises explicitly stated (in so-called "reproduction calculations") that affected workers had been redeployed. Together with the provision of Labour Law which made it illegal to dismiss those older than five years below retirement age for "reasons of ill-health or age", state policies effectively guaranteed older workers the opportunity of employment if they wanted it.

The fact that even as late as 1989 about 11 per cent of those of pensionable age were in paid employment (*Altenreport*, 1990) is empirical evidence for this regulatory framework. This statistic does not, however, tell us why so many pensioners opted to continue working and whether they were employed in activities appropriate to their age. Based on evaluations of empirical studies Schwitzer (*Altenreport*, 1990) gives *four motives for old-age pensioners to continue working*:

1.   The desire to supplement pension income.
2.   Job satisfaction.
3.   The feeling of being useful, needed.
4.   Social and communicative relations in the labour process.

Given the fact that in 1989 about two thirds of all old-age pensioners received the minimum pension of between 330 and 470 Marks, it seems that the desire for pension supplementation must have ben dominant in many cases. Even allowing for the fact that goods meeting basic needs, housing rents, transport fares etc. were heavily subsidised at the time, pension incomes were relatively low compared with average gross income of full-time blue and white-collar workers of the GDR, averaging 1280 Marks monthly (*Sozialreport*, 1990: 224, 336; cf. also section 1).

A constituent part of *state policy – which was aimed at integrating older workers rather than externalising them –* was the provisions, taken into Labour Law in 1977, on the creation of employment opportunities suited (in terms of working conditions etc.) to older workers. While the vast majority of enterprises kept to the statutory provisions concerning dismissal protection for and continued employment of older workers, the creation of jobs suited to older workers within enterprises was something the state found very difficult to monitor with the result that it was only very infrequently realised in practice. This is largely due to the fact that *the "social quality" of work was not the prime interest of economic and social policy*, as can be seen from the fact that enterprises were oriented exclusively to fulfilling purely economic coefficients (targets) selected by the state, many of which were in fact substantively unsuitable to the task of providing a true reflection of the state of the economy.

The final decade of the existence of the GDR saw a deterioration in working conditions and job contents, so that it seems plausible to assume that many older workers – in view of their lower skill levels on average – found themselves confronted with simple but often physically demanding tasks (Fischer, 1984).

2.1.2 Age-Relevant State Action within the Framework of Social Policy

Social policy, as part of the overall social concept oriented towards the realisation of the "basic economic law of socialism", played a central role in age-relevant state action. The GDR's theoretical conception of social policy was completely different from that favoured by the Federal Republic (risk compensation and prevention, cf. Lampert, 1985 and Brück, 1988). In line with the overall social concept just mentioned, social policy in the GDR was to "realise the social aims of the working class and its allies" (*Lexikon der Sozialpolitik*, 1987: 347).

This covered a multiplicity of tasks and goals with the aim of providing social security for, and promoting the interests of certain social groups. Social policy aimed to reinforce the "socialist way of life", maintain social security and stability (including the right to work), raise the standard of living and improve living and working conditions (cf. Manz and Winkler, 1988: 12ff.). This concept of social policy had its beginnings in a theoretical re-evaluation of practical social policy in the GDR which occurred at the end of the 1960s and beginning of the 1970s. For many years before, with the exception of a number of measures introduced shortly after the end of the Second World War, social policy in general had been considered irrelevant to the needs of a socialist society. This, at least, is a plausible conclusion to be drawn from the range and content of the few publications on this subject at that time: socialism was itself social policy and so did not require a specific system of social security to deal with social problems (cf. Lampert, 1989: 2). Despite this, practical social policy did exist, particularly in the fields of educational and family policy. By 1971 at the latest, a corresponding reorientation of official policy had taken place. Since then, with the "unity of economic and social policy" a social concept was officially established which was based on the a priori assumption that social policy and social security have a motivating effect on individual and worker performance. In other words, an increase in economic performance was, alongside other factors, expected from an instrument which should have the effect of reducing social differentiation. In many instances, wage and salary differentials which were related to differences in performance levels were offset by transfers from the so-called "social fund".

The primary orientation of social policy towards reinforcing the "socialist way of life" and improving economic performance levels may help explain why it was tailored more closely to the needs of younger workers and their families than to older employees. This was particularly the case for those older workers who left the employment system at the regular retirement age (on pension insurance cf. section 2.2). The concept of "the old person" on which practical policy in the GDR was based, was largely determined by the idea of his/her continued integration into the employment system.

Deficit-models of old age were rejected by state policy makers, who favoured the maintenance of the full-employment goal based on the right to work even for the end-phase of workers' occupational lives. Clearly this was a reflection of a classic "coupling" of progressive views on health and well-being in old age (Eitner, 1960; Schmidt, Schwitzer and Runge, 1982) with economic requirements (the apparent labour shortage). This is one of the main explanations for the lack of state policies providing pathways out of the employment system before standard retirement age.

To sum up, age-relevant state action in the centrally planned economic system of the former GDR can be described as work-oriented and internalising. Taking account of psycho-social changes which occur during the aging process, it was based not on deficit models but was oriented, for the reasons give, towards the creation of working conditions suitable for older workers, the statutory legal framework for which was established.

In current practice amongst firms and enterprises, however, state conceptions were only fulfilled to the extent that this was a legal requirement and could be monitored and enforced. As we will see in section 4, economic practice and general consciousness were largely determined by deficit models (*Altenreport*, 1990). This fact is of considerable significance in view of the new opportunities for individual strategies of action provided by the transformation process.

2.2   Instruments of State Age-Structure Policy in the Centrally Planned Economy

Age-relevant strategies and instruments are to be sought within the tension between the requirements of economic policy and the aims of social policy. We use the verb "to seek" deliberately as we believe that the GDR lacked a conscious age-structure or retirement-age policy. However, *strategies were pursued within the frameworks of social, population and labour-force policies,* and these can be expected to have had comparable effects.

These three policy areas which could be expected to exert effects on workforce age structures will now be briefly described. In each case they can be considered as consisting of *a network of legal, financial and organisational instruments.*

One feature distinguishing *population policy* from the other two areas is that it is very largely oriented towards future developments. Population and family policy in the GDR, with its decidedly pro-natalist components, exerted age-structural effects to the extent that it attempted to take account of the course of secular age-structural change. The policy was primarily adressed at younger age groups and attempted, by creating favourable conditions for child-birth and child-care, to ensure – for "national-interest" reasons – a relatively balanced demographic trend. One of the most important aims of this relatively comprehensive policy was to attenuate the ageing process of the population resulting from increasing life expectancy which was seen as leading to "unfavourable age structures".

It was an explicit aim of *social policy* in the GDR to "provide special care for senior citizens" (Manz and Winkler, 1988: 65). This aim, derived from the "work principle", was realised in a number of ways. To the extent that elderly people were still in paid employment the legal and organisational provisions of health and safety at work regulations oriented specifically to older workers were relevant to social policy in old age. The *Labour Law* (AGB, enacted in 1977), alone, contained 13 paragraphs dealing specifically with the position of older workers in production, including those of pensionable age. According to these provisions it was one of the enterprises' most important tasks to "secure for workers of pensionable age continuing occupational activity according to their abilities and wishes" (§ 5), to offer workers special protection from dismissal once they reached five years below retirement age (§ 59), to create suitable jobs of older workers (§ 74) and to offer old-age and disabled pensioners part-time work should they so desire (§ 160). Particularly significant in this context were the paragraphs 208 and 209 which incorporated workers of "pre-retirement age" (5 years before regular retirement) into plant-level medical provisions and which mandated the enterprises to offer older workers who for health reasons wished to be transferred to another job the chance to do so. In addition, workers in this upper age group were entitled to longer holidays.

Clearly, the large number of such specific provisions for older workers, not all of which are mentioned here, inevitably led to conflicts of interest between enterprises' efficiency targets and their duties under labour law. Despite this, firms did not pursue age-selective strategies. This can only be explained with reference to overall social and economic policies against the background of the permanent labour shortage (cf. 2.1).

While this side of the policies oriented towards older workers aimed to support those of pensionable age who wished to continue in paid employment, social policy for the elderly outside the labour process was clearly oriented towards care, support and medical attention. The services required in this sphere were provided by the state, the churches, by institutions sponsored by the trade unions and, in particular, by the "Volkssolidarität", a national charitable organisation. East German Labour Law also mandated enterprises to see to the well-being of former employees in retirement.

The mainstay of state provision for the elderly, though, was the pension system, in particular old-age and disability pensions. *The East German pension system* developed gradually after the Second World War as a constituent part of the unitary social insurance system, evidently on the Soviet model. Nevertheless, the pensions paid by the GDR's social-insurance system in fact exhibited greater similarities to the West German system than to that of the other East European countries. Hentschel (1983) explains this with reference to the common history and the lack of clear conceptions in the GDR until the 1960s. The differences from the systems in the other formerly socialist countries are to be seen above all in the way in which it is financed (in the GDR by contributions from firms, workers and the state; in the Soviet Union exclusively by the state) and in the linkage between earned income and the pension level (although the degree of differentiation was much less than in the FRG).

Until 1971 the pension-insurance scheme, based as it was on the principle of minimal social security, consisted solely of a compulsory insurance, for which contributions were paid amounting to 10 per cent of income up to an income level of 600 Marks. This led to an ever-widening gap between income during working life and expected pension entitlements. It was to meet this problem that, in 1971, the voluntary supplementary pension insurance (FZR) system was established, which organised contribution payments for incomes above 600 Marks. By paying additional contributions workers could gain entitlements to a higher old-age pension and higher benefits in case of sickness.

In addition to this system, there also existed pension schemes, comparable with the system of insurance for civil servants in the Federal Republic, in which were organised those working in the state apparatus, the military, the police force and teachers, etc. Such groups were entitled to substantially higher pensions than those of the "average pensioner", often without having to make contributions – or only at a reduced rate – during working life. In 1988 some 250 000 pensioners were in one of these special schemes (*Sozialreport*, 1990: 225). The majority of pensioners in the GDR (about two thirds in 1989) received the minimum pension. Only one third had gained extra entitlements under the FZR, with women clearly underrepresented.

The relatively low level of average pensions (cf. also 2.1) is due to the fact that, in contrast to the Federal Republic, there was no provision for an automatic linkage between pension and wage levels over time. An increase in pensions required an appropriate decision by the state and the trade union. While pensions were increased with some degree of regularity, the gap between benefits and average earned incomes grew ever wider.

The third relevant policy area – alongside the underlying mechanisms set out in 2.1 – were the strategies and instruments of so-called *"labour-force policy"*. This policy area was charged with the problem of the so-called "locational distribution of the productive forces". At least in theory, the aim was to ensure a distribution of resources – in this case labour – among different regions and branches which was commensurate with economic and social goals. This process was planned and steered by institutions specifically charged with the task, whereby quotas and balance-sheets were used as regulatory instruments. Where it proved impossible directly to steer and control such process a number of indirect forms of steering and regulation were developed and applied in various combinations. These indirect steering mechanisms included the so-called "wage-policy measures", i.e., specific occupational groups, industries and regions were favoured with higher wages and salaries, higher bonuses were paid, or housing was provided.

Such instruments affected age structures in two ways. Firstly, certain planning and steering mechanisms were directly age-related. For instance, balances were drawn up in which all school-leavers and their distribution among the various training institutions were recorded; a similar balance existed for those leaving universities and colleges. Secondly, the indirect instruments had age-selective effects to the extent that either certain age categories were explicitly named as representing a labour-force potential for the solution of a particular problem (e.g., by setting age limits, or stipulating membership of a youth organisation) or by selecting the forms of regulation in such a way that a particular age group would be more likely than others to respond.

A practical example of such forms of regulation is provided by the so-called "youth objects" of the FDJ, the GDR youth organisation. Under this system special economic tasks were placed in the hands of the youth organisation, with the effect that young people from all over the GDR came to participate in their realisation. A specific example was the so-called "FDJ-Initiative Berlin" with the aim of realising complex construction projects.

This method of realising specific projects – mandating individual administrative districts to provide material, financial or personnel resources – had extremely negative consequence for the areas making such resources available: as far as our context is concerned it led in particular to an acceleration of the aging process within the resident population and labour force.

Similar effects in principle, although in some ways the reverse of those just mentioned, were induced by the creation of large-scale industrial sites, which were usually led to an influx of people from outside the area and the founding of new cities or the expansion of existing ones into previously "green-field" areas. The best-known examples here are the founding of Eisenhüttenstadt around a new iron and steel combine in 1950 (Eisenhütten-stadt translates roughly as "Steel-works City") and the massive migration into cities such as Schwedt and Hoyerswerda as a result of the development of industrial production there. That the population of these cities exhibited a significantly younger age structure due to the planned influx of workers and that as a result of natural demographic developments they have experienced rapid population growth are trends which can be seen in the labour-force potential of these areas to this day.

2.3   Upheaval and Transformation: The New Role of Retirement-Age Policies

Not at least as a result of the breakneck pace of the process of German unification all the changes seem to have been one single event. While subjective experience might lead to such an impression, closer observation and analysis show that the process did occur in a succession of distinct phases, characterised by different political and economic intentions and by different phenomena and constraints (cf. Wetzker, 1990). The different phases are also distinguished by different age-relevant strategies and regulatory mechanisms implemented by the state.

The First Period from October to November 1989

The *first period* of the transformation was between *October 7th to November 11th, 1989*. During this period the political situation rapidly came to a head due, not least, to the activities of citizens' groups. There was a change of leadership in the Central Committee of the SED. Promises of political and economic changes were made, but neither realised nor accepted by the East German population. The wave of emigrants leaving the GDR had been growing since August (opening of the Hungarian border). The subsequent opening of the Wall and thus all the borders for individual travel provided, on the one hand, an important safety valve for the political situation, but did not succeed in stemming the flood of East Germans leaving for the Federal Republic (in November this amounted to some 73 400 people). As most of these were either young or middle-aged, this migration process had the effect of shifting the age structure of the population in favour of the upper age groups. By the end of 1989 a total of 300 000 people had left the GDR, leading to insufficiencies in the service sector. In manufacturing, however, production was maintained due to the existence of hidden unemployment.

The Second Period, from Mid-November 1989 to Mid-March 1990

The period in office of the government under Modrow was characterised by the fact that great attempts were made – for the first time including social scientists from the GDR – to draw up and implement concepts for economic reforms. The aim was to link elements of the planned economy with those of the social market economy and can be described as the attempt to find a "Third Way". But these efforts only got as far as the drawing-board. In practice it became clear that the attempts at reform taking the planned economy as their point of departure were confronted with inherent, systemic limitations, such as the dominant role of state-run industry.

Due to the breakneck pace of events and the realisation just how quickly the political and economic situation was deteriorating after the borders were opened, not to mention the situation in the socialist block as a whole and in particular in the Soviet Union, the reform process never got off the ground. By the beginning of February at the latest, it was clear that German unification was very much on the agenda. It was thus useless to reflect further on the socio-economic conditions for reform in the GDR within some form of political alliance (confederation) with the FRG.

Although the foreign trade monopoly of the state was still formally in place, the shift in consumer demand to West Germany (accompanied by severe problems for the East German currency) led to tough competitive pressure in a number of sectors, particularly those, such as the electronics industry, producing consumer goods. Overall output was on the decline.

Unemployment began to be a problem, primarily as a result of the reform of economic organisation and cutbacks in the state apparatus (of the 50 former GDR-ministries, 25 were scrapped under a decree enacted 21/12/89). In our context it is interesting to note that, as unemployment threatened, workers who had already reached pensionable age were "sent into retirement", while the first pre-retirement provisions were established – coming into force in February 1990 – for older workers who had not yet reached retirement age (cf. section 2.4).

In other words, increasing rates of unemployment immediately gave rise to age-selective policies by the state and (as we shall see later) by firms, in order to ease the pressure on the labour market.

Meanwhile the methods of central planning were steadily losing their influence. In January 1990 the enterprises and industrial combines were granted far greater room for manoeuvre in all spheres of managerial activity.

Finally, a decree announced on March 8th gave firms the legal right to make their own decisions regarding workforce levels and development. The state ceased to have the power to mandate firms to take on workers and the special provisions protecting older workers from dismissal were no longer valid.

That these new possibilities were immediately used by firms as tools of age-selective policy was merely the logical consequence of the deteriorating economic situation (cf. section 3). It was during this period that the "Treuhandanstalt" was established (March 1st) and given responsibility for privatising the formerly state-run enterprises of the GDR. In the course of subsequent events the Treuhandanstalt exerted a major influence on individual firms: its decisions as to whether enterprises should continue operations or not determined by how much workforce levels were cut, with corresponding repercussions for older workers.

All this time migration to West Germany continued at a high level – some 40 000 per month – particularly of younger people. 76.7 per cent of all persons leaving the GDR in 1989 were younger than 40 years. Especially concerned was the age group of 25 to 40 years, comprising 37 per cent of all emigrants. (*Sozialreport*, 1990: 38).

The Third Period, from March 1990 to July 1990

Although the de Maiziere government was in power from 18th March 1990 until the 2nd October 1990 we will restrict the *third period* from *18th March 1990 to 1st July 1990* as the introduction of economic, monetary and social union at the beginning of July brought with it fundamental changes, particularly in the economic sphere.

Until then the government under de Maiziere attempted to bring political, economic and social conditions in the GDR into line with those in the FRG as quickly as possible. An independent economic policy was lacking during this period: certain elements of the centrally planned economy continued to exist against the background of falling output levels. Import restrictions were lifted, intensifying competition on the East German market. Unemployment continued to rise steadily as firms pursued – differentiated – strategies of workforce reduction. In particular, firms attempted to publish opening balances (the first accounts to be published in D-Mark) showing the lowest possible wage costs. As a result, many workers were made redundant on June 30th, in many cases on a "voluntary" basis with generous compensation payments. As expected this affected older workers particularly (cf. sections 1 and 3). On top of this, large numbers of workers were made redundant from the state administrative apparatus, the armed forces, political parties and mass organisations (e.g., trade unions).

The Fourth Period, from July to October 1992

The *fourth period* from *July 1st to October 2nd 1990* brought about fundamental economic changes as a result of the introduction of the D-Mark as legal tender in the GDR. Overnight the East German economy was exposed to world-market competition. The massive shift in price and cost structures led to an immediate deterioration on the sales side. From the beginning of July on the GDR's internal market was dominated by goods – particularly daily necessities – "made in West Germany".

The collapse of markets in Eastern Europe, which had been the GDR's major export area, was the logical consequence of the introduction of the D-Mark, although until the end of 1990 certain transactions at least could be cleared on the basis of the transfer rouble.

Beginning in July and continuing until the present day, the combined effect of this was a rapid rise in unemployment, resulting both from job cuts in enterprises seeking to cut personnel costs and from the liquidation of entire firms, particularly in the consumer-good sector.

For the agricultural sector, too, immediate adjustment to the EC agricultural market and the falling level of demand (and in some cases the deliberate blockage of such demand for such East German products as existed) had grave consequences.

The state reacted with regulatory instruments aimed at easing the pressure on the labour market: short-time working provisions were introduced which went considerably beyond the regulations prevailing in the old federal states (e.g., the possibility of "zero-hour short-time working"). Short-time working was also used by firms in order to externalise older workers from their workforces before entitlement to, for example, early retirement (cf. section 3). The course of this process of contraction is shown mostly clearly on the *labour market*:

	July 1990	November 1990
Unemployment	272 017	589 178
Workers on short time	656 277	1 773 866

In November a further 80,000 workers were in further training programmes, while public job-creation measures began to make themselves felt, starting with 14 500 workers. The labour-market situation was further eased by the continuing migration of East German citizens – an additional 265 000 between January and November 1990.

The Fifth Period, from 3rd October until the End of December 1991

The trends which set in after the introduction of monetary union have continued, indeed the effects have been more severe than had been forecast. It has proved unexpectedly difficult to find the necessary investors for firms in the new federal states. There are a number of reasons for this, the most important of which are disputes over property rights, the "ecological debt" (environmental pollution damage) of many East German firms and the sometimes obscure and oft criticised approach adopted by the Treuhandanstalt to the reprivatisation, and either refinancing or liquidation of formerly state-run enterprises. The overall result has been job-losses on a scale unprecedented in post-war Western Europe.

The state has implemented regulatory measures in an attempt to ease the pressure on the labour market. The provisions governing *short-time working*, for instance, were renewed several times. As has already been mentioned, this instrument is often used to externalise older workers, without them having to register as unemployed or to enter early retirement straight away. Massive resources have been made available for *job-creation measures*. The response to the public programmes has been unexpectedly positive with the result that the planned total for the end of the year (of 180 000 jobs) had already been exceeded by the Summer. In addition, the state enacted further *forms of age-selective regulation*. From the second half of 1991 on both men and women were entitled to a "transition pension" (Altersübergangsgeld) on reaching the age of 55.

Current prognoses of coming economic trends in the new federal states point to continued rising unemployment rates, or, at best, stagnation at its present very high levels. The following figures indicate the dimension of the problem. It is to be expected that unemployment trends will lead to an intensification of age-limit policies.

Labour-Market Figures as of December 1991

Unemployed	On short time	In early retirement	In job-creation programmes	Further education & retraining
1 037 709	1 034 543	700 000	389 861	435 200

In other words, in December 1991 about 3.6 million persons out of a potential working population of about 8 million were affected by unemployment in one form or another. The Federal Labour Office expects a further decrease in working population from 6.8 million at the end of 1991 to 6.3 million in 1992.

We can summarise these developments as follows: the transition from the centrally planned to the market economy has led directly to the progressive creation of forms of state regulation which together can be termed "state age-structural policies". The approach characteristic of the planned economy – the integration of older workers – was abandoned as soon as dirigiste methods of labour-force policy were dropped and replaced by a labour market in the genuine sense of the term.

2.4   Age-Relevant Instruments Employed by the State during the Transformation Process and Their Effects

The described increase in unemployment, some of it as a result of the "uncovering" of previously hidden unemployment, led to the *introduction of social security programms against unemployment* at the beginning of 1990 which, until then, had been unknown in the GDR. A decree was enacted on "the provision of public support and compensation by the employer to those seeking employment". This official description of the decree clearly points to the overall context of the transformation from one economic system to another: coming from the full-employment guarantee of the centrally planned economy, the legislators clearly balked at the use of the word "unemployment", although it is perfectly obvious that the decree represents a form of state regulation securing the payment of unemployment benefit to those out of work.

A further decree, enacted in February 1990, was also designed to ease the pressure on the nascent labour market: the "Decree on the provision of pre-retirement pensions" represented the first step towards the *provision of social security for older workers leaving the labour force before standard retirement age.*

On June 22nd 1990, an important set of provisions on the labour market were enacted under the Labour Promotion Law of the GDR. Due to the early subsequent unification (3rd October 1990) of the two German states, however, most of the provisions contained in the Law were only valid for a short period. We, therefore, provide a summary of the age-structurally important provisions in the following table 8.

In principle, the Labour Promotion Law of the Federal Republic also applies to the new federal states, although a number of exceptions have been made (under the Unification Treaty signed between the two German states) and the Law has been modified to the extent that some provisions of the GDR-version remain valid in the new federal states and will remain so for a limited period. The same is true of the laws regulating old-age pensions; which are regulated by a uniform system from the beginning of 1992.

The pre-retirement provision enacted by the Modrow government in 1990 permitted workers to withdraw from the labour force five years before standard retirement age, i.e., at 55 for women, at 60 for men. Those retiring early were entitled to 70 per cent of their average net income during the previous 12 months.

Under immense pressure to cut staffing levels, many firms developed their own "early pre-retirement" schemes, often unaware of the long-term financial commitments they were making. This became clear when, on October 3rd 1990, the pre-retirement provisions of the former GDR were rescinded and replaced by a new pre-retirement scheme, the so-called "*Transition*

Table 8: Pathways into (Early) Retirement 1980–1991

Scheme	Period	Age of Entrance	Target Group/ Conditions
Old Age Pension	−31. 12. 1991[1]	Women 60 Men 65	Every Citizen after 15 Years of Employment/Contribution; Women with 5 and more Children without Employment
Disability Pension	−31. 12. 1991[1]	No Limit after School-Leaving	Every Citizen with lost of 2/3 of Work Capacity after 5 Years of Paid Employment/Contr.; Special Prov. for those who Had Never Been Able to Work

Pre-retirement Schemes for Particular Groups[2]

Scheme	Period	Age of Entrance	Target Group/ Conditions
Miner's Pension	−31. 12. 1991[1]	Women 55 Men 60	Miners After 15 Years of Employment/Contributions, whereby at Least 6 Years in the Mining Industry
Miner's Full Pens.	−31. 12. 1991[1]	Women 50 Men 50	Miners after 25 Years of Empl./Contr., of which 15 Years Underground
Dancer's Pension	−31. 12. 1991[1]	Women 35 Men 35	Dancers after 15 Years of Professional Activity for Health Reasons or after Quitting Profession
Pension for Resistors Against the Nazi Regime	−31. 12. 1991[1]	Women 55 Men 60	Resistors Against and those who were Persecuted by the Nazi Regime and their Natives
Pre-retirement Scheme	02. 01. 1990 – 02. 10. 1990	Women 55 Men 60	Every Citizen after 20 (Women) and 25 (Men) Years of Empl./Contr.
Transitional Old-Age Pension	0.3 10. 1990 – 31. 12. 1991	Women 55 Men 55	Every Unemployed Full-Filling the Conditions for Unemployment Benefit for 832 Days

(1) With modifications of the Unification Act (Einigungsvertrag)
(2) Other Schemes (Army, Customs etc.) are not Reconstructable.

Pension" (Altersübergangsregelung) applicable only in the new federal states.

This new provision was closely oriented to the conditions of entitlement to unemployment benefit, in particular, to the fact of unemployment itself. In other words, payment of benefit under this provision is not the decision of the individual worker alone; it is normally necessary for the worker to be made redundant by his employer, whereby this may occur by mutual agreement, made attractive to the employee by severance pay.

In 1991 workers of both sexes were eligible under this scheme on reaching the age of 55. Those retiring under these provisions receive 65 of previous net income, i.e., somewhat less than under the preceding system. On the other hand, these benefits are paid exclusively by the employment office, whereas pre-retirement pensions were financed jointly by the state and firms.

The moral pressure on older workers to opt for one of the schemes available was, and remains very great. Moreover, it seems that large numbers of older workers are worried that they will not be able to meet performance requirements in future and, therefore, leave the employment system of their own accord. In many cases, decisions are made without adequate consideration of the legal and, above all, financial consequences. In addition, entitlement conditions have been altered *retrospectively*, e.g., an assessment limit has been introduced and limits placed on the amount of additional money pensioners can earn through paid employment.

Those who withdrew from the labour market before the substantial pay increases are now confronted with rising rents and prices, which they could not have foreseen when they decided to leave employment. During the first half of 1990 the average monthly gross income (used as the basis for calculating pension levels) was, at DM 1 150 only marginally higher than in 1989. Compensation payments which in West Germany sometimes amount to 100 per cent of previous net incomes are financially beyond the reach of the large majority of firms in the former GDR. For all these reasons, the level of social security provided, even when allowance is made for other transfer benefits and provisions for automatic "dynamisation" of pre-retirement benefits, is incomparably lower than in the old federal states.

In addition, the moral and psychological consequences for the individual must be taken into account. The sudden stop of working life leads to losses of values and total breaks in biographies which could not be imagined before. The complexity of these problems disallows more than cursory comment here.

The age-selective effects of pre-retirement are considerable, as is illustrated both by macroeconomic data and our firm case studies. To some extent these effects are reinforced by the short-time working provisions. In line with the stipulations made in the Unification Treaty, the period for which workers on short-time working can claim state benefits has been extended to allow for the specific conditions of restructuring in the wake of economic, monetary and social union (§ 63 of the Labour Promotion Law of the GDR). Even more important, in contrast to the situation in the old federal states, up to the end of 1991 workers were entitled to benefits under the short-time working scheme even if they were on "zero hours" and there were no prospects of regaining full-time employment within the enterprise.

These provisions, linked to a number of collectively negotiated agreements which offer workers a high degree of protection from dismissal and enable them to draw short-time pay of up to 90 per cent of previous earnings, presented firms with the opportunity – in line with the wishes of the workforce – to exploit this regulatory framework (primarily) for older workers. Often they are in this way forced into a sort of "preliminary unemployment" without, in many cases, actually being aware of the fact.

Finally, the transformation process – taking the relevant instruments into account – can be characterised as follows. Despite some minor exceptions, our main findings confirm that there was a *definite type of transfering* of the labour-market and social policy instruments. These instruments were developed within a long period. They were well working under the conditions given in the old federal states. Initially, some of the instruments were copied by the former GDR labour legislation. But later on it became obvious, that general copying and taking over was impossible, since the conditions in the East were very different from those in the West. Therefore, *adaptation to the specific economic conditions* of the former GDR had to be made, and this is still occuring.

The aim of all these instruments was to ease the pressure on the labour market by offering certain socio-demographic groups the option of withdrawing from the labour force under conditions suited, more or less, to their needs. Social-policy instruments, provided by the pension-insurance system for instance, did not play any part in 1991, inducing early retirement by older workers.

3   Age-Related Policies by Firms

3.1   Case Studies

We conducted case studies of six firms from July 1990 to October 1991. The analysis includes both the recent history of the firms and "accompanies" them through the transformation process since then.

The sample is random and makes no claims to be representative. This is due to the fact that only a small number of firms were prepared during such a complicated and difficult phase to grant us an insight into intra-firm relations. We would like to thank the firms for this willingness and wish though the following description that their identity may remain anonymous.

The firms studied are presented in the table 9. According to our typology

Table 9: Overview of Sample Firms

Firm	Industry	Workforce	
		before 1989[1]	after 1989[2]
Firm A	Engineering (Batch Prod.)	1.800	1.000
Firm B	Engineering (Batch Prod.)	2.100	1.200
Firm C	Services (Transport)	7.200	2.500
Firm D	Services (Transport)	15.000	15.000
Firm E	Basic Chemicals	8.500	6.600
Firm F	Electrical Eng. (Mass & Batch Prod.)	1.000	600

(1) Average of the Years 1980–1989
(2) At the Time of the last Survey made during our Study

they are all to be considered as large firms. The fact that two firms belong each to the engineering and the transport sector affords the opportunity for comparison.

3.2   The Logic of Age-Related Policies by Firms in the Centrally Planned Economy

The logic of age-related policies by firms in the centrally planned economy can, and indeed must be seen within the context of the logic of state strategies.

In the state system of labour-force planning and accounting older workers were seen as a potential labour reserve. The ruling party, the SED, aimed, at least according to its party-political programme, to facilitate the participation of older workers in social life and to secure their social, cultural and medical well-being. Consequently, and as a result of the comprehensive provisions laid down in the GDR's Labour Law (cf. section 2.2), firms were oriented to offering older workers who so desired the opportunity of working within the existing labour process and, in some cases, to creating jobs tailored to their needs (e.g., part-time work). Where this was not possible firms were mandated to find alternative employment for older workers.

This integrative policy with respect to older workers was not, as might be expected, implemented by the personnel but rather by the "social policy" department within the firm. This is primarily to be explained by the fact that firms in the centrally planned economy lacked the extensive personnel departments responsible, among other things, for age-selective strategies, typical of firms in the market economy. Personnel matters were dealt with in various departments. The "labour economics" department, for example, was responsible for quantitative aspects such as personnel planning, pay structures etc. Its strategies were age-related with regard to the provision of jobs and pay for older workers. Qualitative aspects were planned, realised and controlled by the so-called "cadre department". This was dominated by the ruling party and its policies were oriented towards the Party-line. A major component of its work was the selection, development and deployment of the "cadres", based largely on political criteria. Its strategies affect age structures through the selection of young cadres, cadre development and withdrawal, particularly of leaders and specialists.

Another reason is that the task of integrating and supporting older workers was assigned to the "social department" (which was often a subsidiary of the labour economics department) *because age-related behaviour by firms was seen primarily as a matter of social policy and much less as a matter of enterprise efficiency.*

This view is supported by the poor attention the problem received in the specialised literature in the GDR. The last edition of the handbook *Leiter-Kollektiv-Persönlichkeit* (Autorenkollektiv, 1982), for instance, describes the principles on which the "leader's" (enterprise director etc.) actions towards older workers should be based in terms of considerate behaviour with regard to their needs and welfare. At the same time, the authors of the book tend to lean, in contrast to the official line, to the deficit model of old age.

Questions regarding the efficiency of the labour of older workers were apparently considered irrelevant. However, this should not be taken to mean that firms' age-specific policies in practice always followed these guide-lines. The social orientation of age-specific practices by firms leads to a potential conflict of interests facing enterprise management with regard to the fulfillment of the economic plan targets. These conflicts, however, are not mentioned in the literature, although they were part of the day-to-day experience of those involved in the former GDR.

At the same time, it is indisputable that the socially-oriented strategy of age-related behaviour by firms was of great practical benefit to older workers. In addition to job security, on reaching "pre-retirement age" (five years before statutory retirement) they were integrated into the enterprise's dispensary health service, were entitled to a week's extra holiday per year and enjoyed special protection under labour law, even from the negative effects of rationalisation measures.

Various welfare facilities were also available once the older worker retired from the firm. They were allowed to eat in the works' canteen, for example, could participate in the holiday and tourism programmes run by the firm and often received other forms of support such as when moving house, for example, or house repairs. In this field – the so-called "care for veterans" – the local trade union bodies were particularly active. Collective agreements negotiated with management included stipulations on services such as those just described, and the union organised personal care for retired workers. This covers the entire field of age-relevant practices by the unions: due to the comprehensive protection afforded older workers by the GDR's labour laws, the union was not required to perform further age-relevant tasks.

We conclude that *age-relevant practices by firms in the context of the planned economy were primarily socially-oriented and were not aimed at the exclusion but rather at the integration of older workers.*

3.3   Age-Relevant Trends in Workforce Structures in the Centrally Planned Economy

Workforce levels and structures in the six firms in our case study remained remarkably constant during the 1980s. *The size of the workforce* in each firm oscillated only marginally around its average value, with a slight expansionary trend. None of the firms experienced major restructuring. *Skill structures* changed gradually, with rising proportions of university and college graduates, although this was not always reflected in the work actually performed. The share of unskilled workers fell (with the exception of firm D) to significantly less than 10 per cent. *Gender structure* was such that men accounted for between 60 and 75 per cent in all firms, whereby women were usually employed in white-collar areas.

In view of the fact that *age structures* changed only slightly during the 1980s, with a slight increase in average workforce age reflecting demographic trends, the situation as it existed in 1989 can be taken as representing the "centrally planned period" in our study.

A comparison of age structures in the six firms reveals a relatively homogeneous picture (cf. figure 3).

Very pronounced in each case is the demographic break in the 40–44 year-old age group, the so-called post-war generation. Also typical is the higher share in the groups between 45 and 54 and the low percentage shares of the age groups above 55. So, the age structure of the case-study firms corresponds with that of the whole population.

Deviations in some age groups from the standard profile were registered (apart from the somewhat more pronounced spread in firm F) in firms C and D, both firms in the transport sector.

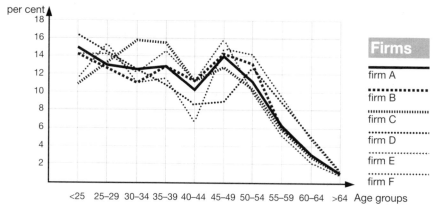

Figure 3: Age Structures of the Case-Study Firms, 1989

Firm D has an age-structure characteristic of those firms in which the age groups above 55 make up a comparatively large proportion of the workforce (15 per cent). Of the younger age groups, only that of the under 24 year olds was comparatively well represented, with the figures falling for subsequent groups. This seems to be the result of planned labour-force management: in view of its economic importance, every year the firm received 400 to 500 trainees with an equal proportion of young men and women (women accounted for only 33 per cent of the rest of the workforce). The difficult working conditions in many area of the firm's activities, including the need to work shifts meant that continued employment in the firm after completing training was unattractive for many young workers, particularly women. Thus many left the firm immediately or relatively soon after completing their training.

Firm C, by contrast, also active in the transport sector, has a young workforce structure. This is due to specific working conditions in a number of areas of activity which led the firm to pursue a conscious policy aimed at attracting younger workers. The result: high employment shares for the age groups under 45.

These exceptions do not allow us to draw conclusions on the possible influence of production regimes on workforce age structures. It is interesting, however, to note the high degree of homogeneity between the age structures of firms A and B, which operate in the same industry and under the same production regime.

Table 10: Employment Shares of Older Workers in Case-Study Firms 1989 (in percent)

Firm/ Age Group	A	B	C	D	E	F	GDR
55 – 59 Years	6.1	5.9	5.7	8.9	4.9	9.6	8.7
60 – 64 Years	3.2	3.3	2.7	5.2	2.1	4.7	3.0
> 64 Years	0.9	0.6	0.6	0.8	0.4	1.4	3.3
3 Groups	10.2	9.8	9.0	14.9	7.4	15.7	14.2
Working Pensioners	1.4	1.2	1.2	1.9	0.1	2.8	3.3

3.3.1 Employment of Older Workers

While all the firms employed workers who had reached retirement age (i.e., were over 60 – female workers – or 65 – male workers), closer study reveals a number of minor differences (table 10).

Firm E employed the lowest proportion of workers below the age of 55. This can be explained with reference to the catchment area surrounding this firm. The firm was founded as a result of state "locational policy" and its age structure is merely a reflection of the relatively young population structure in the surrounding region. This is also the reason behind the small proportion of working pensioners in the firm.

Of our sample firms, only firms D and F had employment shares of older workers approximating to average figures for the GDR economy as a whole. It would, however, be a mistake to deduce from this that the remaining firms had pursued age-selective strategies, as will become clear from the following.

3.3.2 Age-Relevant Labour-Market Withdrawal in the Sample Firms

Until 1989 the only pathway out of employment before statutory retirement age which was supported by state transfer benefits was via a disability pension. As we have already shown at macroeconomic level, this led to early-retirement rates of around 30 per cent, substantially lower than in the old Federal Republic. This finding is supported by the following data which, unfortunately, were not available for all the sample firms (table 11).

This trend towards early retirement, relatively weak and usually based on individual decision by the worker concerned must be compared with the stronger trend towards continued employment beyond pensionable age. This is indicated by the table 12 showing average age of workers when receiving their old-age pension in firm C (with its overall young age structure).

Table 11: Exits from the Firm via Disability Pension as a Proportion of all Retirements in the Sample Firms, 1980–1989 (%)

Year	Firm			
	A	B	C	F
1980	24.1	12.5	17.1	8.3
1981	12.9	28.6	17.1	33.3
1982	39.1	15.0	23.8	14.3
1983	20.0	33.3	11.6	23.1
1984	24.0	13.3	20.1	22.2
1985	16.7	14.3	23.1	11.1
1986	12.5	–	13.8	33.2
1987	7.4	–	25.0	20.0
1989	37.5	42.1	27.6	21.0
1990	21.0	28.6	19.2	20.0

Clearly, macroeconomic trends of continuing working after standard retirement age are closely reflected in retirement trends in firm C. There has been a decline in the duration of paid employment after retirement age during the 1980s. On the average women worked longer after their retirement age than men.

In general terms, the trends identified in the firms with regard to changing age structures confirm the hypotheses regarding the logic of enterprise behaviour in the context of the planned economy. There is no evidence of a strategy to stimulate early retirement.

Where firms faced a partial conflict of interest between workforce performance potential and economic requirements, they opted – given the regulatory framework provided by the state and the nature of their economic problems – for different solutions than those selected by firms working in a market environment (cf. 3.2). Most importantly, they did not opt for the externalisation of the "problem group". The rise in disability pensions in recent years can not be characterised as an overall exit strategy of firms like

Table 12: Average Actual Retirement Age in Firm C

Year	Total	Male	Female
1983	65.9	66.7	64.5
1984	64.2	65.3	63.4
1985	65.2	65.9	63.7
1986	64.2	65.4	62.2
1987	63.9	65.2	62.8
1989	63.5	65.8	61.9
1990	63.7	65.5	62.0

in some Western countries. This becomes clear if we see that in some firms
exit by disability is combined with continued employment beyond pensionable age.

3.4   The Logic, Instruments and Results of Age-Relevant Practices by Firms during the Transformation Process

The logic of age-relevant practices by firms during the transformation process has been influenced, on the one hand, *by the factors, which affected all the
firms in East Germany* during the successive stages of the transition process
since the Autumn of 1989 (cf. section 2.3). On the other hand, empirical
analysis of concrete cases reveals *significant differences* both regarding initial
conditions and the further development of different firms. Consequently,
closer analysis also reveals a degree of differentiation between firms' strategies within the framework set by the process of fundamental economic and
political change. This will be illustrated in this sub-section with reference to
selected "firms' histories". Subsequently we will return to the macro level to
look at the results, i.e., the age-structural effects, of these strategies.

3.4.1 The Engineering Firm A

In the GDR the firm was a reputed mechanical engineering firm, the sole
producer of a number of types of lathes, enjoying guaranteed sales in Eastern
Europe and the GDR. The transition to the market economy (monetary
union) led directly to the loss of sales markets and a drop in output.

The firm tried to respond to the rapidly worsening crisis with a programme
of structural adjustment (some departments were shed, plant closed and the
main plant reorganised) and changes in the product range (consumer-good
production previously required of the firm by the state was abandoned and
a new product was adopted).

The primary aim of the firm was to reach the – in international terms –
normal "efficiency coefficient" of DM 200 000 turnover per employee per
year as quickly as possible. In 1989 turnover per employee amounted to
GDR-Mark 129 000.

Despite the attempts made by the firm at structural and demand-side
adjustment to the new competitive conditions, it proved impossible to
prevent a substantial fall in output during 1990. The conclusion drawn from
this was that by reducing the workforce the firm gradually tried to reach the
coefficient mentioned above in order to make the firm an attractive object
for foreign investors (from an early date firms in the old Federal Republic
and Switzerland had expressed interest in buying the firm). However, the

process of selling the firm – which was placed under the auspices of the Treuhandanstalt for the purposes of privatisation – proved very complicated for reasons which are far from clear. To our knowledge, the process of privatisation remains unfinished. The aim of the *job-cutting programme* was to reduce the workforce from 1 826 in 1989 to 900 in 1991, whereby the reductions were to be concentrated in the main plant.

The following *instruments* were used for this purpose: further hiring was stopped, working time reduced from 42 to 40 hours, shift-work was cut back, short-time working affecting the entire workforce was introduced, redundancies made and, last but not least the conscious use of age-selective instruments (described in detail below) was begun.

The use of these instruments of personnel reduction have already had *age-structural* effects. Firstly, the rapid deterioration of the economic situation led to high rates of fluctuation among younger workers, who, as a consequence of the cessesion of hiring, were not replaced. Secondly, the closure of the firm's vocational training establishment shut off this source of workforce rejuvenation. Moreover, the "social selection" of those to be made redundant had the effect that younger workers left the firm, while middle-aged and older workers remained. Overall this led to an increase in the average age of the workforce, a trend which was not fully offset, as we shall see, by the age-selective policy of labour-market withdrawal of older workers and those of pensionable age.

These age-structural effects of the process of job-losses are having serious *consequences* for the enterprise because it now lacks the potential of high-performance younger workers, a vital factor in personnel development. Moreover, on a long-term view, the "bunching" of the workforce in the age groups prior to retirement age represents a potential for further job losses rather than a "performance potential" for the firm. This is a *trend* which is evident *in all the firms studied*: the massive pressure to reduce staffing levels has led to job losses among key personnel of vital importance for the future of the firm. Firm A, for example, suddenly found itself without any skilled foremen (Meister).

The use of *intentional age-selective instruments of workforce reduction* is to be seen in the fact that first of all working pensioners were "induced" to leave the firm. The "success" of this strategy is clear from the following figures:

	Dec. 1989	June 1990	Nov. 1990 (main plant)
Employees over 60	93	10	0
of which women	17	0	0

From an early stage Firm A made use of the pre-retirement instrument. Incentives were offered to those workers eligible in the form of enterprise compensation payments linked to length of tenure (amounting to between DM 1 000 and DM 8 000). This was preceded by personal discussions with the relevant superior in each case: the intensity of use of this approach, generally referred to as a "soft measure", varied greatly from case to case. While we know of no representative survey on this question, our interviews indicate that some degree of moral pressure was exerted on the workers eligible for pre-retirement. Firstly, they were not presented with an alternative, and, secondly, they were confronted with the argument that older workers would, by taking pre-retirement – which, at that point in time, appeared to be a relatively favourable option – be helping to secure the jobs of younger workers.

Before monetary union, the material consequences of this decision were unclear to most of those affected, particularly with regard to the extent to which pensions would increase in future (in the Spring of 1990 it was generally assumed that pre-retirement pensions would keep pace with wage and salary incomes). Still, 139 workers left the firm for pre-retirement before monetary union under these conditions. A further 23 followed between July 1st and October 3rd. Most of these left under the threat that the pre-retirement provision was only to apply until October 2nd to be replaced by the Transition Pension (Altersübergangsgeld, cf. table 8).

The number of workers of pre-retirement age employed by the firm changed as follows:

	Dec. 1989	June 1990	Nov. 1990 (main plant)
Employees 56-60	128	100	33
of which women	41	7	0
Employees 61-65	93	10	0
of which women	17	0	0

In other words, here, too, there was a regular "clear-out" as a result of the use of age-selective instruments of staff reduction. It is also interesting to note that 32 of the 33 employees still on the payroll in Firm A and of pre-retirement age were on "zero-hour" short-time working in November 1990.

The overall effect of the strategy of workforce reduction in firm A described above has led to a *substantial age-structural change in the direction of an aging of the workforce* despite of the early exit of the 55 and over age

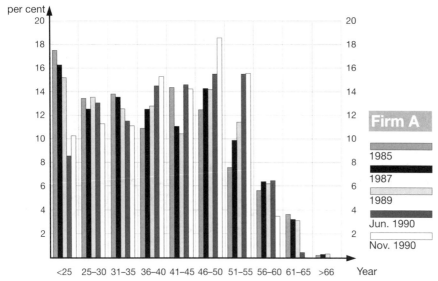

Figure 4: Age Structural Change in Firm A

groups (cf. figure 4). This represents a less favourable point of departure for future development than previously. On the other hand, it also provides further potential to reduce the workforce through early retirement in the coming years. Whereas in the context of the centrally planned economy withdrawals from firm A before retirement age were restricted to disability pension (2 to 6 workers per year), the transition to the market economy led immediately to the intensive use of age-selective instruments.

In October 1991 it became public knowledge, that the firm A had been sold with only 500 workers.

3.4.2 The Service Firm C

The initial position facing this transport firm was such that the opening of the borders led to an immediate and drastic fall in demand, with the result that already by the first half of 1990 trading profit was down to half its level of the previous year. Monetary union in the Summer of 1990 effectively threatened the very existence of the firm. German unification finally, with its effects on transport infrastructure, made fundamental restructuring unavoidable; the result was the shedding of a large number of former "departments" of enterprise C. This process of splitting up the firm proved to be long and complex, not least due to disputes about ownership rights. *The result of the restructuring process* in employment terms was that only 3,467 out of an original workforce of 8 204 remained in firm C itself. The management concept for the future of the enterprise foresaw, alongside changes in the profile of services offered by the firm and restructuring measures, a reduction in the workforce by the end of June 1991 to 1 200 employees.

In addition to the conditions just described arising from the transition to the market economy, firm C is also distinguished by a workforce of below-average age, resulting from the regular influx of younger workers under the planned economy and the working conditions in the firm. The employment share of working pensioners had been relatively low (1.3 per cent). As in other firms, withdrawal from the employment system before statutory retirement age was only possible via a disability pension: in firm C this accounted for about 3 per cent of all withdrawals. Until 1989 labour turnover had been relatively low and constant, linked, so it was claimed, to high wages and a high degree of job satisfaction: in 1989 it increased to 4.6 per cent (largely due to emigration to the FRG.).

The workforce-reduction strategies employed by firm C differ fundamentally from those used in firm A. Firstly, as early as January 1990 a strong works council was constituted which, together with management, developed a programme of action to save and modernise the firm. In the course of 1990 agreements were reached on dismissal protection and protection from the effects of rationalisation, on the mode of filling vacancies; negotiations commenced on pay and conditions. Secondly, all the actors concerned were convinced that the firm could be sold as several interested buyers were on hand.

Under these conditions the company's strategies can be termed cautious and "socially acceptable". One of the main aims was clearly to ensure that highly skilled personnel were not lost to the firm (and to the subsequent buyer). This is why even as late as the Spring of 1990 substantial new recruits were taken on and until October 1990 while the firm as a whole was split up no organisational and few personnel changes were made within the core operations of the firm itself.

This also applies to the *use of age-selective instruments*. Material incentives were provided for the 97 working pensioners to leave the firm during 1990; 71 of them left before it was split up, the remaining 26 at the end of the year. An "incentive" for the latter group was not least the fact that proposals for a collective agreement for the branch as a whole came out in December under which the employment contract would be declared invalid at the latest one month after the worker reached retirement age. Voluntary early retirement from the firm entitled those leaving to compensation payments amounting, in most cases, to DM 20 000.

The use of the pre-retirement provision (GDR) was completely different from that employed in firm A. Despite substantial offers of compensation, by

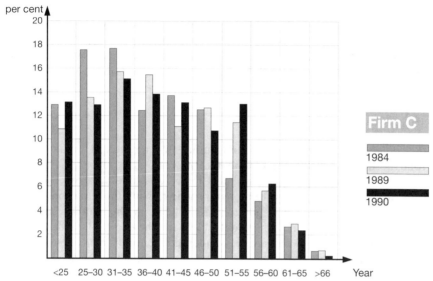

Figure 5: Age Structural Change in Firm C

the end of 1990 only 17 of the 184 workers eligible had left the firm. This can only be explained by the prevailing optimism at that time that the firm would survive (be sold), the expected wage and salary increases during 1991 and, apparently, the fact that less severe moral pressure was exerted on the employees affected. The net result was that at the end of 1990 211 workers aged between 55 and 60 (49 of them women), and 42 between 60 and 65 (none of them women) were still employed with the firm. Together with the entire workforce (2 839 persons) the older workers had to undergo a selection procedure by applying for a specific job within the firm. The aim was to reduce the workforce to 1 200 by June 1991. In contrast to the sole use of "social criteria" sometimes practiced, this approach was designed to take account of both social and performance criteria. An additional age-selective effect was produced by the fact that 435 workers were taken on by a West German firm, largely young and highly skilled workers. A further 193 young, skilled employees left the firm to take a secure position in another firm.

Despite the different firm strategies, *the age-structural change* in firm C as in firm A characterised by a shift from younger to middle aged and older workers, despite the fact that there has been an early exit of the older age groups. In other words: the (unhindered) exit of younger age groups is even stronger than of the older age groups. (cf. figure 5).

Our empirical investigation of firm C ended at the end of 1990. The attempts made to pursue a socially and performance-oriented strategy of workforce reduction could not be completed as, contrary to expectations, the firm was not sold and was closed in April 1991. A so-called Training and Employment Company was founded for the workers made redundant, with the aim of providing them with further training or re-training opportunities.

3.4.3 The Chemical Firm E

The initial economic conditions confronting firm E differed fundamentally from those facing firms A and C in that it was able, even after monetary union, to maintain output levels almost intact. Just one area of production was shut down to coincide with monetary union, while those responsible for the production of consumer goods were split from the mother company. The most important products manufactured in the main plant had had a stable position on the world market under the centrally planned economy, and this was held by and large even after the introduction of the D-Mark.

Production by the firm as a whole fell from 1988 = 100 to 96 per cent in 1989 and 80 per cent in 1990. The firm continues to operate at a profit under the new market-economic conditions so that it is no surprise that it has now been successfully privatised. At the same time, firm E is producing at a wage-cost rate of 4.98 per cent, indicating the excessive use of "living labour", as comparable firms in the old federal states operate with a coefficient of 4.5 per cent. The firm's management deduces from this the need to cut manning levels in the longer term.

Management strategies with their age-relevant effects will now be presented with reference to workforce trends from August 1989 to April 1991. During the 1980s the firm had employed around 8 500 workers, with only small variations around this figure. In August 1989, the employment level began to decline as a result of the opening of the border to Hungary in that month and the resulting migration to the West. In a continuation of the strategic paradigm "learned" in the context of the planned economy, up until March 1990 the firm attempted to offset this process by increasing recruitment. It was not until April 1990 that hiring was restricted to in-firm apprentices and a few university or college graduates. As a result the decline in the workforce during 1989 was very minor, from 8 431 to 8 350 employees.

In April 1990, firm E changed its personnel policy in such a way that *instruments designed to limit workforce size* began to be implemented: no attempt was made to restrain labour turnover, new recruitment was restricted to isolated cases, some departments were shed from the main firm and early retirement began to receive management support. Evidently, the firm placed a premium on conducting the process of workforce reduction in a "socially acceptable" way, as personnel policy aimed not to resort to redundancies: workers who lost their jobs were to be offered alternative employment. The staff of the in-firm fire-brigade, for instance, which was shed by the firm, were offered jobs in plant security, which many of the workers involved (70) accepted. It is of note that the firm's strategy aimed to cause as little disturbance as possible within the firm. Structural changes in the organisational sphere, for example, were not implemented, presumably in the expectation that the future owners would bring their own concepts. Cooperation between the plant-level organs of the trade union – and later the works council (established in September 1990) – and management was apparently lacking in major conflict, with both sides attempting to maintain the level of output and to make the firm attractive to a potential buyer.

Despite these efforts, at the turn of the year (1989–90) *labour turnover* increased markedly, particularly among younger skilled workers, only to decline in the run-up to monetary union, to rise once more in September 1990 and finally to return to a value which was considered "normal" before the onset of the economic and political upheavals. This was evidently the result of the optimistic forecast made by the firm's management and also due to the fact that the demand for chemical workers on the labour market in the old federal states was relatively weak. The fact that the workforce shared the optimistic views of management, this much is revealed by our studies, was vital in influencing workforce developments.

How did the firm go about realising the necessary *cuts in staffing levels* ?

One method was the removal of 465 jobs from the payroll by *excising* consumer-good *production*, vocational training etc. from the firm. This process is to be continued (300 employees during 1991).

Another strategy, found, to this degree of intensity, only in this firm, was the conscious *internal re-allocation of jobs* which, through fluctuation or, as we shall see, through age-selective instruments of staff reduction, had become vacant but which were considered necessary for production. The firm's strategy aimed to redeploy workers who had lost their original job due to the requirements of rationalisation to new jobs within the firm. During the course of 1990 this strategy affected 336 workers, whereby it is important to note that this process was not without conflict: it often proved difficult to match workers' expectations with the job-requirements of the tasks available.

It is also of note that from an early stage management adopted a clear, *new personnel concept*, including a purposeful strategy of offering further training to key staff together with more general human-resource development. This limited the damage done by the withdrawal of younger, high-performance and flexible workers. It is not insignificant in this context that the firm had greater opportunities for such a strategy given its dominance of the local economy (in contrast to the other sample firms which are located in large cities).

Another principle pursued by management was that of "mutual agreement to end the employment contract". Financial resources were made available to induce workers to leave the enterprise where there was no chance of continued employment: this strategy was employed with 200 staff during 1991.

We now turn to *the use of age-selective instruments* of personnel reduction.

Only 44 employees of pensionable age were working in the firm in 1989: they all left in the course of 1990 on the basis of mutual agreement.

At first, the employees eligible were reluctant to take early retirement: from February to May only a small number of workers accepted the offer of early retirement, as the prospect of 70 per cent of previous income was not a sufficient stimulus and because older workers apparently enjoyed the favourable working conditions offered by the firm. Only when in June the firm began to offer substantial bonuses did larger numbers of older employees begin to opt for early retirement. Compensation amounted to a one-off payment of between 70 and 100 per cent of last net pay depending on length of tenure.

In addition, the firm offered an "early pre-retirement" scheme under which workers could retire for health reasons on reaching the age of 55 (and even earlier in some cases). This in contrast to the former social-oriented approach in the GDR: under the economic pressure to reduce its workforce firm C used deliberately this form of exit to separate itself from employees expected not to be able to meet the future needs of efficiency. The overall effect of these measures was that by the end of 1990 almost the entire age group in pre-retirement age had taken advantage of one of the options. During the first four months of this year, however, none of the workers eligible for early retirement has taken it as it had become known that on April 1st wages were to be raised by a not inconsiderable margin. The 380 workers affected do not intend to retire until the end of June in order to benefit from a higher pension entitlement. Apparently, they are not under pressure from the company to retire earlier.

The overall effect of the strategies described has been *a drop in the workforce* from 8 350 in 1989 to 7 121 workers in 1990 and 6 748 in April 1991. By the end of year 1990, staffing levels were planned to fall further to 5 709 employees.

Regarding the use of age-selective instruments we conclude, as with firms A and C, that, in contrast to the previous economic regime under which early retirement was only possible via a disability pension, the transition to the market economy has led the firm to make full use of the new forms of state regulation on offer, and indeed to extend their coverage by offering enterprise-specific compensation payments to those retiring early.

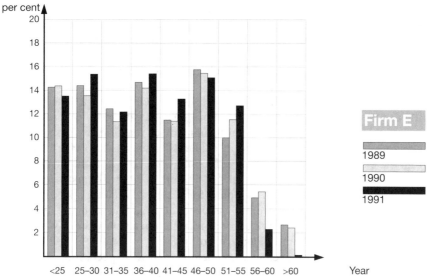

Figure 6: Age Structural Change in Firm E

In firm E, too, the net result has been a "clear-out" of the age groups eligible. As figure 6 shows, the net result has been that the enterprise age structure has remained fundamentally unchanged.

This is not to say that corporate development and the process of workforce reduction in the firm are complete. On the contrary, following the sale of the firm to three different buyers and in the light of the results of an analysis performed by a renowned firm of management consultants it is clear that by 1995 the workforce will be cut back further to around 2 600, this despite considerable planned investment (capital-intensive) and expanding production. The cuts in staffing levels are to proceed in stages, whereby the policy of "mutual agreement to end the employment relation" is to be maintained. The majority of the redundant workers are, however, to be integrated into a "Structural Promotion Company" (Strukturförderungsgesellschaft), financed jointly with local government, which will provide a framework for large-scale job-creation measures and which will aim to open up new locations for both research and production in the field of ecology and pharmaceuticals.

3.4.4 Corporate Age-Structural Strategies: Overall Trends and Effects

To conclude, we now present the strategies adopted by our 6 sample firms in terms of those trends and effects which can be generalised and with regard to the effect of state regulation on firms' behaviour.

All the sample firms found it necessary, confronted with the fundamental political and socio-economic changes resulting from the transition from the centrally planned to the market economy, *to reduce the size of their workforce.* The pace of staff reduction and the strategies adopted, however, were subject to significant differences which can be explained with reference to the following factors.

The pressure of competition from the market environment faced by the firms, especially after monetary union, was clearly most severe in the engineering firms (A and B). It led to immediate reactions by management including the use of age-selective instruments. This was also true of firm F from the electrical engineering/electronics industry. Firm E, from the chemical industry, on the other hand, was under less pressure on the markets for its most important products and so opted for a staged, gradual approach. The service firms C and D apparently believed at first that demand for their services would remain high and this was reflected in a slow pace of workforce reduction, even among the older age groups.

A further factor influencing firms' behaviour was expectations regarding privatisation,,and is thus linked to the *behaviour of the Treuhandanstalt.*

Last but not least, *the influence of management consultants* and their orientation toward certain indicators of efficiency have clearly made their influence felt. These were active in the engineering industry from the beginning of 1990, whereas they were not called into chemical enterprises, until 1991. This had corresponding effects on the process of personnel reduction in each case.

Our sample is too small to determine whether different fundamental human-resource conceptions were being employed. It is significant, though, that even under the planned economy the chemical firm E had been well known for its intensive enterprise social policy and its worker-oriented forms of work organisation. In addition, service firm C had always employed a "holistic" labour-force strategy with regard to the high skill level and development potential of its workforce, compared to what was possible (and necessary) in "classical" production plants utilising Taylorist forms of the division of labour. To some degree this explains the more socially-oriented concept underlying workforce reduction in firms C and E. The use of management conceptions along the lines practiced in market economies was only identified in firm E, and then only embryonically.

The excessive manning levels originating from the planned economy and the economic pressure to rationalise induced by the transition to the market economy prompted all the firms studied *to employ the full range of instruments suited to the aim of personnel reduction* which they found at their disposal, especially those which allowed the firm to externalise staff without legal difficulties. To this end both state labour-market policy instruments were employed (pre-retirement, short-time working) and in-firm instruments

Table 13: Workers in Upper Age Groups as a Proportion of the Total Workforce in the
Sample Firms, 1989 and 1990/91

Age Group		55−59	60−64	>64	3 Groups	Working Pensioners
Firm	Year					
A	1989	6.1	3.2	0.9	10.2	1.4
	1990	3.4	−	−	3.4	−
B	1989	5.8	3.3	0.6	9.8	1.2
	1990	2.1	−	−	2.1	−
C	1989	6.1	2.7	0.6	9.0	1.2
	1990	5.7	2.2	0.1	8.4	1.0
D	1989	8.9	5.2	0.8	14.9	1.9
	1990	6.1	2.4	0.1	8.6	0.1
E	1989	4.9	2.1	0.4	7.4	0.1
	1991	2.1	−	−	2.1	−
F	1989	9.6	4.7	1.4	15.7	3.3
	1990	7.7	1.8	−	9.5	0.1

and strategies developed (in-house pre-retirement schemes, social plans etc.).

All these instruments must be considered age-relevant, and this in a double sense: On the one hand, the *state* provides a set of instruments with which the employer incurs relatively minor costs and which can be used in the knowledge that they enjoy a relatively high degree of both social and individual acceptability as they provide at least a minimum of social security: this is the case with pre-retirement schemes of various types.

These instruments, modeled on those in the old Federal Republic are *deliberately age-selective* in their effects. For reasons of labour-market policy, they induce a specific group of workers to withdraw from the labour force before reaching statutory retirement age. Of course, this begs the question as to the justification for the continued employment of those of pensionable age which may be superfluous to the requirements of the enterprise, but where working life remains important to the individual workers concerned.

It is our view that *corporate strategies* were primarily aimed at personnel reduction; the *age-selective aspect was subordinate* to this aim, not to say somewhat random. Random to the extent that the new forms of state regulation prescribe such a personnel approach without firms having the chance or the time to ascertain which groups of workers are indispensable to performance levels or future enterprise strategies. An approach of this type was identified in only a small number of cases, and was usually restricted to managerial levels (firm F).

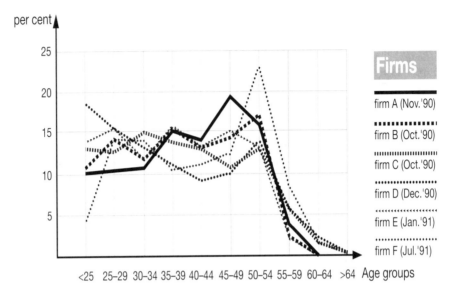

Figure 7: Age Structures of the Case-Study Firms, 1990/91

On the other hand, the age-structural effects observed were not merely the result of specific instruments but *the entire process of workforce reduction had an age-selective aspect*. This process was not consciously steered by the firms with an eye to age structures. This is why age structures in all firms – with the exception of firm E – have changed in an unfavourable way in the course of workforce cuts: unfavourable because not only the upper age groups but also young workers have left the firms, leaving the middle-age categories to dominate (cf. figure 7).

The overall result of this process in terms of the employment shares of older workers with respect to the overall workforce in the sample firms can be summarised as follows (table 13).

As early as November 1990, two of the sample firms were no longer employing workers of pensionable age. The two pre-retirement schemes contributed to workforce reduction in all the firms among the over-55 age groups. Due to the fact that the entitlement conditions were modified by the state several times and a number of firms (B, D, E) also initiated "early pre-retirement" schemes of their own it is not possible to make clear calculations of percentage effects. But it can be seen that, with the exception of firm C, between 75 to 99 per cent of all employees in pre-retirement age made use of this regulation. The result of this trend has been a marked fall in the employment shares of the over-55 age groups. The changing age structures of the sample firms between 1989 and 1990/91 provide an good overview of the marked changes which have occurred (cf. figures 7 and 3).

Overall, the extent of differentiation between the employment shares of the age groups between 25 and 45 years of age has decreased. The demographic "dip" in the 40–45 year age group is scarcely recognisable. This reveals all the more clearly the similarities and differences between the firms regarding the way in which they have "dealt" with the other age groups. Common to all firms is a shift in employment shares in favour of the 50–54 year-olds (in firm C, the emphasis is on the age group below this).

These tendencies were confirmed by a survey of the Treuhandanstalt conducted in May 1991 comprising 5 269 assigned firms (Wahse et. al., 1991). According to the results of this survey between 17.2 per cent (Mecklenburg-Vorpommern) and 20.3 per cent (Sachsen) of all work force were in the age of 50–56, while between 3 per cent (Mecklenburg-Vorpommern) and 5 per cent (Berlin-East) were in the age of 57–65 years.

At least *two reasons* can be put forward for this effect. Firstly, the approach based on "social criteria" has particularly affected treatment of the age group between 50 to 54. Given that the chances of finding alternative employment for workers over 50 were almost nil, social plans and other enterprise strategies of workforce reduction were usually conceived in such a way that workers in this age group were able to remain within the firm.

The consequence of this strategy is that since 1989 the average age of the workforce has increased in all the firms studied, despite the reduction in employment shares of working pensioners and the over 55s. At the same time the concentration of the workforce in the 50–54 year age group represents a potential for personnel reduction which can be successively exploited in the coming years, provided that state instruments remain available.

This approach to the 50–54 year-olds, identified in all the sample firms, must be conceived as a policy of social security for older workers, protecting the interests of individual workers in this – vulnerable – age group.

Secondly, firms did not appear to be pursuing active strategies with regard to younger workers. Labour turnover of younger workers was either actively supported, or at the very least was left unhindered. In other words, the sample firms are failing to tie to the enterprise the personnel they will need to cope with the coming challenges. The lack of an overall enterprise concept for the future was, of course, hardly conducive to preventing this trend.

4   Conclusion

Though our study on the age-structural change in the GDR only comprises a very short historical period of the transformation from the centrally planned to the market economy several transformations in state-firm interaction could be identified. The most significant of these can be described as follows:

(1) The transformation in the former GDR (under the specific conditions of the GDR's accession to the FRG) has been accompanied by fundamental changes in ideology and practice of labour-force participation in particular with respect to the older age groups.

(2) The process as a whole can be characterised as a change from a policy of integrating older workers in the former GDR to an age-limit policy in the five new federal states, i.e., in respect of older age groups a change from internalisation to externalisation.

(3) This process has been supported by the state as well as by firms trying to meet the challenges of the market economy.

The *state*, first the GDR, later the FRG, was confronted with the tasks of creating a framework for the developing labour market *and* supporting firms in managing their economic problems. The various methods and measures employed by firms in this transfer and transition included an identifiable assumption of preexisting regulations of the former FRG as well as gradual and stepwise adaptations from conditions and situations existing in the ex-GDR. As a result of this transition in state economic strucure of the ex-GDR, an employment system with scarcely any available exit routes prior to official retirement age (barring disability) evolved quickly into a system encompassing constantly changing variety of exit pathways. Adaptations in exit routes and conditions were realised mainly due to the rapid deteriorating labour-market situation. The number of peoply possibly addressed by one pathway or another was increasing up to the end of 1991. As a part of these changes, the preference given to women in the former GDR (they had retirement options five years before men) has been abandoned. Both men and women are enabled to make use of pre-retirement schemes at 55.

Firms came under pressure from rapidly changing market conditions. In contrast with their experience in the planned economy, they had to develop their own firm strategies in view of the fact that a viable workforce in volume, structure, training and motivation would be essential for future productivity and profitability. Thus, workforce reduction, by using the deliberately age-selective instruments provided by the state, has been the first step taken in this direction by most of the enterprises studied. In addition, we could identify further firm strategies aimed at early exit of certain (older) age groups. The overall firm strategy in our firms we can be described as a change from the former combination of social policy and internalisation of the older age groups to the "new" combination of personnel policiy and externalisation. However, in light of the spectrum of personnel-policy requirements, companies often failed to develop a sense of firm loyalty in younger people through for example, incentives for them to stay on. Thus, despite the early exit of the older age groups the overall result of the whole process was a shrinking working population and at the same time an aging workforce in 6 firms studied. Accordingly, one is brought to question the logic and rationality of the corporate strategies described.

This development of an aging workforce has its equivalent on the macro level. The ongoing emigration and mobility of especially younger age groups accelerates the demographically determined process of aging population and workforce. This problem and its further consequences have not yet found the same attention in the public debate as in the western part of Germany, although the consequences in the eastern part are expected to be much more serious.

The overall socio-economic effects of the new form of state-firm interaction towards older employees in the new federal states differ greatly from those in the old Federal Republic. This is because, firstly, they were implemented by firms in the context of a generalised, rapid and, as a consequence, usually ill-thought out reduction in workforce levels, whereby the future development of the firms remained clouded in obscurity: secondly, because they are being implemented on the basis of a lower material and financial standard of living than in the FRG. The social and economic consequences of this will have to be steadily overcome through the continuing reconstruction and development of the new federal states in the coming years.

Appendix

Table A: Age Structure of Employment by Sector, GDR 1989 (in percent)

Age Group Sector	GDR-economy	Industry	Construc-tion	Agricul-ture	Transport
<25	12.9	13.3	14.9	13.2	13.9
25–29	13.2	13.0	14.2	13.2	13.6
30–34	13.0	12.7	13.5	13.0	13.0
35–39	12.8	12.9	13.6	11.6	12.1
40–44	8.8	8.8	8.7	7.1	8.3
45–49	12.1	12.1	11.9	9.7	11.6
50–54	12.2	12.3	11.4	12.7	12.3
55–59	8.7	8.6	7.1	11.5	8.8
60–64	3.0	3.4	3.1	4.3	4.3
>64	3.3	2.9	1.7	3.4	2.2

	Post and Tele-Communic.	Trade	Other Product. Sectors	Non-Productive Sectors
>25	12.0	14.4	10.7	10.9
25–29	11.7	13.2	12.5	13.4
30–34	10.9	12.5	12.7	13.6
35–39	11.1	12.3	14.0	13.2
40–44	8.1	8.9	10.0	9.4
45–49	12.7	12.1	13.9	13.4
50–54	14.1	11.8	12.7	12.0
55–59	10.7	8.2	8.1	8.3
60–64	2.7	1.7	2.7	2.1
>64	6.0	4.9	2.8	3.7

Source: Sozialstatistik (Official Statistics), own Calculations.

Table B: Age Structure of Disability Pensioners (in percent)

Age Group	Total	Women	Men
65 and over	0.5	0.9	0.2
60 to 65	21.2	1.0	38.9
50 to 60	45.0	59.6	32.2
40 to 50	14.1	18.2	10.4
below 40	19.2	20.3	19.3
Total	100.0	100.0	100.0

Source: Figures Provided by the Social-Insurance Authorities.

References

Altenreport (1990). In: *Blätter der Wohlfahrtspflege* 10/11. Stuttgart: Verlag Wohlfahrtswerk.

Arbeitsgesetzbuch der DDR (1977). Berlin: Verlag Tribüne.

Autorenkollektiv (1982). *Leiter-Kollektiv-Persönlichkeit.* Berlin: Verlag Die Wirtschaft.

Brück, G. W. (1988). *Allgemeine Sozialpolitik.* Köln: Bund-Verlag.

DIW (1990). *An der Schwelle zur sozialen Marktwirtschaft – Ergebnisse aus der Basiserhebung des Sozio-ökonomischen Panels in der DDR im Juni 1990.* In: *Beiträge zur Arbeitsmarkt- und Berufsforschung* 143. Nürnberg: Bundesanstalt für Arbeit.

Einigungsvertrag (1990). Sonderdruck aus der Sammlung Das deutsche Bundesrecht, Baden-Baden: Nomos Verlagsgesellschaft.

Eitner, Siegfried (1960). *Gerohygiene. Hygiene des Alterns als Problem der Lebensgestaltung.* Berlin: Akademie-Verlag.

Fischer, Peter (1984). *Sozialökonomische Aspekte der Berufstätigkeit von Produktionsarbeitern in der zweiten Hälfte des Arbeitslebens unter besonderer Beachtung einer altersdispositionsgerechten Gestaltung ihrer Arbeitsaufgaben und Arbeitsplätze.* (Diss.) Berlin: Hochschule für Ökonomie.

Frauenreport (1990) (ed. by Gunnar Winkler). Berlin: Verlag Die Wirtschaft.

Hentschel, Volker (1983). *Geschichte der deutschen Sozialpolitik 1880–1980.* Frankfurt a.M.: Suhrkamp Verlag.

Institut für Angewandte Sozialwissenschaften (IASW) (1991). *Frauen in den neuen Bundesländern im Prozeß der deutschen Einigung.* Bad Godesberg.

Lampert, Heinz (1985). *Lehrbuch der Sozialpolitik.* Berlin: Springer Verlag.

Lampert, Heinz (1989). *Theorie und Praxis der Sozialpolitik in der DDR.* (Arbeitsberichte zum Systemvergleich Nr. 13). Marburg: Philipps-Universität.

Lexikon der Sozialpolitik (1987) (ed. by Gunnar Winkler). Berlin: Akademie Verlag.

Manz, Günter and Gunnar Winkler (eds.) (1988). *Sozialpolitik.* Berlin: Verlag Die Wirtschaft.

Naschold, Frieder (ed.) (1985). *Arbeit und Politik. Gesellschaftliche Regulierung der Arbeit und der sozialen Sicherung.* Frankfurt a.M.: Campus Verlag.

Schmidt, U. J.; Schwitzer, Klaus-P. und Irene Runge (1982). *Altern in der sozialistischen Gesellschaft.* Jena: S. Fischer Verlag.

Schuldt, Karsten (1991). *Arbeitsmarktbilanz.* In: Gerda Jasper und Elke Wendt, *Veränderungen in der Arbeitsmarkt- und Lebenslage der Frauen in den neuen Bundesländern.* Berlin: Projektgemeinschaft Sozialforschung.

Sozialistische Volkswirtschaft (1989). Berlin: Verlag Die Wirtschaft.

Sozialreport (1990) (ed. by Gunnar Winkler). Berlin: Verlag Die Wirtschaft.

Statistisches Jahrbuch der DDR (sev. years). Berlin: Staatsverlag der DDR.

Wahse, Jürgen (1991). *Beschäftigungsperspektiven von Treuhandunternehmen.* In: *Beiträge zur Arbeitsmarkt- und Berufsforschung* 152. Nürnberg: Bundesanstalt für Arbeit.

Wetzker, Konrad (ed.) (1990). *Wirtschaftsreport. Daten und Fakten zur wirtschaftlichen Lage Ostdeutschlands.* Berlin: Verlag Die Wirtschaft.

8 Great Britain: Firm Policy, State Policy and the Employment of Older Workers[1]

Bernard Casey and Stephen Wood

1   Introduction

One of the more remarkable features of the British labour market in the first part of the 1980s was the sharp fall in the proportion of older men who were participating in the labour market. Whereas in 1979 as many as 91 per cent of men aged 55–59 and 73 per cent of men aged 60–64 were economically active, by 1986 their activity rates had dropped to 80 per cent and 53 per cent respectively. The objective of this chapter is to examine the contribution of firm policies and practices to the decline and stagnation in the proportion of older people in work which was observed in the 1980s and to assess whether these policies and practices were induced or encouraged by particular interventions on the part of the state. Of especial concern is whether the developments of the last decade have led to fundamental changes in the labour market for older workers, and in particular to the institutionalisation of a new age of retirement.

As figure 1 shows, the fall in older men's participation rates occurred simultaneously with a severe deterioration in the overall labour market.

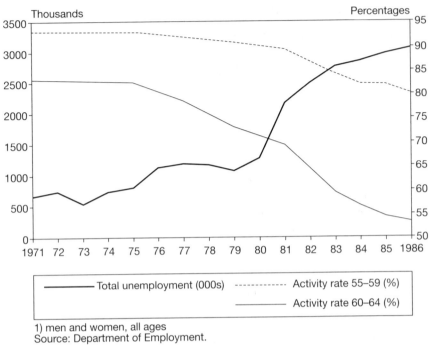

1) men and women, all ages
Source: Department of Employment.

Figure 1: Total Unemployment[1] and Activity Rates of Older Men, Great Britain 1971–1986

Registered unemployment, which stood at 1.1 mill. in 1979, had risen to 3.1 mill. by 1986. As this sequential presentation of the facts implies, the growth in the proportion of older men ceasing to work or to look for work appears to have been very much a consequence of the worsening of the labour market. Econometric analysis has suggested that each 1 mill. rise in the number of unemployed results in a fall in the participation rate of 55–59 year olds of 3 percentage points in the short run and 6 percentage points in the long run, and equivalent falls in the participation rate of 60–64 year-old men of 4 per cent and 9 per cent. If this is indeed so, then almost all of the exit from the workforce amongst the two groups of older men under discussion is to be ascribed to the worsening situation on the labour market (*see* Casey and Laczko, 1989).

The net result of this was that by 1986 less than three- quarters of men aged 55–59 years old, and less half of men aged 60–64 years old, were actually in paid employment. A few of the remainder were unemployed; most of the rest occupied an intermediate status between "hidden unemployment" and "early retirement".

Older women had experiences broadly similar to those of older men, although the fact that a higher proportion of each cohort of women was working than the one preceding it prevents this from being observed in time series data on activity rates. Thus, the number of women aged 55–59 who were in employment in 1984 was 23 per cent lower than the number of 50–54 year old women who were in employment in 1979. Comparing the same age groups over the period 1984 to 1989 suggests a net fall in the employment rates of 18 per cent. The equivalent figures for men in the same age groups are 19 per cent and 14 per cent.

A further symptom of the difficulty older workers were experiencing at that time was the growth in the number of older men and women who were in receipt of an invalidity pension. Between spring 1981 and spring 1990 the number of men aged 55–59 who were deemed unable to work because of disability rose by nearly two-thirds whilst the number of disabled men aged 60–64 rose by just over a half (*Social Security Statistics*, 1991, table D2.06). This increase does not appear to have been a consequence of an increase in the number of older men *becoming disabled*, rather it was a consequence of those who were disabled *staying disabled longer*. Average durations of disability rose by over a quarter for both 55–59 year olds and 60–64 year olds (*Social Security Statistics*, 1991, table D1.14). Older invalidity benefit recipients who experienced an improvement in their health and who, in a more favourable environment would have been able to return to work, found the labour market closed to them. There is anecdotal evidence from those who administer or experience the invalidity benefit system that sympathetic doctors continued to certify as disabled those whom they recognised as standing little chance of finding a job.[2]

Between 1986 and the end of the decade unemployment fell rapidly, to a low point of 1.5 mill. in 1990. There was, however, no corresponding upturn in older men's participation or employment rates; rather a further gradual decline was observable. In other words, older people continued to leave employment and the labour market at at least the same rate as they had in the mid-1980s. Moreover, the incidence of disability continued to rise, suggesting either that the unemployment-disability relationship is strongly lagged, or that the improvement in job opportunities did not favour older workers to anything like the extent it favoured other groups. Only at the end of the 1980s, in the context of labour supply constraints consequent upon a decline in the number of young entrants to the labour market, did attention focus on the issue of older people's retention in, or return to, employment rather than their exit from it. Yet even in this changed environment, no significant impact on older people's activity rates was to be discerned.[3] An important explanation for this was that it proved to be a very temporary environment, so that any new practices and opportunities to which it gave rise were of highly limited, short-term interest. At the start of the 1990s, as the short-lived upturn on the labour market gave way to recession and unemployment reached in excess of 2.5 mill., the employment chances of older people started to deteriorate once more.

To obtain a better understanding of firm policies and state policies and how they contributed to the large-scale withdrawal of older people from employment a number of approaches were adopted. The existing literature on older people in the labour market in Britain was consulted and a number of national data sets – especially the 1984 Workplace Industrial Relations Survey and the 1990 Labour Force Survey – were analysed. In addition, a postal survey of some 180, mainly larger, firms from all sectors of the economy was carried out in the summer of 1991, asking mainly about their retirement and redundancy policies. Lastly, a series of interviews were undertaken over the years 1989 to 1991 with senior personnel managers in a total of 30 firms in the public and private sector.

The close relationship between the fall in older men's participation rates and the rise in unemployment in the first part of the decade can be explained in either or both of two ways. First, it could be the consequence of employers pursuing age-specific dismissal practices; second it could be the consequence of their pursuing age-specific recruitment policies. These issues are addressed in parts 2 and 3 of the chapter respectively.

Part 2 looks at (2.1) the institution of "voluntary redundancy" in Britain and the implications it has for the older members of a firm's workforce, (2.2) the motives employers may have for choosing to dismiss older rather than other categories of worker, (2.3) the packages they construct in order to induce older workers to leave, (2.4) the way in which smaller firms might be expected to differ in their behaviour from larger firms, and thus the extent to which labour market segmentation has an impact on older people's labour market experiences, and (2.5) the extent to which employers' redundancy policies are shaped or reinforced by the state's labour market or social security policies.

Part 3 discusses (3.1) employer's recruitment practices in times of recession and labour market surplus, (3.2) the way in which employers regard age when they are recruiting and the ways in which job structures and promotion procedures might be disadvantageous to older workers, (3.3) the recruitment patterns of smaller firms, (3.4) the impact of demographic change and economic recovery upon practices and attitudes, and, again, (3.5) the extent to which firms' policies have been influenced by policies of the state.

Lastly, part 4 of the chapter summarises and draws out some conclusions. It suggests that the policies and practices which contributed to the decline in older people's employment rates were the responsibility of firms themselves; there exist no regulations in labour law which directly encourage firms to engage in age- specific dismissals, nor any provisions in tax or social security law which subsidise them. It also suggests that the economic circumstances in which they find themselves has not only been an important determinant of firms' behaviour but also of the way in which they assess the merits and demerits of older people and act upon these assessments. Accordingly, the chapter rejects the proposition that firms have developed a permanent interest in the exclusion of older people from their workforces. The contingent nature of firm policy, and the absence of significant state policy, means that prospects for older workers in the coming decade will, as in the past decade, be governed primarily by the state of the labour market for all workers.

2   Employers' Redundancy Practices

The extent to which older workers are vulnerable to job loss can be considered in two ways. If inflows into unemployment are taken as a proxy for vulnerability to job loss, then in the first three months of 1989 about 15 older workers (workers aged 55 and over) in every thousand registered as unemployed. By comparison, the rate of inflow into unemployment amongst 20–24 year-olds in the same period was 60 per thousand, whilst even those in the "prime" 35–45 year age-range had a higher incidence – 19 per thousand – of becoming unemployed than did older workers. If, however, attention is paid to employers' redundancy practices, a rather different picture emerges. In the first three months of 1990 a total of 180 000 people were declared redundant, that is to say dismissed as a result of there being no work available for them to do. Nearly one in six of them was aged over 55. As table 1 shows, the incidence of redundancy rises sharply once this age is past, and for 60–64 year-old men it is well over twice the rate for "prime-age" (25–54 year old) men. This second set of statistics suggests that older workers are one of the groups which bears a disproportionate share of the burden of dismissals. The reasons for this must be sought in the nature of employers' redundancy practices.

Table 1: Age-Specific Redundancy Rates, Great Britain 1990

	All	>25	25–49	50–54	55–59	60–64	65+
Men	10	13	8	8	11	18	3
Women	6	7	6	5	12	3	5
All	8	10	7	7	11	13	4

The Age Specific Redundancy Rate is Defined as the Number of People Reporting they had been Made Redundant in the Last three Months per 1000 Dependent Employees. Source: 1990 Labour Force Survey; own Calculations.

2.1   The Practice of "Voluntary Redundancy"

The British Employment Protection (Consolidation) Act of 1978 makes reference to the procedures to be used in selecting candidates for redundancy (*see* IDS, 1987). However, the extent of such regulation is quite limited. Selection must be "fair", and fairness is defined by reference to "customary agreement" or "agreed procedure". The meaning of these terms is not specified by the legislation, only by the courts (industrial tribunals and higher instances) when particular selections have been challenged. In general, customary agreements and agreed procedures are taken to mean any agreements or procedures which are known or reasonably ascertainable by the workforce. In their absence, the employer has an almost entirely free hand.

As well as the rather vague requirements on redundancy procedures contained in law, firms are also subject to an obligation to compensate all workers with more than two years' service whom they dismiss as a consequence of a lack of work. Although the principle of compensation was already contained in collective agreements entered into by a minority of firms (some 7 per cent, but 21 per cent of large ones, according to Parker et. al., 1971), it was not generalised until the passing of the Redundancy Payments Act of 1965. The Act followed the earlier collective agreements in linking compensation to length of service, but it added an additional element to the formula – age. Thus, each week of service from the age of 18 to 20 entitled the person declared redundant to half a week's pay, each week from the age of 21 to 40 to one week's pay and each week above 40 to one and a half week's pay. A proportion of the costs to the firm of making the compensation payment could be refunded from a national redundancy fund, financed by employer and employee contributions.

The redundancy payments legislation is widely agreed to have had a major impact on employment practices: "Managers found that when lump sum payments were available to workers then many individual workers were not adverse to the idea of redundancy" (Daniel, 1985: 73). Under such circumstances, trade unions often found it difficult to maintain their traditional hostility to redundancy and to fight dismissals. Instead, their concern became as much one of ensuring that those who were adversely affected were compensated as generously as possible. This was the genesis of the peculiarly British practice of "voluntary redundancy", whereby enhanced levels of redundancy payment, sometimes two or more times that specified in law, are negotiated or offered unilaterally, in order to buy industrial peace. The gearing of the size of statutory payments to age and length of service already meant that the largest payments were available to older workers, and the practice of enhancement exaggerated this effect. Within a few years of the passage of the Redundancy Payments Act, it had become clear that age had become an important factor in redundancy. This is not

Table 2: Methods Used to Effect Workforce Reductions by Characteristic of Workplace,
Great Britain 1984

	Row Percentages			
	Compulsory Redundancies	Voluntary Redundancies	Early Retirement	Vol. Reds. or E. R.
Industry/Ownership				
Priv. Manuf.	52	37	38	51
Priv. Servs.	32	16	21	29
Nat. Incls.	9	32	49	53
Pub. Admin.	6	11	41	43
Size (No. of Employees)				
25 – 99	24	13	27	33
100 – 199	27	26	48	52
200 – 499	32	44	59	64
500 – 1.999	23	56	72	79
2.000 or more	15	69	88	91
Union Recognition				
Any Recog.	19	21	40	45
No Recog.	45	15	19	31
All Workplaces	25	20	35	41

Note: Base = Workplaces which Reduced Workforce in Previous 12 Months; More
than one Method Could be Used; Other Methods (not Reported here) Include
Natural Wastage and Redeployment within Establishment.
Source: WIRS 1984; Own Calculations.

because firms had started forcibly to dismiss older workers[4], but because,
through a judicious use of compensation payments, they were able to
induce them to volunteer themselves to leave. This does not mean either
that older workers were the only ones affected by redundancy; other
categories of worker, including those who perceived their chances on the
external labour market as good, would also volunteer. Nor does it mean
that compulsory redundancies were avoided; in cases of total closure they
were unavoidable, whilst in smaller, non-unionised firms they still tended to
prevail.

Table 2, which is drawn from the 1984 Workplace Industrial Relations
Survey covering some 2 000 establishments, makes clear the varying patterns of practice adopted by firms reducing their labour forces. It shows that
it is in large firms, in firms in the manufacturing sector and in the public
sector, and in firms where trade unions have a significant presence, that
voluntary redundancies and particularly early retirement is most frequently
practised. By contrast, it is in small firms, in the service sector and in the

Table 3a: Mechanical Engineering Company, Destinations of those Made Redundant by Age

Destination	Age				
	25 or Under	26−35	36−45	46−55	56 or Over
Transferred	50	38	50	57	14
Employed Elsewhere	43	53	37	31	15
Self-Employed	6	5	8	*	3
Unemployed	1	1	3	7	16
Retired	0	0	0	1	50

private sector, and in firms where trade unions have little, if any presence, that compulsory redundancies are most frequently practised.

Table 3a shows what happened at a mechanical engineering company studied during the research when it closed one of its establishments in the late 1980s and offered voluntary redundancy/early retirement or transfer to other establishments to its employees. Almost all those who were old (56 or above) accepted severance, whilst those in their later middle age were much more inclined to stay. Those in their "prime" (26–35), who were particularly confident of being able to find alternative jobs, also opted to leave. Table 3b reproduces the age-specific redundancy rates for a steel company that was investigated. They relate to the running down of two of its major works earlier in the 1980s and the picture given is very similar to that given by the mechanical engineering company.

Table 3b: Steel Company, Age-Specific Reduncancy Rates at Two Plants Subject to Restructuring

Age	Redundant (%)
<20	13.6
20−29	43.0
30−39	38.5
40−49	29.0
50−54	29.3
55−59	86.0
60+	100.0
All	45.0

Source: Harris, 1987.

In more recent years, the steel company had continued to make a steady reduction of its labour force across all establishments as new technologies were introduced. In most cases, it was not the employees directly affected by this process of change who lost their jobs; rather they were transferred within the establishment and leavers were selected from a list of volunteers. The generous nature of the company's early retirement arrangements meant that these volunteers were largely those aged 55 and above.

2.2   The Motives for Age-Specific Redundancies

Having presented evidence in support of the thesis that firms engage in redundancy practices which have a major impact on older workers, it becomes necessary to give some indication as to why they do so. A study of the workings of employment protection laws conducted in the late 1970s (Daniel and Stilgoe, 1978) provides an initial answer to this question. It showed that managers tended to construct voluntary redundancy schemes to attract workers who were less fit/healthy as well as those who were older. There is no doubt that there is an overlap between these two groups. Moreover, as far as many employers are concerned, there is a tendency to equate age with diminishing ability. Of employers surveyed, between half and two thirdss regarded older workers as less adaptable than younger or prime- age workers, and about three quarters regarded them as less trainable. The interviews with personnel managers gave examples of what was meant thereby.

The steel company management saw older workers as potentially problematic in terms of their "adaptability". In an industry where technology is developing very fast, older workers are thought not to be able to learn and adapt quickly enough to the new technology. A similar argument was advanced by the retail bank, where management commented that the rapid spread of electronic data processing technology created problems for many of its older managers, who saw traditional ways of conducting business usurped. In the view of many respondents, "adaptability" cuts across a whole range of issues, from work attitudes, to using new equipment in the current job, to changing job activities altogether. "Change" is something that older people are often believed to be poor at; indeed, a number of the managers interviewed recognised that they, too, were not without criticism. However, whether lack of "adaptability" is a consequence of age *per se*, is less clear. Managers in a health authority, where age and long service were by no means as highly correlated as in some other firms studied, had a rather different perception of the situation. It was less age they saw as the problem than long service. It was those who had been doing the same job for a long time who were seen as resistant to change, regardless of their age.

Linked to "adaptability" is the perception of decreased "trainability". In this context some personnel managers suggested that their organisations tended to see older workers as a poor long-term investment. This was because they will supposedly have fewer years of service than the younger members of the workforce. In addition, and as the personnel manager at the mechanical engineering company emphasised most clearly, retraining, even of middle-aged employees, is frequently hindered by demarcation lines, company culture and an attitude that workers were thought to have, that you were trained once to do some thing and then you did it for the rest of your life.

A part of the "trainability" aspect is the irrefutable fact that some groups of older workers, by the fact that they are old, also possess "older", in other words, dated, skills. In an electrical engineering company, mechanical engineers, who were older workers, were being superseded by electronic engineers, who were younger workers. In a newspaper company, the traditional compositor (who sets and corrects type and assembles the plating for printing) tends to be older – no apprentices had been taken on for several years. Compositors have been replaced by younger people with keyboard input skills. In cases such as these, it seems that it is less because they are old and more because they have redundant skills that older workers are vulnerable to redundancy.

Set against all these negative perceptions were, however, certain positive perceptions. All managers recognised the greater maturity, experience and stability of their older workers. Three quarters of the employers surveyed claimed them to be more reliable than younger workers, and a third more reliable than prime-age workers. The health authority personnel manager made mention of cases where workers in their fifties had been successfully retrained to perform jobs very different from those they had held previously. Equally, a dockyard personnel manager recognised that, in the absence of special redundancy schemes, it was not older workers who were most likely to leave, and thereby give rise to a loss of any investments in training that might be made in them, but rather younger workers, including those who had just completed their apprenticeships.

Assessing managers' overall views, it did not appear that the intrinsic attributes of older workers were always such that younger workers would always be favoured for retention if workforce reductions had to be made, even if under some circumstances this might be the case. Other reasons gave them at least as much cause to encourage older workers' departure. Every manager recognised and admitted that targeting older workers, was the "softest" way of carrying out redundancies. Older workers, given their longer service, are likely to receive the highest severance payments, and their exit will often be further cushioned by some kind of early pension. Middle-aged and younger workers are still forced to seek work. For the rest

Table 4: Main Reason for Using Early Retirement (%s)

to Reduce Workforce	77
to Clear Promotion Blockages	3
to Ease out Employees with Outdated Skills	7
Other	13

Source: LSE Survey of Employers.

of the workforce, shifting the burden of job loss on to older workers seems to be the "least misery" approach. As the personnel manager in an engineering company put it:

"If there have to be redundancies, we talk to the unions about it and see how we can deal with it. We first look to see if early retirement is possible, and then maybe ask for volunteers. Why do we prefer early retirement? It is more acceptable to the workforce if those who leave are those who are going to finish work in a few years time in any case."

Equally, early retirement is seen as offering older workers themselves the opportunity to take life more easily, coupled with the financial support to enjoy other activities. At the retail bank, where it was the middle- or branch-management tier which was being severely rationalised, and where older workers in particular were vulnerable to job loss, the personnel managers interviewed claimed that this argument was particularly relevant. They suggested that the long service which most older bank employees have put in takes its toll on them. The physical exertion, often a twelve hour day, and the intensity of the work, was argued to mean that most senior staff are happy to leave when still in their early fifties.

The survey of firms illustrated the importance of industrial relations considerations in causing firms to resort to early retirement. As table 4 shows, three-quarters of respondents who had instituted early retirement programmes said that their main reason for doing so was to effect workforce reductions. Only one in twenty said that it was to ease out employees with outdated skills.

2.3   The Nature of Compensation Packages

The Redundancy Payments Act sets out the legal minima for sums payable, but more importantly, sets out the criteria for their calculation. Of the companies studied which had been making redundancies, almost all used age and length of service criteria as the conceptual basis on which to build their own levels of benefit. Accordingly, the Act could be said to have set basic standards of fairness or to have formed notions of what were acceptable principles to employ. Nevertheless, the level at which these larger organisations set their severance payments was considerably higher than the Act specified. The survey of firms showed that nearly 80 per cent of the sample paid more than the statutory minimum: a third paid up to 50 per cent above the statutory level, a quarter up to double the statutory level and nearly 40 per cent more than double the statutory level. Of the firms visited, a local authority and the electrical engineering company were examples of firms paying double the statutory requirement, the retail bank of a firm paying three times and the steel company of a firm paying as much as four times. Whether or not they were specifically intended to appeal to older workers, because of the greater sums of money they involved, enhanced redundancy payments, constituted an even greater incentive to them to volunteer to leave than did statutory redundancy payments.

In addition, most of the larger organisations studied grafted additional, age-related components on top of the sort of enhanced severance payments just described. Such enhancements took one of two forms: first, further, age-related lump sums for (late) middle-aged workers (usually those aged 40 or 45 to 50 or 55); and second, continuing payments for older workers (usually those aged 55 or over). The rationale behind the first form of enhancement was that, in many ways, the (late) middle aged were in the most difficult situation should they be made redundant. They lacked the mobility, and often also the skills, of their younger colleagues, but they did not have open to them, as did their older colleagues, the opportunity to retire. Thus, they were accorded additional compensation, the amount of which increased until the age of eligibility for an early pension was reached and then stopped or tailed off equally rapidly.

The second form of enhancement was the early pension itself. Under normal circumstances early retirement results in a considerable loss of benefit as an "actuarial reduction" is made to take account of the fact that the pension will be paid out over a greater number of years.[5] For example, under a typical pension scheme with a normal retirement age of 65 a man aged 58 who retires after twenty years service will receive one third (20/60ths) of his final salary. With an actuarial reduction of 5 per cent for each year by which he retired early, this becomes a mere 22 per cent (65% of 1/3) of final wage. By comparison, had he continued working until 65, his pension would have been worth 45 per cent (27/60ths) of final wage.

A pension which is more likely to attract older workers to leave, is one with no, or less than a full, actuarial reduction. Often such pensions are available from the age of 60, sometimes from 55 and sometimes even from 50. Obviously, the earlier the availability, the larger the target group. However, take-up of such schemes need not be purely a function of the generosity of the scheme. The retail bank scheme permits early retirement at age fifty with a non-reduced pension to all staff whose jobs are affected by reorganisation or rationalisation measures. The acceptability of early retirement is increased by the employment histories of its senior staff. Many have been with the bank since leaving school at 16 or 18 and so, on reaching age fifty, have completed service of thirty years or more. Thus, the pension to which they will be entitled is already close to the maximum (40/60ths) achievable, and is sufficient to permit them to leave their employment with the assurance of a reasonable level of income. Indeed, management suggested that the major restructuring which the bank had been pursuing over the last decade, coupled with the nature of its pension arrangements, had resulted in a situation in which age fifty had effectively become the "normal" retirement age.

Given the size of some of compensation payments firms made, redundancy costs could be substantial. However, mainly because the organisations studied were unwilling to divulge the necessary information, it was normally impossible to say exactly what the costs of individual redundancy exercises were, or to give a breakdown of the early pension as opposed to the severance payments element. In one of the firms for which sufficient information was available, a rough estimate suggested that the cost of compensating a man leaving in his mid-fifties after thirty years' service would have the equivalent of just over three years' pay, of which redundancy payments accounted for just under two thirds and the enhancement of the pension entitlement for the remainder. Over and above the unwillingness of firms to disclose the relevant information, there was often the problem of distinguishing the real nature of the costs of enhancing pension benefits. In theory, an account should have been submitted by the pension fund to the firm; in practice, and as a consequence both of large-scale labour force reductions in the early part of the decade, that had reduced the value of their future obligations, and of a booming stock market that had appreciated the value of their assets, many pension funds had established a considerable surplus over the 1980s and this surplus could be used to cover the costs of redundancy exercises (*see* NAPF, 1987).

On the other hand, there was little doubt that firms gave full consideration to the cost implications of what they were doing. Normally a cost-benefit analysis was undertaken, and the maximum payback period (time by which sufficient benefits had accrued to offset costs) used by the organisations studied seemed to lie between eighteen months and two years. On some occasions, firms could have afforded to be much more generous than they had been; the personnel manager of one firm admitted that the gains to efficiency from a particular rationalisation were more than ten times the costs of making compensation payments to those who lost their jobs. On other occasions, the serious financial difficulties in which they found themselves meant that the costs were not really affordable. Nevertheless, even in such cases, personnel managers recognised it would have been impossible to implement large-scale cuts in employment without making substantial severance payments.

From the point of view of the worker taking early retirement, total value of the compensation package was not as considerable as the size of the redundancy payment made might suggest. A calculation which assumes that the employee is male, has had twenty years service with the firm, receives an unreduced pension (i.e., no actuarial reduction) and retires early at the age of 55 suggests that the pension and unemployment compensation received is the equivalent of 39 per cent of last gross income in the first year of retirement. When unemployment compensation is exhausted after one year the gross replacement rate falls to 33 per cent. If assumed length of service is increased to thirty years, the gross replacement rate rises to 50 per cent (*see* Casey, 1992). On to this could be added the value of the lump sum redundancy payment received. A payment worth one and a half years wages would, if converted into a stream of income to last twenty years, increase the gross replacement rate by about 12 percentage points.[6]

2.4   The Practices of Smaller Firms

As is the case with almost all empirical studies of industrial relations and personnel practices the research on which this chapter is based largely upon developments in larger firms. Yet, as table 2 illustrates, the redundancy practices of such organisations differ substantially from those of small organisations. In particular, resort to voluntary redundancy and early retirement is much less common in small firms. An important reason for this is that they are much less likely to have the resources which would enable them to finance enhanced redundancy payments. Equally, few small organisations have a pension scheme upon which early retirement benefits might be based. Survey evidence illustrates the latter, revealing that, for example, only half of firms with less than 25 employees have occupational pension schemes, but as many as 96 per cent of those with more than 100 employees do so (calculated from *General Household Survey*, 1987, table 7.8).

Just as important, however, are the different turnover patterns of small firms. As analysts of small firms generally agree (*see*, for example, Storey and Johnson, 1987), such organisations, in response to the relative unpredictability of the environment in which they operate, are more likely to recruit those forms of labour which have a more marginal attachment either to the labour force or to any individual employer. Moreover, they tend to complement this by emphasising the contingent nature of the employment relationships which they offer. Unlike large firms, small firms are argued to be less likely to seek to generate expectations of long-term employment. And for this reason, too, they are not obliged to develop the institutions, such as pension schemes and compensation systems which are necessary to sustain such relationships or to permit their premature termination (Casey, 1992). Special analysis of the Labour Force Survey confirms the consequent differences. Well over a quarter of employees in establishments with less than 25 employees had been with their present employer for less than a year, and only a fifth for over 10 years, whilst the comparable proportions for employees in establishments with more than 25 employees were less than a fifth and as much as a third.[7]

To an extent, and in so far as they do experience higher levels of labour turnover, small firms are less likely to have to resort to redundancy to cope with downturns in demand for their output. Natural wastage will provide a greater part of the solution. To the extent, however, that their activities are subject to greater volatility, they are more likely to have to shed labour. When they do, the procedures adopted are likely to be different from those adopted in larger firms. It has already been shown that voluntary forms of redundancy are less often found, whilst the frequent absence of structures of collective representation in small firms would lead one to expect that it is management alone which determines who is to leave. This could well mean that individual performance and health considerations are given greater weight. On the other hand, it has often been commented that small firms have their own culture of paternalism and reciprocal loyalties which serve to protect those who have been with them a long time (Ingham, 1970). Thus, older workers with considerable seniority might be expected to enjoy reasonable employment security, even if those with little or no seniority do not.

Nevertheless, the fragility of the mixture of personal and employment relationships which produces this latter outcome has also to be stressed. The authors of one of the few empirical investigations of industrial relations in small firms record visiting one organisation where, on the first visit, a number of older workers were fondly referred to by management. By the second visit, however, declining demand for its output had obliged that organisation to cut back its labour force, and the older workers had been amongst the first to be dismissed. Management not only showed no regrets about this but now went so far as to make highly derogatory comments about their capabilities and qualities (Scott et. al., 1989: 50).

The difference between larger and smaller firm responses to the requirement to impose workforce reductions, in so far as these impact upon older workers, can therefore be summed up as follows. In both types of organisation, older workers with short service are likely to be dismissed and to receive only the minimum level of compensation. For many, of course, this will be nothing at all. In large firms, older workers with long service are more likely to be amongst the first to leave, having been encouraged to accept redundancy by the offer of an early pension and/or a relatively generous compensation. In small firms, they occupy a much more uncertain position. Where management behaves according to the patterns associated with the paternalist stereotype, they are more likely to be able to stay whilst other, less-well-integrated groups are dismissed. Where management instead behaves according to the patterns associated with the unrestrained entrepreneur, they are likely to be amongst the most vulnerable members of the workforce, and again to leave with only the minimum level of compensation.

2.5   The Role of the State

The practice of resolving situations of labour surplus by voluntary redundancy and early retirement was one that was initiated by employers and unions in large companies, not one which was prescribed by an outside source. Although the Redundancy Payments Act is credited with giving the impetus to age-selective redundancy practices, this was in no way one of its objectives. The purpose of the Act, which was introduced at a time of full employment, was to aid labour market flexibility and transfers between growing and declining sectors of industry by removing barriers to necessary dismissals. If anything, it was feared that the higher compensation paid to older workers might *discourage* employers from dismissing them, and for this reason a higher level of refund on the redundancy payment could be claimed by employers dismissing them – for those aged 41 and above, a refund of 7/9 instead of 2/3 (Hansard, 1965). As far as the government was concerned, the ensuing age-specific redundancy practices were unintended and undesired, and it was for this reason that it moved to a uniform level of refund – 50 per cent – when it amended the Act in 1969 (Jolly et. al., 1980). However, as the evidence above suggests, this attempt at restraint failed.[8]

Whatever its intent in the Redundancy Payments Act, in the late 1970s, the state introduced a new labour market measure which suggested it was not unsupportive of early retirement as an instrument of personnel policy. This was the Job Release Scheme, a scheme which allowed men and women to retire a year before the state pension age (and, under its most extensive terms at the start of the 1980s, disabled men to retire at 60 and non-disabled men to retire at 62) so long as the employer filled the vacancy created with a previously unemployed person. Participants in the scheme received a flat rate allowance, paid directly by the state. The Job Release Scheme was never large, but at its peak in 1984, there were about 88 000 male Job Release allowance beneficiaries, which equalled about one eighth of the number of non-working men aged sixty to sixty-four. At the end of 1987, the programme closed for further applications, the government being of the opinion that the resources it consumed would be better spent on training measures for the unemployed (*see* DE, 1989).

The government's acceptance and active promotion of early retirement as a means of relieving unemployment problems was further underlined by a succession of changes which were made in the early 1980s to the rules of entitlement to the welfare benefits system as these affect older people. The most important has affected Income Support, a means-tested benefit payable to those whose net income is less than a specified level. Many claimants of Unemployment Benefit are also claimants of Income Support, and those unemployed who have no rights to Unemployment Benefit or who have exhausted their year's entitlement to Unemployment Benefit are in receipt of Income Support. In 1981 unemployed men over the age of sixty who had been out of work for at least one year were made eligible for a higher level of Income Support, known as the "long-term" rate (25% higher than the "short-term" rate). In addition, they were freed from the obligation to register as job seekers. In 1983 the requirement of one year's unemployment was dropped. At the same time the dispensation from registration as a job seeker was extended to all over-60-year-old unemployed except those actually in receipt of Unemployment Benefit. Thus, in terms of benefit entitlement, the oldest unemployed were placed on an effective par with old- age pensioners, whilst by counting them as out of the labour market, the government could also be seen as sanctioning the use of "early retirement".

Lastly, it must be recognised that, as an employer of labour, the state has operated workforce reduction policies very similar to, and often modelled upon, those found in private firms. In the National Health Service, and in anticipation of a major, nation-wide reorganisation of administrative structures in 1982, a "Premature Retirement Scheme" was negotiated with health service unions as a way of avoiding redundancy. The age at which early retirement is available, fifty (with a minimum of five years service), is relatively low. What is more, the National Health Service scheme is generous. Employees receive an immediate pension and lump sum based on accrued service, which is enhanced by the crediting of additional service. Those with 10 or more years' service receive 10 extra years, giving them the same pension as had they retired at 60. Other public sector organisations have established similar arrangements. The civil service employment terms and conditions provide for early retirement in cases of redundancy, and they too permit a pension to be granted at 50 with up to 10 years' additional service being credited. These terms had applied in the dockyard studied, and when it passed into private ownership it did so on condition they continued to be applied to existing employees.

3   Employers' Recruitment Practices

Although the beginning of the 1980s saw an absolute fall in the level of dependent employment, in the years thereafter dependent employment grew, if only slowly. Between 1981 and 1988 dependent employment increased by 0.4 mill. compared to a fall of 1.2 mill. in the years 1979 to 1981. This growth compensated for the job losses that were continuing to occur (although not those that had occurred), but it did so only partially. There were three reasons for this. First, the rate of growth of the labour force outstripped the ability of firms to create jobs. The labour force, even after taking account of early retirements, grew by 1.4 mill. between 1981 and 1988. Second, the new jobs were often in places far removed from the old ones. For example, dependent employment in the north and north west of Britain fell by 3 per cent between 1981 and 1988, but it increased in the south east of Britain by 9 per cent. Third, the new jobs were often very different from the old ones. One illustration of this is the fact that production industry employment fell a further 1.2 mill. between 1981 and 1988; it was service sector employment which grew – by 1.7 mill.

For each of these three reasons, the prospects for those seeking jobs have often been difficult. Moreover, the prospects for those who were "older" have been more difficult still. They have tended to experience long durations of unemployment, and the proportion of them which returns to work has been low. Data from the Labour Force Survey shows that only 11 per cent of 54–58 year-old men who were out of employment in 1989 were in employment in 1990, and for 59–63 year-old men the proportion was only 9 per cent. In contrast, for men aged 25–34 the proportion was 40 per cent. If consideration is restricted to those who were actively seeking jobs – a third of the 55–59 year olds and just over 10 per cent of the 60–64 year olds – the outcome improves somewhat, but the proportion returning to work still remains small. Eighteen per cent of unemployed 54–58 year-old men and 29 per cent of unemployed 59–63 year-old men were back in work one year later.

To understand why older people out of work have such difficulties returning to employment requires an understanding of employers' recruitment practices, and in particular of employers' recruitment practices in time of recession and of labour market surplus. Recession might have characterised only the start of the 1980s, but as figure 1 indicates, unemployment did not fall below 2 mill. until the end of 1988. At the same time, and as figure 2 shows, the rate of engagement (new hirings as a proportion of the workforce) fell dramatically at the start of the decade – from two per cent in 1979 to one per cent in 1980. Although it rose thereafter, it did not recover its initial level until 1989. Consequently, the opportunities for those under notice of dismissal and those who had already lost their jobs to apply for alternative

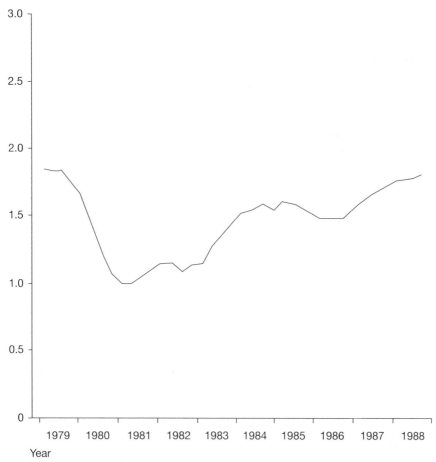

Figure 2: Engagement Rate (4 quarter moving average) in Manufacturing Industry, Great Britain 1979–1988

work were greatly reduced, and the competition between job-seekers for any vacancy was greatly increased. Even without changing their hiring proce-dures or criteria, in such a climate firms are able to be more selective in whom they recruit (*see* Wood, 1986). This greater selectivity tends to disad-vantage older workers.

3.1   The Attitude of Employers to Older Applicants

A number of commentators have pointed to the reluctance employers, or at least employers in the "primary" sector show towards recruiting from the unemployed (*see* Windolf and Wood, 1988: 74–75). This attitude does not appear to change in times of recession. Although many managers recognise that economic downturns have their impact on all workers, many retain a perception of unemployment as a sign of personal shortcomings. This is reinforced by their awareness that, when making redundancies, they try to dismiss, or encourage to leave, those whom they regard as the "least productive" members of the workforce. On top of this, however, managers who have been implementing workforce reductions which have included incentives to encourage the departure of older workers, will be reluctant to be seen recruiting the very categories they have been persuading to resign or retire.

The self-same arguments about "trainability" and "adaptability" which were used to justify the dismissal of older workers can also be used to justify a reluctance to hire them. Moreover, managers recruiting manual workers often make reference to the diminished physical capabilities of older workers. They question their ability to cope with heavy tasks or tasks requiring sustained periods of intensive effort, and will normally seek to fill such jobs with those in the "prime" age range. By the time these recruits have aged, the operation of more or less informal seniority systems has usually ensured that they have moved on to the less physically demanding jobs within the firm. The steel company provided a good example of this, where recruits started in the hardest jobs, manning the blast furnaces, but progressed as internal vacancies arose to sedentary jobs such as crane driver. Where no such paths exist, it is usual for at least some allowance to be made for older workers on the basis of their seniority, so that a slower pace of working is accepted than would otherwise be the case.

As well as there being doubts about their productivity which serve to discourage firms in recruiting older workers, there are other reasons why some managers might be sceptical of their cost effectiveness. A study of manufacturing plants conducted in 1990 confirmed (Wood, 1992) that almost no payments systems Britain pay workers on an age-related basis and thereby make the recruitment of an older person into any given job more costly.[9] Nevertheless, there are other elements of labour costs which might discourage older applicants from being hired. Employers frequently mention the costs of training and/or the returns to it. For older workers, they argue, training costs will be increased, whilst the time in which these can be recouped is curtailed by the relatively short time that the older person will be employed. Given the speed at which skills become obsolete, and the high rate of turnover amongst young employees, the validity of this line of reasoning is open to question. Yet this did not prevent it from being advanced by almost all employers spoken to. A further cost barrier, although one which is less frequently recognised is that set by occupational pension schemes. Under typical actuarial assumptions the costs of "buying" the pension entitlement earned by a year's service rises with age. For a man aged 55 they are over 250 per cent of those for a man aged 30, assuming that both are doing the same job and earning the same wage or salary.[10] Since the employer would normally pay the same contribution for both employees – a fixed percentage of the wage – the costs associated with the younger worker contain an element of subsidy for the older worker. This subsidy could be regarded as unfair. It is largely for this reason that a substantial proportion of pension funds – half, according to a recent survey (National Association of Pension Funds, Annual Survey 1988, table 10) – refuse entry to those over a certain age, and this becomes the firm's maximum recruitment age.

More frequently cited as a disincentive by the managers who were interviewed, and an issue where the cost difference is more apparent, is the higher sickness and absence rates of older workers. Reference to the Labour Force Survey shows some substance to this claim; the sickness absence rate does rise with age. However, only amongst over 60 year olds is it higher than the average for all ages. What is more noteworthy is the way in which the duration of absence increases with age. Younger workers are often absent, but only for a short period; older workers are infrequently absent, but when they are they are away for longer periods.[11] On the other hand, most employers will also concede that the incidence of casual absence amongst older workers is lower than it is amongst younger workers. This could be seen as compensating, in part or in full, for older workers' higher absence for other reasons. As already suggested, it is with respect to more arduous or intensive jobs that the health status of the job applicant is of greater importance and for which older workers are less likely to be considered. Whilst firms are sometimes able to make special arrangements to accommodate long-serving older workers whose health has deteriorated (although pressures to rationalise in the 1980s have led to the disappearance of many of the "retraite" jobs they utilised for such ends), managers tend to regard recruiting categories with a potential for absence as a risky practice, to be avoided as far as possible. Older applicants who have been in receipt of invalidity benefit are likely to be amongst those who are most disadvantaged by such an attitude, as the statistics on disability cited earlier testify.

Lastly, account needs be taken of the way in which considerations of "social acceptability" influence recruitment as well as redundancy practices. Although management prerogative is much stronger in recruitment than dismissal matters, and decisions are seldom subject to formal processes of joint negotiation or control, firms still need to be sensitive to the concerns both of the community in which they operate and of their workforce. In the face of persistently high levels of unemployment, personnel managers often see themselves expected to give greater priority to those who have a lifetime of employment ahead of them, or to those who have responsibilities to provide for spouses and children, than to those who are at the end of their working lives and would, in any case, be retiring before very long. What is more, the conventions about who it is more acceptable to dismiss overturn the argument that is often advanced by the advocates of older workers – namely, that once recruited they are likely to stay longer with firm than most other categories of worker. Although this might be true under normal circumstances (*see* Dalessio et. al., 1986), it ceases to be when firms find themselves required to make workforce reductions and are under pressure to do this in a way which places much of the burden of adjustment upon the older members of the labour force.

3.2 The Role of Internal Labour Markets

In addition to their (not always well substantiated) views about older workers capabilities or costs, or because of their (certainly questionable) perceptions of what constituted fairness, employers have other reasons to be reluctant about hiring workers. In almost all firms, at least some jobs are constructed around age, in that it is expected they will be occupied by someone of a given age band[12], and this is particularly the case in firms which seek to create career structures for their employees or with respect to jobs which are part of a "formal hierarchy" within a firm. In such firms recruitment to vacancies is, in the first instance, from amongst current employees. Only once a chain of transfers or promotions has occurred will a recruitment be made on the external labour market, and this will be at a considerably lower level than was the position for which the initial vacancy occurred. The retail bank provided an extreme example of a firm with such recruitment practices; managerial staff were recruited direct from school and (increasingly) university and promoted upwards. Almost no managerial vacancies were filled by outsiders.

Although examples like the retail bank might be taken as suggesting that internal labour markets are more frequently found operating for white collar/managerial jobs than for blue collar jobs (skilled or otherwise), many firms put a premium on experience and commitment, and seniority rules operate on an informal, if not a formal, basis for many blue collar jobs, too (Windholf and Wood, 1988, chapter 8). The earlier example of the steel company showed how seniority brought access to more pleasant, or lighter tasks; in many firms it also leads to the acquisition of tasks incorporating a degree of supervision or guidance. Beyond this, it has to be recognised that both managers and employees, either implicitly or explicitly, tend to make an equation of age and seniority. Recruiting older workers into work groups where such an equation is made might be considered inadvisable. Were it to occur, the expectations of group members could well be confounded.

3.3   The Practices of Smaller Firms

It is important to recognise that not all managers have the same perceptions of older workers, or that, if they do, not all are able to act in accordance with them. Just as employers in tight labour markets cannot afford to be as selective as employers in slack labour markets, so employers in the "second-ary" sector cannot afford to be as selective in their recruitment practices as those in the "primary" sector. A study of the unemployed (Daniel, 1990) has shown that small firms provide a disproportionate number of the jobs into which people leaving unemployment go, and that these jobs are often poorly paid and insecure. By analogy, it is likely that "secondary" sector firms will be disproportionate employers of older workers.

Defining "secondary" sector firms in such a way as to permit substantia-tion of this assertion by reference to available statistics would have been beyond the scope of the research as it had been conceived. An operationalisation based upon size alone failed to show any real difference between small firms and the remainder in terms of the proportion of their workforce which was "old".[13] However, a plastics factory studied fell very clearly into the "secondary" sector. It was small, offered rather low wages and rather poor conditions of employment, and it was not competitive within the labour market in which it was situated. Its labour force constituted a disproportionate number of older workers (50 per cent), since these were one of the few categories management could expect to recruit or retain.

3.4   The Impact of Demographic Change

In tight labour markets, employers in the "primary" sector have also proved willing to take on older applicants. A local authority which was studied had been experiencing difficulties in recruiting at all levels, and had recently hired people into quite senior positions who were only a few years from retirement. The personnel manager made reference to the wealth of expe-rience they would bring to the job and to the fact that, in a tight labour market where turnover was high, they at least could be relied upon to stay "for three or four years" (!). Indeed, at the end of the 1980s interest in the potential offered by "older workers" became quite widespread. Between 1985 and 1990, the number of young people of school-leaving age (16–19) had fallen by a 15 per cent. At the same time, in the South East and East Anglian regions labour surpluses had largely been replaced by labour short-ages. Firms in these regions which in the past had been major recruiters of young people – retailers, insurance companies, caterers – found themselves in especial difficulties, and looked around for alternative sources of supply. Older people, including the older unemployed, the early retired and those over the state pension age were targeted (*see* Casey and Wood, 1990).

Employers who adopted such practices chose to stress the positive qualities of older workers. Two large retailing firms and a second local authority pointed out many of their jobs involved customer or client contact, and they often saw older people as far better than young people in situations where these interpersonal skills are required. Similarly, one of the large retailing firms stressed older people's reliability, and suggested that, if they are not always as fast as their juniors, they are more thorough and need less supervision.

Such attitudes and such behaviour was the exception rather than the rule. The number of firms that were driven to introduce recruitment policies explicitly favouring older people seems to have been small, and even the number that have been less explicit in their actions cannot have been so large. Although the decline in the number of people of school-leaving age will continue into the middle of the 1990s, the onset of recession in autumn 1990 shifted the balance of advantage back in the direction of employers and many of the "older worker" initiatives were dropped.

3.5   The Role of the State

It would be a reasonable reaction to categorise many of the employers' attitudes which have been described so far as discriminatory. However, it would appear that age discrimination is viewed by British employers as something different from sex or race discrimination. For example, whilst a considerable number of larger firms and organisations have formal "equal opportunities" policies, only a small proportion of these policies make any reference to age (EOR, 1989). The implication is that, in many cases, companies describe themselves as "equal opportunities" employers, and at the same time impose explicit age barriers when recruiting.

A number of attempts were made at the end of the 1980s to complement existing sex and race discrimination legislation with a prohibition of age discrimination. Two bills were tabled in the House of Commons, one in the House of Lords, but none came close to enactment into law. Despite concern of possible labour shortage, the government maintained a scepticism of the value of a legal approach to the problem, seeing the outcome as unworkably complex. In any case, and more generally, it regarded the employment relationship, and so recruitment decisions, as better determined privately than subjected to external intervention. The House of Commons Committee on Employment, which reported in spring 1989 on the employment patterns of the over 50s, was considerably more sympathetic to the objectives of age discrimination legislation than the government. Nevertheless, it recommended that one last chance be given to "persuasion" and "encouragement" (*see* Employment Committee, 1989: xi).

Age discrimination legislation could have been expected to address the utilisation of age limits in job advertisements, the extent and possible impact of which has been subject to considerable analysis in recent years (*see*, for example, Tillsley, 1990). Through the operation of its own network of employment offices, the government has effectively participated in the perpetuation of the practice of excluding applications from those outside predetermined age ranges, since these offices have accepted employers' vacancy notices and respected the preferences they contain. To a considerable degree, this is understandable. The employment offices are dependent upon employers to supply them with the vacancies which will enable them to fulfil their responsibility to help the unemployed. They cannot lightly ignore an employer's wishes and send applicants who do not conform to specifications laid down, whether or not they regard these specifications as reasonable (Barugh, 1990). Nevertheless, the House of Commons Employment Committee recommended that employment offices question the necessity of explicit age requirements more closely. In the summer of 1991, this recommendation was translated into a formal directive from the employment ministry to all employment offices (*Financial Times*, 14.8.91). What impact this directive will have remains to be seen.

The remaining interventions made by the state in its capacity as a setter of norms were limited to exhortations. Thus, government ministers made a number of statements in the course of 1988 and 1989 calling upon employers to reassess the value of older people, and reconsider their qualities as workers. On top of this, special studies were commissioned by the labour ministry (Department of Employment) and the national planning council (the National Economic Development Office) to report on employers' policies and initiatives and give examples of "best practice" (for example, NEDO, 1989; Metcalf and Thompson, 1990).[14]

As an employer, the state shared the concern of its private sector counterparts that it too might suffer the affects of labour shortages or otherwise fail to attract the best quality recruits. This led it in the course of the 1980s to revise upwards the age limits that it imposes for various branches of government and for various occupations. The outcome was often the replacement of a limit of (for example) late 20s with one of mid 30s or early 40s, so that the result has been to give greater opportunities to middle-aged candidates, rather than to old candidates (*see* Treasury, 1989). It certainly does not appear to be the case that the civil service has established itself as significantly more inclined to hiring the older unemployed than any other major employer, or than it was in the past.

4   Conclusions

This chapter has sought to show how firms' employment policies have contributed to the substantial fall in the proportion of people in the decade before the "normal" retirement age who are no longer in the labour force. It has done so by illustrating the way in which firms – particularly larger firms – place considerable reliance upon encouraging the departure of older workers when trying to resolve problems of labour surplus, and the way in which they tend not to recruit from amongst older applicants when they have vacancies to fill. Some of the older workers who are displaced through redundancy leave the labour force immediately, encouraged to do so by the lump-sum payments and early occupational pensions offered them. Others, especially those who are younger and those who are less generously compensated, try to find new employment, but many fail either to locate vacancies at all or to be selected for those for which they apply. After repeated negative experiences, they become "discouraged" and drop out of the labour force. Such an unfavourable environment, of course, also has negative consequences for those older workers whose health is less good. Employers encourage their departure in particular, and equally they are likely to place them at the end of the queue when they are making recruitment decisions.

In portraying firms' redundancy and recruitment practices, the context in which these occur and thus their contingent nature should be emphasised. Firms seek to encourage the exit of older workers in a particular situation, that of an excess of manpower. This was the impression gained from the interviews carried out; it was also the impression given by the survey of firms. The corollary was that very few employers appeared to have a strong wish to rid themselves of older workers simply because, as members of a particular age range, they saw them as having certain negative qualities. Indeed, in many cases they appeared to respect the elderly and, in an ideal world, would have liked them to have had a choice about whether they worked or not. However, their exit facilitated the resolution of the problem of labour surplus. It provided an "efficient" solution, in that it removed those who were less "adaptable" or "trainable", and it provided a "socially acceptable" solution, in that it removed those who were entitled to the most generous levels of compensation and who had at their disposal the "alternative role" (Offe and Hinrichs, 1977) of "early retirement". Firms were prepared to pay to achieve this twin objective – some as much as three years' pay.

In the same vein, it would be wrong to suggest that at the end of the 1980s, when recession employers fundamentally revised their attitudes to older workers. It might be that a small number of employers, in a limited number of sectors, "discovered" the potential of older workers, but they "discovered" it only in exceptional circumstances. Traditional sources of recruitment had been exhausted and they were forced to turn to those whom they had previously rejected as inferior. To put it bluntly, older workers were what they came up with when they started to scrape towards the bottom of the barrel. It is only once these employers found themselves obliged to recruit older workers that they began to give express appreciation of their qualities. As with employers who had been initiating age-specific redundancies, they were able to satisfy themselves that they had taken appropriate means to resolve the problems they were encountering. In both cases, behaviour and thinking might be expedient rather than reflecting a change in employers' conceptions or firms' culture.

In the pursuit of their age-related redundancy and recruitment policies firms received, in the 1980s, neither direct encouragement nor discouragement from the state. The state did not subsidise the extra costs which arose from making dismissals more socially acceptable and thus incite firms to adopt a solution they would, perhaps, otherwise not have chosen. Admittedly, in certain of its labour market and social security policies it has taken steps which could be seen as sanctioning early retirement as a means of resolving problems of oversupply on the labour market, but it cannot thereby be inferred to be encouraging them. The state had, of course, established a system which supported workers certified as disabled, but it did not take any steps to make access to that support system easier or the benefits it provided more generous. As an employer, the state has behaved like other employers, but there is no indication that these other employers, although they recognise the need to offer "competitive" benefits, have felt pressure to emulate specifically its practices. Rather, the state as an employer seems to have followed "standard practice", not to have promoted innovative solutions in the management of redundancy.

This is not to say that state policy has had no bearing at all on the way in which firms implement workforce reductions. As has been shown, some commentators (for example, Daniel, 1985) regard the Redundancy Payments Act as one of the most important pieces of employment legislation of the post-war era. In its first years, the act seems substantially to have altered employers' behaviour. It enabled the development of the practice of "voluntary redundancy", and thereby made it possible and acceptable for employers to move away from procedures which, by primarily affecting younger workers, could both damage their reputation internally and externally and produce an undesirable ageing of their workforces. Today, "voluntary redundancy" has become institutionalised, with the consequence that the Redundancy Payments Act's influence seems largely unrecognized by the main actors in the labour market. Instead, they acknowledge the existence of a broad set of principles which should be followed if redundancies are to be implemented.

The employment policy of the state in the 1980s was very different from that of the state in the 1960s and 1970s. In many areas, its influence was at least as strong, although it operated through a process of a withdrawal rather than an enhancement of rights. With respect to firms' redundancy policies, and their age-specific character which contributed to the exodus of older people from the labour market, the state made no attempt to intervene. To have done so would have been contrary to the non- interventionist stance espoused by the government of the day. Moreover, this philosophy meant that even the actions and pronouncements made by the state at the end of the 1980s were not directed at promoting the employment opportunities of older workers, but rather at effecting an adequate supply of manpower. This limited its intervention to responding favourably to representations from business interests for the relaxation of those regulations – under labour or social security law – which impeded the employment of any group. Promotion of the rights of any one group – be it older workers, women, ethnic minorities or the handicapped – through anti-discrimination legislation or, as had sometimes been proposed, by quotas, was alien to a government committed to deregulation of the labour market. Recruitment was a matter that was better left to managers, and redundancy practices, if not settled unilaterally were better the subject of collective bargaining than rules laid down by the state. Lastly, unlike youth unemployment, which was politically sensitive and thus demanded some form of governmental response, older-worker unemployment was more tolerable, for the very same reasons which made age-specific redundancy practices acceptable in the first place.

The way in which employers seem motivated as much by pragmatism as anything else, and the absence of significant state involvement in the mechanisms by which older workers are encouraged to leave the labour market, suggests that what came to pass in the 1980s is unlikely to become a permanent feature of the labour market. Certainly, it does not seem as if firms were strategically committed to reducing the employment opportunities they offered older people. Moreover, in pursuing the practices they did, firms appeared to take care to avoid establishing expectations of a right to leave early that they might later be unwilling to satisfy. This is evidenced by the way in which most facilitated early retirement through special, one-off arrangements, outside the terms of their regular pension scheme, and the way in which those that did use the regular scheme awarded "conditional" rather than "final" benefits.

This care to avoid establishing expectations is also evidenced by the way in which, faced with the threat of labour shortages, certain firms have been prepared to embrace older workers as offering at least a partial solution. These firms, which proclaimed older workers' advantages with an enthusiasm more than equal to that with which firms making age-specific redundancies proclaimed their shortcomings, were interested in discouraging early retirement and even with promoting delayed retirement. However, the personnel policy of both types of firm had a common feature. In both cases, the firms sought to maximise their freedom to determine the extent and nature of the employment of older workers. In both cases, they aimed to determine the effective retirement age, and in both cases they sought to exercise a veto over who left and who stayed.

A telling illustration of the contingent nature of firms' policies and practices with respect to older workers is provided in two articles authored by the Personnel Director of IBM (UK) and former Director of Personnel of the National Health Service, Britain's and Europe's largest employer. In the first, written in 1989, he argued that, in pursuing early retirement policies over the 1980s, firms may have made it more difficult for themselves to handle the assumed to be emerging problem of labour shortage. This was because future cohorts of older workers might expect to have the same opportunities to leave the labour force early as had their immediate predecessors (Peach, 1989). Subsequent events have shown that his concern was to a large extent misplaced. The recession of the early 1990s removed any immediate prospects of labour shortage, but it also forced IBM (UK) to initiate its own workforce rationalisation programme which included generous early retirement provisions. These were described by the Personnel Director as enabling "parting by mutual agreement" (Peach, 1992). It is, perhaps, this feeling of mutuality, and the perception (illusion in some cases) of voluntariness implied by practices like early retirement – linked as they are to the British liberal tradition – which makes them likely to remain a prominent feature of workforce management in the coming decade. It is precisely because of this that a *de jure*, or even *de facto*, institutionalisation of a new retirement age is unlikely.

Notes

1   Bernard Casey's participation in the production of this chapter was funded by a grant from the Leverhulme Trust. The research assistance of Sonia Edwards was made possible by a grant from the Anglo-German Foundation for the Study of Industrial Society which also covered fieldwork and survey expenses.

2   There has been some interest in recent years in the relationship bet-ween disability and the state of the labour market. For example, Disney and Webb (1991), pooling cross-sectional data for the years 1979-1984, found a strongly positive relationship between the local unemployment rate and the rate of receipt of a disability pension, with this relationship operating first and foremost through increased durations of benefit receipt rather than increased inflows into benefit receipt. Equally, Piachaud (1986) showed that over half the increase in

disability retirement among older men between 1971 and 1981 was attributable to the rise in unemployment over that period.

3   The activity rates of 65-69 year-old men rose slightly in 1989 and 1980, but those of other older men were unchanged or continued to fall.

4   Nevertheless, according to one contemporary survey, whereas before the passage of the Act 19 per cent of firms used age as a criterion for selection in redundancy, five years after its passage 38 per cent did (Parker et. al., 1971).

5   Actuaries calculate the amount of years the average person is likely to live after the normal retirement age (NRA) of 65 or 60 and divides the lump sum accrued through an employee's contributions into annual pension payments. If the employee retires before the NRA, there are more years over which payments have to be made, and, therefore, a percentage reduction is made in the pension to balance this out.

6   This assumes a real interest rate of 5 per cent.

7   Of course, these proportions are also influenced by the fact that, in general, smaller establishments have existed less time than larger establishments.

8   The size of the refund was reduced further in the following year, to 41 per cent in 1977 and to 35 per cent in 1983 cent, before being abolished for all but the smallest firms in 1986. Since the refund applied to statutory payments only, not to enhanced payments, the effective rate of refund was much lower than the Act prescribed. It is therefore not surprising that the abolition of the refund in 1986 is claimed to have had no impact on firm's redundancy practices (IDS, 1986).

9   The almost universal exception to the absence of any age based differential in pay is the distinction made by almost all payments systems between "juveniles" (aged under 18) and "adults".

10   The real rate of growth is assumed to exceed the real rate of increase of wages or salaries by three percentage points.

11   The Labour Force Survey shows an absence rate for 50-59 year-old men of 4.8 per cent and one for 60-64 year-old men of 6.3 per cent. The overall absence rate for men is 4.2 per cent. However, whilst only 55 per cent of all sickness absences among men exceeded 3 days, 80 per cent of those for men 55-59 and 75 per cent of those for men 60-64 were longer than this.

12   Such a structuring of jobs on the basis of age is analogous the their structuring on the basis of sex or race. It is, however, one to which industrial sociologists have devoted scarcely any attention. Thus, one of the "standard" sociological works on employment in Britain in the 1980s (Gallie, 1989) makes only one reference to age in some 500 pages.

13   Special analysis of the Labour Force Survey revealed an almost identical proportion of workers aged 55 and above in establishments with less than 25 employees as in establishments which were larger.

14   Aimed at the supply side rather than the demand side, in 1989 the government abolished the so-called "earnings rule" which reduced on a £ for £ basis the state pension of those within the age range 65-70 (60-65 women) who earned £80 or more per week. The extent to which this has influenced pensioners to return to the labour market is argued to be questionable (Whitehouse, 1990).

References

Barugh, J. (1990). *A Question of Age: Wearside Employers and Older Workers*. Wearside Training and Enterprise Council and Sunderland Health Authority.

Casey, B. (1992). *Redundancy and Early Retirement: The Interaction of Public and Private Policy in Britain, Germany and the USA*. In: *British Journal of Industrial Relations* 30 (3): 425–443.

Casey, B. and F. Laczko (1989). *Early Retired or Long-Term Unemployed*. In: *Work, Employment and Society* 3 (4): 509–526.

Casey, B. and S. Wood (1990). *Firm Policy, State Policy and the Recruitment and Retention of Older Workers*. Paper presented to the Conference "The Firm, the State and the Older Worker", held in Berlin, September.

Dalessio, A. et. al. (1986). *Paths to Turnover: A Re-Analysis and Review of Existing Data on the Mobley, Horner and Hollingsworth Turnover Model*. In: *Human Relations* 39 (3): 245–264.

Daniel, W. (1985). *The United Kingdom*. In: M. Cross (ed), *Managing Worforce Reduction: An International Survey*. London: Croom Helm: 67–90.

Daniel, W. (1990). *The Unemployed Flow*. London: Policy Studies Institute.

Daniel, W. and E. Stilgoe (1978). *The Impact of Employment Protection Laws*. London: Policy Studies Institute.

DE (1989). *Memorandum by the Department of Employment*. In: *List of Memoranda Included in the Minutes of Evidence*. No. 8: 83–95.

Disney, R. and S. Webb (1991). *Why are There so Many Long-Term Sick in Britain*. In: *Economic Journal* 101 (405): 252–263.

EOR (1989). *Age Discrimination: Over the Hill at 45*. In: *Equal Opportunities Review* 25 (May/June): 10–15.

Employment Committee (1989). *The Employment Patterns of the Over-50s*. London: HMSO.

Gallie, D. (ed.) (1989). *Employment in Britain*. Oxford: Basil Blackwell.

Hansard (1965). *Second Reading of the Redundancy Payments Bill*. In: *House of Commons Hansard 26/4/65*.

Harris, C. (1987). *Redundancy and Recession*. Oxford: Basil Blackwell.

IDS (1986). *Redundancy Terms*. Incomes Data Services (Study No. 369), London.

IDS (1987). *Redundancy*. Incomes Data Services (Employment Law Handbook 37), London.

Ingham, G. (1970). *Size of Industrial Organisation and Worker Behaviour*. Cambridge University Press.

Jolly, J. et. al. (1980). *Age as a Factor in Employment*. Department of Employment (Research Paper No. 11), London.

Metcalf, H. and M. Thompson (1990). *Older Workers: Employers' Attitudes and Practices.* Institute of Manpower Studies (Report No. 194). University of Sussex.

NAPF (1987). *Pensions – The Opportunity for Employer Action.* London: National Association of Pension Funds.

NEDO (1989). *Defusing the Demographic Time Bomb.* London: National Economic Development Office.

Offe, C. and K. Hinrichs (1977). *Sozialökonomie des Arbeitsmarktes und die Lage 'benachteiligter' Gruppen von Arbeitnehmern.* In C. Offe et. al. (eds.), *Opfer des Arbeitsmarktes.* Darmstadt: Neuwied: 3–61.

Parker, S. et. al. (1971). *Effects of the Redundancy Payments Act.* London: HMSO.

Peach, L. (1989). *A Practitioner's View of Personnel Excellence.* In: *Personnel Management* 21 (9): 37–41.

Peach, L. (1992). *Parting by Mutual Agreement: IBM's Transition to Manpower Cuts.* In: *Personnel Management* 24 (3): 40–43.

Piachaud, D. (1986). *Disability, Retirement and Unemployment of Older Men.* In: *Journal of Social Policy* 15 (2): 145–163.

Scott, M. et. al. (1989). *Management and Industrial Relations in Small Firms.* Department of Employment (Research Paper No. 70), London.

Storey, D. and S. Johnson (1987). *Job Generation and Labour Market Change.* London: Macmillan.

Tillsley, C. (1990). *The Impact of Age upon Employment,* University of Warwick (Warwick Papers in Industrial Relations No. 33).

Treasury (1989). *Evidence of HM Treasury.* In: *Employment Committee,* op cit.

Windolf, P. and S. Wood (1988). *Recruitment and Selection in the Labour Market.* London: Gower.

Whitehouse, E. (1990). *The Abolition of the Pensions 'Earnings Rule'.* In: *Fiscal Studies* 11 (3): 55–70.

Wood, S. (1986). *Recruitment Systems in the Recession.* In: *British Journal of Industrial Relations* 24 (1): 103–120.

Wood, S. (1992). *Human Resource Management, Payment Systems and Paying for Productivity.* London School of Economics, Department of Industrial Relations, mimeo.

9 The United States: Employer Policies for Discouraging Work by Older People

Robert Hutchens

Employers in the United States pursue a diversity of policies toward older workers. Some seek out older workers, often adapting work schedules to their needs. Others encourage early retirement and focus their recruiting efforts on younger workers, thereby discouraging work by older people. Such a diversity of employer policies produces a labor market for older workers that is characterized by both opportunities and barriers. This paper examines the diversity of policies. In particular, it examines how and why large bureaucratic firms often discourage work by older people.

Sections 1 and 2 establish a context for understanding employer policies toward older workers. The first section traces trends in the work behavior of older Americans. As in most developed economies, these trends are dominated by the continuing shift toward earlier retirement. Section 2 discusses institutions that surround and support the U.S. labor market for older workers. In particular, it reviews the social security system, private pensions, and government regulation of employer hiring and retirement practices.

Section 3 addresses the central issue in the paper: employer policies that discourage work by older Americans. It describes these policies, examines their incidence across types of jobs, and sketches an explanation for why firms utilize such policies.

Section 4 inquires into an important issue associated with these employer policies. Over the past decade the U.S. federal government has essentially prohibited employers from imposing mandatory retirement on employees. Since several countries are contemplating a similar prohibition, it is useful to review the U.S. experience in this area. Did the prohibition against mandatory retirement alter firm behavior toward older workers? What happened to employment of older workers in firms that formerly used mandatory retirement? Section 4 reviews the available evidence, and presents new data from the Current Population Survey.

1   Establishing the Context: Retirement Trends in the U.S.

In the United States, as in many other countries, retirement is occurring at younger ages. Figure 1 indicates that male labor force participation dropped precipitously since 1948. At age 65 and older, male labor force participation rates declined by almost thirty percentage points, and at age 55–64 the rates declined by 22 percentage points. As indicated in figure 2, the time trends are much less dramatic for women. Female labor force participation rates increased for almost all age groups since 1948. The major exception is

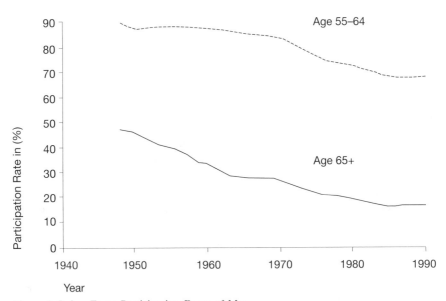

Figure 1: Labor Force Participation Rates of Men

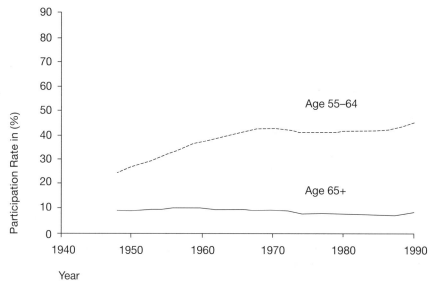

Figure 2: Labor Force Participation Rates of Women

women over 65. For this group labor force participation decreased slightly from 9.1 to 7.9 percent.

Not only have older workers tended to withdraw from the labor force, but when they work, they increasingly work part-time. As indicated by table 1, this is particularly true for people over age 65. U.S. labor statistics classify people as part-time workers if they worked 1 to 34 hours per week.In 1960, 35 percent of the male workers age 65 and over worked part-time; in 1989 almost half worked part-time. Over the same period part-time employment for female workers over 65 increased from 48 to 58 percent.

Older workers in the U.S. tend to be concentrated in certain types of jobs. In particular, they are much more likely than not to be self-employed. According to the March 1990 Current Population Survey, 12 percent of the male workers and 7 percent of the female workers were self employed. At ages 55 to 64 these fractions are 21 percent for males and 11 percent for females, and above age 65 they are 42 percent and 17 percent respectively. Interestingly, the fraction of employed older males that are self-employed has tended to decline with time. This is largely due to the decline in self-employed farmers. The fraction of employed older women that are self-employed has remained about the same for the last twenty years (Sum and Fogg, 1990: 51).

Older workers also tend to find employment in smaller firms. Table 2 indicates that the fraction of workers over 60 in small firms (under 100

Table 1: Part Time (PT) and Full Time (FT) Older Workers by Age, 1989

Age	Males			Females		
	%PT	%FT	Total	%PT	%FT	Total
All Ages						
+16	10.0	90.0	100.0	25.5	74.5	100.0
55−59	6.0	94.0	100.0	24.9	75.1	100.0
60−64	14.4	85.6	100.0	33.6	66.4	100.0
65−69	41.0	59.0	100.0	54.1	45.9	100.0
70+	53.7	46.3	100.0	64.9	35.1	100.0

Source: U.S. Bureau of Labor Statistics, Special Tabulations.

workers) is almost double that found in large firms (over 500).[1] And a similar relationship holds true irrespective of major industry. As discussed below, small firms are less likely than large firms to pursue policies that discourage work by older people.

Older workers tend to be employed in specific occupations. The broad occupational category with the highest fraction of older workers is, "farming, forestry, and fishing"; in 1989 15.2% of the people in this occupation were over age 60 and 8.7% were over 65. White collar occupations also tend to employ comparatively high fractions of older workers. Seven percent of the workers in white collar occupations (for example, managers or technicians) were over age 60 compared with 5.3% in blue collar occupations (for example, operative or laborer). At age 65 these percentages are 3.1% for white collar and 1.7% for blue collar. Such numbers are consistent with the finding – often based on multivariate statistical models – that white collar males tend to retire later than blue collar males (Hayward and Hardy, 1985; Mitchell, Levine, and Pozzebon, 1988).

Finally, older workers tend to locate employment in specific industries. When the employment share of males over 65 is compared to the employment share of all males, we find that the older males are over-represented in three major industry groups: agriculture; services; and finance, insurance, and real estate. They are under-represented in three others: construction; manufacturing; and transport, communications, and other public utilities. Similar lists apply to women over 65. They too are over-represented in agriculture and services (but not in finance, insurance, and real-estate); they too are under-represented in manufacturing and in transport, communications, and other public utilities (but not in construction). In 1989, two industries – miscellaneous services (primarily business and repair and professional services) and trade (primarily retail) – employed about half of the men and more than two-thirds of the women over 65.

Table 2: Persons 60 or Older as a Percentage of Employment, by Industrial Sector and
Size of Firm, 1988 (in percent)

Industrial Sector	Older Persons Employed in All Firms	Older Persons Employed in Firms with		
		Under 100 Workers	100 – 499 Workers	500 or More Workers
All Industries	5.7	7.4	5.3	4.2
Durable Manufacturing	4.8	7.4	4.0	3.9
Nondurable Manufacturing	5.4	6.3	6.2	4.6
Wholesale Trade	6.2	8.9	2.4	2.5
Retail Trade	5.4	7.5	3.4	3.3
Finance, Insurance, Real Estate	4.8	8.4	3.3	2.8
Miscellaneous Services	6.8	8.3	6.3	5.4

Sources: Tabulations from the May 19888 Current Population Survey Using Supplement
Weights. Sample Size = 24682.

The above statistics hint at the possibility that retirement in the U.S. does
not always mean moving from full-time work to full-time nonwork. Recent
studies of panel data shed light on this. They indicate that retirement often
involves a period of partial retirement. In the Retirement History Survey,
a ten year study of a national sample of older workers approaching retirement age, 17 percent of the white males between 65 and 69 and 11 percent
of white males between 62 and 64 report themselves as "partially retired".[2]
The same data indicate that by age 69, more than a third of white males
have experienced a spell of self-reported partial retirement (Gustman and
Steinmeier, 1984a, table 2).

Although in most cases, this partial retirement involves a new job at a
new firm, there are many exceptions. It is not uncommon for males between
the ages of 55 and 62 to report movement from non-retirement to partial
retirement without changing employers. Table 3 presents a useful illustration drawn from Gustman and Steinmeier (1984a). The table was constructed by first estimating a multivariate logit model and then computing
retirement status probabilities for an individual with specific demographic
and job characteristics. Note that prior to age 63 the probabilities in column
(3) are larger than those in column (4). That means that prior to age 63
most partial retirement occurs for people who remain in their "main job"
(the main job is defined as a full time job held at age 55). From age 63 on,
partial retirement usually involves a new job.

Not only is this self-reported partial retirement associated with reduced
hours worked per week and weeks worked per year, it is also associated

Table 3: Estimated Probabilities of Retirement Outcomes for an Individual in Good Health, Without a Pension and Not Facing Mandatory Retirement

Age	Retirement Status				
	Not retired	Partially Retired in Main Job[a]	Partially Retired Outside Main Job[a]	Retired	Total
(1)	(2)	(3)	(4)	(5)	(6)
58 – 59	.988	.033	.001	.008	1.000
60 – 61	.970	.012	.011	.007	1.000
62	.865	.047	.036	.052	1.000
63	.827	.035	.054	.085	1.000
64	.616	.048	.088	.249	1.000
65	.396	.099	.089	.417	1.000
66 – 67	.218	.075	.129	.578	1.000
68 – 69	.099	.064	.117	.720	1.000

(a) The "Main Job" is Defined as a Full Time Job Held at Age 55.
Source: Gustman and Steinmeier (1984a, Table 4).

with reduced hourly wage rates. According to Gustman and Steinmeier (1985), while people who become partially retired on a new job suffer the greatest wage loss, declines also occur for those who partially retire without changing jobs. They estimate that partial retirement causes about a 20 percent drop in the hourly wage.

One can reasonably question the validity of such self-reported retirement numbers. Self reports may not reflect actual behavior; for example, actual partial retirees may be embarrassed by their status and report themselves as fully employed. However, studies that use more objective measures of partial retirement come to conclusions that are qualitatively similar to those based on self-reports. For example, in their study of males, Honig and Reimers (1987a) define a transition from non-retirement to partial retirement as a sudden decline in monthly earnings followed by a period in which monthly earnings are well below the individual's peak monthly earnings.[3] Over the ten years of the Retirement History Survey, they find that of the 1735 transitions out of non-retirement, fully 31 percent were transitions into partial retirement. The remaining 69 percent were transitions into full-retirement with zero monthly earnings. Many of these partial retirements involved a reduction in wages but not hours, a phenomenon that is consistent with people moving to less demanding jobs. The main point, however, is that retirement in the U.S. cannot simply be characterized as a jump from full-time work to full-time non-work. An intermediate step – partial retirement – is quite common.

As implied by the above discussion, much of what we know about partial retirement focuses on males. At least two studies have examined partial retirement by unmarried women (Honig, 1985; Ruhm, 1990), and they indicate that female behavior is quite similar to male behavior. For example, according to Ruhm's analysis of heads of households in the 1969–1979 Retirement History Survey, 45.7 percent of the males and 43.3 percent of the females report themselves as partially retired in at least one of the interviews.[4] To my knowledge, there are no studies of partial retirement by married women.

There remains the question of whether some kinds of people are more likely than others to take the intermediate step of partial retirement. The available literature (Gustman and Steinmeier, 1984a; Ruhm, 1990; Honig and Hanoch, 1985) points to low income as a key determining factor. For example, Ruhm's multivariate models indicate that people with no pensions or with comparatively low income over their lifetimes are more likely to experience partial retirement. People with higher incomes – especially pension incomes – tend to move directly from full-time work to full-time non-work without entering partial retirement.

That result is consistent with the principal theme of this paper. U.S. employers pursue a diversity of policies toward employment of older workers. Some employers discourage work by older people while others encourage it. As a result there is a diversity of paths to retirement. Some people move to partial retirement without changing employers, some partially retire by changing jobs, and some simply jump from full-time work to full-time non-work.

2   Establishing the Context: Institutions Associated with Retirement

The retirement process not only involves movement from work to non-work, it also involves movement from earned income to non-earned income. This section first discusses the sources from which the elderly draw incomes, and then examines the institutions associated with key income sources.

Table 4 presents data on the income of people over 55 in 1988. Note the age-related shift from earned to nonearned income. Whereas 80 percent of the 55-61 year olds have earned income, this number drops to 22 percent for those over 65. Income shares decline in a parallel fashion, going from 78 percent for 55-61 year olds to 17 percent for those over 65. This decline is offset by sources of non-earned income, the most important being federal social security benefits. Fully 38 percent of the income received by the age 65+ units comes from social security. Also important is asset income. A surprising 68 percent of the age 65+ units have asset income (largely

Table 4: Percentage of Aged Units[a] with Income from Various Sources and Shares of Aggregate Income from these Sources, 1988

Income Source	Age		
	55 – 61	62 – 64	65 or Older
Percentage of Units with Income from:			
Earnings	80	61	20
Social Security	13	53	92
Pensions[b]	21	35	42
Assets	65	68	68
Share of Aggregate Income Provided by:			
Earnings	78	56	17
Social Security	2	13	38
Pensions[b]	8	15	18
Assets	10	14	25
Other[c]	2	3	3

Source: U. S. Department of Health and Human Services, Social Security Administration, Office of Research and Statistics, Office of Policy, *Income of the Population 55 and Over, 1988*, SSA Publication No. 13-11871, June 1990, Tables 1 and 47.

(a) An Aged Unit is a Married Couple Living Together — at Least one of whom is over 55 — or a Nonmarried Person. The Unit May Reside within a Larger Household.

(b) Includes Private Pensions and Annuities, Government Pensions, Railroad Retirement Benefits.

(c) Includes Public Asistance, Veteran's Benefits, Unemployment Insurance, Workers' Compensation, and Personal Contributions.

interest from savings accounts), which accounts for 25 percent of their aggregate income. Finally, although not as significant as social security or asset income, pensions also help to offset the age-related decline in earnings.

2.1   Income from the Government: The Social Security System in the U.S.

The United States' social security system was introduced in 1935, well after most European countries introduced such programs. The initial legislation envisioned a fully funded program that simply paid cash benefits to older workers. Very quickly, however, a more complex program emerged. In 1939, benefits were extended to dependents and survivors, and full funding gave way to pay-as-you-go financing. The system expanded to include programs for the disabled during the 1950s, medical insurance benefits for the elderly and disabled in 1965, and automatic cost of living adjustments in 1972. In 1987, this "Old Age, Survivors, Disability, and Health Insurance System" paid $288 billion in benefits to 38 million recipients.

The present social security system is financed out of a payroll tax on employees, employers and the self-employed. In 1989 employees paid 7.51 percent of their first $48 000 in annual earnings, and employers matched that. Although the system has historically operated on a pay-as-you-go basis, an effort is currently underway to build up trust funds in anticipation of the large cohorts of workers who will retire early in the 21st century. Thus, current revenues are more than sufficient to cover current expenditures.

In order to focus on older workers, the following discussion concentrates on the primary retirement program (and largest component of the social security system), Old Age Insurance (OAI). In 1987, 27 million people receive $147 billion in retirement benefits from OAI. Due to 1983 legislation, over the next several years OAI will change so as to encourage the elderly to work more. As such, I first describe the OAI program as of 1989, and then describes the planned changes.

To be eligible for social security retirement benefits, an individual must reach age 62 and earn a minimum amount of income in "covered employment" over a minimum number of quarters. (One year of work in covered employment yields four "quarters of coverage".) The minimum number of quarters has increased with time. A person reaching age 62 after 1991 needs 40 quarters to qualify for benefits; a person reaching 62 in 1981 needed only 30 quarters. Fifty years ago, several types of jobs were excluded from covered employment (e.g., self-employment, employment in the federal government). Today almost all jobs are included.

The level of OAI retirement benefits received by an eligible worker depends on four factors:

(1) *The worker's earnings record.* The Social Security Administration computes a Primary Insurance Amount (PIA) by applying a benefit formula to the worker's average indexed monthly earnings in covered employment. (The indexing is complicated; it essentially adjusts for historical changes in the average wage level in the economy.) Although the benefit formula dictates larger benefits for larger average monthly earnings, the formula is weighted in favor of low earners in the sense that the ratio of the benefits to monthly earnings falls as monthly earnings increase.

(2) *The worker's marital status and number of dependents.* Workers with a spouse and/or dependent children receive additional benefits. For example, the additional benefits from a spouse age 65 are equal to 50 percent of the worker's PIA.

(3) *The age at which the worker begins receiving benefits.* Workers obtain

their full PIA if they begin receiving benefits at age 65. This is cut to 80 percent of the PIA if receipt begins at age 62 (the youngest allowable age). If a worker delays benefit receipt until after age 65, his or her benefits are increased by 3 percent of the PIA per year of delay.

(4) *The worker's current earnings.* Earned income can lead to reduced benefits. For example, in 1989, a 63 year old beneficiary could earn up to $6480 without a benefit reduction. If earnings exceed the exempt amount of $6480, benefits are reduced by $1 dollar for each $2 dollars in earnings. Benefit levels do not vary with nonearned income like dividends or pensions.

It should, perhaps, also be noted that benefits received by upper income families are subject to the federal income tax. For example, a retired couple with income in excess of $32 000 may pay income taxes on as much one-half of their social security benefits.

In part due to the declining labor force participation of older workers, the work disincentives inherent in the U.S. Social Security program have recently come under intense scrutiny. Two disincentives are particularly important. First, the way in which benefits are reduced for younger retirement ages (item 3 above) encourages early retirement. This is because an additional year of work results in a smaller expected value of lifetime social security benefits. Although an additional year of work may bring a higher annual benefit, that higher benefit does not fully compensate for the decrease in the individual's expected duration of social security receipt. Thus, to delay retirement is to essentially forego a portion of social security benefits. Second, the treatment of current earnings, whereby a worker loses $1 in benefits for each $2 in earnings, is the equivalent of a 50 percent tax rate. It reduces the financial gains from continued work. The 63 year old in item 4 above is encouraged to earn $6480 per year in a part-time or part-year job and then stop working.[5] Thus, not only does the social security program encourage early receipt of benefits, but – once receipt begins – it discourages continued work.

In 1983, the U.S. federal government enacted legislation that partially addressed concerns about the work disincentives inherent in social security. The primary motivation behind the 1983 legislation was the threatened collapse of the social security system in the early 21st Century. Projections of future revenues and benefit payments indicated that, under reasonable assumptions, there would be insufficient funds to pay benefits to the large cohorts of workers who will retire between 2010 and 2030. In order to build up trust funds in anticipation of those large cohorts, the government both raised future payroll taxes and cut future benefits.

The benefit cuts were designed to encourage work by the elderly. In particular, the normal retirement age – the age at which the worker receives the full PIA – will increase from its current age 65 to age 67. This change will occur slowly; the normal retirement age will begin to rise in the year 2000 and not be fully implemented until 2027. Although covered workers will still be able to receive benefits at age 62, they will only receive 70 percent of their PIA (as opposed to the current 80 percent). In addition, by the year 2004, workers who delay benefit receipt until after the normal retirement age will enjoy an 8 percent increase in benefits (as opposed to the current 3 percent) per year of delay. Finally, whereas benefits were reduced by $1 for each $2 of earnings over the annual exempt amount, beginning in 1990 workers who are at or above the normal retirement age (currently age 65) will have benefits reduced by $1 for each $3 of earnings over the exempt amount. Each of these changes increase the incentives for healthy older people to continue working rather than choose retirement. There remains, of course, the question of whether older people will have an opportunity for continued work.

2.2   Income from Pensions: The Private Pension System in the U.S.

Although the government does not mandate pensions in the U.S., employers often voluntarily provide pensions as a fringe benefit. Indeed, over the past forty years pension coverage has doubled; whereas 25 percent of the labor force had some form of pension in 1950, today the number is almost 50 percent. Moreover, the fraction of retirees with pension income has expanded rapidly. In 1950, fewer than 5 percent of the population over age 55 received pension income. In 1986 that was 34 percent[6], and given the increase in coverage, this percentage will continue to grow in the future as more and more workers acquire pension rights.

Since pensions are voluntary, some workers are more likely to be covered than others. Pension coverage is, "... most prevalent for government workers (roughly 90 percent are covered), union workers (about 80 percent coverage), and employees of large firms (75+ percent covered in firms with 500 or more workers)" (Mitchell, 1988: 152). Furthermore, workers with more education, higher wages, and longer job tenure are more likely to be covered by a pension plan. In general, the people who receive lesser rewards in the labor market are also the people who tend to not have a pension (Wise, 1984).

Unlike social security benefits, pension benefits usually do not fully adjust for inflation. Thus, an inflationary period can seriously damage the economic well being of pension recipients. Interestingly, cases have been documented where employers responded to inflation by voluntarily increasing retiree pension benefits.

Most U.S. workers with pensions are covered by "defined benefit" pensions. Such pensions are based on the employer's promise to pay benefits according to a specific formula. For example, the employer may promise that employees with 20 years of experience who retire at age 65 will receive annual benefits equal to 60 percent of final salary. A characteristic of a defined benefit pension is that the employer may fail to set aside sufficient funds to make good on promised benefits. For example, although an employer may promise retirement benefits to today's forty year-old worker, in the event of bankruptcy that promise may be broken.

This cannot happen with the alternative "defined contribution" pension. Under a defined contribution pension, the employer essentially makes a contribution to an individual savings account for each employee. The contribution may depend on salary, profits, or both. Employees may also make contributions to the account. In a defined contribution pension, the employee's retirement benefit depends solely on the amount of funds contributed to the account, the investment performance of those funds at the time of retirement, and the worker's age of retirement. The employer does not promise a specific level of benefits, but rather only promises to pay an annuity based on the funds in the account. Thus, "unlike the defined benefit plans, defined contribution plans can never have too few assets to meet liabilities since, by definition, liabilities are equal to assets" (Mitchell, 1988: 153).

For purposes of this paper, it is important to distinguish between these two types of pensions because they can have different retirement effects. Employers can manipulate defined benefit pensions in ways that influence the age of retirement. As discussed in section 3, that is less the case with defined contribution plans.

Although defined benefit plans are the most common form of pension in the United States (about three-fourths of the workers with a pension plan are in a defined benefit plan), defined contribution plans are increasingly popular. Between 1975 and 1985 the number of participants in defined contribution plans grew by almost two hundred percent, while the number in defined benefit plans grew by a mere seven percent (Beller, 1989: 39).

Private pensions are subject to regulation by the U.S. federal government. This regulation in part arises because defined benefit plans sometimes collapse; employers do not set aside sufficient assets to meet liabilities. Over the past two decades, a sequence of legislative initiatives sought to raise the probability that covered workers actually receive promised benefits. Certainly the centerpiece of these initiatives is the Employee Retirement Income Security Act of 1974 (ERISA). ERISA established funding requirements, vesting standards, and criteria for prudent management of pension assets. It also established the Pension Benefit Guarantee

Corporation (PBGC), which pays benefits to workers when underfunded defined benefit plans collapse.[7]

Government regulation also places some, rather limited, restrictions on benefit levels and structures. For example, employers cannot use age as a basis for stopping pension accruals. In addition, the benefit paid to a 65 year-old employee in a defined benefit plan must not exceed 100 percent of the average of the three highest years of compensation, or $90 000 (the latter figure is adjusted each year for changes in the cost of living). These maximums are actuarially reduced for workers who retire before age 65. Subject to such maximums the employer is free to design a benefit formula which influences worker retirement and quit decisions.

The federal government's principal weapon for enforcing such regulations is the tax code. Pensions enjoy considerable tax advantages in the United States. Like other labor costs, employer pension contributions are deductible from the federal corporate income tax, and employees do not pay personal income taxes on them until benefits are received. Moreover, income earned on pension assets is allowed to accumulate within the pension fund free of taxes. Government regulations are often tied to these tax advantages; a pension plan that violates government regulations may lose its tax exempt status.

2.3   Income from Work

Income from work is another important financial resource for the elderly. Since we observe people working well after age 65, it is clear that some older people can choose between working and not working. Less clear are the constraints on those choices. How do the work opportunities confronting older people differ from those confronting younger people? Both private and public policies shape the opportunities confronting older people in ways that are, as yet, poorly understood. Section 3 examines private sector policies in detail. Here we focus on government policies.

A structure of government regulations surrounds the U.S. labor market for older workers. In most cases the regulations apply to workers of all ages. For example, the Fair Labor Standards Act sets minimum wage and maximum hour requirements. Other regulations, like the federal Age Discrimination in Employment Act (ADEA) of 1967, focus on older workers.

The ADEA is perhaps best known for its treatment of mandatory retirement; with a few minor exceptions the ADEA prohibits age-based mandatory retirement. But the Act encompasses more than retirement policy. It prohibits covered employers from using age as a basis for hiring, discharge, or compensation. It also prohibits employers from publishing advertisements that imply discrimination based on age. For example, a help wanted notice that includes phrases like "age 25 to 35", "young", or "recent college graduate", violates the ADEA unless certain exceptions apply. The original 1967 Act only covered workers between the ages of 40 and 65, but the 1978 and 1986 Amendments greatly extended coverage. Today the Act protects almost all workers over the age of 40.

The principal exception to the Act occurs when age is a "bona fide occupational qualification." For example, in 1974 the courts permitted a large bus company (Greyhound Lines) to impose a maximum hiring age of 35. The company successfully argued that new drivers face strenuous driving assignments, and also presented evidence that less experienced older drivers pose a safety risk. This was, however, an unusual case. In general, the courts require employers to demonstrate that they must use age – instead of an observable medical or physical condition – when making personnel decisions. Employers rarely succeed in demonstrating this. Most employers either do not claim that age is a bona fide occupational qualification, or do not litigate such claims if challenged (Rosenblum, 1983).

The extent of age discrimination and the impact of legislation like ADEA remains almost wholly unknown. It is difficult to measure age discrimination, and, in consequence, it is difficult to know whether government policies have altered discrimination over time. As described below, we do know that the ADEA provisions on mandatory retirement affected employer retirement policies. We also know that litigation has increased. There were 26 549 age-bias suits filed in 1986, which is more than double the number filed in 1980 (Bureau of National Affairs 1987: 124). This may, however, simply reflect greater awareness of the law.

3   Employer Policies for Discouraging Older People from Working

U.S. employers pursue a diversity of policies toward older workers. Some seem thoroughly indifferent to a worker's age; they hire and compensate older workers in a manner identical to younger workers. Other employers use a broad array of policies for discouraging work by older people. Included here are pensions, policies against hiring older workers, limitations on flexible retirement, and (prior to 1986) mandatory retirement. Why do we see such a striking diversity of policies?

This section grapples with that question. It begins with a discussion of the variety of policies that some employers use to discourage work by older people. It then examines the characteristics of employers that use such policies. Finally, it speculates about why some employers adopt such policies and others do not.

3.1   The Policies

A subset of employers use an array of personnel practices to discourage work by older people. The most obvious practice is mandatory retirement, whereby an employer can force a worker who has reached a specific age (e.g., 65) to retire.[8] Although mandatory retirement policies are now largely prohibited in the U.S., prior to 1978 approximately 35 percent of the workforce was subject to mandatory retirement, with 65 being the most common age of employment termination. Other practices include pensions that make it costly for a person to continue working, restrictions on flexible retirement, and policies that discourage hiring of older workers. Since the next section discusses mandatory retirement in some detail, this section focuses on the other practices.

Pensions. Employers often use pensions to discourage work by older people. In particular, employers can structure a defined benefit pension plan so that workers lose money if they delay retirement past a certain age. Such plans usually designate an age at which the worker is entitled to full benefits, for example age 65. This is termed the "normal retirement age". The plans also designate a younger age – the early retirement age – at which retirees can receive reduced benefits, for example age 55. This is, of course, similar to social security Old Age Insurance with its normal retirement age of 65 and its early retirement age of 62.

The employer can structure the pension so that once a worker has reached the age of normal retirement, an additional year of work results in a smaller expected value of lifetime pension benefits. Although an additional year of work may bring a higher annual benefit, that higher benefit does not fully compensate for the decrease in the individual's expected duration of pension receipt. Thus, much as with Old Age Insurance, an extra year of work results in a smaller expected value of lifetime pension benefits. This is called an "actuarially unfair" pension. Defined benefit pensions can be actuarially unfair after the early retirement age, after the normal retirement age, or both.

Note that defined contribution pensions cannot be structured in this way. In a defined contribution plan, the retiring worker receives the amount of money deposited in his or her pension account. An additional year of work can only increase this amount of money. Thus, defined contribution pensions cannot be actuarially unfair.

We have solid evidence that actuarially unfair defined benefit pensions exist.[9] For example, Kotlikoff and Wise (1987) describe a large corporation (identified only as "the FIRM") with a pension plan that encourages early retirement. The normal retirement age in this plan is 65, and the early retirement age is 55. Workers who take early retirement receive generous benefits. Indeed, in some cases an individual who takes early retirement can

410

receive the full (age 65) benefit. Moreover, since early retirees cannot obtain government social security benefits until age 62, the FIRM pays them extra pension benefits in the form of a "social security offset". As a result, if employees with thirty years of service at age 60 work an additional year, they lose compensation that is equivalent to a wage cut of about 14 percent. The actual numbers can be quite dramatic. For example, "the typical manager in the FIRM, making about $48 000 per year in wage earnings at age 60, would lose about $42 000 in pension wealth were he to continue working until age 65" (1987: 81). And were this typical manager to work beyond age 65, he or she would continue to lose pension benefits.

One would expect such incentives to influence retirements, and they do. "Over 50 percent of the 50-year-old employees of the FIRM leave before age 60, and 90 percent leave before age 65. Moreover, the jumps in departure rates at specific ages coincide precisely with the discontinuities (kink points) in pension and social security accrual" (1987: 5).

Kotlikoff and Wise (1987) also examine data on pensions in 1469 establishments covering 3.386.121 participants. They conclude that "in most firms with defined benefit plans, pension accrual gives workers a very substantial incentive to leave the firm after the age of early retirement and an even greater incentive to leave after normal retirement age" (1987: 4). Moreover, private pension plans typically contain work disincentives that exceed those in the social security program.

Employers can also encourage retirement through early retirement incentive plans (ERIPs). These plans usually offer a more generous pension to employees who choose to retire during a specific time interval. Some plans also offer continued health insurance coverage to retired workers. Hewlett-Packard Corporation provides an example of an ERIP. In 1986, the corporation offered employees who were age 55 or older and had at least 15 years of service a bonus for voluntary retirement. The bonus equalled one-half of a month's salary for each year of service up to a maximum of one year's salary. Of course, this was in addition to promised pension and profit sharing benefits. Fully 46 percent of the eligibles accepted (Bureau of National Affairs, 1987: 76).

We know very little about ERIPs. In particular, we do not know to what extent separations under ERIPs are voluntary. Although we know there is a carrot in the form of a more generous pension, we do know not whether there is also a stick. If the worker decides to not an accept an ERIP, what happens? Furthermore, we do not know how prevalent they are. A 1983 survey by the Conference Board indicated that of the 363 companies responding, 36 percent had offered an ERIP since 1970 (Rhine, 1984). However, the survey sample focused on large firms, and was, in consequence, not representative.

Restrictions on Flexible Retirement. Another way to discourage work by older people is to restrict their choices. As workers age, they often wish to remain with their firm but move to less demanding jobs. It is not difficult to imagine how employers could accommodate such preferences. For example, they could offer (perhaps at a reduced salary) part-time work; flexibility in work scheduling and job assignments; and longer vacations, leaves, and sabbaticals. When firms are unwilling to structure jobs in this way, they encourage older workers to either withdraw from the labor force or find employment elsewhere. Available data indicate that although workers often want some form of flexible retirement, most employers do not offer the option. Several surveys have asked whether, at normal retirement age, people would prefer to work part-time instead of retiring completely. About 80 percent of the respondents state a preference for some form of part-time work.[10] Yet, it is unusual for employers to accommodate this preference. Gustman and Steinmeier (1983: 81) present striking evidence on this. They discuss a 1979 survey of 267 organizations.

Approximately one-half of the responding establishments were manufacturing companies, one-third nonmanufacturing businesses, and about one-fifth nonbusiness organizations (hospitals, universities, government organizations, etc.). According to the survey, while over half of the firms made arrangements for some employees to stay on as consultants – and sometimes recalled retirees for temporary assignment – only 15 percent of the responding firms and only 10 percent of the manufacturing firms had a "tapering off" program in which at least some employees could reduce their work time as they approached retirement. Only 7 percent had such programs covering all employees. The percentages were similar among large firms (more than 1 000 employees) and small firms (fewer than 1 000 employees).

As best can be determined, this situation has not changed since 1979. It remains the case that many large employers force workers to choose between full time work and retirement.

Policies that Discourage Hiring. Yet, another way for employers to discourage work by older people is to not hire them. Prior to the 1967 Age Discrimination in Employment Act, many employers had explicit policies against hiring older workers. A 1965 survey (U.S. Department of Labor, 1965) provides a striking illustration of this. The survey asked employers in five cities whether they impose upper age limits on new hires. In fact, almost three out of five did, with most of the limits lying between ages 45 and 55. Moreover, data on actual hiring behavior indicate that these limitations had teeth. Employers with such policies tended to not hire older workers.

Although such explicit policies against hiring older workers are now illegal, something like them almost certainly continues to influence hiring decisions. It is still possible for employers to avoid hiring older workers; they simply must not use age in justifying their decisions. For example, they can justify not hiring an older worker by claiming that the person's personality traits are inappropriate for the job.

And there is good reason to think that this goes on. When they look for jobs, old workers tend to find them in a smaller subset of industries and occupations than young workers. Moreover, old workers are less likely than otherwise identical young workers to move from unemployment to employment, and to reap a wage gain once they have found a job (Hutchens, 1988). Finally, despite federal legislation against age discrimination, employers often respond to surveys by indicating a preference for hiring younger workers (Collins, 1975; Rosen and Jerdee, 1985). Thus, several pieces of evidence are consistent with the claim that many employers continue to avoid hiring older workers.

3.2   What Kinds of Employers Use these Policies?

Of course, not all employers discourage older people from working. Indeed, some employers appear to be indifferent to a worker's age. A recent study of an industrial area in Massachusetts describes a set of firms that rarely discriminate against the old. These are usually small low-wage employers in retail trade, services, furniture manufacturing, plastics, and apparel. They offer jobs with flexible hours that require little training. Moreover, the firms need labor badly "because they serve as a feeder or labor pool for higher-paying and more selective firms" (Doeringer and Terkla, 1990: 159). What distinguishes such firms from those that discourage work by older people?

Due to incomplete data, we can only provide a partial answer to this question. Our best information concerns mandatory retirement prior to 1978. We have solid data on the incidence of mandatory retirement across firms and workers. Less adequate is the information on hiring policies, flexible retirement, and pensions. Here the data tend to be either old, unrepresentative, or lacking in detail. Despite their limitations, however, the available data point to the following hypothesis:

The employers that impose mandatory retirement also use several other policies to discourage work by older people. In particular, they offer actuarially unfair pensions, impose bars against hiring older workers, and provide few opportunities for flexible retirement.

Our information on mandatory retirement comes from surveys of employers and employees prior to the 1978 ADEA Amendments. Simple univariate cross-tabulations indicate that,

– Larger employers were more likely to impose mandatory retirement. In one survey, 86 percent of the older workers in firms with 100 000 or more employees were subject to mandatory retirement; the corresponding number for older workers in firms with fewer than 200 employees was 21 percent. As indicated by the fact that mandatory retirement tended to be more likely in firms that utilized formal personnel policies[11], these firms were likely to be bureaucratic and perhaps hierarchical.

- The incidence of mandatory retirement varied dramatically across industries. Workers were more likely to be subject to mandatory retirement if they worked in transportation, communications, chemicals, rubber, petroleum, and the federal government. They were unlikely to be subject to mandatory retirement if they worked in apparel manufacture, retail or wholesale trade, or the service sector (Urban Institute, 1981: 50-52).
- Roughly speaking, the incidence of mandatory retirement increased with skill level and decreased with physical requirements. Professional and other white collar workers were more often subject to mandatory retirement than blue collar workers. More skilled blue collar workers (like craftsmen) were more often subject to mandatory retirement than less skilled blue collar workers (like laborers) (Urban Institute, 1981: 55).
- Consistent with the results on skill levels, workers subject to mandatory retirement tended to have higher wages and longer job tenures than those not subject to mandatory retirement (Hutchens, 1987b).

Multivariate analysis of data on individual workers yields evidence that is consistent with the univariate cross-tabs. Lazear (1979) estimates a logit model of the probability that an older individual faced mandatory retirement, and finds that males, more educated workers, and urban workers were more likely to face mandatory retirement. Hutchens (1987b) obtains similar results. He estimates a probit model of the probability that an older male confronted mandatory retirement, and obtains positive and statistically significant coefficients on education, union status, and marriage. He also finds that after controlling for other factors, jobs that were repetitive tended to not involve mandatory retirement. In summary, the workers that were subject to mandatory retirement were among the more privileged in the American labor market. They were male, comparatively well-educated, well-paid, and unionized. Moreover, they tended to spend much of their career working in a large bureaucratic firm.

But these firms did not simply impose mandatory retirement. They evidently pursued additional policies that discouraged work by older people. First, they probably offered actuarially unfair pensions. We know that the firms that imposed mandatory retirement also provided pensions to their retired workers[12], but are less certain about the characteristics of those pensions. Since the firms that imposed mandatory retirement were comparatively large, and since large firms often have actuarially unfair defined benefit pensions, it is likely that the pensions offered by firms with mandatory retirement were actuarially unfair defined benefit pensions.

Second, the firms that imposed mandatory retirement also tended to not hire older workers. From Hutchens (1986) we know that firms with mandatory retirement tended to employ older workers but not hire them. These firms concentrate their hiring efforts on young workers. They employ older workers – workers who were hired when young and are completing the final years of a long-term attachment – but they do not hire *new* older workers. Consistent with this, the previously noted 1965 Department of Labor survey found that a major reason for explicit employer policies against hiring older workers was "promotion from within". Policies against hiring older workers were part of a policy for maintaining promotion ladders.

Third, the firms that imposed mandatory retirement also offered few opportunities for partial retirement. Our best evidence on this comes from Gustman and Steinmeier (1984a). Using multivariate models estimated in data from the early 1970s, they find that, holding demographic factors constant, self-reported partial retirement on the main job was least common among those workers in jobs with pensions and mandatory retirement. In order to partially retire, these workers usually moved to a new job.

In summary, employers in the U.S. exhibit a diversity of policies toward older workers. Those that discourage work by the old tend to be large and bureaucratic. At one time these firms often imposed mandatory retirement. Today they tend to offer actuarially unfair pensions, impose bars against hiring older workers, and provide few opportunities for flexible retirement. Interestingly, these policies tend to be targeted on some of the most privileged workers in the U.S. labor market.

3.3   An Explanation for the Existence of such Policies

What causes some firms to adopt policies that discourage work by older people while others do not? Do some employers discriminate in the sense that they possess a "taste" that favors young over old workers, or is another economic force operative? Here I sketch one possible answer – an answer that focuses on long term contracts and fixed costs. Since the ideas sketched here are not fully developed, this should be viewed as preliminary notes toward a theory.

There is good reason to argue that long-term contracts influence the way firms behave toward older workers. Firms differ in their propensity to enter into long-term relationships. Some employers essentially provide life-time employment to workers who successfully complete a probationary period (which may extend over several years). These long-term contracts are tied to promotion ladders and hierarchical structures. Workers who receive timely promotions can be reasonably confident that they will not be fired or suffer a permanent layoff. They are assured that the firm will find a place for them. To lose their job they must commit a serious crime (e.g., theft). Workers may join such firms when they are young and remain there until retirement.

At least in the U.S., these long-term contracts are usually implicit in the sense that they are not enforceable in the courts. The parties understand their promises to each other, and they have a self interest in keeping those promises. In particular, the firm is bound to the implicit contract through reputation effects. To cheat on the contract (for example, to lay off an older person without appropriate compensation) is to suffer a loss of reputation that may hurt the firm when hiring workers in the future. Of course, these contracts can also be explicit. In particular, unions may negotiate seniority provisions that both have the effect of a long-term contract and are enforceable in the courts.

Not all firms offer long-term contracts. For example, fast food chains or retail clothing stores have considerable turnover in their workforces; layoffs and quits are common. In such cases neither the firm nor the workers anticipate long-term relationships.

Why do some firms provide long-term contracts and others not? The principal explanation is "fixed costs of hiring". Some firms bear considerable costs when they hire a worker. Included here are training costs, search costs, and costs associated with monitoring worker effort (Hutchens, 1986). Firms can minimize such costs by entering into long-term contracts that minimize turnover. Some firms do not offer long-term contracts because they do not confront large fixed costs. Moreover, firms that are more likely to fail (i.e., more likely to suffer bankruptcy) are less likely to offer long-term contracts since they are unable to make a credible long-term commitment to young workers. Since bankruptcy rates decline with firm size, long-term implicit contracts should primarily be associated with large firms.

Firms that rely on long-term contracts are unlikely to hire *new* old workers. Even if old workers are as skilled and productive as young workers, old workers have a distinct disadvantage relative to the young: they do not have the potential to remain with the firm for twenty or thirty years. Thus, firms that rely on long-term contracts will tend to concentrate their hiring efforts on younger workers. They are looking for people who, after completing a probationary period, will remain with the firm for a very long time.

But why would these firms also pursue policies that encourage retirement – policies like mandatory retirement, actuarially unfair pensions, and few opportunities for partial retirement? One very good answer posits that under these long-term contracts, employers pay the average older worker a wage that exceeds his or her value of marginal product (Lazear, 1979). Alternatively stated, the wage cost of older workers exceeds the value of what they produce. In this case the profit maximizing firm encourages retirement through mechanisms that do not violate the long-term contract.

Mandatory retirement is one of these mechanisms. This is not an arbitrary or capricious policy. Workers are aware of it well before retirement age. Indeed, the age of mandatory retirement could be thought of as a provision that is agreed to at the time that the young worker enters into the long-term contract. Moreover, it is almost always tied to a pension – a particularly generous form of severance pay.

Early retirement plans and actuarially unfair pensions are yet another mechanism that the firm uses to encourage departure at the end of the contract. When the wage exceeds the value of marginal product, there is a price at which the profit maximizing firm is willing to "buy out" the long-term contract. Those workers who find the price acceptable take the money and terminate the contract prior to the normal retirement age.

Finally, in order to encourage exits by older workers, the firm does not offer opportunities for partial retirement. When wages are above marginal product, the profit maximizing firm will be uninterested in adapting the job to the wishes of its older workers. The firm only accommodates their wishes when older workers are unusually valuable (e.g., when they have unusual skills) or when they are willing to accept a considerable drop in wages.

Firms without long-term contracts (e.g., small firms) do not pursue such policies. They are pleased to hire older workers because they do not seek long-term relationships. Moreover, they tend to pay wages equal to value of marginal product, and thus have no reason to encourage early retirement.

A key question remains in this line of logic: why do firms with long-term contracts pay older workers a wage greater than value of marginal product? The question is key because if the wage were no greater than the marginal product, there would be no reason for the firms to encourage retirement. An institution like mandatory retirement would be irrational in the sense that it would imply foregone profits.

There now exist several plausible theories that address the question of why wages exceed value of marginal product for older workers.[13] At present, none of these rest on a solid empirical footing. A full understanding of why (and whether) older workers are paid a wage greater than marginal product must await further empirical work.

Although these ideas are rather abstract, they are quite compatible with more concrete notions of industrial relations. For example, Kochan, Katz and McKersie (1986) describe the work organization associated with "job control unionism". Here the union and firm agree to a highly formalized contract with sharply delineated jobs. Tied to each job are specific wages and employment rights. Since jobs are structured in promotion ladders, workers and firms are engaged in a long-term relationship. Kochan and his coauthors emphasize that this bureaucratic form of work organization arises in nonunion as well as union settings.

The workplace depicted by Kochan, Katz, and McKersie is quite compatible with theories of long-term implicit contracts.[14] They are describing
large organizations that make implicit (and sometimes explicit) promises to
workers who are hired at young ages. Sometimes these promises are
concerned with matters that only arise after several years with the firm
(e.g., pensions, or promotion opportunities). Moreover, wages rise with
seniority. The firms depicted by Kochan, Katz and McKersie can be viewed
as concrete examples of firms with implicit contracts. There remain, however, a key set of questions; and these are the same questions that lead to
the above abstractions. Specifically, if these firms maximize profits, why
would they discourage work by older people? Why would they impose
mandatory retirement and provide pensions that encourage early retirement? Why would a profit maximizing firm try to rid itself of productive
workers?

Since Kochan, Katz, and McKersie do not address retirement issues, they
do not seek to answer such questions. One could, however, imagine them
arguing that as workers gain seniority and move up promotion ladders,
there comes a time when, on average, the wages paid to older workers
exceed the value of their product. A profit maximizing firm will want to
limit that. Although the firm could solve its problem by simply dismissing
older workers or by arbitrarily cutting the wages of less productive workers,
such behavior is inconsistent with the highly formalized rules and procedure
that govern work in this firm. Alternatively stated, such behavior is inconsistent with the implicit contract. A better (less arbitrary) solution is to
impose mandatory retirement and to offer pensions that encourage early
exit.

To conclude, one way to "make sense" of employer behavior toward
older workers is to invoke theories of long-term implicit contracts. Such
theories provide an explanation for why a profit maximizing firm would
discourage work by older people. Moreover, since long term contracts will
not occur in all firms, these theories help to explain the diversity of policies
across employers. Of course, such theories are not without disadvantages.
They are often quite abstract and built around unobserved variables (e.g.,
value of marginal product). As such, they are not easily translated into
concrete situations. In addition, they are largely untested. At present they
are simply a source of interesting hypotheses.

4   The U.S. Experience with Regulating Mandatory Retirement

In recent years the U.S. federal government has moved toward regulating
employer policy toward older workers. The most dramatic effort to date
takes the form of regulating mandatory retirement. The 1978 ADEA

Amendments raised the minimum mandatory retirement age from 65 to 70, and the 1986 ADEA Amendments prohibited firms from using mandatory retirement for all but a handful of workers. These amendments provide insights into the current level of U.S. government influence over employer policy toward older workers.

4.1   Early Results

Around the time that the 1978 ADEA Amendments were under debate, several researchers sought to estimate their impact on labor force participation of older workers. All concluded that the effect would be minimal. This was primarily because mandatory retirement forced very few workers out of their jobs. As indicated above, firms have several tools for inducing older workers to leave their jobs. Mandatory retirement serves as a "backstop" that only influences behavior when all else fails. Figure 3 illustrates.

The data for figure 3 come from a 1968 survey of people who recently began receiving social security benefits. They therefore exclude retirees in groups that were not then covered by social security (e.g., federal and certain state and local government workers), and pertain to people who are aged 65 or less. Figure 3 makes two important points. First, most of the men who were subject to mandatory retirement left their jobs *before* the age of mandatory retirement; whereas 54 percent were subject to mandatory retirement, fully 30 percent retired before the age of mandatory retirement. Second, only a small fraction of the men (10 percent) were willing and able to work and were forced out of their job by a mandatory retirement rule. As documented in Halpern (1978), other surveys yield similar results.

Numbers like those in figure 3 can be used to estimate how a change in the age of mandatory retirement will affect the labor force participation of older workers. For example, on the basis of similar data Halpern (1978) determined that if the mandatory retirement age were raised from age 65 to 70, an additional 11 percent of males and 7 percent of females aged 65-69 would continue to work. If all worked continuously from age 65 to 69, that translates into a labor force increase of 375 000 workers. Since some of these people would almost certainly retire after a year or two of work and not work continuously from age 65 to 69, Halpern viewed an increase of 200 000 as more realistic. In the U.S. labor market, that is a small number. Since the size of the labor force exceeds 100 million, a 200 000 increase in the labor force represents a 0.2 percentage point increase.

There are, however, problems with this approach to studying the effect of raising the mandatory retirement age. In particular, Halpern's estimates are based on retiree responses to a survey rather than actual behavior. Some of the people who *say* they would have continued working may actually not

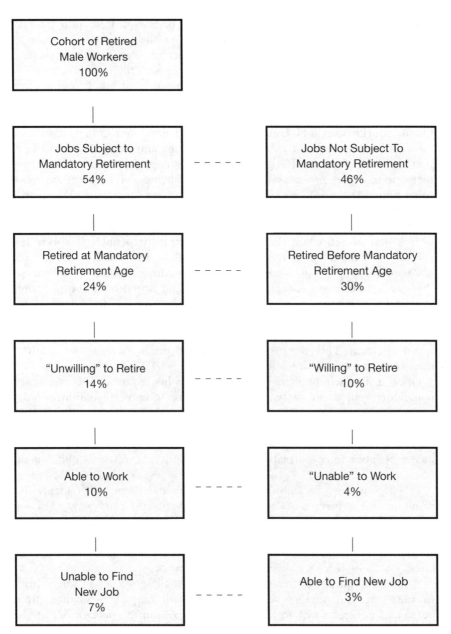

Source: Schulz (1976: 81) and Levine (1988: 28).

Figure 3: Mandatory Retirement and Labor Force Participation have done so. In addition, this approach does not take into account employer responses to a legislated increase in the mandatory retirement age. If employers use other mechanisms to encourage early retirement (e.g., pensions), then Halpern's estimates are too large. Other studies, some of which were commissioned by the U.S. Department of labor, partially address this issue.[15]

An excellent example is a 1983 paper by Richard Burkhauser and Joseph Quinn (Burkhauser and Quinn, 1983). Burkhauser and Quinn investigate the relationship between mandatory retirement and labor force participation using data from the Retirement History Survey. They use a multivariate methodology that indicates the effect of mandatory retirement on labor force participation holding constant pension characteristics, social security benefits, and other measured variables.

The Burkhauser-Quinn analysis begins with estimation of a linear regression model of retirement behavior in a sample of people who *were not* subject to mandatory retirement. The model is then used to predict the behavior of people who *were* subject to mandatory retirement. Of course, there is a difference between the predicted and actual behavior of people subject to mandatory retirement. For example, the predicted labor force participation rate of men aged 64-66 who were subject to mandatory retirement in 1975 was 37 percent; their actual labor force participation rate was 17 percent. This gap between actual and predicted behavior is attributed to mandatory retirement rules.

Once again, such numbers can be used to estimate how an increase in the mandatory retirement age will affect the labor force participation of older workers. The results of this exercise were remarkably close to the 200 000 person increase predicted by Halpern and others.[16] Thus, the evidence indicated that although raising the mandatory retirement age from 65 to 70 increases labor force participation of the elderly, the effect is quite small.

In light of the "backstop" role played by mandatory retirement, this result is not surprising. As we have seen, there are many ways in which employers induce early retirement, and some are quite effective (e.g., pensions). Most workers retired before reaching the age of mandatory retirement. As such, an increased mandatory retirement age has but a small effect on labor force participation by older workers.

A plausible question remains in all of this. If the government forces firms to raise their mandatory retirement age, will employers change other personnel policies so as to counteract the government policy? All of the estimates of the impact of the 1978 ADEA Amendments made a key assumption: employers will do nothing in response to a forced increase in the mandatory retirement age. This seems quite implausible. Elimination of mandatory retirement should increase worker control over the retirement process; workers should have more power to negotiate the terms under which they leave the firm. Since that will affect costs, one would think that firms would respond. For example, the firm could manipulate pensions, performance evaluations, or working conditions. Given the many ways in which employers can influence retirement behavior, it seems unlikely that firms will passively accept a forced increase in the mandatory retirement age.

The Department of Labor was aware of this issue and tried to address it through a survey of 6 000 randomly selected workers and their employers (*see* U.S. Department of Labor, 1982). In order to focus on people who were likely to be affected by the change in mandatory retirement, the sample excluded federal workers, workers in firms with less than 20 employees, and people younger than 40 and over 69. Data collection occurred in early 1980, about a year after implementation of the 1978 ADEA Amendments.

Perhaps the most surprising result from the survey was the fact that many employers seemed unconcerned about the ADEA Amendments. Although firms raised their mandatory retirement age as required by the law, only 8 percent of the sampled workers were employed at a firm that had changed *other* retirement policies. These changes were usually in the direction of encouraging earlier retirement.[17] Most employers evidently adopted a "wait and see" attitude; before making changes they wanted to determine whether workers would react to the ADEA Amendments by delaying retirement. Some employers indicated that if the Amendments caused large numbers of employees to delay retirement, then they would alter their retirement policies. Yet even here, there is no evidence of a dramatic response. The survey revealed that 65.2 percent of the older workers could expect their employers to make no policy changes, even if significant numbers of workers delayed retirement.[18]

For those few employers who expressed concern about the ADEA Amendments, the most common reaction was to liberalize retirement benefits. For example, they would provide pension incentives for early retirement and improve post-retirement health and welfare benefits. These employers evidently hoped to encourage older workers to leave their workforce by enhancing the financial attractions of retirement. Few spoke of making work less attractive. For example, only 8 percent of the workers had an employer who would respond to a sharp rise in retirement ages by discontinuing pension contributions for workers over 65. Only a few employers spoke of using stricter performance evaluations.

To conclude, research on mandatory retirement flourished around the time of the 1978 ADEA legislation. That research speculated that an increase in the age of mandatory retirement would have little effect on retirement behavior. Although employers may respond to this legislation with more generous incentives for early retirement, even that would be a rather weak response.

4.2   Later Results

It is interesting that today, more than 13 years after passage of the 1978 ADEA Amendments, we have very little evidence on the *actual* effects of the change in mandatory retirement policy. Almost all of the research on the effects of the Amendments occurred prior to (or shortly after) passage, and is thereby speculative. Of course, such gaps in the literature are also an opportunity. What does the recent evidence indicate?

First, the evidence indicates that employers may, in fact, have responded to the 1978 ADEA legislation by providing more generous incentives for early retirement. Lazear (1983), Mitchell and Luzadis (1988), and Ippolito (1990) examine changes in pension characteristics around the time of the 1978 legislation. All find evidence (albeit not conclusive evidence) indicating that pensions put greater emphasis on encouraging early retirement. Another source of information is a 1983 survey of employers (Morrison, 1985). The survey asked whether there had been any change in employer policies toward early retirement between 1978 and 1983. Fourteen percent of the employers said they were providing more encouragement for early retirement, 4 percent said they were providing less encouragement, and the remaining 82 percent said no change. The fact that 14 percent were providing more encouragement for early retirement is interesting. It is conceivable that this was due to the 1978 legislation.

Second, there is some evidence indicating that medium and large size firms are increasingly likely to provide retirement assistance programs to older workers (Morrison, 1985: 13). These programs usually supply information that eases the transition from work to retirement. For example, these programs might deal with financial planning, physical fitness, travel, or educational assistance.

Third, a recent paper by Krueger and Pischke presents evidence indicating that the 1978 legislation increased the labor force participation rate of older males by one or two percentage points. Although this result is not strictly comparable to the earlier work on mandatory retirement, it is consistent with the claim that the 1978 legislation had a very small impact.[19]

Finally, Tables 5 and figures 4 and 5 present new data on the effect of the 1978 ADEA legislation. Table 5 presents new data on males over 65 from

Table 5: Employed Males over 65 as a Percent of Employed Males over 50

Industry Group			
Year	(1) [%]	(2) [%]	(3) [%]
1974	2.84	8.30	11.20
1978	2.64	8.17	12.53
1983	4.63	8.01	11.18
1987	4.04	7.88	11.32

Source: Current Population Survey Computer Tapes, March 1974, January 1978, March 1983, January 1987.

the Current Population Survey. The Current Population Survey is a national survey of approximately 150 000 people age 14 and older. I separated out the employed males over age 50 and classified them into three industry groups:

(1) Industries with a high incidence of mandatory retirement. In these industries more than 70% of the workers age 58-61 were subject to mandatory retirement.[20] Included were chemicals, petroleum, rubber, transport, instruments, communications, federal government, public utilities, and state government.
(2) Industries with a medium incidence of mandatory retirement. In these industries between 30% and 70% of the workers age 58-61 were subject to mandatory retirement. Included were foods, paper, lumber, primary metals, fabricated metals, machinery, electrical machinery, railroads, local transit, motor freight, finance, insurance, hospital services, and local government.
(3) Industries with a low incidence of mandatory retirement. In these industries less than 30% of the workers age 58-61 were subject to mandatory retirement. Included were mining, oil and gas, construction, apparel, leather, furniture, wholesale and retail trade, business services, repair services, personal services, medical services, welfare, religious, and other services.

One would expect the 1978 ADEA Amendments to primarily affect the employment of workers in the first group of industries. And that is evidently what happened. The percentage for the first group increases between 1978 and 1983, and that for the second and third group decreases. But note how small the numbers are. Although the elimination of mandatory retirement evidently caused more work by males over 65, the effect appears to be quite small.

Figures 4 and 5 present CPS data on what could be thought of as the four year "survival rate" for males in 1974 and 1983. Here the survival rate in year t for males in industry i who are age j equals,

$$\frac{\text{\# Males in industry i age j+4 in year t+4 with job tenure} > 4 \text{ years}}{\text{\# Males in industry i age j in year t all job tenures}}$$

To compute the 1974 survival rate, the numerator is obtained from data in the January 1978 CPS, while the denominator is obtained from the March 1974 CPS. For example, suppose that the March 1974 Current Population Survey indicated that there were 100 000 males who were age 55 and working in manufacturing, and that the January 1978 Current Population Survey indicated 50,000 males with tenure greater than four years who were age 59 and working in manufacturing. In this case we would estimate that 50% of the original 100 000 males had "survived" for four years in their jobs. The 1983 survival rate is computed in similar fashion from the March

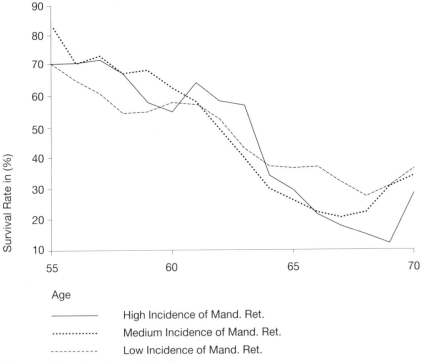

Figure 4: "Four Year Survival Rate"
Age Relationship in 1974 for Three Industry Groups

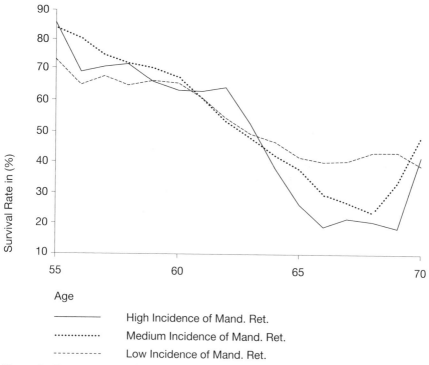

Figure 5: "Four Year Survival Rate"
Age Relationship in 1983 for Three Industry Groups

1983 and January 1987 CPS.[21] Figure 4 presents the 1974 relationship
between age and survival rates for the previously described three industry
groups. As one would expect, for workers in industries that tended to use
mandatory retirement in 1974, survival rates dropped precipitously in the
age range 62-65. Between 1974 and 1978 these workers were quite likely to
leave their jobs. Note that the drop in the age-survival rate relationship is
much more gradual for the other industry groups. A reasonable hypothesis
would be that after the 1978 ADEA Amendments, the age-survival rate
relationship for the mandatory retirement industries became flatter and
more like that for the non-mandatory industries. Figure 5 examines this.
There was obviously not a major change. Although close examination
reveals some support for the hypothesis, the 1983 age-survival rate relationships look surprisingly similar to the 1974 relationships.

5   Conclusion

This paper argues that employers in the United States pursue a diversity of policies toward older workers. Although some firms seem indifferent to a worker's age, others – particularly those that are large and bureaucratic – pursue an array of policies aimed at discouraging work by older people. Included in that array are actuarially unfair defined benefit pensions that encourage early retirement, bars against hiring older workers, limited opportunities for flexible retirement, and prior to the 1986 ADEA Amendments, mandatory retirement. Interestingly, these policies tend to be targeted on some of the most privileged workers in the U.S. labor market.

Why large bureaucratic firms tend to pursue such policies is something of a mystery. This paper speculates that part of the answer lies in hiring costs, implicit contracts, and older workers that are "overpaid" in the sense that their wage lies above their marginal product. But that is speculation. At present we do not have sufficient evidence to draw strong conclusions.

How can governments affect employer behavior in this area? This paper reviews the U.S. experience with prohibiting mandatory retirement. Although the prohibition succeeded in dramatically reducing the incidence of mandatory retirement, it had minimal effects on employment of the elderly. This is in part because large bureaucratic firms discourage work by older people in a variety of ways; mandatory retirement is only one of these ways, and it is comparatively unimportant.

If the U.S. government hopes to prod firms into providing greater work opportunities for older people, then it will have to take a serious look at regulating pensions. A prohibition against actuarially unfair defined benefit pensions would probably have an effect. An alternative, perhaps complementary, policy would be to encourage development of private institutions (like Japan's "Shukko") that smooth the transition of older workers out of large firms.

Notes

1   As indicated by the following all-industry numbers, this firm size relationship is strongest for people over 65.

	Firm Size		
	Under 100	100–499	500+
Age 60-64	3.86%	3.50%	3.04%
Age 65+	3.56%	1.80%	1.13%

The May 1988 Current Population Survey indicates that the fraction employed does not decline with firm size for people age 55-59. For earlier data on the population over 65 (with similar results) see Sum and Fogg (1990: 50).

2   Computed from Gustman and Steinmeier (1984a, table 1). These white males were not self-employed in their main job.

3   More precisely, they define partial retirement as positive monthly earnings that are less than 80 percent (in real terms) of the individual's maximum annual earnings divided by 12, and, if the person was classified as non-retired in the previous month, a decline in nominal earnings of at least 20 percent from the previous month.

4   Ruhm's multivariate models (*see* his table 8) indicate that after controlling for income, education, and race, partial retirement is less likely for females (Ruhm, 1990).

5   Yet another disincentive is the "recalculation effect." Prior to 1977 benefits were calculated on the basis of *nominal* earnings. By working an additional year, a prospective retiree could raise benefits by replacing a previous year of inflation-eroded earnings with current earnings. This work incentive was partially eliminated when, in 1977, the social security program began calculating benefits on the basis of *real* earnings prior to age 60. *See* Ippolito (1990) for a detailed discussion.

6   Computed from U.S. Department of Health and Human Services (1988, table 1).

7   The PBGC may have contributed to recent growth in defined contribution pensions. Benefits paid by the PBGC are partially financed out of a tax on defined benefit pension plans. Since this tax has grown in the past and is likely to grow in the future, and since it is not levied on defined contribution plans, the tax may encourage growth of defined contribution plans.

8   Kittner (1977) presents a useful description of different types of mandatory retirement policies. In most cases the employer had the option of forcing a worker to retire. In some cases, however, retirement was automatic in the sense that the employer was not permitted to retain the older worker.

9   Lazear (1983), Mitchell and Fields (1985), Kotlikoff and Wise (1987).

10   Levine (1988: 33). Also *see* Louis Harris and Associates (1989).

11   U.S. Department of Labor (1982, table 17 and table 20). Older workers in this context are between 40 and 70.

12   *See* Levine (1988: 101), Morrison (1988: 390), and Lazear (1979).

13   For example, Freeman (1977), Lazear (1979), Harris and Holmstrom (1982), Carmichael (1983), and Malcolmson (1984).

14   This is not to say that the other forms of industrial relations described by Kochan, Katz, and McKersie are incompatible with long-term implicit contracts. Their book primarily deals with large firms. Even the more modern forms of industrial relations involve long-term attachments, promotion ladders, and wages that increase with seniority.

15   For a list of other studies see U.S. Department of Labor (1982: 148, table 14). Also *see* Morrison (1988).

16   *See* Urban Institute (1981, chapter 5 and table 24).

17   U.S. Department of Labor (1982: 51). Focusing only on workers subject to mandatory retirement, the fraction is 10 percent.

18   Similar evidence was obtained in independent surveys of employers. *See* American Society for Personnel Administration and the Bureau of National Affairs (1978, 1980).

19   *See* Krueger and Pischke (1991, table 6). Since they do not interact their mandatory retirement variable with their age variables, we can not assess the extent to which the change in mandatory retirement policy differentially affected workers over 65.

20   These are 1969 figures from the Retirement History Survey. *See* Urban Institute (1981: 49-52).

21   Figures 4 and 5 present data that were "smoothed" by taking three year moving averages. Of course, it would be better to compute survival rates from panel data on the same population of people. The survival rates presented here are computed with different populations of people. They essentially employ the method of independent cross-sections.

References

American Society for Personnel Administration and Bureau of National Affairs Survey No. 36 (1978). *Impact of the New Mandatory Retirement Age Provisions*. No. 1497, Part II. Washington, D.C.: Bureau of National Affairs.

American Society for Personnel Administration and Bureau of National Affairs Survey No. 39 (1980). *Retirement Policies and Programs*. No. 1559, Part II. Washington, D.C.: Bureau of National Affairs.

Beller, Daniel J. (1989). *Coverage and Vesting Patterns in Private Pension Plans, 1975–1985*. In: John A. Turner and Daniel J. Beller (eds.), *Trends in Pensions* . Washington, D.C.: U.S. Department of Labor: 39-66.

Bureau of National Affairs (1987). *Older Americans in the Workforce: Challenges and Solutions*. Washington, D.C.: Bureau of National Affairs.

Burkhauser, Richard and Joseph Quinn (1983). *Is Mandatory Retirement Overrated? Evidence from the 1970s*. In: *Journal of Human Resources* 18 (3): 337-358.

Carmichael, H. Lorne (1983). *Firm-Specific Human Capital and Promotion Ladders*. In: *Bell Journal* 14 (Spring): 251-258.

Collins, H. G. (1975). *Age Discrimination Comes Home to Roost*. In: *Personnel Management* 7 (April): 24-26.

Doeringer, Peter B. and David G. Terkla (1990). *Business Necessity, Bridge Jobs, and the Nonbureaucratic Firm*. In: Peter B. Doeringer (ed.), *Bridges to Retirement: Older Workers in a Changing Labor Market*. Ithaca, N.Y.: ILR Press: 146-171.

Freeman, Smith (1977). *Wage Trends as Performance Displays Productive Potential: A Model and Application to Academic Early Retirement*. In: *Bell Journal* 8 (Autumn): 419-443.

Gustman, Alan L. and Thomas L. Steinmeier (1983). *Minimum Hours Constraints and Retirement Behavior.* In: *Contemporary Policy Issues,* supplement to Economic Inquiry 3 (April): 77-91.

Gustman, Alan L. and Thomas L. Steinmeier (1984a). *Partial Retirement and the Analysis of Retirement Behavior.* In: *Industrial and Labor Relations Review* 37 (3): 403-415.

Gustman, Alan L. and Thomas L. Steinmeier (1984b). *Modeling the Retirement Process for Policy Evaluation and Research.* In: *Monthly Labor Review* 107 (July): 26-33.

Gustman, Alan L. and Thomas L. Steinmeier (1985). *Partial Retirement and Wage Profiles of Older Workers.* In: *Industrial Relations* 24 (2): 257-265.

Halpern, Janice (1978). *Raising the Mandatory Retirement Age.* In: *New England Economic Review* (May–June): 23-35.

Harris, Milton and Bengt Holmstrom (1982). *A Theory of Wage Dynamics.* In: *Review of Economic Studies* 49 (July): 315-333.

Hayward, Mark D. and Melissa A. Hardy (1985). *Early Retirement Processes Among Older Men.* In: *Research on Aging* 7 (4): 491-515.

Honig, Marjorie (1985). *Partial Retirement Among Women.* In: *Journal of Human Resources* 20 (4): 613-621.

Honig, Marjorie and Giora Hanoch (1985). *Partial Retirement as a Separate Mode of Retirement Behavior.* In: *Journal of Human Resources* 20 (1): 21-46.

Honig, Marjorie and Cordelia Reimers (1987a). *The Labor Market Mobility of Older Workers.* New York, N.Y.: Department of Economics, Hunter College.

Honig, Marjorie and Cordelia Reimers (1987b). *Retirement, Re-entry, and Part-Time Work.* In: *Eastern Economic Journal* 13 (4): 361-371.

Hutchens, Robert M. (1986). *Delayed Payment Contracts and a Firm's Propensity to Hire Older Workers.* In: *Journal of Labor Economics* 4 (4): 439-457.

Hutchens, Robert M. (1987a). *Do Monitoring Difficulties Cause Specific Training?* Ithaca, N.Y.: NYSSILR, Cornell University.

Hutchens, Robert M. (1987b). *A Test of Lazear's Theory of Delayed Payment Contracts.* In: *Journal of Labor Economics* 5 (4): 153-170.

Hutchens, Robert M. (1988). *Do Job Opportunities Decline with Age?* In: *Industrial and Labor Relations Review* 42 (1): 89-99.

Ippolito, Richard A. (1990). *Toward Explaining Earlier Retirement After 1970.* In: *Industrial and Labor Relations Review* 43 (5): 556-569.

Kittner, Dorothy R. (1977). *Forced Retirement: How Common is it?* In: *Monthly Labor Review* 100 (December): 60-61.

Kochan, Thomas A.; Harry C. Katz, and Robert B. McKersie (1986). *The Transformation of American Industrial Relations.* New York: Basic Books.

Kotlikoff, Laurence J. and David A. Wise (1987). *The Incentive Effects of Private Pension Plans*. In: Zvi Bodie, John B. Shoven and David A. Wise (eds.), *Issues in Pension Economics*. Chicago/London: University of Chicago Press: 283-340.

Kotlikoff, Laurence J. and David A. Wise (1989). *The Wage Carrot and the Pension Stick: Retirement Benefits and Labor Force Participation*. Kalamazoo, M.I.: W. E. Upjohn Institute for Employment Research.

Krueger, Alan B. and Jorn-Steffen Pischke (1991). *The Effect of Social Security on Labor Supply: A Cohort Analysis of the Notch Generation*. Working Paper No. 3669. Boston, Mass.: National Bureau of Economic Research.

Lazear, Edward (1979). *Why Is There Mandatory Retirement?* In: *Journal of Political Economy* 87 (6): 1261-1284.

Lazear, Edward P. (1983). *Pensions as Severance Pay*. In: Zvi Bodie and John Shoven (eds.), *Financial Aspects of the U.S. Pension System*. Chicago, I.L.: University of Chicago Press: 57-85.

Levine, Martin Lyon (1988). *Age Discrimination and the Mandatory Retirement Controversy*. Baltimore, M.D.: Johns Hopkins University Press.

Louis Harris and Associates (1989). *Older Americans: Ready and Able to Work*. New York, N.Y.: Louis Harris and Associates, Inc.

Malcomson, James M. (1984). *Work Incentives, Hierarchy, and Internal Labor Markets*. In: *Journal of Political Economy* 92 (3): 486-507.

Mitchell, Olivia S. (1988). *Pensions and Older Workers*. In: Michael E. Borus, Herbert S. Parnes, Stephen Sandell and Bert Seidman (eds.), *The Older Worker*. Madison, Wisconsin: Industrial Relations Research Association: 151-166.

Mitchell, Olivia S. and Gary S. Fields (1985). *Rewards for Continued Work: The Economic Incentive for Postponing Retirement*. In: Martin David and Timothy Smeeding (eds.), *Horizontal Equity, Uncertainty, and Economic Well-Being*. Chicago, I.L.: National Bureau of Economics Research: 269-292.

Mitchell, Olivia; Phillips Levine and Sylvana Pozzebon (1988). *Retirement Differences by Industry and Occupation*. In: *Gerontology* 28 (4): 545-551.

Mitchell, Olivia S. and Rebecca Luzadis (1988). *Changes in Pension Incentives Through Time*. In: *Industrial and Labor Relations Review* 42 (October): 100-108.

Morrison, Malcolm H. (1985). *The Transition to Retirement: the Employer's Perspective*. Washington, D.C.: Bureau of Social Science Research.

Morrison, Malcolm H. (1988). *Changes in the Legal Mandatory Retirement Age: Labor Force Participation Implications*. In: Rita Ricardo-Campbell and Edward P. Lazear (eds.), *Issues in Contemporary Retirement*. Stanford University, C.A.: Hoover Institution Press: 378-405.

Rhine, Shirley (1984). *Managing Older Workers: Company Policies and Attitudes*. Conference Board Report No. 860. New York, N.Y.: The Conference Board, Inc.

Rosen, Benson and Thomas H. Jerdee (1976). *The Nature of Job-Related Stereotypes*. In: *Journal of Applied Psychology* 61 (2): 180-183.

Rosen, Benson and Thomas H. Jerdee (1985). *Older Employees: New Roles for Valued Resources*. Homewood, I.L.: Dow Jones-Irwin.

Rosenblum, Marc (1983). *ADEA: The Role of Technology in Enforcement*. In: *Aging and Work* 6 (4): 303–311.

Ruhm, Christopher (1990). *Bridge Jobs and Partial Retirement*. In: *Journal of Labor Economics* 8 (4): 482-501.

Sandell, Steven H. (1988). *Public Policies and Programs Affecting Older Workers*. In: Michael E. Borus, Herbert S. Parnes, Stephen Sandell and Bert Seidman (eds.), *The Older Worker*. Madison, Wisconsin: Industrial Relations Research Association: 207-227.

Schulz, James H. (1976). *The Economics of Aging*. Belmont, C.A.: Wadsworth Publishing Company, Inc.

Sum, Andrew M. and W. Neal Fogg (1990). *Profile of the Labor Market for Older Workers*. In: Peter B. Doeringer (ed,), *Bridges to Retirement: Older Workers in a Changing Labor Market*. Ithaca, N.Y.: ILR Press: 64-91.

Urban Institute (1981). *Mandatory Retirement Study: Final Report; The Effects of Raising the Age Limit for Mandatory Retirement in the Age Discrimination in Employment Act*. Washington, D.C.: The Urban Institute.

U.S. Department of Health and Human Services, Social Security Administration, Office of Policy, Office of Research and Statistics (1988). *Income of the Population 55 or Older, 1986*. SSA Publication No. 13-11871, Washington, D.C.

U.S. Department of Labor (1982). *Interim Report to Congress on Age Discrimination in Employment Act Studies, Report to the Congress Required by Section 5 of the Age Discrimination in Employment Act*. Washington, D.C.: U.S. Government Printing Office.

U.S. Department of Labor (1965). *The Older American Worker*. Report of the Secretary of Labor to the Congress Under Section 715 of the Civil Rights Act of 1964, Washington, D.C.: GPO.

Warshawsky, Mark J. (1989). *The Institutional and Regulatory Environment of Private Defined Benefit Pension Plans*. In: John A. Turner and Daniel J. Beller (eds.), *Trends in Pensions*.Washington, D.C.: U.S. Department of Labor: 29-38.

Wise, David A. (1984). *Pensions and the Labor Market*. National Bureau of Economic Research, Summary Report.

10 Regulating Employment and Retirement: An International Comparison between Firms and Countries

Frieder Naschold, Bert de Vroom and Bernard Casey

1   The Dialectics of Industrial Work, the Welfare State and Age Structure
2   The Early Exit/Entry Mix and Productivity/Welfare Combinations: Trends and Patterns
3   The Employment/Retirement Mix and Labour-Market and Demographic Developments
4   The National Body Policy and the Employment/Retirement Mix: Strategies and Instruments Affecting the Early Exit/Entry Mix
5   Enterprise Production Regimes and the Employment/Retirement Mix
6   The Governance of the Employment/Retirement Mix
7   Future Prospects for the Governance of the Employment/Retirement Mix

The problems surrounding the trend towards early exit from paid employment of older male workers in industrialised societies represented the point of departure for our international research network (cf. Kohli et. al., 1991). Our basic assumption that country-specific patterns of externalisation and integration of older workers could only be explained as the result of the dialectical relationship between production regimes and country-specific welfare state regimes has been supported by the results of the various national reports.

In the first part of this concluding chapter, we shall return to our dialectical model of work and welfare (part 1) and relate it to the global characteristics of the countries. Against this background we then present in brief some of the most significant empirical findings, the trends and patterns of the transition from work to welfare, their similarities and differences (part 2). This is followed by the central sections of this summary, those dealing with the various approaches – mostly neo-institutional-historical in nature – which seek to explain this empirical variation. Specifically, we look at the importance of the labour market (part 3), the strategies and instruments employed by national governments (part 4), and the role of enterprise production regimes (part 5). We then, (in part 6) turn to the governance of the mode of employment-retirement regulation in the countries studied. We conclude by looking at the current tensions within the dominant patterns of regulation of employment and retirement, arising largely out of far-reaching demographic developments, in an attempt to determine the conditions necessary for, and the opportunities provided by a strategic shift in the policies governing the relationship between industrial employment and the welfare state (part 7).

A caveat needs to be made concerning the analyses which follow. Wherever possible we have tried to put forward arguments which are both systematic and comparative in support of our interpretations. Yet, despite the fact that our international research network was relatively homogeneous and was able to pursue its studies over several years, the support for the arguments presented here remains, in some cases, exemplary rather than systematic, suggestive rather than conclusive. Nevertheless, the preceding chapters have provided a "structural anchorage" for the most important empirical findings pertaining to the regulatory dynamic of the various social systems.

1   The Dialectics of Industrial Work, the Welfare State and Age
     Structure

The seven countries studied illustrate different types of welfare states. Sweden, Germany and the Netherlands represent the characteristic continental European answer to the industrial revolution. The historical mix of social-democratic and conservative regime traits have resulted in a highly differentiated social insurance system with relatively high levels of benefit. The UK, and in particular the USA, represent the liberal welfare state, characterised by its primary reliance on the market. Since these welfare state regimes support only those who are unable to provide for themselves in the market place, they have resulted in a less differentiated system of social insurances. At the same time the levels of benefit are low. The former East Germany and Japan are particular cases. The official East German policy was dominated by the concept of full-employment for everyone and every age group. Externalisation was effectively defined out of the system. As a result, a welfare state regime (in the western sense) was not very well developed. Japan once set itself the task of establishing a continental European welfare state regime, but the idea was modified during the 1980s in favour of establishing a liberal regime with a less differentiated social security system and correspondingly lower levels of benefit.

Apart from intra-national sectoral differences – to which we shall return – differences can be identified between dominant patterns of industrial production regimes. The dominant production regimes in the USA are

Table 1: Country-Specific Constellations of Industrial Employment and Welfare Provision

		Welfare State	
		Relatively Low Level of Provision and Differentiation	Relatively High Level of Provision and Differentiation
Industrial Systems	Taylorism/ Fordism	USA Great Britain GDR	
	Diversified Quality Production		Netherlands Germany Sweden
	Toyotism/ Lean Production	Japan	

those based on "Taylorism" and "Fordism". In the European countries, production regimes vary between the American model and the diversified, quality production model. Japanese production regimes were originally influenced by organisational models imported from the USA, but subsequently they developed into a specifically national model of "Toyotism" or "lean production".

The wide diversity of industrial systems and forms of public welfare provision suggest a considerable degree of heterogeneity between country-specific contexts. This diversity is summarised – at a high level of aggregation and in an ideal-typical manner – in table 1.

In all the countries studied, the dialectical relationship between industrial production and the welfare state involves two points of transition. These two interfaces are of critical importance as they determine – with reference to both individual workers and benefit-recipients – both the quantity and quality of the exchange relations between the two systems.

The mode of entry into paid employment regulates the age-selective volume, and, in conjunction with the education and training system, the human-resource skills and qualifications of the workforce. Clearly this has repercussions for the "inputs" provided by the state and by society at large, and the expectations held by firms.

In 1945, 80 per cent of 25–35 year old Germans had only minimum school leaving qualifications, by 1985 this had fallen to only 50 per cent and by 2025 it is projected to stand at only 20 per cent (Working paper of the conference "Erwerbsarbeit der Zukunft" in Berlin, 1992).

The second interface, namely the exit of older workers out of the employment system and into the state welfare system, is subject to regulation by both the state and firms themselves. The trends and changing problem

Table 2: Age-Selective Problem Constellations in the Context of Industrial Employment
and the Welfare State

Functional Relationship Between Industrial Employment and the Welfare State	Social Problem Constellation
Supply of Labour	
Quantitatively	Distribution of Employment Between Younger and Older Age Groups
Qualitatively	Problems of Productivity, Innovation and Mobility
Economic Growth	Quantitative and Qualitative Importance of the Input of Labour on Growth Rates
Social Consumption	Possibilities and Difficulties of Financing Systems of Social, Inter-Personal, Inter-Temporal and Inter-Sectoral Redistribution
Social Integration	Quantitative and Qualitative Regulation of Exit in Old Age Affect Constellations of Consensus and Conflict within the Firm, Impacting on Wages, Productivity and the Whole Area of Personnel Management
Externalisation	Quantitative and Qualitative Regulation by the Welfare State both Supports and Restricts Firms in Their Aim of Externalising the Negative Effects of Production

constellations in and around this interface, and their modes of regulation, have been a central topic of this study, and will be recapitulated in the following sections.

Clearly, both interfaces exert a profound influence on the interrelations between the two systems, affecting a wide range of social and corporate problem areas. Table 2 illustrates, by way of example, the way in which the interface of age-selective exit affects a large number of highly relevant problems, touching on all the functional relationships between industrial employment and welfare-state systems.

All the functional relationships and problem areas identified so far within the dialectical relationship between industrial employment and the welfare state have been described with respect to the reference model of the "standard" age distribution (seen both as an empirical fact and a social norm). This age-structural reference model, whose origins go back to the 19th century, can be summarised as follows:
- a social age structure in the form of an "age pyramid";
- higher turnover rates (high rates of occupational disability and death) among both younger and older workers, a concomitant of the phase of extensive population growth;

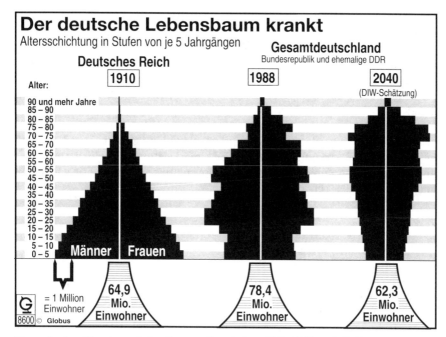

Figure 1: Age Structure of the German Population, 1910, 1988 and 2040

– rigid age limits and mechanisms regulating the transition between the three "life-phases" linked to, and an expression of, the mode of state regulation in old age.

The age-structural reference model applies at both national and firm level, a fact which can be nicely illustrated by two (exemplary) empirical findings (Working paper of the conference "Erwerbsarbeit der Zukunft" in Berlin, 1992).

First, as figure 1 shows, changes have occurred in the age structure of the German population over a period of some 80 years, and the prospects for the coming half century. A conventional, pyramidal age structure obtained before the First World War; there were already signs of erosion among younger age cohorts in the 1980s; and a reversal of the pyramid can be expected for the year 2040.

Second, as studies made of the Japanese corporate context (cf. Kimura et. al., 1990; Oka, 1992) have clearly shown at the level of the individual firm, the empirical and normative significance of a pyramidal age mix of the workforce in Japanese firms. A number of important mechanisms, serving the aims of social and systemic integration within Japanese firms are based on such a pyramidal age-structural reference model. From our analysis of the trend age structure of the German population – a trend which is matched more or less closely in all the countries considered here – it is clear that the reference model of a "standard" age distribution is being steadily eroded, as the social age pyramid begins, from the mid 1990s, to, as it were, stand on its head. The already extremely complex constellation constituted by the interaction of industrial employment and state welfare is thus gradually being overdetermined by a secular, demographic trend towards aging workforce structures. The added complications to which this trend gives rise are the subject of the more speculative analysis with which our analysis concludes (cf. part 7).

2   The Early Exit/Entry Mix and Productivity/Welfare Combinations: Trends and Patterns

To begin this concluding summary, we wish to establish a quantitative frame of reference and a statistical point of departure for the comparative analysis of the early exit/entry mix and the productivity/welfare combination on which it is based. This represents both a temporal and a geographical extension of the statistical analyses already conducted in this field (Kohli et. al., 1991; Jacobs and Rein in this volume). We start by looking at the trend changes in the male labour force aged between 60 and 64 in each of the seven countries (figure 2).

A very clear picture emerges from the time-series data on labour-force participation rates – an indicator of the quantitative relationship between paid employment and the welfare state among older workers – for the countries studied over the observation period. In 1970 labour-force partici-pation rates for men aged between 60 and 64 in the seven countries were relatively high and the inter-country differences relatively low. Participation averaged 75% for this group as a whole, ranging between the two extremes of 69% for West Germany and 83% for the UK. This picture changed dramatically in the two decades which followed: firstly, the average level fell sharply to 54%; secondly, the gap between the two extremes widened substantially to 23% for the Netherlands and 73% for Japan (78% for the GDR before its inclusion into the Federal Republic).

To illustrate the current extent of the divergence between countries and the changes of older workers' participation rates over time, i.e., the diver-gences and convergences between the different national trends, a static indicator (labour-force participation in 1990) must be combined with a dynamic indicator (changes in participation rates from 1970 to 1990). And to

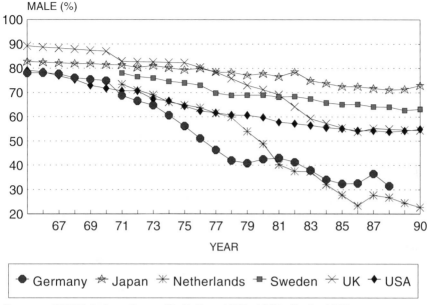

Source: OECD Labor Force Statistics 1970–1990, Paris 1992.

Figure 2: International Comparison of the Participation Rates of Men Aged 60–64

complete the picture, we have added some aggregate indicators characterising the pattern of transition from work to welfare, and the different productivity/welfare combinations indicating both the supportive and limiting conditions for the employment/exit relationship. The transition pattern can either be a single movement from employment to non-employment or a series of movements involving a greater or lesser level of part-time and/or occasional working (figure 3).

On the basis of this analysis, we can distinguish between three different types of country, two extreme and one "middle-of-the-road". The extreme types are represented by the Netherlands and, to a lesser degree, Germany on the one hand, and Japan, the former GDR, and, to a lesser degree, Sweden, on the other. The Netherlands, which takes pole position in the trend towards early exit/entry, had the fastest decrease in participation rates over time (-69%), resulting in a very low final rate (23% in 1990). Japan and the former GDR can be seen as the exact opposites of the Dutch pattern: both countries are characterised by a relatively low rate of decline in participation rates over time; consequently participation by older workers was still relatively high in 1990.

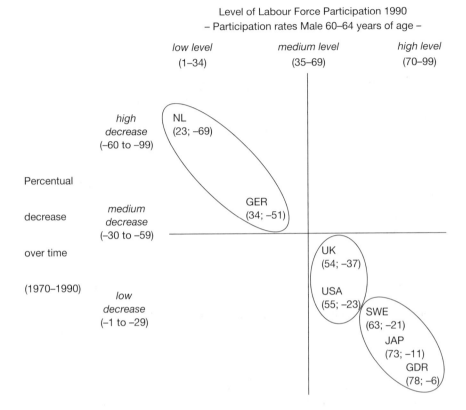

Figure 3: Country-Specific Trends and Patterns of Participation by Older Workers

Note: The first number indicates the participation rate in 1990, the secong the percentage decrease over time.

Source OECD Labour Force Statistics 1970–1990; for GDR data see Figure 2, cf. Schuster/Sthieler in this volume; own calculations.

The former GDR must be considered a special case. Until 1990 labour-force participation was high for all groups of workers, and especially so – in comparison to other countries – for workers in the 65–69 year age group. Since 1990, however, the situation has changed radically and remarkably quickly. Within the space of a year East Germany virtually moved from the one extreme – high and stable participation rates – to the other, the continental externalisation type.

The two English-speaking countries, the UK and the USA are located between the two extreme types: intermediate participation rates (54% and

Table 3: Country-Specific Forms of Transition from Employment to Retirement

		Labour Force Participation Rate		
		Low	Medium	High
Transition Pattern	Gradual		USA	Japan Sweden GDR
	Immediate	Germany Netherlands		

55%) go hand in hand with am average rate of decrease over time (37% and 23%).

In addition to the quantitative distribution of the employment/retirement mix in the countries studied, we can also distinguish between two patterns of transition from work to retirement: the one-step movement from the employment to the welfare system, and the gradual, staged transition. The distribution of the two forms of transition across the countries is as follows:

Table 3 indicates two centres of gravity and a consistent and uniform developmental logic across the seven countries. Countries with low labour-force participation rates, such as the Netherlands and Germany, are characterised by a one-stage transition pattern, whereas those with high labour-force participation rates, such as Japan, the GDR and Sweden, all exhibit a gradual, staged pattern of transition. The two countries with intermediate participation rates, Great Britain and the USA, are consistent with both types of transition. At the empirical level at least, national constellations characterised by low participation rates and a staged transition, and high rates and a one-off transition do not occur. Here the former GDR can be taken, as in other respects, as an historical "guinea pig" which, by virtue of its sudden "leap" from the one predominant employment/welfare constellation to the other, serves to confirm the above statements.

So far we have taken males and their exit behaviour as the point of departure and reference. Any attempt to explain gender-specific differences – of both a qualitative and quantitative nature – in early exit/entry patterns must take account of the socially dominant mode according to which women are integrated into the labour market, and the way female employment interacts with the provisions governing retirement.

Figure 4 shows that female participation rates rose in all the countries studied during the observation period.

The leading country in this international trend towards greater female participation in the labour market is clearly Sweden, just ahead of the GDR. By contrast, the increase in participation rates was very limited in (West) Germany and the Netherlands (cf. Olofsson and Petersson in this volume).

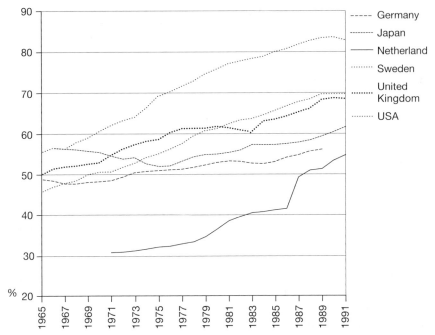

Source: OECD Labour Force Statistics, different volumes, Paris.

Figure 4: Female Participation Rates in the Selected Countries

This overall pattern does conceal a number of, in some cases contradictory
trends, however:
– female employment in Sweden and the GDR is/was closely oriented
  towards standard, male, full-time employment;
– in the other countries, women's employment has tended to remain
  discontinuous and primarily short-term oriented, despite the rise in the
  overall level of participation;
– in all the countries studied, part-time work constitutes a very significant
  component of female employment. Unlike for males, part-time work for
  women is far more readily accepted socially. This is not to ignore the
  considerable differences in the role played by part-time work in the
  different countries. Germany, for instance, where part-time employment
  accounts for just 14% of total employment, lags far behind the
  Scandinavian countries and the Netherlands with figures of over 25%,
  and Great Britain with 23% (Federal Ministry of Labour, 1992).

Let us now turn to a direct comparison of early exit/entry patterns between
male and female workers aged 55 to 64 (table 4).

Despite significant quantitative differences in absolute level, older male

Tab. 4: Labour-Force Participation Rates for Men and Women Aged between 55 and 64 in Selected Countries — 1970 to 1991

Country	Gender	(Participation Rats in Percent)					(in Percent Points)
		1970	1975	1980	1985	1991	1970—1991
Germany	Male	80.7	69.8	67.3	60.1	57.7	−23.0
	Female	42.2	25.4	28.9	23.8	25.3	−16.9
Japan	Male	86.6	86.0	85.4	83.0	84.5	− 2.1
	Female	44.4	43.7	45.3	45.3	48.5	4.1
Netherlands	Male	80.8	72.2	63.2	47.0	43.4	−37.4
	Female	13.8	14.2	14.4	12.3	15.3	1.5
Sweden	Male	85.4	82.0	78.7	75.9	75.5	− 9.9
	Female	44.5	49.6	55.3	59.9	66.9	22.4
United	Male	91.3	87.6	81.6	68.8	67.5	−23.8
Kingdom	Female	39.3	40.1	39.1	35.1	39.2	− 0.1
USA	Male	80.7	74.6	71.2	67.3	66.3	−14.4
	Female	42.2	40.7	41.0	41.7	45.0	2.8

Notes: The Data for Germany 1991 Refer to 1989.
         The Data for the Netherlands 1970 Refer to 1971.
Source: OECD Labour Force Statistics 1970—1990, Paris 1992.

workers in all the selected countries exhibit the well-known and unambiguous trend towards sinking participation rates. For women workers the picture is far more complex. Although in the majority of countries declining participation rates are to be observed for women workers, too, this trend occurs at a considerably lower absolute level. Moreover, in the case of Sweden we find a substantial increase in rates, while in the GDR and, to a lesser extent, in Japan participation by older women has remained relatively constant. Both these findings suggest that exit behaviour for male and female workers differs in significant ways.

A more subtle analysis – differentiating between two age groups (55–59 years and 60–64 years) – reveals that in some countries the overall participation trend for older women conceals contradictory age-group-specific developments (table 5).

– For the 55–59 year olds, female participation rates increased in all the selected countries, with the highest growth rates in Sweden, the lowest in Great Britain, and relatively constant values in the GDR.

– Among the 60–64 year olds, on the other hand, participation declined in all the countries – with the exception of Sweden – with the fastest rate of decline recorded in Germany, the lowest in Japan. Sweden is again the

Table 5: Percentage of Older Women in the Labour Force by Age Group

Country	Age Group	(Participation Rates in Percent)			(in Percent Points)
		1970	1980	1991	1970−1991
Germany	55−59	37.2	39.9	40.7	3.5
	60−64	22.5	12.5	10.7	−11.8
Japan	55−59	48.7	50.5	55.5	6.8
	60−64	39.1	38.8	40.7	1.6
Netherlands	55−49	17.7	18.5	22.8	5.1
	60−64	11.9	9.5	7.8	− 4.1
Sweden	55−59	65.0	68.8	79.4	14.4
	60−64	44.5	41.0	54.7	10.2
United Kingdom	55−59	50.1	53.6	54.5	4.4
	60−64	28.0	22.4	24.1	− 3.9
USA	55−59	48.8	48.1	55.4	6.6
	60−64	34.8	32.9	34.8	0.0
(German Democratic Republic)	55−59	62.0	70.0	77.0	15.0
	60−64	22.0	13.0	13.0	− 9.0

Notes: The Data for Germany 1991 Refer to 1989.
The Data for the Netherlands 1970 Refer to 1971.
The Data for GDR 1970 Refer to 1972; the Data for 1991 Refer to 1989.
Source: OECD Labour Force Statistics 1970−1990, Paris 1992. For GDR Data See Figure 1, cf. Schuser/Stiehler in this Volume.

exception which proves the rule; even for this age group participation rates increased. The Swedish special case might well be due to the overwhelming importance of part-time work for women (cf. Olofsson/ Petersson in this volume).

The relevance of social stratification – in terms of income, educational level etc. – to issues of social concern is in most cases readily apparent, and is usually well documented. In looking at age-selective aspects of the transition from industrial employment to the welfare state from an international perspective, however, a number of problems arose, not only of an empirical, but also of a conceptual and methodological nature. For this reason, we can do no more at this point than to present a number of selected findings pointing to configurations which are specific to social strata and which differ from the overall trends described above. They are in most cases derived from our case studies and must be considered as being exemplary in nature.

- In contrast to our initial supposition, we found little significant difference, particularly in the German data, in the early exit/entry patterns of the broad mass of blue-collar as against those of white-collar workers.
- At the same time, it was a feature common to all the countries analysed that high-level management tends to spend considerably longer within the employment system than the broad social strata covering the majority of blue- and white-collar workers. This reflects not only a simple extension of full-time work beyond normal retirement age, but sometimes part-time work, but often part-time activity or suitable outplacements for this group. Clearly, the fate of such workers contrasts starkly with that of unskilled and semi-skilled workers whose labour often becomes superfluous as firms seek to make their production "leaner", and who consequently come under heavy pressure to withdraw completely from paid employment.
- In practically all the countries studied, we continue to find a socio-structural constellation in which workers of above average age and below-average skill levels and wages, together with discontinuous employment biographies stand in a symbiotic relationship to firms operating at the profitability margin. We will look at firms in the secondary labour market, and the considerable international variation in this more closely in the context of our analysis of production regimes.
- Another social group differing from the overall trend consists of a complex sub-group of women workers for whom early retirement does not constitute a feasible option. In Germany and Great Britain, for example, some women, although employed, are not entitled to pension benefits of their own; either because they have paid contributions for an insufficient number of years, or because, on marriage, they opted to be insured through their husband or to receive their pension entitlements as a lump sum. In some countries, women are, for similar reasons, only entitled to a pension if they continue to work until the age of 65. Finally, some women are forced – due to an inadequate level of social-security provision – simply to continue to work for as long as possible. Of course, it must also be mentioned that for many women withdrawal from paid employment does not mean a simultaneous entry into retirement, but a return to "the family" and thus, as far as pension entitlements are concerned, to a state of limbo, which may come to an end through entitlement to an early-retirement benefit or to a standard pension at 65.

It goes without saying that the quantitative trends and qualitative patterns of early exit/entry examined so far are embedded in a more general economic and political context. Early exit/entry both constitutes one, alongside countless other elements, of an overall social context and is itself conditioned by this framework. As we have already seen, the dominant influences on the interface between employment and retirement are exerted by, on the one hand, economic growth and productivity trends, and, on the other, changing state welfare policies (in the widest sense of the word): long-term economic productivity trends are essential to provide sufficient resources for redistributive social policies, as most clearly seen in the structured financial benefits provided by the welfare state; at the same time, the services offered and the benefits provided by the welfare state affect the cost structures of both the private and public sectors, the level of aggregate demand, and, in the final analysis, the conditions for economic growth via their effects on the supply of labour (Fujii, 1992)[1].

In the following we shall attempt, on the basis of selected indicators, to sketch at least the contours of the political and economic context which, in each country, sets the conditions for the early exit/entry mix. The limited reliability and solidity of some of these indicators, in particular the welfare benefit level, should be apparent enough. Equally obviously, in the real world the relationships between the micro variables and the overall context are not one-way and causal but complex interactions.

Figure 5 brings together the various relationships between the early exit/entry mix, productivity trends and the level of welfare benefit identified in our seven countries.

The first point shown by the figure is that there are no linear, causal relationships between the three groups of variables. Nevertheless, three national constellation types emerge relatively clearly, each with varying degree of homogeneity and differing relationships between the three variables.

- The most homogeneous group is that consisting of the two continental European countries, Germany and the Netherlands, in which relatively low activity rates go hand in hand with rapid productivity growth and a high level of welfare benefit. These two countries can be seen as prototypical "non-working, high productivity, high welfare" societies.
- A relatively high degree of homogeneity exists between the two English-speaking countries, Great Britain and the USA. Here an intermediate level of activity and welfare are associated with relatively slow long-term productivity growth.
- Heterogeneity characterises the group of countries with high rates of labour-force participation: Japan, the GDR and Sweden. In Japan very rapid productivity growth is associated with a relatively low level of public welfare provision; in Sweden an intermediate rate of productivity growth is linked to a high level of welfare-state benefit; in the GDR slow productivity growth went along with a low level of welfare benefit.

Besides determining the nature of the statistical relationship between the three variable-complexes for the various countries, two, more systematic statements can be derived from our empirical findings: on both the demand

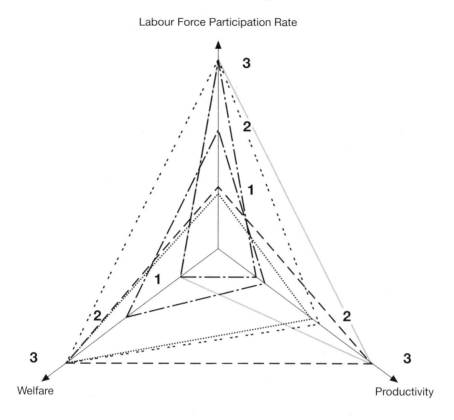

Labour Force Participation Rate

		Labour Force Participation Rate	Productivity	Welfare
Germany	— — — —	low	high	high
GDR	—·—·—	high	low	low
Japan	————	high	high	low
Netherland	················	low	medium	high
Sweden	—··—··—	high	medium	high
UK/USA	—·—·—	medium	low	medium

high	3
medium	2
low	1

Figure 5: Early Exit/Entry Mix, Prductivity Trends and the Level of Welfare Benefit

and the supply side, they stake out the possible "spread" of national development paths.

As far as the supply side is concerned it is probable that, without medium to high productivity growth over the longer term, no country can afford to generate high early exit rates and high levels of benefit. The converse is not true, however: relatively high rates of long-term productivity growth do not necessarily lead to high benefit levels and early-exit rates.

On the demand side, our empirical findings show that a high level of social consumption, such as exists in the Netherlands and Germany, i.e., relatively low activity rates and high levels of welfare provision, can clearly be beneficial to productivity; conversely though, a constellation involving high levels of social consumption with mediocre productivity growth can, despite high activity rates, lead to massive productivity problems in the longer term, as recent developments in Sweden have shown.

In the case of the GDR, two contra-intentional effects can be observed on the supply and demand sides: high and stable activity rates produce very limited levels of welfare-state benefits; a low level of social consumption does not necessarily lead to more rapid productivity growth.

3   The Employment/Retirement Mix and Labour-Market and Demographic Developments

The quantitative and statistical analyses described in the first two sections have enabled us to identify a number of sub-trends diverging from the homogeneous basic trend, and a limited number of different, but clearly defined constellations of the employment/retirement mix and the productivity/welfare combination at national level. It is the task of the analyses which follow to identify the social factors which offer plausible explanations for this statistical and empirical variation.

The academic and political discussion in this field is dominated by three explanatory approaches.

- The "classical" debate on the early-exit problematic seeks to identify the central explanatory factors for early retirement patterns in changing external variables, such as labour market trends and demographic developments (cf. among others Kohli et. al., 1991 and Schmähl, 1988, 1989): early retirement is seen as a reflection of labour market trends at the macro level.

- The Titmussian view sees the welfare state as the regulator of the retirement process (cf., in addition to Kohli et. al., 1991; Esping Andersson, 1985, 1990, and Heinelt, 1991), and early retirement is seen as a particular steering problem for the welfare state.

- The supply side approach, in so far as it is concerned with the problems of mandatory retirement, long-term employment contracts and firm-specific early retirement provisions, is based on an extension of neoclassical theories of the firm (cf. the bibliography in Hutchens in this volume), and decisions on older workers' exit from employment are seen here primarily as a consequence of individual firms' marginal-cost calculations.

Taking these theoretical traditions as a point of departure, we will initially examine the role played by the labour market and demographic trends – factors usually considered as exogenous – in determining the employment/ retirement relation. We then turn to institutional-political factors situated within the national body politic, and, finally, to institutional-economic factors linked to firms' production regimes. The limitations inherent in such partial approaches will then lead us to the more complex theoretical constructs of the governance-school (cf. Campbell, Hollingsworth and Lindberg, 1991).

Labour market trends are very often put forward to explain the early-exit trend, the former being seen as a variable exogenous to the latter (Kohli et. al., 1991), and, at first sight, a whole body of empirical findings can undoubtedly be adduced in support of such a macro-level, labour-market-oriented approach. Econometric analyses, for example, suggest that in Britain over the 1970s and 1980s each 1% rise in unemployment led, in the short term, to a 3% fall in activity rates among 55–59 year olds, and a 6% fall among 60–64 year olds, and in the longer-term to falls of 4% and 9% respectively (cf. Casey and Wood in this volume). And indeed, the labour-market constellations prevailing in the countries examined in our study tend to support this approach, at least for the two extreme groups – Germany and the Netherlands with long periods of relatively high unemployment, and Japan, Sweden and the GDR in which labour was in short supply for most of the observation period.

Table 6: State of the Labour Market and Labour-Force Participation Rates

		Early-Exit Level (as Measured by Participation rates)		
		High	Medium	Low
Unemployment Level	Persistently High	FRG NL	GB USA	
	Low			Japan GDR Sweden

Table 6 illustrates the – provisional – finding of a relationship between the state of the labour market and early retirement trends.

However, a more thorough analysis of labour market conditions and labour-force participation rates in the various countries over a longer period, taking in several business-cycle swings, produces a far more diffuse picture, one indicating that the labour market exerts very different effects on the early exit/entry mix.
Let us take Germany as the point of departure for this closer analysis (figure 6).

What is true of the German early retirement trend between 1970 and 1973 applies more or less equally to all the countries studied: the trend to early retirement unambiguously preceded the changes on the labour market which occurred in the mid-1970s. Neither in those countries which have experienced high and lasting unemployment since the mid 1970s, nor in those with a quasi permanent labour shortage, such as Japan, Sweden and the former GDR, can labour market developments be seen as the initiator

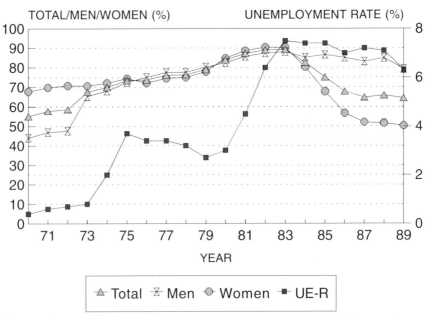

Source: Association of German Pension Insurers, annual statistics and own calculation.

Figure 6: Early Retirement as a Share of Total Retirements in Germany, 1970–1989 of the trend towards early exit/entry. Initially, at least, labour-market and early exit/entry trends were not linked.

Equally, there can be no doubt that, after this initial phase, events on national labour markets exerted a profound effect on the relationship of employment to retirement. In countries such as Germany and the Netherlands – and, after the start of the 1980s, Great Britain – mass unemployment undoubtedly gave a considerable boost to the already discernible trend towards early retirement, whereas in countries with low exit rates the attempts at integration were intensified. To put it another way: at this historical phase the worsening state of the labour market exerted a supportive effect on early exit/entry in the countries studied, establishing a link between the labour market and the employment/retirement relationship.

Analysis suggests a third constellation characterising the relationship between the labour market and early exit/entry, at least in the Netherlands, Germany and Great Britain, with their high rates of unemployment. As the trend to early retirement persisted, it increasingly took on institutional forms and became increasingly autonomous, enabling it to endure phases of relatively full employment such as the early to mid 1980s.

To sum up, contrary to the view that the relationship between labour market trends and early exit/entry is of a global and generalised nature, we have identified three distinct types of impact: in the initial phase the two areas were "decoupled"; this was followed in the mid 1970s by very strong supportive effects, which subsequently, in the course of the institutionalisation of the early retirement regime, played the role of catalyst. This historical variation in the relationship between the labour market situation and the employment biographies of older workers is true of both high-unemployment countries and, conversely, of those affected by labour shortages. Looked at historically from its initial phase, early exit/entry clearly has a secular trend component. This might well reflect a historical reduction in the overuse of productive potential which characterised the period during and after the Second World War, a view supported by longitudinal studies from the USA (Sheppard in Kohli et. al., 1991). The dominant effects in the more recent early-exit developments are supportive labour-market and institutionalisation effects. From the mid 1990s these will increasingly be superseded by demographic trends. That demographic trends have had little effect in the countries studied during the post-war period is due to the fact that the (roughly) pyramidal age structure of the labour force has remained intact in these countries. In the decades to come, though, demographic developments will constitute a serious structural problem to the employment/retirement relationship (cf. section 6).

4   The National Body Politic and the Employment/Retirement Mix:
     Strategies and Instruments Affecting the Early Exit/Entry Mix

As we have seen, the empirical variation with regard to the different levels
and rates of early exit/entry, both between the different countries and over
the 20–year observation period, can be partly explained by changes in the
state of national labour markets. However, not only does this approach
leave a considerable proportion of such variation unexplained, the more
important point is that national labour-market trends clearly cannot be
treated as merely reflecting higher-order economic forces on national and
international goods and financial markets; in other words, the national
labour market cannot be seen purely as an exogenous variable as it is itself
partly dependent on national and supranational political strategies (cf.
Therborn, 1985).

At the same time, the international variation in national labour-market
situations clearly provides the macroeconomic backdrop against which
national governments pursue a greater or lesser degree of regulatory
activity. At the microeconomic level, the justification for government regulation of the early exit/entry mix, of the transition from work to welfare –
and a determinant of its intensity – is to be found in market failure at the
age-selective point of transition. The constellation of transaction costs
borne by firms in personnel recruitment, implicit long-term contracts,
seniority rules and variations in productivity and value generates systematic
problems of asymmetric information and negative external effects which
together justify systematic political intervention (cf. the theoretical debate
which followed Lazear, 1979). And, if nothing else, our national studies
show unambiguously that all national governments intervene in and regulate the transition process from employment to retirement; only the extent
to which they do so varies.

The empirically and theoretically relevant question is, thus, not whether
state regulation of the employment/retirement interface is necessary, or
whether it in fact exists. The existence and relevance of government
regulation should rather be taken as a point of departure from which to
consider the differences in regulatory patterns between countries which,
together with labour market effects, can explain national trends and patterns in the early exit/entry mix.

In seeking to conceptualise state regulation of the employment/retire-
ment interface our analysis draws on two eminent theoretical traditions:
– the approach in the tradition of Heimann and Titmus, a theory of the
   welfare state in terms of a classical and comprehensive theory of state
   intervention in the economy and working life (Heimann, 1980; Titmuss,
   1950);
– the modern theory of regulation, which conceives state intervention in

the context of a complementary relationship between the state and markets, rather than an hierarchical view of governmental steering [cf. the modified statism approach of Ikenberry (Hall and Ikenberry, 1989) and Samuels (1987) and also the French "Regulation School"].

The first step in the comparative analysis of national political regimes is to establish the extent to which clearly identifiable national strategies and instrument-profiles exist at national level which correlate closely with the rates and levels of early exit/entry observed. In line with the traditions just mentioned, we understand by the term "strategy" a relatively consistent and stable pattern of action implemented by collective actors, which is either based on more or less discursive and explicit intentions, or which at least induces intentional causal chains. Instruments are the immediate and concrete means of action employed in the course of such strategies, so designed as to realise strategic aims.

On the surface, the strategic approaches implemented in the seven countries over the past twenty years constitute a prodigious diversity of forms of state regulation. Yet, this plethora can be relatively easily reduced to three underlying strategic functions of state employment/retirement policies.

- First, the social-policy and redistributive function: state employment/ retirement policies serve to redistribute life chances (employment, income, education and training, health) interpersonally and intertemporally. All state policies which affect the labour market and demographic trends must be taken into account here, to the extent that the accent is on social-policy, transfer and compensatory functions.

- Second, the supply-side, productivity-raising function of age-selective policies aims to bring about as comprehensive a development of human-resource potential as possible, its most cost-effective and efficient implementation in, and exit from the employment system, all with a view to maximising macroeconomic growth.

- Third, the procedural-cooperation function of state employment/retirement policy aims to influence the form in which leading social actor-systems deal with human-resource issues in the various "arena-structures".

By means of this distinction between three underlying functions of state employment/retirement policies, it is possible through comparative analysis to identify and specify quite distinct national strategies.

The following typological summary of the central dimensions of state employment/welfare policies in the seven countries (table 7) points to the existence of two distinct, quasi "natural" basic types: on the one hand, a social-policy, demand-side orientated, state externalisation strategy, based on

Table 7: State Strategies Affecting the Employment/Retirement Mix in the Selected Countries

Dimensions of State Strategies	USA	GB	NL	FRG	Japan	Sweden	GDR
Growth/Productivity Function: Work Principle	+	–	–	–	+++	+++	++
Social-Policy/ Redistributive Function: Transfer Principle	–	+	+++	+++	+	++	++
Cooperation Function	–	–	++	++	++	+++	++
Role of the State	Market Facilitators Deregu-lation	Orga-nisation	Cooperative Welfare State: Intertemporal Redistribution		Administrative Guidance	Cooperative Regulating Involving Entire State Apparatus	Centralised State Planning
Role of (Age-Selective) Human Ressources	Production Factor Steered by Market Forces		Flexibility Potential for Social Policy		Strategic Competitive Factor	Production Factor Protected by Welfare State Regulation	Mainstay of Production and Welfare

an interpersonal and intertemporal transfer principle, in which the government offers incentives to firms and workers to transfer the employment-linked risks of older workers to the welfare state system, usually, but not necessarily, with a parallel shift in the cost burden; on the other, a supply-side, internalisation strategy based on the "work (for everybody) principle", in which growth and productivity effects are seen as of central importance and as a necessary precondition for the attempts made to integrate older workers.

Germany and the Netherlands can be considered as typical representatives of state externalisation strategies. Our comparative analysis clearly shows that the Dutch and German political regimes concentrate heavily – with long-term, broad-based and intensive strategies – on the redistributive and cooperative functions, while ignoring the productivity function. The dominance of the transfer principle and procedural cooperation is a typical characteristic of employment/retirement policies in Germany and Holland. The differences which do exist between the two countries at this level, in particular the more clearly "statist" tradition in Germany as opposed to the meso-corporatist tradition in the Netherlands, need not concern us at present.

Japan, Sweden and the former GDR embody the second type of strategy, dominated by governmental efforts at integration. Especially in Japan, throughout the entire postwar period (at least until 1989 and the change of course in favour of expanding domestic demand) both the state and the leading collective organisations pursued growth, productivity and active labour market policies which, based as they were on the work principle, both set the framework, and provided the prerequisites for the integrationist strategies pursued by the corporate sector. Government policies aimed at redistribution were concentrated on providing a minimum level of security, with the greatest stress accorded a "reciprocal consensus" (Samuels) between all the actors involved in this policy arena.

At first sight, the strategy pursued in Sweden would appear, with its emphasis on the work principle, its labour-market, growth and productivity policies, and the cooperative style adopted by all those involved in the political process, to correspond perfectly with the ideal-typical integration strategy. The report on Sweden, however, (Olofsson/Petersson, which comes to rather different conclusions than those drawn by Wadensjö in his analysis in Kohli et. al., 1991) reveals a second, often covert strategic approach, one termed "accommodation", tantamount to externalisation. As will become clear when we turn our attention to the instruments employed, the Swedish state has in fact developed a whole range of instruments – flexible retirement pension, partial pensions etc. – which, together with the underlying political aim of achieving a high degree of distributive justice, are capable of setting powerful incentives. In a context of unfavourable economic and labour market developments these can also serve as mechanisms of externalisation as well as of internalisation. All the same, despite this ambivalence, from an international perspective Swedish policy is dominated by the integration strategy.

The former GDR can also be considered as a clear case of the dominance of an integration strategy, one in line with the social consensus on the desirability of full employment, whereby work in the GDR was seen not only as a right but also as a duty. The difference between this political strategy and those pursued by Japan and Sweden – in addition, of course, to the fundamental questions of planning and public ownership vs. market and private ownership – can be found in two factors: the pursuit of the prime aim of full employment to the detriment of productivity growth, and a distributive policy which bore no relation to productivity. In the final analysis it was these two elements which destroyed the economic basis for the GDR's integration policy.

The USA and Great Britain, on the other hand, cannot be classified by means of the externalisation/internalisation dichotomy. Neither country has developed long-term and – more or less – explicit policies reflecting a desire on the part of the state to actively influence the employment/retirement interface. In neither country can the early exit/entry mix be interpreted as resulting from an active strategy pursued by the state. Increasingly regulation has been left to the market.

Our analysis of state employment/welfare policies thus reveals three distinct strategy types: externalisation, internalisation and market-oriented strategies, with one of these strategy types dominating the approach taken in each of our seven countries (table 8).

Further analysis indicates that these strategy types are based in each case on differing views of the role to be played by the state and the role ascribed to (age-selective) human resources (cf. table 9). Extending the line of enquiry pursued by Samuels (1987), it is apparent that in Germany and the Netherlands, the two representatives of the externalisation strategy, the state brings together other social actors, ensures their cooperation and redistributes life chances, while (age-selective) human resources are seen largely as offering a flexibility potential which can be drawn on when required. Japan and Sweden, although they both pursue a strategy of internalisation, differ considerably as regards both the role played by the state and that accorded to human resources. While the Swedish state is entrusted with the task of macroeconomic and political regulation, the role of the Japanese state centres on so-called "administrative guidance". In Japan the workforce is seen as a strategic competitive factor, whereas in Sweden workers are seen as a factor of production (among others), one entitled to protection by the welfare state.

These two characteristics are different again in the USA and Great

Tab. 8: Strategy by Country

Strategy type	Country
Externalisation Strategy	NL
	Germany
Internalisation Strategy	Japan
	GDR
	Sweden
Market-oriented Strategie	USA
	Great Britain

Britain, both of which pursue a market-oriented age-selective strategy. In both cases the state plays the role of "market facilitator": in the USA this tends to take the form of an active policy of deregulation and privatisation; in Great Britain the state fulfills an "orientation function" for the corporate sector. Human resources are seen first and foremost merely as factors of production which can be steered by market forces without state intervention to facilitate cooperation etc.

If political strategies are to go beyond mere symbolic proclamation and are to have an impact on the real world, they require appropriate and effective instruments to ensure their implementation. Accordingly, the next step is to examine whether such instruments are in fact in operation in the various countries in support of their respective strategy types. Three types of instrument can be distinguished, consistent with each of the strategy types.

Externalisation strategies contrast three types of provision to facilitate early exit (these are the central topic of the study by Kohli et. al., 1991):
- disability pension permitting early retirement as a consequence of deteriorating health and work performance;
- unemployment pension linked to the level of demand for labour on the labour market, covering early retirement schemes and special measures implemented by the unemployment insurance system;
- flexible pension linked to stipulations on the length of time for which social-insurance contributions have been paid, offering a number of ways of entering retirement before standard retirement age.

The most important instruments within an internalisation strategy are:
- active labour-market, market-expansion and full-employment policies;
- measures designed to improve health and safety at work, often in conjunction with cost subsidies, information services and counselling;
- partial retirement models, coupled with the provision of part-time jobs, i.e., instruments offering a staged transition from employment to retirement in its various forms.

A market-oriented strategy can be based on:
- diverse forms of deregulation and privatisation;
- an "active rejection" of interventionist market regulation.

On the basis of our seven country reports, we examined national strategy regimes with a view to their instrumentation; the results are summarised in table 9.

From the mass of information presented in the above figure a number of significant similarities and dissimilarities can be distinguished.

The instrumentation of the German and Dutch states, the two classic representatives of the externalisation strategy, is very clear: both provide a wide range of externalisation incentives and options within the national and sectoral social-insurance systems, and the level of income-replacement is high. Equally striking is the absence of active labour-market and employment policies for older workers in these countries. There is a total lack of attractive partial retirement models coupled with part-time employment opportunities in Germany, while in the Netherlands they are only at an early stage of development. Health and safety at work, and supportive information and advisory service are, however, relatively highly developed in both countries. With the possible exception of a limited flexibilisation of the retirement age in Germany, instruments of deregulation are also few and far between. Clearly, the externalisation strategy characteristic of both countries is strongly underpinned with a wide range of instruments, while alternative instrumental options are almost entirely lacking.

Equally consistent is the complementary relationship between state strategy and instruments in the Japanese and Swedish internalisation regimes. The system of state regulation in Sweden combines a long tradition of active labour market and employment policies with the aim of maintaining the level of employment and improving its quality – and which thus effectively reduces the risks facing older workers – with a strategic orientation on the part of social policy which aims less at the ex post financial compensate of risks than to avoid such (age-selective) risks altogether. Relevant to Swedish regulation in this area are both financial incentives for firms to employ older workers and the institutional arrangements which seek to bring about cooperation between the labour market authorities, firms/employers' organisations and trade unions in developing measures to integrate those groups of workers at greatest risk from corporate adjustment processes. Particularly characteristic of Swedish policy are the long-term programmes in the field of health and safety at work and work organisation within the firm, and the provision of partial retirement pensions with a system of incentives for firms to offer part-time employment. It is equally apparent, however, that the Swedish system is somewhat Janus-faced: the high net compensation level of the early retirement provisions,

Table 9: National Strategies and their Instrumentation

Early Exit/Entry Employment/Retirement Instruments	FRG	NL	USA	GB	JAP	SWD	GDR
I. Externalisation Strategy							
1) Retirement Linked to Specific Number of Years' Insurance	++	++	+	+	+	++	+
2) Early Retirement in Connection with Level of Demand for Labour	++	++	−	−	−	++	
3) Early Retirement for Health and Work-Performance Reasons	++	++	+		−	++	+
II. Internalisation Strategy							
4) Active Labour Market and Employment Policy	−	−	+	−	++	++	++
5) Market Expansion Policy	−	−	+	−	++	+	−
6) Information and Consultancy Services	+	+	−	−	+	++	+
7) Health and Safety at Work Programmes	++	++	−	−	−	+++	++
8) Cost Subsidies	−	−	++	−	+	+	+++
9) Staged Retirement in Conjunction with Part-Time Employment Opportunites	−	(+)	+	−	+	++	+
III. Market-Oriented Strategy							
10) Instruments of Deregulation	−	−	++	+	+	−	−

and the flexibilisation of the retirement pathways can, in an economically unfavourable climate, be so employed as to effectively externalise older workers.

The Japanese approach combines an expansive economic and labour market policy, one which has had a positive impact on employment, with a state age-structure policy. The latter has promoted the employment of older workers by means of specific programmes – financial incentives, and "legislative orientation" (e.g., raising the compulsory retirement age and plans to raise the age for pension entitlement) – and, more generally, through administrative guidance. Liberal labour laws promote the creation of diverse employment relations steered from the supply side. This is reinforced by Japanese social policy, which, by virtue of the relatively low levels of net income compensation in case of unemployment and old age, and the almost complete absence of a disability pension, offers little incentive to retire early. On the contrary, the system exerts substantial pressure on Japanese workers to remain in the economically active population for as long as possible and to save a considerable proportion of their earnings, and substantial pressure on firms to employ older workers.

Clearly, in both countries the dominant internalisation strategy is well supported by a corresponding instrumentation. In the case of Sweden, though, certain instruments can be said to have a latent or potential externalising function.

Characteristic of the two countries pursuing a market-oriented strategy is that, while they have, of course, developed systems of social insurance and welfare, they tend to offer a minimum coverage with regard both to the level of compensation and the diversity of measure available for older workers expelled from the employment system (especially, compared with those in Germany and the Netherlands). Equally, compared with the internalisation regimes of Japan and Sweden, the two English-speaking countries lack the typical instruments of an active labour market and employment policy, and partial retirement coupled with part-time employment opportunities. In Great Britain the state has largely retreated from the interventionist role it played during the 1960s and 1970s to an "observer status", while in the USA government policies in the 1980s were actively oriented towards deregulation and privatisation (the anti-discrimination law and financial support for company and private pension schemes, for instance). We can conclude that the instrumentation of countries pursuing age-selective strategies largely via market forces is also broadly in line with their strategic programme.

Let us now recapitulate our findings on the significance of national strategies and instruments as a means of explaining temporal and geographical similarities and variation in employment/retirement patterns.

(1) Throughout the 20–year observation period three distinct strategies relating to the employment/retirement mix can be identified in our seven countries: an externalisation strategy (Netherlands, Germany), an internalisation strategy (Japan, Sweden, GDR) and a market-oriented strategy (USA, Great Britain). Each strategy is accompanied by a well-defined package of appropriate instruments. In each case, the strategy-instrumentation combination proves to be very homogeneous.

(2) Comparing our institutional findings on strategy-instrument combinations and the various national early exit/entry mixes, their quantitative rates and levels, and their qualitative patterns, reveals a clear correlation between institutional and quantitative findings: the institutional

framework is closely reflected in the quantitative outcomes in the employment/retirement system in each case.

(3) Correlation need not imply causation, however. If, with a view to establishing causal relationships, the constellations of political power and interest underlying these strategy-instrument combinations are analysed, a distinct finding emerges, which can, for present purposes, be summarised as follows. In all the countries pursuing externalisation and internalisation strategies, we find some form of "grand coalition" consisting of all the leading political parties and interest groups which has jointly developed a national strategy and supported the deployment of its instruments. This is true in particular of Germany, the GDR and the Netherlands, and scarcely less so of Sweden and Japan. Great Britain is characterised by a "non-policy" in this arena, while the USA was marked by conflicting political constellations with regard to the market-oriented strategy during the 1980s.

(4) We are now in a position to ask how, in the light of these findings, the relationship between labour market trends and state strategies can best be evaluated. Clearly, it is extremely difficult to estimate the relative importance of the "labour market effect" and the "strategy effect" empirically, and, in conceptual terms, it is all but impossible in view of the systematic interdependence of both factor-complexes. A historical, comparative approach can at least provide two insights, however. It can be unambiguously shown that in those countries pursuing an externalisation strategy the relevant strategies and instruments were developed long before the onset of mass unemployment, and that the motives for their development were primarily linked to social-policy aims. In other words, state externalisation strategies were not dependent on the labour market for their genesis and initial implementation. For the countries dominated by a strategy of internalisation, on the other hand, it can be shown that the labour market trends in the two countries with relatively low unemployment rates and relatively high participation rates were not merely a consequence of exogenous market forces or demographic developments, but were very largely the product of specific labour-market, employment, growth and productivity policies, pursued consciously and over a long period. Thus age-selective trends on the labour market cannot merely be considered as an exogenous variable, but are also, to a very considerable extent, strategically determined.

(5) We are now in a position to draw a provisional resume: without wishing to deny the role played by labour market trends and demographic developments, there is considerable evidence for the view that the strategic regimes pursued by the state with their specific packages of instruments played a considerable and autonomous role in fashioning

the employment/retirement mix in each country. At the same time, the significance of the role played by the state varies between the different strategic orientations: an internalisation strategy require a highly complex arrangement consisting of both internalising and externalising instruments; externalisation strategies, on the other hand, are able to concentrate largely on developing and implementing instruments of externalisation; for a market-oriented strategy all that is required are measures of deregulation.

(6) This provisional conclusion leaves two questions unanswered: a considerable degree of variation at firm level remains to be explained, while the question as to the causal factors behind the employment/retirement mix has as yet been only partially answered. Our findings on the role played by state strategies have gone some way to resolving the causality question, but it remains to be seen whether or not the policies pursued by national political regimes were merely a direct reflex of corporate strategies, i.e., whether the preceding analysis has been, to some extent at least, a victim of the well-known "chameleon effect" (Dahl, cf. Samuals, 1987). For these reasons, we must now focus our analysis on the production regimes within which firms operate, and the strategies and instruments employed by firms in the context of employment and retirement.

5   Enterprise Production Regimes and the Employment/Retirement Mix

We have so far examined employment/retirement patterns at the aggregate level of the nation state, and from the perspective of labour market trends and the institutional framework in the seven countries. We now pursue the analysis further by turning to a question which has received considerable attention in the debates in this field; the importance of economic sector for the employment/retirement patterns. The findings of Jacobs, Rein and Kohli (1987), based on their "industry-mix hypothesis", are ambivalent on this question. The authors identify both a secular trend transcending sectoral boundaries and a degree of age-selective differentiation between individual sectors. Our findings are broadly in line with this view. We identified, for instance, very slight differences in all seven countries between the public and private sectors, with average ages higher and early-exit rates somewhat lower in the former. In general, though, we consider the discussion on sectoral differentiation to have been relatively unproductive. The central problem confronting research on this question lies in the conceptualisation of its analytical unit, the economic sector. The term "economic" or "structural" sector can be taken to mean an area of production producing an

homogeneous range of goods or services, a statistical entity, a political unit
of organisation, or as a combination of several of these dimensions. The
conclusion drawn from our research is that as a statistical entity, particularly
at the two-digit level, "the sector" is little more than a statistical artifact,
unsuited to distinguishing between the apples and pears – the very different
areas of economic activity. Equally, economic sector understood as an area
of homogeneous production does not reveal extant externalising or internalising consequences. The sectoral concept is, however, of relevance where,
as in the Netherlands, it depicts a political form of organisation which, at
the four-digit level, groups together relatively homogeneous conditions of
production. It is in this form that we will now consider sector-specific
differentiation. Any other form of sectoral analysis we consider unproductive, preferring instead to analyse effects either at firm or at national level.

Against this background it should now be easy to see why we consider
that it is firms, seen as socio-economic institutions incorporating the behavioural patterns of both managements and workforces with their various
forms of interest representation, which are the central actors responsible for
early exit/entry trends and patterns. It is within the firm, a fundamental
organisational unit of socio-economics and political economy, that the
central interface between industrial employment and state welfare is situated. And yet it is here also that we identify the strategic deficiency, the
blind spot, of much of the research which has so far been undertaken in this
field.

At the same time, the firm-level approach taken by the research network
not only constitutes a strategic research opportunity, but also represents an
enormous challenge. In the seven countries with their six sectors, the
research network conducted more than thirty intensive case studies covering a period of up to twenty years. This naturally renders the subsequent
task of analysis highly complex.

Moreover, the huge diversity at the empirical level is matched by the
breadth of widely differing theoretical conceptualisations of the firm, ranging from the representative competitive firm (Marshall, 1981), the vertically
integrated firm (Galbraith, 1982), and the transactions-cost model
(Williamson, 1985) to Japanese Toyotism concepts.

Following the pattern employed in the preceding analysis at national
level, our evaluation of the case-study material starts by identifying structural patterns and strategies, and then proceeds to analyse the packages of
instruments deployed within the context of these strategies. At the methodological level, the central problem lies in the systematic interaction
between corporate strategies and the context set by the national state. A
firm's behaviour must be seen not only in terms of quasi-autonomous
corporate strategies, but also, and significantly, as an adaptive reaction to a
framework of economic and political conditions which can be considered

Table 10: Firms' Motives and Externalisation/Internalisation Elements

Externalisation	Internalisation
1) Need to Reduce the Size of the Overall Workface	1) Social Integration
2) Need to Rid Themselves of Obsolete Workforce Skills	2) Life-Long-Employment Systems
3) Coping with Workers to Longer Able to Withstand the Pace of Work	3) Compensating for Labour Shortages
4) Maintaining for Smooth Functioning of the Managerial System	4) Need to Supplement Pension and other Forms of Income
5) Managing the Effective Performance of Long-Term Employment Contracts	
6) Meeting Workers' Aspirations	

exogenous to the firm. For this reason, we will be forced throughout this section to work with a ceteris paribus assumption as regards the political context when evaluating the case-study material. The interactive relationship between the political and economic context and corporate strategies will be dealt with explicitly within our analysis of the governance of employment/retirement trends (section 6). For the present we will concentrate on the characteristics of a relatively endogenous logic of firms' behaviour, in other words, on an analysis of what might be though of as potential corporate strategies.

All thirty case studies reveal more or less distinct elements of internalisation or externalisation and a wide variety of hybrid strategies at firm level. Let us first examine, in line with the logic of standard economics, whether it is possible to identify a universal economic logic amongst the diverse corporate strategies observed, one which transcends national boundaries. Our findings on firms' motives for pursuing externalisation or internalisation strategies are summarised in table 10.

Is it possible, on the basis of the mass of information from our case studies and the condensed findings presented above, to identify an endogenous profile of a quasi-universal economic logic of corporate behaviour? Initially it should be noted that certain findings, consistent across all firms and national boundaries, effectively refute two views which are frequently put forward in the discussions on employment/retirement trends (cf. for a guide to the literature Dohse, Jürgens and Russig, 1982).

(1) On the supply side, it is frequently argued that the productivity of older workers tends to decline with increasing age, and that this constitutes a universal incentive for their externalisation. Our findings furnish the

following – exemplary – counter-evidence. The literature contains numerous examples of performance-level differences between older and younger workers – in both directions. Our explorative analysis of wage/performance data in German firms was unable to detect any systematic relationship. Even more significant is the following, international finding: if productivity differential between older and younger workers were really so relevant, the internalisation strategies which dominate Japanese and Swedish corporate policies in this area would make no economic sense whatsoever. The Japanese instrument of "elderly workers' firms" would be inconceivable on competitive markets. It would therefore seem far more plausible to interpret the data the other way around: the supposed existence of a productivity differential, based on a "deficit model" of older workers' capabilities, is in fact an ex post justification of existing externalisation practices (this interpretation is elaborated in the Dutch and British reports).

(2) On the demand side, older workers are frequently claimed to be physically and mentally "worn out"; externalisation strategies thus reflect the physical and mental wear and tear to which (older) workers are exposed in the production process. In support of this view, the increasing rates of retirement for reasons of disability in Germany, Holland or Sweden are put forward. Yet here too, an international, comparative perspective leads to rather different conclusions: as was demonstrated in section 2, high-performance countries such as Japan or the USA exhibit low rates of retirement for reasons of disability (and, in the case of Japan, the highest life expectancy), whereas the reverse is trues of countries such as Germany and the Netherlands. Given that it is implausible to argue that Japanese employment relations are less demanding than those in Europe, or that significant differences in rates of occupational illness are at work (cf. Karasek and Theorell, 1990), the huge difference in the level of early exit are unlikely to be the result of variations in the "wear and tear" to which workers are exposed in the production process.

(3) At the same time, on the basis of our case-study material, it is possible to isolate two other factors which enter the economic calculations of virtually all the firms studied:

– older workers have one systematic disadvantage compared with their younger colleagues: their expected future service is shorter in so far as there is less time until they reach retirement age;

– in all countries and almost all firms, the dominant normative conception of "fairness" as far as the labour-market and social context is concerned in any trade off between younger and older workers calls for the withdrawal of older workers from the labour market provided this can be achieved under socially acceptable conditions.

In practice there is a systematic link between these two features. The overwhelming majority of our case studies involved firms in which, at least implicitly, long-term employment relations and, linked to this, implicit or explicit seniority regulations are predominant. In both cases the two conditions just mentioned are fulfilled. Such firms are subject to an endogenous logic of externalisation: the overall costs of older workers, with respect to their performance level, and allowing for the higher transaction costs resulting from longer job tenure, are higher than for younger workers. At the same time, seniority provisions ensure that older workers enjoy a higher degree of job security. As a consequence, the exit of older workers from the workforce can only occur under socially acceptable conditions, bearing in mind the costs of conflict and loss of reputation for the firm. Given the prevailing social norms, it is the combination of retirement and monetary compensation for older workers in favour of continued employment and wage income for younger workers which is most often seen as a socially acceptable solution. The endogenous trend towards the externalisation of older workers is thus economically rational and socially acceptable.

This provisional conclusion requires qualification in two respects. Firstly, even in the case of this, the empirically dominant logic of firms' behaviour, there is always at least a minimal degree of interaction with welfare-state structures. Secondly, in all countries this firm-type is complemented by a very different type of enterprise, one dominated by a very different economic rationality with distinct age-selective consequences.

Such differences between firm strategies are revealed by our second analytical approach, undertaken in order to explain inter-firm variation. It examines the influence of firm size on early exit/entry patterns. The findings for the USA and Great Britain indicate clear differences in early exit/entry behaviour between firms of different size categories. It is primarily large firms which, by means of a variety of instruments, release older workers before retirement age, whereas smaller firms and, by extension, branches dominated by such firms frequently recruit older workers in so-called "bridging jobs" as a second career opportunity; consequently the upper age groups usually account for a higher proportion of the workforce in smaller than in larger firms. However, more detailed analysis reveals that the factor "firm size" is often merely a proxy for different production regimes. On the one hand, medium-sized and large firms, with (frequently implicit) long-term employment relations and seniority rules, interest-representation structures etc., make widespread use of early retirement practices; on the other, small, often marginal enterprises, in the lower regions of the pyramid of supplier firms, with low-pay jobs, low-skill, often older employees, and often no structures of interest representation, frequently have high rates of labour turnover as a functional equivalent of early retirement practices.

This firm-level dichotomy finds its clearest structural expression in Japan. Japan's dual economic structure still maintains an extensive small-firm sector, with a vast potential for integrating older workers, although at comparatively poor working conditions. In times of labour market difficulties, however, such firms constitute a reservoir from which (older) workers can be released into marginal forms of employment or into non-employment.

Although corporate structure in Germany, the Netherlands and Sweden is fairly similar, the size-specific effects are rather different. The analysis of enterprise-size effects in Germany, for instance, reveals a broadly homogeneous trend with only limited segmentation: large firms, and sectors dominated by them, have greater recourse to early retirement practices than small firms and sectors dominated by small enterprises. The differences can be explained with reference to organisational and regulatory conditions, linked to the norms of industrial relations and state intervention in countries like Germany. However, our analysis also reveals that workforce age structures scarcely differ at all between small and large firms. The differences in early retirement behaviour are thus insufficient to offset other social trends whose impact on workforce age structures (at least with respect to the over 55s) is one of harmonisation.

Although in both Germany and the Netherlands size-specific differences in corporate regulatory systems do exist, the interaction with the national externalisation regimes would appear to overdetermine such firm-level differentiation.

In a third analytical step, we examined the possible effects of different production regimes on the age structure and early exit/entry mix in firms.

"The research conducted by industrial sociologists and personnel experts has shown that it is primarily the firm's personnel-development strategies, which are linked to the firm's production regime, that are of decisive importance for the firm-specific way in which older workers, and the workforce at large are treated, and early retirement and workforce age structures are regulated." (Weber, 1986).

Unless such strategies are overdetermined by other factors, they generate specific age-selective risk effects. The different production regimes and their associated personnel-development strategies can be expected to go hand in hand with heterogeneous development opportunities and heterogeneous age-specific risks for workers, and thus to give rise to heterogeneous early retirement practices. In order to ascertain the significance of this effect we investigated and compared the employment and early retirement practices of firms located in a variety of different production regimes. The case studies presented in this book can be classified in terms of three different types of production regimes: (1) Taylorism/Fordism or Mass Pro-

Table 11: Firms by Production Regime, Supposed and Actual Effects on Externalisation and/or Internalisation

Country/No. of Firms	Production Regime	Work Organisation and Qualification	Age-Specific Risks	Supposed Effect	Actual Effect
FRG 2	Taylorism Fordism	Extreme Division of Labour; Polarisation of the Workforce; Intensive Production: High Performance and Low Skill Requirements: High Labour Force Turnover	Decreasing Labour Power and Skill Level for Aging Workers	High Externalisation or Turnover	FRG A/E
JAP 1	Mass Production				JAP E
FRG 3	Diversified Quality Production	Relative Cooperative and Innovative Work Structure; Moderate Work and Performance Requirements; High Skill Requirements: Low Labour Force	Relatively Low Risk of Decreasing Labour Power + Skill for Aging Workers	Quasi Life-Time Employment; Low Risk of Externalisation for Elderly Workers	FRG I/I/I
JAP 1					JAP I
FRG 1	Innovation Oriented Market-Expansion Strategy	Permanent Improvement of Work Structure; Permanent Upgrading of Skills by Job Rotation, Polyvalent Use of Labour Force; Polarisation into Stable Core Workforce and Flexible Peripheral Workforce	Risk of High Stress Load	Life-Time Work/ Low Risk for Externalisation of Core Group	FRG E
JAP 3					JAP I/I/I

duction, (2) Diversified Quality Production and Flexible Specialisation, and (3) Innovation-Oriented Market-Expansion.

In table 11 the case studies have been classified according to both the assumed and the actual practice of externalisation and internalisation of older workers.

The German firms are concentrated within the diversified quality production regime, although they are also to be found in both the other regime types. Yet almost all the firms exhibit practically indistinguishable behaviour patterns with regard to early exit. An examination of their workforce statistics reveals extremely high early retirement shares in all the German firms, 95% of older workers leaving before 65. The figures for early exit before the age of 63 are analogously high. The findings from our German case studies thus refute, at least for Germany's externalisation regime, one of the project's most important initial hypotheses; namely that the firm's production regime determines its strategy of workforce selection. Irrespective of differences between production regimes and, in some cases, a considerable potential for internalisation, all the firms studied exhibit a uniform pattern of early exit from the workforce. Despite the potential for internalisation offered by the dominant production regime, older workers are not seen as a human resource critical to the success of the firm but – consistently – as a "flexibility potential" by means of which necessary personnel adjustment can be implemented more smoothly. The strategy adopted by all the German firms studied to cope with age-selective personnel problems is one of externalisation. In none of the production regimes were internalisation strategies employed to cope with potential age-selective risks. With the exception of a few, and limited, efforts to establish age-specific working structures and labour redeployment between departments or establishments, the German case-study firms had not even begun to consider a systematic policy aimed at integrating older workers or the creation of new and age-specific tasks through product diversification or systematic labour redeployment. Clearly then, the policies pursued by German firms vis a vis older workers are not significantly influenced by the firm-specific production regime, but are rather the expression of a regulatory framework at a higher – namely national – level.

The findings from Japanese firms reveal a rather similar picture with regard to the potential for internalisation, but a very different one with regard to actual personnel policies compared with German firms. Our Japanese case-study firms are also to be found in all three production regimes, whereby their centre of gravity is located in the innovation-oriented, market-expanding regime. The majority of firms in this production regime have actually realised the main characteristics of Japanese internalisation potential, from staged transition and reemployment to "elderly workers' firms". The one Japanese firm with a Taylorist production regime, on the other hand, did lay off workers, while the firm located between the Taylorist and the diversified quality production regimes was pushing for voluntary early exit by a number of white-collar workers. Thus in Japan the internalisation or externalisation potential of different production regimes is actually reflected in a firm-specific variation in age-selective effects: Japan's national internalisation regime also contains corporate segments pursuing personnel strategies based on externalisation.

The difference in the impact of production regimes in Germany and Japan is, however, not only linked to variation in the production-regime-specific potential for externalisation or internalisation in conjunction with strategy regimes at the national level. The differences in firms' strategies also point to differences of corporate structure between the Japanese and western economies.

There is, namely, a significant structural difference between Japanese firms, with their horizontal and vertical linkages and network structures ("keiretsu"), and western "stand-alone" firms. Irrespective of national strategy regimes, network firms possess a significantly greater potential for internalisation than the typically isolated, western firm (for further details *see* the paragraphs dealing with instrumentation and Abegglen and Stalk, 1986).

The preceding analysis of the endogenous strategic logic pursued by firms with respect to their externalisation and internalisation potential at the employment/retirement interface can be summarised in the form of a diagram (see table 12).

The analysis presented so far, together with the findings summarised in the above figure, enable us to draw the following – exemplary – conclusions.

(1) It is not individual economic sectors, as postulated by the main body of research, but rather firms which are the strategic economic actors in early exit/entry practices.

(2) In the overwhelming majority of medium-sized and large firms in all the countries studied, it is the economic rationale of externalisation which predominates over the strategy of internalising older workers. This is not a consequence of productivity levels or wear and tear on older employees, however. It results from the combination of differing transaction-cost structures – due to the shorter further tenure of older workers – and the availability of socially acceptable instruments by which older workers can be externalised in return for the continuing provision of employment for younger workers. Moreover, this is consistent with the currently dominant social norm of what is "right and proper".

Table 12: Corporate Externalisation and Internalisation Potentials

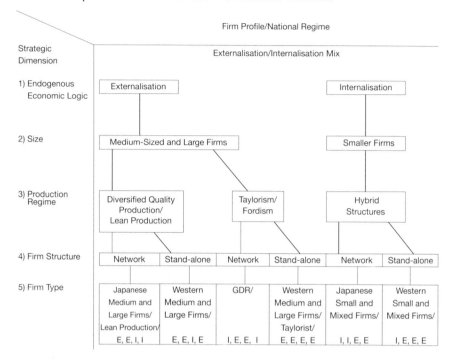

(3) In all the seven countries, smaller firms frequently exhibit a different age-selective personnel strategy: high rates of labour turnover, as a functional equivalent to early retirement strategies, are coupled with higher recruitment rates for older workers. The resulting age-structural effects vary according to the relevant strategic regime at national level.

(4) By combination a total of six firm types can be distinguished, each with a different potential for externalisation or internalisation:

– Medium-sized or large firms with an endogenous logic of externalisation, production regimes based on lean production and network structures;

– Medium-sized and large firms with an endogenous logic of externalisation, diversified quality production and stand-alone firm structures;

– Medium-sized and large firms with an endogenous logic of internalisation, Taylorist production system and network structures (the "deviant case" of the GDR);

– Smaller firms with an endogenous logic of internalisation, mixed production regimes and network structures;

– Smaller firms with an endogenous logic of internalisation, mixed production regimes and stand-alone structure.

The differences in externalisation and internalisation potential corresponding to these firm-types have already been described, see above.

(5) It is important to reemphasise that the endogenous firm-level strategies identified here only hold if other factors are held constant. As such strategies are only finally constituted in a real-world constellation profoundly influenced by nationally specific forms of regulation. Consequently, corporate strategies must, in the final analysis, be considered in terms of their interaction with such national frameworks.

Against the background set by these selected strategic logics of corporate behaviour in early exit/entry practices, we now turn to the set of instruments, the "box of tools", used by firms to implement their strategies. The aim is to provide a more comprehensive explanation of inter-firm variation both within and between countries.

At first sight, the diversity of instruments emerging from the thirty case studies – for both externalisation and internalisation strategies – is overwhelming. If this complexity is condensed down to fundamental instrument-types, however, the findings for the seven countries are as follows (table 13):

(1) The instruments at firms' disposal for the purposes of externalisation/ internalisation in each country are broadly in line with the strategy which dominates the relevant national political and economic context. The clearest example of this is the intensive use of internalising instruments by Swedish and Japanese firms (firms in the former GDR concentrated their internalisation efforts on the provision of age-selective job structures and requirements). Such instruments are lacking in Germany and, to a lesser degree. in Holland. In the countries pursuing market-oriented strategies, firms have developed part-time, "bridging" jobs and company retirement schemes as partial instruments of integration.

(2) A significant exception to the general rule concerning internalising measures was identified in the area of health and safety at work, and job restructuring. Here Swedish firms are the leading exponents, followed, surprisingly, by Dutch and German firms. Japanese firms, by contrast, are relatively reticent in employing this strategy, although it is not one from which trenchant age-selective effects can be expected. Working conditions in Japanese firms are highly segmented, while particularly striking in the case of the former GDR was the huge discrepancy between the state's programmatic aims and real-world working conditions.

(3) The "tool box" of Dutch and German firms is particularly well stocked with instruments of externalisation, far better so than in the other countries. It should be recalled, however, that a number of purportedly

Table 13: Employment/Retirement Instruments by Firm and Contry

Instruments Used by the Firms Studied in:	FRG	NL	JAP	SWD	GDR	UK	USA
I. Internalisation							
1) Part-Time Jobs	−	(+)	+	+	−	+	+
2) Occupational Pension/ Partial Pension	−	+	+ +	+	−	+ +	+ +
3) Redeployment within Enterprises or Overall Organisation (Shukko)	−	−	+ +	−	+	−	−
4) Reemployment	−	−	+ +	−	−	−	+
5) Health and Safety Measures, Work Restructuring	+ +	+ +	+/−	+ + +	+/−	−	−
6) Sheltered Jobs	−	−	+ +	−	+ +	+	−
II. Externalisation							
1) Age-Selective Redundancies with or without Compensatory Measures (Social Plan)	+ +	+ +	−	+	−	+	+ +
2) Active Disincentives for Older Workers	−	−	(−)	−	−	−	+
3) Financial Incentive Programe	+ +	+ +	+/−	+	−	+	+
4) No Attempt Made to "Humanise" Working Conditions	+	+	+(−)	−	−	+	+
5) Early Retirement after a Given Number of Years' Insurance Contrib's	+ +	+ +	+	+ +	+	+	+
6) Retirement Provisions Linked to Overall State of Demand for Labour	+ +	+ +	−	+ +		−	−
7) Retirement Linked to Health and Performance Level	+ +	+ +	−	+ +	+	+	
III. Market-Oriented Strategies							
1) Plant-Level Anti-Discrimination Regulations	−	−	+/−	−	+/−	−	+/−

internalising instruments can, in fact, be used multi-functionally depending on the current state of the labour market. Instruments such as partial retirement/part-time work, of great relevance in Sweden and the USA, are not merely an internalising instrument, but can also be used as a means of regulating the size of the workforce according to age-structural requirements. And even shukko, the instrument so characteristic of Japanese firms has been used as a means of externalising middle management from core firms in recent years.

(4) International comparison of the instruments employed in externalisation vis a vis internalisation strategies reveals that the latter require a more complex instrumentation than the former. Firstly, they require a complex bundle of in-plant measures in the field of personnel policy and work organisation; secondly, such firms must also always have instruments of externalisation at their disposal – as a "fall-back position". Thus internalisation strategies in practice always demand a combination of internalisation and externalisation instruments. As we will see in the next section, this instrumental diversity calls for a multitude of social actors, all which must be effectively coordinated if an internalisation strategy is to be successful.

(5) There is also a huge divide in personnel-management strategies separating both externalising and internalising firms, on the one hand, and British and American companies, on the other. Large Japanese firms, in particular, have much more highly differentiated personnel-management structures, characterised by relatively long-term planning horizons. In Swedish and, although less pronounced, in German and Dutch firms, too, we identified a complex personnel-management regime and at least a medium-term planning perspective. This is in stark contrast to the relatively underdeveloped state of personnel management in US and British companies, a finding which can be summed up in two phrases from the research literature: "extreme short-termism" (Thomas, Pearson and Meegan, 1992) and the "contingent nature of personnel policy" (Casey and Wood in this volume).

Yet the way in which these instruments are deployed in practice and their relative significance within the framework of plant-level externalisation and internalisation strategies will only become fully apparent when corporate behaviour is set in the context of the different forms of political regulation furnished by the state at national level. Corporate action and state regulation are complementary values. It is only on the canvas spanned by interaction between firms, the state, collective organisations, and markets that the full picture of employment/retirement activity can be depicted.

6   The Governance of the Employment/Retirement Mix

The task of the preceding analysis has been to explain – in terms of labour market developments, state strategies at national level, and the strategies pursued by firms – the empirical variation and similarities in early exit/entry trends and patterns in the seven countries, all against the background of an unchanged demographic constellation. The various complexes of explanatory factors had to be isolated from one another by means of ceteris paribus clauses, in order to ascertain the direction and strength of their specific endogenous effects. Yet, on completing each analytical step it was all too apparent that market developments cannot be examined in isolation from state regulation, corporate behaviour from the institutional framework established by the state and collective organisations, and state strategies and instruments without markets and firms. In the final analysis, early exit/ entry activity, the volume and structure of employment and retirement, the relationship between industrial employment and state welfare, are constituted within a systematic interactive context involving markets and firms, the state, collective organisations and networks. We are now in a position to examine this context, the governance of the employment/retirement interface. Table 14 provides an overview and synopsis of the findings of the various steps of the analysis so far.

In evaluating these overall findings, the first task is to identify the various governance regimes as nationally specific constellations. We then proceed to select and examine a number of cross-sectional aspects which have often been the subject of theoretical and strategic interest. The last section deals with the impact of demographic trends for the governance regime of the employment/retirement mix in the context of possible changes in the productivity/welfare trade-off and a shift in age structures. In other words, we will be considering the future prospects for the relationship between industrial employment and state welfare.

The specific profile of the employment/retirement pattern in the Netherlands, its poll position in international comparisons of early-exit rates and levels, is a result of the interaction of four modes of regulation which together constitute the specific essence of Dutch governance in this area. First, the Dutch state has implemented a large number of measures, motivated by social-policy considerations, with a high monetary compensation level and significant effects in initiating the trend towards early exit/entry; this has occurred in the context of a change in value systems with respect to the trade-off between work and leisure.

Second, no attempt was made to counter the – largely exogenous – trend towards rising unemployment from the mid 1970s with active employment and growth policies. Third, endogenous, firm-specific incentive structures are overwhelmingly oriented towards externalisation, so that the endogenous adjustment behaviour of firms coincides with the incentive structures set by the state and collective organisations. Lastly, the country's highly differentiated meso-corporatist system has given the early-exit system its distinctive form and its dynamic of development. Not only do sectoral collective organisations dominate the structures by which the statutory

Table 14: Governance of the Employment-/Retirement-mix

Countries	Netherlands	Germany	Sweden	Japan	USA	Great Britain	GDR
Governance Mechanism and Employment/Retirement-Mix							
Labour Market Trends and Policies	Persistent Over-Supply of Labour; no Active Labour Market and Employment Policy for Older Workers	Persistent Over-Supply of Labour; no Active Labour Market and Employment Policy for Older Workers	Persistent Labour Shortage; Intensive Use of Active Labour Market Policies	Persistent Labour Shortage; Active Growth and Industrial Policies	Persistent Over-supply of Labour; no Active Labour Market Policy, but Commitment to Growth	Increasing Over-Supply of labour; no Active Labour Market Policy	Structural Labour Shortage in Economy Dominated by Shortage
State Early Exit Policy	Externalisation	Externalisation	Internalisation, but Potential for Externalisation	Internalisation	Market-Oriented, Deregulatory	Market-Oriented, Non-Interventionist	Internalisation
Significance of Influence Exerted by Collective Organisations	Highly Differentiated and Potent National and Mesocorporatist Regimes, Controlling and in many Cases (Partly) Substituting for State Policies	Highly Differentiated, Centralised Collective Organisations; only Minor Role Played by Sectoral Regimes	Highly Differentiated, Centralised Collective Organisations; Tripartite Constellation Under State Leadership	Limited Role for Collective Organisations at Sectoral and National Level	Policies Pursued by Collective Organisations of Low Importance	Policies Pursued by Collective Organisations of Low Importance	Policies Pursued by Collective Organisations of Low Importance and Little Differentiated

Firm Policies	Larger Firms More Likely to Use Semi-Private, Sectoral Early Retirement Schemes, Small Firms to Use State Schemes	Large Firms More Likely to Pursue Externalisation, Small Firms to Have Some Potential for Internalisation	Large Firms More Likely to Pursue Externalisation, Small Firms to Have Some Potential for Internalisation	Large Firms Medium Potential, Small Firms Large Potential to Pursue Internalisation	Large Firms Most Likely to Pursue Externalisation, Small Firms Somewhat Less Likely	Large Firms Most Likely to Pursue Externalisation, Small Firms Somewhat Less Likely	Unequivocal Predominance of Internalisation Potential
Early Exit Rate	High	High	Low	Low	Medium	Medium	Low
Early Exit Transition Patterns (One-Step vs. Staged)	One-Step	One-Step	One Step and Staged	Staged	One Step and Staged	One-Step	Staged
Productivity-Growth	Medium	High	Medium	High	Low	Low	Low
Level of Welfare State Provision	High	High	High	Low	Medium	Medium	Low

early-exit pathways are implemented, in times when public resources are in short supply, they develop a parallel system of early exit through collective bargaining. The highly differentiated public/private mix of different compensation programmes used for early exit, with relatively high levels of benefit and low thresholds for entrance, has resulted in a relative autonomous social process for early exit, which is out of direct control. Medium rates of productivity growth in the Netherlands, together with the high welfare-benefit levels generated by this constellation clearly set strict limits on this productivity-welfare mix.

The Federal Republic of Germany exhibits early-exit patterns similar both in principle and, at first sight, in structure to those in Holland. The two externalisation regimes do differ, however, in two respects. First, early-exit rates and levels in Germany, while very pronounced, are still significantly below those in the Netherlands. Second, this difference may well be linked to the different steering-structure characteristic of the German political system; the predominance of early-exit instruments within an overall externalisation strategy is, in the final analysis, a result of coordination by the state and is based on relatively high rates of productivity growth. Although collective institutions do play a significant role in drawing up and implementing statutory measures, and in economic and labour market policy, this does not take the form of a substitute for state activity, nor imply that they seek to control state policy. While in the Netherlands the social partners represent an important controlling mechanism in the implementation of statutory early exit/entry pathways, and even perform a substitutive function in generating pathways of their own, in Germany the state remains the leading protagonist with respect to all the most significant measures: early exit/entry activity remains firmly within the state arena. The German equivalent to Dutch meso-corporatist dominance within the governance regime is a state-centred externalisation regime with support from collective organisations.

Sweden constitutes, alongside Japan, the avant garde in the development of internalisation strategies, despite the fact that its pathways also contain a potential for externalisation; Swedish governance consists of an asymmetric combination of an internalisation regime with externalisation potential. The decisive determining factor for the Swedish internalisation regime does not lie, as the conventional wisdom has it, in specific, endogenous incentive structures within Swedish firms. The endogenous logic at firm level is in no way different to that in Germany or Holland. Decisive for the mode of governance in Sweden is the specific relationship between the political regime and labour market trends. As is well known, for decades Sweden has pursued a highly differentiated and far-reaching active labour market and employment policy, together with work restructuring, training and preventative health and safety measures, which, until the start of the 1990s,

effectively countered any cyclical or structural threats to the smooth running
of the labour market. The strategic capability of the political system, comparable only with that of Japan, is based on the decades-long hegemony of the
ruling social-democratic party and on the tripartite association of the state
with the – highly centralised – employers' organisations and trade unions.
Such long-term strategic capability and compact, heavily centralised political
structures ensure deep penetration and a firm basis for the state in the
employment/retirement field, and lead to a very high degree of socialisation
of early exit/entry activity. The high rates of productivity growth experienced
until the 1960s, together with the dominance of the work principle, enabled
Sweden to afford both a high wage and welfare level until the end of the
1980s.

Japan, the country with the lowest rates and level of early exit in our
study, can be interpreted as the other prototype of an internalisation
strategy. The volume and structure of employment and retirement in Japan
are, however, based on a fundamentally different governance regime to that
in Sweden. The distinctive characteristic of the Japanese mode of regulation
is to be seen in the unidirectional interactive effect of all the relevant social
actors and markets: the persistently high level of demand for labour conditioned by the unusually broad-based and aggressive expansion of the
leading economic sectors and firms; support for such market developments
from a consistent policy of administrative guidance on the part of the state,
in the form of growth, employment, and active labour market and technology policies; the comparatively high endogenous internalisation potential of
Japan's industrial structure, based on networks and a dual firm-structure;
the social consensus, maintained until the 1980s, on the trade-off between
high productivity and a relatively underdeveloped welfare provision. It is
not Japan's central state as a social and market-steering mechanism, but
rather in the unidirectionality of the various strategies, the networking
between the various actor-systems together with the supportive and conducive development of its markets which constitutes the characteristic elements of the governance of the employment/retirement mix in Japan.

The picture in the two English-speaking countries is, of course, very
different. Both the USA and Great Britain exhibit intermediate levels and
rates of early exit. This quantitative outcome is based, in both countries, on
a market-oriented strategy in which the state attempts, via deregulation, to
stimulate market forces on goods, financial and labour markets. This, at
least, is the conclusion drawn if the two countries are set against those with
a clear strategy of externalisation or internalisation. A comparison between
the two countries, however, reveals a number of significant differences
within the overall market-orientation.

First, the state in the USA pursued (at least during the 1980s) an active policy of deregulation, whereas in Great Britain the policy was one of non-intervention. Second, American firms exploit the scope offered by government policy to take active early-exit measures, according to their respective corporate logic. Deregulated labour markets with relatively low welfare income-replacement effects respectively allow for, and make necessary second career paths and bridging jobs, thereby establishing a counter trend towards internalisation. British firms, on the other hand, are characterised by the short-termism and the contingent nature of their personnel policy referred to above, particularly in the field of age-selective policies. Third, in Great Britain the relationship between the state and the corporate sector with regard to early-exit policies can be described as uncoordinated and indifferent. In the USA, on the other hand, firms and the state have opposing interests and conflicting policies; statutory incentives to raise the retirement age and the explicit abolition of mandatory retirement limits in firms are at odds with the incentives provided by company occupational pension schemes, which, as a rule, foresee one-step and early transition to retirement in line with firms' cost-benefit calculations.

The two countries do have an additional aspect in common, however; their relative productivity-welfare position. The predominance of traditional production regimes in British and American firms, the back-seat regulatory role played by the state and the lack of coordination, if not actual conflict, between state and corporate policies combine to produce a productivity-welfare mix at a low, at best mediocre, level.

The diametric opposite to the two countries pursuing market-oriented strategies is, of course, the GDR, with its high employment level, not least among older workers, many of whom stayed on beyond the official retirement age. The consistent strategy pursued by all social actor-systems, the unidirectional interactive effect of all regulatory mechanisms provide a solid basis for this employment/retirement pattern. Permanent labour shortage, not least a consequence of systematic labour hoarding, bears witness to the consistent pursuit and realisation of a major aim of central-state planning – full emplyoment. This strategy could count on firms realising in full their high internalisation potential. However, this constellation correlated directly with a productivity-welfare mix at a comparatively low level.

If we abstract from country-specific features, it is possible at the international comparative level to identify five basic governance regimes for the employment/retirement mix (table 15).

Against the background of our characterisation of national governance regimes and their condensation down to five basic types, we now proceed to examine a number of questions which lie tangential to national profiles, which play an important role in current political and academic discussions. to

Table 15: Five Basic Forms of Governance of Employment/Retirement Practices

Countries	Forms of Governance
Japan	Unidirectional Interaction Effects from the Labour market, State, Collective Organisations and Firms
USA Great Britain	Deregulated Labour Markets Predominate, Firms and State Pursue Conflicting/Uncoordinated Policies
Netherlands Germany	Regulated Labour Markets; High Level of Welfare-State Compensation in Cases of Externalisation via Welfare-State Policies Organised Through Meso-Corporatist/Central-State Dominated Regimes
Sweden	Overdetermination of Firms in the Fields of Labour Market and Social Policy by a Corporatist Steering Mechanism Dominated by the Central State and Highly Centralised Collective Organisations
GDR	Central-State Regulation of External and Internal Labour Markets

and relate to our initial line of enquiry into the role played by firms in the regulatory context, and their relationship to statutory and collective arrangements.

The Interactive Relationship between Firms, the State and Collective Organisations

Two findings from the comparative study are relevant to the question of the relationship between firms and the state and collective organisations. First, the six types of firm are distributed very unevenly over the seven countries (cf. table 14); second, the sectoral spread in early-exit rates varies considerably between countries. We have already drawn one conclusion from these findings in our analysis of firm behaviour: national (state) and sectoral institutions exert a systematic mediation or contextual effect on firms and early-exit patterns. This is consistent with the findings of international, comparative analyses of competitiveness which point to the relevance of the national "home environment" (Porter, 1985) in determining firms' competitiveness. Our findings go beyond this, however, and suggest a more far-reaching interpretation: the significance of the national home environment varies with respect both to the strength of interaction and the extent of cooperation between firms and the state depending on the nature of the national institutional framework:

– In countries such as the Netherlands, Germany and Sweden we identified only a narrow (sectoral) spread in firms' early exit/entry activities, due to the dominance of state or corporatist labour-market regulation at this interface, with a significant role also played by intermediate (collective) groups. The overdetermination of firm policies by the actions of the state (and collective organisations) is supported by a high degree of cooperation between these micro- and macro-level actors.

- In the USA, and also in Great Britain, on the other hand, the spread of corporate early-exit activity is substantially greater; the market-oriented strategies pursued by the state – collective organisations play only a limited role – aim to decouple firms and the state, and involve non-cooperative relations at the employment/retirement interface.
- Japan exhibits the greatest inter-firm spread in early-exit activity. This is a reflection of Japan's dual economic structure, the lack of labour market regulation, state intervention in the form of "non-binding legislation" and administrative guidance, and the fact that collective organisations play a limited, coordinating role. The relationships between firms and the state are characterised by interaction based on "reciprocal consensus" (Samuels, 1987) in the transition from employment to retirement.
- The exact opposite case, namely an extreme lack of differentiation in firms' early-exit behaviour, is that of the former GDR. Centralised state economic and social planning attempted not only to regulate external labour markets, but also to exert strict control on internal labour markets. The non-existence of intermediary social groups, and the very limited autonomy enjoyed by firms – which were little more than subordinate economic-administrative bodies – meant that firm-state relations were both very close and clearly asymmetrical.

Firms' Potential to Control their Own Early-Exit Outcomes

The interaction between firms, on the one hand, and the state and collective organisations, on the other, can also be illuminated by examining the "control potential" of individual firms in early-exit activity (cf. de Vroom and Trommel in this volume). A substantial volume of data emerges from our case studies concerning the extent to which firms are able to shape the means of exit and to which they are able to select how many and which workers actually exit. Figure 7 summarises, albeit tentatively and in an aggregated way for each country, the control potential of the case-study firms.

Here as elsewhere, Japan and the GDR form the two extreme types. Japanese firms enjoy a relatively high control potential with regard both to the way pathways are constructed and selection by personnel management. East German firms, by contrast, have relatively little control over both variables. Compared with Japanese companies, US and British firms have a very much more limited control potential: instrumental control by firms was in some cases "externalised" onto external labour markets. What is remarkable about both Sweden and the Netherlands and Germany is the split in their control potential. While firms exert considerable control with regard

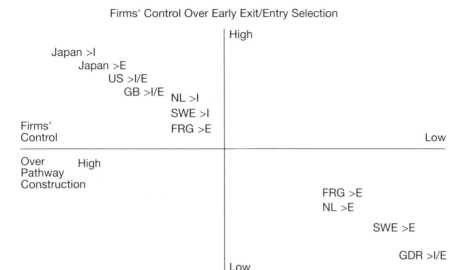

Firms' Control Over Early Exit/Entry Selection

Legenda
E = Externalisation
I = Internatisation

Figure 7: Firms' Control over Pathway Construction and Early Exit/ Entry Selection

internalising instruments, albeit constrained by the demands of the industrial relations system, the scope left to individual firms in constructing externalising pathways and in selecting personnel for such pathways is very limited. Unless they are very large, and themselves dominate these, they are heavily dependent on other actor-systems.

Let us summarise the results of our analysis of the various national governance regimes of the employment/retirement mix. In order to explain the substantial national differences in the level and rates of early exit/entry, we isolated analytically and examined labour-market developments, state strategies and instruments, and production regimes and their potential and actual impact. We were able to demonstrate that the early exit/entry regime in the different countries can only be explained with reference to an entire framework of interaction between markets and the various social actor-systems. We identified for each of our seven countries nationally specific governance profiles. In a further step, these were condensed to five basic forms of governance of the employment/welfare interface:
- the unidirectional interaction regime with reciprocal consensus between firms and the state in Japan;
- the labour market-oriented regime with non-cooperative dislocation between firms and the state in Great Britain and the USA;

- a correspondence relationship between a highly regulated labour market and a welfare-state or meso-corporatist cooperation strategy, with extensive cooperation between firms, the state and collective organisations in continental European countries such as Germany and the Netherlands;
- the overdetermination of markets by labour-market and social policies by means of a centralised corporatist network in Sweden; and
- the marginal case of intensive central-state regulation of both internal and external labour markets, an asymmetric relationship between the state and subordinate economic units in the context of the planned economy of the GDR.

In most countries, the regime governing the transition from employment to welfare established itself from the 1960s on, and the regimes have shown themselves to be remarkably stable up until the beginning of the 1990s. We must now consider whether these governance regimes were appropriate only to the demographic distribution in which they developed, namely the standard age pyramid discussed earlier, and whether they are suited only to phases of mass unemployment. The concluding section discusses the stability of these governance regimes over time, attempting – rather speculativly – to evaluate the development dynamic of early exit/entry activity in the coming years.

7   Future Prospects for the Governance of the Employment/Retirement Mix

The analysis of early exit behaviour and governance regimes in the seven selected countries was situated within the historical context of the mid 1960s to the late 1980s. Since the mid 1980s, however, the evidence has been mounting that far-reaching changes in this context, beginning in the last decade of the 20th century, is bound to occur. In this final section, we turn to this changing context, to the new problems it will give rise to, and to the stability of the dominant national governance regimes over time, and the prospects for the different productivity/welfare mixes.
    The country chapters and current analytical and political discourse point to four major trends affecting, mutatis mutandis, all the selected countries.
- Important demographic changes leading to a reversal of the age-structure pyramid of national labour forces. This reversal will be most acute in Japan, followed by Germany; Great Britain will experience the least demographic distortion.
- Large scale labour shedding, a result of either longer-term stagnation or global corporate strategies of "lean production".
- A substantial intensification of the demands and pressures of work, in

consequence of both "lean production" techniques and demands for greater employee "flexibility".
- The threat of refusal by taxpayers, employers and employees to contemplate the increase in tax and social insurance contribution rates necessary to sustain benefits paid to a growing retired population.

The ramifications of these trends are again likely to be similar in nature, if not in quantitative importance, across all the seven countries, and all western industrial, too. Already a number of responses are being developed and some have been enacted. In some cases these responses have been strategic, in others they have been more ad hoc. In some cases the state has taken the lead, in others lower level bodies – collective organisations or firms. By no means always has there been a harmony of objective between all relevant levels. The responses can be summarised as follows.
- Raising the "normal" retirement age. The USA took the lead back in 1983, albeit phasing in the change over many years and well into the future; (West) Germany followed suit in 1989; the issue is being actively discussed in Japan.
- Cutting state benefits paid to the retired and early retired. This has occurred, to a greater or lesser extent, in Great Britain, the Netherlands and Germany.
- Redefining the definition of "disability" to exclude labour market considerations from being taken into account. The two countries where disability pensioning has been of greatest importance, Sweden and the Netherlands, have already taken the necessary steps; in Germany they are under consideration.
- Greater reliance on non-state benefits (benefits financed by employers either individually or collectively). This has occourred in countries where state provision is already less generous, Great Britain and the USA, and seen as a likely development in countries where a more generous state provision is being reduced, such as Sweden.
- Greater reliance on affiliates and subcontractors to absorb unwanted older workers. This response remains peculiar to Japan.

From among the heterogeneous strategic and instrumental adjustment measures implemented or planned in the seven countries, we can draw two conclusions regarding the stability of governance regimes over time.
- With the exception of the former GDR, where the previously dominant internalisation regime has been rapidly replaced by the (West) German externalisation regime, the existing governance regime in each country is destined to remain in place. Despite considerable activity at all levels, the basic orientation of each form of governance – externalisation, internalisation or market-orientation – will be retained.

– This persistence of existing governance structures, despite far-reaching contextual changes, is, however, the result of very different factor-complexes and development dynamics in each case: the institutionalisation of an exit regime which has escaped the direct control of the state (Netherlands); the momentum of a strategy pursued by a grand coalition of parties and collective organisations (Germany); the delicate balance between firms and the state within a system of reciprocal consensus (Japan); an unstable "lowest common denominator" in the dislocated interaction between the state and firms (USA and Great Britain); the resilience of deeply-rooted structures and established institutions and norms, even following a major shift in political regime (Sweden).

The homogeneous development of the underlying structure of governance in the seven countries should not be allowed to conceal the wide diversity of modifications and adjustments to these structures currently under way. Yet even allowing for these modifications, the common ground between all the governance regimes studied remains considerable. Each of the countries is experimenting with ways to render the transition from employment to retirement more flexible, with ways to shift the burden of costs away from the state and onto private firms (and from firms on to workers). Equally, none of the countries is making innovations which seem likely to generate novel and original patterns within the employment/ retirement mix. Early exit remains dominated by the inertia of structural conservatism.

Even more importantly, in none of the seven countries is there a sign of a governance regime capable of generating a "Kaldor-optimal" overall constellation, i.e., one in which the productivity gains of the consistent use of potential labour capacity, within the framework of an internalisation strategy and based on the "work principle", are at least equal in value to the sum of the social-compensation benefit payments made to the potential victims of an externalisation regime. Given this, the following three problems, each related to the other, are likely to characterise the interface between employment and retirement in the 1990s and the decades which follow:

– Pressure on production costs from the rising costs of seniority systems and the growth of indirect wage costs, both consequent on an increasingly selective approach in personnel-management strategies;
– Pressure on the value (measured as a replacement rate) of welfare-state benefits claimed by those who are de jure or de facto retired;
– An increasingly unequal distribution of income amongst those who have retired, either early or at the "normal" age.

Whether these three problems degenerate into a vicious circle or are countered by innovative developments within governance regimes, will be of decisive importance for the relationship between industrial employment and state welfare at the start of the new millennium.

Notes

1   For data cf. chapter by Jacobs and Rein; for figures in the GDR *see* the chapter by Schuster and Stieler; *see* also figure 5.
     Productivity trends between 1950 and 1986 (cf. Maddison, 1989) are classified as low (5% or less), medium (5 to 7.9%) or high (8% and above). The level of welfare is defined in terms of the level of income replacement provided in the case of early exit; here we distinguish between low (up to 35%), medium (36% to 59%) and high (60% and above). Cf. the case studies in this volume.

References

Abegglen, James C. and George Stalk (1986). *Kaisha*. Düsseldorf: Econ Verlag.

Campbell, John L.; Hollingsworth, Roger J. and Leon N. Lindberg (eds.) (1991). *Governance of the American Economy*. Cambridge, N.Y.: Cambridge University Press.

Conference *"Erwerbsarbeit der Zukunft"* (Berlin 1992). GfAH-Working Paper, Dortmund: GfAH (mimeo).

Dohse, Knut; Jürgens, Ulrich and Harald Russig (eds.) (1982). *Ältere Arbeitnehmer zwischen Unternehmensinteressen und Sozialpolitik*. Frankfurt a.M.: Campus: 467–503.

Esping-Andersen, Gösta (1985). *Politische Macht und wohlfahrtsstaatliche Regulation*. In: Frieder Naschold (ed.), *Arbeit und Politik*. Frankfurt a.M.: Campus: 467–503.

Esping-Andersen, Gösta (1990). *The Three Worlds of Welfare Capitalism*. Cambridge: Polity Press.

Federal Ministry of Labour, Great Britain (1992). *Part-Time Work 1992*.

Fujii, Hidehiko (1992). *Japan's Economy Amidst the Manpower Shortage*. In: *Japan Research Review* (Spring): 38–52.

Galbraith, Kenneth (1982). *Designing the Innovating Organization*. In: *Organizational Dynamics* 10 (3): 5–25.

Hall, John A. and G. John Ikenberry (1989). *The State*. Minneapolis: University of Minnesota Press.

Heimann, Eduard (1980). *Soziale Theorie des Kapitalismus. Theorie der Sozialpolitik.* Frankfurt a.M.: Suhrkamp.

Heinelt, Hubert (1991). *Frühverrentung als politischer Prozeß.* Wiesbaden: Deutscher Universitätsverlag.

Jacobs, Klaus; Rein, Martin and Martin Kohli (1987). *Testing the Industry Mix Hypothesis of Early Exit.* Discussion Paper IIVG/dp 87–229, Wissenschaftszentrum Berlin für Sozialforschung.

Karasek, Robert and Töres Theorell (1990). *Healthy Work.* New York: Basic Books.

Kimura, Takeshi et. al. (1990). *The Companies, the State and the Changing Age-Structure in Japan: A Profile Report.* Discussion Paper FS II 90–201. Berlin: Wissenschaftszentrum für Sozialforschung.

Kohli, Martin et. al. (eds.) (1991). *Time for Retirement.* Cambrigde, N.Y.: Cambridge University Press.

Lazear, Edward (1979). *Why is there Mandatory Retirement?* In: *Journal of Political Economy* 87 (6): 1261–1284.

Maddison, Angus (1989). *The Word Economy in the 20th Century.* In: *OECD Development Centre Studies.* Paris: OECD.

Marshall, Alfred (1981). *Principles of Economics.* London: Macmillan.

Oka, Shinichi (1992). *Older Workers: Conditions of Work and Transition to Retirement.* In: *Country Report: Japan.* Working Papers, Geneva: International Labour Office: 101–130.

Porter, Michael E. (1985). *Competitive Advantage of Nations. Creating and Sustaining Superior Performance.* New York: Free Press.

Samuels, Richard J. (1987). *The Business of the Japanese State.* Ithaca: Cornell University Press.

Schmähl, Winfried (1988). *Verkürzung oder Verlängerung der Erwerbsphase?* Tübingen: Mohr.

Schmähl, Winfried (1989). *Retirement at the Cross-Roads.* In: Winfried Schmähl (ed.), *Redefining the Process of Retirement. An International Perspective.* Berlin: Springer: 50–78.

Sheppard, Harold L. (1991). *The United States: The Privatisation of Exit.* In: Kohli et. al. (eds.), *Time for Retirement.* Cambridge, N.Y.: Cambridge University Press: 252–283.

Therborn, Göran (1985). *Arbeitslosigkeit.* Hamburg: VSA.

Thomas, Andrew; Pearson, Maggie and Richard Meegan (1992). *Older Workers: Conditions of Work and Transition to Retirement.* In: *Country Report: United Kingdom.* Working Papers. Geneva: International Labour Office.

Titmuss, R. (1950). *Problems of Social Policy.* London: Her Majesty's Treasure Office (HMSO)

Weber, W. (1986). *Der Einfluß demographischer Veränderungen auf Arbeitsorganisation und Beschäftigungsstrategien – Empirisch-theoretische Analyse des Unternehmensverhaltens.* In: Antrag auf Einrichtung eines Sonderforschungsbereichs "Organisation der Arbeit", Paderborn/Hannover.

Williamson, Oliver E. (1985). *The Economic Institutions of Capitalism.* New York: Free Press.

Contributors

Bernard Casey is a Senior Research Fellow at Policy Studies Institute, London. He started doing research on age and employment in 1980, whilst at the Wissenschaftszentrum Berlin, when he was the co-author of a five country study of labour market and social policy for older workers produced for the Federal German Labour Ministry. In recent years he contributed to the *Carnegie Trust's Inquiry into the Third Age* and was a consultant to the OECD social affairs direcorate's investigation into the *Transition from Work to Retirement*. In 1993, he completed a project for the Department of Social Security on employer's practices and policies with respect to company pensions.

Robert Hutchens is Professor of Labor Economics at the School of Industrial and Labor Relations, Cornell University. His publications have examined the economics of government transfer programmes, long-term implicit contracts, and the labour market for older workers.

Klaus Jacobs is a researcher at the Institute of Health and Social Resarch, Berlin (IGES). His research activities center around health economics, systems of social insurance and labour market and social policy.

Takeshi Kimura is Professor of Public Finance at the Faculty of Literature and Social Sciences, Yamagata University. He has done research on public finance and social security in Japan. He is co-author of *Gaisetsu Nihon no Shakai Seisaku* (Social Policy in Japan) with Ikuro Takagi.

Frieder Naschold is director of the Research Unit II, Technology-Work-Environment, at the Science Center Berlin (WZB). His research interests are development trends in the industrial and public sectors, labour and industrial policy from an international, comparative perspective and applied research in the field of innovation development.

Masato Oka is Associate Professor at the Economic Research Institute, Yokohama City University. He has been doing research on the Fabian Socialism and Japanese Fabians. His current research interests are in the field of social policy and regional economic development.

Gunnar Olofsson, Associate Professor in Sociology at the Department of Sociology, University of Lund, specialises in economic and political sociology, social and labour market policy. He has written on the Swedish labour movement, Social Democracy and the Swedish model and also on housing and unemployment. He does reserch (with Jan Petersson) on the fate of older workers in Sweden during high unemployment.

Maki Omori is Professor of Social Policy and Administration at the Faculty of Economics, Rikkyo University. She is author of *Gendai Nihon no Josei Rodo* (Women at Work in Japan). Her research activities center around the economic effects of labour law and administration on the labour market.

Maria Oppen is senior sociologist at the Research Unit II, Technology-Work-Environment, of the Science Center Berlin (WZB). Her current research interests focus on the interplay of state (labour and social) policy and organisational innovation policy in the sector of public and private services, with a particular interest in the development of services' quality and the 'gendered' quality of work life.

Holger Peinemann is a graduate of political science and economics at the Free University of Berlin. His research interests centres on the question of the regulation of employment through the interaction of the two major actors, firms and the state. Since 1990 he has worked as a research assistant at the Research Unit II, Technology-Work-Environment, of the Science Center Berlin (WZB). He is currently writing his dissertation on the subject of 'employment companies' within the network of social actors.

Jan Petersson, Associate Professor in Economics and Social Policy at the School of Social Work, University of Lund, specialises in social and labour market policy and the history of economic thought. He has written on the pricing of social services, the care of the elderly and the Stockholm School in Economics. He is at the time still occupied with the theme of this book together with Gunnar Olofsson.

Martin Rein is Professor at the Department of Urban Studies and Planning at Massachusetts Institute of Technology (M.I.T.). His current professional activities include a comparative study of the role of social policy in industrial reorganisation in Eastern Europe; a study of the role of the firm in promoting early retirement; and a comparative study of the abortion controversy in West Germany and the United States.

Joachim Rosenow is senior sociologist at the Research Unit II, Technology-Work-Environment, of the Science Center Berlin (WZB). His current research interests and publications focus on corporate strategies of human-resource utilisation and their interaction with regulation by systems of social security and welfare.

Martina Schuster was leader of a research project in the "a&o research GmbH" until April 1991. She has been working in the area of demographical and structural analysis of enterprises during the transformation process in the GDR. She has mainly published on demographical problems. Since 1990 she has been working on the changes in regulatory conditions and their effects in the process of transformation from planned to the market economy in the former GDR. She is currently working in the personnel department of the Dresdner Bank in Leipzig.

Brigitte Stieler is manager and director of the "a&o research GmbH" – (Institute for labor-psychological and organizational research). Her current research interests are directed on human ressources management, qualification research and participational labour organisation. She has published many articles in these fields. Since 1990 she has been working on the changes in regulatory conditions and their effects in the process of transformation from planned to the market economy in the former GDR.

Ikuro Takagi is Professor of Political Economy and Social Policy at the Faculty of Home Economics, Nippon Women's University. He is active in research on industrial relations, especially the unions' attituide in Japan. He is author of many books in this area.

Willem Trommel studied sociology at the University of Leyden. Since 1984 he has published in the area of work and organisation. From 1990 he works at the Leyden Insitute for Law and Public Policy, University of Leyden, writing his PhD on early exit of older workers in the Netherlands.

Bert de Vroom is senior sociologist at the Leyden Institute for Law and Public Policy, University of Leyden. His research interest is concentrated on regulation at the intermediary level of societies (between the market and the state). He did research and published on neo-corporatist patterns, arrangements and self-regulation of organised business interests. Current research and recent publications deal with an international comparison of the organisational response on the AIDS-epidemic and different international comparative projects on the role of firms and intermediary organisations in regulating labour markets.

Stephen Wood is Reader in Industrial Relations at the London School of
Economics. He has published widely in the areas of industrial relations,
industrial sociology and organisation theory. He has written or edited
several books including *The Transformation of Work* (Unwin Hyman,
1989), and *The Car Industry* (Tavistock, 1985) (with D. Marsden, T.
Morris and P. Willman). He is currently researching on developments
in Human Resource Management and payment systems in British
manufacturing. He is an editor of the *British Journal of Industrial
Relations*.